NOAH, THE FLOOD
AND THE
FAILURE OF MAN
ACCORDING TO THE MIDRASH RABBAH

NOAH, THE FLOOD AND THE FAILURE OF MAN

according to the
MIDRASH RABBAH

Rabbi Dr.
WILFRED SHUCHAT

DEVORA
PUBLISHING
NEW YORK◆JERUSALEM◆LONDON

Noah, the Flood and the Failure of Man
According to the Midrash Rabbah
by Wilfred Shuchat

Copyright © 2013 by Wilfred Shuchat

Typeset by Ariel Walden

Printed in Israel

First Edition
ISBN 978-965-524-128-0

Urim Publications
P.O.Box 52287
Jerusalem 91521 Israel

Lambda Publishers, Inc.
527 Empire Blvd.
Brooklyn, NY 11225 U.S.A.
Tel: 718-972-5449
Fax: 718-972-6307

www.UrimPublications.com

To my dear grandchildren

AYALA SARA BRACHA SCHWARTZ

ARIELLE JUDITH LANDES

ELI JACOB LANDES

DANIEL MEIR LANDES

In Memoriam – Miriam Sochet Shuchat

It is my sad duty to report the death of my beloved wife,

MIRIAM SOCHET SHUCHAT,

which took place May 3rd, 2012, 11 days in Iyar 5772. We had been together in marriage for fifty-eight years and for both of us, it was by the far the best period of our lives. Unfortunately, MIRIAM was very sick toward the end, but she was a person of great courage and never complained, despite her suffering.

As the wife of a Rabbi, she gladly undertook whatever congregational responsibilities were requested of her, but she wanted more. When her children were of the age when they could go to school by themselves, she re-entered university and, with her post-graduate degree, received an appointment of PROFESSOR OF HUMANITIES at VANIER COLLEGE in MONTREAL, a position which she occupied for twenty-five years. Many of her students have told us what a wonderful teacher she was and how she helped them not only in their studies, but also in their choice of careers.

That which she considered her main joy and her main responsibility was being involved in the lives of her children, who loved her very much and whom she loved with a full heart – MARGOLA SHUCHAT, ELIZABETH SHUCHAT-SCHWARTZ of blessed memory, Rabbi Dr. BERNARD RAPHAEL SHUCHAT, BRYNA SHUCHAT-LANDES.

We lose, in her passing, a woman who combined beauty with dignity, elegance and good deeds. We lose, in her passing, a woman who observed the TORAH COMMANDMENTS with great love. We lose, in her passing, a woman of worth – the model *Eshet Chayil*.

In Memoriam

MARVIN SOCHET

A few years ago, as this manuscript was originally being prepared, I was saddened to learn of the passing of my brother-in-law, MARVIN SOCHET, who was close to so many people involved with this volume. MARVIN was a person who loved life and did everything in his power to awaken among his friends and associates a feeling that being a human being is the greatest possible gift. He leaves behind him his dear wife, MARY; his children, MELORA and DAVID; his son-in-law, JOSH SCHAFF; his grandson, MICAH and his granddaughter, ESME. His sister, MIRIAM SHUCHAT, z"l, was his lifetime sibling and friend. It is our hope that all who love Marvin will find a measure of comfort in the beautiful memories they shared together.

CONTENTS

Contents

PREFACE

Although I have studied Midrash for many years, the decision to publish has helped me very much. It has forced me to keep a regular daily schedule of study and challenged me to meet not only deadlines of publication, but also higher standards, not only of the text but of my own commentaries to the text.

This is my third volume of Midrash commentary. I was very happy with the publication of *The Creation* as well as the publication of *The Garden of Eden*. This kind of work cannot, of course, become a bestseller. On the other hand, I received many responses from readers who felt that my work had helped and inspired them for which I am very grateful.

The publication of *The Garden of Eden* coincided with the sixtieth anniversary of my rabbinate at Congregation Shaar Hashomayim. Although I had actually retired in 1993, after forty-seven years, and am looked upon as Rabbi Emeritus, the congregation insisted that the sixtieth anniversary had to be celebrated. At the tribute dinner in connection with this event, I was taken by surprise to discover that every family that attended that dinner was presented with a copy of *The Garden of Eden: The Struggle to be Human*. I am very grateful for that surprise.

I want to thank the Shaar Hashomayim, not only for that gesture, but for so many of their efforts to make my retirement from the congregation a positive event and with every possibility to continue my midrashic work. They have made my retirement both comfortable and functional. I have a beautiful study, secretarial help whenever needed and many other privileges. I greatly appreciate the friendship that the congregation shared with me and my family circle.

Regarding the publication of my previous works *The Creation* and *The Gate of Heaven*, I was able to prepare those manuscripts entirely on my own, including the computer work and everything associated with this kind of preparation. Unfortunately, I have developed low vision in recent years and it has made my use of the computer more difficult. I can do the work, but very slowly. However, both in Israel and in Montreal,

I was able to find young people to help me very much in this regard. I should like to express my thanks to Yarom Pinckovich of Montreal. Yarom typed and proofread the entire manuscript trying to keep a consistency in the formatting and transliterations, thus attemping to make it easier for the editor to function. He is also a lover of Midrash and has offered many insights, some of which have been included in this volume. I also wish to thank Daniel Lallouz for the technical advice in arranging the transmission of the digital content to the publisher in Jerusalem.

I wish to acknowledge my indebtedness to a number of individuals whose contribution to my work has been of a permanent nature. First and foremost I remember with gratitude my indebtedness to my late cousin by marriage, Jack Goldman, president of Judaica Press, for permission to use the Soncino translation of the *Midrash Rabbah*. He was the first person whom I showed my work and he was the one who encouraged me to publish.

I wish to thank my dear friend Rabbi Avraham Steinberger, editor and publisher of the *Midrash HaMevo'ar*, who allowed me to use his vocalized Hebrew text. This has saved me many hours of work. My teacher and friend Prof. David Weiss-Halivni, one of the world's great Talmudists, who authored the "blurb" for the *Garden of Eden* volume, has been honored as of this writing with the Israel prize for his original and pioneering work in understanding how the Talmud was created in all of its many details. We extend our heartiest congratulations to him.

I also want to thank my former publisher, Yaacov Peterseil of Devorah Publications, and my present publisher, Tzvi Mauer, and his editor Sara Rosenbaum, whose encouragement has been very important to me. I also want to thank my son, Rabbi Dr. Bernard Raphael Shuchat, for his contribution to the final editing of the book. Finally, I should like to express my deepest appreciation to R. Yitz and Blu Greenberg for the blurb which they forwarded that is now included in the cover of this volume. They themselves are among the finest interpreters of classical Judaism and their blessing is most generous. After the publication of *The Garden of Eden*, one of my grandchildren approached me with a complaint. I had dedicated my previous volumes to my dear wife, Miriam, and my children. But what about them? I promised that I would do my best to honor them also with the forthcoming volume and it is my pleasure to dedicate this volume to them; their names are listed on the dedication page. May the Midrash with their names in it always encourage them to study the Torah, to lead a religious life and always to be associated with the doing of good deeds.

I am sorry to add that our family suffered a serious loss in the passing of Miriam's brother, Marvin Sochet. He was a remarkable human being. Interested in every aspect of life and every aspect of the problems of the Jewish people. He loved America, particularly New York City, and once served as a councilor for the West Side. We miss his original ideas and his dedication to values. Throughout the past year he kept asking me about the progress of my most recent work. I am honored to dedicate it to his memory.

The first volume in this series, *The Creation*, ended with *Midrash Rabbah* 11:6 of *Genesis Rabbah*. The second volume, *The Garden of Eden and the Struggle to be Human*, begins with parashah 11, *midrash* 7 and continues until the end of parashah 24. The present volume, *Noah, the Flood and the Failure of Man*, begins where the last one left off, parashah 25, and ends with parashah 38, inclusive, which prepares us for the coming of Abraham. Everything in *Genesis Rabbah* has been included and explanations and interpretations will be found with as much detail as is necessary. We are in the process of preparing an index for this volume, which we expect to be ready in time for its publication.

We have also made every effort to follow the editorial principles of the previous volumes, which can be summarized as follows: In order to facilitate easy reading, we have provided the text of the Midrash in vocalized Hebrew and the translation immediately following; the rest, in normal characters, is my contribution. In translating biblical verses I have generally followed the Jewish Publications Society of America's translation (Philadelphia,1962), except when that translation does not agree with the midrashic context.

This is my third volume of commentary to the *Midrash Rabbah*. Nevertheless, I would have to add that I have merely scratched the surface. At the rate at which I study and work, it would take me a quarter of a century to complete the *Midrash Rabbah* and it is something not to be expected. On the other hand, even scratching the surface is not to be minimized. When the Midrash is studied intensively, one derives an insight into Judaism that is very unique.

In the Midrash every one of the sages is looked upon as valuable and important and it is not necessary to come to a conclusion of which opinion is correct, as is done in the Talmud. This freedom of expression and opinion is one of the most important learning devices, and I am most grateful for the experience. I thank the Holy One Blessed be He for the privilege of learning this material and will continue to do so for as long as He makes it possible. May the publication of this work be a blessing to my family and an *aliyat neshama* (ascent of the soul) to my dear wife, Miriam, *z"l*.

INTRODUCTION

A short review of the important themes in the Midrash on Noah: Those who are unfamiliar with Midrash, including many good Jews who love the Torah and practice it, find it hard to understand what attracts so many of us to midrashic literature. The truth of the matter is that, for the modern reader, there are many sections of the Midrash in which some of the ideas just seem ordinary. Many of the behavioral practices of previous generations and centuries seem irrelevant to today's world. There are also sections that seem to testify that at least some of the sages, though not many, were influenced by doctrines that have no meaning for any of us today.

What, then, is the great attraction? The answer is that the Midrash also has secret treasures, which sometimes come to the open and are revealed in all their brilliance. When that happens, the reader becomes captivated and all the other irrelevancies are immediately swept away.

One of these brilliant gems occurs toward the end of the portion of Noah in *Midrash Rabbah*, dealing with the generation of Division, דר הפלגה – *dor haflagah*. The Midrash asks a very important question. The generation of the Flood sinned terribly and were punished terribly. They were exterminated by a flood. What about the generation of Division, who planned and executed the Tower of Babel? Were they not in rebellion against God? In connection with the worship of idols, did it not say in later generations יהרג ואל יעבור – *yehareg ve'al ya'avor*, that one should rather be killed than transgress this commandment?

Why were they not punished in equal measure?

They were banished from their homes and dispersed to many parts of the world. But, as we learn in later chapters, particularly the opinion of R. Nechemiah, all of them eventually return to where they were formerly living because the power of attraction of their homes was very great. Compared to the punishment of the generation of the Flood, this should not even be considered a punishment. How is this explained?

The answer is that while this generation was in rebellion against God, at the same time, they practiced שלום – Shalom, they loved each other.

They helped each other, they encouraged each other. Satan, himself, is quoted as saying, "How could you punish a generation that practices Shalom?" Or, as the great editor of the *Mishnah*, Rabbi Yehudah Ha-Nassi, put it: "Rabbi said: 'Great is peace, for even if Israel practice idolatry but maintain peace amongst themselves, the Holy One, Blessed be He, says, as it were, "I have no dominion over them"'" (38:06). Does this mean that the commandments between man and man are greater than the commandments between man and God? Not necessarily. Ordinarily, one does not generalize from one law to another. But at this moment, the love of *shalom* took precedence even over the love of God. Can there be anything more tolerant than what we have just read and learned? Are we aware of any other religious tradition that can make this kind of statement? But the Midrash has this kind of moral vision and it is this kind of brilliance that illumines this great text from time to time.

One of the remarkable sections of this particular Midrash is the vehement criticism of excessive drinking. The object of the criticism regarding the excessive drinking was wine, although the term שכר – *shekhor* is also used. The latter is probably not what we today would call whiskey, but the name itself implies something that can contribute to intoxication.

I am not aware of any other place in rabbinic literature where the problem of drinking was discussed, or rather attacked, in such a forceful manner as appears in these pages. The provocation of this whole discussion is the incident in Noah's life when, after leaving the ark, he became drunk. The Midrash details Noah's problem, describing in detail what provoked him to engage in drink and the consequences of his behavior. This is not the place to review those matters other than to point out that this was the event that contributed to the attack in the Midrash on drunkenness and excessive drinking. As great a scholar as Rabbi, who was not only head of the academy of his generation, but the person who edited the *Mishnah*, was quoted as saying the following: "R. Judah b. R. Simon and R. Hanan in the name of R. Samuel b. R. Isaac said: 'Not "vayigal" is written, but "vayitgal"; he was the cause of exile for himself and subsequent generations.'" (36:04)

These are very strong words. It would have helped us a lot had we known what events in particular R. Judah had in mind in charging that excessive drinking contributed to both exiles. Before reading this material, I had assumed, along with so many others, that drinking was not a Jewish problem. During the years of the exile, the only Jewish contact with wine had to do with religious occasions such as קידוש – Kiddush and הבדלה – Havdalah. However, it was a little more than that since Jews

were encouraged to celebrate with wine. As it says in "Tzur Mishelo," a
traditional Sabbath hymn, הרחמן הנקדש יתברך ויתעלה על כוס יין מלא כברכת ה'
– *Harachaman Hanikdash yitbarekh veyitaleh al kos yayin maleh kevirkat
Hashem*. In other words, it is as though celebration with wine is part of
God's blessing. So long as the Jews lived a more or less separate existence,
this kind of drinking was easily controlled. We even have a collection of
folk songs that rejoice in the fact that Jews were sober while members
of other cultures were subject to drunkenness. When the emancipation
came, however, Jews were not only able to assimilate the good things in
the modern, but also the bad things such as excessive drinking. In our
day and age, there are many Jews who are subject to alcoholism and are
spending the best years of their lives trying to combat it.

The big question facing all of us in the light of this criticism is how we
are to react in the light of the fact that so much in the scriptural and rabbinic writings, especially the psalms, praise the drinking of wine? The
answer, of course, is moderation. One of my colleagues had a problem
with a young man who could not control his drinking. When he was
asked how he first started drinking wine in this fashion, his answer was,
in the Kiddush of the shul that he attended. These are unexpected developments and require our utmost care and concern. Maybe the criticism
of the Midrash, now before us, will help us take the problem of drinking
more seriously than in the past.

In the overall picture, I would have to admit that the Midrash on
Noah is not a happy document. In going over many themes from which
to choose a title for this volume, one of the themes that I thought of
discarding was the failure of man. I hesitated because "failure" does not
look good in the title. But it does seem to me that the outstanding lesson
to be learned from these pages is about the failure of man.

We are dealing with two time slots, very close to each other, but
slightly differentiated: the generation of the Flood and the generation of
the Tower of Babel. In the case of the latter period, it contained people
who were saved from the Flood. One would imagine that they, of all
people, would be overflowing with thanksgiving, grateful for the gift of
life that was denied to so many others. But this was not so. It was not
so because they did not see the hand of God in what was happening
to the world and to them. They saw, in the events surrounding them,
purely natural phenomenon. This held them back from acknowledging
the miracles and feeling the thankfulness that should have ensued.

Mankind of the twentieth century cannot feel superior to the generation of the Flood because of the fact that it was the generation that
perpetrated the Holocaust. Can it be that man has continued to fail?

What the Midrash has to say after speaking of the generation of Noah is not a secret to any of us. We know what is coming. It is Abraham and the possibility of a nation called the Jewish people, through whom God hoped to redeem the world. Has it happened? As we approach those forthcoming chapters, this is the serious question we will have to reflect upon. Can we eliminate the failure of man? Can we bring forward the possibility of redemption?

The Midrash of Noah concludes in a very beautiful way. It focuses on the word עקרה – *akarah*, which refers to a woman who is barren. Sarah was so described. So was Hannah. But our Midrash points out that these were not absolute descriptions. They were temporary descriptions of these women at the time. Sarah ultimately gave birth to Isaac and therefore was no longer barren. Hannah gave birth to Samuel and others, so that she was no longer barren. The Midrash then goes on to point out that the word *akarah* is often used by the prophets to describe the the the land of Israel. We have to learn from the midrashic lesson that barrenness is only temporary. The prophet Isaiah calls out, "Sing, O! you barren one, because your children will yet come from afar." What a beautiful message of hope to all of us. These words are being written on the occasion of the sixtieth anniversary of the State of Israel.

The ingathering of the exiles of which the prophets spoke has not been completed, but it is very much alive and ongoing. One million Jews have come to Israel from the Soviet Union. Many thousands have come from Ethiopia and many hundreds have come from various other parts of the world and are continuing to come despite the many challenges that Israel is facing. Let the once barren land rejoice. Let us hope that the prediction of the prophet will come to pass and we will open our mouths in praise and rejoicing as we experience the fulfillment of this new dream. "May God bless you from Zion, and may you gaze upon the goodness of Jerusalem, all the days of your life. And may you see children born to your children, peace upon Israel" (Psalms, 128:6).

א. (ה, כד) 'וַיִּתְהַלֵּךְ חֲנוֹךְ אֶת הָאֱ־לֹהִים, וְאֵינֶנּוּ, כִּי לָקַח אֹתוֹ אֱ־לֹהִים' אָמַר רַבִּי חָמָא בַּר הוֹשַׁעְיָא, אֵינוֹ נִכְתָּב בְּתוֹךְ טִימוֹסָן שֶׁל צַדִּיקִים, אֶלָּא בְּתוֹךְ טִימוֹסָן שֶׁל רְשָׁעִים. אָמַר רַבִּי אַיְבוּ, חֲנוֹךְ, חָנֵף הָיָה, פְּעָמִים צַדִּיק פְּעָמִים רָשָׁע, אָמַר הַקָּדוֹשׁ בָּרוּךְ הוּא, עַד שֶׁהוּא בְצִדְקוֹ אֲסַלְּקֶנּוּ, אָמַר רַבִּי אַיְבוּ, בְּרֹאשׁ הַשָּׁנָה דָּנוֹ, בְּשָׁעָה שֶׁהוּא דָן כָּל בָּאֵי עוֹלָם.

1. AND ENOCH WALKED WITH GOD, AND HE WAS NOT; FOR GOD TOOK HIM (V. 24). R. HAMA B. R. HOSHAYA SAID: [AND HE WAS NOT MEANS] THAT HE WAS NOT INSCRIBED IN THE ROLL OF THE RIGHTEOUS BUT IN THE ROLL OF THE WICKED. R. AIBU SAID: ENOCH WAS A HYPOCRITE, ACTING SOMETIMES AS A RIGHTEOUS, SOMETIMES AS A WICKED MAN. THERE-FORE THE HOLY ONE, BLESSED BE HE, SAID: WHILE HE IS RIGHTEOUS, I WILL REMOVE HIM. R. AIBU ALSO SAID: HE JUDGED [I.E., CONDEMNED] HIM ON NEW YEAR, WHEN HE JUDGES THE WHOLE WORLD.

The verse in question does not follow the usual style describing the death of a person. As a result, R. Hama points out that Enoch was not counted among the good people, but among the bad ones. He had his ups and downs. When he climbed up to a good category, God decided to remove him from the earth quickly so that he could merit the World to Come. When it says "God took him," it meant quickly, before he would descend to a lower level.

אֶפִּיקוֹרְסִים, שָׁאֲלוּ לְרַבִּי אַבָּהוּ, אָמְרוּ לוֹ, אֵין אָנוּ מוֹצְאִין מִיתָה לַחֲנוֹךְ, אָמַר לָהֶם, לָמָּה, אָמְרוּ לוֹ, נֶאֶמְרָה כָּאן לְקִיחָה, וְנֶאֶמְרָה לְהַלָּן, (מ"ב ב, ה) 'כִּי הַיּוֹם ה' לֹקֵחַ אֶת אֲדֹנֶיךָ מֵעַל רֹאשֶׁךְ', אָמַר לָהֶם, אִם לִלְקִיחָה אַתֶּם דּוֹרְשִׁים, נֶאֱמַר כָּאן לְקִיחָה, וְנֶאֶמַר לְהַלָּן, (יחזקאל כד, טז) 'הִנְנִי לֹקֵחַ מִמְּךָ אֶת מַחְמַד עֵינֶיךָ', אָמַר רַבִּי תַּנְחוּמָא, יָפֶה הֵשִׁיבָן רַבִּי אַבָּהוּ.

SOME SECTARIANS ASKED R. ABBAHU: WE DO NOT FIND THAT ENOCH DIED! HOW SO? INQUIRED HE. 'TAKING' IS EMPLOYED HERE, AND ALSO IN CONNECTION WITH ELIJAH, SAID THEY. IF YOU STRESS THE WORD 'TAKING,' HE ANSWERED, THEN 'TAKING' IS EMPLOYED HERE, WHILE IN EZEKIEL IT IS SAID, "BEHOLD, I TAKE AWAY FROM THEE THE DESIRE OF THINE EYES," ETC. (EZEK. 14:16) R. TANHUMA OBSERVED: HE ANSWERED THEM WELL.

The *apikorsim*, heretics, question R. Abbahu claiming that nowhere does it say that Enoch died an earthly death. Based on a comparison with the prophet Elijah, the word לקיחה – *lekichah*, meaning to be removed from the earth, is similar to the expression used in connection with Enoch. Therefore, earthly death is not intended. R. Abbahu's response is that this should be compared with the word *lekichah* in the writings of Ezekiel, where it means earthly death. Moshe Aryeh Mirkin (1896–1964) notes that the heretics at this time were probably the early Christians, for whom it was important that Enoch should not have an earthly death, to fit in with their Christian theology.

מַטְרוֹנָה, שָׁאֲלָה אֶת רַבִּי יוֹסֵי, אָמְרָה לוֹ, אֵין אָנוּ מוֹצְאִין מִיתָה בַּחֲנוֹךְ, אָמַר לָהּ, אִלּוּ נֶאֱמַר, 'וַיִּתְהַלֵּךְ חֲנוֹךְ אֶת הָאֱ-לֹהִים', וְשָׁתַק, הָיִיתִי אוֹמֵר כִּדְבָרַיִךְ, כְּשֶׁהוּא אוֹמֵר, 'וְאֵינֶנּוּ כִּי לָקַח אֹתוֹ אֱ-לֹהִים' וְאֵינֶנּוּ בָּעוֹלָם הַזֶּה, כִּי לָקַח אוֹתוֹ אֱ-לֹהִים.

A MATRON ASKED R. JOSE: WE DO NOT FIND DEATH STATED OF ENOCH! SAID HE TO HER: IF IT SAID, AND ENOCH WALKED WITH GOD, AND NO MORE, I WOULD AGREE WITH YOU. SINCE, HOWEVER, IT SAYS, AND HE WAS NOT, FOR GOD TOOK HIM, IT MEANS THAT HE WAS NO MORE IN THE WORLD [HAVING DIED], FOR GOD TOOK HIM.

A similar answer is given to the distinguished lady, who also felt that an earthly death did not seem to apply to Enoch. The answer, however, was that the Hebrew word איננו – *einenu*, indicates that he was removed (from this world to the next). That is what death is all about.

—

Seed Thoughts

This is another occasion where the Midrash opposes the usual interpretation of a biblical verse and offers its own unique explanation. All the translations seem to indicate the virtue of the unusual expressions by which the life of Enoch is terminated. But he did not die the usual death. In some fashion, he seemed to have been transported to a heavenly sphere, similar to Elijah. The Midrash completely opposes this kind of interpretation. In the case of Elijah, he was worthy of such an esteemed spiritual deliverance. In the case of Enoch, we have no knowledge of any special worthiness. Some of the sages thought he had moments of good behavior, while others thought that he was in the category of the wicked. It was also very important to them that it should have been understood as having died a natural death, and thus removing all possibilities of any other interpretation. The note by Moshe Aryeh Mirkin, which will appear in the Additional Commentary section, that the fear of the rabbis of how this verse could be misinterpreted was very justified. Enoch was not Elijah. He died as every other human being dies. This is how the biblical verse should be interpreted.

—

Additional Commentary

Apikorsim – *heretics*

This expression probably refers to the early Christians, who felt that it was important to prove that immortality happened with others as well. This would help them in interpreting their own concept of the Christian messiah, of having experienced resurrection, and therefore, immortality. (Mirkin)

In the role of the righteous and the role the wicked

The entire Hebrew verse reads, ויתהלך חנוך את הא-להים ואיננו כי – *Vayithalekh Chanokh et HaElokim v'eineno ki* ... The expression *v'eineno ki* is completely unnecessary, for it could have simply said that Enoch walked with God and God took him. That is why R. Hama feels that an interpretation is necessary. It was meant to indicate that Enoch was also in the role of the wicked. The word כי – *ki* has the meaning of כאשר – *ka'asher*. It was meant to indicate that when God took him, he was on a high moral level. Other times, he was not. (*Tiferet Tzion*)

Enoch as a righteous person

R. Aibu accepted the fact that there is a גזירה שוה – *gzeirah shavah* (a parallelism) between the verb לקח – *lakach* as applied to Enoch and *lakach* as it appears in Ezekiel. In Ezekiel, his wife was described as מחמד עיניך – *machmad eineiha* (the precious one). Since the verse spoke in praise of the wife of Ezekiel, the parallelism should apply to Enoch that he was a very good person. In this respect, the word *ki* is interpreted as nevertheless. That would mean that although he was a good person, God took him before he descended to a lower level. Even though R. Hama did not accept this parallelism, they both agreed that the word *einenu* means that he was taken quickly before descending to a lower level. (*Tiferet Tzion*)

ב. (כט) 'וַיִּקְרָא אֶת שְׁמוֹ נֹחַ, לֵאמֹר', רַבִּי יוֹחָנָן, וְרַבִּי שִׁמְעוֹן בֶּן לָקִישׁ, רַבִּי יוֹחָנָן אָמַר, לֹא
הַמִּדְרָשׁ הוּא הַשֵּׁם, וְלֹא הַשֵּׁם הוּא הַמִּדְרָשׁ, לָא הֲוָה צָרִיךְ קְרָא לְמֵימַר אֶלָּא נֹחַ זֶה יְנִיחֶנוּ, אוֹ,
נַחְמָן זֶה יְנַחֲמֵנוּ, אֶלָּא, בְּשָׁעָה שֶׁבָּרָא הַקָּדוֹשׁ בָּרוּךְ הוּא אֶת אָדָם הָרִאשׁוֹן, הִשְׁלִיטוֹ עַל הַכֹּל,
הַפָּרָה הָיְתָה נִשְׁמַעַת לַחוֹרֵשׁ, וְהַתֶּלֶם נִשְׁמָע לַחוֹרֵשׁ, כֵּיוָן שֶׁחָטָא אָדָם, מָרְדוּ עָלָיו, הַפָּרָה לֹא
הָיְתָה נִשְׁמַעַת לַחוֹרֵשׁ, וְהַתֶּלֶם לֹא הָיָה נִשְׁמָע לַחוֹרֵשׁ, כֵּיוָן שֶׁעָמַד נֹחַ נָחוּ, וּמִנָּא לָן, נֶאֱמַר כָּאן,
נְיָחָה, וְנֶאֱמַר לְהָלָן, (שמות כג, יב) 'לְמַעַן יָנוּחַ שׁוֹרְךָ וַחֲמֹרֶךָ', מַה נְיָחָה שֶׁנֶּאֱמַר לְהָלָן נְיָחַת שׁוֹר,
אַף נְיָחָה שֶׁנֶּאֱמַר כָּאן נְיָחַת שׁוֹר.

2. AND HE CALLED HIS NAME NOAH, SAYING: THIS SAME SHALL COMFORT US [YENAHAMENU FR. NAHEM] IN OUR WORK, ETC. R. JOHANAN SAID: THE NAME DOES NOT CORRESPOND TO THE INTERPRETATION [GIVEN TO IT], NOR DOES THE INTERPRETATION CORRESPOND TO THE NAME. THE TEXT SHOULD EITHER HAVE STATED, "THIS SAME SHALL GIVE US REST [YANIHENU]," OR, "AND HE CALLED HIS NAME NAHMAN, SAYING: 'THIS SAME YENAHAMENU . . .'"; BUT DOES NOAH CORRESPOND TO YE-NAHAMENU? THE TRUTH IS THAT WHEN THE HOLY ONE, BLESSED BE HE, CREATED ADAM, HE GAVE HIM DOMINION OVER ALL THINGS: THE COW OBEYED THE PLOUGHMAN, THE FURROW OBEYED THE PLOUGHMAN. BUT WHEN HE SINNED, HE MADE THEM REBEL AGAINST HIM: THE COW DID NOT OBEY THE PLOUGHMAN, NOR DID THE FURROW OBEY THE PLOUGH-MAN. BUT WHEN NOAH AROSE, THEY SUBMITTED; EASE IS MENTIONED HERE, AND EASE IS MENTIONED ELSEWHERE, VIZ. "THAT THINE OX AND THINE ASS MAY BE AT EASE" (EX. 23:12): JUST AS THE EASE STATED THERE MEANS THE EASE OF THE OX, SO THE EASE MENTIONED HERE IMPLIES THE EASE OF THE OX.

This *Midrash* begins by questioning the grammatical interpretation of the name נֹחַ – *Noach*. The text reads that he was called Noah because he will comfort us. Consolation or comfort might, indeed, be the role of Noah. However, grammatically, it is not derived from his name. The *Midrash*, as consolation, is not derived from the name Noah, which really is related to the word מנוחה – *menuchah*, meaning rest. The name Noah cannot be truly derived from the word "consolation," which in Hebrew is נחמה – *nechamah*. If the derivation is consolation, Noah's name should have been Nahman. R. Yochanan brings an example that when the first man, Adam, occupied supremacy in the world, everything from man to beast was disciplined. But when Adam sinned, the discipline broke down. It was only recaptured with the emergence of Noah, who brought peace into the world. The Hebrew uses ניחא – *neicha* from which the name Noah is derived.

רַבִּי שִׁמְעוֹן בֶּן לָקִישׁ אָמַר, לֹא הַשֵּׁם הוּא הַמִּדְרָשׁ, וְלֹא הַמִּדְרָשׁ הוּא הַשֵּׁם, וְלֹא הֲוָה צָרִיךְ
קְרָא לְמֵימַר אֶלָּא, אוֹ, נֹחַ זֶה יְנִיחֵנוּ, אוֹ נַחְמָן זֶה יְנַחֲמֵנוּ, אֶלָּא, עַד שֶׁלֹּא עָמַד נֹחַ, הָיוּ הַמַּיִם,
עוֹלִים וּמְצִיפִים אוֹתָם בְּתוֹךְ קִבְרֵיהֶם, שְׁתֵּי פְעָמִים כְּתִיב, (עמוס ה, ח; ט, ו) 'הַקּוֹרֵא לְמֵי הַיָּם',
כְּנֶגֶד שְׁתֵּי פְעָמִים שֶׁהָיוּ הַמַּיִם עוֹלִים, וּמְצִיפִין אוֹתָן בְּתוֹךְ קִבְרֵיהֶם, אַחַת בְּשַׁחֲרִית, וְאַחַת
בְּעַרְבִית, הֲדָא הוּא דִכְתִיב, (תהלים פח, ו) 'כְּמוֹ חֲלָלִים שֹׁכְבֵי קֶבֶר', שׁוֹכְבִים שֶׁלָּהֶם חֲלָלִים הָיוּ,
כֵּיוָן שֶׁעָמַד נֹחַ נָחוּ, נֶאֱמַר כָּאן, נְיָחָה, וְנֶאֱמַר לְהַלָּן נְיָחָה, (ישעיה נז, ב) 'יָבוֹא שָׁלוֹם, יָנוּחוּ עַל
מִשְׁכְּבוֹתָם', מַה נְיָחָה הָאָמוּר לְהַלָּן נְיָחַת קֶבֶר, אַף נְיָחָה הָאֲמוּרָה כָּאן נְיָחַת קָבֶר.

RESH LAKISH SAID: THE NAME DOES NOT CORRESPOND TO ITS INTERPRE-
TATION, NOR DOES THE INTERPRETATION CORRESPOND TO THE NAME.
SCRIPTURE SHOULD HAVE WRITTEN EITHER, "THE SAME YANICHENU
[SHALL GIVE US REST]" OR "... NAHMAN ... THE SAME YENACHAMENU
[SHALL COMFORT US]." THE FACT IS THAT BEFORE NOAH AROSE, THE
WATERS USED TO ASCEND AND INUNDATE THEM [THE DEAD] IN THEIR
GRAVES. FOR IT IS TWICE STATED, HE CALLETH FOR THE WATERS OF
THE SEA (AMOS 5:8, 9:6), CORRESPONDING TO THE TWO TIMES [DAILY]
THAT THE WATERS CAME UP AND INUNDATED THEM IN THEIR GRAVES,
ONCE IN THE MORNING AND ONCE IN THE EVENING, AS IT IS WRITTEN,
LIKE THE SLAIN THAT LIE IN THE GRAVE (PS. 88:6), I.E., EVEN THOSE
WHO HAD DIED NATURALLY WERE LIKE THE SLAIN. BUT WHEN NOAH
AROSE, THEY HAD REST; FOR 'RESTING' IS MENTIONED HERE, AND ALSO
ELSEWHERE, VIZ. HE ENTERETH INTO PEACE, THEY REST IN THEIR BEDS
(ISA. 57:2): JUST AS THERE THE REST OF THE GRAVE IS MEANT, SO HERE,
TOO, THE REST OF THE GRAVE IS MEANT.

Resh Lakish, who debates with R. Yochanan throughout the Talmud, agrees with his conclusion, but offers a different illustration. Before the time of Noah, the waters of the sea used to remove bodies from their graves. With the advent of Noah, everything came to its proper rest.

רַבִּי אֱלִיעֶזֶר אָמַר, לְשֵׁם קָרְבָּנוֹ, נִקְרָא, שֶׁנֶּאֱמַר (בראשית ח, כא) 'וַיָּרַח ה' אֶת רֵיחַ הַנִּיחֹחַ', רַבִּי
יוֹסֵי בַּר רַבִּי חֲנִינָא אָמַר, לְשֵׁם נַחַת הַתֵּבָה, נִקְרָא, דִּכְתִיב, (שם שם, ד) 'וַתָּנַח הַתֵּבָה'.

R. ELIEZER SAID: HE WAS SO NAMED ON ACCOUNT OF HIS SACRIFICE, AS
IT IS WRITTEN, AND THE LORD SMELLED THE SWEET [NICHOACH] SAVOR

(GEN. 8:21). R. JOSE B. R. HANINA SAID: ON ACCOUNT OF THE RESTING
OF THE ARK, AS IT IS WRITTEN, AND THE ARK RESTED [VATTANACH]
(IBID., 4).

Other interpretations of the name Noah make reference to the sacrifice that Noah made when the ark alighted. It says that God smelled a sweet savor. In Hebrew, sweet is ניחוח – *nichoach*. The *Tiferet Tzion* adds the beautiful thought that it was not the offering that had the sweet savor, but the person who brought the offering with character and good deeds was the real sweet savor that pleased God. From this, Noah was derived. A further interpretation relates the name Noah to the moment when the ark alighted, which in Hebrew is rendered as נחת התיבה – *nachat hateivah*.

אָמַר רַבִּי יוֹחָנָן, לֹא שִׁמְּשׁוּ הַמַּזָּלוֹת, כָּל אוֹתָן שְׁנֵים עָשָׂר חֹדֶשׁ, אָמַר לוֹ רַבִּי יוֹנָתָן, שִׁמְּשׁוּ, אֶלָּא שֶׁלֹּא הָיָה רְשׁוּמָן נִכָּר. (שם שם, כב) 'לֹא יִשְׁבֹּתוּ' רַבִּי אֱלִיעֶזֶר וְרַבִּי יְהוֹשֻׁעַ, רַבִּי אֱלִיעֶזֶר אָמַר, 'לֹא יִשְׁבֹּתוּ' מִכָּאן שֶׁלֹּא שָׁבָתוּ, וְרַבִּי יְהוֹשֻׁעַ אוֹמֵר, 'לֹא יִשְׁבֹּתוּ' מִכָּאן שֶׁשָּׁבָתוּ.

R. JOHANAN SAID: THE PLANETS DID NOT FUNCTION THE ENTIRE TWELVE MONTHS [OF THE FLOOD]. SAID R. JONATHAN TO HIM: THEY DID FUNCTION, BUT THEIR MARK WAS IMPERCEPTIBLE. R. ELIEZER SAID: THEY SHALL NOT CEASE [IBID., 22] IMPLIES THAT THEY NEVER CEASED. R. JOSHUA DEDUCED: "THEY SHALL NOT CEASE": HENCE IT FOLLOWS THAT THEY HAD CEASED.

The difference of opinion between the sages as to whether the constellations did not function during the twelve months that the ark was functioning is also related to the name Noah. If they did not function, it would mean that they rested, which in Hebrew is rendered as נחו – *nachu*, from which the name Noah is derived. If one takes the position that the constellations did function but was not visible because of the clouds, that, too, would be a form of rest and rendered as *nachu*.

Seed Thoughts

Grammatically speaking, the *midrash* is correct. The name נח – *Noach* is not derived from the root of נחמה – *nechamah*. If it were so, the appellation would have been נחמן – *Nachman*. On the other hand, as an interpretation, the *midrash* is very beautiful. The emergence of Noah and his career during the Flood was a tremendous source of consolation and inspiration, both to his generation and all others. That should not stop us from examining the real grammatical root of the name Noah, because that is also replete with meaning. Grammatically, *Noach* is derived from the word מנוחה – *menuchah,* which means rest – physical and spiritual. In this respect, *menuchah* is also a form of consolation. However, *menuchah* is much more. It is the goal of the Sabbath.

Indeed, in one of the Sabbath prayers at the time of מנחה – *Minchah* (the afternoon prayer), there is a beautiful interpretation of what *menuchah* really means. This is how it is expressed: מנוחת אהבה ונדבה, מנוחת אמת ואמונה, מנוחת שלום ושלוה ושקט ובטח – *menuchat ahavah undavah, menuchat emet ve'emunah, menuchat shalom veshalvah vehashket vavetach;* this translates to, "a rest of love and magnanimity, a rest of truth and faith, a rest of peace and serenity and tranquility and security." The concept of *menuchah* as spiritual rest begins with love and reaches out in compassion and giving. Spiritual rest is also a search for truth, which reaches out to faith and belief. It is to be identified with a desire for that wholesomeness and inner peace, as well as that confidence that leads to inner security. Thus, we see that *menuchah* as spiritual rest is a tremendous moral concept. So is *nechamah,* consolation, and this *midrash* helps us appreciate both.

—

Additional Commentary

He was so named on account of his sacrifice

He was named Noah because of the fact that the ark alighted on the ground and the Hebrew for alighted is נחת – *nachat.* God always allows a father and a mother to name their child in association with that which is most suitable to that child. Lemech, the father of Noah, might have called his son *Nachman,* the consoler. But God influenced him to name his son in terms of that which most affected his life, which was the alighting of the ark on the ground.

R. Eliezer and others claimed that Noah did most of his good deeds through his own inner conviction. Therefore, they maintained that the name Noah reflects those good deeds, as a result of which, God inhaled (so to speak) the ריח ניחוח – *reiyach nicho'ach,* the sweet savor. ("Sweet" is the word from which Noah is derived.) The main teaching of ריח ניחוח has nothing to do with the offering or sacrifice, but rather with the person who brings the sacrifice. The sweet perfume represents the sweetness of his character.

R. Jose b. R. Hanina and others maintain that not all of Noah's good qualities came from himself, but rather that the Holy One, Blessed be He, helped him. Thus, the name Noah does not reflect his own doing, but God's love and help for him. God's greatest gift to Noah was the fact that the ark alighted on Mount Ararat. Otherwise, it would have remained on the waters until the Flood waters would have disappeared, by which point it would have been in danger from damages. Therefore, he was called Noah, to remind him of God's great love that He alighted the ark on its proper place. (*Tiferet Tzion*)

ג. 'מִן הָאֲדָמָה אֲשֶׁר אֵרְרָהּ ה'', עֲשָׂרָה שְׁנֵי רְעָבוֹן בָּאוּ לָעוֹלָם, אֶחָד בִּימֵי אָדָם הָרִאשׁוֹן,
שֶׁנֶּאֱמַר (בראשית ג, יז) 'אֲרוּרָה הָאֲדָמָה בַּעֲבוּרֶךָ', וְאֶחָד בִּימֵי לֶמֶךָ, שֶׁנֶּאֱמַר 'מִן הָאֲדָמָה אֲשֶׁר
אֵרְרָהּ ה'', וְאֶחָד בִּימֵי אַבְרָהָם, שֶׁנֶּאֱמַר (שם יב, י) 'וַיְהִי רָעָב בָּאָרֶץ', וְאֶחָד בִּימֵי יִצְחָק, שֶׁנֶּאֱמַר (שם כו,
א) 'וַיְהִי רָעָב בָּאָרֶץ, מִלְּבַד הָרָעָב הָרִאשׁוֹן', וְאֶחָד בִּימֵי יַעֲקֹב, שֶׁנֶּאֱמַר (שם מה, ו) 'כִּי זֶה שְׁנָתַיִם
הָרָעָב', וְאֶחָד בִּימֵי שְׁפֹט הַשּׁוֹפְטִים, שֶׁנֶּאֱמַר (רות א, א) 'וַיְהִי בִּימֵי שְׁפֹט הַשֹּׁפְטִים וַיְהִי רָעָב
בָּאָרֶץ', וְאֶחָד בִּימֵי דָוִד, שֶׁנֶּאֱמַר (ש"ב כא, א) 'וַיְהִי רָעָב בִּימֵי דָוִד שָׁלֹשׁ שָׁנִים', וְאֶחָד בִּימֵי
אֵלִיָּהוּ, שֶׁנֶּאֱמַר (מ"א יז, א) 'חַי ה' אֱלֹהֵי יִשְׂרָאֵל, אֲשֶׁר עָמַדְתִּי לְפָנָיו, אִם יִהְיֶה הַשָּׁנִים הָאֵלֶּה
טַל וּמָטָר כִּי אִם לְפִי דְבָרִי', וְאֶחָד בִּימֵי אֱלִישָׁע, שֶׁנֶּאֱמַר (מ"ב ו, כה) 'וַיְהִי רָעָב גָּדוֹל בְּשֹׁמְרוֹן',
שֶׁהוּא מִתְגַּלְגֵּל וּבָא לָעוֹלָם

3. [WHICH COMETH] FROM THE GROUND WHICH THE LORD HATH CURSED (5:29). FAMINE VISITED THE WORLD TEN TIMES. ONCE IN THE DAYS OF ADAM: CURSED IS THE GROUND FOR THY SAKE (GEN. 3:17); ONCE IN THE DAYS OF LAMECH: WHICH COMETH FROM THE GROUND WHICH THE LORD HATH CURSED; ONCE IN THE DAYS OF ABRAHAM: AND THERE WAS A FAMINE IN THE LAND (GEN. 12:10); ONCE IN THE DAYS OF ISAAC: AND THERE WAS FAMINE IN THE LAND, BESIDE THE FIRST FAMINE THAT WAS IN THE DAYS OF ABRAHAM (IBID., 26:1); ONCE IN THE DAYS OF JACOB: FOR THESE TWO YEARS HATH THE FAMINE BEEN IN THE LAND (IBID., 45: 6); ONCE IN THE DAYS WHEN THE JUDGES JUDGED: AND IT CAME TO PASS IN THE DAYS WHEN THE JUDGES JUDGED, THAT THERE WAS A FAMINE IN THE LAND (RUTH 1:1); ONCE IN THE DAYS OF ELIJAH: AS THE LORD, THE GOD OF ISRAEL, LIVETH, BEFORE WHOM I STAND, THERE SHALL NOT BE DEW NOR RAIN THESE YEARS (I KINGS 17:1); ONCE IN THE DAYS OF ELISHA: AND THERE WAS A GREAT FAMINE IN SAMARIA (II KINGS 6:25); ONE FAMINE WHICH TRAVELS ABOUT IN THE WORLD;

The listing of these ten forms of famine describes ten different types of famine. Not all of them had the same character. The main reason behind all of these famines was the fact that the earth was cursed during the days of Adam. Furthermore, God does not continue these famines permanently. Otherwise, the world could not survive. The earth was not

cursed during the time of Lemech; however, he suffered from the afteref-
fects of the previous famine. The *Midrash* lists these famines in detail:

וְאֶחָד לֶעָתִיד לָבוֹא, שֶׁנֶּאֱמַר (עמוס ח, יא) 'לֹא רָעָב לַלֶּחֶם וְלֹא צָמָא לַמַּיִם, כִּי אִם לִשְׁמֹעַ אֵת
דְּבַר ה''

... AND ONCE IN THE MESSIANIC FUTURE: NOT A FAMINE OF BREAD,
NOR A THIRST FOR WATER, BUT OF HEARING THE WORDS OF THE LORD
(AMOS 8:11).

The reference to a famine that travels through different parts of the
world probably refers to a permanent famine that takes place in the
world, although not localized in one place (Mirkin). The reference to
the World to Come is not part of the ten, but an additional one, quite
different from the rest, since it is not a famine based on material needs,
but on spiritual hopes. Even though there will be a real famine in the
world, the people will not pay attention to it because they will prefer to
listen to the words of the Lord (Mirkin). More on this subject will be
detailed in further paragraphs.

רַבִּי הוּנָא, וְרַבִּי יִרְמְיָה בְּשֵׁם רַבִּי שְׁמוּאֵל בַּר רַב יִצְחָק, עִקַּר אַוְתֶּנְטְיָא שֶׁלּוֹ, לֹא הָיָה רָאוּי לִהְיוֹת
בִּימֵי דָוִד, אֶלָּא בִּימֵי שָׁאוּל, אֶלָּא, עַל יְדֵי שֶׁהָיָה שָׁאוּל גְּרוֹפִית שֶׁל שִׁקְמָה, גִּלְגְלוֹ הַקָּדוֹשׁ בָּרוּךְ
הוּא, וֶהֱבִיאוֹ בִּימֵי דָוִד, מַתְלָא אָמְרִין, שִׁילוֹ חָטָא, וְיוֹחָנָא מִשְׁתַּלְמָא, אַתְמְהָא, אָמַר רַבִּי חִיָּא
רַבָּה, מָשָׁל לְזַגָּג שֶׁהָיָה בְיָדוֹ קֻפָּה מְלֵאָה כוֹסוֹת וּדְיַאטְרוֹטִין, בְּשָׁעָה שֶׁהָיָה מְבַקֵּשׁ לִתְלוֹת אֶת
קֻפָּתוֹ, הָיָה מֵבִיא יָתֵד וּתְקָעָהּ, וְנִתְלָה בָהּ, וְאַחַר כַּךְ הָיָה תוֹלֶה אֶת קֻפָּתוֹ, לְפִיכַךְ לֹא בָאוּ, בִּימֵי
בְּנֵי אָדָם שְׁפוּפִים, אֶלָּא בִּימֵי בְּנֵי אָדָם גִּבּוֹרִים, שֶׁהֵן יְכוֹלִין לַעֲמֹד בָּהֶן. רַבִּי בֶּרֶכְיָה הֲוָה קְרֵי
עֲלֵיהוֹן, (ישעיה מ, כט) 'נֹתֵן לַיָּעֵף כֹּחַ'.

R. HUNA AND R. JEREMIAH IN THE NAME OF R. SAMUEL AND R. ISAAC
SAID: ITS OCCURRENCE OUGHT PROPERLY TO HAVE BEEN NOT IN THE
DAYS OF DAVID, BUT IN THE DAYS OF SAUL, BUT BECAUSE SAUL WAS A
SHOOT OF A SYCAMORE TREE, THE HOLY ONE, BLESSED BE HE, POST-
PONED IT AND BROUGHT IT IN THE DAYS OF DAVID. SHILA SINS AND
JOHANAH IS PUNISHED! SAID R. HIYYA: IT IS LIKE THE CASE OF A GLASS-
WORKER HOLDING A BASKET FULL OF GOBLETS AND CUT GLASS, WHO,
WHEN HE WISHED TO HANG THE BASKET UP, BROUGHT A NAIL, DROVE
IT [INTO THE WALL], SUSPENDED HIMSELF THEREBY, AND THEN HUNG
UP HIS BASKET. FOR THAT REASON, ALL THESE [FAMINES] CAME NOT IN
THE DAYS OF LOWLY [WEAK] MEN, BUT IN THE DAYS OF MIGHTY MEN,
WHO COULD WITHSTAND IT. R. BEREKIAH APPLIED TO THEM THE VERSE,
HE GIVETH POWER TO THE FAINT (ISA. 40:29).

The famine that came during the reign of King David was supposed to happen during the time of the King Saul. However, King Saul was weak and would not have been able to withstand the famine, so it was postponed to the time of King David. In general, God tests a generation that He knows would withstand the ordeal given.

רַבִּי בֶּרֶכְיָה בְּשֵׁם רַבִּי חֶלְבּוֹ, אָמַר, שְׁנַיִם בָּאוּ בִּימֵי אַבְרָהָם, רַבִּי הוּנָא בְּשֵׁם רַבִּי אַחָא, אָמַר, אֶחָד בִּימֵי לֶמֶךְ, וְאֶחָד בִּימֵי אַבְרָהָם. רָעָב שֶׁבָּא בִּימֵי אֵלִיָּהוּ רָעָב שֶׁל בַּצֹּרֶת הָיָה, שָׁנָה עָבְדָה שָׁנָה לֹא עָבְדָה, רָעָב שֶׁבָּא בִּימֵי אֱלִישָׁע רָעָב שֶׁל מְהוּמָה הָיָה, שֶׁנֶּאֱמַר (מ"ב ו, כה) 'עַד הֱיוֹת רֹאשׁ חֲמוֹר בִּשְׁמֹנִים כָּסֶף'. רָעָב שֶׁהָיָה בִּימֵי שְׁפֹט הַשּׁוֹפְטִים, רַבִּי הוּנָא בְּשֵׁם רַבִּי דוֹסָא, אָמַר, אַרְבָּעִים וּשְׁתַּיִם סְאִין הָיוּ, וְנַעֲשׂוּ אַרְבָּעִים וְאֶחָת, וְהָא תְנֵי, לֹא יֵצֵא אָדָם לְחוּצָה לָאָרֶץ אֶלָּא אִם כֵּן הָיוּ סָאתַיִם שֶׁל חִטִּים הוֹלְכוֹת בְּסֶלַע, אָמַר רַבִּי שִׁמְעוֹן, אֵימָתַי בִּזְמַן שֶׁאֵינוֹ מוֹצֵא לִקַּח, אֲבָל אִם הָיָה מוֹצֵא לִקַּח, אֲפִלּוּ, סְאָה בְּסֶלַע לֹא יֵצֵא לְחוּצָה לָאָרֶץ, וְאִלּוּ אֱלִימֶלֶךְ, יָצָא לְפִיכָךְ נֶעֱנָשׁ.

R. BEREKIAH SAID IN R. HELBO'S NAME: THERE WERE TWO FAMINES IN THE DAYS OF ABRAHAM. R. HUNA SAID IN R. AHA'S NAME: THERE WAS ONE IN THE DAYS OF LAMECH AND ONE IN THE DAYS OF ABRAHAM. THE FAMINE OF ELIJAH'S TIME WAS ONE OF SCARCITY, ONE YEAR YIELDING AND ONE YEAR NOT YIELDING. THE FAMINE IN THE DAYS OF ELISHA WAS ONE OF PANIC, "[U]NTIL AN ASS'S HEAD WAS SOLD FOR FOURSCORE PIECES OF SILVER," ETC. (II KINGS 6:25). AS FOR THE FAMINE DURING THE DAYS OF THE JUDGES, R. HUNA SAID IN R. DOSA'S NAME: FROM THE PRICE OF FORTY-TWO SE'AHS [OF WHEAT PER SELA], IT ADVANCED TO FORTY-ONE SE'AHS [PER SELA], AND IT WAS TAUGHT: "A MAN MUST NOT EMIGRATE ABROAD UNLESS TWO SE'AHS COST A SELA." R. SIMEON OBSERVED: THAT IS ONLY WHEN IT IS ALTOGETHER UNOBTAINABLE, BUT IF IT IS OBTAINABLE, EVEN AT A SE'AH PER SELA, ONE MUST NOT GO ABROAD.

The famine during the time of Elijah is called בצורת – *batzoret*. The explanation is that it was not a permanent famine. During one particular year, the earth can be very fruitful and in the next year, it can be devastated and produce no crops at all. The word *batzoret* comes from the Aramaic root *batzor*, which means to lessen.

The famine during the time of Elisha is called מהומה – *mehumah*, which means confusion. The reason for this was that Shomron (Samaria) was occupied by the Syrian army and farmers were afraid to harvest their crops for fear of being attacked by occupational forces.

During the time of what is called שפוט השופטים – *shfot hashoftim,* the period of the Judges, mentions the book of Ruth that we are not dealing so much with famine but the high cost of living. The wealthy were able to survive, as opposed to the poor, who had great difficulty. The *Midrash* mentions the increase in the cost of living from forty-two se'ah per sela to forty-one. This is a relatively minor increase in cost. Nevertheless, it was after such an increase that Elimelech left the land of Israel to go to Moab. No Jew is allowed to leave the land of Israel merely because of the high cost of living, so long as produce is available in markets to be sold, even at a high price. This was a rule strongly enforced upon the rich. It was their duty to remain in the land of Israel, not only to perform those commandments having to do with the holiness of the land, such as the tithing, but also to support the poor under these strenuous circumstances. Elimelech rejected these principles, left the land of Israel and, as the Book of Ruth mentions, he was punished for this behavior.

Seed Thoughts

The *Tiferet Tzion*, quoted later in these pages, seems to have a different concept of the meaning of the World to Come (עתיד לבא – *atid lavo*). Ordinarily, the concept of the "future world," the World to Come, is part and parcel of a syndrome that includes the coming of the Messiah, immortality, resurrection and the day of judgment. The order of these categories differs according to different sages.

The *Tiferet Tzion*, however, seems to think differently concerning the terms עולם הבא – *olam habah*, the World to Come, and עתיד לבא – *atid lavo*, the future world. The World to Come refers to a world beyond this world. The future world is a time that will take place just before the גאולה – *geulah*, which is the coming of the Messiah. The future world will not apply everywhere at once. Just as there can be a material famine in one place and not another, so there can be a spiritual famine (a search for God) in one place before it reaches another. According to this theory, the future world is a preparatory concept which paves the way for the coming of Messiah and all those other wonderful things that have to do with immortality in the World to Come.

Additional Commentary

One famine that travels about in the World to Come

As it is written, "it is not a famine for bread," etc. The meaning is that the famine mentioned above would not occur at one time, everywhere in the world, but would travel from one place to another. In one year the famine could be in one country, and the next year, in another country. Finally, the famine would reach the whole world and the text proves this point: "Behold, days will come and I will send a famine to the land." The implication is that first, there will be a material famine, and afterward, a famine for the word of the Lord. The point of the verse is to show that the real famine will not be for bread, because people can migrate to where there is food. Thus, it is a famine for the word of the Lord. All of this will happen before the coming of the redeemer (Messiah) in order to bring attention to those people who are giving their lives to the Torah, even in those difficult times. This confirms what *Song of Songs Rabbah* says, that before the redemption, there will be great spiritual cleansing. (*Tiferet Tzion*)

א. (א, לב) 'וַיְהִי נֹחַ בֶּן חֲמֵשׁ מֵאוֹת שָׁנָה', כְּתִיב, (תהלים א, א) 'אַשְׁרֵי הָאִישׁ אֲשֶׁר לֹא הָלַךְ בַּעֲצַת
רְשָׁעִים', 'אַשְׁרֵי הָאִישׁ' זֶה נֹחַ, 'אֲשֶׁר לֹא הָלַךְ בַּעֲצַת רְשָׁעִים, וּבְדֶרֶךְ חַטָּאִים לֹא עָמָד

1. AND NOAH WAS FIVE HUNDRED YEARS OLD; AND NOAH BEGOT SHEM,
HAM, AND JAPHETH (5:32). IT IS WRITTEN, HAPPY IS THE MAN THAT
HATH NOT WALKED, ETC. (PS. 1:1); "HAPPY IS THE MAN" REFERS TO
NOAH, "THAT HATH NOT WALKED IN THE COUNSEL OF THE WICKED."

The reason for this midrashic interpretation is the fact that in the
first Psalm, the word אִישׁ – *ish* does not appear by itself, but with the
descriptive ה – *heh* preceding it. It reads, אשרי האיש – *ashrei ha-ish*, happy
is the man. Without the *heh*, the psalm could apply to anyone. With it,
however, there is a specific reference. The sages chose to interpret that
heh refers to Noah.

רַבִּי יְהוּדָה וְרַבִּי נְחֶמְיָה, רַבִּי יְהוּדָה אוֹמֵר, בִּשְׁלֹשָׁה דוֹרוֹת, בְּדוֹר אֱנוֹשׁ, וּבְדוֹר הַמַּבּוּל, וּבְדוֹר
הַפְלָגָה, רַבִּי נְחֶמְיָה אוֹמֵר, בְּדוֹר הַמַּבּוּל, וּבְדוֹר הַפְלָגָה, אֲבָל בְּדוֹר אֱנוֹשׁ הָיָה קָטָן. עַל דַּעְתֵּהּ
דְּרַבִּי יְהוּדָה דַּאֲמַר, 'אַשְׁרֵי הָאִישׁ, אֲשֶׁר לֹא הָלַךְ בַּעֲצַת רְשָׁעִים' זֶה דוֹר אֱנוֹשׁ, 'וּבְדֶרֶךְ חַטָּאִים
לֹא עָמָד' זֶה דוֹר הַמַּבּוּל, 'וּבְמוֹשַׁב לֵצִים לֹא יָשָׁב' זֶה דוֹר הַפְלָגָה

R. JUDAH AND R. NEHEMIAH DIFFER ON THIS. R. JUDAH SAID: IT MEANS
THROUGH THREE GENERATIONS, VIZ. OF ENOSH, THE FLOOD, AND THE
DIVISON [OF TONGUES]. R. NEHEMIAH SAID: DURING THE GENERATION
OF ENOSH HE WAS BUT A CHILD. ACCORDING TO R. JUDAH'S VIEW,
[THE VERSE IS TO BE INTERPRETED THUS:] "IN THE COUNSEL OF THE
WICKED" REFERS TO THE GENERATION OF ENOSH; "NOR STOOD IN THE
WAY OF SINNERS," TO THAT OF THE FLOOD; "NOR SAT IN THE SEAT OF
THE SCORNFUL," TO THAT OF THE DIVISON [OF TONGUES].

The sages interpret the rest of the psalm as being identified with the
career of Noah. The psalm is talking about a *tzaddik* and in the Torah
it says, "*Noach ish tzaddik.*" It mentions the fact that the good man is
confronted by רשעים – *resha'im*, evil ones, חטאים – *chata'im*, sinners and
לצים – *letzim*, scoffers. There are different opinions among the sages as

to which part of Noah's life was identified with these verses. However, all agree that over three generations, he was confronted first with the evildoers. One view is that the generations involved were that of Enosh, that of the Flood and the generation of the Division of the world (Tower of Babel). Another view is that Noah was too young to have been influenced by the generation of Enosh, but in the generation of the Flood and of the division of the world, he was confronted by evildoers, sinners and scoffers.

((שם שם, ב) 'כִּי אִם בְּתוֹרַת ה' חֶפְצוֹ', אֵלּוּ שֶׁבַע מִצְוֹות שֶׁנִּצְטַוָּה, (שם שם, שם) 'וּבְתוֹרָתוֹ יֶהְגֶּה יוֹמָם וָלָיְלָה', שֶׁהָגָה דָבָר מִתּוֹךְ דָּבָר, אָמַר, מַה טַּעַם רִבָּה הַקָּדוֹשׁ בָּרוּךְ הוּא בְּטְהוֹרִים יוֹתֵר מַטְּמֵאִים, לֹא שֶׁהוּא רוֹצֶה לְהַקְרִיב מֵהֶן קָרְבָּן, מִיָּד, (בראשית ח, כ) 'וַיִּקַּח מִכֹּל הַבְּהֵמָה הַטְּהוֹרָה, וְגו''

BUT HIS DELIGHT WAS IN THE LAW OF THE LORD (PS. 1:2) ALLUDES TO THE SEVEN PRECEPTS WHICH HE WAS COMMANDED. BUT IN HIS LAW DOTH HE MEDITATE: HE INFERRED ONE THING FROM ANOTHER, ARGUING, WHY DID THE HOLY ONE, BLESSED BE HE, ORDER MORE CLEAN ANIMALS [TO BE SAVED] THAN UNCLEAN ONES? SURELY BECAUSE HE DESIRES THAT OFFERINGS SHOULD BE MADE TO HIM OF THE FORMER. FORTHWITH, HE TOOK OF EVERY CLEAN BEAST, ETC. (GEN. 8:20).

The interesting part to note here is the fact that it says that he studied the Torah day and night. What Torah did he study (since he preceded the giving of the Torah at Sinai)? The answer is that he was given seven commandments, six of which he inherited from Adam, and a seventh prohibition, אבר מן החי – *ever min hachai,* tearing a limb from an animal. This section indicates that Noah thought very carefully about the commandments given to him in the instructions about the ark and tried to find meaningful interpretations to what he was doing.

((תהלים שם, ג) 'וְהָיָה כְּעֵץ שָׁתוּל עַל פַּלְגֵי מָיִם' שֶׁשְׁתָלוֹ הַקָּדוֹשׁ בָּרוּךְ הוּא בַּתֵּבָה, (שם, שם, שם) 'אֲשֶׁר פִּרְיוֹ יִתֵּן בְּעִתּוֹ', זֶה שֵׁם (שם שם, שם) 'וְעָלֵהוּ לֹא יִבּוֹל', זֶה חָם, (שם שם, שם) 'וְכֹל אֲשֶׁר יַעֲשֶׂה יַצְלִיחַ', זֶה יָפֶת.

AND HE SHALL BE LIKE A TREE PLANTED BY STREAMS OF WATER (PS. 1:3): THE LORD PLANTED HIM [I.E., SAVED HIM] IN THE ARK; THAT BRINGETH FORTH ITS FRUIT IN ITS SEASON: THIS ALLUDES TO SHEM; AND WHOSE LEAF DOTH NOT WITHER: TO HAM; AND IN WHATSOEVER HE DOETH, HE SHALL PROSPER: TO JAPHETH. THUS IT IS WRITTEN, AND NOAH BEGOT SHEM, HAM, AND JAPHETH.

Noah's fruitfulness had to do with the birth of his sons, which the *Midrash* identifies with the closing words quoted from the first psalm, "The tree that is planted by streams of water gives beautiful fruits," as happened in the time of Noah, with the birth of his three sons.

—

Seed Thoughts

A beloved daughter of mine, who passed away several years ago, loved to study Torah and share her interpretations with her friends and often with her clients. Whenever she was faced with a difficult problem in the ways of God and man, she often used the expression, "You have to try to figure it out. Even if there is no solution, something good happens."

We have a beautiful example of this in the life of Noah. The first psalm says, "In His Torah, he reflected day and night." That is interpreted as meaning that Noah has studied the commandments given to him, and from them, he learned the different principles that were later revealed in the Torah. One of the problems that bothered him was, why there was one couple of ritually unclean animals and seven ritually clean ones? Why was there a difference? In trying to figure it out, Noah came to the conclusion that the additional animals were meant to be offered as sacrifice to God in terms of thanksgiving after the Flood. As a result of this thinking, the moment the ark alighted on Mount Ararat, he immediately offered a sacrifice to God as a token of his own thanksgiving.

There is more to this than the story of Noah. Every Jew who tries to come close to God and His Torah has to try to be creative. That means that when faced with a problem of interpretation, he has to try to figure it out. We have the intellectual capacity to do so, and though our answers may not always be correct, they will help us become better Jews and more fulfilled human beings.

—

Additional Commentaries

Happy is the man

The verse in Psalms could have said, "happy is *a* man" but instead it says, "happy is *the* man," interpreted to refer to Noah. It also describes three categories – evildoers, sinners and scoffers. This can be interpreted as three generations (in which Noah was righteous). It also says about

Noah that he was a righteous man and wholehearted in his generation. In the time of Enosh, he was only 84 years old, which was considered young since in those days, no one under 100 was eligible for punishment. R. Judah feels that the generation of Enosh does apply to the category of evil ones and that the Flood applies to the generation of sinners and the generation of Division applies to the scoffers, who said terrible things about God. (Mirkin)

Happy is the man

The identification with the first psalm is to look for a reason why Noah did not father children until he reached the age of 500 (later than others before him). Since the word *ish* is written with an additional *heh*, it implies that it is dealing with a particularly well-known person. The *Midrash* identifies this psalm with Noah, about whom it said that he was a righteous man and lived within the three generations of evildoers, sinners and scoffers. This can refer only to Noah and none of the other righteous, who did not have such connections to these generations. (*Tiferet Tzion*)

הגה דבר מתוך דבר – higah davar mitokh davar

Because he was able to deduce one principle from another, it is appropriate that when the psalm says he meditated on his Torah, that it should apply to Noah, who created new ideas with his intelligence. The *Midrash* brings an illustration of this in terms of why he offered sacrifices even though he was not commanded to do so. Furthermore, we have to infer from this that he acted that way toward each of the seven commandments that he inherited. He looked upon those seven commandments as being the fundamental principles of the entire Torah and by virtue of the fact that he thought about them, he was able to learn from them almost the whole Torah. That is why the sages say that Noah studied the Torah even before it was given. (*Tiferet Tzion*)

ב. (ו, י) 'וַיּוֹלֶד נֹחַ שְׁלֹשָׁה בָנִים אֶת שֵׁם אֶת חָם וְאֶת יָפֶת', כְּתִיב (תהלים צב, יד) 'שְׁתוּלִים בְּבֵית
ה', בְּחַצְרוֹת אֱלֹהֵינוּ יַפְרִיחוּ', 'שְׁתוּלִים בְּבֵית ה'' זֶה נֹחַ, שֶׁשְּׁתָלוֹ הַקָּדוֹשׁ בָּרוּךְ הוּא בַּתֵּבָה,
'בְּחַצְרוֹת אֱלֹהֵינוּ יַפְרִיחוּ', 'וַיּוֹלֶד נֹחַ אֶת שֵׁם אֶת חָם וְאֶת יָפֶת', (שם שם, טו) 'עוֹד יְנוּבוּן בְּשֵׂיבָה,
דְּשֵׁנִים וְרַעֲנַנִּים יִהְיוּ', עוֹד יְנוּבוּן' זֶה נֹחַ, (שם שם, שם) 'דְּשֵׁנִים וְרַעֲנַנִּים יִהְיוּ', 'וַיּוֹלֶד נֹחַ'.

2. PLANTED IN THE HOUSE OF THE LORD, THEY SHALL FLOURISH IN THE
COURTS OF OUR GOD (PS. 92:14). "PLANTED IN THE HOUSE OF THE LORD"
ALLUDES TO NOAH, WHOM THE HOLY ONE, BLESSED BE HE, PLANTED IN
THE ARK; "THEY SHALL FLOURISH IN THE COURTS OF OUR GOD," AS IT
IS WRITTEN, AND NOAH BEGOT, ETC.; "THEY SHALL STILL BRING FORTH
FRUIT IN OLD AGE" (IBID., 92:15) ALLUDES TO NOAH. "THEY SHALL BE
FULL OF SAP AND RICHNESS" (IBID.), AS IT IS WRITTEN, AND NOAH BE-
GOT SHEM, HAM, AND JAPHETH. AND NOAH WAS FIVE HUNDRED YEARS
OLD, ETC. (5:32).

The main point of this quotation is to examine the question of why
Noah fathered children at the age of five hundred, which was an elderly
age even in those days. Others gave birth, on average, between the ages
of 100 and 200. The *Tiferet Tzion* quotes the Zohar, which states that
Noah's Ark had the spiritual status of the *Mishkan* – the tabernacle,
and was considered as the house of God. The area in front of the Ark
was considered the חצר – *chatzer*, meaning the courtyard of the Ark.
Thus, the verse that is being quoted from Psalms applies appropriately
to Noah. "Planted in the house of the Lord [which was the Ark] and
he blossomed in the courtyard of the Lord [which is where he and his
family lived until the ark was completed]."

אָמַר רַבִּי יוּדָן, מַה טַּעַם, כָּל דּוֹרוֹת הוֹלִידוּ לְמֵאָה שָׁנִים וּלְמָאתַיִם שָׁנָה, וְזֶה הוֹלִיד לַחֲמֵשׁ
מֵאוֹת שָׁנָה, אֶלָּא אָמַר הַקָּדוֹשׁ בָּרוּךְ הוּא, אִם רְשָׁעִים הֵם, אֵין רְצוֹנִי שֶׁיֹּאבְדוּ בְּמַיִם, וְאִם
צַדִּיקִים הֵם אַטְרִיחַ עָלָיו וְיַעֲשֶׂה לָהֶם תֵּבוֹת הַרְבֵּה, וְכִיבֵּשׁ הַקָּדוֹשׁ בָּרוּךְ הוּא מַעְיָנוֹ, וְהוֹלִיד
לַחֲמֵשׁ מֵאוֹת שָׁנָה, רַבִּי נְחֶמְיָה בְּשֵׁם רַבִּי אֱלִיעֶזֶר בְּנוֹ שֶׁל רַבִּי יוֹסֵי הַגְּלִילִי, אָמַר, אֲפִלּוּ יֶפֶת
שֶׁהוּא הַגָּדוֹל, לִכְשֶׁיָּבוֹא הַמַּבּוּל, אֵינוֹ בֶן מֵאָה שָׁנָה, שֶׁרָאוּי לָעוֹנָשִׁים.

R. JUDAN OBSERVED: ALL HIS CONTEMPORARIES BEGOT AT A HUNDRED OR TWO HUNDRED YEARS, WHILE HE BEGOT AT FIVE HUNDRED YEARS! THE REASON, HOWEVER, IS THAT THE HOLY ONE, BLESSED BE HE, SAID: "IF THEY [NOAH'S SONS] ARE TO BE WICKED, I DO NOT DESIRE THEM TO PERISH IN THE FLOOD; WHILE IF THEY WILL BE RIGHTEOUS, AM I TO PUT HIM TO THE TROUBLE OF BUILDING MANY ARKS?" THEREFORE THE LORD STOPPED HIS FOUNTAIN AND HE BEGOT AT FIVE HUNDRED YEARS. R. NEHEMIAH SAID IN THE NAME OF R. ELIEZER THE SON OF R. JOSE THE GALILEAN: EVEN JAPHETH, WHO WAS THE ELDEST, WAS NOT AT THE TIME OF THE FLOOD A HUNDRED YEARS OLD SO AS TO BE LIABLE TO PUNISHMENT.

As to the question of why Noah's having children was delayed until he was five hundred years old, the *Midrash* answers that it was God's decision. The *Midrash* states that God was uncertain as to whether Noah's children would be evil or good. Here we have to understand that while God knows everything, He deliberately gives man the freedom of choice and allows this freedom to play itself out in extreme fashion. If, therefore, it turned out that the children would be evil, they would have to be destroyed in the Flood. God did not want that to happen. If they turned out to be good, more than one Ark would have to be prepared by Noah for them because they would be adding to the population. By having children at the age of five hundred, and in light of the fact that the Ark would be completed by the age of six hundred, Noah's oldest child, Japheth, would be under one hundred years old by the time of the Flood. Therefore, he, along with the rest of Noah's younger offspring, would not be subject to punishment according to the tradition of those days.

אָמַר רַבִּי חֲנִינָא, אֵין מִיתָה לֶעָתִיד לָבוֹא, אֶלָּא בְּעוֹבְדֵי כּוֹכָבִים בִּלְבָד, רַבִּי יְהוֹשֻׁעַ בֶּן לֵוִי אָמַר, לֹא בְיִשְׂרָאֵל וְלֹא בְעוֹבְדֵי כּוֹכָבִים, שֶׁנֶּאֱמַר (ישעיה כה, ח) 'וּמָחָה ה' אֱ-לֹהִים דִּמְעָה מֵעַל כָּל פָּנִים', מֶה עָבֵד לֵהּ רַבִּי חֲנִינָא 'מֵעַל כָּל פָּנִים', מֵעַל פְּנֵיהֶם שֶׁל יִשְׂרָאֵל, וְהָכְתִיב (שם סה, כ) 'כִּי הַנַּעַר בֶּן מֵאָה שָׁנָה יָמוּת', וְהָא מְסַיֵּיעַ לֵהּ לְרַבִּי חֲנִינָא, מֶה עָבֵד לֵהּ רַבִּי יְהוֹשֻׁעַ בֶּן לֵוִי, רְאוּיִ לְכָל עוֹנְשִׁים.

R. HANINA SAID: IN THE MESSIANIC AGE, THERE WILL BE DEATH AMONG NONE, SAVE THE CHILDREN OF NOAH. R. JOSHUA B. LEVI SAID: NEITHER AMONG ISRAEL NOR AMONG THE OTHER NATIONS, FOR IT IS WRITTEN, AND THE LORD GOD WILL WIPE AWAY TEARS FROM OFF ALL FACES (ISA. 25:8). HOW DOES R. HANINA EXPLAIN THIS? FROM OFF ALL FACES OF ISRAEL. YET SURELY IT IS WRITTEN, FOR THE YOUNGEST SHALL DIE A HUNDRED YEARS OLD (IBID., 65:20), WHICH SUPPORTS R. HANINA; HOW

THEN DOES R. JOSHUA EXPLAIN IT? THAT MEANS THAT HE WILL THEN BE
LIABLE TO PUNISHMENT.

(Note: Soncino's translation of "children of Noah" is "non-Israelite.")
According to the *Tiferet Tzion* on this *Midrash*, the difference in opinion between R. Hanina and R. Joshua centers around the following
question: Was the first man created in order to be mortal or immortal?
If he was created to be mortal, then at the end of days, only the idol-
worshiping inhabitants would be subject to death. Israel would not be
subject to death as a reward for their dedication to the commandments
of God's law. However, if man was created to be immortal, then there
would be no death for Israel or for the nations of the world. However,
they would all be subject to the day of judgment.

וְהָא כְתִיב (תהלים מט, טו) 'כַּצֹּאן לִשְׁאוֹל שַׁתּוּ, מָוֶת יִרְעֵם, וַיִּרְדּוּ בָם יְשָׁרִים', וְהָא מְסַיֵּיע לֵהּ
לְרַבִּי חֲנִינָא, מֶה עָבֵד לֵהּ רַבִּי יְהוֹשֻׁעַ בֶּן לֵוִי, לְפִי שֶׁבְּעוֹלָם הַזֶּה, פַּרְעֹה בִּשְׁעָתָן, סִיסְרָא בִּשְׁעָתָן,
סְנַחֲרִיב בִּשְׁעָתָן, אֲבָל לֶעָתִיד לָבוֹא, הַקָּדוֹשׁ בָּרוּךְ הוּא עוֹשֶׂה מַלְאַךְ הַמָּוֶת סְטַטְיוֹנַר שֶׁלָּהֶם,
הֲדָא הוּא דִכְתִיב, (שם שם, שם) 'וַיִּרְדּוּ בָם יְשָׁרִים לַבֹּקֶר, וְצוּרָם לְבַלּוֹת שְׁאוֹל מִזְּבֻל לוֹ', מְלַמֵּד,
שֶׁשְּׁאוֹל בָּלֶה, וְגוּפָן אֵינָה בָלֶה, וְכָל כָּךְ לָמָּה, עַל שֶׁפָּשְׁטוּ יְדֵיהֶם בִּזְבוּל, הֲדָא הוּא דִכְתִיב, (מ"א
ח, יג) 'בָּנֹה בָנִיתִי בֵּית זְבֻל לָךְ'.

BUT IT IS WRITTEN, LIKE SHEEP THEY ARE APPOINTED FOR THE
NETHER-WORLD; DEATH SHALL BE THEIR SHEPHERD (PS. 49:15), WHICH
SUPPORTS R. HANINA: HOW, THEN, DOES R. JOSHUA EXPLAIN IT? THUS:
WHEREAS IN THIS WORLD PHARAOH [WAS PUNISHED] IN HIS TIME AND
SISERA IN HIS TIME; IN THE MESSIANIC ERA, HE WILL APPOINT THE
ANGEL OF DEATH THEIR [SC. PHARAOH AND SISERA'S] OFFICER, AS IT
IS WRITTEN, AND THE UPRIGHT SHALL HAVE DOMINION OVER THEM IN
THE MORNING, AND THEIR FORM SHALL BE FOR THE WEARING AWAY
OF THE NETHER-WORLD ON ACCOUNT OF HIS HABITATION (IBID.): THIS
TEACHES THAT SHEOL [THE NETHER-WORLD] WILL BE DESTROYED, YET
THEIR BODIES WILL NOT BE DESTROYED. AND WHY SUCH SEVERITY?
"ON ACCOUNT OF HIS HABITATION," I.E., BECAUSE THEY STRETCHED
OUT THEIR HANDS AGAINST HIS HABITATION [SC. THE TEMPLE], AS IT
IS WRITTEN, I HAVE SURELY BUILT THEE A HOUSE OF HABITATION (I
KINGS 8:13).

The last section briefly describes the punishment meted out to those
responsible for the destruction of the Temple over the years. Their vil-
lainy will never be forgotten and they will be punished at the end of
days.

Seed Thoughts

The *Midrash* and the commentators are astonished at the fact that God seemed to have doubts whether the children of Noah would be wicked or good. But how could God have doubts? Does not God of all the world know everything? The answer is (and repeated many times throughout rabbinic literature) that God created this world in such a manner that man was given freedom. Of course, God knows everything, but He deliberately puts this knowledge aside so that the human being can be free. Whatever God's purpose in creating the world, the method He chose was to grant the human being the freedom not only to observe the commandments, but to reject them as well. As it says, הכל בידי שמים חוץ מיראת שמים, "everything is in the hand of God except for the fear of God" (*Brakhot* 33b). God does not interfere with man's choices. That is the beauty of the Creation story. It is also its challenge and terrible risk.

Even though God knows in advance whatever is going to happen, not only is that information not revealed to us, but it never will be. This is similar to a remarkable principle of physics in which Einstein introduced to us that if we could know the exact position and momentum of a particle at one given time, we would be able to calculate all events from that time and until the end of time. This gives us the idea that everything has a destiny. However, another physicist, Werner Heisenberg, backed by Neils Bohr, discovered that it is not possible to know such information. This is known as the Heisenberg Uncertainty Principle and is elaborately explained in most physics sources. Einstein used to say that God never plays with dice. What He planned, shall be. Bohr answered him by saying that he shouldn't tell God what to do. Anything can happen and can only be described with probabilities rather than certainties. Here, physics tells us that the future must be inscribed in the fabric of the universe, but it can never be completely revealed to us.

—

Additional Commentary

אם רשעים הם – *If they are wicked*

Even though the Holy One, Blessed be He, knows everything about the world from beginning to end, nevertheless, He does not reveal this knowledge to the heavenly court. As it is written in the Tractate *Nidah*, that the good person and the evil person are not listed so that the human being would be free to make choices in life, because God's knowledge does not lessen human choices. It continues that because the choice of past, present and future are equal to God, He is able to see everything from the beginning and also knows what will come at the end; however, if such knowledge were ever to be revealed, the human being would be forced to behave as God wanted him to behave. Therefore, when God speaks about the behavior of man, in the future, He uses the language of doubt, even though the Holy One, Blessed be He, knows everything clearly from beginning to end. (*Tiferet Tzion*)

This is Noah, who was planted in the house of God

As written in the previous *Midrash*, 'As a tree planted by riverlets of water,' for the Ark was a home that God commanded to be built, so it, therefore, was the house of God; as for the courtyard in front of the house, this is a symbol of the world outside the Ark. As for the fact that Noah had his children before they entered the Ark of the courtyard, planted near the Ark, who would eventually enter the Ark, which is the house of the Lord, that is the meaning of the verse that says, 'He will renew himself in old age,' referring to the fact that he fathered his children at the age of five hundred. That is also the meaning in the same verse, דשנים ורעננים יהיו, meaning that from his children, the entire world was populated. (Maharzu)

ג. 'וַיּוֹלֶד נֹחַ שְׁלֹשָׁה בָנִים, אֶת שֵׁם אֶת חָם וְאֶת יָפֶת' וַהֲלוֹא יֶפֶת הוּא הַגָּדוֹל, אֶלָּא, בַּתְּחִלָּה אַתָּה דוֹרֵשׁ שֶׁהָיָה צַדִּיק וְנוֹלַד כְּשֶׁהוּא מָהוּל, וְשֶׁיִּחֵד הַקָּדוֹשׁ בָּרוּךְ הוּא שְׁמוֹ עָלָיו, וְשֶׁאַבְרָהָם עָתִיד לָצֵאת מִמֶּנּוּ, שֶׁשִּׁמֵּשׁ בִּכְהֻנָּה גְדוֹלָה, וְשֶׁנִּבְנָה בֵּית הַמִּקְדָּשׁ בִּתְחוּמוֹ

3. SHEM, HAM AND JAPHETH. SURELY JAPHETH WAS THE ELDEST? [SHEM,
HOWEVER, IS WRITTEN] FIRST BECAUSE HE WAS [MORE] RIGHTEOUS
[THAN THE OTHERS]; ALSO, BECAUSE HE WAS BORN CIRCUMCISED, THE
HOLY ONE, BLESSED BE HE, SET HIS NAME PARTICULARLY UPON HIM;
[OTHER REASONS FOR HIS PRIORITY ARE THAT] ABRAHAM WAS TO ARISE
FROM HIM, HE WAS MINISTER IN THE HIGH PRIESTHOOD, AND BECAUSE
THE TEMPLE WOULD BE BUILT IN HIS TERRITORY.

The question that the *Midrash* raises is why, in the order of Noah's
children, Shem is always mentioned first, whereas, Japheth was the oldest. Six reasons are offered in this *Midrash* on why this is so. The general
principle is that the order is the order of importance and not the order
of chronology. Shem was righteous over and above the others. One of
the interpretations is that Shem was born circumcised. Why was this
not mentioned as the first of the six reasons, since it was the fact most
obvious at the beginning of Shem's life? Here, too, righteousness was
more important than chronology.

שִׁמְעוֹן בַּר חוּטָה אָמַר, שֶׁמִּנְיַן אוֹתִיּוֹתָיו, תָּלָה הַקָּדוֹשׁ בָּרוּךְ הוּא לַדּוֹרוֹת מִן הַמַּבּוּל וְעַד הַפְּלָגָה, שְׁלֹשׁ מֵאוֹת וְאַרְבָּעִים שָׁנָה.

SIMON THE SON OF HUTA SAID: [SHEM IS WRITTEN FIRST] BECAUSE
THE HOLY ONE, BLESSED BE HE, SUSPENDED [PUNISHMENT] FOR THE
GENERATIONS FROM THE FLOOD UNTIL THE DIVISON ACCORDING TO
THE NUMERICAL VALUE OF HIS NAME, VIZ. THREE HUNDRED AND FORTY
YEARS.

R. Shimeon b. Huta points out that the numerical value of the letters
in the name of Shem, 340, represents the years between the Flood and
the story of the Tower of Babel. The commentary of Mirkin details these

years very explicitly: "From the Flood until the death of Peleg, from which we get the Hebrew term דר הפלגה [*dor haflagah*], the generations of Peleg, which is used to describe the generation of the Tower of Babel, there were three hundred and forty years. This is how it is calculated: Two years from Shem to the birth of ארפכשד, thirty-five from ארפכשד to שלח, thirty years from שלח to the birth of עבר, thirty-four years from the birth of עבר to the birth of פלג, two hundred and thirty-nine years in which פלג lived. Thus, the total is three hundred and forty years. At the time of Peleg it was written that in his days, the earth was destroyed and it used the term נפלגה הארץ – *niflegah ha'aretz*. Since God calculated the years according to the numerical value of the name of Shem, this proves that he was, indeed, a very great tzaddik and because of him, the Holy One, Blessed be He, delayed the punishment of the Tower of Babel for three hundred and forty years.

Seed Thoughts

The question of the first born and the status seems to be a concern, not only in the *Midrash*, but in the Pentateuch and for many of the writers in the world of the Oral Law as well. The biblical rule is that the first born inherits a portion double the size of that of the other siblings. On the other hand, when we examine the stories of the patriarchs, we realize that all kinds of squabbles and quarrels emerge because of the question of the first born. It began with Cain and Abel. Cain was the eldest and killed his brother out of jealousy. Ishmael was Abraham's first born but was replaced by Isaac, the first born of Sarah (and not of Abraham). Jacob and Esau quarreled most of their lives about who was the first born and deserved the birthright. Joseph was the first born of Rachel and not of Jacob, but in the blessing he received far more credit than Reuben, who was Jacob's first born.

We can detect from these passages that the rabbis were uncomfortable with the status given to the first born. As we can see from the present *Midrash, it seems* that being righteous is more important than being first.

Additional Commentary

Is not Japheth the oldest?
One would have thought that it would have been best to begin the

various explanations with the fact that Shem was born circumcised, which was known from the time of his birth, and even before he had yet become righteous. Nevertheless, the answer is that we begin with the fact that he was righteous. (*Tiferet Tzion*)

PARASHAH TWENTY-SIX, *Midrash Four*

ד. (ו, א) 'וַיְהִי כִּי הֵחֵל הָאָדָם', אָמַר רַבִּי סִימוֹן, בִּשְׁלֹשָׁה מְקוֹמוֹת, נֶאֱמַר בַּלָּשׁוֹן הַזֶּה, לְשׁוֹן מֶרֶד, (בראשית ד, כו) 'אָז הוּחַל', 'וַיְהִי כִּי הֵחֵל', (שם י, ח) 'הוּא הֵחֵל לִהְיוֹת גִּבֹּר בָּאָרֶץ', אֲתִיבָן לֵהּ, וְהָכְתִיב (שם יא, ו) 'וְזֶה הַחִלָּם לַעֲשׂוֹת', אָמַר לָהֶם, קִיפַּח עַל רֹאשׁוֹ שֶׁל נִמְרֹד, וְאָמַר לָהֶם, זֶה, הִמְרִידָן עָלַי. 'לָרֹב עַל פְּנֵי הָאֲדָמָה', שֶׁהָיוּ שׁוֹפְכִים אֶת זַרְעָם עַל הָעֵצִים וְעַל הָאֲבָנִים, וּלְפִי שֶׁהָיוּ שְׁטוּפִים בִּזְנוּת, לְפִיכָךְ הִרְבָּה לָהֶם נְקֵבוֹת, הֲדָא הוּא דִכְתִיב, 'וַיְהִי כִּי הֵחֵל הָאָדָם וּבָנוֹת יֻלְּדוּ לָהֶם'.

4. AND IT CAME TO PASS WHEN MAN REBELLED, E.V. 'BEGAN' (GEN. 6:1). R. SIMON SAID: IN THREE PLACES THIS TERM IS USED IN THE SENSE OF REBELLION [AGAINST GOD]: THEN THEY REBELLED [HUCHAL] TO CALL UPON THE NAME OF THE LORD (IBID., 4:26); AND IT CAME TO PASS, WHEN MAN REBELLED; HE [NIMROD] REBELLED WHEN HE WAS A MIGHTY ONE IN THE EARTH (IBID., 10:8). AN OBJECTION WAS RAISED: BUT IT IS WRITTEN, AND THIS IS WHAT THEY HAVE REBELLED TO DO? (IBID., 11:6). HE REPLIED: [GOD] SMOTE NIMROD'S HEAD, EXCLAIMING, 'IT IS HE WHO HAS INCITED THEM TO REBEL AGAINST ME! TO MULTIPLY ON THE FACE OF THE EARTH.' THIS TEACHES THAT THEY SPILLED THEIR SEMEN UPON THE TREES AND STONES, AND BECAUSE THEY WERE STEEPED IN LUST, THE HOLY ONE, BLESSED BE HE, GAVE THEM MANY WOMEN, AS IT IS WRITTEN, AND IT CAME TO PASS, WHEN MAN BEGAN TO MULTIPLY . . . AND DAUGHTERS WERE BORN UNTO THEM.

The literal meaning of החל – *heichel* in our text is "beginning," as in, "Then they began to call upon the name of the Lord" (Gen. 4:26), which is mentioned in connection with the generation of Enosh. However, in each of the three cases where this word is used, the event led to rebellion, as the Midrash points out; therefore, it is translated here as "rebellion" instead. In the case of the generation of Enosh, where the word *heichel* is also used, their rebellion was that they used to worship idols and call them by the name of God. In that case, the rebellion was the sin of עבודת כוכבים – *avodat kokhavim*, meaning the worship of idols.

Our text, which is a precursor to the generation of Noah, states that men began (*heichel*) to multiply on the earth and took women regardless of whether they were permitted or prohibited to them. This was a sin of גלוי עריות – *gilui arayot*, meaning sexual immorality. Similarly, in connection with the third text above, "He began to be a mighty one in the earth," this refers to Nimrod, whose rebellion consisted of murder and pillage. This is the sin of the spilling of blood.

These were and are the three cardinal sins of Judaism. The question was then raised about another verse with the word *heichel*, which appears in Genesis 11:6: " . . . this is what they began to do." However, since this reference also concerns Nimrod, who was included in the third reference, this was not regarded as a separate category.

The explanation here seems to be that men engaged in immoral sexual behavior such as masturbation and other forms of inappropriate sexual activity, which is probably meant in the expression that their seed was spilled on trees and stones. The implication seems to be that this was not because men were intrinsically evil, but because not enough women were in existence to allow them to have a sexual life under normal or legitimate conditions. Therefore, "the Holy One Blessed Be He gave them many women" (ibid.), changing the numerical balance. Could this have been one of the reasons for polygamy in ancient times? It is an interesting source of speculation. Nevertheless, the conclusion of this verse seems to be that the addition of so many women on the earth does not seem to be a good thing. In the above text, the word *heichel* is interpreted not as a "beginning," but as in the expression, "they defiled that which is holy," namely the sexual behavior of the human being.

רַבִּי שִׁמְעוֹן בַּר אַמֵּי, יָלְדָה אִשְׁתּוֹ נְקֵבָה, חֲמָתֵהּ רַבִּי חִיָּא רַבָּה, אָמַר לֵהּ, הִתְחִיל הַקָּדוֹשׁ בָּרוּךְ הוּא לְבָרֶכְךָ, אָמַר לֵהּ מְנָא לָךְ הָא, אָמַר לֵהּ דִּכְתִיב, 'וַיְהִי כִּי הֵחֵל הָאָדָם לָרֹב, וְגוֹ'', עָלָה אֵצֶל אָבִיו, אָמַר לוֹ, שֶׁמַחֲךָ, הַבַּבְלִי, אָמַר לוֹ כֵן, וְכֵן אָמַר לִי, אָמַר לוֹ, אַף עַל פִּי כֵן, צֹרֶךְ לַיַּיִן וְצֹרֶךְ לַחֹמֶץ, צֹרֶךְ יַיִן יֹתֵר מִן הַחֹמֶץ, צֹרֶךְ לַחִטִּין וְצֹרֶךְ לַשְּׂעוֹרִים, צֹרֶךְ לַחִטִּין יוֹתֵר מִן הַשְּׂעוֹרִים

THE WIFE OF R. SIMEON B. RABBI GAVE BIRTH TO A DAUGHTER. WHEN R. HIYYA THE ELDER MET HIM, HE SAID TO HIM: 'THE HOLY ONE, BLESSED BE HE, HAS BEGUN TO BLESS YOU.' 'WHAT IS THE PROOF?' INQUIRED HE. 'BECAUSE IT IS WRITTEN, AND IT CAME TO PASS, WHEN MAN BEGAN TO MULTIPLY . . . AND DAUGHTERS WERE BORN UNTO THEM,' (GEN. 6:1) HE REPLIED. WHEN HE [R. SIMEON] WENT TO HIS FATHER, HE ASKED HIM, 'DID THE BABYLONIAN CONGRATULATE YOU?' 'YES,' HE ANSWERED, 'AND HE SAID THUS TO ME.' 'NEVERTHELESS,' HE [RABBI] OBSERVED, 'BOTH WINE AND VINEGAR ARE NEEDED, YET WINE IS MORE NEEDED THAN VINEGAR; BOTH WHEAT AND BARLEY ARE NEEDED, YET WHEAT IS MORE NEEDED THAN BARLEY.'

In this section we will notice a difference of opinion in the evaluation of the birth of sons as compared to daughters. When R. Simeon's wife gave birth to a daughter, R. Hiyya said that this was a great blessing. This is indicated by the verse that says when people multiplied, daughters were born. However, when R. Simeon went to visit his father, R. Yehudah the Prince, he was told that this was not necessarily a blessing. He used two parables to explain what he meant, that sons are better than daughters. The first is wine and vinegar. Both are needed, but wine is more important than vinegar. He went on to say that wheat and barley are both important, but wheat is more important than barley. Similarly, sons are more important than daughters.

מִשֶּׁהָאָדָם מַשִּׂיא אֶת בִּתּוֹ וּמוֹצִיא יְצִיאוֹתָיו, הוּא אוֹמֵר לָהּ, לֹא יְהִי לִיךְ מַחֲזוֹרִי לְהָכָא. רַבָּן גַּמְלִיאֵל, אַסֵּב בְּרַתֵּהּ, אֲמַרָה לֵהּ, אַבָּא צַלִּי עֲלַי, אֲמַר לָהּ לָא יְהִי לִיךְ מַחֲזוֹרִי לְהָכָא, יָלְדָה בֶן זָכָר, אֲמַרָה לֵהּ, אַבָּא, צַלִּי עֲלַי, אֲמַר לָהּ, לָא יִשְׁלֵה וַי מִפֻּמִּיךְ, אָמְרָה לוֹ, אַבָּא, שְׁתֵּי שִׂמְחוֹת שֶׁבָּאוּ לִי, אַתָּה מְקַלְלֵנִי, אֲמַר לָהּ, תַּרְתֵּיהֶן צְלָוָנֶן, מִן גּוֹ דְּאַתְּ הָוְיָא שְׁלָם בְּבֵיתֵךְ, לָא יְהִי לִיךְ מַחֲזוֹרִי לְהָכָא, וּמִן גּוֹ דְּהָוֵי בְּרִיךְ קַיָּם לָא יִשְׁלֵה וַי מִפֻּמִּיךְ וַי דְּלָא שָׁתֵי בְּרִי, וַי דְּלָא אָכַל בְּרִי, וַי דְּלָא אָזֵל בְּרִי לְבֵי כְנִשְׁתָּא.

WHEN A MAN GIVES HIS DAUGHTER IN MARRIAGE AND INCURS EXPENSE, HE SAYS TO HER, 'MAY YOU NEVER RETURN HITHER.' 'R. GAMLIEL GAVE HIS DAUGHTER IN MARRIAGE. 'FATHER,' SHE REQUESTED, 'PRAY FOR ME.' 'MAY YOU NEVER RETURN HITHER,' SAID HE TO HER. WHEN SHE GAVE BIRTH TO A SON SHE AGAIN BEGGED HIM, 'FATHER, GIVE ME YOUR BLESSING.' 'MAY "WOE" NEVER LEAVE YOUR MOUTH,' REPLIED HE. 'FATHER,' SHE EXCLAIMED, 'ON BOTH OCCASIONS OF MY REJOICING YOU HAVE CURSED ME!' 'BOTH WERE BLESSINGS,' HE REPLIED. 'LIVING AT PEACE IN YOUR HOME, YOU WILL NOT RETURN HERE, AND AS LONG AS YOUR SON LIVES, "WOE" WILL NOT LEAVE YOUR MOUTH; "WOE THAT MY SON HAS NOT EATEN," "WOE THAT HE HAS NOT DRUNK," "WOE THAT HE HAS NOT GONE TO SCHOOL."'

The *Midrash* continues the tendency of showering daughters with what we today would call left-handed compliments. Thus, a father's hope when he marries off his daughter is that she should never return to his home. This means, after a possible divorce. This is illustrated in the story told about R. Gamliel. His daughter, who was about to be married asked for his blessing and prayers. He answered, "Let us hope and pray that you never return to my home." When she gave birth to a son and asked for a blessing, he answered, "May 'Oy Vay' never part from your lips." The daughter said to him, "My dear father, I have come for your blessings and you gave me curses." "Not at all," replied her father. "I prayed that your marriage should be very happy, so that it should never end in divorce and force you to come back to live in my home. And as for my saying, 'Oy Vay, my children did not drink enough, eat enough or go to synagogue enough, should not leave your lips,' all these are wonderful forms of worries that I pray you should have."

—

Seed Thoughts

In studying *Midrash,* we have many examples of the fact that the sages reflected the moods and attitude of the environment and majority culture in which they lived. We saw this with many examples in the area of science where the *Midrash* accepts the science of their age, whereas we know in modern times that those facts were outlived and changed. Similarly, in our present *Midrash* we are dealing with attitudes toward men and women, referred to in this case as sons and daughters. Fashions change when it comes to these attitudes. Although, for generations, mothers generally preferred to have sons over daughters. This is not only a Jewish feeling, but something that can be seen in many cultures of nations that Jews have lived among. There are also people who feel this way in modern times. These views are gradually changing.

I have heard it said that when you educate a boy, you educate an individual. But when you educate a girl, you eventually educate a family. This is because in most home situations, the mother is the key to the family circle, its education and upbringing. Today, we would have to say that the Torah looks upon the men and women as being of equal worth. We have that beautiful line in Genesis that says, "Male and female created He them and He called their [plural] name Adam [one human being]." Men and women together share the highest qualities of being a human being.

—

Additional Commentary

When human beings began to multiply (A)

It says in the text that as human beings began to multiply on the earth, daughters were born unto them. (Gen. 6:1) The reason is that when God wishes to bless human beings that they should multiply, he provides them with women, because it is their responsibility to raise the children in a proper way. (*Tiferet Tzion*)

When human beings began to multiply (B)

In order for the *Midrash* to prove that sons are better than daughters, the interpretation is as follows: The great assets of a daughter are two-fold. For one thing, they raise children. Secondly, through them, the population increases. It is in this connection that the *Midrash* offers the two parables. The fact that the daughter is the one that raises children is acknowledged in the parable as vinegar. The difference between vinegar and wine is that wine, by itself, makes God and man rejoice, whereas vinegar is only of value when it is mixed with something else. That is the difference between sons and daughters. The sons on their own make God and man rejoice by virtue of learning Torah and their *avodah*, whereas in the case of daughters, their values are in their relationship to others, namely raising children. It is added to note that in this con-nection, the home of R. Judah the Prince, there were many servants to raise the children and therefore, daughters were not needed for this particular role. As for their need in terms of population, the parable of wheat and barley is looked upon. Wheat is an absolute need of the human body. But barley is only good when mixed with other things. That is the difference between sons and daughters; the daughters follow their husbands and take over their family name. All those born to the daughters are attributed to the fathers. (*Tiferet Tzion*)

ה. (ב) 'וַיִּרְאוּ בְנֵי הָאֱ־לֹהִים', רַבִּי שִׁמְעוֹן בֶּן יוֹחַאי קָרֵא לְהוֹן בְּנֵי דַיָּנַיָּא, רַבִּי שִׁמְעוֹן בֶּן יוֹחַאי
מְקַלֵּל לְכָל מַאן דְּקָרֵא לְהוֹן בְּנֵי אֱלָהַיָּא, תָּנֵי רַבִּי שִׁמְעוֹן בֶּן יוֹחַאי, כָּל פְּרָצָה שֶׁאֵינָהּ מִן
הַגְּדוֹלִים, אֵינָהּ פְּרָצָה, כְּמָרַיָּא גָּנְבוּ אֱלָהַיָּא, מַאן מוֹמֵי בֵהּ אוֹ מַאן מְקָרֵב.

5. THAT THE SONS OF GOD [BNEI ELOKIM] SAW THE DAUGHTERS OF MEN,
ETC. (6:2). R. SIMEON B.YOHAI CALLED THEM THE SONS OF NOBLES;
[FURTHERMORE,] R. SIMEON B. YOHAI CURSED ALL WHO CALLED THEM
THE SONS OF GOD. R. SIMEON B. YOHAI SAID: IF DEMORALIZATION DOES
NOT PROCEED FROM THE LEADERS, IT IS NOT REAL DEMORALIZATION.
R. AZARIAH SAID IN R. LEVI'S NAME: WHEN THE PRIESTS STEAL THEIR
GODS, BY WHAT CAN ONE SWEAR OR TO WHAT CAN ONE SACRIFICE?

The problem facing the *Midrash* is why the word *Elokim*, which implies a relationship to God, is used. The first response is that this word
is used very often in the Torah text to mean a judge or a judgment. (It
is pronounced as "elohim" and spelled without a capital "E" when used
in this context.) Therefore, here it refers to those who are in position of
leadership. On the other hand, R. Shimon b. Yohai cursed those who
used this terminology because it brings one very close to blasphemy
and taking the name of God in vain. The conclusion of this section is
that the real responsibility for the moral condition of a people depends
upon its leadership. The leadership of the generation of the Flood were
corrupt and immoral and they influenced all the people.

וְלָמָּה קוֹרֵא אוֹתָן, 'בְּנֵי הָאֱ־לֹהִים', רַבִּי חֲנִינָא וְרַבִּי שִׁמְעוֹן בֶּן לָקִישׁ, תַּרְוֵיהוֹן אָמְרִין, שֶׁהֶאֱרִיכוּ
יָמִים בְּלֹא צַעַר וּבְלֹא יִסּוּרִין, רַבִּי חָנָא בְּשֵׁם רַבִּי יוֹסֵי, אָמַר, כְּדֵי לַעֲמֹד עַל הַתְּקוּפוֹת וְעַל
הַחֶשְׁבּוֹנוֹת, רַבָּנָן אָמְרִין, כְּדֵי שֶׁיִּטְּלוּ שֶׁלָּהֶם, וְשֶׁל דּוֹרוֹת הַבָּאִים אַחֲרֵיהֶם.

NOW WHY ARE THEY CALLED THE SONS OF GOD? R. HANINA AND RESH
LAKISH SAID: BECAUSE THEY LIVED A LONG TIME WITHOUT TROUBLE
OR SUFFERING; R. HUNA SAID IN R. JOSE'S NAME: IT WAS IN ORDER THAT
MEN MIGHT UNDERSTAND [ASTRONOMICAL] CYCLES AND CALCULA-
TIONS. THE RABBIS SAID: IT WAS IN ORDER THAT THEY MIGHT RECEIVE

THEIR OWN PUNISHMENT AND THAT OF THE GENERATIONS THAT FOL-
LOWED THEM.

This is a most unusual interpretation. The real question is, why were
such leaders allowed to remain in power so many years before the Flood?
The answer is that they seem to have had some special knowledge of as-
tronomy, which requires many generations and many opportunities to
observe the constellations in order to extract meaningful information.
They were given the opportunity to live in luxury during this period, but
would ultimately receive their just punishment.

'כִּי טֹבֹת הֵנָּה' אָמַר רַבִּי יוּדָן, 'טֹבֹת' כְּתִיב, מְשֶׁהָיוּ מְטִיבִין אִשָּׁה לְבַעְלָהּ, הָיָה גָדוֹל נִכְנַס וּבוֹעֲלָהּ
תְּחִלָּה, הֲדָא הוּא דִכְתִיב 'כִּי טֹבֹת הֵנָּה', אֵלּוּ הַבְּתוּלוֹת, 'וַיִּקְחוּ לָהֶם נָשִׁים מִכֹּל אֲשֶׁר בָּחָרוּ'
אֵלּוּ נְשֵׁי אֲנָשִׁים, 'מִכֹּל אֲשֶׁר בָּחָרוּ', זֶה זָכָר וּבְהֵמָה, רַבִּי הוּנָא בְּשֵׁם רַבִּי, אָמַר, דּוֹר הַמַּבּוּל, לֹא
נִמּוֹחוּ מִן הָעוֹלָם, עַד שֶׁכָּתְבוּ גְמוֹמְסִיּוֹת לַזָּכָר וְלַבְּהֵמָה

THAT THEY WERE FAIR [TOVOT]. R. JUDAN SAID: ACTUALLY TOVAT IS
WRITTEN: WHEN A BRIDE WAS MADE BEAUTIFUL FOR HER HUSBAND, THE
CHIEF [OF THESE NOBLES] ENTERED AND ENJOYED HER FIRST. HENCE IT
IS WRITTEN, FOR THEY WERE FAIR, WHICH REFERS TO VIRGINS; "AND
THEY TOOK THEM WIVES" REFERS TO MARRIED WOMEN. "WHOMSOEVER
THEY CHOSE": THAT MEANS MALES AND BEASTS. R. HUNA SAID IN R.
JOSEPH'S NAME: THE GENERATION OF THE FLOOD WERE NOT BLOTTED
OUT FROM THE WORLD UNTIL THEY COMPOSED NUPTIAL SONGS IN
HONOR OF PEDERASTY AND BESTIALITY.

The word טבת – *tovot* in the Torah is written without the two appearances of the letter ו – *vav*. According to Aryeh Mirkin, the Torah usually
uses the expression *tovot mareh*, meaning the beauty of a person's appearance. Since it is not written that way, it must have a different meaning. According to the *Midrash Hamevo'ar* it really means הטבה – *hatavah*,
which means that they tried to make themselves look beautiful by arti-
ficial means. That generation was rife with sexual immorality, including
first-night sexual privileges of the dominant group whenever there was
a marriage, and sexual behavior without rules affecting married women,
same-sex relationships and even bestiality. All of this behavior was completely in the open and nothing was hidden.

אָמַר רַבִּי שְׂמְלַאי, בְּכָל מָקוֹם שֶׁאַתָּה מוֹצֵא זְנוּת, אַנְדְּרוֹלוֹמוֹסְיָאה בָּאָה לָעוֹלָם, וְהוֹרֶגֶת
טוֹבִים וְרָעִים, רַבִּי עֲזַרְיָה, וְרַבִּי יְהוּדָא בַּר רַבִּי סִימוֹן, בְּשֵׁם רַבִּי יְהוֹשֻׁעַ בֶּן לֵוִי, אָמַר, עַל הַכֹּל
הַקָּדוֹשׁ בָּרוּךְ הוּא מַאֲרִיךְ אַפּוֹ, חוּץ מִן הַזְּנוּת, מַאי טַעְמָא, 'וַיִּרְאוּ בְנֵי הָאֱ-לֹהִים וְגוֹ'', וּמָה
כְּתִיב בָּתְרֵהּ, (בראשית ו, ז) 'וַיֹּאמֶר ה' אֶמְחֶה אֶת הָאָדָם'. רַבִּי יְהוֹשֻׁעַ בַּר לֵוִי בְּשֵׁם רַבִּי פְּדָיָה, אָמַר,

כָּל אוֹתוֹ הַלַּיְלָה, הָיָה לוֹט מְבַקֵּשׁ רַחֲמִים עַל הַסְּדוֹמִיִּים, וְהָיוּ מְקַבְּלִין מִיָּדוֹ, כֵּיוָן שֶׁאָמְרוּ לוֹ,
(שם יט, ה) 'הוֹצִיאֵם אֵלֵינוּ וְנֵדְעָה אֹתָם', לְתַשְׁמִישׁ אָמְרוּ לוֹ, (שם שם, יב) 'עֹד מִי לְךָ פֹה', לְלַמֵּד
סֵנֵגוֹרְיָא עֲלֵיהֶם, מִכָּאן וְאֵילַךְ אֵין לְךָ לְלַמֵּד עֲלֵיהֶם סֵנֵגוֹרְיָא.

R. SAMILAI SAID: WHEREVER YOU FIND LUST, AN EPIDEMIC VISITS THE
WORLD THAT SLAYS BOTH GOOD AND BAD. R. AZARIAH AND R. JUDAH
B. R. SIMON IN R. JOSHUA'S NAME SAID: THE HOLY ONE, BLESSED BE HE,
IS LONG-SUFFERING FOR EVERYTHING SAVE IMMORALITY. WHAT IS THE
PROOF? THE SONS OF MEN SAW, ETC., WHICH IS FOLLOWED BY, AND THE
LORD SAID: I WILL BLOT OUT MAN (GEN. 6:7). R. JOSHUA B. LEVI SAID
IN BAR PADIAH'S NAME: THE WHOLE OF THAT NIGHT LOT PRAYED FOR
MERCY FOR THE SODOMITES. THEY [THE ANGELS] WOULD HAVE HEEDED
HIM, BUT AS SOON AS THEY [THE SODOMITES] DEMANDED, BRING THEM
OUT UNTO US, THAT WE MAY KNOW THEM (IBID., 19:5) – FOR INTER-
COURSE – THEY [THE ANGELS] SAID, 'HAST THOU HERE ANY BESIDES?
(IBID., 12). HITHERTO YOU MAY HAVE PLEADED IN THEIR DEFENSE, BUT
YOU ARE NO MORE PERMITTED TO DO SO.'

In God's eyes, sexual immorality is the worst of all forms of immorality.
The biblical proof is that the moment God perceived sexual immorality, He made His decision to remove the generation from the earth by
means of the Flood. However, even the terrible calamity of the Flood
does not necessarily change the moral challenges, because human
nature does not change. We then find the story of Lot praying for the
people of Sodom. However, the behavior of the people of Sodom was
almost a carbon copy of that of the generation of the Flood. Since they
demanded that the visitors, described as angels, be turned over to them
for sexual purposes.

Seed Thoughts I

The interpretation of Bnei Elokim, meaning sons of God, as bnei dayy-
ana, meaning sons of nobles, indicates that the leadership of a people,
a society or a civilization is responsible for its moral condition. The
leadership has the power to influence the majority, and usually does.
This is the great responsibility, not only of government, but of the social
behavior of every community. Everything depends upon leadership.
When Moses asked that special representatives be chosen to lead the
community, he gave a definition of the kind of people he wanted: וְאַתָּה
תֶחֱזֶה מִכָּל-הָעָם אַנְשֵׁי-חַיִל יִרְאֵי אֱלֹהִים אַנְשֵׁי אֱמֶת שֹׂנְאֵי בָע – "And you shall choose
out of all the people able men, such as fear God, men of truth, hating

unjust gain . . ." (Exodus 18:21). This is the ideal concept of leadership and it is a goal for which all societies should strive. Such leaders are not easily available. Even Moses had to compromise when he was choosing those who would represent the people. He described them as *anshei chayil*, able men, but he left out the other criteria, presumably because he found difficulty in finding personalities who lived up to that beautiful definition. The lesson is that the key to a just society is a just leadership.

⁓

Seed Thoughts II

The word "immorality" covers a wide area of human concerns and human delinquency. However, of all the forms of immorality, sexual immorality seems to be of the greatest concern to the biblical writers. Scripture never gives reasons for these values, but it is obvious that sexual immorality is the great concern. Rabbinic teaching also found a way of incorporating this value system into the personal behavior of individuals. Of all the commandments of Judaism, there are only three that can be described as cardinal sins, of which it has been said, "יהרג ואל יעבור – *yehareg ve'al ya'avor*", meaning allow yourself to be killed if necessary, but never transgress these prohibitions; they are (1) *avodat kokhavim* – idolatry, (2) *shfikhat damim* – murder and (3) *gilui arayot* – sexual immorality. In this definition, sexual immorality is equated with murder.

The rabbis believed that when sexual immorality becomes widespread, it becomes the beginning of the end of a society, culture or civilization. If we are sensitive to what is happening in the Western world and the various forms of sexual permissiveness, we have reason to be very much concerned. Let us hope that we can take a lesson from our past and raise ourselves to a higher level.

PARASHAH TWENTY-SIX, *Midrash Six*

ו. (ג) 'וַיֹּאמֶר ה'', לֹא יָדוֹן רוּחִי בָאָדָם' אָמַר רַבִּי יִשְׁמָעֵאל בְּרַבִּי יוֹסֵי, אֵינִי נוֹתֵן רוּחִי בָּהֶם,
בְּשָׁעָה שֶׁאֲנִי נוֹתֵן מַתַּן שְׂכָרָן שֶׁל צַדִּיקִים לֶעָתִיד לָבוֹא, שֶׁנֶּאֱמַר (יחזקאל לו, כז) 'וְאֶת רוּחִי אֶתֵּן
בְּקִרְבְּכֶם'.

6. AND THE LORD SAID: 'MY SPIRIT SHALL NOT ABIDE [YADON] IN MAN
FOREVER [LE'OLAM] (6:3). R. ISHMAEL INTERPRETED THIS: I WILL NOT
PUT MY SPIRIT IN THEM WHEN I GIVE THE RIGHTEOUS THEIR REWARD.

The sages were attracted to the word *yadon*, from the root meaning
"to judge." Their immediate reaction was that there was only one day
of judgment and this comes at the end of days. Therefore, the Divine
statement that He will not judge the human being again forever applies
not to this world, but to the end of days. In this first interpretation, it
means that the generation of the Flood will not be resurrected and will
not participate in the revival of the dead.

רַבִּי יַנַּאי וְרַבִּי שִׁמְעוֹן בֶּן לָקִישׁ, תַּרְוֵיהוֹן אָמְרִין, אֵין גֵּיהִנָּם לֶעָתִיד לָבוֹא, אֶלָּא, יוֹם הוּא שֶׁמְּלַהֵט
אֶת הָרְשָׁעִים, מַה טַּעַם, (מלאכי ג, יט) 'כִּי הִנֵּה יוֹם בָּא בֹּעֵר כַּתַּנּוּר, וְהָיוּ כָל זֵדִים וְכָל עֹשֵׂי רִשְׁעָה
קַשׁ, וְלִהַט אֹתָם הַיּוֹם הַבָּא', וְרַבָּנָן אָמְרִי, יֵשׁ גֵּיהִנָּם, שֶׁנֶּאֱמַר (ישעיה לא, ט) 'נְאֻם ה', אֲשֶׁר אוּר לוֹ
בְּצִיּוֹן וְתַנּוּר לוֹ בִּירוּשָׁלַםִ'. רַבִּי יְהוּדָה בַּר רַבִּי אִילְעַי אָמַר, לֹא יוֹם וְלֹא גֵּיהִנָּם, אֶלָּא, אֵשׁ הִיא
שֶׁתִּהְיֶה יוֹצֵאת מִגּוּפוֹ שֶׁל רָשָׁע וּמְלַהַטְתּוֹ, שֶׁנֶּאֱמַר (שם לג, יא) 'תַּהֲרוּ חֲשַׁשׁ, תֵּלְדוּ קַשׁ, רוּחֲכֶם
אֵשׁ תֹּאכַלְכֶם'. אָמַר רַבִּי יְהוּדָה בַּר אֶלְעַי, מַהוּ 'לֹא יָדוֹן רוּחִי', עוֹד אֵין הָרוּחוֹת הַלָּלוּ, נְדוֹנוֹת
לְפָנַי לְעוֹלָם.

R. JANNAI AND RESH LAKISH SAID: THERE IS NO OTHER GEHENNA [IN
THE FUTURE] SAVE A DAY WHICH WILL BURN UP THE WICKED. WHAT
IS THE PROOF? AND THE DAY THAT COMETH SHALL SET THEM ABLAZE
(MAL. 3:19). THE RABBIS MAINTAIN: THERE WILL BE A GEHENNA, FOR
IT SAYS, WHOSE FIRE IS IN ZION, AND HIS FURNACE IN JERUSALEM (ISA.
31:9). R. JUDAH B. R. ILAI SAID: THERE WILL BE NEITHER A DAY NOR A GE-
HENNA, BUT FIRE SHALL COME FORTH FROM THE BODY OF THE WICKED
HIMSELF AND BURN HIM UP. WHAT IS THE PROOF? YE CONCEIVE CHAFF,
YE SHALL BRING FORTH STUBBLE, YOUR BREATH IS A FIRE THAT SHALL
DEVOUR YOU (IBID., 33: 11). [R. JUDAH SAID: THE MEANING OF LO YADON,

I WILL NOT JUDGE, IS THAT THE SPIRITS OR SOULS OF THE GENERATION
OF THE FLOOD BE ELIGIBLE FOR JUDGMENT IN THE END OF DAYS. (THIS
SECTION IS NOT TRANSLATED BY THE SONCINO MIDRASH)]

The view here is that the generation of the Flood will be in *Gehinnom*
from the time that they perish, but not in a future world, when the day
of judgment will be rendered. One view is that there will be no *Gehinnom* and they will simply disappear; another view is that the *Gehinnom*
refers to one day of tremendous heat by the sun, which will burn all the
evildoers, including the generation of the Flood, and a final view is that
the fire will come from within their own bodies and destroy them.

רַבִּי הוּנָא בְּשֵׁם רַב אַחָא, אָמַר, בְּשָׁעָה שֶׁאֲנִי מַחֲזִיר הָרוּחַ לְנָדָנָהּ, אֵינִי מַחֲזִיר רוּחָן לְנָדְנֵיהֶן.
R. HUNA INTERPRETED IN R. AHA'S NAME: WHEN I RESTORE THE SPIRIT
TO ITS SHEATH [NADAN], I WILL NOT RESTORE THEIR SPIRIT TO THEIR
SHEATH.

Up to this point, the *Midrash* was dealing with the interpretation of
the meaning of *yadon*, referring to judgment. From this point on, the
rabbis deal with the word *ruach* and attempt to discover what its meaning is. The first observation is that at the end of days, the soul would
return to its space in the human body. That will not apply to the generation of the Flood.

אָמַר רַבִּי חִיָּא בַּר אַבָּא, אֵינִי מְמַלֵּא רוּחִי בָהֶן בְּשָׁעָה שֶׁאֲנִי מְמַלֵּא רוּחִי בָאָדָם, לְפִי שֶׁבָּעוֹלָם
הַזֶּה, הָרוּחַ הִיא נִבְזֶקֶת בְּאֶחָד מֵאֵבָרָיו, אֲבָל לֶעָתִיד לָבוֹא הִיא נִבְזֶקֶת בְּכָל הַגּוּף, הָדָא הוּא
דִכְתִיב, (יחזקאל ל, כו) 'וְאֶת רוּחִי אֶתֵּן בְּקִרְבְּכֶם'.
R. HIYYA B. ABBA INTERPRETED: I WILL NOT FILL THEM WITH MY SPIRIT
WHEN I FILL ALL OTHER MEN WITH MY SPIRIT, BECAUSE IN THIS WORLD
IT [MY SPIRIT] SPREADS ONLY THROUGH ONE OF [THE MAIN] LIMBS,
BUT IN THE FUTURE IT WILL SPREAD THROUGHOUT THE BODY, AS IT IS
WRITTEN, AND I WILL PUT MY SPIRIT WITHIN YOU (EZEK. 36: 27).

The only innovation of this addition is the fact that the soul will not
return to one particular space in the body, whether that would be the
heart or the brain, but that it would spread throughout the human body.

אָמַר רַבִּי יוּדָן בֶּן בְּתֵירָה, עוֹד אֵינִי דָן אֶת הַדִּין הַזֶּה, לְעוֹלָם, רַבִּי הוּנָא בְּשֵׁם רַבִּי יוֹסֵף, אָמַר,
(בראשית ח, כא) 'לֹא אֹסִף' (שם שם, שם) 'לֹא אֹסִף', לְסַגֵּי לְסַגֵּי, רַבָּנָן אָמְרֵי, 'לֹא אֹסִף' לִבְנֵי נֹחַ,
'לֹא אֹסִף' לַדּוֹרוֹת.

R. JUDAN B. BATHYRA INTERPRETED IT, NEVER [LE'OLAM] AGAIN WILL
I JUDGE [DAN] MAN WITH THIS JUDGMENT. R. HUNA COMMENTED IN R.
JOSEPH'S NAME: I WILL NOT AGAIN CURSE . . . I WILL NOT AGAIN SMITE
(GEN. 8: 21): [THE REPETITION IMPLIES], LET THIS SUFFICE. THE RABBIS
SAID: "I WILL NOT AGAIN CURSE" REFERS TO THE CHILDREN OF NOAH;
"I WILL NOT AGAIN SMITE," TO FUTURE GENERATIONS.

T he phrase that repeats 'I shall not continue' twice, refers in one case
to the generation of Noah and that this punishment will not be repeated.
The repetition in the verse refers to all other generations, who will not
suffer the same punishment.

אֲנִי אָמַרְתִּי שֶׁתְּהֵא רוּחִי, דָּנָה בָהֶן, וְהֵן לֹא בִקְשׁוּ, הֲרֵי אֲנִי מְשַׁגְּמָן בְּיִסּוּרִין. אֲנִי אָמַרְתִּי שֶׁתְּהֵא
רוּחִי דָנָה בָהֶן, וְהֵן לֹא כְחָשׁוּ, הֲרֵינִי מְשַׁגְּמָן אֵלּוּ בְאֵלּוּ, דַּאֲמַר רַבִּי אֶלְעָזָר, אֵין לְךָ, שֶׁהוּא
מִתְחַיֵּב בְּאָדָם הַזֶּה, אֶלָּא אָדָם כַּיּוֹצֵא בּוֹ

I INTENDED THAT MY SPIRIT SHOULD JUDGE [I.E., RULE AND GUIDE]
THEM, BUT THEY REFUSED; BEHOLD, THEREFORE, I WILL BEND THEM
[MESHAGGEMAN] THROUGH SUFFERING. I INTENDED THAT MY SPIRIT
SHOULD JUDGE THEM, BUT THEY REFUSED; BEHOLD, THEREFORE, I WILL
BEND THEM [BREAK THEIR POWER] THROUGH EACH OTHER, FOR R. EL-
EAZAR SAID: NONE BECOMES ANSWERABLE FOR [INJURY DONE TO] MAN
SAVE ANOTHER MAN LIKE HIMSELF.

M aharzu (the acronym by which R. Zeev Wolf Einhorin is known)
makes the following observation: The word *yadun* always refers to strict
justice because it refers to the day of judgment. The word *ruach* always
refers to *rachamim*, meaning mercy. It was the hope of the Holy One,
Blessed be He, that by returning His *ruach* to man, they would repent.
But it did not happen and therefore, He would punish them with suffering.

רַבִּי נָתָן אוֹמֵר, אֲפִלּוּ זְאֵב וְכָלֶב, רַבִּי הוּנָא בַּר גּוּרְיוֹן אָמַר, אֲפִלּוּ מַקֵּל אֲפִלּוּ רְצוּעָה, הֲדָא הוּא
דִכְתִיב, (ישעיה ט, ג) 'כִּי אֶת עֹל סֻבֳּלוֹ וְאֵת מַטֵּה שִׁכְמוֹ, שֵׁבֶט הַנֹּגֵשׂ בּוֹ, הַחִתֹּתָ כְּיוֹם מִדְיָן', כְּיוֹם
הַדִּין, אָמַר רַבִּי אַחָא, אַף אִילָנֵי סְרָק עֲתִידִין לִתֵּן דִּין וְחֶשְׁבּוֹן, רַבָּנָן אָמְרֵי מֵהָכָא, (דברים כ, יט)
'כִּי הָאָדָם עֵץ הַשָּׂדֶה' מָה הָאָדָם נוֹתֵן דִּין וְחֶשְׁבּוֹן, אַף עֵצִים נוֹתְנִין דִּין וְחֶשְׁבּוֹן.

R. NATHAN SAID: EVEN A DOG OR A WOLF IS ANSWERABLE. R. HUNA
B. GORION SAID: EVEN A STAFF OR A THONG IS ANSWERABLE, AS IT IS
WRITTEN, FOR THE YOKE OF HIS BURDEN . . . THOU HAST BROKEN AS IN
THE DAY OF MIDIAN (ISA. 9: 3). R. AHA SAID: EVEN BARREN TREES WILL
HAVE TO RENDER AN ACCOUNT. THE RABBIS PROVED IT FROM THE FOL-

LOWING: FOR THE TREE OF THE FIELD IS MAN (DEUT. 20: 19); JUST AS
MAN MUST RENDER AN ACCOUNT, SO MUST TREES RENDER AN ACCOUNT.

It was hoped that through mercy and compassion, they would help
each other. But that did not happen and they merited punishment. One
of the phrases, *lo osiph*, refers to man and his punishment and the other
refers to earth and its punishment. Various aspects of earth are personified in this Midrash, such as a dog, a wolf and the trees. All of them have
a responsibility.

אָמַר רַבִּי יְהוֹשֻׁעַ בַּר נְחֶמְיָה, אֵינִי דָן רוּחָן בְּעַצְמָן, שֶׁבָּשָׂר וָדָם הֵן, אֶלָּא, הֲרֵי אֲנִי מֵבִיא עֲלֵיהֶם
מְעוּט שָׁנִים שֶׁקְּצַבְתִּי עֲלֵיהֶם בָּעוֹלָם הַזֶּה, וְאַחַר כָּךְ, אֲנִי מְשַׁגְּמָן בְּיִסּוּרִין.

R. JOSHUA B. NEHEMIAH INTERPRETED: THEIR SPIRIT DOES NOT REA-
SON WITH ITSELF THAT THEY ARE BUT FLESH AND BLOOD; THEREFORE I
WILL REDUCE THEIR YEARS, AS I HAVE DETERMINED FOR THEM IN THIS
WORLD, AND THEN I WILL BEND THEM THROUGH SUFFERING.

אָמַר רַבִּי אַיְבוּ, מִי גָּרַם לָהֶם שֶׁיִּמְרְדוּ בִּי, לֹא עַל יְדֵי שֶׁלֹּא שִׁגַּמְתִּי אוֹתָם בְּיִסּוּרִין, הַדֶּלֶת הַזּוֹ מִי
מַעֲמִידוֹ, שְׁנָמָיו. אָמַר רַבִּי אֶלְעָזָר, בְּכָל מָקוֹם שֶׁאֵין דִּין יֵשׁ דִּין, רַב בֵּיבִי בְּרֵהּ דְּרַבִּי אַמִּי בְּשִׁטַּת
רַבִּי אֶלְעָזָר, 'לֹא יָדוֹן רוּחִי', אָמַר רַבִּי מֵאִיר, הֵן לֹא עָשׂוּ מִדַּת הַדִּין לְמַטָּה, אַף אֲנִי אֵינִי עוֹשֶׂה
מִדַּת הַדִּין לְמָעְלָה, הֲדָא הוּא דִכְתִיב, (איוב ד, כא) 'הֲלֹא נִסַּע יִתְרָם בָּם, יָמוּתוּ וְלֹא בְחָכְמָה'
בְּלֹא חָכְמַת הַתּוֹרָה, (שם שם, כ) 'מִבֹּקֶר לָעֶרֶב יֻכַּתּוּ מִבְּלִי מֵשִׂים לָנֶצַח יֹאבֵדוּ', וְאֵין 'מֵשִׂים',
אֶלָּא דִין, הֵיךְ מַה דְּאַתְּ אָמַר, (שמות כא, א) 'וְאֵלֶּה הַמִּשְׁפָּטִים אֲשֶׁר תָּשִׂים לִפְנֵיהֶם', אָמַר רַבִּי
יוֹסֵי הַגְּלִילִי, עוֹד אֵינִי דָן, מִדַּת הַדִּין כְּנֶגֶד מִדַּת רַחֲמִים, רַבִּי אוֹמֵר, 'וַיֹּאמֶר' דּוֹר הַמַּבּוּל לַה',
'לֹא יָדוֹן', אָמַר רַבִּי עֲקִיבָא, (תהלים י, יג) 'עַל מֶה נִאֵץ רָשָׁע אֱ-לֹהִים, אָמַר בְּלִבּוֹ לֹא תִדְרֹשׁ',
לֵית דִּין וְלֵית דַּיָּן, אֲבָל אִית דִּין וְאִית דַּיָּן. אָמַר רַבִּי חֲנִינָא בַּר פָּפָּא, אֲפִלּוּ נֹחַ, שֶׁנִּשְׁתַּיֵּר מֵהֶם,
לֹא שֶׁהָיָה כְדַי, אֶלָּא, שֶׁצָּפָה הַקָּדוֹשׁ בָּרוּךְ הוּא שֶׁמֹּשֶׁה עָתִיד לַעֲמֹד מִמֶּנּוּ, שֶׁנֶּאֱמַר 'בְּשַׁגַּם' זֶה
מֹשֶׁה, דְּחָשְׁבְּנֵהּ דְּדֵין הוּא חָשְׁבְּנֵהּ דְּדֵין, רַבָּנָן מַיְיתוּ לַהּ מֵהָכָא, 'וְהָיוּ יָמָיו מֵאָה וְעֶשְׂרִים שָׁנָה'
וּמֹשֶׁה חַי מֵאָה וְעֶשְׂרִים שָׁנָה.

R. AIBU INTERPRETED: WHAT WAS THE CAUSE THAT THEY REBELLED
AGAINST ME? WAS IT NOT BECAUSE I DID NOT BEND THEM THROUGH
SUFFERING? WHAT KEEPS A DOOR IN POSITION? ITS HINGES. R. ELEAZAR
SAID: WHEREVER THERE IS NO JUDGMENT [BELOW] THERE IS JUDGMENT
[ABOVE]. R. BIBI, THE SON OF R. AMMI, INTERPRETED, FOLLOWING R. EL-
EAZAR: IF THEY HAVE NOT JUDGED, THEN MY SPIRIT [WILL JUDGE MAN].
R. MEIR SAID: IF THEY DID NOT PERFORM JUDGMENT BELOW, AM I, TOO,
NOT TO PERFORM JUDGMENT ABOVE! THUS IT IS WRITTEN, IS NOT THEIR
TENT-CORD PLUCKED UP WITHIN THEM? THEY DIE, AND THAT WITHOUT
WISDOM (JOB 4: 21): I.E., THROUGH LACKING THE WISDOM OF THE TO-
RAH. BETWIXT MORNING AND EVENING THEY ARE SHATTERED; THEY
PERISH FOREVER WITHOUT ANY REGARDING [MESIM] IT (IBID., 20).

NOW 'MESIM' CAN ONLY REFER TO JUDGMENT, AS YOU READ, NOW THESE
ARE THE ORDINANCES [JUDGMENTS] WHICH THOU SHALT SET [TASIM]
BEFORE THEM (EX. 21:1). R. JOSE THE GALILEAN INTERPRETED: NO MORE
SHALL MY ATTRIBUTE OF JUSTICE BE SUPPRESSED [LIT. 'JUDGED'] BEFORE
MY ATTRIBUTE OF MERCY. RABBI INTERPRETED: AND THE GENERATION
OF THE FLOOD SAID, 'THE LORD WILL NOT JUDGE MY SPIRIT.' R. AKIBA
CITED: WHEREFORE DOTH THE WICKED CONDEMN GOD, AND SAY IN HIS
HEART, THOU WILT NOT REQUIRE (PS. 10:13), MEANING THAT THERE IS
NO JUDGMENT OR JUDGE? [IN TRUTH,] THERE IS JUDGMENT AND THERE
IS A JUDGE. R. HANINA B. PAPA SAID: EVEN NOAH WHO WAS LEFT OF
THEM WAS LEFT NOT BECAUSE HE MERITED IT, BUT BECAUSE THE HOLY
ONE, BLESSED BE HE, FORESAW THAT MOSES WAS DESTINED TO DESCEND
FROM HIM, 'BESHAGAM' AND 'MOSHE' [MOSES] BOTH HAVING THE SAME
NUMERICAL VALUE. THE RABBIS ADDUCED IT FROM THE FOLLOWING:
AND HIS DAYS SHALL BE A HUNDRED AND TWENTY YEARS.

The main point here is that there is a Judge, there is justice and there
is a judgment. What will not be accomplished in this world will be accomplished in the World to Come. The Holy One, Blessed be He, will
not allow any evil doing to escape its proper punishment. The *Midrash*
ends with a beautiful interpretation of God's relationship to Noah.
Noah was never an ideal person. There is even a debate as to the degree
of his righteousness. But God foresaw that one of his descendants will
be Moses, the leader of the Jewish people and the deliverer of God's
Torah. That gave Noah the authority and the prestige of the mission to
save the world.

—

Seed Thoughts I

The other day, I was watching a television program that featured psychics. A psychic is person who claims to have certain ways of foreseeing
the future and the ability to interpret events in the past of certain individuals. The panel also contained a person who disagreed vehemently
with them and maintained that the only thing that counts is to lead a
good life in this world. The things the psychics were talking about were
not even important. He was probably right. But that is not the way
people act. Human beings are extremely curious. They tend to want to
know everything that one can possibly know, not only about the future,
but their own immediate past.

When I listened to this panel, I thought of this *Midrash*. Our sages were not psychics, but had a tremendous desire to know as much as one could know. They sought not only the meaning of life, but the ultimate meaning of existence. They wanted to know as much as one could know, including information about the end of days, the resurrection of the dead, the nature of the reward to the righteous and the nature of the punishment to the wicked. As we have seen, their responses were not uniform and there was no consensus. The struggle for ultimate meaning will continue, but it seems doubtful that it will ever fully be resolved by man in this world. In the meantime, the best we can do is try to observe the Torah, try to lead a good life and leave everything else to the will of God.

Seed Thoughts II

The *Midrash* notes that Noah's character and achievement was less than perfect, but that God retained his leadership because God foresaw that Moses will be one of his descendants. The verse that it refers to is as follows, "And the Lord said: 'My spirit shall not abide in man for ever, for that he also is flesh; therefore shall his days be a hundred and twenty years' (Genesis 6:3)." This is related to the verse in Deuteronomy 34:4, giving the age of Moses as 120 years when he died. This is embellished by a most interesting גימטריא – *gimatria*, that בשגם – *beshagam*, (from בשגם הוא בשר – *beshagam hu basar*, "for that he is also flesh"),has the same numerical value asמשה – "*Moshe*," (Moses); both are 345.

Of course, only God is able to tell who our future generations will be. Nevertheless, there is a lesson that we can learn from this episode and I would describe it as tolerance. Let me tell you a little story. A young Jewish man and woman were about to be married. Since they were secularist, not only in behavior but in principle, they decided that they would not have the usual *chuppah*, but they would appear for a civil ceremony. One of their closest relatives, who was religious, was appalled by this decision and announced that under no circumstance would he attend this ceremony. A week before this ceremony, a close friend of the protestor paid a visit. He said, "If you stay away from the ceremony, what will you achieve? They already know your views and principles as you know theirs. On the other hand, if you are present at their ceremony, they would only be shocked and grateful and maybe something good will come of it."

Six months later, the relative and the friend met on the street. "There is something I have to tell you," said the friend. "Last Friday night I was at Josh's home [the groom] for dinner and guess what? He made *Kiddush*."

Said the relative, "I am amazed, he never did that in his entire life." The friend retorted, "I am not claiming that your attending the wedding produced the *Kiddush,* since I have no proof. What I am saying, however, is that sometimes, the most important motivation in life is tolerance."

—

Additional Commentary

Moses descended from Noah

Why was Noah chosen as the vehicle through whom to save the world? It is because it says, *"Beshagam hu basar."* This means that although he was just ordinary flesh and blood, there was going to be descended from him a person, who also shall be a person of flesh and blood, but nevertheless, as a result of his effort, he merited to become *ish Elokim,* a man of God. He lived to the age of 120, which is interpreted as meaning that not even one minute of that time was empty of the service of God. That is why all the 120 years are considered as years of dedication and because of his merit, he rescued Noah from the generation of the Flood.

Noah was a remnant of the generation of the Flood. Since he completed the redemption of the world, it could only have been Moses that rescued Noah. The question may be asked, why could not Abraham have been chosen to save Noah, since he was also a descendant? This is explained earlier in *Midrash Rabbah* 19:13 (according to the *Tiferet Tzion* numbering). It says as follows:

The fundamental place for the Heavenly presence is on Earth (בתחתונים – *batachtonim*). However, when Adam, the first man, sinned, the Heavenly presence ascended to the first Heaven. When Cain sinned, it ascended to the second Heaven. At the sin of the generation of Enoch, the presence ascended to the third Heaven. The sin of the generation of the Flood projected the Heavenly presence to the fourth Heaven. The Tower of Babel projected the *shekhina* to the fifth Heaven. The sinners of Sodom projected the presence to the sixth Heaven. Finally, as a result of the Egyptians during the time of Abraham, the Heavenly presence ascended to the seventh Heaven. [The Egyptians were guilty of sexual immorality.] By contrast of the above, seven righteous people emerged who changed the spiritual balance of the world. As a result of the life of Abraham, the Heavenly presence was lowered from the seventh to the sixth Heaven. The life of Isaac brought the presence from the sixth to the fifth. Jacob lowered it from the fifth to the fourth, the behavior of Levi brought it down from the fourth to the third. Kehot brought it from the third to the second. Amram brought it from the second to the first. Finally, when Moses appeared at the scene of history, the Heavenly presence returned to the world. It was at that moment that the redemption of Noah was completed and Moses made it be possible for Noah to be chosen to save the world. (*Tiferet Tzion*)

ז. (ד) 'הַנְּפִלִים הָיוּ בָאָרֶץ בַּיָּמִים הָהֵם', שִׁבְעָה שֵׁמוֹת נִקְרְאוּ לָהֶם, אֵימִים, רְפָאִים, גִּבּוֹרִים,
זַמְזֻמִּים, עֲנָקִים, עַוִּים, נְפִילִים. 'אֵימִים' שֶׁכָּל מִי שֶׁרָאָה אוֹתָן הָיְתָה אֵימָתָן נוֹפֶלֶת עָלָיו.
'רְפָאִים' שֶׁכָּל מִי שֶׁרָאָה אוֹתָן הָיָה לִבּוֹ רָפֶה כַּשַּׁעֲוָה. 'גִּבּוֹרִים', רַבִּי אַבָּא בַּר כַּהֲנָא בְּשֵׁם רַבִּי
יוֹחָנָן, אָמַר, מֹחַ קוּלִיתוֹ שֶׁל אֶחָד מֵהֶם הָיְתָה נִמְדֶּדֶת שְׁמוֹנֶה עֶשְׂרֵה אַמָּה. 'זַמְזֻמִּים' אָמַר
רַבִּי יוֹסֵי בַּר חֲנִינָא, מְנַטְרוֹמִין, מְגִיסְטֵי מִלְחָמָה. 'עֲנָקִים' רַבָּנָן וְרַבִּי אַחָא, רַבָּנָן אָמְרוּ, שֶׁהָיוּ
מַרְבִּים עֲנָקִים עַל גַּבֵּי עֲנָקִים, רַבִּי אַחָא אָמַר, שֶׁהָיוּ עוֹנְקִים גַּלְגַּל חַמָּה וְאוֹמְרִים, הוֹרֵד לָנוּ
גְשָׁמִים. 'עַוִּים' שֶׁצָּדוּ אֶת הָעוֹלָם, וְשֶׁהֻצְדוּ מִן הָעוֹלָם, שֶׁגָּרְמוּ לָעוֹלָם שֶׁיָּצוּד, הֵיךְ מַה דְּאַתְּ
אָמַר, (יחזקאל כא, לב) 'עַוָּה עַוָּה עַוָּה אֲשִׂימֶנָּה', אָמַר רַבִּי אֶלְעָזָר בְּרַבִּי שִׁמְעוֹן, שֶׁהָיוּ בְּקִיאִים
בַּעֲפָרוֹת, כַּנְּחָשִׁים, בַּגָּלִילָא צֻוְּחִין לְחִוְיָא אִוְיָא. 'נְפִילִים' שֶׁהִפִּילוּ אֶת הָעוֹלָם, וְשֶׁנָּפְלוּ מִן
הָעוֹלָם, וְשֶׁמִּלְּאוּ אֶת הָעוֹלָם נְפִלִים בַּזְנוּת שֶׁלָּהֶם.

7. THE NEPHILIM WERE IN THE EARTH . . . THE SAME WERE THE GIBBORIM
(E.V. 'MIGHTY MEN') THAT WERE OF OLD (6:4). THEY WERE CALLED
BY SEVEN NAMES: NEPHILIM, EMIM, REFAIM, GIBBORIM, ZAMZUMIM,
ANAKIM, AND AWIM. EMIM SIGNIFIES THAT THEIR DREAD (EMAH) FELL
UPON ALL; REFAIM, THAT ALL WHO SAW THEM MELTED (NIRPEH) LIKE
WAX. GIBBORIM: R. ABBA SAID IN R. JOHANAN'S NAME: THE MARROW
OF EACH ONE'S THIGH BONE WAS EIGHTEEN CUBITS LONG. ZAMZUMIM:
R. JOSE B. R. HANINA SAID: THEY WERE THE GREATEST OF ALL MASTERS
OF THE ARTS OF WAR. ANAKIM: THE RABBIS EXPLAINED IT AS SIGNIFY-
ING THAT THEY WERE LOADED WITH CHAINS (ANAKIM) UPON CHAINS.
R. AHA SAID: THEIR NECKS REACHED (ONKIM) THE GLOBE OF THE SUN
AND THEY DEMANDED, "SEND US DOWN RAIN." AWIM DENOTES THAT
THEY CAST THE WORLD INTO RUINS, WERE THEMSELVES DRIVEN FROM
THE WORLD IN RUIN, AND CAUSED THE WORLD TO BE RUINED, AS YOU
READ, A RUIN, A RUIN, A RUIN [AVAH, AVAH, AVAH] WILL I MAKE IT (EZEK.
21:32). R. ELEAZAR B. R. SIMEON SAID: "IT SIGNIFIES THAT THEY WERE
AS EXPERT IN THE KNOWLEDGE OF DIFFERENT KINDS OF EARTH AS A
SERPENT, FOR IN GALILEE A SERPENT IS CALLED AVIAH. NEPHILIM DE-
NOTES THAT THEY HURLED (HIPPILU) THE WORLD DOWN, THEMSELVES
FELL (NAFLU) FROM THE WORLD, AND FILLED THE WORLD WITH ABOR-
TIONS (NEPHILIM) THROUGH THEIR IMMORALITY.

The *Midrash* noticed that there are two verses that mean the same but
are separated from each other. The first verse said, "And the Lord said:
'My spirit shall not abide in man forever, for that he also is flesh; therefore shall his days be a hundred and twenty years'" (Genesis 6:3). The
second expression is similar in tone and reads, "And the Lord saw that
the wickedness of man was great in the earth, and that every imagination
of the thoughts of his heart was only evil continually" (Genesis 6:5).
These two expressions are separated by a description of the *nephilim*,
who are known by several names. Why was this done? The answer is
that the text is trying to mitigate the responsibility of the descendants
of Cain. They were not the only ones who were corrupt and immoral.
There were others, who had seven different names, who were just as
corrupt and just as immoral. That is what the text is trying to tell us.
(*Tiferet Tzion*)

'וְגַם אַחֲרֵי כֵן' יְהוּדָה בַּר רַבִּי אִמִּי אָמַר, אֲחָרָאֵי לָא יִלְפוּן מִן קַדְמָאֵי, דּוֹר הַמַּבּוּל לֹא לָקְחוּ
מוּסָר מִדּוֹר אֱנוֹשׁ, וְדוֹר הַפְּלָגָה, מִדּוֹר הַמַּבּוּל.

AND ALSO AFTER THAT. JUDAH B. RABBI COMMENTED: THE LATER
GENERATIONS WOULD NOT LEARN FROM THE EARLIER ONES, I.E., THE
GENERATION OF THE FLOOD FROM THAT OF ENOSH, AND THE GENERA-
TION OF THE DIVISION FROM THAT OF THE FLOOD.

Mirkin adds the following interesting observation. It is not only the
generation of Babel that did not learn from the generation of the Flood.
No generation appears willing to learn from the previous. All of us,
especially when young, are arrogant to feel that our answers are better.
This is something that we have to remember at all times.

'וְגַם אַחֲרֵי כֵן אֲשֶׁר יָבֹאוּ בְּנֵי הָאֱ-לֹהִים אֶל בְּנוֹת הָאָדָם', אָמַר רַבִּי בֶּרֶכְיָה, הָיְתָה אִשָּׁה יוֹצֵאת
בַּשּׁוּק, וְהָיְתָה רוֹאָה בָחוּר וּמִתְאַוָּה לוֹ, וְהָיְתָה הוֹלֶכֶת וּמְשַׁמֶּשֶׁת אֶת מִטָּתָהּ, וְהָיְתָה מַעֲמֶדֶת
בָּחוּר כַּיּוֹצֵא בּוֹ.

AND ALSO AFTER THAT, WHEN THE SONS OF GOD CAME IN UNTO THE
DAUGHTERS OF MEN. R. BEREKIAH SAID: A WOMAN WOULD GO OUT
INTO THE MARKETPLACE, SEE A YOUNG MAN, AND CONCEIVE A PASSION
FOR HIM, WHEREUPON SHE WOULD GO, COHABIT, AND GIVE BIRTH TO A
YOUNG MAN LIKE HIM.

This story demands an explanation. Let us begin with a biblical interpretation. The verse does not say, נולדו מהם – *noldu mehem*, born from
them, but says נולדו להם – *noldu lahem*, were born to them, namely, to

the women and their husbands. The claim is made that in some fashion, the child that was born looked like the young man for whom she had passion for at the market place. This is regarded in Talmudic literature as a serious sexual offense, which is very disturbing, because nowhere is a person charged with sexual sinfulness merely by the sinfulness of one's thought. Our tradition says that your deeds will bring you closer to God and your deeds will bring you farther away from God.

Aryeh Mirkin, in his commentary to this section in *Midrash Rabbah*, notes that stories like this are rampant in Greek mythology. Since we know that some of the Greek philosophers had a close relationship with the Jewish sages, this might explain how such a story might enter the *Midrash*.

'אַנְשֵׁי הַשֵּׁם' אָמַר רַבִּי אַחָא, (איוב ל, ח) 'בְּנֵי נָבָל, גַּם בְּנֵי בְלִי שֵׁם', וְאַתְּ אָמַרְתְּ, 'אַנְשֵׁי הַשֵּׁם', אֶלָּא, שֶׁהֵשִׂימוּ אֶת הָעוֹלָם, וְשֶׁהוּשְׁמוּ מִן הָעוֹלָם, וְשֶׁגָּרְמוּ לָעוֹלָם שֶׁיִּשּׁוֹם. רַבִּי לֵוִי בְּשֵׁם רַבִּי שְׁמוּאֵל בַּר נַחְמָן, אָמַר, אֲנָשִׁים שֶׁנִּתְפָּרְשׁוּ שְׁמוֹתָן לְמַעְלָן, דַּאֲמַר רַבִּי יְהוֹשֻׁעַ בֶּן לֵוִי, כָּל הַשֵּׁמוֹת הַלָּלוּ, לְשׁוֹן מַרְדּוּת הֵן, 'עִירָד', עוֹרְדָן אֲנִי מִן הָעוֹלָם, 'מְחוּיָאֵל', מוֹחָן אֲנִי מִן הָעוֹלָם, 'מְתוּשָׁאֵל', מַתִּישָׁן אֲנִי מִן הָעוֹלָם, מַה לִי לְלֶמֶךְ וּלְתוֹלְדוֹתָיו. אָמַר רַבִּי יוֹחָנָן, 'הֵמָּה הַגִּבֹּרִים אֲשֶׁר מֵעוֹלָם, אַנְשֵׁי הַשֵּׁם', וּמִי פֵּרֵשׁ מַעֲשֵׂיהֶן, אֱלִיפַז הַתֵּימָנִי, וּבִלְדַּד הַשּׁוּחִי, וְצוֹפַר הַנַּעֲמָתִי, רַבִּי אוֹמֵר, אִלּוּ לֹא בָא אִיּוֹב לָעוֹלָם אֶלָּא לְפָרֵשׁ לָנוּ מַעֲשֵׂה הַמַּבּוּל דַּיּוֹ. אָמַר רַבִּי חֲנִין, אִלּוּ לֹא בָא אֵלְיָהוּ אֶלָּא לְפָרֵשׁ לָנוּ מַעֲשֵׂה יְרִידַת הַגְּשָׁמִים דַּיּוֹ, דַּאֲמַר רַבִּי יוֹחָנָן, כָּל אוֹרָה שֶׁנֶּאֱמַר בָּאֱלִיָּהוּא, אֵינָהּ אֶלָּא בִּירִידַת גְּשָׁמִים, רַבִּי הוֹשַׁעְיָה רַבָּה אָמַר, אֵינָהּ אֶלָּא בְּמַתַּן תּוֹרָה, כְּמָה דְּאַתְּ אָמַר, (משלי ו, כג) 'כִּי נֵר מִצְוָה, וְתוֹרָה אוֹר'. רַבִּי אַחָא בְּשֵׁם רַבִּי יְהוֹשֻׁעַ בֶּן לֵוִי, אָמַר, קָשָׁה הִיא הַמַּחֲלֹקֶת כְּדוֹר הַמַּבּוּל, נֶאֱמַר כָּאן, 'אַנְשֵׁי הַשֵּׁם', וְנֶאֱמַר לְהַלָּן, (במדבר טז, ב) 'קְרִאֵי מוֹעֵד אַנְשֵׁי שֵׁם', מָה 'אַנְשֵׁי הַשֵּׁם' שֶׁנֶּאֱמַר לְהַלָּן מַחֲלֹקֶת, אַף 'אַנְשֵׁי שֵׁם', שֶׁנֶּאֱמַר כָּאן מַחֲלֹקֶת.

THE MEN OF RENOWN ["HASHEM"]. R. AHA QUOTED: THEY ARE THE CHILDREN OF CHURLS, YEA, CHILDREN OF IGNOBLE MEN – BELI SHEM (JOB 30: 8), YET YOU SAY THAT THEY WERE MEN OF RENOWN! BUT IT MEANS THAT THEY LAID THE WORLD DESOLATE (HESHIMU), WERE DRIVEN IN DESOLATION FROM THE WORLD AND CAUSED THE WORLD TO BE MADE DESOLATE. R. LEVI EXPLAINED IN THE NAME OF R. SAMUEL B. NAHMAN: IT MEANS THE MEN WHOSE NAMES ARE SPECIFIED ABOVE, FOR R. JOSHUA B. LEVI SAID: ALL THESE NAMES SIGNIFY CHASTENING: IRAD: I SHALL DRIVE THEM (ORDAN) OUT OF THE WORLD; MEHUJAEL: I SHALL WIPE THEM (MOHAN) OUT OF THE WORLD; METHUSHAEL: I SHALL WEAR THEM OUT (MATISHAN) FROM THE WORLD: WHAT HAVE I TO DO WITH LAMECH AND HIS DESCENDANTS? R. JOHANAN INTERPRETED: THE SAME WERE THE MIGHTY MEN THAT WERE OF OLD, THE MEN OF NAME: AND WHO ENUMERATES THEIR DEEDS? THE MEN ENUMERATED BY NAME, VIZ. ELIPHAZ THE TEMANITE, BILDAD THE SHUHITE, AND ZOPHAR THE NAAMATHITE. FOR RABBI SAID: HAD JOB COME FOR NO OTHER PURPOSE

BUT TO ENUMERATE FOR US THE DEEDS OF THE GENERATION OF THE
FLOOD, IT WOULD HAVE SUFFICED HIM. R. HANAN SAID: HAD ELIHU
COME FOR NO OTHER PURPOSE BUT TO DESCRIBE TO US THE ACTION OF
THE RAIN-FALL, IT WOULD HAVE SUFFICED HIM. FOR R. JOHANAN SAID:
EVERY TIME ORAH (LIGHT) IS STATED IN CONNECTION WITH ELIHU,
IT REFERS TO THE DESCENT OF RAIN. R. HOSHAYA THE ELDER SAID: IT
REFERS TO NOUGHT ELSE BUT REVELATION. R. AHA SAID: DISSENSION IS
AS GREAT AN EVIL AS THE GENERATION OF THE FLOOD: IT SAYS HERE,
MEN OF RENOWN, WHILST ELSEWHERE IT SAYS, THEY WERE PRINCES
OF THE CONGREGATION, THE ELECT MEN OF THE ASSEMBLY, MEN OF
RENOWN (NUM. 16: 2).

The *Midrash* is concerned with the expression *anshei hashem,* notable
men. How could they be notable when the generation can be so corrupt and immoral? Several explanations are offered. The first is that the
word *shem* should not be translated as "name," but as coming from the
expression שממה – *shemamah,* meaning desolation or destruction. All
the names quoted had this kind of meaning. The second interpretation
is that *anshei hashem* refers to the friends of Job who, in the Book of
Job, came to comfort him from his bereavement and losses. They were
Eliphaz, Elihu, Bildad and Tzophar. The Book of Job contains many
references and many interpretations of the Flood and its generation.

According to Aryeh Mirkin, there is a connection between the Book
of Job and our text in the from of a גזרה שוה – *gzeirah shavah,* which means
a similarity in expression. In our text we have the expression ויבואו בני
אלוהים – *vayavo'u bnei Elokim,* "and the sons of God came." In the Book
of Job (1:6), we have the expression, ויראו בני אלוהים – *vayiru bnei Elokim,*
"and the sons of God saw." The third interpretation of *anshei hashem*
connects it to the story of Korach and the theme of *machloket,* which
means controversy or dissension. The *Midrash* asserts that controversy
was the bane of social existence during the time of the Flood and one of
the causes of its destruction.

—

Seed Thoughts

The theme of controversy is a difficult and serious one. People have a
right to have differences of opinion and to fight for their views. On the
other hand, there are issues that cannot always be resolved and have
to be tolerated. How do we know the differences between the two?
Probably the best treatment of this subject is found in the Ethics of the

Fathers (5:20): "Any argument that is for the sake of Heaven will have a constructive outcome; but one that is not for the sake of Heaven will not have a constructive outcome."

The *Mishnah* then goes on to give their example of a controversy for the sake of Heaven as the ones between the followers of Hillel and those of Shammai. They disagreed with each other on many issues. In most cases, the law follows Hillel and in some, the law follows Shammai. Both sides always respected the law and each other. They honored each other and intermarried with each other. As for the controversy that is not for the sake of Heaven, the example given is that of Korach in his relation to Moses. The goal of Korach was not principle, but power. He wanted the status and the authority of Moses. It was for this that he was punished.

The argument in the *Mishnah* is beautifully stated. The problem is that the human being does not always act in this spirit. They all too often seem to think that their own opinion is for the sake of Heaven and that the opinion of their opponents are strictly for power and not for the sake of Heaven. How to sort out the authenticity of these claims is one of the great challenges of the ethical life.

⁓

Additional Commentary

The meaning of עווים – avim

There is a word like that in the text of Ezekiel where the meaning is desolation. It is also said about this people that they specialized in their knowledge of the earth like serpents. They knew what was the right place for planting, the right place for seeding and the best place for fruit. The serpent was told that he would eat earth his entire life. But not all earth is edible and a serpent is forced to know the difference. It so happens that in the Galilee, one of the names for a serpent is עיוויא – *ivaiya'a*, which is probably the source of the name עווים. (Aryeh Mirkin)

The men of renown

In connection with the expression אנשי השם – *anshei hashem*, the men of renown, the *Midrash* makes reference to the friends of Job who came to comfort him the time of his distress. They were Eliphaz HaTeimani, Bildad HaShuchi and Tzophar HaNa'amati. In the process of comforting him, they criticized him, argued and debated with him and expressed remarkable insights, many aspects into nature and human nature, all of which are included in the Book of Job. One of the special interpretations from which all of us have benefited is the special interpretation of the generation of the Flood and the specific nature of their evil doings. It was in this connection that Rabbi said that if the Book of Job had only offered us interpretations on the details of the Flood, it would have been worthy to include it in the biblical canon. As a matter of fact, many *midrashim* in this volume are based on interpretations by the friends of Job. In addition, another friend of Job's, Elihu, was responsible for interpreting the various rains in connection with the Flood and other phenomena. (*Midrash HaMevo'ar*)

א. (ו, ה) 'וַיַּרְא ה' כִּי רַבָּה רָעַת הָאָדָם', כְּתִיב, (קהלת ב, כא) 'כִּי יֵשׁ אָדָם שֶׁעֲמָלוֹ בְּחָכְמָה וּבְדַעַת וּבְכִשְׁרוֹן

1. AND THE LORD SAW THAT THE WICKEDNESS OF THE MAN WAS GREAT
IN THE EARTH, AND THAT EVERY IMAGINATION OF THE THOUGHTS OF
HIS HEART WAS ONLY EVIL ALL DAY (6:5). IT IS WRITTEN, FOR THERE IS
A MAN WHOSE LABOR IS WITH WISDOM, ETC. (ECCL. 2:21).

The *Midrash* is slightly astonished that the text should say that God
suddenly discovered that there was wickedness in the earth. After all,
did it not say in the previous verse that men took wives, some of whom
were already married? What evil can be greater than this? That answer
is not that God suddenly beheld a new development; it is that God has
given man free will in ethics and morality. What God wanted to discover was the reason why human beings were behaving in this manner.
(*Tiferet Tzion*)

אָמַר רַבִּי יוּדָן, גָּדוֹל כֹּחָן שֶׁל נְבִיאִים שֶׁמְּדַמִּין צוּרָה לְיוֹצְרָהּ, שֶׁנֶּאֱמַר (דניאל ח, טז) 'וָאֶשְׁמַע קוֹל
אָדָם בֵּין אוּלַי', אָמַר רַבִּי יְהוּדָה בַּר סִימוֹן, אִית לָן קְרָיָא אוֹחֲרָן דִּמְחַוַּר יַתֵּר מִן דֵּין, שֶׁנֶּאֱמַר
(יחזקאל א, כו) 'וְעַל דְּמוּת הַכִּסֵּא דְּמוּת כְּמַרְאֵה אָדָם עָלָיו מִלְמָעְלָה', 'שֶׁעֲמָלוֹ בְּחָכְמָה', שֶׁנֶּאֱמַר
(משלי ג, יט) 'ה', בְּחָכְמָה יָסַד אָרֶץ', 'וּבְדַעַת', שֶׁנֶּאֱמַר (שם שם, כ) 'בְּדַעְתּוֹ תְּהוֹמוֹת נִבְקָעוּ'.
'וּבְכִשְׁרוֹן'

R. JUDAN SAID: GREAT IS THE POWER OF THE PROPHETS, WHO COMPARE
THAT WHICH IS CREATED TO ITS CREATOR, AS IT IS WRITTEN, AND I
HEARD THE VOICE OF A MAN BETWEEN THE BANKS OF THE ULAI, ETC.
(DAN. 8:16). R. JUDAH B. R. SIMON SAID: WE HAVE OTHER VERSES WHICH
DISPLAY THIS MORE CLEARLY THAN THIS ONE: AND UPON THE LIKENESS
OF THE THRONE WAS A LIKENESS AS THE APPEARANCE OF A MAN UPON
IT ABOVE (EZEK. 1:26). "WITH WISDOM," AS IT IS WRITTEN, THE LORD BY
WISDOM FOUNDED THE EARTH (PROV. 3:19); "AND WITH KNOWLEDGE"
(ECCL. LOC. CIT.), AS IT IS WRITTEN, BY HIS KNOWLEDGE THE DEPTHS
WERE BROKEN UP (PROV. 3: 20). "AND WITH SKILL" (ECCL. LOC. CIT.):

$\rm T$ he *Midrash* then proceeds to respond to this problem in a series of steps. It acknowledges at first that the prophets had special privileges in relationship to the Holy One, Blessed be He. They were allowed to describe God by means of allegories and parables. Thus, they would make statements about man by reference to God – the created in relationship to its Creator; for example, that man was created in the image of God. But it works in reverse also. God is sometimes described in terms which are more related to humans; for instance, the verse in Daniel, when he heard the voice of God as a human voice, or, more dramatically, from Ezekiel, when the presence of God seemed to be apprehended in the figure of a man. Sometimes, these relationships, which attempt to identify the created with its Creator, can have very negative consequences.

רַבִּי בֶּרֶכְיָה בְּשֵׁם רַבִּי יְהוּדָה בַּר סִימוֹן, לֹא בְעָמָל וְלֹא בִיגִיעָה בָּרָא הַקָּדוֹשׁ בָּרוּךְ הוּא אֶת
עוֹלָמוֹ, אֶלָּא, (תהלים לג, ו) 'בִּדְבַר ה' שָׁמַיִם נַעֲשׂוּ', 'בִּדְבַר ה'' וּכְבָר שָׁמַיִם נַעֲשׂוּ, (קהלת שם, שם)
'וּלְאָדָם שֶׁלֹּא עָמַל בּוֹ יִתְּנֶנּוּ חֶלְקוֹ' זֶה דּוֹר הַמַּבּוּל, (שם שם, שם) 'גַּם זֶה הֶבֶל וְרָעָה רַבָּה', 'וַיַּרְא
ה' כִּי רַבָּה רָעַת הָאָדָם בָּאָרֶץ'.

R. BEREKIAH SAID IN THE NAME OF R. JUDAH B. R. SIMON: NOT WITH LA-
BOR OR TOIL DID THE HOLY ONE, BLESSED BE HE, CREATE THE WORLD,
BUT "BY THE WORD OF THE LORD" (PS. 33: 6), AND STRAIGHTWAY, THE
HEAVENS HAVE BEEN MADE (IBID.). YET TO A MAN THAT HATH NOT
LABORED THEREIN SHALL HE LEAVE IT FOR HIS PORTION (ECCL. 2:21):
THAT REFERS TO THE GENERATION OF THE FLOOD. THIS ALSO IS RARITY
AND A GREAT EVIL (IBID.): THUS IT IS WRITTEN, AND THE LORD SAW
THAT THE WICKEDNESS OF THE MAN WAS GREAT.

$\rm R.$ Judah makes the point, which was elaborated upon in earlier *midrashim,* that God created this universe without any real effort or labor on His part, but simply on His word. However, when human beings tried to do the same or pretend that they could do the same, the result was catastrophic. And so we have the *midrash* saying that the description of the human being who does not really work and receives everything without effort, applies in a very special way to the generation of the Flood. This was the reason for their catastrophe. That is the reason it says, "And God beheld that there was wickedness on the part of man." The reference to this is that the human being was idle and idleness ultimately contributes to delinquent behavior.

Seed Thoughts

There is a beautiful saying, that a human being needs three things for a fulfilled life: Something to do, someone to love, and something to live for. All three of these goals are of maximum importance. But it would also have to be said that without something to do, the other goals in life would be very much affected. It was said of the generation of the Flood that they would seed for one season and it would last for forty years. They were privileged to experience four to five generations before dying (*Midrash Tanhuma*). We might think that such privileges and such an easy lifestyle would be a good thing. But its consequences were disastrous and always are. Based on the reasoning of the Book of Ecclesiastes, the *Midrash* explains what had happened to the generation of the Flood and what made them behave as they did, the subject of idleness is tremendously important. Its importance goes beyond the generation of the Flood because it can be applied to the many problems of modern life. People resort to drugs when they have nothing else to do. People resort to crime when they have no work and no income and no vision of a future that might be better for them. This does not apply merely to young people. Having something to do is indispensable. Many people who have retired from their professions and business responsibilities thinking that relaxation would be the best for them, have discovered to their chagrin that without something significant to do, even retirement can have its share of misery. We would be a much better society if a good proportion of the energies of governments, education and social scientists would be concentrated on the goal of creating something to do for every individual in our society.

⁓

Additional Commentary

The prophets

The prophets were given permission that was not given to anyone else – namely, to describe God with physical expressions that were also used to describe man. The prophets used allegory and symbolism as a way not to have to describe God in too much detail. The Torah tell us that God has no image (Deut. 4:15) but the one place where you do find attempts to describe God as an image is found in the prophets. However, this is only done by them to give us a concept or a description of God, Who in fact has no human description. They used human concepts and adjectives to describe God, only so that we may be able to understand them. However, only the prophets are allowed to do this. We ordinary human beings do not have this right. (Mirkin)

PARASHAH TWENTY-SEVEN, *Midrash Two*

ב. דָּבָר אַחֵר, 'וַיַּרְא ה' כִּי רַבָּה רָעַת הָאָדָם בָּאָרֶץ', כְּתִיב, (קהלת ב, כג) 'כִּי כָל יָמָיו מַכְאוֹבִים,
וָכַעַס עִנְיָנוֹ, גַּם בַּלַּיְלָה לֹא שָׁכַב לִבּוֹ, גַּם זֶה הֶבֶל הוּא', 'כִּי כָל יָמָיו מַכְאוֹבִים' זֶה דּוֹר אֱנוֹשׁ וְדוֹר
הַמַּבּוּל, שֶׁהָיוּ מַכְאִיבִים לְהַקָּדוֹשׁ בָּרוּךְ הוּא בְּמַעֲשֵׂיהֶן הָרָעִים, 'וָכַעַס עִנְיָנוֹ' שֶׁהָיוּ מַכְעִיסִים
לְהַקָּדוֹשׁ בָּרוּךְ הוּא בְּמַעֲשֵׂיהֶן הָרָעִים, 'גַּם בַּלַּיְלָה לֹא שָׁכַב לִבּוֹ' מִן הָעֲבֵרוֹת, וּמִנַּיִן אַף בַּיּוֹם,
תַּלְמוּד לוֹמַר, (בראשית ו, ה) 'וְכָל יֵצֶר מַחְשְׁבֹת לִבּוֹ רַק רַע כָּל הַיּוֹם'.

A DIFFERENT INTERPRETATION, AND THE LORD SAW THAT THE WICKED-
NESS OF THE MAN WAS GREAT IN THE EARTH. AS IT IS WRITTEN FOR
ALL HIS DAYS ARE PAINS, AND HIS LABOR GRIEF; EVEN IN THE NIGHT
HIS HEART DOES NOT REST. THIS ALSO IS VANITY (ECCLESIASTES 2:23).
WITH REFERENCE TO THE VERSE FOR ALL THE DAYS ARE PAINS, THIS
REFERS TO THE GENERATION OF ENOCH AND THE GENERATION OF THE
FLOOD, WHO SADDENED THE HOLY ONE, BLESSED BE HE, BY VIRTUE
OF THEIR EVIL DEEDS. AS FOR THE EXPRESSION AND HIS LABOR GRIEF
(VEXATION), IT MEANS THAT THEY WERE ANGERING THE HOLY ONE,
BLESSED BE HE, BY THEIR TERRIBLE DEEDS. THE EXPRESSION, EVEN IN
THE NIGHT HIS HEART DOES NOT REST, IT MEANS THAT MAN DID NOT
REST FROM SIN. HOW DO WE KNOW THAT THIS INCLUDES THE DAY? BE-
CAUSE OF THE VERSE WAS ONLY EVIL ALL DAY (GENESIS 6:5).

There is no way in which the verse, "All the days were marked by
pain," could refer to the generation of either Enoch or the Flood. This is
because they lived in relative prosperity and an easy type of living as is
indicated in earlier *midrashim*. It could only refer to God, Who is sensitive to their moral laxity and evil ways, which marked their lives. This is
what was meant in saying that God saw how prevalent evil was and that
He understood the reasons for it, as indicated in earlier *midrashim*.

דָּבָר אַחֵר, 'גַּם בַּלַּיְלָה לֹא שָׁכַב לִבּוֹ', זֶה הַקָּדוֹשׁ בָּרוּךְ הוּא, מִלְּהָבִיא עֲלֵיהֶם פֻּרְעָנִיּוֹת בַּיּוֹם
וּפֻרְעָנִיּוֹת בַּלַּיְלָה, דִּכְתִיב (שם ז, כג) 'וַיִּמַח אֶת כָּל הַיְקוּם'. דָּבָר אַחֵר, 'כִּי כָל יָמָיו מַכְאוֹבִים',
אֵלּוּ סְדוֹמִיִּים, שֶׁהָיוּ מַכְאִיבִים לְהַקָּדוֹשׁ בָּרוּךְ הוּא בְּמַעֲשֵׂיהֶם הָרָעִים, 'וָכַעַס עִנְיָנוֹ' שֶׁהָיוּ
מַכְעִיסִין לְהַקָּדוֹשׁ בָּרוּךְ הוּא בְּמַעֲשֵׂיהֶם הָרָעִים. 'גַּם בַּלַּיְלָה לֹא שָׁכַב לִבּוֹ', זֶה הַקָּדוֹשׁ בָּרוּךְ

הוּא מֵלְהָבִיא עֲלֵיהֶם פֻּרְעָנוּת בַּיּוֹם וּפֻרְעָנוּת בַּלַּיְלָה, הָדָא הוּא דִכְתִיב, (שם יט, כד) 'וַה' הִמְטִיר עַל סְדֹם'.

A DIFFERENT INTERPRETATION, EVEN IN THE NIGHT HIS HEART DOES NOT REST, REFERS TO THE HOLY ONE, BLESSED BE HE, WHO BROUGHT PUNISHMENT UPON THEM IN THE DAY TIME AND THE NIGHT, AS IT IS WRITTEN: AND EVERY LIVING SUBSTANCE WAS DESTROYED WHICH WAS UPON THE FACE OF THE GROUND (GENESIS 7:23). A DIFFERENT INTERPRETATION: FOR ALL HIS DAYS ARE PAINS, THE REFERENCE IS OF THE SODOMITES, WHOSE BEHAVIOR SADDENED THE HOLY ONE, BLESSED BE HE, VERY MUCH. THEIR EVIL BEHAVIOR WAS AT NIGHT TIME AND DAY TIME. AND HE DETERMINED TO BRING PUNISHMENT UPON THEM EVEN BY DAY AND EVEN BY NIGHT, AS IT IS WRITTEN: THEN THE LORD RAINED UPON SODOM (GENESIS 19:23).

This section does not require clarification, as it is straightforward.

דָּבָר אַחֵר, 'כִּי כָל יָמָיו מַכְאוֹבִים' אֵלּוּ הַמִּצְרִים, שֶׁהָיוּ מַכְאִיבִים לְהַקָּדוֹשׁ בָּרוּךְ הוּא בְּמַעֲשֵׂיהֶם הָרָעִים, 'וָכַעַס עִנְיָנוֹ', שֶׁהָיוּ מַכְעִיסִים לְהַקָּדוֹשׁ בָּרוּךְ הוּא בְּמַעֲשֵׂיהֶם הָרָעִים, 'גַּם בַּלַּיְלָה לֹא שָׁכַב לִבּוֹ', מֵאַחַר שֶׁהָיָה בֶּן יִשְׂרָאֵל גּוֹמֵר אֶת מְלַאכְתּוֹ, הָיָה אוֹמֵר לוֹ, עֲדוֹר לִי שְׁתֵּי עֲדָרִיּוֹת, בְּקַע לִי שְׁתֵּי בְקָעִיּוֹת. דָּבָר אַחֵר, 'גַּם בַּלַּיְלָה לֹא שָׁכַב לִבּוֹ', זֶה הַקָּדוֹשׁ בָּרוּךְ הוּא מֵלְהָבִיא עֲלֵיהֶם פֻּרְעָנִיּוֹת בַּיּוֹם וּפֻרְעָנִיּוֹת בַּלַּיְלָה, הָדָא הוּא דִכְתִיב, (שמות יב, כט) 'וַיְהִי בַּחֲצִי הַלַּיְלָה', (קהלת שם, שם) וְ'גַם זֶה הֶבֶל הוּא'.

A DIFFERENT INTERPRETATION, FOR ALL HIS DAYS ARE PAINS. THESE ARE THE EGYPTIANS WHO PAINED THE HOLY ONE, BLESSED BE HE, FOR THEIR EVIL DOINGS AND VEXATIONS. EVEN IN THE NIGHT HIS HEART DOES NOT REST, THIS IS EXPLAINED IN THE FACT THAT WHEN AN ISRAELITE SLAVE FINISHED A DAY'S WORK, HIS SUPERVISOR WOULD SAY TO HIM, "PREPARE FOR ME TWO VINE TREES AND TAKE DOWN TWO TREES." A DIFFERENT INTERPRETATION FOR EVEN IN THE NIGHT HIS HEART DOES NOT REST REFERS TO THE HOLY ONE, BLESSED BE HE, FOR BRINGING UPON THEM PUNISHMENTS IN THE DAY AND PUNISHMENTS IN THE NIGHT, AS IT IS WRITTEN, AND IT CAME TO PASS, THAT AT MIDNIGHT (EXODUS 12:29). THIS TOO IS VANITY.

God saw that their evil was very great and therefore, the punishment had to be very great. Not only the generation of Enoch and the generation of the Flood, but also the generation of Egypt before the exodus.

Seed Thoughts

The use of the Hebrew word מכאוב – *makhov*, meaning pain, is used very often in this *Midrash*. When it takes the form of מכאובים – *makhovim*, it means the kind of pain that is brought upon by others. So, in our *Midrash*, it is God, the Holy One, Blessed be He, Who experiences great pain, because of the evil done by the human beings whom He had created.

Why does God suffer this pain? It is because He loves man. He loves the human being that He created. He loves them even after they sin because He knows that it is a result of their freedom and free will, which He has given as the great mark of being a human being.

At which point in time does God suffer? He suffers not only when an individual sins, but especially when an entire generation acts in a corrupt way. He does everything possible to motivate them, change them and have them repent. When that process is successful, it brings great joy to the Holy One, Blessed be He (so to speak). We apply human emotions to God, only for us to understand His nature and the process with which He relates to the world. In this way, God suffers when man sins and He grieves very much when it happens. But there is one other process of experience that causes God to be full of sadness. That is when He realizes that the person, or the generation, are way beyond the possibility of repentance. There is no way in which they can change for the better, or repent or transform themselves. They have to be blotted out and removed from the cycle of life. This punishment is a terrible experience for the Holy One, Blessed be He. It saddens Him and, as we will see in a few verses later on, it makes Him have doubts as to whether the creation of the human being was worthwhile.

God loves man, especially when man is good. But He also loves the sinners. His goal is not punishment. His goal, to paraphrase the *Ne'ilah* service, is to redeem the human being so that he might return to God, permanently.

—

Additional Commentary

This too is vanity

Even though the verse in Ecclesiastes says that anger is better than laughter – which the sages explain as meaning, better is the anger that God sometimes directs to man than the good times that life occasionally brings forward – nevertheless, the verse also said that suffering is also vanity and meaningless. After all, the main good that arises out of God's anger is to motivate a person to do *tshuvah*, which is penitence. But in connection with the terrible punishment that was wreaked upon all the earlier generations, all of whom went up in smoke (so to speak) and in whose case their punishment did not bring any penitence, there is no vanity and meaningless greater than this. The main point of this text is to inform us that we are duty bound to give thanks to God for His great love, to Him Who pays us back through punishment for our misdeeds only gradually, little by little. This makes it possible for us to arouse ourselves to penitence. This is what the verse really means when it says anger is better than laughter. Through this kind of anger, a person can be granted a life in this world and eternal life in the next. Those generations who were punished at one time instead of little by little, like the generation of Enoch and the generation of the Flood, were able to find no healing and no extenuating circumstances. He who heals the sickness of his people Israel, He will also heal our soul and we will be able to experience the light of His Torah and the light of His holiness. May His name grow in sanctity in the world. (*Tiferet Tzion*)

ג. 'וַיַּרְא ה' כִּי רַבָּה וְגוֹ'', רַבִּי חֲנִינָא אָמַר, רַבָּה וְהוֹלֶכֶת, רַבִּי בֶּרֶכְיָה בְּשֵׁם רַבִּי יוֹחָנָן, אָמַר, שָׁמַעְנוּ בְּדוֹר הַמַּבּוּל שֶׁנִּדּוֹנוּ בַּמַּיִם, וְהַסְּדוֹמִים שֶׁנִּדּוֹנוּ בָאֵשׁ, וּמַנַּיִן לִתֵּן אֶת הָאָמוּר כָּאן, לְהַלָּן, וְאֶת הָאָמוּר לְהַלָּן, כָּאן, תַּלְמוּד לוֹמַר, 'רַבָּה' 'רַבָּה' לִגְזֵרָה שָׁוָה.

3. AND THE LORD SAW THAT THE WICKEDNESS OF MAN WAS GREAT. R. HANINA INTERPRETED: IT WAXED EVER GREATER. R. BEREKIAH SAID IN R. JOHANAN'S NAME: WE KNOW THAT THE GENERATION OF THE FLOOD WAS PUNISHED BY WATER AND THE SODOMITES BY FIRE: WHENCE DO WE KNOW TO APPLY WHAT IS STATED HERE TO THE CASE BELOW [SC. THE SODOMITES], AND THE REVERSE? BECAUSE "GREAT" IS MENTIONED IN BOTH PLACES, AFFORDING AN ANALOGY.

The sages of the *Midrash* saw a connection between the generation of the Flood and the generation of Sodom and Gemorah, as reflected in the texts associated with them. They discovered a שוה גזרה – *gzeirah shavah*, which means a correspondence in literary style. They discovered not one, but two. In the case of the Flood, the word רעה – *ra'ah*, is mentioned, meaning "evil." This appears also in the story of Sodom and Gemorah. At the same time, in both texts, the word *ra'ah* is related to the word רבה – *rabbah*, which means an evil that not only continues, but gets worse and worse. They also saw a correspondence in the fact that the generation of the Flood was punished by extermination and so was the generation of Sodom and Gemorah.

'וְכָל יֵצֶר מַחְשְׁבֹת לִבּוֹ רַק רַע כָּל הַיּוֹם', מִשֶּׁהָיְתָה חַמָּה זוֹרַחַת, וְעַד שֶׁהָיְתָה שׁוֹקַעַת לֹא הָיְתָה בָהֶם תּוֹחָלֶת, הֲדָא הוּא דִכְתִיב (איוב כד, יד) 'לָאוֹר יָקוּם רוֹצֵחַ, יִקְטָל עָנִי וְאֶבְיוֹן, וּבַלַּיְלָה יְהִי כַגַּנָּב', וְהָא כְתִיב (שם שם, טז) 'חָתַר בַּחֹשֶׁךְ בָּתִּים', לָמָּה, (שם שם, שם) שֶׁ'יּוֹמָם חִתְּמוּ לָמוֹ', מֶה הָיוּ עוֹשִׂים, הָיוּ מְבִיאִים אֲפוֹפוֹלְסִימוֹן, וְשָׁף בְּאֶבֶן, וּבָאִים בַּלַּיְלָה, וּמְרִיחִים וְחוֹתְרִים, כָּךְ דָּרַשׁ רַבִּי חֲנִינָא, בְּצִפּוֹרִין, אִתְעֲבֵד הַהוּא לֵילְיָא תְּלָת מְאָה מָאָה חֲתָרִין, הֲוָה לְהוֹן אֲפוֹפוֹלְסִימוֹן, מַה הֲוָה צִפּוֹרָאֵי עָבְדִין, בִּתְמִיהָה.

WAS ONLY EVIL ALL DAY. FROM THE RISING UNTIL THE SETTING OF THE SUN THERE WAS NO HOPE [OF GOOD] IN THEM, AS IT IS WRITTEN, THE MURDERER RISETH WITH THE LIGHT (JOB 24:14). BUT IT IS WRITTEN, IN

The *Midrash* now specifies the manner in which the evil deeds grew from day to day and moment to moment. Not only was there stealth at night, but all kinds of stratagems were used for burglary to take place even in the light of day. They even went to the extreme of making burglary at night more accessible by placing material in places in the various homes that appear to be very lucrative, a material whose odor would be strong and therefore lead the robber to where he wanted to go.

Seed Thoughts I

The sages of the *Midrash* were very disturbed by what they perceived as an absence of Divine justice. Granted, the generation of the Flood was sinful. However, could every individual, man and woman, including the children, have been equally guilty? Surely, every "bell curve," includes those who are better and also those who are worse. Even in the case of Sodom and Gemorah, Abraham's questions to God about saving the city ended at number ten. But what of the individuals under the number ten; could they not have been good people? And as Abraham put it, would not the Judge of all the earth do justly?

The answer of the *Midrash* is in the correspondence between the story of the Flood and the story of Sodom and Gemorah: the term *ra'ah* is used in each case twice, demonstrating that the evil would not only continue, but that even the average, so-called good people would be swept in torrent of delinquency that would prevail their generation.

Seed Thoughts II

The *Tiferet Tzion* has a quite different interpretation. Of the problems dealt with in our text, he writes that sin is usually motivated by two factors or phenomena. The first is described in Hebrew as תאוה – *ta'avah*, meaning lust or desire. This is usually a sexual lust, but not necessarily. It could be a lust for power, domination, wealth, popularity and many such elements that motivate individuals in society. When sin is motivated by this kind of lust, which is animalistic and has to do with the human body and material things, it is possible for an individual to repent. He can either recognize the evil of his ways, or he can mature in years and reach an age where these desires lose importance. There is the possibility of a person becoming a *ba'al tshuvah*, meaning one who repents.

However, there is a second motivation for sin. This is ideological, that is, if the person believes that what he is doing is right, because in his view, God and morality do not exist; such a view is beyond redemption. The use of the term *ra'ah*, evil, in the case of the stories of the Flood and Sodom and Gemorah, seems to indicate that the individuals were in the grip of an ideological commitment to evil and there was no hope for their repentance.

―

Additional Commentary

There was no hope

For as long as a person engages in sin, there is no hope that he will repent. The reason for this is that he has distanced himself from holy things. Since they were engaged in sin all day long, there is really no hope that they would repent. (*Tiferet Tzion*)

ד. (ו) 'וַיִּנָּחֶם ה' כִּי עָשָׂה אֶת הָאָדָם בָּאָרֶץ', רַבִּי יְהוּדָה וְרַבִּי נְחֶמְיָה, רַבִּי יְהוּדָה אָמַר, תֹּהוּת הָיְתָה לְפָנַי, שֶׁבְּרָאתִי אוֹתוֹ מִלְמַטָּה, שֶׁאִלּוּ בְרָאתִי אוֹתוֹ מִלְמַעְלָה, לֹא הָיָה מוֹרֵד בִּי, רַבִּי נְחֶמְיָה אָמַר, מִתְנַחֵם אֲנִי, שֶׁבְּרָאתִי אוֹתוֹ מִלְמַטָּה, שֶׁאִלּוּ בְרָאתִי אוֹתוֹ מִלְמַעְלָה, כְּשֵׁם שֶׁהִמְרִיד בִּי אֶת הַתַּחְתּוֹנִים, כָּךְ הָיָה מַמְרִיד בִּי אֶת הָעֶלְיוֹנִים.

4. AND THE LORD REGRETTED (VAYINACHEM) THAT HE HAD MADE MAN
ON THE EARTH (6:6). R. JUDAH SAID: [GOD DECLARED:] 'IT WAS A RE-
GRETTABLE ERROR ON MY PART TO HAVE CREATED HIM OUT OF EARTHLY
ELEMENTS, FOR HAD I CREATED HIM OUT OF HEAVENLY ELEMENTS, HE
WOULD NOT HAVE REBELLED AGAINST ME.' R. NEHEMIAH INTERPRETED
IT: I AM COMFORTED (MITNACHEM) THAT I CREATED HIM BELOW, FOR
HAD I CREATED HIM ABOVE, HE WOULD HAVE INCITED THE CELESTIAL
CREATURES TO REVOLT, JUST AS HE HAS INCITED THE TERRESTRIAL BE-
INGS TO REVOLT.

This *midrash* addresses a very serious question. If the verse truly says
that God regretted the creation of man, how could this have even been
said? If God created a universe in which man is to seek out his Creator,
then man is not an insignificant part of creation, but rather the center
of creation. That having being said, how could the verse speak of God
regretting creating man if this is the primary goal of creation? A number
of sages now try to approach this question and to change the focus of
the verse. R. Judah responds by saying that God merely regretted the
creation of man on earth. Whereas had the location been in the heavens,
it would have been a terrific idea. R. Nehemiah interprets the word *vayinachem* not as "regret," but as "comfort." God is saying that at least He
feels good that He created man on earth, because had he lived in Heaven,
then with his free will, he may have started a rebellion in Heaven.

אָמַר רַבִּי אַיְבוּ, תֹּהוּת הָיְתָה לְפָנַי, שֶׁבְּרָאתִי בוֹ יֵצֶר הָרָע, שֶׁאִלּוּלֵי לֹא בָרָאתִי בוֹ יֵצֶר הָרָע, לֹא הָיָה מוֹרֵד בִּי, אָמַר רַבִּי לֵוִי, מִתְנַחֵם אֲנִי שֶׁעֲשִׂיתִי אוֹתוֹ, וְנִתַּן בָּאָרֶץ.'

R. AIBU INTERPRETED: IT WAS A REGRETTABLE ERROR ON MY PART TO
HAVE CREATED AN EVIL URGE (YETZER HARA) WITHIN HIM, FOR HAD

I NOT CREATED AN EVIL URGE WITHIN HIM, HE WOULD NOT HAVE RE-
BELLED AGAINST ME. R. LEVI INTERPRETED: I AM COMFORTED THAT I
MADE HIM FROM THE EARTH.

R. Aibu also interprets it as being comforted, in that God did not
regret creating man, but that He had put the evil inclination within him.
This view is quite a puzzle itself, since the evil inclination has to do with
the creation of free will, which has to do with the creation of man. This
requires further interpretation.

R. Levi says that by being created from the earth, man is mortal and
therefore, his evil ways will be limited and eventually ended as man
returns to the earth.

אָמַר רַבִּי בֶּרֶכְיָה, מָשָׁל לְשַׂר שֶׁבָּנָה פָּלָטִין עַל יְדֵי אַדְרִיכָל, רָאָה אוֹתָהּ וְלֹא עָרְבָה לוֹ, עַל מִי,
אָמַר רַבִּי אַסִּי, מָשָׁל לְשַׂר שֶׁעָשָׂה סְחוֹרָה עַל יְדֵי סַרְסוּר, וְהִפְסִיד, עַל מִי יֵשׁ לוֹ לְהִתְרָעֵם,
לֹא עַל הַסַּרְסוּר, כָּךְ, 'וַיִּתְעַצֵּב אֶל לִבּוֹ'.יֵשׁ לוֹ לְהִתְכַּעֵם, לֹא עַל אַדְרִיכָל, כָּךְ, 'וַיִּתְעַצֵּב אֶל
לִבּוֹ'

AND IT GRIEVED HIM AT HIS HEART. R. BEREKIAH SAID: IF A KING HAS A
PALACE BUILT BY AN ARCHITECT AND WHEN HE SEES IT, IT DISPLEASES
HIM, AGAINST WHOM IS HE TO COMPLAIN? SURELY AGAINST THE AR-
CHITECT! R. ASSI SAID: IF A KING DID BUSINESS THROUGH A MEDIATOR
AND LOST, AGAINST WHOM WOULD HE COMPLAIN, NOT THE MEDIATOR?
SIMILARLY, IT GRIEVED HIM AT HIS HEART.

Notice that the Hebrew says, אל לבו and not בלבו – in other words,
these reflections were not said in His heart, but to His heart. It is as
though the heart were personified, as if it were another being with
whom God could communicate from time to time. In an earlier *Midrash*, when the question was raised about with whom God discussed
the creation of man (since it said, "Let us make man," in the plural), the
answer given is that God reflected with His own wisdom, knowledge
and know-how. This is what is meant when it says "to His heart," meaning to His understanding. Another interpretation is that it says 'at his
heart,' meaning 'about his heart,' referring to man. God grieved at man's
having evil thoughts in his heart. (Maharzu)

אֶפִּיקוֹרֹס אֶחָד, שָׁאַל אֶת רַבִּי יְהוֹשֻׁעַ בֶּן קָרְחָה, אָמַר לוֹ, אֵין אַתֶּם אוֹמְרִים שֶׁהַקָּדוֹשׁ בָּרוּךְ
הוּא רוֹאֶה אֶת הַנּוֹלָד, אָמַר לוֹ, הֵן, וְהָא כְתִיב 'וַיִּתְעַצֵּב אֶל לִבּוֹ', אָמַר לוֹ, נוֹלַד לְךָ בֶּן זָכָר מִיָּמֶיךָ,
אָמַר לוֹ, הֵן, אָמַר לוֹ, מֶה עָשִׂיתָ, אָמַר לוֹ, שָׂמַחְתִּי וְשִׂמַּחְתִּי אֶת הַכֹּל, אָמַר לוֹ, וְלֹא הָיִיתָ יוֹדֵעַ,
שֶׁסּוֹפוֹ לָמוּת, אָמַר לוֹ, בִּשְׁעַת חֶדְוָתָא חֶדְוָתָא, בִּשְׁעַת אֲבֵלָה אֲבֵלָה, אָמַר לוֹ, כָּךְ מַעֲשֶׂה לִפְנֵי
הַקָּדוֹשׁ בָּרוּךְ הוּא, דַּאֲמַר רַבִּי יְהוֹשֻׁעַ בֶּן לֵוִי, שִׁבְעָה יָמִים נִתְאַבֵּל הַקָּדוֹשׁ בָּרוּךְ הוּא עַל עוֹלָמוֹ,

קֹדֶם שֶׁלֹּא יָבוֹא מַבּוּל לָעוֹלָם, מַאי טַעְמָה, 'וַיִּתְעַצֵּב אֶל לִבּוֹ', וְאֵין עֲצִיבָה אֶלָּא אֲבֵלוּת, הֵיךְ
מַה דְּאַתְּ אָמַר, (שׁ"ב יט, ג) 'נֶעֱצַב הַמֶּלֶךְ אֶל בְּנוֹ'.

A CERTAIN GENTILE ASKED R. JOSHUA B. KARHAH: 'DO YOU NOT MAIN-
TAIN THAT THE HOLY ONE, BLESSED BE HE, FORESEES THE FUTURE?'
'YES,' REPLIED HE. 'BUT IT IS WRITTEN, AND IT GRIEVED HIM AT HIS
HEART!' 'HAS A SON EVER BEEN BORN TO YOU?' INQUIRED HE. 'YES,'
WAS THE ANSWER. 'AND WHAT DID YOU DO?' – 'I REJOICED AND MADE
ALL OTHERS REJOICE,' HE ANSWERED. 'YET DID YOU NOT KNOW THAT
HE WOULD EVENTUALLY DIE?' 'GLADNESS AT THE TIME OF GLADNESS,
AND MOURNING AT THE TIME OF MOURNING,' REPLIED HE. 'EVEN SO
WAS IT WITH THE HOLY ONE, BLESSED BE HE,' WAS HIS REJOINDER, 'FOR
R. JOSHUA B. LEVI SAID: SEVEN DAYS THE HOLY ONE, BLESSED BE HE,
MOURNED FOR HIS WORLD BEFORE BRINGING THE FLOOD, FOR IT IS
SAID HERE, AND IT GRIEVED HIM, WHILE ELSEWHERE IT SAYS, THE KING
GRIEVETH FOR HIS SON' (II SAM. 19:3).

The final interpretation is that God mourned for the creation of the
world. He mourned before the Flood took place and while it took place.
He hoped that the one who remained, namely Noah, who is the progenitor of Abraham, would restore the world to its original purpose.

—

Seed Thoughts I

This *Midrash* gives us an opportunity to analyze how the sages of the
Midrash confronted what they found to be a difficulty in the text. Let us
begin with the problem. The problem is that God regretted the creation
of man. How is it possible for God, The Perfect One, to regret the central
goal of creation? The first approach is to examine the verse that is the
source of the difficulty. This was done by R. Judah, who pointed out that
it was not the creation of man, per se, that was the problem, but the fact
that he was created from the earth of this world. R. Aibu offers a similar
interpretation that it was not the creation of man but the evil inclination
of man that was the source of the problem. None of these explanations
was completely satisfactory, and so various approaches were attempted.

The second approach was to question the translation of the verb
vayinachem. It need not be translated as coming from "regret." It could
also be translated as "comforted." Thus, God was relieved, as it were, that
man was created on earth, because, had he been created in Heaven, he
would have started a rebellion there, and that would have been much
worse. But even with the midrashic interpretations, none of these expla-

nations give a satisfactory answer to the philosophical question of how a perfect God can regret something He did. This is why a commentator like the *Tiferet Tzion* moves into the area of Jewish mysticism, interpreting that God has limited His power in this world due to His own decree. This can sometimes cause regret. But the absolute infinite power of God in all areas of the universe makes regretting impossible.

Seed Thoughts II

The *Midrash* includes a parable of an employer who uses an agent to sell his goods. If the agent fails to do his job well, the responsibility is that of the agent. Conversely, if the agent is very successful, it is he who deserves the credit. R. Ami makes the point that man is God's agent in the universe. Whereas he deserved the punishment meted out with the generations of the Flood and Sodom and Gemorah, he still has a responsibility of being God's agent on earth. All of us are meant to be God's agents and our responsibility to do His work should be our priority. Later on, the Torah establishes this teaching as one of the most important principles of the Jewish religion. We have a covenant with God and that covenant is to be a kingdom of priests and holy nation. This makes the teaching that we are God's agents a central principle of the Jewish religion and one that we should hold aloft at all times.

Additional Commentary

Questions from a gentile

A gentile once asked a couple of questions on a couple of matters: The first was, since God knows everything that happened before and everything to come, and knew that man's behavior would produce death, why did He create man in the first place? The second question was, why was God saddened at the death of the generation, since he knew all of this was to be, from the very onset? To these questions, two answers were forthcoming.

On the first question, the answer was rejoicing. You rejoice at such a creation as you would rejoice at the birth of an infant, even with the knowledge that it will ultimately die, because of the years for which it will live. That is why God created man. Even though He knew that his behavior contributed to his death. He wanted the נחת רוח that he would achieve in this world before the Flood. Furthermore, as will be learned later, the people of the generation of the Flood were entitled to the World to Come.

In connection with the question of God's sadness, the word ויתעצב should not be interpreted as sadness, but אבילות – mourning. The Torah tells us that God acted as a mourner. In the same way one sits shivah for seven close relationships (father, mother, brother, sister, son, daughter or spouse), one reason for which is to safeguard the dead from punishment in the World to Come, so, too, did God sit shivah for the generation of the Flood to spare them from suffering after death. (*Tiferet Tzion*)

It grieved Him at His heart

R. Assi interprets, "And it grieved Him in His heart" as a parable of the agent who is given goods to sell by an employer. When the agent was not successful, then he would be blamed. What R. Assi is trying to tell us is that man, the human being, is the agent of the Holy One, Blessed be He. Man was given control over the whole universe on God's behalf. If his conduct is good, if his behavior is on a high level, the whole universe ascends to greater heights. When it says that God put sadness into the hearts of man, it was because during the generations of the Flood and of Sodom and Gemorah, the role of the agent was unsuccessful.

The parable of the builder, mentioned later in the midrash, has the same meaning as the one about the agent. As the saying goes, אחת דיבר אלוקים שתים זו שמעתי – sometimes, you can have two teachings for the same lesson. (*Tiferet Tzion* on 8:3)

It was a regrettable error

On the question of תווהות היתה לפניו – *tavhut haiytah lefanav*: the meaning of this expression is one of regret. In our verse we have the expression *vayinachem Hashem*, and elsewhere it says, על הרעה – *al hara'ah*, God was comforted "on the evil" that was done. The meaning is that whenever God decrees a difficult punishment, it is always based on one particular condition. If man repented and prayed, the decree would be annulled. That is the meaning of the expression *vayinachem*. By means of prayer and repentance, *nichum* as comfort was achieved. Similarly, in our case, God created man on condition that He would obey the commandments; when they transgress the commandments, it turns out that God's regret was caused by their behavior and they were the ones who created the regret, not God. (Maharzu)

א. (ו, ז) 'וַיֹּאמֶר ה', אֶמְחֶה אֶת הָאָדָם', (איוב לד, כה) 'לָכֵן יַכִּיר מַעְבָּדֵיהֶם וְהָפַךְ לַיְלָה
וְיִדַּכָּאוּ', רַבִּי חֲנִינָא שְׁאֵלָה לְרַבִּי יוֹנָתָן, אָמַר לֵהּ מַהוּ דִכְתִיב, 'לָכֵן יַכִּיר מַעְבָּדֵיהֶם,
וְגוֹ'', אָמַר לוֹ, אֵין הַקָּדוֹשׁ בָּרוּךְ הוּא נִפְרָע מִן הָרְשָׁעִים, עַד שֶׁהוּא קוֹרֵא אַגָּלִיגִין שֶׁלָּהֶן
מִלְמַעְלָן, וְאַחַר כָּךְ הוּא פּוֹרֵעַ מֵהֶן, שֶׁהַקָּדוֹשׁ בָּרוּךְ הוּא הוֹפֵךְ אֶת יוֹם לְלַיְלָה, וְהִקְשִׁיטָן
לְפָרְעָנוּת

1. AND THE LORD SAID: I WILL BLOT OUT MAN WHOM I HAVE CREATED
(6:7). IT IS WRITTEN, THEREFORE HE TAKETH KNOWLEDGE OF THEIR
WORKS, AND HE TURNETH [DAY] TO NIGHT, SO THAT THEY ARE CRUSHED
(JOB 34:25). R. HANINA ASKED R. JONATHAN: WHAT DOES 'THEREFORE
HE TAKETH KNOWLEDGE OF THEIR WORKS,' ETC. MEAN? HE ANSWERED:
AFTER THE HOLY ONE, BLESSED BE HE, HAS TURNED DAY INTO NIGHT
AND PUT THEM AT THEIR EASE, TO BE READY FOR PUNISHMENT, HE
THEN PUNISHES THEM.

The *Midrash* begins by asking a question that repeats many times for
various *midrashim*. To whom was God speaking when He made the
remark of His intention to destroy man? In order to answer, the *Midrash*
reverts to a verse in *Job*, which is a continuation of one that began several
midrashim ago, and which has been interpreted as referring exclusively
to the generation of the Flood and its problems. It is interesting to note
that even the sages of the *Midrash* found the verse in *Job* difficult to
interpret.

When R. Hanina asked for an explanation, R. Jonathan answered
that the meaning of the word יכיר – *yakir*, in the text means that God
does not punish man unless and until He has a detailed description of
their sins, so that He recognizes the problem. This is made possible,
since everything that a human being does is recorded by a Heavenly
court. Therefore, He is able to recognize each one's deeds and mete out
punishment.

וְאַחַר כָּךְ הוּא פּוֹרֵעַ מֵהֶם, כָּךְ, בַּתְּחִלָּה, 'וַיַּרְא ה' כִּי רַבָּה רָעַת הָאָדָם', וְאַחַר כָּךְ, 'וַיִּנָּחֶם ה' כִּי
עָשָׂה אֶת הָאָדָם בָּאָרֶץ', וְאַחַר כָּךְ, 'וַיֹּאמֶר ה' אֶמְחֶה אֶת הָאָדָם אֲשֶׁר בָּרָאתִי'.

SIMILARLY, AT FIRST, THE LORD SAW THAT THE WICKEDNESS OF MAN
WAS GREAT; THEN, IT REPENTED THE LORD, ETC.; AND FINALLY, AND
THE LORD SAID: I WILL BLOT OUT MAN.

When it says, "The Lord saw that the wickedness of man was great," it
means He could see because the Heavenly court showed Him the documents that prove the sinfulness of man. After that it says *vayinachem*,
that God regretted the creation of man, and finally, it says *emcheh et
ha'Adam*, wipe out mankind.

—

Seed Thoughts

In the collection of the *midrashim* that we are now studying, there is one
basic concern on the part of the *midrashic* scholars. It can be stated in
the form of Abraham's question: "Shall not the God of all the earth do
justly?" They were concerned about the punishment meted out to an
entire generation. How could they have all been bad? They were also
concerned about the destruction of Sodom and Gemorah. How could
everyone have been equally guilty? This *midrash* tries to mitigate some
of this concern.

God would never punish anyone unless He would have a detailed
description of a person's sins and inadequacies. These records are kept
by the Heavenly court and readily available only to God. Since God has
accepted the Oral Law, which He had commanded to man, He also accepted the task of making sure that whatever punishment is meted out is
definitely deserved. It is as though the *Midrash* is saying, yes, the Judge
of all the earth is expected to do justly.

—

Additional Commentary

He reads from the record אנאלוגין *– analagin*

(Found only in the Hebrew content.) God does not punish any evildoer
without examining all of his deeds very carefully. As it is written, "The
rock whose work is perfect and all of His ways are just" (*Deut.*32:4). He
reads the book of "*analagin*" and examines the list of deeds after which
He issues punishment. The entire verse in *Job* deals with the generation of the Flood. There it says that the people of the generation of the
Flood were very special. How come they were not punished until after

many centuries? It was only now that God examined a summary of their deeds, as written in a special record, to make sure that the punishment would be authentic and well deserved, not dependent upon guesswork.

The word *analagin* comes from Greek and it refers to a list of complaints. When it says that God turns their day into night, it is referring to the verse in *Job*, describing the punishment meted out. (Aryeh Mirkin)

PARASHAH TWENTY-EIGHT, *Midrash Two*

ב. רַבִּי בֶּרֶכְיָה בְּשֵׁם רַב בֵּיבַי, (בראשית א, ט) 'יִקָּווּ הַמַּיִם' יֵעָשֶׂה מִדָּה לַמַּיִם, כְּמוֹ שֶׁנֶּאֱמַר (זכריה
א, טז) 'וְקָו יִנָּטֶה עַל יְרוּשָׁלָם', רַבִּי אַבָּא בַּר כָּהֲנָא בְּשֵׁם רַבִּי לֵוִי, אָמַר, יִקָּווּ לִי הַמַּיִם, מַה שֶּׁאֲנִי
עָתִיד לַעֲשׂוֹת בָּם

2. AND THE LORD SAID: I WILL BLOT OUT MAN. R. BEREKIAH SAID IN THE
NAME OF R. BEIVAI: IT IS WRITTEN, LET THE WATERS BE GATHERED TO-
GETHER (YIKAVU) UNTO ONE PLACE (GEN. 1:9): THAT MEANS, LET THERE
BE A MEASURE SET FOR THE WATER, AS YOU READ, AND A LINE (KAV)
SHALL BE STRETCHED FORTH OVER JERUSALEM (ZECH. 1:16). R. ABBA
B. KAHANA EXPLAINED IT IN R. LEVI'S NAME THUS: LET THE WATERS
BE GATHERED TOGETHER FOR MY PURPOSE [SO AS TO PERFORM WHAT I
WILL ONE DAY DO WITH THEM].

The actual text is one that applies to several of the earlier *midrashim* in parashah 28: אמחה – *emcheh*, "I will blot out the man whom I have created." The *Midrash* was bothered by a number of aspects of this verse. In the first place, it does not say to whom it was said. Secondly, it has the phrase "the man whom I have created," which is self-explanatory and unnecessary. Also, it says, "I will blot out man from off the earth," which is also self-explanatory, since from where else can he be blotted out? In response to these concerns, R. Berekiah brought down the verse wherein God said, "Let the waters be gathered." The ordinary word for "gathered" would be יאספו – *ye-'asfu*. The use of the term יקוו – *yekavu* probably implies additional teachings that come from the word *yekavu* itself. One of them is the word קו – *kav*, which is a boundary or a measure, and the commandment would imply that the waters would require a measure or a boundary so that they would not overflow the banks and Flood the world.

Another interpretation notes that *yekavu* has the word תקוה – *tikvah*, which means "hope," and it is as though God said to the waters, "Even though you are restricted, some day you will help me when I will need you to punish mankind."

מָשָׁל לְשַׂר שֶׁבָּנָה פָּלָטִין, וְהוֹשִׁיב בָּהּ דִּיוֹרִים אִלְּמִים, וְהָיוּ מַשְׁכִּימִים וְשׁוֹאֲלִים בִּשְׁלוֹמוֹ שֶׁל
שַׂר בִּרְמִיזָה וּבְאֶצְבַּע וּבְמַנְוָולִים, אָמַר הַשַׂר, מָה הֵם אֵלּוּ, שֶׁהֵם אִלְּמִים, מַשְׁכִּימִים וְשׁוֹאֲלִים
בִּשְׁלוֹמִי בִּרְמִיזָה וּבְאֶצְבַּע, אִלּוּ הָיוּ פִּקְחִים, עַל אַחַת כַּמָּה וְכַמָּה, הוֹשִׁיב הַשַׂר בְּתוֹכָהּ דִּיוֹרִים
פִּקְחִים, עָמְדוּ וְהֶחֱזִיקוּ בַּפָּלָטִין, אָמְרוּ, אֵין פָּלָטִין זוֹ שֶׁל שַׂר, שֶׁלָּנוּ הִיא, אָמַר הַשַׂר, תַּחֲזֹר
הַפָּלָטִין לְכָמוֹת שֶׁהָיְתָה, כָּךְ מִתְּחִלָּה, לֹא הָיָה קִלּוּסוֹ שֶׁל הַקָּדוֹשׁ בָּרוּךְ הוּא עוֹלֶה, אֶלָּא מִן
הַמַּיִם, הֲדָא הוּא דִכְתִיב, (תהלים צג, ד) 'מִקֹּלוֹת מַיִם רַבִּים, וְגוֹ'', מָה הֵן אוֹמְרִים, (שם שם, שם)
'אַדִּיר בַּמָּרוֹם ה'', אָמַר הַקָּדוֹשׁ בָּרוּךְ הוּא, מָה אֵלּוּ שֶׁאֵין לָהֶם לֹא אֲמִירָה וְלֹא דִבּוּר, הֲרֵי הֵן
מְקַלְּסִין אוֹתִי לִכְשֶׁאֶבְרָא אָדָם, עַל אַחַת כַּמָּה וְכַמָּה, עָמַד דּוֹר אֱנוֹשׁ וּמָרַד בּוֹ, דּוֹר הַמַּבּוּל וּמָרַד
בּוֹ, דּוֹר הַפְלָגָה וּמָרַד בּוֹ, אָמַר הַקָּדוֹשׁ בָּרוּךְ הוּא, יִפָּנוּ אֵלּוּ וְיָבוֹאוּ אוֹתָן, הֲדָא הוּא דִכְתִיב,
'וַיֹּאמֶר ה', אֶמְחֶה אֶת הָאָדָם אֲשֶׁר בָּרָאתִי', מָה הֵם סְבוּרִים, אַרְיוֹת, גַּסְטְרָיוֹת אֲנִי צָרִיךְ, הֲלֹא
בִדְבָר בְּרָאתִי אֶת הָעוֹלָם, דָּבָר אֲנִי מוֹצִיא, וּמְכַלֶּה אוֹתָן מִן הָעוֹלָם

IT IS AS IF A KING BUILT A PALACE AND TENANTED IT WITH DUMB
PEOPLE, WHO USED TO RISE EARLY AND PAY THEIR RESPECTS TO THE
KING WITH GESTURES, WITH THEIR FINGERS AND WITH THEIR HAND-
KERCHIEFS. SAID THE KING: 'IF THESE, WHO ARE DUMB, RISE EARLY
AND PAY THEIR RESPECTS WITH GESTURES, HOW MUCH MORE ZEALOUS
WOULD THEY BE IF THEY POSSESSED ALL THEIR FACULTIES!' THERE-
UPON THE KING TENANTED IT WITH MEN GIFTED WITH SPEECH, WHO
AROSE AND SEIZED THE PALACE, ASSERTING, 'THIS PALACE IS OURS.'
'THEN LET THE PALACE RETURN TO ITS ORIGINAL STATE,' THE KING OR-
DERED. SIMILARLY, AT THE BEGINNING, THE PRAISE OF THE ALMIGHTY
ASCENDED FROM NAUGHT BUT THE WATER, AS IT IS WRITTEN, FROM
THE VOICES OF MANY WATERS, THE MIGHTY BREAKERS OF THE SEA (PS.
93:4); AND WHAT DID THEY PROCLAIM? THE LORD ON HIGH IS MIGHTY
(IBID.). SAID THE HOLY ONE, BLESSED BE HE: 'IF THESE, WHICH HAVE
NEITHER MOUTH NOR SPEECH, DO THUS, HOW MUCH MORE WILL I BE
PRAISED WHEN I CREATE MAN!' BUT THE GENERATION OF ENOSH AROSE
AND REBELLED AGAINST HIM; THE GENERATION OF THE FLOOD AND
THAT OF THE DIVISION [OF TONGUES] AROSE AND REBELLED AGAINST
HIM. THEREUPON THE HOLY ONE, BLESSED BE HE, SAID: 'LET THESE
BE REMOVED AND THE FORMER COME [IN THEIR PLACE].' HENCE IT IS
WRITTEN, AND THE LORD SAID: I WILL BLOT OUT MAN. 'WHAT DO THEY
THINK? THAT I NEED ARMIES [TO COMBAT THEM]? DID I NOT CREATE
THE WORLD WITH A WORD? I WILL UTTER A WORD AND DESTROY THEM!'

This parable is used to indicate that the deterioration that comes
to the world and to society becomes the responsibility of man. The
inanimate objects, such as water, are personified as obeying God in all
respects. The destruction of the world was not merely the behavior of
one generation, but at least three. The generation of Enosh, that of the
Flood and that of the Division of tongues (the Tower of Babel).

אָמַר רַבִּי בֶּרֶכְיָה, כְּלוּם בְּרָאתִי אוֹתוֹ אֶלָּא מִן הֶעָפָר, מִי מַמְחֶה אֶת הֶעָפָר הַמָּיִם.

R. BEREKIAH SAID: SURELY I CREATED THEM FROM THE EARTH; WHAT
DISSOLVES EARTH? WATER. THEN LET THE WATER COME AND DISSOLVE
THE EARTH.

In the last section, R. Berekiah explained why the original verse
included the phrase, "which I have created from upon the face of the
earth." It stands as a reminder that the human being was created from
earth and it is the earth that will be used as the instrument through
which water will engulf mankind.

—

Seed Thoughts

The *Midrash that* we are now studying (28:2 and 28:1) contains famous
parables. One has to do with a palace inhabited by handicapped people
who could praise the Lord, and the other, with an agent who was au-
thorized to sell certain merchandise and did not succeed. Both of these
parables were first mentioned in 8:3 of *Midrash Rabbah* and the contrast
in which they are handled in those sections are very revealing and very
instructive. In the *midrashim* that we are now studying, man is described
as most responsible for the deterioration of the world. Inanimate water
knew how to serve the Lord better than the human being. Generation
after generation suffered because of the evil powers of man. On the
other hand, in the earlier chapters of *Midrash Rabbah*, a very opposite
teaching emerges. As can be seen by the additional commentary, the
human being is the greatest creation. He can reach the highest heights,
well beyond any other being in the universe. When he makes mistakes,
he can correct them. He can change them and improve. He can make
the right choices.

The remarkable thing about the treatment in both these *midrashim*
is that both are correct. Man can destroy the universe. That was correct,
not only in ancient times, but remains so also in modern times, as can
be evidenced from the Holocaust and other modern-day wars. On the
other hand, man and only man is the hope of the world. Only man can
live according to values Only man can commit himself to commandments. Only he can sacrifice himself for what he considers good in life.
That man can be evil is a true possibility, but he can also be a צדיק – *tzaddik*, a righteous person. That is our hope and that should determine our
life. Only man is capable of *imitatio Dei*, imitation of God, which is a
great aim of religion. The *Midrash* helps us move in that direction.

Additional Commentary

Consulted with His own heart (A)

One of the questions raised by the *Midrash* in the early chapters of Genesis is the response that says, "Let us make man in our image." One of the reasons offered, by R. Levi, in an early *midrash,* was that God wanted to create a being who could experience not only that of the עליונים, but also of the תחתונים. The creation of man fulfilled both of these purposes, because he had the values of this world, which were materialistic and animalistic, as well as the upper worlds, which had to do with the mind and intelligence (parashah 8, *midrash* 3). Another great rabbi has the thought, האדם הוא עולם קטן – the makeup of man represents the entire world; he is the only creature that is not subject entirely to the laws of nature. He has the ability to change, the ability to repent and start over again. Only the human being can do this. (*Yefei To'ar*)

Consulted in His own heart (B)

Commenting on the view of *midrash* 8:3, that God consulted with His own heart, it should be pointed out that the greatest aspect of man as a human being is the fact that he has the ability to choose. He could choose the good and he could choose the bad. In order for this to happen, however, he must have the ability to think. He has to think through the meaning of happiness. He has to think through the meaning of suffering. All these are dependent upon the heart. So when it says, *vayitatzev el libo,* it is to teach us to reflect in our hearts, being the most important thing that a human being is capable of doing. (Maharzu)

ג. 'וַיֹּאמֶר ה' אֶמְחֶה אֶת הָאָדָם', רַבִּי לֵוִי בְּשֵׁם רַבִּי יוֹחָנָן, אָמַר, אֲפִלּוּ אִסְטְרוֹבִּלִין שֶׁל רֵחַיִם נִמְחָה.

3. (AND GOD SAID: I WILL BLOT OUT THE HUMAN BEINGS.) R. LEVI SAID IN R. JOHANAN'S NAME: EVEN THE NETHER STONE OF A MILLSTONE WAS DISSOLVED.

The *Midrash* is concerned with the article *et,* which is often used in conjunction with "the," and which doesn't seem necessary here. Usually this article is used to add something that would not otherwise be there. Here the *Midrash* has added *et* to include the idea of a heavy stone, such as the millstone, to express that even such objects as that will be destroyed and reduced to water as a result of the Flood.

רַבִּי יְהוּדָה בַּר סִימוֹן בְּשֵׁם רַבִּי יוֹחָנָן, אָמַר, אֲפִלּוּ עֲפָרוֹ שֶׁל אָדָם הָרִאשׁוֹן נִמְחָה. כַּד דְּרָשָׁהּ רַבִּי יְהוּדָה, בְּצִפּוֹרִי בְּצִבּוּרָא, וְלָא קִבְּלוּ מִנַּהּ, רַבִּי יוֹחָנָן בְּשֵׁם רַבִּי שִׁמְעוֹן בֶּן יְהוֹצָדָק, אָמַר, אֲפִלּוּ לוּז שֶׁל שִׁדְרָה, שֶׁמִּמֶּנּוּ הַקָּדוֹשׁ בָּרוּךְ הוּא מֵצִיץ אֶת הָאָדָם לֶעָתִיד לָבוֹא, נִמְחָה.

R. JUDAH B. R. SIMON SAID IN THE NAME OF R. JOHANAN: EVEN THE DUST OF ADAM WAS DISSOLVED. R. JUDAH LECTURED THUS, BUT THE CONGREGATION WOULD NOT ACCEPT IT. R. JOHANAN SAID IN THE NAME OF R. SIMEON B. JEHOZADAK: EVEN THE NUT (LUZ) OF THE SPINAL COL-UMN, FROM WHICH THE HOLY ONE, BLESSED BE HE, WILL CAUSE MAN TO BLOSSOM FORTH IN THE FUTURE, WAS DISSOLVED.

Another interpretation of the article *et and its presence in this verse is* that even the first remains will be destroyed and eliminated, referring to the remains of the very first human being, entirely created by God. The comment that R. Judah's lecture in Zippori was not accepted means that it was not accepted by the sages of the community because the first Adam had nothing to do with the Flood and could not be held responsible for it. (Mirkin)

אַדְרִיָאנוֹס, שְׁחִיק עֲצָמוֹת, שָׁאַל אֶת רַבִּי יְהוֹשֻׁעַ בֶּן חֲנַנְיָא, אָמַר לוֹ, מֵהֵיכָן הַקָּדוֹשׁ בָּרוּךְ הוּא
מֵצִיץ אֶת הָאָדָם לֶעָתִיד לָבוֹא, אָמַר לוֹ, מִלּוּז שֶׁל שִׁדְרָה, אָמַר לוֹ, מִנַּיִן אַתָּה יוֹדֵעַ, אָמַר לֵהּ
אַיְתֵיתֵהּ לִידִי, וַאֲנָא מוֹדַע לָךְ, טְחָנוֹ בָרֵחַיִם, וְלֹא נִטְחַן, שָׂרְפוֹ בָאֵשׁ, וְלֹא נִשְׂרָף, נְתָנוֹ בַמַּיִם,
וְלֹא נִמְחָה, נְתָנוֹ עַל הַסַּדָּן, וְהִתְחִיל מַכֶּה עָלָיו בַּפַּטִּישׁ, נֶחֱלַק הַסַּדָּן, וְנִבְקַע הַפַּטִּישׁ, וְלֹא חָסַר
כְּלוּם.

HADRIAN – MAY HIS BONES ROT! – ASKED R. JOSHUA B. HANANIA:
"FROM WHAT PART WILL THE HOLY ONE, BLESSED BE HE, CAUSE MAN
TO BLOSSOM FORTH IN THE FUTURE?" "FROM THE NUT OF THE SPINAL
COLUMN," HE REPLIED. "HOW DO YOU KNOW THAT?" HE ASKED. "BRING
ME ONE AND I WILL PROVE IT TO YOU," HE REPLIED. HE THREW IT INTO
THE FIRE, YET IT WAS NOT BURNT; HE PUT IT IN WATER, BUT IT DID
NOT DISSOLVE; HE GROUND IT BETWEEN MILLSTONES, BUT IT WAS NOT
CRUSHED; HE PLACED IT ON AN ANVIL AND SMOTE IT WITH A HAMMER;
THE ANVIL WAS CLEFT AND THE HAMMER SPLIT, YET IT REMAINED IN-
TACT.

Another interpretation of *et* and its inclusive power is the fact that it
refers to that part of the human body known as לוז – *luz,* which is a section of the spinal cord that is very small and indestructible. Through the
luz, God will recreate the human body and the human being in the time
of the resurrection. However, the *luz* will be destroyed for the generation of the Flood, who did not deserve resurrection. It would remain for
all the rest of humanity.

The section on the emperor Hadrian is brought in to indicate that
et refers to the spinal area known as *luz, and that it* still retains indestructible power. When he raised the point, by asking R. Joshua how
the *luz* could survive while everything else in the body rots over the
centuries, the answer by R. Joshuah was to bring a sample of this *luz*
and to try to destroy it in any manner. All methods used had no effect. In
one instance, the hammer was destroyed, while the *luz* was still intact.
In other words, the *luz* remains the vehicle within the human that will
allow for the resurrection to take place.

⁓

Seed Thoughts

One of the special concerns of this *Midrash* is the use of the term אמחה
– *emcheh,* meaning to destroy, rather than more popular words, such
as להשמיד – *lehashmid* or להרוס – *leharos.* It goes on to respond that the
reason for this is that the word *emcheh* has the special meaning of being
blotted out or obliterated, particularly by water. It is for this reason that

the vocalization is changed so that it is not read as *emcheh* but *amacheh*, "I will obliterate you" into earth and water, which is really mud. This conveys the meaning in a more specific way.

Another fascinating aspect of this *Midrash* is the use of the term *luz*. The reference here is to that small object or bone in the spinal area, which apparently is indestructible and through which God will restore the body of mankind in the time of resurrection. Let us reflect for a moment on what this means. It means that the resurrection will produce men and women of flesh and blood, and not some spiritual entity. It also means that the World to Come is something that will happen right here and not in some spiritual universe. This would probably happen after the coming of Messiah. We do not know how long it will last, nor whether it will be forever. There are differences of opinion where this is discussed. Nevertheless, one would have to say that in this *Midrash*, something new has been added to the literature of resurrection. That is to say that the World to Come will take place right here on earth, with human beings like you and me, but coming after the age of the Messiah, it would be a world without persecution – without war but with all the other challenges of being a human being.

—

Additional Commentary

Even the great stone known as estrobulin

The *Midrash* is interpreting the fact that the word *et* appears in the verse, "I will blot out the man." because every time *et* or *gum* would appear, the intention of them is to multiply whatever the theme is. What is happening here is that the *Midrash is* providing different meanings that *et* might include. The first is what is known as *estrobulin,* which is a very heavy rock and is the base for millstone. It can be eaten away and destroyed by water. The second interpretation has to do with the earth from which the first man was created, and that also will be destroyed by water. The third has to do with the body part known as *luz*. This is what the Holy One, Blessed be He, established into our nature so that human beings will have an opportunity to live forever. This can never be destroyed by fire, nor by water. The *luz*, therefore, is a sign to all human creatures that the time will come when resurrection will take place and human beings will have a chance to be reborn. (*Yefei To'ar*)

Estrobulin *or heavy stone*

Here, the Midrash points out that the verb *emcheh* has to be understood as "destroyed" or "dissolved" by water. When the term *et is* used in *et ha'adam*, it should be understood as *im ha'adam,* meaning "with" the human being. In other words, everything belonging to the human being has to be destroyed in the generation of the Flood. (Maharzu)

ד. 'אֶמְחֶה', אֲנִי מַמְחֶה עַל בְּרִיּוֹתַי, וְאֵין בְּרִיּוֹתַי מַמְחִים עַל יָדִי.

4. I WILL BLOT OUT [EMCHEH]MAN WHOM I HAVE CREATED. I CAN
IMPOSE AN INTERDICT [MEMACHEH] UPON MY CREATURES, BUT MY
CREATURES CANNOT IMPOSE AN INTERDICT UPON ME.

What is being said here is that God will now assert His will over human beings. They will not be permitted to assert their will over Him.
This was the behavior of the generation of the Flood. They thought that
the world was theirs and that they were the dominant ones. This would
not happen again.

אָמַר רַבִּי אֶלְעָזָר, מָשָׁל לְמֶלֶךְ שֶׁהָיוּ לוֹ אוֹצָרוֹת בְּלוּסִים, וְהָיוּ בְּנֵי הַמְּדִינָה מְלִיזִין אַחֲרֵי הַמֶּלֶךְ
לֵאמֹר, מִזְגּוֹ שֶׁל מֶלֶךְ רָעָה, מֶה עָשָׂה הַמֶּלֶךְ, פָּתַח לָהֶם הַמְאֻשָּׁרִים שֶׁבָּהֶם, וּמִלְאוּ אֶת כָּל
הַמְּדִינָה סַרְיוּת, הִתְחִילוּ גוֹרְפִים וּמַשְׁלִיכִים לַיְאוֹר, כָּךְ, אֵלּוּ הַחֲשׁוּבִים שֶׁבָּהֶם כָּךְ עָשׂוּ,
הַגְרוּעִים שֶׁבָּהֶם עַל אַחַת כַּמָּה וְכַמָּה.

R. ELEAZAR SAID: THIS MAY BE COMPARED TO A KING WHO POSSESSED
MIXED STORES, AND HIS SUBJECTS CRITICIZED HIM, SAYING, 'THE KING
IS MISERLY.' WHAT DID THE KING DO? HE OPENED UP FOR THEM THE
BEST, AND THEY FILLED THE COUNTRY WITH STENCH, SO THAT THEY
HAD TO SWEEP IT OUT AND CAST IT INTO THE FIRE.

R. Eleazar has a different interpretation of the word אמחה – *emcheh*.
It could be translated as "destroy" or "protest," as suggested above, or it
could also mean "erase." For example, if in Hebrew one wanted to erase
chalk from a blackboard, one would use the term למחוק – *limchok*, which
would mean "to erase." This is now the meaning of the parable. It was
God's intention to create 1000 generations as part of His plan for the
world. It was an intention, not an actual fact that happened. But He was
concerned about the quality of the generations. He had therefore started
with what seemed to be the best, namely, the generation of the Flood.
This is like the king in the parable who was critical about the quality of
his fruits, which turned out to be a great failure when he distributed

them to the world. Similarly, the generation of the Flood, which seemed it would have been the best, failed miserably through their sinfulness.

(קהלת ז, כח) 'אָדָם אֶחָד מֵאֶלֶף מָצָאתִי', כְּהָדָא דִתְנַן, אַלְפָא לְיַיִן, 'אָמְחָה אֶת הָאָדָם אֲשֶׁר בָּרָאתִי', אֶלֶף דּוֹר עָלוּ בַּמַּחֲשָׁבָה לְהִבָּרֹאת, וְכַמָּה נִימוֹחוּ מֵהֶם, רַבִּי הוּנָא בְּשֵׁם רַבִּי אֱלִיעֶזֶר בְּנוֹ שֶׁל רַבִּי יוֹסֵי הַגְּלִילִי, אָמַר, תְּשַׁע מֵאוֹת וְשִׁבְעִים וְאַרְבָּעָה דּוֹרוֹת, מַאי טַעֲמֵהּ, (תהלים קה, ח) 'דָּבָר צִוָּה לְאֶלֶף דּוֹר', זֶה הַתּוֹרָה. רַבִּי לֵוִי מְשׁוּם רַבִּי שְׁמוּאֵל בַּר נַחְמָן, תְּשַׁע מֵאוֹת וּשְׁמוֹנִים, מַאי טַעֲמֵהּ, 'דָּבָר צִוָּה לְאֶלֶף דּוֹר', זוֹ הַמִּילָה.

SIMILARLY, THESE WERE THE BEST OF THEM, YET ONLY "ONE MAN [SC. NOAH] AMONG A THOUSAND [ELEF] HAVE I FOUND" (ECCL. 7:28), [ELEF BEING USED IN THE SAME SENSE] AS WHEN WE LEARNED, "BEST QUALITY [ALFA] WINE," AND THEY HAVE ACTED THUS; THEREFORE I WILL BLOT OUT MAN, THE BEST (ASHER) THAT I HAVE CREATED. [GOD] CONTEMPLATED CREATING A THOUSAND GENERATIONS, AND HOW MANY OF THEM WERE BLOTTED OUT? R. HUNA SAID IN THE NAME OF R. ELIEZER, THE SON OF R. JOSE THE GALILEAN: NINE HUNDRED AND SEVENTY-FOUR. WHAT IS THE PROOF? THE WORD WHICH HE COMMANDED AFTER [E.V. 'TO'] A THOUSAND GENERATIONS (PS. 105:8), WHICH REFERS TO THE TORAH. R. LEVI SAID IN THE NAME OF R. SAMUEL B. NAHMAN: NINE HUNDRED AND EIGHTY. WHAT IS THE PROOF? 'THE WORD WHICH HE COMMANDED AFTER A THOUSAND GENERATIONS' REFERS TO CIRCUMCISION.

R. Huna elaborates that it was God's intention to create 1000 generations before the giving of the Torah. What happened to them? Nine hundred seventy-four generations were erased. What, then, happened to the twenty-six generations that were created? There were ten generations from Adam to Noah, followed by ten generations from Noah to Abraham. The crowning achievement were the six generations from Abraham to Moses, climaxed by the giving of the Torah.

The main conclusion of this *Midrash* is that the world cannot survive and, in particular, the Jewish people cannot survive, without a moral commitment. One view states that the moral commitment is dramatized by the covenant of circumcision, which appeared at the time of Abraham. Another view is that the full moral commitment was taken six generations later, at the time of Moses at the receiving of the Torah. The question that would be raised is why would God not wait the whole thousand years? It is because the human being could not survive without it.

Seed Thoughts

The *Tiferet Tzion* makes reference to the Zohar where it says that God was not satisfied with the leadership of Noah. Why was He not satisfied? Because in Noah's case, *lo bikesh rachamim*, meaning he did not use his leadership to beseech God to have mercy on the generation, to eliminate the decree of destruction and give the people another chance. By contrast, the leadership of Abraham was quite remarkable. Even though he knew that the people of Sodom and Gemorah were sinners, he did everything possible to see to it that the innocent would not suffer with the guilty. The same comparison can be made with Moses. After the terrible incident of the golden calf, Moses knew that the people were guilty and had sinned, yet he did everything possible to find arguments that would defend their behavior, which he attributed partly to their fear and their insecurity and other arguments listed in the rabbinical literature. After all, what is leadership? It has to do with having a vision for a community, for a people, for a society that would rehabilitate the people if they required it and would raise them to a higher level of accomplishment. In light of these facts, why did God choose Noah? Because He knew that ten generations later, Abraham would appear and Abraham would justify the creation of the world.

—

Additional Commentaries

Torah as the goal

R. Levi interpreted that 980 generations were eliminated from the 1000 that God
intended, and the remaining 20 were created. What was the source of this? It was the following verse" זכר לעולם בריתו דבר צוה לאלף דור – *zekher le'olam berito davar tzivah le'elef dor*. Notice that this verse contains the world *brit*, which is the commandment of circumcision, and the word *davar*, which is the commandment of the Torah. The commandment of circumcision was given to Abraham at the close of the twentieth generation, and the Torah itself, six generations later through Moses. (*HaMidrash HaMevo'ar*)

ה. אָמַר רַבִּי אַבָּא בַּר כָּהֲנָא, נַעֲשָׂה בַּעֲשֶׂרֶת הַשְּׁבָטִים מַה שֶׁלֹּא נַעֲשָׂה בְּדוֹר הַמַּבּוּל, כְּתִיב
בְּדוֹר הַמַּבּוּל, (בראשית ו, ה) 'וְכָל יֵצֶר מַחְשְׁבֹת לִבּוֹ, רַק רַע כָּל הַיּוֹם', וּבַעֲשֶׂרֶת הַשְּׁבָטִים כְּתִיב,
(מיכה ב, א) 'הוֹי, חֹשְׁבֵי אָוֶן וּפֹעֲלֵי רָע עַל מִשְׁכְּבוֹתָם', הֲרֵי זֶה בַּלַּיְלָה, וּמִנַּיִן אַף בַּיּוֹם, תַּלְמוּד
לוֹמַר, (שם שם, שם) 'בְּאוֹר הַבֹּקֶר יַעֲשׂוּהָ', אוֹתָן לֹא נִשְׁתַּיֵּר מֵהֶן פְּלֵיטָה, וְאֵלּוּ נִשְׁתַּיֵּר מֵהֶן,
אֶלָּא בִּזְכוּת הַצַּדִּיקִים וְהַצַּדִּיקוֹת שֶׁהֵן עֲתִידִין לַעֲמֹד מֵהֶן, הֲדָא הוּא דִכְתִיב, (יחזקאל יד, כב)
'וְהִנֵּה נוֹתְרָה בָּהּ פְּלֵטָה, הַמּוּצָאִים בָּנִים וּבָנוֹת', הִנֵּה מוֹצִיאִים בָּנִים וּבָנוֹת אֵין כְּתִיב כָּאן, אֶלָּא
'הַמּוּצָאִים בָּנִים וּבָנוֹת', בִּזְכוּת הַצַּדִּיקִים וְהַצַּדִּיקוֹת הָעֲתִידִים לַעֲמֹד מֵהֶן.

5. FROM THE FACE OF THE EARTH. R. ABBA B. KAHANA SAID: THE TEN
TRIBES DID WHAT WAS NOT DONE EVEN BY THE GENERATION OF THE
FLOOD. WITH REFERENCE TO THE GENERATION OF THE FLOOD, IT IS
WRITTEN, AND EVERY IMAGINATION OF THE THOUGHTS OF HIS HEART
WAS ONLY EVIL ALL DAY (GEN. 6:5), WHEREAS WITH REFERENCE TO
THE TEN TRIBES IT IS WRITTEN, WOE TO THEM THAT DEVISE INIQUITY
AND WORK EVIL UPON THEIR BEDS (MICAH 2:1), IMPLYING, AT NIGHT.
AND HOW DO WE KNOW THAT THEY DID SO BY DAY TOO? BECAUSE IT
IS STATED, WHEN THE MORNING IS LIGHT, THEY EXECUTE IT (IBID.).
YET OF THOSE [THE GENERATION OF THE FLOOD] NOT A REMNANT WAS
LEFT, WHILE OF THESE A REMNANT WAS LEFT. IT WAS LEFT ONLY FOR
THE SAKE OF THE RIGHTEOUS MEN AND WOMEN THAT WERE DESTINED
TO ARISE FROM THEM, AS IT IS WRITTEN, AND, BEHOLD, THERE SHALL
BE LEFT A REMNANT THEREIN THAT SHALL BE BROUGHT FORTH, BOTH
SONS AND DAUGHTERS (EZEK. 14:22): MEANING, FOR THE SAKE OF THE
RIGHTEOUS MEN AND WOMEN THAT WERE TO ARISE FROM THEM.

This *Midrash* is another interpretation of the verb *emcheh*, from the
root meaning "to destroy." The text mentions with surprise that the behavior of the ten tribes who were exiled after the destruction of the First
Temple was even more evil than that of the generation of the Flood. The
prophet Micah is the source of showing that the evil of the ten tribes was
done by night and even by day, while the evil of the generation of the
Flood was done only by day. Another surprise to the sages was the fact
that despite their evil, a remnant of the ten tribes remained and lived

on into the future, whereas the generation of the Flood was completely obliterated. The answer that they presented was the fact that the ten tribes had a population of young people who were ethically and morally of high quality and that justified their special treatment.

אָמַר רַבִּי בֶּרֶכְיָה, נַעֲשָׂה בְּשֵׁבֶט יְהוּדָה וּבִנְיָמִין, מַה שֶׁלֹּא נַעֲשָׂה בַּסְּדוֹמִיִּים, בַּסְּדוֹמִיִּים כְּתִיב, (בראשית יח, כ) 'וְחַטָּאתָם כִּי כָבְדָה מְאֹד', וּבְשֵׁבֶט יְהוּדָה כְּתִיב, (יחזקאל ט, ט) 'עֲוֹן בֵּית יִשְׂרָאֵל וִיהוּדָה, גָּדוֹל בִּמְאֹד מְאֹד', וְאוֹתָן לֹא נִשְׁתַּיֵּר מֵהֶם פְּלֵיטָה, וְאֵלּוּ נִשְׁתַּיֵּר מֵהֶם פְּלֵיטָה, אֶלָּא, אוֹתָה (איכה ד, ו) 'הַהֲפוּכָה כְמוֹ רָגַע', לֹא פָשְׁטוּ יְדֵיהֶם בַּמִּצְוֹת, (שם שם, שם) 'לֹא חָלוּ בָה יָדַיִם', אָמַר רַבִּי תַּנְחוּם, לֹא חָלַת יָד לְיָד, אֵלּוּ פָשְׁטוּ יְדֵיהֶם בַּמִּצְוֹת, (שם שם, י) 'יְדֵי נָשִׁים רַחֲמָנִיּוֹת בִּשְּׁלוּ יַלְדֵיהֶן', כָּל כָּךְ לָמָּה, 'הָיוּ לְבָרוֹת לָמוֹ, עַל שֶׁבֶר בַּת עַמִּי'.

R. BEREKIAH SAID: THE TRIBES OF JUDAH AND BENJAMIN DID WHAT WAS NOT DONE EVEN IN SODOM. WITH REFERENCE TO SODOM IT IS WRITTEN, AND, VERILY, THEIR SIN IS EXCEEDING GRIEVOUS (GEN. 18:20), WHEREAS OF THE TRIBES OF JUDAH AND BENJAMIN IT SAYS, THE INIQUITY OF THE HOUSE OF LSRAEL AND JUDAH IS MOST EXCEEDING GREAT (EZEK. 9:9); YET OF THE LATTER NOT A REMNANT WAS LEFT, WHILE OF THE FORMER A REMNANT WAS LEFT. BUT THE REASON IS: THE LATTER, THAT WAS OVERTHROWN AS IN A MOMENT (LAM. 4:6), NEVER STRETCHED FORTH THEIR HANDS TO GOOD DEEDS, AS IT IS WRITTEN, HANDS THEREIN AC-CEPTED NO DUTIES (IBID.), WHICH R. TANHUMA INTERPRETED: HAND DID NOT JOIN HAND. BUT THE FORMER STRETCHED FORTH THEIR HANDS TO GOOD DEEDS, AS IT IS WRITTEN, THE HANDS OF WOMEN FULL OF COMPASSION HAVE SODDEN THEIR OWN CHILDREN AND PROVIDED THE MOURNER'S MEAL.

The *Midrash* now finds a second illustration of unequal treatment. Their point is that the tribes of Judah and Benjamin were guilty of worse behavior than the generation of Sodom and Gemorah. Yet Sodom and Gemorah were completely obliterated, while the tribes of Judah and Benjamin were given a future. The answer of the *Midrash* is that Sodom and Gemorah lacked *mitzvot* and generally speaking, when the term *mitzvah* is used in a general way, and not referring to a specific commandment, it usually has the meaning of Tzedakah, or charity. The *Midrash* points out that Sodom and Gemorah lacked this concept of charity. However, there were those in Judah and Benjamin who prac-ticed charity in a very exceptional way.

אָמַר רַבִּי חָנִין, נֶאֱמַר בְּכַרְכֵּי הַיָּם, מַה שֶׁלֹּא נַעֲשָׂה בְּדוֹר הַמַּבּוּל, (צפניה ב, ה) 'הוֹי, יֹשְׁבֵי חֶבֶל הַיָּם, גּוֹי כְּרֵתִים', גּוֹי שֶׁהָיָה רָאוּי לִכָּרֵת, וּבְאֵי זוֹ זְכוּת הֵן עוֹמְדִין, בִּזְכוּת גּוֹי אֶחָד, בִּזְכוּת יְרֵא

שָׁמַיִם אֶחָד, שֶׁהָיוּ מַעֲמִידִין בְּכָל שָׁנָה. רַבִּי לֵוִי פָּתַר לָהּ לִשְׁבַח, גּוֹי שֶׁכָּרַת בְּרִית, הֵיךְ מַה דְּאַתְּ
אָמַר, (נחמיה ט, ח) 'וְכָרוֹת עִמּוֹ הַבְּרִית'.

R. HANIN SAID: WHAT WAS PERPETRATED BY THE COASTAL CITIES WAS
NOT PERPETRATED EVEN BY THE GENERATION OF THE FLOOD, FOR IT
IS WRITTEN, WOE UNTO THE INHABITANTS OF THE SEA-COAST, THE
NATION OF THE CHERETHITES (ZEPH. 2:5), WHICH MEANS THAT THEY
DESERVED TO BE ANNIHILATED (KARETH). YET FOR WHOSE SAKE DO
THEY STAND? FOR THE SAKE OF ONE NATION AND ONE GOD-FEARING
PERSON WHOM THE HOLY ONE, BLESSED BE HE, RECEIVES FROM THEIR
HANDS. 'THE NATION OF THE CHERETHITES': [OTHERS] INTERPRET IT
IN A LAUDATORY SENSE, AS YOU READ, THAT MAKETH (KORETH) THE
COVENANT.

A third example is now brought. The behavior of the coastal cities was
also worse than that of the generation of the Flood. The answer of the
Midrash as to why this was so is that those in the coastal cities whose majority population was not Jewish, from time to time, produced a convert
of the highest quality. That phenomenon saved the coastal cities from
the punishment that would have otherwise been theirs.

—

Seed Thoughts I

As a reader and student of the *Midrash*, I am always impressed with the
sensitivity of the sages of the *Midrash* to the concept of justice and in
particular to the dimension of Divine Justice. If it is true, as the prophets
quoted maintain, that there were situations and people in biblical history whose behavior was worse than the generation of the Flood, how
could that have been tolerated by the Master of the universe? Where is
the justice? As Abraham himself put the question, "Shall not the Judge
of the world do justly?" The *Midrash* attempts to answer this problem:
the justice is in the great potential of the future generations. But can we
not say the same thing of the generation of the Flood? Maybe they also
had great potential and maybe they too could have had offspring that
would eventually would redeem the world.

One gets the impression that the sages of the *Midrash* understood
that the answers that they offered were not nearly as powerful as the
questions they raised. It seems to this reader that the real goal was to
raise the question and make all of us sensitive to the fact that justice
should always prevail, even though we may not know the full answer to

these problems. Maybe some day the Almighty will share these secrets with all of us.

—

Seed Thoughts II

When the word "*mitzvah*" is used in rabbinic writings, simply in a general sense, without specifying a particular commandment, itis always referring to charity. Charity is the greatest of all the commandments.

The word *Tzedakah*, biblically speaking, means righteousness. The rabbis offered a shortcut to righteousness in suggesting that charity is the highest form of *mitzvah* and one of the important roads leading to righteousness.

This is especially true in modern times. Even more so than in the ancient world. When the Temple in Jerusalem was in operation, the various offerings, particularly those related to the individual, offered a remarkable outlet for the expression of an individual's emotional life. There was a sin offering for when some sin or other had occurred. There was a peace offering, usually done to mark a positive celebration. There was a thanksgiving offering, a guilt offering when the person thought he had sinned without being sure of it, and even a doubt offering when the person was uncertain of his next move in life. These outlets are not available today, but charity replaces them all. In times of trouble, we give charity. As the saying goes, צדקה תציל ממות – *tzedakah tatzil memavet*, which means that charity can contribute to a better life. In times of thanksgiving, it is best to give charity. When you are uncertain as to having to thank someone, give charity under their name. No matter what the emotional situation, no matter the purpose or frustration, giving charity is the one tangible, relevant, positive religious act available to all of us in this contemporary world. It is available to all human beings, Jew or non-Jew. But only to Jews is it a *mitzvah*, a commandment. As the saying goes, *stam mitzvah perusho tzedakah*: the highest form is the giving of charity.

—

Additional Commentaries

More about charity (A)

In the rabbinical text known as the ספרי – *Sifre*, it is written, "A good deed for a bad deed and vice versa" (זכות לחובה וחובה לזכות – *zekhut lechovah vechovah lezekhut)*. If someone does something good, he receives that reward which is associated with that commandment. If he does something bad, he receives that punishment which has to do with that particular sin. As it is written in the *Midrash* known as שוחר טוב, – shocher tov, this interpretation is very important for the development of a human being. The reward of a *mitzvah* remains forever and is eternal. But the punishment for a sin is only temporary. Therefore, God would not reduce the eternal reward of a good deed for the sake of punishing a bad deed, which only brings a temporary penalty unless it is the kind of a sin which merits that level of punishment. It so happens that the people of Sodom כפרו – *kafru*; rejected the principle of faith in God. That is why it describes them as not stretching forth their hands to good deeds, because they figured, "What good is it anyway if we become righteous?" But as for Israel, even though their sins may be many, they believe in God and never betrayed their belief in God, and always engaged in charity. (*Yefei To'ar*)

More about charity (B)

It is written, "The hands of compassionate women have boiled their own children; they were their food in the destruction of the daughter of my people" (Lamentations 4:10). This means that the women took the one morsel of bread that they had, deprived their husbands and children of it and gave it to a neighbor who required it for the meal of condolence. This comforted the neighbor. God looked upon this as though they were actually boiling their children. This kind of lovingkindness was done while their children were starving. (Rashi)

So desperate was their situation that even their charity contributed to their ruination (to explain the severity of boiling children.")

ו. רַבִּי יוּדָן, וְרַבִּי פִּינְחָס, רַבִּי יוּדָן אָמַר, מָשָׁל לְמֶלֶךְ שֶׁמָּסַר אֶת בְּנוֹ לְפַיְדָגוֹג, וְהוֹצִיאוֹ לְתַרְבּוּת רָעָה, כָּעַס הַמֶּלֶךְ עַל בְּנוֹ וַהֲרָגוֹ, אָמַר הַמֶּלֶךְ, כְּלוּם הוֹצִיא אֶת בְּנִי לְתַרְבּוּת רָעָה, אֶלָּא זֶה, בְּנִי אָבַד הוּא וְזֶה קַיָּם, לְפִיכָךְ 'מֵאָדָם עַד בְּהֵמָה, עַד רֶמֶשׂ וְעַד עוֹף הַשָּׁמָיִם'.

BOTH MAN, AND BEAST, AND CREEPING THING, AND FOWL OF THE AIR.
R. JUDAN SAID: THIS MAY BE ILLUSTRATED BY THE CASE OF A KING
WHO ENTRUSTED HIS SON TO A TEACHER WHO LED HIM INTO EVIL
WAYS, WHEREAT THE KING BECAME ANGRY WITH HIS SON AND SLEW
HIM. SAID THE KING: 'DID ANY LEAD MY SON INTO EVIL WAYS SAVE THIS
MAN: MY SON HAS PERISHED AND THIS MAN LIVES!' THEREFORE [GOD
DESTROYED] BOTH MAN AND BEAST.

T his *Midrash* is a continuation of the verse in which God declares that
He will destroy the entire world during the generation of the Flood.
Indeed, He did destroy man as well as the beasts of the field. The *Talmud*
asks the question, if a man sins, why should the animals be treated as
though they had also sinned? The *Midrash* tries to respond to this concern. The first answer is that there was a role for the animal in the world
to influence the human being for good. Since that did not happen, they,
too, deserved destruction.

רַבִּי פִּינְחָס אָמַר, מָשָׁל לְמֶלֶךְ שֶׁהָיָה מַשִּׂיא אֶת בְּנוֹ, וְעָשָׂה לוֹ חֻפָּה, סִיְּדָהּ וְכִיְּרָהּ וְצִיְּרָהּ, כָּעַס הַמֶּלֶךְ עַל בְּנוֹ וַהֲרָגוֹ, מֶה עָשָׂה, נִכְנַס לְתוֹךְ הַחֻפָּה, הִתְחִיל לְשַׁבֵּר אֶת הַקַּנְקַנִּים, וּמְפַקִּיעַ בַּחֲצָאוֹת, וּמְקָרֵעַ בַּכִּילָיוֹת, אָמַר הַמֶּלֶךְ, כְּלוּם עָשִׂיתִי זוֹ, אֶלָּא בִּשְׁבִיל בְּנִי, בְּנִי אָבַד, וְזוֹ קַיֶּמֶת, לְפִיכָךְ 'מֵאָדָם עַד בְּהֵמָה עַד עוֹף הַשָּׁמָיִם'.

R. PHINEHAS SAID: A KING GAVE HIS SON IN MARRIAGE AND PREPARED
A NUPTIAL CHAMBER FOR HIM, PLASTERING, PAINTING, AND DECORAT-
ING IT. SUBSEQUENTLY, THE KING WAS ANGRY WITH HIS SON AND SLEW
HIM, WHEREUPON HE ENTERED THE NUPTIAL CHAMBER AND BROKE
THE [SUPPORTING] RODS, TORE DOWN THE PARTITIONS, AND RENT
THE CURTAINS, EXCLAIMING: 'MY SON HAS PERISHED: SHALL THESE
REMAIN!' THEREFORE [GOD DESTROYED] BOTH MAN AND BEAST.

The same holds true for the second parable. God expected man to be protected by the world. When this did not happen, there was no reason to protect this environment, which was, therefore, destroyed.

הֲדָא הוּא דִכְתִיב, (צפניה א, ב-ג) 'אָסֹף אָסֵף כֹּל, מֵעַל פְּנֵי הָאֲדָמָה, נְאֻם ה', אָסֵף אָדָם וּבְהֵמָה, אָסֵף עוֹף הַשָּׁמַיִם וּדְגֵי הַיָּם, וְהַמַּכְשֵׁלוֹת אֶת הָרְשָׁעִים', הֵם הִכְשִׁילוּ אֶת הָרְשָׁעִים, כַּד הֲוָה צָיֵד עוֹפָא, וְאָמַר לֵהּ זִיל וְאִשְׁתַּמֵן וְאָתֵי, וְהוּא אָזֵל וּמִשְׁתַּמֵן וְאָתֵי.

AS IT IS WRITTEN, I WILL CONSUME MAN AND BEAST, ETC. (ZEPH. 1:3). [THE VERSE CONTINUES,] AND THE STUMBLING BLOCKS WITH THE WICKED (IBID.): IT WAS THEY [THE ANIMALS, ETC.] WHICH CAUSED THE WICKED TO STUMBLE, FOR ONE WOULD CATCH A BIRD AND SAY TO IT, 'GO, FATTEN THYSELF, AND THEN RETURN,' WHEREUPON IT WOULD GO, FATTEN ITSELF, AND THEN RETURN.

This last section should be understood as relating to the views of R. Huna, who maintains that it was the goal of the animal world to protect the human being and lead him to a better life. The text here says that when hunting birds, the man would say to the bird, "Go fatten yourself up and then return to me." They would do so, meaning they did everything man commanded and fulfilled his every whim.

—

Seed Thoughts

The last section of this *Midrash* is most intriguing. Why was the influence of the animal world on man so destructive? The answer is that they did for man everything that he wanted and there is no greater recipe for disaster than that. What is there about having only good things happen to you that is so disastrous? Let us be clear that it is not so much good things in general, but those areas that are in man's power to control. When that control is lost or compromised or rejected, only destruction can result. What is this destruction being talked about and how does it happen? When a person's every wish and whim is satisfied, there can be no such thing as morality. How do we differentiate between right and wrong? If a person gets everything, how could there be a conception of wrong or anything being described as wrong when all the things that happen to you are either right or made to look right?

The second terrible consequence of experiencing only good and happy things is that the creation of character is at stake. Character depends on responsibility, self-control, reflection, etc. – all of which depend upon human reason and the very limitations of being a human being. The third area of human life that suffers much when only good things are allowed to happen is the lack of challenge. Challenge is the key ingredient to the formation of character and the elevation of the human personality to his highest capacity. Sometimes, challenge involves taking risks. Sometimes challenge involves failure and the need to accept failure as a possibility of human life. But sometimes also, challenges can help us surmount many difficulties and lead us to experiences of satisfaction and fulfillment.

Two children were arguing about the existence of God, one denying His existence and one affirming it. They decided to put their beliefs to the test. They would ask for ice cream and return after two hours to see if their prayers were answered. Two hours later, they met again. The first child said, "You see? God does not answer our prayers, we do not have our ice cream." The second child says, "God does answer our prayers. He said, 'No you cannot have it.'"

The ability to say, 'No you cannot have it' is one of the most important lessons of the moral life. Without it, there is devastation. With it, much can be accomplished.

—

Addtional commentary

The disagreement between R. Judan and R. Phinehas (A)

According to R. Judan, the human being has to achieve whatever it is that he can achieve through the use of his talents and behavior. The human being needs help in this kind of fulfillment. This is why the animals were created. When their help fails, man also fails and all have to be destroyed together. R. Phinehas explains that the natural world is dependent on man and man has to function within it. Therefore, when he fails, everything else fails. (*Tiferet Tzion*)

The disagreement between R. Judan and R. Phinehas (B)

The reason why R. Judan and R. Phinehas disagree may be stated as follows: It was the view of R. Judan that every aspect of creation has its own individuality, not necessarily connected to man. Therefore, one has to look for a reason why the animals of that generation were being destroyed. The only reason he could think of was that the animals had misled man. R. Phinehas, on the other hand, maintains that everything was created for the sake of man and no special reasons or interpretations are necessary to explain why the animals were punished. When man is eliminated, everything else is eliminated. Everyone, including the animals are left without a role. (*Yefei To'ar*)

ז. אָמַר רַבִּי אֶלְעָזָר, (איוב כב, כ) 'אִם לֹא נִכְחַד קִימָנוּ', בַּתְּחִלָּה אִבֵּד הַקָּדוֹשׁ בָּרוּךְ הוּא אֶת
מָמוֹנָן, שֶׁלֹּא יִהְיוּ אוֹמְרִים לְמָמוֹנֵנוּ הוּא צָרִיךְ. (שם שם, שם) 'וְיִתְרָם אָכְלָה אֵשׁ', שֶׁהָיוּ רוֹאִים
בּוֹלָרִיּוֹת שֶׁל זָהָב נִתָּרוֹת בָּאֵשׁ.

7. R. ELEAZAR QUOTED: SURELY THEIR SUBSTANCE IS CUT OFF (JOB 22:20).
FIRST THE HOLY ONE, BLESSED BE HE, DESTROYED THEIR WEALTH, LEST
THEY SHOULD SAY, 'HE NEEDS OUR WEALTH.' AND THEIR ABUNDANCE
THE FIRE HATH CONSUMED (IBID.): THEY SAW THEIR CHAINS OF GOLD
MELTED IN THE FIRE.

The text of this passage has to be understood as similar to the preceding *midrashim*, namely, "I will destroy man." At the same time, the article את – *et*, used with "the," has to be understood as being inclusive. What the *et* comes to include in this *Midrash* is their wealth, which also had to be destroyed. The fact that they thought that God needed their wealth for His purposes is quite outrageous. What it probably means (see additional commentary) is that God was reserving their wealth for Noah and his family because He loved them more.

אָמַר רַבִּי עֲקִיבָא, הַכֹּל קָרְאוּ תֶגֶר, עַל הַכֶּסֶף וְעַל הַזָּהָב שֶׁיָּצָא עִמָּהֶם מִמִּצְרָיִם, שֶׁנֶּאֱמַר (ישעיה
א, כב) 'כַּסְפֵּךְ הָיָה לְסִיגִים', (הושע ב, י) 'וְכֶסֶף הִרְבֵּיתִי לָהֶם, וְזָהָב עָשׂוּ לַבַּעַל', (שם ח, ד) 'כַּסְפָּם
וּזְהָבָם עָשׂוּ לָהֶם עֲצַבִּים לְמַעַן יִכָּרֵת', רַבִּי הוּנָא וְרַבִּי יִרְמְיָה בְּשֵׁם רַבִּי שְׁמוּאֵל בַּר רַב יִצְחָק,
לְמַעַן יִכָּרְתוּ, אֵין כְּתִיב כָּאן, אֶלָּא, 'לְמַעַן יִכָּרֵת'. כְּאִינִישׁ דְּאָמַר, יִתְמְחֵק שְׁמֵהּ דִּפְלָן, דְּאַפְקֵהּ
לִבְרִי לְתַרְבּוּת בִּישָׁא.

R. AKIBA SAID: ALL [THE PROPHETS] COMPLAINED OF THE GOLD AND
SILVER WHICH WENT FORTH WITH THEM FROM EGYPT: E.G., THY SILVER
IS BECOME DROSS (ISA. 1:22); AND MULTIPLIED UNTO HER SILVER AND
GOLD, WHICH THEY USED FOR BAAL (HOS. II, 10); OF THEIR SILVER AND
THEIR GOLD HAVE THEY MADE THEM IDOLS, ETC. (IBID., 8:4). R. HUNA
AND R. JEREMIAH IN THE NAME OF R. SAMUEL B. ISAAC SAID: IT IS NOT
WRITTEN, VTHAT THEY MAY BE CUT OFF,' BUT THAT IT MAY BE CUT OFF
(IBID.), AS A MAN SAYS: 'I WILL BLOT OUT THE NAME OF SO-AND-SO WHO
LED MY SON INTO EVIL PATHS.'

R. Akiva makes an important point, which will be developed shortly. He uses the wealth acquired in Egypt as a way of proving the risks that are involved in having too much material wealth. The prophets have pointed out that the wealth that they brought out of Egypt was a great contributing factor to the creation of the golden calf. Therefore, it is a great warning of the risks that are involved in having too much in terms of material things.

—

Seed Thoughts

The *Tiferet Tzion* (28:07) has a beautiful interpretation of the verse from Isaiah, כספך היהלסיגים – *kaspekh hayah lesigim*, which means, "Your silver has become dross." It does not mean that the silver was mixed together with other minerals, such as copper or nickel, but rather that the currency itself became dross, meaning that it lost its value and meaning. Money can be looked at from two points of view: quantitative and qualitative. The value of currency has very little to do with one particular individual, but has to do with economic factors that relate to a particular society. However, from the qualitative point of view, money depends entirely on the behavior of the individual. In the first place, it has to be acquired legitimately, honestly and without harming any other element of society. In the second place, it can and should be used for the highest purposes in the area of גמילות חסדים – *gmilut chasadim*, acts of charity and lovingkindness.

As these words are being written, the two richest men in the world, Bill Gates and Warren Buffett, are combining their resources so that their fortunes can be dedicated to charitable purposes of the highest sort. This is surely a קדוש השם – *kiddush hashem*. On the other hand, it is possible for too much wealth to lead to the deterioration of human behavior, either through conceit, selfishness, arrogance, the use of power to oppress others or the use of personal anger and temperament to control others. Material wealth by itself is a neutral factor. How it can be used is one of the great tests of mankind. The generation of the Flood failed that test. We still have a chance to pass that test if the best part of our character will come forward to lead us and bless the world.

—

Addtional Commentary

The article et *is meant to be inclusive*

In the case of this *Midrash*, the article *et* is meant to include the wealth of that generation. A reason is offered as to why God preferred to destroy the wealth and not to keep it as a legacy for Noah and his family: it was a sign of His love for them. The reason was that He never wanted it to seem as though He destroyed the generation of the Flood simply for this kind of reason, so that it would favor Noah and his family. If that were so, the generation of the Flood would resent it very much and every opportunity for *tshuvah*, penitence (even after their death), would have been destroyed. It was, therefore, important to get rid of their material substance in an obvious way so that everyone would understand that their punishment was due to the evil behavior of the generation of the Flood. (*Tiferet Tzion*)

Said R. Akiva

R. Akiva offers more evidence that their evil behavior was due to the abundance of their wealth, which influenced every aspect of their temptation for evil. He brings a powerful example from what happened in Egypt: One can say about the generation of the Flood that they acquired their wealth via sinful behavior, deceit, cheating, etc. Nothing of this sort happened in Egypt. One can even say that the money that the Jews acquired was a direct commandment from God, Who advised them to request it of their Egyptian neighbors, who owed them so very much. Despite the honorable beginning, this wealth had a terrible effect on the people – how much more so for the generation of the Flood, who acquired the funds in a sinful manner. (*Tiferet Tzion*)

ח. רַבִּי עֲזַרְיָה, בְּשֵׁם רַבִּי יְהוּדָה בַּר סִימוֹן, אָמַר, הַכֹּל קִלְקְלוּ מַעֲשֵׂיהֶן בְּדוֹר הַמַּבּוּל, הַכֶּלֶב הָיָה
הוֹלֵךְ אֵצֶל הַזְּאֵב, וְהַתַּרְנְגוֹל הָיָה מְהַלֵּךְ אֵצֶל הַטַּוָּס, הָדָא הוּא דִכְתִיב, (בראשית ו, יב) 'כִּי הִשְׁחִית
כָּל בָּשָׂר' הִשְׁחִית כָּל אָדָם אֵין כְּתִיב, אֶלָּא, 'כִּי הִשְׁחִית כָּל בָּשָׂר.' רַבִּי לוּלְיָאנִי בַּר טַבְרִין בְּשֵׁם
רַבִּי יִצְחָק, אָמַר, אַף הָאָרֶץ זִנְּתָה, הָיוּ זַרְעִין לָהּ חִטִּין, וְהִיא מַפְקָא זוּנִין, אִלֵּין זוּנַיָּא רַבָּה מִן
דָּרָא דְּמַבּוּלָא אִנּוּן.

8. R. AZARIAH SAID IN R. JUDAH B. SIMON'S NAME: ALL ACTED COR-
RUPTLY IN THE GENERATION OF THE FLOOD: THE DOG [COPULATED]
WITH THE WOLF, THE FOWL WITH THE PEACOCK; HENCE IT IS WRITTEN,
FOR ALL FLESH HAD CORRUPTED THEIR WAY, ETC. (GEN. 6:12). R. JULIAN
[LULIANUS] B. TIBERIUS SAID IN R. ISAAC'S NAME: EVEN THE EARTH
ACTED LEWDLY; WHEAT WAS SOWN AND IT PRODUCED PSEUDO-WHEAT,
FOR THE PSEUDO-WHEAT WE NOW FIND CAME FROM THE AGE OF THE
DELUGE.

This *Midrash* is self-explanatory. For reasons not given and, therefore,
probably not known, everything in creation acted unnaturally and in
corrupt fashion. One species copulated with another species. In actual
fact, the *Midrash* does indicate that those species that had similar appearances copulated with each other. This probably means that like
creatures had the ability to do so and that unlike creatures did not. It
was not only animal life that acted in this extraordinary fashion; so did
the earth itself. Seeds of one kind were planted, but blossoms or fruit
of another kind responded to the planting. Everything was unnatural,
illogical, incomprehensible, and The Creator felt that this could not go
on in this manner, so it was destroyed.

—

Seed Thoughts I

A reader of the *Midrash* is impressed by the fact that the sages were
very sensitive to Divine Justice. Of course they accepted the story of

the Flood in the Bible. However, its implications bothered them very much. For one thing, how could every human being be equally sinful? Secondly, if man sinned, why should animals pay the penalty? Several of the *midrashim* just concluded dealt with these questions and have offered answers that seemed to be acceptable. A similar notion can be found in this *midrash*. Granted that domestic animals were involved with man and were, therefore, doomed to suffer the same fate as man, but could that be said of the wild beast of the field? This sensitivity is something that is very commendable and should be learned to understand and appreciate. The answer of the *Midrash* may or may not be acceptable. Do we really know that the wild beasts were provoked into corruption by human beings? The important point here is not that the answer is convincing, but that the sages of the *Midrash* were asking the right questions. Divine Justice has to be clear. When it is not clear, we should do our best to try to understand it.

Seed Thoughts II

One might ask if this *midrash, in talking of the corruption of the animals and plants,* is opposed to the achievements of modern scientific research. After all, modern botany works on the modification of fruits and vegetables to produce new varieties, and modern zoology in the breeding of certain animals, in order to produce a higher quality of offspring, some for personal benefit and others for social benefits. Many such things are also done in the medical milieu. Much is happening today in the area of genetics as it concerns animals, crops and humans – can it be that the *Midrash* is speaking against such innovations? Does this mean that what we are engaged in today is prohibited?

I think that this actually is not the point of this midrash; the midrash here is trying to stress the idea that when man falls into moral corruption, so does all of creation, whether it be the animal kingdom or the plant world. All are linked, as in a domino effect, to man, who is the center of creation. The midrash is dealing with the issue of *moral* corruption and not the scientific quest of how to benefit man and plant life by horticulture or interbreeding.

Addtional Commentary

Everybody was corrupt

That is why it says, "Everyone was eliminated, including animals, creeping things, etc." All of them behaved corruptly. However, if the animals were punished because of the sins of man, the only ones that should have been punished were those related to man, such as sheep and birds (namely, domesticated animals), but not the wild beasts or wild birds and the various creeping things, which were not connected to the human being at all. They are usually hidden in forests, deep valleys, high mountains or jungles. The only answer is that human beings tried to motivate them to copulate with each other and thus, even the wild beasts became involved in the corruption. (Maharzu)

ט. אָמַר רַבִּי יוֹחָנָן, מִשְׁפַּט דּוֹר הַמַּבּוּל שְׁנֵים עָשָׂר שָׁנִים עָשָׂר חֹדֶשׁ, נָטְלוּ דִינָם וְיִהְיֶה לָהֶם חֵלֶק לָעוֹלָם הַבָּא, דַּאֲמַר רַבִּי יוֹחָנָן, כָּל טִפָּה וְטִפָּה שֶׁהַקָּדוֹשׁ בָּרוּךְ הוּא מוֹרִיד עֲלֵיהֶם הָיָה מַרְתִּיחָהּ בְּגֵיהִנָּם, וּמוֹצִיאָהּ וּמוֹרִידָהּ עֲלֵיהֶם, הָדָא הוּא דִכְתִיב, (איוב ו, יז) 'בְּעֵת יְזֹרְבוּ נִצְמָתוּ', זְרִיבָתָם, לַחֲלֻטָנִית הָיְתָה.

9. R. JOHANAN SAID: WE LEARNT: THE JUDGMENT OF THE GENERATION OF THE FLOOD LASTED TWELVE MONTHS: HAVING RECEIVED THEIR PUNISHMENT, ARE THEY TO ENJOY A PORTION IN THE WORLD TO COME? SAID R. JOHANAN: THE HOLY ONE, BLESSED BE HE, WILL BOIL UP IN GEHENNA EVERY SINGLE DROP WHICH HE POURED OUT ON THEM, PRO-DUCE IT AND POUR IT DOWN UPON THEM. THUS IT IS WRITTEN, WHAT TIME THEY WAX HOT, THEY VANISH (JOB 6:17), WHICH MEANS, THEY WILL BE DESTROYED ABSOLUTELY BY SCALDING WATER.

The idea that the Flood lasted for twelve months is based on the fol-lowing verses. It says in Genesis 7:10 that Noah was 600 years old when the Flood started. It then says in Genesis 8:13 that when he was 601 years old, this is the source of the Flood lasting for twelve months. If, dur-ing this period of time, the generation of the Flood received their due judgment and punishment, does that not mean that they were eligible for the World to Come? At this point, some of the commentators have different views. The text interprets R. Yochanan's view that the drops of water that created the Flood were tremendously hot and burning like the fires of hell. It can be interpreted as either completely eliminating that generation from existence, or completing their punishment, which would enable them to have a share in the World to Come. The *Tiferet Tzion* makes the point that those who lived during the generation of the Flood but died before the Flood would not inherit the World to Come. However, those who experienced the Flood did have a share in the World to Come. This is how the *Tiferet Tzion* interprets the *Mishnah* in *Sanhedrin* 10:3, which asserts that the generation of the Flood had no share in the World to Come. Another commentator, Aryeh Mirkin, maintains that the severity of the Flood was so intense that a greater punishment for them was not on the agenda and therefore, they had a share in the World to Come.

(קהלת ט, ו) 'גַּם אַהֲבָתָם' שֶׁהָיוּ אוֹהֲבִים לַעֲבוֹדַת כּוֹכָבִים שֶׁלָּהֶם, (שם שם, שם) 'גַּם שִׂנְאָתָם' שֶׁהָיוּ שׂוֹנְאִים לְהַקָּדוֹשׁ בָּרוּךְ הוּא, (שם שם, שם) 'גַּם קִנְאָתָם' שֶׁהָיוּ מְקַנְאִים לְהַקָּדוֹשׁ בָּרוּךְ הוּא, בַּעֲבוֹדַת כּוֹכָבִים שֶׁלָּהֶם, (שם שם, שם) 'כְּבָר אָבָדָה', (שם שם, שם) 'וְחֵלֶק אֵין לָהֶם עוֹד לְעוֹלָם', עַל דְּבָרַת (שם שם, שם) 'בְּכֹל אֲשֶׁר נַעֲשָׂה תַּחַת הַשָּׁמֶשׁ'.

AS WELL THEIR LOVE (ECCL. 9:6)– I.E., THEY LOVED IDOLATRY; AS THEIR HATRED (IBID.): THEY HATED THE HOLY ONE, BLESSED BE HE, AND PROVOKED HIS JEALOUSY; IS LONG AGO PERISHED, NEITHER HAVE THEY ANY MORE A PORTION IN THE WORLD [TO COME] ON ACCOUNT OF EVERYTHING THAT WAS DONE [BY THEM] UNDER THE SUN (IBID.).

This section continues to assert that the generation of the Flood was so evil that even though the Flood was great and terrible punishment, their evil was such that it even denied them a share in the World to Come.

אָמַר רַבִּי אַבָּא בַּר כָּהֲנָא, 'כִּי נִחַמְתִּי כִּי עֲשִׂיתִם, וְנֹחַ מָצָא חֵן' אַתְמְהָא, אֶלָּא, אֲפִלּוּ נֹחַ שֶׁנִּשְׁתַּיֵּר מֵהֶם, לֹא שֶׁהָיָה כְדַאי, אֶלָּא, שֶׁמָּצָא חֵן.

FOR IT REPENTETH ME, ETC. R. ABBA B. KAHANA OBSERVED: FOR IT REPENTETH ME THAT I HAVE MADE THEM AND NOAH – SURELY NOT! EVEN NOAH, HOWEVER, WAS LEFT NOT BECAUSE HE DESERVED IT, BUT BECAUSE HE FOUND GRACE: HENCE, BUT NOAH FOUND GRACE IN THE EYES OF THE LORD.

The fact that the name of Noah appears very close to the statement that God regretted the creation of the world seems to belittle the status of Noah, suggesting that he, too, left much to be desired from a moral point of view. But Noah found favor in the eyes of God, probably, as the *Tiferet Tzion* suggests, because Moses would be one of his descendants.

—

Seed Thoughts

The sages of the *Midrash* were very much convinced of the existence of the World to Come. They knew very well that this doctrine was not based on knowledge from personal experience, but was a matter of faith. This faith, however, and this belief was so strong that they accepted it as a reality. They spoke about it in terms of its inevitability and also as a factor to be considered very seriously in creating a moral life. To the average reader, it may not seem to matter too much whether the generation of the Flood had a share in the World to Come. To the sages, however, it was of tremendous importance. If, indeed, the generation of the Flood had a share in the World to Come, it meant that the concept of תשובה – repentance, could work even for a generation as evil as that of the Flood, that even they could achieve forgiveness and a rebirth. On the other hand, if they did not have a share in the World to Come, it meant that there were limits to repentance, and that not everyone could achieve forgiveness. The important lesson for all of us who study *Midrash* is to note that the concept of the World to Come and all those issues associated with it was of primary interest to the sages of the *Midrash* and that their spiritual world was largely based upon it.

—

Additional Commentary

And Noah found grace in the eyes of God

Everything about this verse appears to be unnecessary because the story of Noah appears in such detail that everything eventually is revealed in the narrative. Notice that there is a ו – *vav* that preceded the name Noah. It says ונח מצא חן – *veNoach matza chen*, "and Noah found grace." Since this phrase is placed very close to the preceding words, where God says that He regrets having created man, it seems to imply also a regret for having created Noah. This seems to be the impression that the verse was trying to create. Despite all of this, it says that Noah found grace in the eyes of God. (Maharzu)

א. (ו, ח) 'וְנֹחַ מָצָא חֵן בְּעֵינֵי ה'', כְּתִיב (איוב כב, ל) 'יְמַלֵּט אִי נָקִי, וְנִמְלַט בְּבֹר כַּפֶּיךָ

1. BUT NOAH FOUND GRACE IN THE EYES OF THE LORD (6:8). HE DELIV-
ERETH HIM THAT IS INNOCENT (I NAKI), YEA, THOU SHALT BE DELIV-
ERED THROUGH THE CLEANNESS OF THY HANDS (JOB 22:30).

As explained from parashah 26 onward, these verses from the Book
of Job are interpreted as relating to the Flood and the generation of the
Flood. Thus the verse, "He delivered him that is innocent" is interpreted
as referring to God in relationship to the generation of the Flood, and
"thou shalt be delivered . . ." is interpreted as referring to Noah.

אָמַר רַבִּי חֲנִינָא, אִינּוֹנִיתָא, אוּנְקְיָא אַחַת הָיְתָה בְּיַד נֹחַ, אִם כֵּן לָמָה נִמְלָט, אֶלָּא 'בְּבֹר כַּפֶּיךָ',
אַתְיָא, כְּהַהִיא דַאֲמַר רַבִּי אַבָּא בַּר כָּהֲנָא, 'כִּי נִחַמְתִּי כִּי עֲשִׂיתִם וְנֹחַ' אֲפִלּוּ נֹחַ שֶׁנִּשְׁתַּיֵּר מֵהֶן,
לֹא הָיָה כְדַאי, אֶלָּא, שֶׁמָּצָא חֵן בְּעֵינֵי ה', שֶׁנֶּאֱמַר 'וְנֹחַ מָצָא חֵן בְּעֵינֵי ה''.

R. HANINA SAID: NOAH POSSESSED LESS THAN AN OUNCE (UNKIA) [OF
MERIT]. IF SO, WHY WAS HE DELIVERED? ONLY 'THROUGH THE CLEAN-
NESS OF THY HANDS'. THIS AGREES WITH WHAT R. ABBA B. KAHANA
SAID: FOR IT REPENTETH ME THAT I HAVE MADE THEM AND NOAH. BUT
NOAH WAS LEFT ONLY BECAUSE HE FOUND GRACE; HENCE, BUT NOAH
FOUND GRACE IN THE EYES OF THE LORD.

The term אונקיא – *unkia* is used to explain why God selected Noah. It is
not that Noah was so great, but he did have a certain amount of worthiness, even though it might have been minimal as compared to other great
scriptural names. In the Tractate of the *Yerushalmi Peah*, the term *unkia*
is explained as meaning one twelfth of a liter. The same expression can
be found in Latin and it means משהוא – *mashehu*, a very small amount.
In the Book of Job, these words were said by *Eliphaz HaTeimani*, as a
sort of comfort to Job, that God comforts and heals even those who are
אי נקי – *i naki*, not completely pure. The reference in the text refers to Job,
which the *Midrash* transfers to Noah. (Aryeh Mirkin)

Seed Thoughts

You do not have to be a great personality with an overwhelming presence and much charisma in order to be chosen by God for His purposes. You could be a plain, ordinary person with limited good qualities. If God feels that you can fulfill His requirements, then you are chosen. This is an important lesson to all of us, for very few of us can expect to become another Abraham or another Moses. But we could become another Noah. When the text says, 'נח מצא חן בעיני ה – that Noah found favor in the eyes of God, the word *chen* should not be merely understood as meaning "charm" as it is often used in Yiddish. Why would God be interested in charm or anything as superficial as that?! The word *chen* should be understood as meaning "worth." Noah was found worthy. His worthiness may not be as great as some of the more prominent scriptural characters, but he was worthy, and therefore, he was chosen to recreate the world through the ark. Our goal should be worthiness. Of course we are limited by our talents and our disposition, but within those constraints, it should be our goal to make our lives as worthy as possible.

―

Additional Commentary

He delivereth him that is innocent (A)

The Holy One, Blessed be He, will deliver Noah, even though he possesses only a small amount (an ounce, according to Soncino) of merit. This is done to preserve the cleanness of the hands of the Holy One, Blessed be He. The main lesson here is that God will not belittle even the smallest merit that a person demonstrates. (Aryeh Mirkin)

He delivereth him that is innocent (B)

In the *Yalkut* in this section and that of *Job*, they do not use the term אינוניתא – but rather the term אונקיא – *unkia*. The reason for this has to do with the combination of the two words in the term *i naki*: this should not be interpreted as meaning "not clean at all," for if so, neither Job nor Noah would have been delivered; the interpretation, rather, is צדיק קטן – *tzaddik katan*, a small righteous man, whose merits were limited. It was the righteousness of God that insisted that even the small measure of righteousness deserves a reward. (Maharzu)

PARASHAH TWENTY-NINE, *Midrash Two*

ב. רַבִּי סִימוֹן פָּתַח, (ישעיה סה, ח) 'כֹּה אָמַר ה', כַּאֲשֶׁר יִמָּצֵא הַתִּירוֹשׁ בָּאֶשְׁכּוֹל וְאָמַר אַל
תַּשְׁחִיתֵהוּ כִּי בְרָכָה בּוֹ', מַעֲשֶׂה בְחָסִיד אֶחָד שֶׁיָּצָא לְכַרְמוֹ בַּשַּׁבָּת, וְרָאָה עוֹלֵלָה אַחַת, וּבֵרַךְ
עָלֶיהָ, אָמַר, כְּדַאי הִיא הָעוֹלֵלָה הַזּוֹ שֶׁנְּבָרֵךְ עָלֶיהָ, כָּךְ, 'כֹּה אָמַר ה', כַּאֲשֶׁר יִמָּצֵא הַתִּירוֹשׁ
בָּאֶשְׁכּוֹל, וְגו'".

2. R. SIMON QUOTED: THUS SAITH THE LORD: AS, WHEN WINE IS FOUND
IN THE CLUSTER, ONE SAITH: DESTROY IT NOT, FOR A BLESSING IS IN
IT (ISA. 65:8). IT IS RELATED THAT A CERTAIN PIOUS MAN WENT OUT
TO HIS VINEYARD AND SEEING A SINGLE [RIPE] BUNCH, PRONOUNCED
A BLESSING OVER IT, SAYING, 'THIS SINGLE BUNCH MERITS A BLESSING.'
EVEN SO, 'THUS SAITH THE LORD: AS, WHEN WINE IS FOUND IN THE
CLUSTER,' ETC.

This is an additional interpretation of the phrase, "And Noah found
favor in the eyes of God." While the grape has intrinsic value in its own
right, for a wine maker, the grape is only a vehicle for something greater,
namely, the creation of wine. The story of the pious man is a very beautiful one. In visiting his vineyard, he found only one ripe bunch of grapes.
Some owners would simply discard it because the wine production
would be unsuccessful. Not so, the chassid. He thanked God for this
one cluster and looked forward to the wine that would yet be produced.
This is a parable that can be used in many directions. The world has at
times had difficult generations. But man had to be preserved to enable
the many righteous men and women in the future to arise. This is also
a blessing for Noah, because he, too, had great potential. Through his
children emerged Abraham and the nation of Israel.

—

Seed Thoughts

The *midrashim* that we now have studied have a goal, to search for the
merits of Noah. There was a tendency on the part of some of the sages
to belittle Noah. Rashi and other commentators are quick to point out

that Noah may have been righteous in his generation, but would have never appeared in the same capacity were he in the same generation as Abraham. The *midrashim* that we are now studying are to build up a case that would oppose such views. We learned in the previous *midrash* that Noah had worth. It may have been a limited kind of worth. He may have been a small-time tzaddik, but he did have merit and God acknowledged this fact by choosing him. Our present *midrash* moves into a different dimension and sees the importance of Noah as relating to his potential. His potential included Abraham and Moses and the children of Israel. He thus became an important link to the great generations of the founding fathers of mankind and he deserves to be in a category with them.

—

Additional Commentary

The pious man and the grape

The chassid, or pious man, found only one cluster in his vineyard, which rendered the vinyard not of an acceptable caliber. Some owners would decide to destroy the vineyard and start anew. But the chassid did not. He thanked God, even for the one cluster or the one grape, which he knew would someday produce more. His theory was that any יש – *yesh* is better than אין – *ein*. The littlest something is better than nothing. The chassid blessed the grape. He did not eat of the fruit because it was the Sabbath and it was still connected to the branch. But he thanked God for it. This case relates very well to that of Noah, who will be justified by his potential just as wine is justified by the grape. (Maharzu)

ג. אָמַר רַבִּי סִימוֹן, שָׁלֹשׁ מְצִיאוֹת מָצָא הַקָּדוֹשׁ בָּרוּךְ הוּא, אַבְרָהָם, דִּכְתִיב (נחמיה ט, ח)
'וּמָצָאתָ אֶת לְבָבוֹ נֶאֱמָן לְפָנֶיךָ', דָּוִד, דִּכְתִיב (תהלים פט, כא) 'מָצָאתִי דָּוִד עַבְדִּי', יִשְׂרָאֵל,
דִּכְתִיב (הושע ט, י) 'כַּעֲנָבִים בַּמִּדְבָּר מָצָאתִי יִשְׂרָאֵל'.

3. BUT NOAH FOUND GRACE IN THE EYES OF THE LORD. R. SIMON SAID:
THE HOLY ONE, BLESSED BE HE, FOUND THREE TREASURES: AND THOU
FOUNDEST HIS [ABRAHAM'S] HEART FAITHFUL BEFORE THEE (NEH. 9:8);
I HAVE FOUND DAVID MY SERVANT (PS. 89:21); I FOUND ISRAEL LIKE
GRAPES IN THE WILDERNESS (HOS. 9:10).

W e are still dealing with the basic text, which reads that Noah found
favor in the eyes of God. The problem as perceived by the *Midrash* is
that it does not say that God found Noah to be a *tzaddik*, righteous. It
merely says that he found favor in the eyes of God. R. Simon advances
this discussion by asserting that there are three places in Scripture where
the word מוצא – *motze*, from the root "to find," is used, and in each case,
it indicates that something very good was attributed to the individual
concerned. The first was Abraham, where it says specifically that God
found his heart faithful. The second was in the case of David, where
God ordered Samuel to anoint him as king, which, of course, indicates
that he had become an important treasure in the eyes of God. The third
was the case of Israel, who are described as being precious as grapes in
the wilderness, and thus entitled to be the receivers of the Torah.

אֵיתִיבוּן חַבְרַיָּא לְרַבִּי סִימוֹן, וְהָא כְתִיב, 'וְנֹחַ מָצָא חֵן', אָמַר לְהוֹן, הוּא מָצָא, הַקָּדוֹשׁ בָּרוּךְ
הוּא לֹא מָצָא, וְהָא כְתִיב, (ירמיה לא, א) 'מָצָא חֵן בַּמִּדְבָּר', בִּזְכוּת דּוֹר הַמִּדְבָּר, 'וּמָצָאתָ אֶת
לְבָבוֹ נֶאֱמָן לְפָנֶיךָ'.

HIS COLLEAGUES OBJECTED: SURELY IT IS WRITTEN, BUT NOAH FOUND
GRACE IN THE EYES OF THE LORD? HE FOUND, REPLIED HE, BUT THE
HOLY ONE, BLESSED BE HE, DID NOT FIND. R. SIMON INTERPRETED: THE
PEOPLE THAT WERE LEFT OF THE SWORD HAVE FOUND GRACE IN THE
WILDERNESS (JER. 31:2): THAT MEANS, FOR THE SAKE OF THE GENERA-
TION OF THE WILDERNESS.

The question is then asked, is there not a fourth place where the word *motze* is used, where it says that Noah found favor in the eyes of God?! The answer is given on the basis of the literal translation of the text. In the case of the "good" treasures, Abraham, David and Israel, it says that God "found" them. In the case of Noah, it says that he found favor. It was not interpreted as something meritorious, but as receiving a special favor from God. Even though a similar expression, מצא חן – *matza chen*, found favor, is also found in connection with the wilderness, there, at least, it says specifically that Israel was ready to accept the Torah. Such a positive description is not said about Noah at this point.

—

Seed Thoughts

Many years ago, a guest speaker came to my congregation and elaborated upon the fact that from all the peoples who lived in Mesopotamia in those early days, God revealed Himself only to Abraham. God chose Abraham in a very special and personal way. After this presentation, someone from the audience arose and began to debate with the speaker: "This is not how I understand that portion in Scripture. As I understand, it was Abraham who chose God and not vice versa. He had discovered God through his own intellectual capacities. He had discovered the worthlessness of idol worship. That led him to a discovery of the one God."

This kind of debate has gone on for generations and centuries and there are many who argue on each side. Does it make a difference which interpretation is believed? It probably would make a difference that God revealed Himself to Abraham, as He would eventually do this for all of the children of Israel at Sinai. On the other hand, this may seem to take away from the extent to which Abraham reached God on his own accord and through his own intellectual capacities.

Could this be the real interpretation of this *Midrash*? God revealed Himself to Abraham, David and Israel in a very special way, but Noah reached God in terms of his own personal resources and therefore, this approach was found to be of a lesser importance.

—

Additional Commentary

Found favor

This expression, which is found in connection with the Jews while in the wilderness, is one of the three "treasure expressions" described in the *Midrash*. This is so since, in the case of Israel in the wilderness, the expression used was "found favor [*chen*]." But the same expression is found in the case of Noah, where it says that Noah "found favor." He should therefore be included as the fourth among the treasured people. In addition, it so happens that the expression *matza chen* is found in the Book of Jeremiah about his generation, and his generation left much to be desired. The answer is that Jeremiah's generation were called this as a way of receiving encouragement from the generation in the wilderness. As it is written, "I remember the Israel's *love* in its youth" – not that they were of a high level In connection with Noah, it mentions that he found favor, but this does not imply that God found chen, in the sense of goodness, in him. (Maharzu)

ד. רַבִּי הוּנָא, וְרַבִּי פִּינְחָס, וְרַבִּי חָנִין, וְרַבִּי הוֹשַׁעְיָא, לָא מְפָרְשִׁין, רַבִּי יוֹחָנָן, וְרַבִּי שִׁמְעוֹן בֶּן
לָקִישׁ וְרַבָּנָן מְפָרְשִׁין

4. R. HUNA AND R. PHINEHAS, R. HANAN AND R. HOSHAYA DO NOT
EXPLAIN [WHAT GRACE NOAH FOUND]; R. BEREKIAH IN R. JOHANAN'S
NAME, R. SIMEON B. LAKISH, AND THE RABBIS DO EXPLAIN.

The usual style of Scripture is that when the word *chen* appears, it usually explains why the favor was given. In Noah's case, this explanation
does not appear. R. Huna and a few of the other Rabbis listed do not explain why this omission has occurred. On the other hand, R. Yochanan
and his colleagues do try to explain it:

רַבִּי יוֹחָנָן אָמַר, לְאֶחָד שֶׁהָיָה מְהַלֵּךְ בַּדֶּרֶךְ, וְרָאָה אֶחָד וּדְבָקוֹ, עַד הֵיכָן, עַד שֶׁקָּשַׁר עִמּוֹ אַהֲבָה,
כָּךְ, נֶאֱמַר כָּאן 'חֵן', וְנֶאֱמַר לְהַלָּן, (בראשית לט, ד) 'וַיִּמְצָא יוֹסֵף חֵן בְּעֵינָיו'.

R. JOHANAN SAID: IMAGINE A MAN WALKING ON A ROAD, WHEN HE SAW
SOMEONE WHOM HE ATTACHED TO HIMSELF. TO WHAT EXTENT? UNTIL
HE WAS KNIT TO HIM IN LOVE. SIMILARLY, 'GRACE' IS SAID HERE, WHILE
IN ANOTHER PASSAGE WE READ, AND JOSEPH FOUND FAVOR [GRACE] IN
HIS SIGHT (GEN. 39:3).

The idea of a person walking is related to the verse in Scripture where
it says, את האלוהים התהלך נח – *et haElokim hit'halekh Noach*, meaning
Noah walked with, or followed God, and tried to remain together with
Him until together they achieved a bond of love. This achievement of
love was what merited the description of *chen*, favor or grace. In the case
of Joseph, the word *chen* is also used, where he achieved favor in the eyes
of his master. He received no special advantage, but only *chen*, which is
looked upon as an attribute.

רַבִּי שִׁמְעוֹן בֶּן לָקִישׁ אָמַר, לְאֶחָד שֶׁהָיָה מְהַלֵּךְ וְרָאָה אֶחָד וּדְבָקוֹ, עַד הֵיכָן, עַד שֶׁהִשְׁלִיטוֹ, כָּךְ,
נֶאֱמַר כָּאן 'חֵן', וְנֶאֱמַר לְהַלָּן, (אסתר ב, טו) 'וַתְּהִי אֶסְתֵּר נֹשֵׂאת חֵן'.

R. SIMEON B. LAKISH SAID: IMAGINE A MAN WALKING ON A ROAD,
WHEN HE SAW SOMEONE WHOM HE ATTACHED TO HIMSELF. TO WHAT
EXTENT? SO MUCH THAT HE CONFERRED DOMINION UPON HIM. SIMI-
LARLY, 'GRACE' IS SAID HERE, WHILE ELSEWHERE IT SAYS, AND ESTHER
OBTAINED FAVOR IN THE SIGHT OF ALL THEM THAT LOOKED UPON HER
(EST. 2:15),

In a parable, suggested by R. Simeon b. Lakish, the word *chen* implies
the achievement of power or authority. The proof text is the word *chen*
in the Book of Esther, where finding favor let her become queen, with
all the authority that it commanded. Similarly in the case of Noah, it
says in Genesis 9:2 that he was given authority over all the animals and
beasts of the land.

רַבָּנָן אָמְרִי, לְאֶחָד שֶׁהָיָה מְהַלֵּךְ בַּדֶּרֶךְ, וְרָאָה אֶחָד וְדִבְּקוֹ, עַד הֵיכָן, עַד שֶׁנָּתַן לוֹ אֶת בִּתּוֹ, כָּךְ,
נֶאֱמַר כָּאן 'חֵן', וְנֶאֱמַר לְהָלָן, (זכריה יב, י) 'וְשָׁפַכְתִּי עַל בֵּית דָּוִיד וְעַל יוֹשֵׁב יְרוּשָׁלַם רוּחַ חֵן
וְתַחֲנוּנִים'. עַד הֵיכָן עַד שֶׁהָיָה יוֹדֵע לְהַבְחִין, אֵיזֶה בְהֵמָה נִזּוֹנֶת בִּשְׁתֵּי שָׁעוֹת בַּיּוֹם, וְאֵיזוֹ נִזּוֹנֶת
בְּשָׁלֹשׁ שָׁעוֹת בַּלַּיְלָה.

THE RABBIS SAID: IT MAY BE COMPARED TO ONE WHO WAS WALKING
ON A ROAD, WHEN HE SAW A MAN WHOM HE ATTACHED TO HIMSELF SO
STRONGLY THAT HE GAVE HIM HIS DAUGHTER IN MARRIAGE. SIMILARLY,
'GRACE' IS SAID HERE, WHILE ELSEWHERE IT IS SAID, AND I WILL POUR
UPON THE HOUSE OF DAVID AND UPON THE INHABITANTS OF JERUSA-
LEM THE SPIRIT OF GRACE (ZECH. 12:10). HOW FAR [DID GOD'S FAVOR
TO NOAH EXTEND]? UNTIL HE KNEW WHICH ANIMAL WAS TO BE FED AT
TWO HOURS OF THE DAY AND WHICH BEAST WAS TO BE FED AT THREE
HOURS OF THE NIGHT.

In the case of the sages, *chen* is interpreted as the gift of wisdom. The
proof text in Zecharia is that as a result of *ruach chen*, the spirit of grace,
they were able to understand the evil that they had done. The concept
of *chen* is associated with חכמה – *chokhmah*, meaning wisdom. Wisdom
is described as the daughter of God, meaning something that God
treasures very much. This is elaborated upon in parashah 1, midrash 1 of
Midrash Rabbah. Noah had to be blessed with special knowledge; otherwise, how would he have been able to administer all the obligations in
the ark and the creatures that it contained? (Aryeh Mirkin)

Seed Thoughts

Sometimes an individual is described as a loner, which means he is a person who acts on his own most of the time and is not closely connected with intimates in his social world. Noah was a loner. That is why it is so appropriate that the various parables and illustrations in this *midrash* speak of a person who is walking alone on a highway, meeting various people with various consequences, as described.

The more one thinks about it, the more one realizes so many of the great names in Scripture were also loners.

Abraham was a loner. He had family and friends. But in terms of his spiritual discovery of God, his achievements were his alone and as an individual; he did not relate to anyone in his society, as he found none who shared his religious views.

Moses was a loner. He was brought up as an Egyptian prince with the highest social contacts possible. But when he stood at the scene of the burning bush, he was a loner. He was an individual and God spoke to him as an individual. After several *midrashim* that seem to do their best to reduce the importance of Noah, we finally have a text that raises him above so many. Maybe he was not as great as his spiritual successors, but as an individual and as a loner, he was prepared to confront the entire world and do the best he could under special circumstances.

No wonder it is said that Noah found favor in the eyes of God. He deserved it.

ה. אָמַר רַבִּי סִימוֹן, מָצִינוּ שֶׁהַקָּדוֹשׁ בָּרוּךְ הוּא עוֹשֶׂה חֶסֶד עִם הָאַחֲרוֹנִים בִּזְכוּת הָרִאשׁוֹנִים, וּמִנַּיִן שֶׁהַקָּדוֹשׁ בָּרוּךְ הוּא עוֹשֶׂה עִם הָרִאשׁוֹנִים בִּזְכוּת הָאַחֲרוֹנִים, 'וְנֹחַ מָצָא חֵן בְּעֵינֵי ה'', בְּאֵיזוֹ זְכוּת, בִּזְכוּת תּוֹלְדוֹתָיו.

5. R. ABBAHU SAID: WE FIND THAT THE HOLY ONE, BLESSED BE HE, SHOWS MERCY TO THE DESCENDANTS FOR THE SAKE OF THEIR FORBEARS. BUT HOW DO WE KNOW THAT THE LORD SHOWS MERCY TO THE FORBEARS FOR THE SAKE OF THEIR DESCENDANTS? BECAUSE IT SAYS, BUT NOAH FOUND GRACE, WHICH WAS FOR THE SAKE OF HIS OFFSPRING, AS IT IS WRITTEN, THESE ARE THE GENERATIONS OF NOAH.

The problem facing this *midrash* is that the generations of Noah were already listed. For example, "And Noah was 500 years old and gave birth to . . ." This thought is now repeated to explain why Noah found favor in the eyes of God. It is precisely because of the generations that he produced. It was through his son Shem that Abraham ultimately emerged. It was through Abraham that purity and holiness were brought into the material world. It was through Abraham that God's name was sanctified. (*Tiferet Tzion*)

—

Seed Thoughts

The *midrash* asserts very often that God shows mercy to an earlier generation because of the future merits of their descendants. They quote the verse that Noah found favor in the eyes of God because of his descendants. At the same time, the descendants find favor in the eyes of God because of their forbears. For example, "I remember the covenant of Jacob and also the covenant of Isaac and also the covenant of Abraham." (Lev. 26:42). If we were to render this idea into modern terms, it may be that we are often influenced by our history and at the same time, at least in the Bible's perspective, we can be influenced by what was received in prophecy. The fact that the later generations can be

influenced by the former generations is due to history. That is the meaning of history and one of the reasons why it is important to us and why
it is valuable that it is available to us. However, that the earlier generations can be influenced by later ones, that is due to prophecy. Thus, God
favored Noah because He knew that Abraham would be produced from
the generation of Noah. Man cannot know these things. We are capable
of learning from history, but not currently capable of prophecy. Note,
however, the comment by *Yefei To'ar* in the additional commentary: ברא
מזכה אבא ואין אבא מזכה ברא – *bera mezakeh abba v'eyn abba mezakeh bera*.
This quotation from Tractate *Chelek* affirms that the son can add to the
merit of the father but the father cannot add to the merit of the son. In
other words, at least for one generation, this kind of rational policy is
possible, that one generation can influence a previous generation. That
is the most we can say in terms of human behavior. We are left with the
teaching that our role is in history and that we can learn from the past.
As for prophecy, that is in God's hands.

Additional Commentary

The earlier and later generations

One sees that God shows mercy to the later generations because of
the earlier ones, as it is written, "I remember the covenant of Jacob ..."
Also, the verse that says, "I shall show mercy to the thousands ..." On
the other hand, it says, "Noah found favor in the eyes of God ..." and
immediately it follows, "These are the generations ..." This shows that
God shows mercy to the forbears because of the descendants. Something similar is found in the chapter of *Chelek*, ברא מזכה אבא ואין אבא מזכה
ברא – *bera mezakeh abba v'eyn abba mezakeh bera*. Here, however, God is
showing mercy with the descendants because of the forbears. However,
that does not always happen, as in the case of Ishmael and Esav, who
rebelled against the traditions of their fathers. However, when children
honor their parents and live up to the tradition of their parents, families
and the Torah, it can be said of them that the parents can influence the
children and add to the reputation of good. (Yefei To'ar)

אֵ. (ו, ט) 'אֵלֶּה תּוֹלְדֹת נֹחַ נֹחַ אִישׁ צַדִּיק תָּמִים'

1. THESE ARE THE GENERATIONS OF NOAH (6:9).

This *midrash* begins with the same concern as with the previous *midrash*. Since the generations of Noah were already mentioned, why are they repeated here? The answer is that the first reference to generations took place before the Flood, and the second reference took place after the Flood. By the time of the Flood, all of the other generations had ceased to exist, but the generations of Noah had survived because he was אִישׁ צַדִּיק תָּמִים – *ish tzaddik tamim*, he was righteous and wholehearted. (Aryeh Mirkin)

הָדָא הוּא דִכְתִיב, (משלי י, כה) 'כַּעֲבוֹר סוּפָה וְאֵין רָשָׁע, וְצַדִּיק יְסוֹד עוֹלָם', 'כַּעֲבוֹר סוּפָה וְאֵין רָשָׁע' זֶה דוֹר הַמַּבּוּל, 'וְצַדִּיק יְסוֹד עוֹלָם' זֶה נֹחַ

WHEN THE WHIRLWIND PASSETH, THE WICKED IS NO MORE; BUT THE RIGHTEOUS IS AN EVERLASTING FOUNDATION (PROV. 10:25). 'WHEN THE WHIRLWIND PASSETH, THE WICKED IS NO MORE' – THIS REFERS TO THE GENERATION OF THE FLOOD; 'BUT THE RIGHTEOUS IS AN EVERLASTING FOUNDATION' – THIS REFERS TO NOAH, AS IT IS WRITTEN, THESE ARE THE GENERATIONS OF NOAH: NOAH WAS A RIGHTEOUS MAN.

The verse quoted from Proverbs dramatizes what happened. The people of the evil generation were removed by the tempest and the Flood. What remained was the righteous one around whom a future world could be built. This, according to the the *Midrashic* description, describes the position of Noah as the righteous one around whom the world was created.

(שם יב, ז) 'הָפוֹךְ רְשָׁעִים וְאֵינָם, וּבֵית צַדִּיקִים יַעֲמֹד', 'הָפוֹךְ רְשָׁעִים וְאֵינָם' זֶה דוֹר הַמַּבּוּל, 'וּבֵית צַדִּיקִים יַעֲמֹד' זֶה נֹחַ, הָדָא הוּא דִכְתִיב, 'אֵלֶּה תּוֹלְדֹת נֹחַ'.

THE WICKED ARE OVERTHROWN, AND ARE NOT (PROV. 12:7): THIS REFERS TO THE GENERATION OF THE FLOOD; BUT THE HOUSE OF THE

RIGHTEOUS SHALL STAND (IBID.) – THIS REFERS TO NOAH: THESE ARE
THE GENERATIONS OF NOAH.

The continuation of the verse adds the thought that when the evildoers disappear, the house of the righteous remains. This refers to the
family of Noah. This family accepted the obligation to help rebuild the
world.

דָּבָר אַחֵר, 'אֵלֶּה תּוֹלְדֹת נֹחַ', כְּתִיב (שם יד, יא) 'בֵּית רְשָׁעִים יִשָּׁמֵד, וְאֹהֶל יְשָׁרִים יַפְרִיחַ'. 'בֵּית
רְשָׁעִים יִשָּׁמֵד' זֶה דּוֹר הַמַּבּוּל, 'וְאֹהֶל יְשָׁרִים יַפְרִיחַ' זֶה נֹחַ.
THE HOUSE OF THE WICKED SHALL BE OVERTHROWN (PROV. 14:11): THIS
REFERS TO THE GENERATION OF THE FLOOD; BUT THE TENT OF THE
UPRIGHT SHALL FLOURISH (IBID.) – THIS REFERS TO NOAH: THESE ARE
THE GENERATIONS OF NOAH.

There is a contrast here between a house that is firmly built and a tent
that offers only a very loose protection. The generation of the Flood
was prosperous and built fabulous homes that were easily destroyed.
The tent homes of the righteous had no material strength, but were sup-
ported by character and commitment.

One other thought: the expression *toladot* indicates that Noah left
behind him the generations of accomplishment. Nothing, however, was
left of the generation of the Flood. We have no history of any of the
individuals or families, only of Noah, and through him, the world was
renewed.

—

Seed Thoughts

As you go over the various *midrashim* about Noah to this point, it can
become a very intriguing exercise. We began from a comment in the
Zohar that is reproduced in the Talmud, that God was displeased with
the leadership of Noah. Noah made no effort to save his generation, he
neither plead nor prayed for them. By contrast, Abraham moved Heaven
and Earth to convince God to save the cities of Sodom and Gemorah,
if even the slightest positive element could be found. We then find a
midrash that says that Noah did possess a minimum amount of virtue,
which God accepted. A leader does not necessarily have to possess every
possible talent. It then went on to say that Noah found favor in the eyes
of God, but the *Midrash* could not find a reason why. Then something
interesting happened. Suddenly we discover that Noah is identified as

the righteous one upon whose foundation a new world can be built. What happened? One would have to assume that Noah made every effort to improve his character and his righteous deeds and do everything in his power to justify himself in God's eyes. And so the portion of Noah begins by saying that he was righteous and wholehearted in his generation. The climax is reached in this particular *midrash* because he is identified as a righteous one around whom a new world can be built.

We can learn much from this interpretation of Noah. He was not an Abraham, but he did not have to be. It is not our role to be like anyone else. Our goal should be to be ourselves, but we should raise ourselves up to the highest level of which we are capable. That is what Noah tried to do and more than that is not required.

—

Additional Commentary

The righteous person is the foundation of the world.

The term "foundation" refers to the part of a house that would still remain standing even if the entire house is blown away by a hurricane wind. Similarly, Noah was able to survive, not only by himself, but also with his home. Another verse is quoted, which ends with the words "the house of the righteous." The word "house" has three meanings. There is the literal meaning, that being a dwelling, and in this case, it referred to the ark. There is also the expression ביתו זו אשתו, meaning that a person's home is truly his wife. A third meaning is a family; since they are the occupants of a home, a family can also be referred to by this term. With this combination, the world can grow and be sustained. That is why a third verse is brought from Proverbs, that for those who are righteous, even a house as materially weak as a tent can flourish and grow and create. (Maharzu)

ב. דָּבָר אַחֵר, 'אֵלֶּה תּוֹלְדֹת נֹחַ', כְּתִיב (איוב כד, יח) 'קַל הוּא עַל פְּנֵי הַמַּיִם, תְּקֻלַּל חֶלְקָתָם בָּאָרֶץ,
לֹא יִפְנֶה דֶּרֶךְ כְּרָמִים'. 'קַל הוּא עַל פְּנֵי הַמַּיִם', גְּזֵרָה שֶׁנִּגְזְרָה עֲלֵיהֶם שֶׁיֹּאבְדוּ בַּמַּיִם, 'תְּקֻלַּל
חֶלְקָתָם בָּאָרֶץ' כְּלוֹמַר, מִי שֶׁפָּרַע מִדּוֹר הַמַּבּוּל, כָּל כַּךְ לָמָּה 'לֹא יִפְנֶה דֶּרֶךְ כְּרָמִים' שֶׁלֹּא
הָיְתָה כַּוָּנָתוֹ אֶלָּא לְמַטַּעַת כְּרָמִים, אֲבָל נֹחַ, לֹא הָיְתָה כַּוָּנָתוֹ אֶלָּא לְהַפְרוֹת וּלְהַרְבּוֹת בָּעוֹלָם
וּלְהַעֲמִיד בָּנִים, שֶׁנֶּאֱמַר 'אֵלֶּה תּוֹלְדֹת נֹחַ'.

2. HE IS SWIFT (KAL) UPON THE FACE OF THE WATERS (JOB 24:18): A
DECREE WAS PRONOUNCED AGAINST THEM THAT THEY SHOULD PER-
ISH BY WATER; THEIR PORTION IS CURSED IN THE EARTH (IBID.), [AS
PEOPLE CURSE,] HE WHO PUNISHED THE GENERATION OF THE FLOOD
[PUNISH THEM]. AND WHY ALL THIS?BECAUSE, HE TURNETH NOT BY
THE WAY OF THE VINEYARDS (IBID.): THEIR INTENTION WAS NOT TO
PLANT VINEYARDS. BUT NOAH'S ONLY INTENTION WAS TO BE FRUITFUL
AND MULTIPLY IN THE WORLD: HENCE, THESE ARE THE GENERATIONS
OF NOAH.

The second half of the verse from Job states that "their portion is
cursed in the earth." There is a reason for this. Namely, the people of that
generation acted in brutal and immoral ways and seem to have gotten in
the way of everything until their end in the days of the Flood. The line
that says that they did not escape through vineyards requires a special
explanation:

Most of the commentators give this phrase, "the way of the vineyards," a sexual connotation; however, they do not detail the nature of
the parable or show how they come to this special interpretation. One
commentator makes the point that the word *derech*, way, carries the
meaning of *derech eretz*, "the way of the world," and it has to do with
the manner in which a man and woman meet each other in order to
establish a home and a family and their place in society. According to
this interpretation the people of the generation of the Flood had no
interest in subjects like home, family and human relations in general. To
them, the relationship of a man and a woman was sexual only. Some of
the commentators note that their custom was that each man would have

a second wife that would be completely freed from procreation in order to satisfy their passion. Noah, however, had nothing to do with this way of life. At the rebirth of the world, he and his family were interested in the re-population of the world and nothing else. That is why the text emphasizes *toladot*, generations, which were the goal of his endeavors after the Flood.

—

Seed Thoughts

It is somewhat intriguing to note that even in a phrase as innocuous as "by way of the vineyards," the sages of the *Midrash* could detect the sexual imperfections of the generation of the Flood. In fact, the more we read this literature, the more we realize that from the view of the sages, sexual immorality was by far the most crippling sin of the generation of the Flood. Of course, there was also robbery and murder, but these are not discussed nearly as much as their sexual behavior. Someday, I imagine a student will be found who will study this material and discover the exact number of times the sages documented this feeling of theirs, as well as their various interpretations. Their view was that sanctifying sexual behavior is the key to a society, the key to the individual humanization of men and women and the only way that society can grow and improve itself.

In the *Midrash* that follows this one, we will discover the astonishing view that the word *toladot*, meaning "generations," could not be applied to the generation of the Flood. Why? Because the children who were born were not born as a result of the intention to have children, but only accidentally, through some slip-up in what we would call today a lack of birth control. Therefore, they were only offspring by accident, not by choice. This is an extreme view, but it indicates the lengths to which the sages would go to protect sexual morality as the most important element of the ethical life.

—

Additional Commentary

Kal

In the verse quoted from Job, the word *kal* lends itself to many interpretations. The first interpretation is that *kal* comes from the word *kol*, meaning "voice." It may refer to what is known as a בת קול – *bat kol*, voice from Heaven, and probably means *kol gzeirah*, the voice that announced the decree that there would be a Flood that would destroy the sinners. (*HaMidrash HaMevo'ar*)

Another interpretation of the word *kal* is based on the plain and simple Hebrew meaning, which is "light" or "easy." The people in the Flood suffered many difficulties. But for Noah and anyone else who was in the ark, it was simple and easy to remain alive and safe from the destructive waters. (*Matnot Kehuna*)

There is also another possible interpretation of the word *kal* available: When a person drowns, the body immediately descends. After a while, however, it returns to the surface, where it reappears partially, floating on the water, after having become "light." According to this interpretation, the word *kal* refers to those who suffered the fate of the Flood. (*Tiferet Tzion*)

ג. 'אֵלֶּה' אָמַר רַבִּי אַבָּהוּ, בְּכָל מָקוֹם שֶׁנֶּאֱמַר 'אֵלֶּה' פָּסַל אֶת הָרִאשׁוֹנִים, 'וְאֵלֶּה' מוֹסִיף עַל
הָרִאשׁוֹנִים, כָּאן שֶׁנֶּאֱמַר 'אֵלֶּה' פָּסַל אֶת הָרִאשׁוֹנִים, דּוֹר הַמַּבּוּל.

3. THESE: R. ABBAHU SAID: WHEREVER 'THESE' (ELEH) IS WRITTEN, IT
CANCELS THE PRECEDING; 'AND THESE' (VE-ELEH) ADDS TO THE PRE-
CEDING. HERE THAT 'THESE' IS WRITTEN, IT CANCELS THE PRECEDING.
WHAT DOES IT CANCEL? THE GENERATION OF THE FLOOD.

What new thought did the text bring us by "canceling," as it were, the
generation of the Flood, since we already knew specifically and from
the Bible itself that they will be destroyed by the waters?! The intention
of the text was to indicate that the generation of the Flood could not
be described as a people who had a history. Their children could not
be ascribed to the generation of their fathers, since their fathers did not
take seriously the goal of reproduction and had no intention of having
children, as indicated in the previous *Midrash*. This was the fundamental principle that governed the severe judgment rendered against them.
(*Tiferet Tzion*)

Seed Thoughts

Two terrible punishments were experienced by the generation of the
Flood. The first was the extermination of their generation by the de-
structiveness of the Flood itself. The second was that everything that
we know of them or could have known of them was blotted out. That
which we know as history was robbed from the generation of the Flood.
History does not consist merely of countries and peoples. It has to do
also with the personal history of individuals. All of this was "canceled"
or removed from the generation of the Flood. It no longer existed.

In order to appreciate the severity of this historical cancellation, we
can learn much from the mindset of of many of the individuals whose
lives were exterminated in the Holocaust: What bothered so many of

these people, even more than their impending death, was the thought that they would leave this world without anyone knowing about their lives, caring about them or remembering them in any way, shape or form. That is why thousands of pieces of paper were discovered with individual names on them, sometimes addresses as well, sometimes names and addresses of relatives with telephone numbers, sometimes letters written on paper or cigarette boxes, most of them, "To whom it may concern." They wanted urgently to feel that their lives and their deaths would mean something important, at least to the one or more people that would read or discover this material.

Personal history is a very important thing. I recommend that every individual take some time off to write a paragraph about himself. It does not have to be lengthy. The letter should be put in an envelope and left together with one's other precious documents, to be looked at some time in the future when we are not here. It would be even more interesting if such a paragraph could be written more than once during one's lifetime. Imagine how meaningful this would be if, after three generations, a little library of this material would be discovered and read.

I had one grandfather whom I hardly knew. He lived in New York City and I met him only twice as a child. After his death, I was given a present from him of five festival *machzorim*. As I went through this material, I discovered that at least three important prayers in each *machzor* had an important message from him in Yiddish. It contained a brief explanation of something in the prayer followed by a blessing to me. Although the pattern was the same in all of the sections, the words were different and one can see that a serious effort produced these messages. As a result, I always felt closer to this grandfather whom I have rarely seen than to other relatives whom I saw all the time.

Creating a personal history is one of the important things we can do with our lives. I urge everyone to record such a history.

ד. 'אֵלֶּה תוֹלְדֹת נֹחַ, נֹחַ' אָמַר רַבִּי אַבָּא בַּר כַּהֲנָא, כָּל מִי שֶׁנִּכְפַּל שְׁמוֹ, יֶשׁ לוֹ בָּעוֹלָם הַזֶּה וְיֵשׁ
לוֹ בָּעוֹלָם הַבָּא

4. THESE ARE THE OFFSPRING OF NOAH: NOAH [WAS A RIGHTEOUS MAN].
R. ABBA B. KAHANA SAID: WHOEVER HAS HIS NAME THUS REPEATED HAS
A PORTION IN THIS WORLD AND IN THE WORLD TO COME.

The idea of having a share, not only in this world, but in the World to
Come, is based on the fact that the name was mentioned twice. The first
appearance represents this world and the repetition is to represent the
world of the future. Usually when the *Torah* mentions a name twice in
a row, it is referring to a person especially loved by God. In the case of
Noah, this seems to be accidental because his name appears repeated,
but in separate sentences. However, the sages ask a different question:

אֲתִיבוּן לֵהּ, וְהָכְתִיב (בראשית יא, כז) 'תֶּרַח, תֶּרַח' אִם כֵּן יֵשׁ לוֹ חֵלֶק בָּעוֹלָם הַזֶּה וְלָעוֹלָם הַבָּא,
אָמַר לָהוֹן אַף הִיא לָא תַבְרָא, דַּאֲמַר רַבִּי יוּדָן בְּשֵׁם רַבִּי אַבָּא בַּר כַּהֲנָא, (שם טו, טו) 'וְאַתָּה תָּבוֹא
אֶל אֲבֹתֶיךָ בְּשָׁלוֹם' בִּשְּׂרוֹ שֶׁיֵּשׁ לְאָבִיו חֵלֶק בָּעוֹלָם הַבָּא, (שם שם, שם) 'תִּקָּבֵר בְּשֵׂיבָה טוֹבָה',
בִּשְּׂרוֹ שֶׁיִּשְׁמָעֵאל עוֹשֶׂה תְּשׁוּבָה.

THEY RAISED AN OBJECTION TO HIM: BUT IT IS WRITTEN, NOW THESE
ARE THE GENERATIONS OF TERAH. TERAH BEGOT ABRAM, ETC. (GEN.
11:27): HAS HE A PORTION IN THIS WORLD AND IN THE FUTURE WORLD?
EVEN THIS DOES NOT CONTRADICT ME, HE REPLIED, FOR R. JUDAN SAID
IN R. ABBA'S NAME: BUT THOU [ABRAHAM] SHALT GO TO THY FATHERS
IN PEACE (IBID., 15:115): HE [GOD] INFORMED HIM THAT HIS FATHER HAD
A PORTION IN THE WORLD TO COME; THOU SHALT BE BURIED IN A GOOD
OLD AGE (IBID.): HE INFORMED HIM THAT ISHMAEL WOULD REPENT.

The sages wanted to know, in light of this affirmation, how would they
explain the fact that the name *Terach* (the father of Abraham) was written twice in a row, given that he was known as an idolator. The response
is that *Terach* repented toward the end of his life. That is what is meant
by the assurance before Abraham's death that he would live to a "good

old age." The implication is that he would not live to a "good" age had his
father died as an idolator.

―

Seed Thoughts

The *Torah* consists of revealed things and hidden things. The revealed
things, we know about. The hidden things require research and investi-
gation. The hidden things do not necessarily have to refer to philosophical concepts, such as the mystery of the creation of the world or what
happens after death. The hidden things can also refer to simple associa-
tions and very often, they create a challenge for certain people whose
minds tend very much toward confrontation. One of the most important adventures in the study of Judaism is the desire to find meaning.
In our *Midrash*, the sages were challenged by names that appear twice.
They were not challenged by the repetitions of "Abraham, Abraham" or
"Moses, Moses." These were forms of endearment that were obvious to
the reader. God loved Abraham, so He mentioned his name twice, just
as a parent says the names of their children many times as a form of
endearment. But the juxtaposition of the two names of Noah was very
different. Each name appeared in a different sentence. If the name would
not have appeared the second time, the verses would have been just as
good and just as clear. It could have then been translated as, "These are
the generations of Noah, who was a righteous man and wholehearted."
However, now that the second name of Noah did appear, there must
have been a reason. This is the hidden part. But the search for meaning
leads us to the fact that Noah, too, was loved very much by God and that
he too would merit a reward in this world and the next. The same is true
for *Terach*, as the *Midrash* itself indicates, and so too wherever else this
phenomenon would appear.

PARASHAH THIRTY, *Midrash Five*

ה. 'אֵלֶּה תּוֹלְדֹת נֹחַ, נֹחַ', אַתְמְהָא, לָא הֲוָה צָרִיךְ קְרָא לְמֵימַר, אֶלָּא, אֵלֶּה תּוֹלְדוֹת נֹחַ, שֵׁם
5. THESE ARE THE OFFSPRING OF NOAH: NOAH, ETC. SURELY SCRIPTURE
SHOULD HAVE WRITTEN, 'THESE ARE THE OFFSPRING OF NOAH: SHEM,'
ETC.?

One would have expected that a statement saying, "These are the
generations of Noah ..." should be followed by the name Shem, his
oldest son. However, the text, instead, praises Noah, by having his name
appear twice one after the other in the actual statement that follows.
Indeed, from the sound of the two names together, we are able to derive
the word *menuchah*, meaning comfort or well-being. It should also be
added that the expression *toladot* does not always have to refer to descendants. It can also mean "history," as in the phrase from *Genesis 2:4*:
"These are the *toladot* of Heaven and Earth," which can be translated
as "the *history* of Heaven and Earth." Therefore, our verse could mean,
"This is the story of Noah," and could be very appropriately followed by
praise of him.

אֶלָּא, נְיָחָא לוֹ נְיָחָא לָעוֹלָם, נְיָחָא לָאָבוֹת נְיָחָא לַבָּנִים, נְיָחָא לָעֶלְיוֹנִים נְיָחָא לַתַּחְתּוֹנִים, נְיָחָא
בָעוֹלָם הַזֶּה נְיָחָא לָעוֹלָם הַבָּא.
IT TEACHES, HOWEVER, THAT HE WAS A COMFORT TO HIMSELF AND A
COMFORT TO THE WORLD, A COMFORT TO HIS FATHERS AND A COMFORT
TO HIS CHILDREN, A COMFORT TO CELESTIAL BEINGS AND TO MORTALS;
[A COMFORT] IN THIS WORLD AND IN THE WORLD TO COME.

The *Tiferet Tzion*, as will be noted below, interprets these expressions
as describing the preparations that Noah made to safeguard his future
generations. It was only later in life, even by the biblical calculations,
that his children were born. He first had to prepare himself, to control
his own evil inclination and to concentrate on doing good things. As
a result of this preparation, he not only brought well-being to himself,
but he became a very important asset to the world. By the same token,

he had prepared himself to be a caring and morally upright father. Thus, he became an important model for his children. He also did his best to bring to his life a close relationship with God as it is written, "*Et haElokim hit'halekh Noach* – Noah walked with God." Since we are called upon to emulate God's *behavior, as it were, in this world as well* – for example, just as God is merciful, so should we be merciful – Noah was also highly principled in relation to his fellow man. It follows also, therefore, that this kind of behavior in this world earns one admission to the World to Come.

—

Seed Thoughts

The important lesson that we learn from this *Midrash* is that character is the most important aspect of the human personality. It is more important than progeny, more important that wealth and more important than leadership and power. When it says about Noah that he was righteous and wholehearted, it is telling us something about him of the greatest possible importance. Because he was truly righteous and wholehearted, it follows that he was able to control his own desires and passions and dedicate them to higher principles. This gave him an importance in the world at large and rendered him a model to be followed. This same character helped to mold his relationship as parent to his children and as a human being to his fellow man. We should not read these verses with the idea that this teaching is simply relegated to Noah; this should be the goal and the motivation of every human being in this world. Moral character should be the main goal of education and everything should be done to produce a student who will emerge as a citizen with high moral principle.

—

Additional Commentary

These are the toladot *of Noah (A)*

There was no reason for the *Midrash* to be concerned that the phrase "*Eleh toladot Noach* – These are the generations of Noah" should be followed by the mention of his son Shem. We have other verses that show that the concept of *toladot* is not restricted to generations. For example, "These are the *toladot* of Heaven and Earth," which can be translated as "This is the story of Heaven and Earth in their creation." This refers to what happened during the formation of Heaven and Earth and informs us about their natures. By the same token, *"Eleh toladot Noach"* describes something about the nature of Noah. He was blessed with a sense of well-being, contentment and good spirit. He also imbued many with the same feelings, as described by the *Midrash*. (Aryeh Mirkin)

These are the toladot *of Noah (B)*

When it says about Noah that he was righteous and wholehearted, it means that he had self-control over his inner passions and, therefore, was a good influence over his children. He was also *tamim*, which meant that his behavior with people, whether regarding commercial things or personal matters, was done in truthfulness and justice. Another meaning implied in "righteous and wholehearted" is that Noah was righteous in his deeds and wholehearted in his way of life. This means that he was righteous in those things that pertained to his own being, such as his bodily passions, as well as in his behavior, for instance, never interfering with anything that belonged to someone else, and that he was wholehearted in his dealings with people. His well-being as a person extended out to the world. This personal discipline also, of course, had a wonderful effect on his children. As for the midrashic idea that his behavior extended not just to earthly beings but to heavenly celestial beings as well, this meant that he walked with God. He was thus able to influence his fellow human beings. (*Tiferet Tzion*)

ו. 'אֵלֶּה תּוֹלְדֹת נֹחַ, נֹחַ' הֲדָא הוּא דִכְתִיב, (משלי יא, ל) 'פְּרִי צַדִּיק עֵץ חַיִּים', מַה הֵן פֵּרוֹתָיו שֶׁל
צַדִּיק מִצְוֹות וּמַעֲשִׂים טוֹבִים

6. THESE ARE THE OFFSPRINGS OF NOAH: NOAH. THUS IT IS WRITTEN,
THE FRUIT OF THE RIGHTEOUS IS A TREE OF LIFE, AND HE THAT IS WISE
TAKETH SOULS (PROV. 11:30): WHAT IS THE FRUIT OF THE RIGHTEOUS?
LIFE, RELIGIOUS ACTIONS, AND GOOD DEEDS.

The *Tiferet Tzion* was somehow startled by the fact that Proverbs uses
the word "fruit" and then the expression "Tree of Life." After all, a tree
is not a fruit. It seems it should have said the "fruit of life." How, then,
do we explain the use of the term "tree"? A tree does, indeed, produce
fruits. A tree is a symbol of life. Just as a tree produces fruit, so should
we produce good deeds, and the observance of commandments, which
are the true fruits of a moral and ethical life. And, further, we should do
these things without thinking too much of their reward, either in this
world or the World to Come. Just as the goal of a tree is to produce fruit,
so the goal of a good deed should be to produce another good deed. If
one wants to use the word "reward," then the reward would be producing one good deed after another, and may it be so for as long as we live.

(שם שם, שם) 'וְלֹקֵחַ נְפָשׁוֹת חָכָם' שֶׁזָּן וּמְפַרְנֵס כָּל שְׁנֵים עָשָׂר חֹדֶשׁ בַּתֵּבָה

AND HE THAT IS WISE TAKETH SOULS: FOR HE FED AND PROVIDED FOR
[ITS INHABITANTS] THE WHOLE TWELVE MONTHS IN THE ARK.

Noah's responsibility as manager of the ark required knowledge and
great sophistication. Feeding the animals was a major concern and a
major effort that required knowledge. Some animals had to be fed every
two hours, while others had to be fed every six or eight. Noah had to
know these things. There can be no doubt that God endowed him with
that kind of special knowledge to enable him to perform the very sophisticated task of keeping each creation alive for a period of twelve months.
God granted Noah this special wisdom because He had watched Noah

and saw the he was entirely interested in doing good deeds and fulfilling commandments. (*Tiferet Tzion*)

אַחַר כָּל הַשֶּׁבַח הַזֶּה, (שם שם, לא) 'הֵן צַדִּיק בָּאָרֶץ יְשֻׁלָּם' בָּא לָצֵאת וְנִשְׁתַּלֵּם, אִתְמָהָא, דְּאָמַר רַבִּי הוּנָא מְשׁוּם רַבִּי אֱלִיעֶזֶר בְּנוֹ שֶׁל רַבִּי יוֹסֵי הַגְּלִילִי, נֹחַ, כְּשֶׁהָיָה יוֹצֵא מִן הַתֵּבָה הִכִּישׁוֹ אֲרִי וְשִׁבְּרוֹ, וְלֹא הָיָה כָּשֵׁר לְהַקְרִיב, וְהִקְרִיב שֵׁם בְּנוֹ תַּחְתָּיו, קַל וָחֹמֶר (שם שם, שם) 'אַף כִּי רָשָׁע וְחוֹטֵא' זֶה דּוֹר הַמַּבּוּל.

After all this praise, "behold, shall the righteous be requited in the earth?" (ibid. 31). When he was about to leave it [the ark], was he requited? Surely R. Huna said in R. Eliezer's name: When Noah was leaving the Ark a lion set on him and maimed him, so that he was not fit to sacrifice, and his son Shem sacrificed in his stead. Infer from this: 'How much more the wicked and the sinner' (ibid.), which refers to the generation of the Flood.

It seems quite astonishing that after the great praise, he should be punished. After all, no human being is perfect and surely in the twelve months in which the ark was afloat, Noah must have done something to damage or wrong any one of its inhabitants, if but unintentionally. So he was punished for these sins, which were very few. How much more so those whose sins are very many should be punished in terms of what they deserve? The *Midrash* describes one of the ways in which Noah was punished, in light of the fact that he was injured by one of the lions. There is a view that this was done as punishment for the fact that the lions were not given their food on time.

—

Seed Thoughts

In the beautiful interpretation of the *Tiferet Tzion*, the Tree of Life is the tree that produces those moral and ethical principles that are the fruits of the good life. Does a tree demand a reward for its fruits? It does not. Why then should the tree of the life, which is the human being, demand a reward for his ethical behavior either in this world or the next? The ethics of the fathers says that the reward of a commandment is the doing of another commandment. This is really all the reward that is necessary for one who believes that the goal of the religious life is *imitatio dei*, the imitation of God. Just as He is merciful, we should be merciful. Just as He is righteous, so should we be righteous. No reward is required in life other than this. If we could only live this way and help others to live this way, we would be justifying Creation.

—

Additional Commentary

What is the fruit of the righteous?

This question arises when one thinks about the verse quoted from Proverbs, "the fruit of the righteous is a tree of life," and realizes that a tree is not a fruit. It appears that the verse should have really said פרי צדיק פרי חיים – "the fruit of the righteous, the *fruit* of life." Therefore, it can be interpreted as hinting at what the intention of a Tzaddik should be at the time when he performs the religious acts and good deeds. That goal should be to look upon these deeds as fruits of the Tree of Life, meaning that there should be no intention of receiving a reward, either in this world or in the World to Come. The intention should rather be that by means of this particular commandment, God will give him the privilege of doing another mitzvah, as it is written in the *Ethics of the Fathers*, "Do not be as the servants who serve their master in order to receive their reward . . ." Rather, the reward of a *mitzvah* should be gratitude for the privilege of doing another *mitzvah*, and that justifies referring to the *mitzvah* as *eitz chayim*, a tree of life, because in addition to being a "fruit" in itself, it also produces fruit, meaning more mitzvot, as well as the good life that one builds by performing them. This is how we can now translate the verse, "These are the generations of Noah, Noah was a righteous man . . ." This was his entire goal. It can be said that the main goal of his good deeds was that through them, he would be able to do more good deeds and more religious acts. That is why he was called a righteous man. (*Tiferet Tzion*)

Noah and the lion

When Noah left the ark, he was punished. He was attacked by a lion and his limb was broken. This made him handicapped, which meant that he could not proceed with the offering to God that he had planned. This punishment came to him because from time to time, he was late in feeding the lion, as is written in Rashi on the Torah, in connection with the verse in Genesis 7:23. Rashi then goes on to say that Noah's son Shem took his place and continued with the offering. It was said about Malchi Tzedek, in Genesis 14:18, that he was a priest to the Supreme God, meaning that he offered sacrifices. But nowhere in the Torah do we discover offering of sacrifices during the generations from Noah to Abraham, except in the case of Noah. Noah did something wrong and therefore was punished and declared unfit to offer the sacrifice. Malchi Tzedek took his place. It is claimed that Malchi Tzedek is Shem, and that he was the one who took the place of Noah. (Aryeh Mirkin)

ז. 'אִישׁ', כָּל מָקוֹם שֶׁנֶּאֱמַר 'אִישׁ', צַדִּיק וּמוּמְחֶה

7. [NOAH WAS IN HIS GENERATIONS] A MAN [RIGHTEOUS AND WHOLE
HEARTED]. WHEREVER 'A MAN' OCCURS, IT INDICATES A RIGHTEOUS
MAN WHO WARNED [HIS GENERATION].

The question that the *Midrash* raises, by implication, is why the term
ish is used in connection with the name Noah, because it is superfluous.
The statement would have sounded the same without the word *ish*. The
answer is that the word *ish* is a forceful interpretation of a particular
kind of person who was a leader of a community.

שֶׁכָּל מֵאָה וְעֶשְׂרִים שָׁנָה, הָיָה נֹחַ נוֹטֵעַ אֲרָזִים וְקוֹצְצָן, אָמְרוּ, לָמָּה כְדֵין, אָמַר לְהוֹן, כַּךְ אֲמַר
מָארֵהּ דְּעָלְמָא, דְּהוּא מַיְתֵי מַבּוּלָא עַל עָלְמָא, אָמְרוּ לֵהּ אִן אֲתֵי מַבּוּלָא, לָא אָתֵי אֶלָּא עַל
בֵּיתֵהּ דְּהַהוּא גַּבְרָא, כֵּיוָן שֶׁמֵּת מְתוּשֶׁלַח, אָמְרוּ לֵהּ הָא לָא אָתֵי מַבּוּלָא אֶלָּא עַל בֵּיתֵהּ דְּהַהוּא
גַּבְרָא

FOR A WHOLE ONE HUNDRED AND TWENTY YEARS NOAH PLANTED CE-
DARS AND CUT THEM DOWN. ON BEING ASKED, 'WHY ARE YOU DOING
THIS?' HE REPLIED: 'THE LORD OF THE UNIVERSE HAS INFORMED ME
THAT HE WILL BRING A FLOOD IN THE WORLD.' SAID THEY [HIS CONTEM-
PORARIES] TO HIM: IF A FLOOD DOES COME, IT WILL COME ONLY UPON
YOUR FATHER'S HOUSE!'

For 120 years, Noah devoted himself to building the ark. However,
he did more than that. He also used this time to warn his generation
to repent and change their ways. Failing that, they would suffer a great
destruction. Noah would cut down cedar trees and replant them, simply as a delaying action to give the people more time to reflect on his
message and hopefully change their ways. His listeners simply scoffed
at him, saying that if any Flood is going to come, then it would probably
come only upon Noah and not the rest of the people of their generation.
When Metushelah died, the people remarked that the destruction had
actually come upon Noah, since Metushelah was his grandfather and

his father, Lemech, had died five years prior. They did not know that on
the day Metushelah died, the Flood was supposed to begin and that it
was postponed only in honor of Metushelah for the seven days of *shivah*.

הֲדָא הוּא דִכְתִיב, (איוב יב, ה) 'לַפִּיד בּוּז לְעַשְׁתּוּת שַׁאֲנָן, נָכוֹן לְמוֹעֲדֵי רָגֶל', אָמַר רַבִּי אַבָּא בַּר
כָּהֲנָא, כָּרוֹז אֶחָד עָמַד לִי בְּדוֹר הַמַּבּוּל, זֶה נֹחַ, תַּמָּן אָמְרִין, כָּרוֹז לָהּ לַפִּיד לָהּ, 'בּוּז' שֶׁהָיוּ מְבַזִּים
עָלָיו, וְקָרוֹ לָהּ בִּיזַיָּא סָבָא, 'לְעַשְׁתּוּת שַׁאֲנָן' שֶׁהָיוּ קָשִׁים כַּעֲשָׁתוֹת, 'נָכוֹן לְמוֹעֲדֵי רָגֶל', שֶׁהָיוּ
מוּכָנִים לִשְׁנֵי שְׁבָרִים, לְשֶׁבֶר מִלְמַעְלָה וּלְשֶׁבֶר מִלְמָטָה.

THUS IT IS WRITTEN, A CONTEMPTIBLE BRAND (LAPPID BUZ) IN THE
THOUGHT OF HIM THAT IS AT EASE, A THING READY FOR THEM WHOSE
FOOT SLIPPETH (JOB 12:5). R. ABBA INTERPRETED: THE HOLY ONE,
BLESSED BE HE, SAID: 'ONE HERALD AROSE FOR ME IN THE GENERATION
OF THE FLOOD, VIZ. NOAH.' FOR ELSEWHERE PEOPLE SAY, 'AROUSE HIM,
STIR HIM UP!' 'BUZ' (CONTEMPT) INTIMATES THAT THEY DESPISED HIM
AND CALLED HIM, 'CONTEMPTIBLE OLD MAN!' IN THE THOUGHT OF
(LE'ASHTOTH) HIM THAT IS AT EASE: THIS TEACHES THAT THEY WERE
AS HARD AS METAL (ASHTOTH). A THING READY FOR THEM WHOSE FOOT
SLIPPETH: TWO DISASTERS WERE READY FOR THEM: A DISASTER FROM
ABOVE AND A DISASTER FROM BELOW.

The verse from Job reflects this state of affairs, that a feeling of contempt was projected toward Noah. These verses are interpreted in relation to Noah and the people responsible for this derision and contempt,
as those from the generation of the Flood, which eventually destroyed
them, from above and below.

Seed Thoughts

The Hebrew language is not only majorly enriching to know, it is functional in a way that many other languages are not. The letters of the Hebrew alphabet represent a value system and when viewed through the
lens of this system, we can see how certain terms are capable of defining
and redefining important concepts.

In our *Midrash*, one of the most intriguing discussions is the comparison of the words *adam* and *ish*. There is quite a difference between
the two, as our *Midrash* tries to explain. Both mean the human being.
(The fact that *ish* is male is completely irrelevant, for what we are now
discussing implies *ishah, woman, as* well as *ish, man.*) In order to make
this explanation as simple as possible, I will try to make a comparison
in English. There is a difference between a person and a personality.

We are all persons in the sense that we are human beings possessing all those characteristics of uniqueness from other living creatures, such as intelligence, speech, the ability to make choices and the freedom to exercise these choices. A personality is a little bit more than that. Possessing all the already mentioned unique aspects of a human being, someone with "personality" also possess a charisma, often a somewhat forceful demeanor and the kind of presence and articulation of speech that usually leads such a person to a leadership role. That is why the *Midrash* interprets the biblical text expressing the fact that Noah was an *ish*. It was not enough to say that he was a *tzaddik tamim*, it required a special term that said he was a *ish tzaddik*, meaning he had those talents and abilities that qualify him to be a leader. He had to be a leader in order for God to entrust the building of the ark to him.

This does not mean that it should be the goal of all of us to be able to be described as *ish*, meaning people of ability and talent; it should be our goal to become *adam* and realize the great potential of being a human being. But some of us will be leaders and they are those ones who are able to be described as personalities as well as persons – not only *adam*, but *ish*.

—

Additional Commentary

Ish (A)

Whenever the word *ish* (man or person) is used in Scripture seemingly unnecessarily, just as in our text, where it could have said that Noah was righteous without having to say that he was a man of righteousness, it means that the person described as *ish* is not only righteous, but a person whose leadership ability is capable of influencing others. The word *ish* appears with this meaning in many parts of the Torah. For a complete listing of these places, see Aryeh Mirkin in his commentary on this *midrash*. (Mirkin)

Ish (B)

The word *ish* appears to be superfluous in our text. Its purpose in the text was to tell us that Noah was righteous and a leader. There is a difference between the word *adam* and the word *ish*, both of which refer to the human being. The term *adam* is used to describe a person who is still in an earlier stage of moral development and who has not yet been able to conquer his evil inclination. The term *ish*, however, describes one whose personality is fully developed, whose moral behavior is on a high level and whose only desire is to love God. This distinction is reflected in a prayer that we recite on Rosh Hashanah. אשריאיש שלא ישכחך ובן אדם יתאמץ בך – *ashrei ish she-lo yishkachekh u'ben adam yitametz b'kha.* Fortunate is the *ish* who will not forget You and the *adam* who will strengthen himself through You. In other words, the *ish* is only required not to forget God. But the *adam* has to strengthen himself with all his power against his inclination. (*Tiferet Tzion*)

ח. 'תָּמִים הָיָה בְּדֹרֹתָיו' בַּר חֲטָיָּא אָמַר, כָּל מִי שֶׁנֶּאֱמַר בּוֹ 'תָּמִים', הַשְׁלִים שָׁנָיו לְמִדַּת שָׁבוּעַ.

8. WHOLE-HEARTED. BAR HUTAH SAID: EVERY MAN WHOM THE SCRIP-
TURE DESIGNATES 'WHOLEHEARTED' COMPLETED HIS YEARS ACCORD-
ING TO THE MEASURE OF THE SEPTENNATE.

The word שבוע – *shavuah* requires some explanation. In the general
way, it comes from the same root meaning as "completion" or "satisfaction." In relationship to the terminology of years, the word is a symbol
of completion of a seven-year period. Consider the following calculation: The time that Noah left the ark until he died, spanned a period of
350 years; we know this from from Genesis 7:7 and 9:29. This number
consists of fifty seven-year cycles. In the case of Abraham, there was a
period of seventy-seven years from the time of the circumcision of his
son – when God told him to be *tamim*, wholehearted – until his own
death. This is eleven cycles of seven. In the case of David, about whom
the word *tamim* was also used, he lived seventy years, which is ten cycles
of seven years.

'הָיָה' אָמַר רַבִּי יוֹחָנָן, כָּל מִי שֶׁנֶּאֱמַר בּוֹ 'הָיָה', מִתְּחִלָּתוֹ וְעַד סוֹפוֹ הוּא צַדִּיק. הֲתִיבוּן לֵהּ
וְהָכְתִיב, (יחזקאל לג, כד) 'אֶחָד הָיָה אַבְרָהָם, וַיִּירַשׁ אֶת הָאָרֶץ', מֵעַתָּה, הוּא תְּחִלָּתוֹ וְהוּא סוֹפוֹ,
אֲמַר לְהוֹן אַף הִיא לָא תַבְרָא, דְּהָא רַבִּי לֵוִי, בְּשֵׁם רֵישׁ לָקִישׁ אָמַר, בֶּן שָׁלֹשׁ שָׁנִים הִכִּיר
אַבְרָהָם אֶת בּוֹרְאוֹ וְכוּ

WAS. R. JOHANAN SAID: EVERY MAN OF WHOM IT IS SAID THAT HE 'WAS'
(HAYAH) REMAINED UNCHANGED FROM BEGINNING TO END. AN OBJEC-
TION WAS RAISED: BUT IT IS WRITTEN, ABRAHAM WAS ONE, AND HE
INHERITED THE LAND (EZEK. 33:24): WAS HE THEN UNCHANGED FROM
BEGINNING TO END!

The argument that the word *hayah* applies only to one who recognized
God from the beginning to the end of one's life seems to be contradicted
in the Abraham story, because we are told that at the age of three (in

the Hebrew original *Midrash*), he opposed his father's idols. This would seem to mean that until that age, he was an idolator himself! However, this not a real problem since it means that from the age at which he was capable of awareness until the end of his life, he recognized God. In Genesis 26:5, it is written that Abraham hearkened to the voice of God. The word עקב – *ekev* is used to mean "hearken," and its numerical value is 172. This is the same value as the number of years of awareness that Abraham had in his life, beginning at age three, when he first recognized God, which the verse implies as being his full life.

רַבִּי חֲנִינָא וְרַבִּי יוֹחָנָן, תַּרְוֵיהוֹן אָמְרִין, בֶּן אַרְבָּעִים וּשְׁמֹנֶה שָׁנָה הִכִּיר אַבְרָהָם אֶת בּוֹרְאוֹ, וּמָה אֲנִי מְקַיֵּם 'הָיָה' שֶׁהָיָה מְתֻקָּן לְהַדְרִיךְ כָּל הָעוֹלָם כֻּלּוֹ בִּתְשׁוּבָה. (בראשית ג, כב) 'הֵן הָאָדָם הָיָה', מְתֻקָּן לְמִיתָה. נָחָשׁ (שם שם, א) 'הָיָה' מְתֻקָּן לַפֻּרְעָנוּת. קַיִן, (שם ד, ב) 'הָיָה' מְתֻקָּן לַגָּלוּת. אִיּוֹב, (איוב א, א) 'הָיָה' מְתֻקָּן לְיִסּוּרִין. נֹחַ, 'הָיָה' מְתֻקָּן לַנֵּס. מֹשֶׁה, (שמות ג, א) 'הָיָה' מְתֻקָּן לְגוֹאֵל. מָרְדְּכַי, (אסתר ב, ה) 'הָיָה' מְתֻקָּן לַגְּאֻלָּה.

THAT TOO DOES NOT REFUTE ME, HE REPLIED: R. JOHANAN AND R. HANINA BOTH SAID: ABRAHAM WAS FORTY-EIGHT YEARS OLD WHEN HE RECOGNIZED HIS CREATOR. THEN HOW IS 'WAS' TO BE UNDERSTOOD IN HIS CASE? HE 'WAS' DESTINED TO LEAD THE WHOLE WORLD TO RE-PENTANCE. [SIMILARLY,] BEHOLD, THE MAN 'WAS' (GEN. 3:22) MEANS: DESTINED TO DIE. THE SERPENT 'WAS' (IBID., 1): DESTINED TO PUNISH-MENT. CAIN 'WAS' (IBID., 4:2): PREDESTINED TO EXILE; JOB 'WAS' (JOB 1:1): DESTINED TO SUFFERING; NOAH 'WAS': DESTINED FOR A MIRACLE; MOSES 'WAS' (EX. 3:1): DESTINED TO BE A REDEEMER; MORDECAI 'WAS' (EST. 2:5): DESTINED FOR REDEMPTION.

In connection with the argument that Abraham was forty-eight years old when he recognized God, at the time of Tower of Babel, this is answered by R. Yochanan's position that the word *hayah* does not necessarily imply the recognition of God from the beginning of one's life to the end, but rather that the person was destined to proclaim the meaning of God and His importance to the entire world.

רַבִּי לֵוִי וְרַבָּנָן, רַבִּי לֵוִי אָמַר, כָּל מִי שֶׁנֶּאֱמַר בּוֹ 'הָיָה', רָאָה עוֹלָם חָדָשׁ. אָמַר רַבִּי שְׁמוּאֵל, חֲמִשָּׁה הֵן, נֹחַ, אֶתְמוֹל, (איוב יד, יט) 'אֲבָנִים שָׁחֲקוּ מַיִם', דַּאֲמַר רַבִּי לֵוִי בְּשֵׁם רַבִּי יוֹחָנָן, אֲפִלּוּ אִצְטְרוֹבִּילִין שֶׁל רֵחַיִם נִמְחָה בַּמַּיִם, וְהָכָא אַתְּ אָמַר, (בראשית ט, יח) 'וַיִּהְיוּ בְנֵי נֹחַ הַיֹּצְאִים מִן הַתֵּבָה' אַתְמָהָא, אֶלָּא, רָאָה עוֹלָם חָדָשׁ. יוֹסֵף, (תהלים קה, יח) 'עִנּוּ בַכֶּבֶל רַגְלוֹ', וְעַכְשָׁו, (בראשית מב, ו) 'וְיוֹסֵף הוּא הַשַּׁלִּיט', אֶלָּא, שֶׁרָאָה עוֹלָם חָדָשׁ. מֹשֶׁה, אֶתְמוֹל בּוֹרֵחַ מִפְּנֵי פַרְעֹה, וְעַכְשָׁו, הוּא מְשַׁקְּעוֹ בַיָּם, אֶלָּא, שֶׁרָאָה עוֹלָם חָדָשׁ. אִיּוֹב, אֶתְמוֹל, (איוב טז, יג) 'יִשְׁפֹּךְ לָאָרֶץ מְרֵרָתִי', וְעַכְשָׁו, (שם מב, י) 'וַיֹּסֶף ה' אֶת כָּל אֲשֶׁר לְאִיּוֹב לְמִשְׁנֶה', אֶלָּא, שֶׁרָאָה עוֹלָם חָדָשׁ. מָרְדְּכַי, אֶתְמוֹל הָיָה מְתֻקָּן לַצְּלִיבָה, וְעַכְשָׁו, הוּא צוֹלֵב אֶת צוֹלְבָיו, אֶלָּא, שֶׁרָאָה עוֹלָם חָדָשׁ.

R. LEVI SAID: EVERYONE OF WHOM IT IS SAID THAT HE 'WAS' (HAYAH)
SAW A NEW WORLD. SAID R. SAMUEL B. NAHMAN: AND THEY ARE FIVE.
NOAH: YESTERDAY [IT WAS A CASE OF] THE WATERS WEAR THE STONES
(JOB 14:19), FOR R. LEVI SAID IN R. JOHANAN'S NAME: EVEN THE NETHER
MILLSTONE WAS DISSOLVED BY THE WATER; WHEREAS NOW YOU READ,
AND THE SONS OF NOAH THAT WENT FORTH, ETC. (GEN. 9:18)! THUS HE
SAW A NEW WORLD. JOSEPH: YESTERDAY, HIS FEET THEY HURT WITH
FETTERS (PS. 105:18), WHILE NOW, AND JOSEPH WAS THE GOVERNOR
OVER THE LAND (GEN. 42:6)! THUS HE SAW A NEW WORLD. MOSES:
YESTERDAY HE WAS FLEEING FROM PHARAOH, AND NOW HE PLUNGES
HIM INTO THE SEA! THUS HE SAW A NEW WORLD. JOB: YESTERDAY, HE
POURETH OUT MY GALL UPON THE GROUND (JOB 16:13). WHILE NOW,
AND THE LORD GAVE JOB TWICE AS MUCH AS HE HAD BEFORE (IBID.,
42:10)! THUS HE SAW A NEW WORLD. MORDECAI: YESTERDAY HE WAS
READY FOR THE GALLOWS, AND NOW HE EXECUTES HIS EXECUTIONER!
THUS HE SAW A NEW WORLD.

In all of these five illustrations, there is a major change in the status of
the person from slavery, suffering or restriction to an ultimate deliverance. This is described as seeing and experiencing a new world.

רַבָּנָן אָמְרִין, כָּל מִי שֶׁנֶּאֱמַר בּוֹ 'הָיָה', זָן וּמְפַרְנֵס, נֹחַ זָן וּפִרְנֵס כָּל שְׁנֵים עָשָׂר חֹדֶשׁ, שֶׁנֶּאֱמַר
(בראשית ו, כא) 'וְאַתָּה קַח לְךָ. וְגוֹ'', יוֹסֵף, (שם מז, יב) 'וַיְכַלְכֵּל יוֹסֵף אֶת אָבִיו וְאֶת אֶחָיו'. מֹשֶׁה
זָן וּפִרְנֵס אֶת יִשְׂרָאֵל אַרְבָּעִים שָׁנָה בַּמִּדְבָּר, אִיּוֹב (איוב לא, יז) 'וְאֹכַל פִּתִּי לְבַדִּי', שֶׁמָּא (שם שם,
שם) 'לֹא אָכַל יָתוֹם מִמֶּנָּה' אַתְמְהָא, מָרְדְּכַי זָן וּפִרְנֵס, אָמַר רַבִּי יוּדָן, פַּעַם אַחַת חִזֵּר עַל כָּל
הַמֵּינִיקוֹת וְלֹא מָצָא לְאֶסְתֵּר לְאַלְתַּר מֵינִיקָה הוּא, רַבִּי בֶּרֶכְיָה וְרַבִּי אַבָּהוּ, בְּשֵׁם
רַבִּי אֱלִיעֶזֶר, בָּא לוֹ חָלָב, וְהָיָה מֵינִיקָה כַּד דְּרַשׁ רַבִּי אַבָּהוּ בְּצִבּוּרָא, גָּחוּךְ צִבּוּרָא לְקָלֵהּ, אָמַר
לְהוֹן, וְלָא מַתְנִיתָא הִיא, רַבִּי שִׁמְעוֹן בֶּן אֶלְעָזָר אוֹמֵר, חֲלֵב הַזָּכָר טָהוֹר.

THE RABBIS SAID: EVERY MAN OF WHOM IT IS SAID THAT HE 'WAS'
(HAYAH), FED AND SUSTAINED OTHERS. NOAH FED AND SUSTAINED [THE
INMATES OF THE ARK] TWELVE MONTHS, AS IT SAYS, AND TAKE THOU
UNTO THEE OF ALL FOOD THAT IS EATEN (GEN. 6:21). JOSEPH FED AND
SUSTAINED: AND JOSEPH SUSTAINED, ETC. (IBID., 47:12). MOSES FED AND
SUSTAINED [THE ISRAELITES] THE WHOLE FORTY YEARS IN THE WILDER-
NESS. JOB FED AND SUSTAINED: OR HAVE I EATEN MY MORSEL MYSELF
ALONE, ETC. (JOB 31:17)? – DID NOT THE FATHERLESS EAT THEREOF!
BUT DID MORDECAI ACTUALLY FEED AND SUSTAIN? SAID R. JUDAN: ON
ONE OCCASION HE WENT ROUND TO ALL THE WET NURSES BUT COULD
NOT FIND ONE FOR ESTHER, WHEREUPON HE HIMSELF SUCKLED HER. R.
BEREKIAH AND R. ABBAHU IN R. ELEAZAR'S NAME SAID: MILK CAME TO
HIM AND HE SUCKLED HER. WHEN R. ABBAHU TAUGHT THIS PUBLICLY,

This is a very strange teaching that there are instances where a male
can produce milk that would breastfeed an infant. It is enough to note
that the claim was made and we will leave it to the medical researchers
or scientists to explain or deny this phenomenon.

⁓

Seed Thoughts

In connection with five of the great names in the biblical story, it is asserted that they saw or experienced a new world. What does that mean?
It can only mean that as a result of their experience and their circumstances with relation to God, that their character and personality was so
transformed that it is as though they experienced a new world.

There are no new worlds and worlds do not change, but people do.
Their perceptions change and their characters change. But the "new
world" is not the world outside of us, but the world inside of us, having to do with our character and personality. This author just finished
reading a very lengthy volume describing every revolution that took
place in every country in Europe from the eighteenth, nineteenth and
early twentieth centuries. The blood that was spilled, the horrors that
were committed and the tortures, both on the part of the defenders and
protestors, are too horrible to describe in this homily. Unfortunately,
Europe was not improved upon by the various revolutions and only
seemed to find itself after stability returned.

New worlds can not be created by force. They have to do with the development of moral character. Individuals have to transform themselves
into characters of a higher moral level, and this is what would improve
the world.

There was a young child who was annoying his father. In order to
quiet him, the father gave him a puzzle to put together. Within minutes,
the child finished the puzzle. "How did you do it so quickly?" asked
the father. On one side of the puzzle was a picture of a man. The child
answered, "I just put the man together and that put the puzzle together."
What we have to do is put the man together, and that would put the
world together. That would produce the only new world that is possible.

⁓

Addtional Commentary

R. Levi and Rabanan

The purpose of their discussion is to interpret the word *hayah*, which seems quite unnecessary in the verse. (*Tiferet Tzion*)

They saw a new world

The purpose of this discussion is to indicate that the expression *hayah* comes to help us understand the change that took place in the manner in which God conducted the world. In so far as the Holy One, Blessed be He, is concerned, there is no such thing as changing His mind. Therefore, when we say His Divine Supervision changed from what it had been at the beginning, that is due to the change that took place in man, so that he would be able to receive this new type of Divine Supervision. That is why it is said that wherever an expression with *hayah* is used, that person saw a new world. The word *hayah* indicates that the Divine system was changed, but due to the change in man, not a change in God. (*Tiferet Tzion*)

R. Shmuel said that there are five such cases

R. Shmuel said that the Holy One, Blessed be He, conducts this world in five different ways. The first is the special Divine Providence that relates to every individual, such as who will become rich, who will become poor, who will live and who will die, who will be brought down, who will be lifted up, and so on. The second form of Divine Supervision is more general, affecting groups of people all together, and it governs such things as war, famine, etc. Under this type. individuals are usually not taken into account; instead, every member of whatever group is being affected is affected equally. These two forms of supervision function in three different possible ways: The first is the way of nature, the second functions through the use of miracle and the third functions by what should be described as a "hidden miracle," such as the miracle of Mordechai and Esther in the Purim story. This is why R. Shmuel said that there are five forms of supervision or existence, though within these five forms, other forms were included. Only these main five were listed, and from these, we can derive all the others. (*Tiferet Tzion*)

ט. 'בְּדֹרֹתָיו', רַבִּי יְהוּדָה וְרַבִּי נְחֶמְיָה, רַבִּי יְהוּדָה אָמַר, 'בְּדֹרֹתָיו', הָיָה צַדִּיק, הָא אִלּוּ הָיָה בְדוֹרוֹ
שֶׁל מֹשֶׁה אוֹ בְדוֹרוֹ שֶׁל שְׁמוּאֵל לֹא הָיָה צַדִּיק, בְּשׁוּק סַמַיָּא, צָוְחִין לַעֲוִירָא, סַגִּי נְהוֹר
9. IN HIS GENERATIONS. R. JUDAH AND R. NEHEMIAH DIFFERED. R. JU-
DAH SAID: ONLY IN HIS GENERATIONS WAS HE A RIGHTEOUS MAN [BY
COMPARISON]; HAD HE FLOURISHED IN THE GENERATION OF MOSES
OR SAMUEL, HE WOULD NOT HAVE BEEN CALLED RIGHTEOUS: IN THE
STREET OF THE TOTALLY BLIND, THE ONE-EYED MAN IS CALLED CLEAR-
SIGHTED, AND THE INFANT IS CALLED A SCHOLAR.

The concern of the *Midrash* is that the word *bedorotav, meaning "in
his generations,"* is included in the scriptural verse. It was not necessary,
so the *midrashic* writers saw in this word an additional meaning. R.
Yehudah sees in this word a limitation. Noah was righteous *only* in his
generation, but would not have been considered so in the generations of
such great personalities as Moshe and Shmuel. As the folk saying goes,
on the street where everyone is blind, the person of low vision is looked
upon as a person with large vision.

מָשָׁל, לְאֶחָד שֶׁהָיָה לוֹ מַרְתֵּף אֶחָד שֶׁל יַיִן, פָּתַח חָבִית אַחַת, וּמְצָאָהּ שֶׁל חֹמֶץ, שְׁנִיָּה כֵּן,
שְׁלִישִׁית וּמְצָאָהּ קוֹסֵס, אַמְרִין לֵהּ קוֹסֵס הוּא, אֲמַר לְהוֹן, וְאִית הָכָא טַב מְנַהּ, אַמְרוּ לֵהּ לָא.
כָּךְ, 'בְּדֹרֹתָיו' הָיָה צַדִּיק. הָא אִלּוּ הָיָה בְדוֹרוֹ שֶׁל מֹשֶׁה אוֹ בְדוֹרוֹ שֶׁל שְׁמוּאֵל, לֹא הָיָה צַדִּיק.
IT IS AS IF A MAN WHO HAD A WINE VAULT OPENED ONE BARREL AND
FOUND IT VINEGAR; ANOTHER AND FOUND IT VINEGAR; THE THIRD,
HOWEVER, HE FOUND TURNING SOUR. 'IT IS TURNING,' PEOPLE SAID TO
HIM. 'IS THERE ANY BETTER HERE?' HE RETORTED. SIMILARLY, IN HIS
GENERATIONS HE WAS A RIGHTEOUS MAN.

The parable of the wine seems most appropriate. If you cannot produce first-class wine and there is nothing else available, you make do
with what you have. Similarly, God did the best he could with Noah and
with all his limitations.

רַבִּי נְחֶמְיָה אָמַר, וּמָה אִם 'בְּדֹרֹתָיו' הָיָה צַדִּיק, אִלּוּ הָיָה בְּדוֹרוֹ שֶׁל מֹשֶׁה אוֹ בְדוֹרוֹ שֶׁל שְׁמוּאֵל,
עַל אַחַת כַּמָּה וְכַמָּה, מָשָׁל, לִצְלוֹחִית שֶׁל אֲפַרְסְמוֹן מֻקֶּפֶת צָמִיד פָּתִיל, וּמֻנַּחַת בֵּין הַקְּבָרוֹת,
וְהָיָה רֵיחָהּ נוֹדֵף, וְאִלּוּ הָיָה חוּץ לַקְּבָרוֹת, עַל אַחַת כַּמָּה וְכַמָּה, מָשָׁל, לִבְתוּלָה שֶׁהָיְתָה שְׁרוּיָה
בְּשׁוּק שֶׁל זוֹנוֹת, וְלֹא יָצָא עָלֶיהָ שֵׁם רָע, אִלּוּ הָיְתָה בִּשְׁוּקָן שֶׁל כְּשֵׁרוֹת עַל אַחַת כַּמָּה וְכַמָּה,
כָּךְ, וּמָה אִם בְּדוֹרוֹתָיו הָיָה צַדִּיק, אִלּוּ הָיָה בְּדוֹרוֹ שֶׁל מֹשֶׁה אוֹ בְדוֹרוֹ שֶׁל שְׁמוּאֵל עַל אַחַת
כַּמָּה וְכַמָּה.

R. NEHEMIAH SAID: IF HE WAS RIGHTEOUS EVEN IN HIS GENERATION,
HOW MUCH MORE SO [HAD HE LIVED] IN THE AGE OF MOSES. HE MIGHT
BE COMPARED TO A TIGHTLY CLOSED VIAL OF PERFUME LYING IN A
GRAVEYARD, WHICH NEVERTHELESS GAVE FORTH A FRAGRANT ODOR;
HOW MUCH MORE THEN IF IT WERE OUTSIDE THE GRAVEYARD!

The conclusion of R. Nehemiah is quite opposite. If Noah was able to achieve his limited righteousness status in an environment of evildoers, how much higher would he have risen had he been in the time of Moshe and Shmuel, from whom he could have learned. The two parables are also appropriate; how much more effective anything or anyone can be in an environment that is encouraging!

Seed Thoughts

The arguments as to whether the word *bedorotav* should be looked upon as limiting Noah or defining his great potential do not seem terribly relevant. No one is going to be moved from one century to another, even if there was great potential there. Even if Noah had lived during the time of Moshe and Shmuel, would he have been in a position to "compete" with them, and even if so, why should he have done so? The important lesson is what a person can do in his generation. The term *bedorotav* refers to more than one generation. Within an ordinary life span of seventy to eighty years, there could easily be three generations. In the case of Noah, who lived more than five hundred years, there would have been many generations. The great tribute to him was how effective he was in all his generations. The man who built the ark, filled it with the complete cross-section of the animal and plant kingdoms, looked after them while in the ark and removed them safely and securely at the end of the Flood does not need the challenge of additional heroism. He achieved the most important thing a human being can achieve. He was able to achieve the status of a righteous human being, despite all the challenges against him. For this, history will always be grateful.

י. 'אֶת הָאֱ-לֹהִים הִתְהַלֶּךְ נֹחַ', רַבִּי יְהוּדָה וְרַבִּי נְחֶמְיָה, רַבִּי יְהוּדָה אָמַר, מָשָׁל, לְשַׂר שֶׁהָיוּ
לוֹ שְׁנֵי בָנִים, אֶחָד גָּדוֹל וְאֶחָד קָטָן, אָמַר לַקָּטָן, הַלֵּךְ עִמִּי, וְאָמַר לַגָּדוֹל, בּוֹא וְהַלֵּךְ לְפָנַי, כָּךְ
אַבְרָהָם, שֶׁהָיָה כֹחוֹ יָפֶה, (בראשית יז, א) 'הִתְהַלֵּךְ לְפָנַי וֶהְיֵה תָמִים', אֲבָל נֹחַ, שֶׁהָיָה כֹחוֹ רַע, 'אֶת
הָאֱ-לֹהִים הִתְהַלֶּךְ נֹחַ', רַבִּי נְחֶמְיָה אָמַר, מָשָׁל, לְאוֹהֲבוֹ שֶׁל מֶלֶךְ שֶׁהָיָה מִשְׁתַּקֵּעַ בְּטִיט עָבֶה,
הֵצִיץ הַמֶּלֶךְ, וְרָאָה אוֹתוֹ, אָמַר לֵהּ עַד שֶׁאַתָּה, מִשְׁתַּקֵּעַ בְּטִיט, הַלֵּךְ עִמִּי, הֲדָא הוּא דִּכְתִיב,
'אֶת הָאֱ-לֹהִים הִתְהַלֶּךְ נֹחַ'

10. NOAH WALKED WITH GOD. R. JUDAH SAID: THIS MAY BE COMPARED TO
A KING WHO HAD TWO SONS, ONE GROWN UP AND THE OTHER A CHILD.
TO THE CHILD HE SAID, 'WALK WITH ME,' BUT TO THE ADULT, 'WALK
BEFORE ME.' SIMILARLY, TO ABRAHAM, WHOSE [MORAL] STRENGTH
WAS GREAT, [HE SAID,] 'WALK THOU BEFORE ME' (GEN. 17:1); OF NOAH,
WHOSE STRENGTH WAS FEEBLE [IT SAYS], NOAH WALKED WITH GOD.
R.NEHEMIAH SAID: HE MIGHT BE COMPARED TO A KING'S FRIEND WHO
WAS PLUNGING ABOUT IN DARK ALLEYS, AND WHEN THE KING LOOKED
OUT AND SAW HIM SINKING [IN THE MUD], HE SAID TO HIM, 'INSTEAD
OF PLUNGING ABOUT IN DARK ALLEYS, COME AND WALK WITH ME.'

The word *et* may have the meaning of *im*, meaning "with." Therefore
the verse says he walked *with* God, meaning he looked forward to the
assistance that The Divine could offer him. In the case of Abraham and
Isaac, where the expression is "*lifnei Hashem*," meaning that they walked
before God, this means that they did not overly rely upon Him for help
and assistance, but were morally autonomous, knowing intuitively the
right thing to do. Once again, R. Yehudah and R. Nehemiah are divided
in their opinions, in ways that resemble their previously mentioned
original interpretations: R. Yehudah looks upon Noah as being very
limited, even in his potentialities, whereas R. Nehemiah looks upon his
achievements with great approval. Both parables, that of the king who
had two sons, one grown up and one a child, and the parable of the
king who went out of his way to help his friend, reflect the views of R.
Yehudah on one hand and R. Nehemiah on the other.

וּלְמָה אַבְרָהָם דּוֹמֶה לְאוֹהֲבוֹ שֶׁל מֶלֶךְ, שֶׁרָאָה אֶת הַמֶּלֶךְ מְהַלֵּךְ בַּמְּבוֹאוֹת הָאֲפֵלִים, הֵצִיץ אוֹהֲבוֹ, וְהִתְחִיל מֵאִיר עָלָיו דֶּרֶךְ הַחַלּוֹן, הֵצִיץ הַמֶּלֶךְ וְרָאָה אוֹתוֹ, אָמַר לוֹ, עַד שֶׁאַתָּה מֵאִיר לִי דֶּרֶךְ חַלּוֹן, בּוֹא וְהָאֵר לְפָנַי, כָּךְ, אָמַר הַקָּדוֹשׁ בָּרוּךְ הוּא לְאַבְרָהָם, עַד שֶׁתְּהֵא מֵאִיר לִי מֵאַסְפּוֹטַמְיָא, וּמֵחַבְרוֹתֶיהָ, בּוֹא וְהָאֵר לְפָנַי בְּאֶרֶץ יִשְׂרָאֵל, הֲדָא הוּא דִכְתִיב, (שם מח, טו) 'וַיְבָרֶךְ אֶת יוֹסֵף, וַיֹּאמַר, הָאֱ-לֹהִים אֲשֶׁר הִתְהַלְּכוּ אֲבֹתַי לְפָנָיו, וְגוֹ'".

BUT ABRAHAM'S CASE IS RATHER TO BE COMPARED TO THAT OF A KING WHO WAS SINKING IN DARK ALLEYS, AND WHEN HIS FRIEND SAW HIM HE SHONE A LIGHT FOR HIM THROUGH THE WINDOW. SAID HE TO HIM, 'INSTEAD OF LIGHTING ME THROUGH THE WINDOW, COME AND SHOW A LIGHT BEFORE ME.' EVEN SO DID THE HOLY ONE, BLESSED BE HE, SAY TO ABRAHAM: 'INSTEAD OF SHOWING A LIGHT FOR ME FROM MESOPOTAMIA AND ITS ENVIRONS, COME AND SHOW ONE BEFORE ME IN ERETZ ISRAEL.' SIMILARLY, IT IS WRITTEN, AND HE BLESSED JOSEPH, AND SAID: THE GOD BEFORE WHOM MY FATHERS ABRAHAM AND ISAAC DID WALK, ETC. (GEN. 48:15).

Thus, in the case of Abraham, who had the ability to confront the evil inclination, he was told to walk before God. But in the case of Noah, whose character was weaker, he walked hand in hand with God because he needed the Divine assistance.

רַבִּי יוֹחָנָן וְרֵישׁ לָקִישׁ, רַבִּי יוֹחָנָן אָמַר, לְרוֹעֶה שֶׁהוּא עוֹמֵד וּמַבִּיט בְּצֹאנוֹ, רֵישׁ לָקִישׁ אָמַר, לְנָשִׂיא שֶׁהוּא מְהַלֵּךְ וּזְקֵנִים לְפָנָיו, עַל דַּעְתֵּהּ דְּרַבִּי יוֹחָנָן, אָנוּ צְרִיכִים לִכְבוֹדוֹ, וְעַל דַּעְתֵּהּ דְּרַבִּי שִׁמְעוֹן בֶּן לָקִישׁ, הוּא צָרִיךְ, לִכְבוֹדֵנוּ.

R. BEREKIAH IN R. JOHANAN'S NAME AND RESH LAKISH GAVE TWO ILLUSTRATIONS OF THIS. R. JOHANAN SAID: IT WAS AS IF A SHEPHERD STOOD AND WATCHED HIS FLOCKS. RESH LAKISH SAID: IT WAS AS IF A PRINCE WALKED ALONG WHILE THE ELDERS PRECEDED HIM. ON R. JOHANAN'S VIEW: WE NEED HIS PROXIMITY. ON THE VIEW OF RESH LAKISH: HE NEEDS US TO GLORIFY HIM.

In the case of R. Yochanan and Resh Lakish, they, too, engage in the same controversy as R. Yehudah and R. Nehemiah. One acknowledges the limitations of Noah and the other acknowledges his potentialities. They each offer an interesting parable: the shepherd who watches over his sheep and protects them, or the parable of the elders who walk before the king, their role being to add honor to the king. Noah required Divine assistance. Abraham added honor to God by publicizing His Divine guidance.

Seed Thoughts

The *Midrash* ends with a very lovely saying: We need God to guard us so that we do not stumble. This is the view of R. Yochanan. The view of Resh Lakish is that God "needs" us to make His existence known in the world. This comparison reminds us again of the manner of discussion in *Midrashic literature*. In the case of most discussions in *Talmudic* literature, the participants are not satisfied with merely expressing opinions. A decision has to be taken as to which is the proper way, and this becomes the law. The approach of *Midrash* is entirely different. Both sides are right, both sides have merit, both sides should be followed. It is true that we need God to help us, guide us, warn us, so that we should not stumble. It is also true that God needs us, as it were, to stand for Him, to be a witness to His Supreme role in the universe. As the Rabbis put it, "everything is in the hands of Heaven with the exception of fear of Heaven." (*Brakhot* 33b) That means we have the freedom to make the moral decisions of life. These values are profound and complex. We need God, of course, but He also needs us to make the right choices in our lives.

—

Additional Commentary

R. Yehudah and R. Nehemiah

The term *hit'halekh* is used concerning Noah and Abraham, and therefore a comparison is needed. Each of these sages follows his view with great consistency. It is the view of R. Yehudah that Noah was not a completely righteous individual (*tzaddik gamur*). Therefore, he interprets the verse that uses the term *hit'halekh*, meaning that he followed God, as not being able to walk by himself, without the Holy One, Blessed be He, Who guided him. After interpreting the word *lehit'halekh* in connection with Noah to mean that God guided him, he then went on to interpret *lehit'halekh* in connection with Abraham, whom God also guided. It is only because Abraham was a strong person and had a true comprehension of God's will that he was able to walk before God, as the grown-up son who does not need special guidance from his father besides supervision from a distance. However, without some kind of guidance, even Abraham would not have been capable of carrying on in the path of righteousness; therefore, he is still compared to an adult son and not just to an adult.

As for R. Nehemiah, he followed the view that Noah was a completely righteous person, but was inhibited by the people of his generation to follow in God's ways as he would have wanted. Noah's contemporaries would ridicule him and therefore the parable compares him to one who walked in thick mud. Just as the thick mud prevents a person from walking where he wishes to walk, similarly Noah was prevented from following in the ways of righteousness as he would have wanted, until God helped him do so. According to this, in the case of Noah, the word *lehit'halekh* is interpreted to mean that his environment was an important influence over him. (*Tiferet Tzion*)

א. (ו, יג) 'וַיֹּאמֶר אֱ-לֹהִים לְנֹחַ, קֵץ כָּל בָּשָׂר, וְגוֹ'', (יחזקאל ז, יא) 'הֶחָמָס קָם לְמַטֵּה רֶשַׁע', 'הֶחָמָס קָם' אִתְמְהָא, חָס וְשָׁלוֹם, אֵינוֹ קָם, וְאִם קָם 'לְמַטֵּה רֶשַׁע' לְחִיּוּבוֹ שֶׁל רָשָׁע

1. AND GOD SAID UNTO NOAH: THE END OF ALL FLESH IS COME BEFORE ME; FOR THE EARTH IS FILLED WITH VIOLENCE THROUGH THEM (6:13). IT IS WRITTEN, VIOLENCE IS RISEN UP AS A ROD OF WICKEDNESS; NOUGHT COMETH FROM THEM, NOR FROM THEIR TUMULT (HAMONAM), NOR FROM THEIR TURMOIL (HEMEHEM); NEITHER IS THERE EMINENCY (NOHAH) AMONG THEM (EZEK. 7:11). 'VIOLENCE IS RISEN UP' – HEAVEN FORFEND! IT HAS NOT RISEN UP. YET IF IT HAS, IT IS AS 'A ROD OF WICK-EDNESS' – TO PUNISH THE WICKED.

This *Midrash* and several that follow are concerned with the fact that there are two verses that interpret the sinfulness of the Flood. In Genesis 6:1–2, the verse states that the main sin of the generation of the Flood was sexual immorality, despite which their end did not come until the verse says that their society was filled with *hamas*, which means robbery and other forms of delinquency. This seems to be what the prophet Ezekiel had in mind in writing that *hamas*, wickedness, rose up. But how is that possible? How would wickedness rise up, seemingly independently, from its own resources? Can it possibly be that wickedness rises up to help the evildoers? That cannot possibly be. The only explanation is that *hamas* only arises to be used as a force or staff to add to the guilt of the evildoers. The interpretation of the verse is that *hamas* rose up as a criticism and an attack on the generation of the Flood, as a warning to them, not to be influenced by anything that is to be associated with those who do evil, their community, or their money. Despite this, there was no movement on their part to return to God.

(שם שם, שם) 'לֹא מֵהֶם וְלֹא מֵהֲמוֹנָם וְלֹא מֵהֲמֵהֶם' לָא מִנְּהוֹן וְלָא מִמָּמוֹנָם וְלֹא מִן תִּמְהָתְהוֹן, לָמָּה (שם שם, שם) 'לֹא נֹהַּ בָּהֶם'

'NOUGHT COMETH FROM THEM, NOR FROM THEIR TUMULT (HAMONAM).' 'NOR FROM THEIR TURMOIL (HEMEHEM)': I.E., NEITHER FROM THEM

NOR FROM THEIR WEALTH1 NOR FROM THEIR DAZZLING MAGNIFI-
CENCE. WHY SO? BECAUSE 'NEITHER IS THERE NOHAH [E.V. "EMINENCY"]
AMONG THEM.' NO CREATURE EVER ENJOYED SATISFACTION, NOR DID
THE HOLY ONE, BLESSED BE HE, RECEIVE SATISFACTION FROM THEM.
'NEITHER IS THERE NOHAH AMONG THEM': THERE WAS NONE TO SAY TO
THEM: 'LET THERE BE LAMENTING!'

The word *nun'hah* is interpreted as *nun''chet*, since the letters ה and
ח often interchange. This is interpreted as meaning that God derived
no *nachat* from their behavior. Nor did any creature derive *nachat* from
them because all they did was steal and destroy. They were evil to God
and themselves.

הָיָה לְשׁוּם בְּרִיָּה נַחַת רוּחַ מֵהֶם וְלֹא הָיָה לְהַקָּדוֹשׁ בָּרוּךְ הוּא נַחַת רוּחַ מֵהֶם. 'לֹא נֹחַ בָּהֶם'
כְּהַהִיא דְּאָמַר רַבִּי אַבָּא בַּר כָּהֲנָא, (בראשית ו, ז-ח) 'כִּי נִחַמְתִּי כִּי עֲשִׂיתִם וְנֹחַ', אֲפִלּוּ נֹחַ שֶׁנִּשְׁתַּיֵּר
מֵהֶם אֵינוֹ כְדַאי, אֶלָּא שֶׁמָּצָא חֵן, (שם שם, שם) 'וְנֹחַ מָצָא חֵן'. וּלְפִי שֶׁהָיוּ שְׁטוּפִים בַּגָּזֵּה נִמּוֹחוּ
מִן הָעוֹלָם.

AGAIN: 'NEITHER WAS THERE NOHAH AMONG THEM' [IS TO BE EX-
PLAINED] AS R. ABBA B. KAHANA COMMENTED: FOR IT REPENTETH ME
THAT I HAVE MADE THEM AND NOAH (GEN. 6:7). BUT EVEN NOAH, WHO
WAS LEFT, WAS NOT WORTHY, SAVE THAT HE FOUND GRACE AS IT IS
WRITTEN, BUT NOAH FOUND GRACE (IBID.). AND BECAUSE THEY WERE
STEEPED IN ROBBERY, THEY WERE BLOTTED OUT FROM THE WORLD, AS
IT SAYS, AND GOD SAID UNTO NOAH: THE END OF ALL FLESH IS COME BE-
FORE ME, FOR THE EARTH IS FILLED WITH VIOLENCE THROUGH THEM.

There is an interesting "trick," one might say, that is performed by R.
Kahana. The verse says כי נחמתי כי עשיתים – *ki nikhamti ki asitim*, meaning, "I regret that I created [man and the world]." The next verse begins
with the words "And Noah found favor." However, R. Kahana attached
the word "Noah" to the end of the previous verse instead of the beginning of the following one so that it would read, "I regret that I created
man and the world and Noah." The reference here is that even Noah was
not completely righteous and had many limitations. What saved Noah
was the fact that he found favor in God's eyes.

Seed Thoughts I

When the verse says that Noah's only asset was that he found favor in
the eyes of God, there seems to be something missing in the interpreta-

tion of the Rabbis. One gets the impression that Noah was a secondary figure in the eyes of the Rabbis by the way they interpreted what was happening in that generation, but God approved of him for reasons that were not stated and which, therefore, appear to be a complete expression of favoritism. Surely, however, that is not possible. Would one not assume that if Noah found favor in the eyes of God, there must have been a good reason for it? Must it not have been that God found something important, something ethical, something very responsible in the life of Noah to set him aside from others? The mere fact that the Rabbis may not have known all the reasons does not mean that God's position was arbitrary. He must have found Noah to be upright and righteous and wholesome. Those are the reasons for which He may have chosen him.

—

Seed Thoughts II

The Rabbis noted two verses in particular that spoke of the end of the world. The first verse seemed to indicate that the primary sin was sexual immorality. If that were so, why was not the world destroyed at that moment in time, at the first sign of such immorality? In actual fact, we know that the world continued for 120 years until that society succumbed to *hamas* and an all-encompassing wickedness. Why did that happen? Granted that sexual immorality is a very bad thing, but it does not seem to be a satisfactory reason to destroy the whole universe. One can repent from sexual immorality. One can change one's life and one's ways. When that did not happen, and the *znut*, sexual immorality, was accompanied by *hamas,* which is interpreted as any kind of wickedness that is possible, that world must finally be destroyed. God did not want to leave room for anyone who thought the crime did not fit the punishment. But when the *hamas* took over, there existed an all-encompassing evil that justified the destruction of the world.

—

Additional Commentary

There was no satisfaction from him

Because it says לא נה – *lo na* and does not say specifically מהם – *mehem,* from this it was derived that even Noah provided insufficient *nakhat, i.e., favor* in God's eyes. God always favors a tzaddik who does as much as possible to help the world and the people in it. But Noah did not meet this qualification. It was not his goal to protect and defend the world in which he lived. He did not pray for them. As God was quoted as saying to Abraham, "From Noah I did not succeed in producing protectors for the Jewish people because it did not seem to be his goal to pray for mercy for them. But from you," God said to Abraham, "I will create many *tzaddikim* who will protect the Jewish people" – because it was Abraham's goal to pray for all, including the evil ones, such as exhibited in his prayer for Sodom. Noah could not be relied upon to protect his people because he did not pray for them. Therefore, the *Midrash* concludes, "I regret having created the world and Noah." Meaning that even Noah was not sufficient as a leader to be relied upon. That is one of the reasons why the Flood is called מי נח – *mei Noah*, the waters of Noah, because he did not pray that the decree should be removed. However, the conclusion is that God's love was so great that He approved of Noah, despite his limitations. (*Tiferet Tzion*)

ב. 'וַיֹּאמֶר אֱ־לֹהִים לְנֹחַ קֵץ כָּל בָּשָׂר בָּא לְפָנַי'. (איוב כד, יא) 'בֵּין שׁוּרֹתָם יַצְהִירוּ יְקָבִים דָּרְכוּ
וַיִּצְמָאוּ', 'בֵּין שׁוּרֹתָם יַצְהִירוּ' שֶׁהָיוּ עוֹשִׂים לָהֶם בְּדָרִיּוֹת קְטַנּוֹת, 'יְקָבִים דָּרְכוּ וַיִּצְמָאוּ' אֲפִלּוּ
'יְקָבִים דָּרְכוּ וַיִּצְמָאוּ'.

2. THEY MADE OIL WITHIN THEIR ROWS, ETC. (JOB 24:11): THAT MEANS
THAT THEY SET UP SMALL OIL-PRESSES; THEY TREAD THEIR WINE-
PRESSES, AND SUFFER THIRST (IBID.): EVEN WHEN THEY TREAD THEIR
WINE-PRESSES, THEY SUFFER THIRST.

One of the problems bothering the *midrashic* sages here is the fact that
a reason for the destruction of the Flood had already been given by the
present verses. The reason stated above was sexual immorality. Despite
this immoral behavior, they were given an extension of 120 years that
would have enabled them to correct their delinquency, had they chosen
to use that time in that way. When, however, they practiced *hamas*,
which is a high degree of wickedness, their doom was sealed. This interpretation is sustained in the Book of Job, whose verses are regarded as
relating to the story of the Flood in all of its manifestations. In the verse
quoted in our *Midrash*, they had successfully planted vineyards and had
produced an abundance of grapes and wine, only to suffer from the fact
that so much of what they produced was stolen.

אָמַר רַבִּי אַיְבוּ, לָמָּה 'יְקָבִים דָּרְכוּ וַיִּצְמָאוּ' לְפִי שֶׁהָיְתָה מְאֵרָה מְצוּיָה בַּעֲמָלוֹ שֶׁל רָשָׁע, וּלְפִי
שֶׁהָיוּ שְׁטוּפִים בַּזִּמָּה וְגָזֵל, נִמּוֹחוּ מִן הָעוֹלָם.

R. AIBU SAID: WHY DO 'THEY TREAD THEIR WINE-PRESSES, AND SUFFER
THIRST'? BECAUSE A CURSE RESTED UPON THE TOIL OF THE WICKED.
AND BECAUSE THEY WERE STEEPED IN ROBBERY, THEY WERE BLOTTED
OUT FROM THE WORLD: HENCE, AND GOD SAID UNTO NOAH, ETC.

This interpretation is sustained by R. Aibu, who also affirms that
their production of grapes and wine was of great abundance, but the
corruption, particularly in the way of stealing, reduced all of them to

starvation. Nor did the guilty ones repent, even though they were given many opportunities, In terms of time, to do so.

———

Seed Thoughts

There is a special concern in the *midrashim* that we are now studying that is not always stated. That concern is a feeling that there is something unjust in the fact that the world was destroyed by a Flood. How could every individual have deserved this kind of death? The various *midrashim* offer reasons that help them accept the verdict. Judging from our present *midrash*, one might say that the sages were glad that more than one reason was given for the destruction of the Flood. Sexual immorality is a very bad thing; but does it deserve that the entire population be put to death? How is it possible for everyone to have sinned? One senses that the sages were grateful that a second reason was given. The best proof is that the word *hamas*, while it was originally intended to connote stealing, was interpreted to cover every other manifestation of wickedness that they could think of. Only something terrible and all-encompassing would justify the destruction of the world. One senses that they were pleased that such a conclusion was made possible by the scriptural verses themselves.

ג. 'וַיֹּאמֶר אֱ־לֹהִים', (עמוס ה, י) 'שָׂנְאוּ בַשַּׁעַר מוֹכִיחַ, וְדֹבֵר תָּמִים יְתָעֵבוּ', דַּהֲוָה אָמַר לְהוֹן,
רֵיקִים, אַתֶּם מַנִּיחִים מִי שֶׁקּוֹלוֹ שׁוֹבֵר אֲרָזִים, וּמִשְׁתַּחֲוִים לְעֵץ יָבֵשׁ, וּלְפִי שֶׁהָיוּ שְׁטוּפִים בְּגֶזֶל,
נִמּוֹחוּ מִן הָעוֹלָם, שֶׁנֶּאֱמַר 'וַיֹּאמֶר אֱ־לֹהִים לְנֹחַ, קֵץ כָּל בָּשָׂר בָּא, וְגוֹ'".

3. THEY HATE HIM THAT REPROVETH IN THE GATE, AND THEY ABHOR
HIM THAT SPEAKETH UPRIGHTLY (AMOS 5:10). HE [NOAH] REPROVED
THEM: 'YE GOOD-FOR-NOTHINGS! YE FORSAKE HIM WHOSE VOICE
BREAKS CEDARS AND WORSHIP A DRY LOG!' AND BECAUSE THEY WERE
STEEPED IN ROBBERY, THEY WERE BLOTTED OUT FROM THE WORLD:
HENCE, AND GOD SAID TO NOAH, ETC.

The important point that is registered here is that the destruction
came about because of sins other than sexual immorality, which was
the first interpretation. It is as though a certain degree of wickedness
has to be reached before the ultimate disaster can strike. The use of the
term *hamas,* and its application to so many aspects of wickedness, seems
to have pushed that society to reach the high level of wickedness that
merited ultimate destruction. The verse that read, "They hate him that
reproveth in the gate, and they abhor him that speaketh uprightly" refers
to the children of Israel who paid no attention to the preaching of the
prophet. This has been interpreted as referring also to the generation
of the Flood, and the prophet in this case would be Noah. During the
whole 120 years before the Flood, Noah was cutting wood and preparing for the ark in order to arouse the intrinsic concern of the people and
motivate them to repentance. He would say to them, "Foolish people,
who pay no attention to The Voice so powerful as to cut down cedar
trees, but rather paid attention to the wood of the idols, which had no
effectiveness whatsoever." This idol worship was also a manifestation of
hamas, a high degree of wickedness, and pushed the community to that
level of evil that merited their destruction.

Seed Thoughts

As it is stated in the previous Seed Thought, the sages of the *Midrash* seemed very much concerned about the justice of the Flood story. Did that generation really merit complete destruction? Several answers are attempted, and the present *Midrash* is also a focal point for this discussion. It is the *Tiferet Tzion* who raises the question in a very serious way. After all, is not the Almighty a God of mercy and compassion? Surely He would have wanted to do everything to allow that generation to repent. However, here is the problem: It is possible to practice repentance when the sin is sexual immorality, since the sin is practiced on an individual level by individuals. When it comes to the question of stealing and robbery, however, it is possible to steal from individuals, but also from the public, including companies or other various social institutions. How can one repent when it is not always possible to know who all the individuals are that have been wronged, since their forgiveness is an integral part of the function of *tshuvah*? Because this kind of wickedness was rampant and proper *tshuvah* was not possible, all the doors of repentance were closed and destruction was inevitable.

〜

Additional Commentary

Is tshuvah *possible?*

The name of God implies that He is the acme of forgiveness. It would have been expected that He would hold back His anger for as long as possible in order to allow people to do *tshuvah*, to repent. In this respect, the verses in Amos (5:8–11) say, "Who calls for the waters of the sea, and pours them out upon the face of the earth?" It also says, "Who sends forth destruction against the strong?" Furthermore, Amos adds, "They hate him who rebukes in the gate," and goes on to say, " . . . since you trample upon the poor."

These verses are interpreted to mean that the prophet calls upon the waters of the sea because of the destruction that has come to the powerful, and that Noah was already warning them about the impending doom. As they prefer the wooden idols to the voice of God, which is so powerful as to make the cedars tremble, they continue to pay no attention to the prophet.

There are two reasons why repentance was not possible for them. The first was that they paid no attention to the warnings given by Noah and it was obvious that they would never listen to him. Secondly, they stole from the public and behaved wickedly toward them and in such a case, it is impossible to repent.

As the sages of the Talmud say, that which is included in Ethics is far more difficult than sins of sexual immorality. It is possible to repent from sins of the latter, but not so from stealth and robbery, since you never know for sure to whom you can return that which was taken. This is the meaning of the words that God spoke unto Noah, saying that the end of all flesh has come, And the reason he was given was that the world was filled with *hamas*, wickedness, from which it was not possible to repent. (*Tiferet Tzion*)

ד. דָּבָר אַחֵר 'קֵץ כָּל בָּשָׂר', כְּתִיב (איוב לה, ט) 'מֵרֹב עֲשׁוּקִים יַזְעִיקוּ, יְשַׁוְּעוּ מִזְּרוֹעַ רַבִּים', 'מֵרֹב עֲשׁוּקִים יַזְעִיקוּ' אֵלּוּ הַנֶּעֱשָׁקִים, 'יְשַׁוְּעוּ מִזְּרוֹעַ רַבִּים' אֵלּוּ הָעוֹשְׁקִים

4. ANOTHER INTERPRETATION: AND GOD SAID UNTO NOAH: THE END OF ALL FLESH IS COME BEFORE ME; FOR THE EARTH IS FILLED WITH VIOLENCE THROUGH THEM (6:13). BY REASON OF THE MULTITUDE OF (MEROB) OPPRESSIONS THEY CRY OUT; THEY CRY FOR HELP BY REASON OF THE ARM OF THE MIGHTY (JOB 35:9): 'BY REASON OF THE MULTITUDE OF OPPRESSIONS THEY CRY OUT" REFERS TO THE OPPRESSED; "THEY CRY FOR HELP BY REASON OF THE ARM OF THE MIGHTY,' TO THE OPPRESSORS:

The verse from Genesis indicates that because of their wickedness, the generation of the Flood was punished. It would seem, however, that only the oppressors should have been punished. Nevertheless, it says כל בשר – *kol bassar*, meaning all flesh, everyone alive, would be terminated because everyone shared in the wickedness. Not only the oppressors. The verse from Job is quoted because it has been interpreted through-out the recent *midrashim* as referring to the generation of the Flood.

אֵלּוּ רַבִּים עַל אֵלּוּ, וְאֵלּוּ רַבִּים עַל אֵלּוּ, אֵלּוּ רַבִּים עַל אֵלּוּ בְּחִמּוּס מָמוֹן, וְאֵלּוּ רַבִּים עַל אֵלּוּ בְּחִמּוּס דְּבָרִים, עַד שֶׁנִּתְחַתֵּם גְּזַר דִּינָם, וּלְפִי שֶׁהָיוּ שְׁטוּפִים בְּגֶזֶל, נִמּוֹחוּ מִן הָעוֹלָם.

THE LATTER CONTENDED WITH THE FORMER, AND THE FORMER WITH THE LATTER, UNTIL THE DECREE OF THEIR JUDGMENT WAS SEALED. AND BECAUSE THEY WERE STEEPED IN ROBBERY, THEY WERE BLOTTED OUT FROM THE WORLD: HENCE, AND GOD SAID UNTO NOAH, ETC.

The oppressors argued with the oppressed and the oppressed argued with the oppressors. The oppressors argued in terms of money and material things that they wanted. The oppressed argued with the op-pressors in terms of words. They were guilty of words through which they denied God and denied Divine Judgment, לית דין ולית דיין – *let din velet dayan* (Mirkin). Therefore, all flesh were corrupt in the wickedness.

—

Seed Thoughts

This *midrash* begins with the Hebrew wordsדבר אחר – *davar acher*. This can be translated as a new thought, a new opinion or a new interpretation. This expression is one of the hallmarks of the *Midrash*, one of its most popular styles and one of its original contributions to Jewish thought.

In the Talmud and in all *halachic* documents, many opinions are brought forward. But there is always a conclusion that one opinion is decisive, and this becomes the law. This does not exist in *Midrash*. No special opinion is underlined as being the official view. It does not mean that all opinions are acceptable – surely not those that are obviously in contradiction to the Torah. In all other respects, however, new interpretations are sought and almost always discovered.

In the *midrashim* we are now reading, every attempt has been made to find a new interpretation to the verse that says, "The end of all flesh has come before Me." The Rabbis were very sensitive to the fact that an entire generation was destroyed. Could its wickedness have been that terrible? The *Midrash*, therefore, includes many theories demonstrating that their wickedness was far greater than what appears in the biblical text. This is the *davar acher*. The new interpretation always sought in the *Midrash*.

The bottom line of this teaching is not merely that we should be tolerant of many opinions. The real motivation is that we use whatever imagination and brain power we have to add meaning to the biblical text and, therefore, to the life we lead.

———

Additional Commentary

The ones contend with the others

In the verse that is quoted from Job, the word *rabim*, meaning "many," seems to be unnecessary, since the word מרוב – *merov*, which means "multitude," is present in the same verse. For this reason, the word *rabim* is translated as though it came from the word מריבה – *merivah*, which means conflict or difference of opinion. It helps explain why the oppressed and not only the oppressors merited punishment. They were contending (מריבים – *merivim*) and rebelling against God and arguing that the world was הפקר – *hephker*, meaning without a moral law. (Maharzu)

The complaints of the oppressed

As a result of the behavior of their oppressors, the oppressed complained about God and charged that there was no functioning moral law. From the verse in Job, the word *merov* indicates the oppressed who were suffering, and the word *rabim*, the oppressors, who were creating the suffering. The main point to note, however, is that both the former and the latter were terminated as a result of their wickedness. The literalness of the verse comes from the Book of Job, for in Job the character Elihu, who quotes the verse, completely disagrees with Job's theological point of view, as well as with those of his friends, on the meaning of Divine Providence. Elihu asserts that God does not concern Himself with the behavior of the good people, nor with the behavior of the bad people. The Midrash uses this verse, but reinterprets it to show that the oppressed were to blame as well. (Mirkin)

ה. 'קֵץ כָּל בָּשָׂר בָּא לְפָנַי', הִגִּיעַ זְמַנָּם לְהִקָּצֵץ, הִגִּיעַ זְמַנָּן לַעֲשׂוֹת בֹּתָה, הִגִּיעַ קַטֵיגוֹרִים שֶׁלָּהֶן לְפָנַי, כָּל כָּךְ לָמָה 'כִּי מָלְאָה הָאָרֶץ חָמָס מִפְּנֵיהֶם'

5. THE END (KEZ) OF ALL FLESH (BASAR) IS COME BEFORE ME: THE
TIME HAS COME FOR THEM TO BE CUT DOWN (HIKKAZEZ); THE TIME
HAS COME FOR THEM TO BE TREATED AS UNRIPE GRAPES (BOSER); THE
TERM OF THEIR INDICTMENTS HAS COME. WHY ALL THIS? BECAUSE THE
EARTH IS FILLED WITH VIOLENCE (HAMAS) THROUGH THEM.

The *Midrash* notices that the term for ending life on earth is the
word קֵץ – *ketz*, rather than the usual word, סוֹף – *sof*, which is the word
normally used for "the end." It interprets *ketz* as related to the word
קוֹצִים – *kotzim*, which stands for a vegetative debris, such as thorns. This
desolation contributed to the *hamas*, to the wickedness that had perme-
ated every living beingof that generation.

אֵיזֶהוּ חָמָס, וְאֵיזֶה הִיא גָזֵל, אָמַר רַבִּי חֲנִינָא, חָמָס אֵינוֹ שָׁוֶה פְּרוּטָה. וְגָזֵל שֶׁשָּׁוֶה פְּרוּטָה. וְכָךְ הָיוּ אַנְשֵׁי הַמַּבּוּל עוֹשִׂים, הָיָה אֶחָד מֵהֶם, מוֹצִיא קֻפָּתוֹ מְלֵאָה תּוּרְמוֹסִים, וְהָיָה זֶה בָּא וְנוֹטֵל פָּחוֹת מִשָּׁוֶה פְּרוּטָה, וְזֶה בָּא וְנוֹטֵל פָּחוֹת מִשָּׁוֶה פְּרוּטָה, עַד מָקוֹם שֶׁאֵינוֹ יָכוֹל לְהוֹצִיאוֹ מִמֶּנּוּ בַּדִּין, אָמַר לָהֶם הַקָּדוֹשׁ בָּרוּךְ הוּא, אַתֶּם עֲשִׂיתֶם שֶׁלֹּא כַשּׁוּרָה, אַף אֲנִי אֶעֱשֶׂה עִמָּכֶם שֶׁלֹּא כַשּׁוּרָה

WHAT IS 'HAMAS' (VIOLENCE) AND WHAT IS 'GEZEL' (ROBBERY)? SAID R.
HANINA: 'HAMAS' (VIOLENCE) REFERS TO WHAT IS WORTH A PERUTAH;
'GEZEL' (ROBBERY), TO WHAT IS OF LESS VALUE THAN A PERUTAH. AND
THIS IS WHAT THE PEOPLE OF THE AGE OF THE FLOOD USED TO DO:
WHEN A MAN BROUGHT OUT A BASKET FULL OF LUPINES [FOR SALE],
ONE WOULD COME AND SEIZE LESS THAN A PERUTAH'S WORTH AND
THEN EVERYONE WOULD COME AND SEIZE LESS THAN A PERUTAH'S
WORTH, SO THAT HE HAD NO REDRESS AT LAW. WHEREUPON THE HOLY
ONE, BLESSED BE HE, SAID: 'YE HAVE ACTED IMPROPERLY, SO WILL I TOO
DEAL WITH YOU IMPROPERLY.'

The Hebrew text reads as follows: "Said R. Hanina, '*hamas* (violence)
refers to what is worth less than a coin (a *prutah*); *gezel* (robbery) refers

to what is worth at least a coin.'" Because of this definition, many of that
generation would use trickery to transcend the law. For example, a vendor would bring yellow beans, each packet of which is worth less than
a coin, for sale. By mutual agreement, one individual at a time would
remove such a bundle until such time that none were left. They would
thus procure for themselves an income and not be liable to prosecution
under the law. This was regarded as *hamas*, meaning maximum wickedness.

הֲדָא הוּא דִכְתִיב, (איוב ד, כא) 'הֲלֹא נִסַּע יִתְרָם בָּם, יָמוּתוּ וְלֹא בְחָכְמָה' בְּלֹא חָכְמַת הַתּוֹרָה,
(שם שם, כ) 'מִבֹּקֶר לָעֶרֶב יֻכַּתּוּ מִבְּלִי מֵשִׂים לָנֶצַח יֹאבֵדוּ', וְאֵין 'מֵשִׂים', אֶלָּא דַיָן, הֵיךְ מַה דְּאַתְּ
אָמַר, (שמות כא, א) 'וְאֵלֶּה הַמִּשְׁפָּטִים אֲשֶׁר תָּשִׂים לִפְנֵיהֶם'.

2 HENCE IT IS WRITTEN, IS NOT THEIR TENT-CORD PLUCKED UP WITHIN
THEM? THEY DIE, AND THAT WITHOUT WISDOM (JOB 4:21): I.E., WITH-
OUT THE WISDOM OF THE TORAH. BETWIXT MORNING AND EVENING
THEY ARE SHATTERED; THEY PERISH FOR EVER WITHOUT ANY REGARD-
ING (MESIM) IT (IBID., 20). NOW "MESIM' CAN ONLY REFER TO JUDG-
MENT, AS YOU READ, NOW THESE ARE THE ORDINANCES [JUDGMENTS]
WHICH THOU SHALT SET (TASIM) BEFORE THEM (EX. 21:1).

This last section is based on the view that for certain sinners, *Gehinnom* – the punishment in the World to Come – is not the end of it all,
but a form of atonement, after which they are entitled to an eternal life.
However, this would not apply to those who acted as those described
here, in the generation of the Flood. Their behavior would have eliminated *netzakh*, eternity, from their lives.

———

Seed Thoughts

The *Tiferet Tzion* makes the point that what happened in the generation
of the Flood should not be looked upon as punishment or revenge, but
rather as renewal. He bases this opinion on the interpretation of the
word *ketz*. Instead of the word *sof*, usually used to mean "the end of it all,"
he interprets the word *kez* as related to the word *kotzim*, which means a
debris of thorns. He uses an example of a vineyard that is desolate and
where most of the vines have been destroyed. In order for the vineyard
to have a future, all the dead vines have to be removed. Some vines can
be discovered that are still ripe and healthy and, no matter how few they
are, the vineyard can then be renewed. So it is with the world, and so it
was in the time of the generation of the Flood.

The people of the generation of the Flood were sinful, wicked and in some manner, had to be removed for the world to be rehabilitated. When they were removed via the Flood, it was possible to rebuild the world on the basis of the righteous who survived, and in this case, it was Noah and his family. In other words, the purpose of the story of the generation of the Flood was not the punishment of the wicked, but to portray that after their removal, the world was redeemed by those, such as Noah, who were capable of its rehabilitation.

Addtional Commentary

חמס – hamas *as meaning less than the value of a coin*

This is meant to demonstrate that all society in those days was guilty of *hamas*. Even the poor, the weak, were guilty of this kind of behavior. This is quite strange since in most societies, there is always to be found some to way to protect the poor. But in this particular society, using trickery of what is less than the value of a coin, they were able to steal and to rob with impunity. In the case of the lupines (*tarmusim*) sold for less than a coin, individuals could derive much more than they needed through this device without fear of legal action.

Even though the legal custom was that they were not liable for what was taken under the value of a coin, the fact of the matter is that by defining *gezel* as meaning שוה פרוטה – *shaveh prutah*, the value of a coin, it is as though the entire society was generous enough to allow those in need to avail themselves of what is less than a coin. However, by conspiring to exploit this generous custom, they emptied much of the availability of what was less than the value of a coin, so that other poor people could not take advantage of this system. There is no form of social abuse that is worse than this kind of behavior. (Mirkin)

The time has come for them to cut down

Usually, the word *ketz* is associated with a definite time, such as, "And it came to pass after two full years" (Genesis 41:1). The word "year" implies a definite time slot. Furthermore, "And in process of time, it came to pass" (Genesis 4:3) is a reference to days, also being a definite time. It appears, therefore, given the use of the word *ketz* in this verse, that the Almighty had a specific time in view. In those cases where time is not a factor, the word *sof* is usually used, such as, "The end of the matter"

(Ecclesiastes 12:13), meaning that at the end of the matter, everything will be understood. Many other examples like this can be found.

The writers of the *Midrash* had difficulty with the word *ketz* because in connection with the Divine decree, time is not a factor since it has to do with the behavior of man, who might repent, thereby changing the time slot. The use of the term *kol bassar*, "all flesh," is also questionable. Why should it not have been *kol chai*, all who had lived? Even the phrase *ba lefanai* – had come before Me – is questionable. Why could it have not said, "the end of all flesh comes"? Why do we need "before Me"? After all, who is that individual who will come before the King?

In this interpretation of the verse the word *ketz* is to indicate that the important lesson of the Flood was not (ח"ו) that God was involved with some kind of revenge for that generation, but rather, He was interested in תיקון – *tikun*, meaning the repair or renewal of the world. This can be compared to a vineyard that was overgrown with thorns. The owner would have to eliminate the thorns in order for the vineyard to succeed in producing grapes in the future. With the kind of behavior that was rampant during the generation of the Flood, the world would have gone from bad to worse had it continued. The wicked were removed from the world to save and protect the one ripe cluster of grapes that remained, namely, Noah, his family and the generations that were to come from them. (*Tiferet Tzion*)

ו. דָּבָר אַחֵר 'כִּי מָלְאָה הָאָרֶץ חָמָס', אָמַר רַבִּי לֵוִי, 'חָמָס' זֶה עֲבוֹדַת כּוֹכָבִים, 'חָמָס' זֶה גִּלּוּי
עֲרָיוֹת, 'חָמָס' זֶה שְׁפִיכוּת דָּמִים

6. ANOTHER INTERPRETATION: FOR THE EARTH IS FILLED WITH HAMAS
(VIOLENCE), ETC. R. LEVI SAID: 'HAMAS' CONNOTES IDOLATRY, INCEST,
AND MURDER.

R. Levi reiterates a concept that we discussed in the *midrashim* immediately preceding this one. *Hamas*, wickedness, as used in these texts,
is a general concept that includes much more than stealing and robbery.
As interpreted by R. Levi, the sins cover four categories: idolatry, sexual
immorality, murder and an extreme form of robbery.

'חָמָס' זֶה עֲבוֹדַת כּוֹכָבִים, שֶׁנֶּאֱמַר 'כִּי מָלְאָה הָאָרֶץ חָמָס', 'חָמָס', זֶה גִּלּוּי עֲרָיוֹת, שֶׁנֶּאֱמַר
(ירמיה נא, לה) 'חֲמָסִי וּשְׁאֵרִי עַל בָּבֶל', 'חָמָס' זֶה שְׁפִיכוּת דָּמִים, שֶׁנֶּאֱמַר (יואל ד, יט) 'מֵחֲמַס בְּנֵי
יְהוּדָה אֲשֶׁר שָׁפְכוּ דָם נָקִי', 'חָמָס' כְּמַשְׁמָעוֹ.

IDOLATRY, AS IT IS WRITTEN, FOR THE EARTH IS FILLED WITH HAMAS.
INCEST: THE VIOLENCE DONE TO ME (HAMASI FR. HAMAS) AND TO MY
FLESH (SHE'ERI) BE UPON BABYLON (JER. 51:35). MURDER: FOR THE
HAMAS [E.V. 'VIOLENCE'] AGAINST THE CHILDREN OF JUDAH BECAUSE
THEY HAVE SHED INNOCENT BLOOD (JOEL 55:19). IN ADDITION, HAMAS
(VIOLENCE) BEARS ITS LITERAL MEANING ALSO.

The proof texts for R. Levi's claims are not as clear and concise as
one would have hoped. The fundamental point is that *hamas* represents
all four of the fundamental areas of sinfulness that can be found in human life and is interpreted by the Jewish legal tradition. What is the
proof text for idolatry? The fact that the verse says, "The whole earth
was filled with *hamas*." Since God's presence fills the entire earth, that
is the connection. Whoever accepts another God is as though he rebels
against the One God, Whose authority fills the entire world. The proof
text that *hamas* also includes sexual immorality is found in the verse
from Jeremiah 51:35: "The violence done to me (*hamasi*) and to my flesh

(*she'eri*) be upon Babylon." *Hamas* is also applied to blood and murder from the verse from Joel 55:19, "For the violence (*hamas*) against the children of Judah because they have shed innocent blood."

—

Seed Thoughts

The *Midrash* has now concluded a cycle of interpretations having to do with the statement that, "The end of all flesh has come before Me." One might say that this cycle is a crescendo of accusationsagainst the generation of the Flood. They were guilty of idolatry, sexual immorality and murder. Although the first two of these sins had already been alluded to in earlier *midrashim*, their presentation as three together makes a staggering impact.

These three sins are described throughout the Talmud as being the cardinal sins – the Talmud presents these prohibitions as יהרג ועל יעבור – *yehareg ve'al ya'avor*, better allow yourself to be killed rather than transgress these. Did R. Levi and his colleagues believe that all the people of that generation were guilty of these prohibitions? We do not know, but probably not. However, many of the leaders probably were guilty of this kind of behavior and the general population has been sufficiently described in their spiritual weakness for us to know that they, too, shared in the overall guilt.

In a way, this final presentation more or less answers the concern of the sages of the *Midrash*. They were bothered by a concern that God's Justice and Mercy may have been compromised in the destruction of the Flood, for, how could an entire generation be so guilty as to merit this?! When these terrible forms of behavior are added to what has been described previously, the sages must have been satisfied – if not entirely, then at least enough for them to conclude their intensive questioning.

—

Additional Commentary

Why four categories of sin?

R. Levi, to answer the above question, begins by acknowledging that in a previous *midrash*, *gezel*, stealth, is interpreted as a major form of sin. Before that, however, an even earlier *Midrash* asserted that *znut*, sexual immorality, is the sin that sealed the fate of that generation. The verses also said that all flesh was destroyed using the phrase, השחית כל

בשר – *hishchit kol bassar*, implying murder, and this is interpreted to also encompass idolatry and sexual immorality. It is because of this background that R. Levi was able to interpret that *hamas* also refers to these three major categories: idolatry, sexual immorality and murder – all of these are included within the term. (*Tiferet Tzion*)

ז. 'הִנְנִי מַשְׁחִיתָם אֶת הָאָרֶץ' רַבִּי הוּנָא וְרַבִּי יִרְמְיָה בְּשֵׁם רַב כָּהֲנָא בַּר מַלְכִּיָה, אֲפִלּוּ שְׁלֹשָׁה
טְפָחִים, שֶׁהַמַּחֲרֵשָׁה שׁוֹלֶטֶת בָּאָרֶץ נִמּוֹחוּ

7. BEHOLD, I WILL DESTROY THEM WITH THE EARTH – R. HUNA AND
R. JEREMIAH IN R. KAHANA'S NAME SAID: EVEN THE THREE HAND-
BREADTHS OF THE EARTH'S SURFACE WHICH THE PLOUGH TURNS WAS
WASHED AWAY.

Ordinarily, the text should have said מן הארץ – *min ha'aretz, meaning*
"*from* the land," and not את הארץ – *et ha'aretz,* meaning "with" the land.
The way the present text is written can only mean that the people were
destroyed together *with* the land. The term *aretz* in this context refers to
the top three handbreadths of the earth, which is the normal depth of a
plough when it works the fields. In other words, the earth, too, suffers
the results of the sins of mankind. When man sins and is punished, all
living things, whatever grows, and even the inanimate aspects of earth,
all suffer along with mankind.

מָשָׁל, לְבֶן מְלָכִים שֶׁהָיָה לוֹ פֵּידָגוֹג, כָּל זְמַן שֶׁהוּא סוֹרֵחַ הָיָה פֵּידָגוֹג שֶׁלּוֹ נִרְדֶּה, וּלְבֶן מְלָכִים
שֶׁהָיָה לוֹ מֵינִיקָה כָּל זְמַן שֶׁהָיָה סוֹרֵחַ הָיְתָה מֵינִקְתּוֹ נִרְדֵּית, כָּךְ, אָמַר הַקָּדוֹשׁ בָּרוּךְ הוּא, 'הִנְנִי
מַשְׁחִיתָם אֶת הָאָרֶץ', הָא אֲנָא מְחַבֵּל לְהוֹן, וּמְחַבֵּל לְאַרְעָא עִמְּהוֹן.

IT IS AS IF A ROYAL PRINCE HAD A TUTOR, AND WHENEVER HE DID
WRONG, HIS TUTOR WAS PUNISHED; OR AS IF A ROYAL PRINCE HAD A
NURSE, AND WHENEVER HE DID WRONG, HIS NURSE WAS PUNISHED.
SIMILARLY, THE HOLY ONE, BLESSED BE HE, SAID, 'BEHOLD, I WILL DE-
STROY THEM WITH THE EARTH: BEHOLD, I WILL DESTROY THEM AND
THE EARTH WITH THEM.'

The two parables are meant to explain the relationship of earth to
mankind. The first parable has to do with a prince, under supervision
of a pedagogue who was responsible for teaching him the values of life.
When the prince became delinquent, it was the most natural thing that

the pedagogue should be punished, since he was responsible for the prince's moral education.

In the other case, the prince had a nurse or governess who gave way to every one of his wishes and desires, which made him selfish and rebellious and delinquent; therefore, the nurse merited punishment. In a similar fashion, God created the earth as the servant of man. Sometimes it produces beneficial things and sometimes it produces harmful things. It therefore merits punishment when man does.

—

Seed Thoughts

The *Midrash* notices immediately a strange style in the text. One would have thought the text would have read that God would erase man *from* the earth. However, it says that He will destroy him "with" the earth, implying that God destroyed the earth along with man. The question is, why did He do this? The *Midrash* does not use the question "why" in this manner; it never does. Instead, it asks, "Why does the text seem to be different than we would expect, and what does this teach us?"

The answer seems to be that earth is personified to show, on the one hand, how dependent man is upon it, and on the other hand, the responsibility of the earth in providing what mankind needs to sustain himself in this world. Earth is personified in order to make the point that it *wants* to do what it is supposed to do. It wants to produce fruit, vegetables, grains, etc. That is why it is called *aretz*, meaning one who fulfills the wants – *ratzon* – of man.

The *Midrash* becomes very specific in affirming its definition of the word *aretz*. It means a depth of three handbreadths of soil, which represents the depth that a plow reaches in working the fields. The plow, however, is a human invention. Human beings have to work the plow in order to help the earth fulfill its potential. Thus, there is a partnership between human beings and *aretz*, as it is here defined. This partnership evokes a feeling of mutual dependence, but it also implies a mutual responsibility. Therefore, if mankind was to be destroyed in the Flood, the earth (*aretz*, the three handbreadths) also had to be destroyed in order to share the responsibility with man.

—

Additional Commentary

Even as far as three handbreadths

Since the text says *et ha'aretz*, meaning "the earth," and not *min ha'aretz*, meaning "*from* the earth," the implication is that the human beings were destroyed together with the land. It is interesting to note that three handbreadths is a known Talmudic measure and it is those three handbreadths that are defined as *eretz*. The word *eretz*, comes from the word *rotzeh*, meaning "want." It contains what man wants and satisfies these wants through its produce, whether fruit or grain. All the matter beyond three handbreadths is referred to as *adamah*. That is why it says that the earth was destroyed with mankind, even as deep as three hand-breadths. Thought it is called *aretz*, since it satisfies the *ratzon* (wants) of man with its produce, this is also why it was destroyed, because of its relationship to mankind. (*Tiferet Tzion*)

The two parables of this midrash

The pedagogue, or the educator, is responsible for educating the pupil about all the material things in life and their usage, all of which come from the earth. An allusion to this is written in *Tractate Brakhot*, "A child will never know to call his parents *Aba* and *Ima*, until he tastes grain [bread]." In so far as the governess (the nurse) is concerned, it should be noted that the land (*aretz*) gave man the opportunity to taste abundantly in terms of fruit, vegetables, grain, etc., but the governess should have limited the prince's consumption. When, therefore, man sinned, it seemed logical to punish the earth, which bore a share of the responsibility, either in the manner of the pedagogue who allowed him to move to a life of delinquency, or because of an abundance of good things that the nurse or governess allowed him to have without check or limit, as it is written, "When Israel became fat and rebelled . . ." (Deut. 32:15). That is why two parables were needed. The earth can be proven guilty in either (or perhaps both) of two directions: too much bad or too much good. (*Tiferet Tzion*)

ח. (יד) 'עֲשֵׂה לְךָ תֵּבַת עֲצֵי גֹפֶר' אָמַר רַבִּי אִיסִי, בְּאַרְבָּעָה מְקוֹמוֹת נֶאֱמַר בַּלָּשׁוֹן הַזֶּה, 'עֲשֵׂה',
בִּשְׁלֹשָׁה נִתְפָּרֵשׁ וּבְאֶחָד לֹא נִתְפָּרֵשׁ, 'עֲשֵׂה לְךָ תֵּבַת, וְגוֹ'', אָמַר רַבִּי נָתָן, תְּבוֹתָא דְאָעִין
דְּקֶרֶדִינוֹן. (יהושע ה, ב) 'עֲשֵׂה לְךָ חַרְבוֹת צֻרִים', נִתְפָּרֵשׁ, גֻּלְבִּין דְּטִנָּרֵי. (במדבר י, ב) 'עֲשֵׂה לְךָ
שְׁתֵּי חֲצוֹצְרֹת כֶּסֶף', נִתְפָּרֵשׁ. (שם כא, ח) 'עֲשֵׂה לְךָ שָׂרָף', לֹא נִתְפָּרֵשׁ

8. MAKE THEE AN ARK, ETC. (6:14). R. ISSI SAID: IN FOUR PLACES THIS
PHRASE 'MAKE THEE' IS EMPLOYED; IN THREE PLACES IT IS EXPLAINED,
WHILE IN ONE IT IS NOT EXPLAINED. THUS: MAKE THEE AN ARK OF
GOPHER WOOD, ETC. R. NATHAN SAID: THAT MEANS WITH BEAMS OF
CEDAR. MAKE THEE KNIVES OF FLINT (JOSH. V5:2) MEANS FLINT KNIVES.
MAKE THEE TWO TRUMPETS OF SILVER (NUM. 10:2) IS LIKEWISE CLEAR
IN MEANING. BUT THE MEANING OF MAKE THEE A FIERY SERPENT (IBID.,
21:8) IS NOT CLEAR.

The *Midrash* mentions the three other places where the term "Make
thee," is used. What is to be made is usually spelled out in specific terms.
This is not so in one example in our present *midrash*, where we are not
sure of what the term שרף – *seraph* means. In our current text, the tree
that is to be used in the construction of the ark is mentioned by name
and is interpreted as a form of cedar. The tree itself comes from Kurdis-
tan, north of Babylon. In the case of the verse in Joshuah, the material to
be used for the circumcision of his generation was a type of sharp stone.
In Deuteronomy, the trumpets were made of silver, the construction
of which were, therefore, self-explanatory. Two questions now remain:
Why was the term *seraph* not explained, and what is its meaning?

רַבִּי יוּדָן בְּשֵׁם רַבִּי אַיְבּוּ אָמַר, (משלי א, ה) 'יִשְׁמַע חָכָם וְיוֹסִיף לֶקַח' זֶה מֹשֶׁה, שֶׁאָמַר הַקָּדוֹשׁ
בָּרוּךְ הוּא לוֹ לְמֹשֶׁה, 'עֲשֵׂה לְךָ שָׂרָף', וְלֹא פֵּרֵשׁ, אָמַר, אִם אֲנִי עוֹשֶׂה אוֹתוֹ שֶׁל זָהָב, אֵין הַלָּשׁוֹן
הַזֶּה נוֹפֵל עַל לָשׁוֹן זֶה, שֶׁל כֶּסֶף, אֵין הַלָּשׁוֹן הַזֶּה, נוֹפֵל עַל לָשׁוֹן זֶה, אֶלָּא, הֲרֵי אֲנִי עוֹשֶׂה אוֹתוֹ
שֶׁל נְחֹשֶׁת, לָשׁוֹן נוֹפֵל עַל הַלָּשׁוֹן, שֶׁנֶּאֱמַר (במדבר שם, ט) 'וַיַּעַשׂ מֹשֶׁה נְחַשׁ נְחֹשֶׁת'.

6 R. JUDAN SAID IN R. ASSI'S NAME: THE WISE MAN MAY HEAR, AND
INCREASE IN LEARNING (PROV. 1:6) APPLIES TO MOSES, WHO REASONED
THUS: IF I MAKE IT OF GOLD (ZAHAV) OR OF SILVER (KESEF) THESE

WORDS DO NOT CORRESPOND TO THE OTHER. HENCE I WILL MAKE IT OF
NEHOSHETH (BRASS), SINCE THIS WORD CORRESPONDS TO THE OTHER,
VIZ. NEHASH NEHOSHETH A SERPENT OF BRASS (IBID., 9):

The answer of the *Midrash* is that Moses, in his wisdom, figured out
what was intended in the commandment to make a *seraph*. Moses knew
that in the Hebrew language, the correspondence of words to each other
is given great importance. The word *seraph* means snake or serpent.
There would be no correspondence between that word and the words
kesef or *zahav* (silver or gold). However, there is another word that is actually the more common one used to refer to a serpent, *nachash*, which
is very similar to the word *nechoshet*, which means brass. Therefore,
Moses made it out of brass.

מִכָּאן, שֶׁנִּתְּנָה תּוֹרָה בִּלְשׁוֹן הַקֹּדֶשׁ, רַבִּי פִּינְחָס וְרַבִּי חִזְקִיָּה, בְּשֵׁם רַבִּי סִימוֹן, כְּשֵׁם שֶׁנִּתְּנָה
תּוֹרָה בִּלְשׁוֹן הַקֹּדֶשׁ, כָּךְ הָעוֹלָם נִבְרָא בִּלְשׁוֹן הַקֹּדֶשׁ, שָׁמַעְתָּ מִיָּמֶיךָ, אוֹמְרִים גִּינִי, גִּינְיָא,
אַנְתְּרוֹפֵּי, אַנְתְּרוֹפְיָא, גַּבְרָא, גַּבְרְתָא, אֶלָּא, אִישׁ וְאִשָּׁה, לָמָּה, שֶׁהַלָּשׁוֹן הַזֶּה נוֹפֵל עַל לָשׁוֹן
הַזֶּה.

THIS PROVES THAT THE TORAH WAS GIVEN IN HEBREW. R. PHINEHAS
AND R. HEZEKIAH IN R. SIMON'S NAME SAID: JUST AS THE TORAH WAS
GIVEN IN HEBREW, SO WAS THE WORLD CREATED WITH HEBREW: HAVE
YOU EVER HEARD ONE SAY, GINI, GINIA; ITHA, ITTHA; ANTROPI, ANTRO-
PIA; GABRA, GABRETHA? BUT [WE DO SAY] ISH AND ISHA: WHY? BECAUSE
ONE FORM CORRESPONDS TO THE OTHER.

From Moses' decision to create what is described in Hebrew as *nachash nechoshet*, the image of the serpent in brass, the sages concluded
that this is proof not only that the Torah was written in the Hebrew
language, but that God created the world using the Hebrew language as
the vehicle for His commandments to man.

—

Seed Thoughts

In discussing the merits of the Hebrew language, not only here, but also
in Genesis Rabbah parashah 18 Midrash 4, we discover a most unusual
term. In Hebrew it is called לָשׁוֹן נוֹפֵל עַל לָשׁוֹן – *lashon nofel al lashon*,
which means that the language of one word corresponds, with a small
alteration, to the language of another word. The examples brought in
this *Midrash* are words like *ish* and *ishah* (meaning "man" and "woman,"
respectively), which correspond linguistically with each other, as well as

nachash and *nechoshet*. This is of great interest in terms of Hebrew style.

However, the *Midrash* goes much further by making a claim that this proves that the Torah was written in Hebrew and that God created the world using the Hebrew language. Both of these doctrines had been believed by Jews since time immemorial. But they are beliefs, not facts that can be categorically proven logically or scientifically. It is one thing to marvel at the beauty and the resilience of the Hebrew language, but it is another thing to extrapolate beyond what we can comfortably understand.

The Rabbis brought evidence from Greek, where the correspondence of words within the language does not exist. But we are English speakers and we know that terms such as "man" and "woman" are important English words, and they certainly do correspond with each other as well. Can we not claim on the basis of these words that the English language possess the concept of *lashon nofel al lashon*? Whether is does or not, it is clear that the midrash sees 'ish' and 'isha' as a proof that the Torah was written in Hebrew. The Talmud even implies that the Torah was given in the modern Hebrew script referred to as Assyrian or Aramaic script (*Ktav Ashuri*).

—

Additional Commentary

In three places, "Make thee" is used

The *Midrash* quotes three sources where "*asseh lekha*" is used and in those sources, there is no question as to their interpretation; Scripture itself delivers the explanation. However, when it came to "*asseh lekha seraph*" – make for yourself an image of a *seraph* (serpent) – in which the details explaining how to do so are lacking, we would have thought that the details were transmitted orally to Moshe by God, Himself, as Scripture does not state it explicitly. However, precisely because in three other places, Scripture specifies in detail what is meant, we would have to maintain that in connection with *seraph*, Moses received the instruction from God in a general way and that Moses understood the details through inference. (*Yefei To'ar*)

ט. 'קִנִּים תַּעֲשֶׂה אֶת הַתֵּבָה', קֵילִין, וּמְדוֹרִין, אָמַר רַבִּי יִצְחָק, מַה הַקֵּן הַזֶּה, מְטַהֵר אֶת הַמְּצוֹרָע,
אַף תֵּבָתְךָ מְטַהַרְתֶּךָ.

WITH KINNIM [E.V. 'ROOMS'] SHALT THOU MAKE THE ARK: I.E., CELLS
AND CHAMBERS. R. ISAAC SAID: JUST AS A KEN (PAIR OF BIRDS) CLEANSES
A LEPER, SO SHALL THY ARK CLEANSE THEE.

The word *kininm* is interpreted to mean a small room. Such rooms are
usually big enough for eating and drinking, but not to be used as resi-
dence In this case, however, since the ark is definitely being made large
enough to accommodate not only human beings but also all other living
creatures, why was the term *kinnim* used? The reason is that it is meant
to evoke comparison with the of a leper, who would bring a nest ("*ken*,"
related to "*kinnim*") of birds as an offering to signify his purification.

'וְכָפַרְתָּ אֹתָהּ מִבַּיִת וּמִחוּץ בַּכֹּפֶר', הָכָא אַתְּ אָמַר, 'וְכָפַרְתָּ אֹתָהּ, וְגוֹ'', וּלְהָלָן אַתְּ אָמַר, (שמות
ב, ג) 'וַתַּחְמְרָה בַחֵמָר וּבַזָּפֶת', אֶלָּא, לְהָלָן עַל יְדֵי שֶׁהָיוּ הַמַּיִם תַּשִּׁים, 'וַתַּחְמְרָה בַחֵמָר וּבַזָּפֶת'
'בַּחֵמָר' מִפְּנֵי הָרֵיחַ, 'וּבַזָּפֶת' מִפְּנֵי הַמַּיִם.

AND THOU SHALT PITCH IT WITHIN AND WITHOUT WITH PITCH. YET
ELSEWHERE IT SAYS, AND SHE DAUBED IT WITH SLIME AND WITH PITCH
(EX. 2:3)? THERE, SINCE THE WATER [OF THE NILE] WAS GENTLE,' SHE
DAUBED IT WITH SLIME 'ON ACCOUNT OF THE WATER,' AND WITH PITCH
'ON ACCOUNT OF THE ODOR.'

In this section, a comparison is being made between the ark of the generation of the Flood and the little ark used to save the baby Moses from
the cruelty of the Egyptians. Why were different materials used? They
were required for different purposes. In the case of the baby Moses, he
had to be protected on the inside of the ark from the bad smells that he
might breathe and on the outside of the ark from the waters, lest they
enter.

—

Seed Thoughts

One question that arises is, what is the relationship between the ark of Moses and the offering that the leper had to bring to end his purification? This comparison is based on the term *kinnim*, which comes from the singular, *ken*, referring to a bird's nest. We know that the ritual whereby a leper ended his days of purification involved the bringing of birds as a sacrifice. How do we interpret this comparison? Both here and in several other *midrashim*, the point is made that the inhabitants of the ark were not there for a free ride. They had been saved from the terrible catastrophe of the Flood. But their worthiness was not yet completely proven. In many respects, the ark was to be treated like a *Mishkan*, a tabernacle, and the human beings who were in it were to relate to each other with great respect and also to live on as high a level as possible, within the restriction of the ark itself. This applied to the personality of Noah, himself, who was described in many *midrashim* as not being completely righteous, but as a person who had to improve his own relationship with God and man.

—

Additional Commentary

The nest (kinnim) of Noah and the nest (ken) of the leper

The use of the term *kinnim* in the *Midrash* refers to small rooms that generally were used solely for eating and drinking. It was necessary, therefore, to explain that in the case of the ark, this term referred to a dwelling for both man and beast. Why, then, was it called *kinnim*, which implied something quite different?

The answer according to R. Yitzhak is that Noah was being taught that just as the nest (*ken*), i.e., the offering of two birds in the Temple, helped to purify the leper, so would the experience in the ark contribute to improve the behavior of Noah and the others in the ark. Noah did not find the commandment to build the ark difficult, since it was obvious to him that they would all be saved from the terrible Flood to come. More than that, however, was involved, since the experience *in* the ark would also contribute to his own personal rehabilitation. This would be similar to the leper, whose complete purification occurred when he brought the birds as an offering.

In the case of Noah, his rehabilitation began when he started building the ark and throughout this period, he was involved in fulfilling

God's command. He completed his rehabilitation only when he left the ark. It was at that moment, however, that he was attacked by a lion and became injured. This also contributed to his purification, because suffering is also a form of atonement. This also was a hint to Noah that the real conclusion of his rehabilitation would take place at the moment that he offers a sacrifice to God, as did the leper. (*Tiferet Tzion*)

י. (טו) 'וְזֶה אֲשֶׁר תַּעֲשֶׂה אֹתָהּ' אָמַר רַבִּי יוּדָן, זֶה, 'וְזֶה', עָתִיד אֶחָד לָמֹד בְּאַמָּתְךָ, הֲדָא הוּא דִּכְתִיב, (דה"ב ג, ג) 'אֹרֶךְ הָאַמּוֹת, בַּמִּדָּה הָרִאשׁוֹנָה, אַמּוֹת שִׁשִּׁים, וְרֹחַב אַמּוֹת עֶשְׂרִים', וְלָמָּה הוּא קוֹרֵא אוֹתָהּ אַמָּה תְּבִיקוֹן, רַבִּי הוּנָא אָמַר, שֶׁהָיוּ מַתְבִּיאוֹת בָּהּ, רַבָּנָן אָמְרִין, עַל שֵׁם תֵּבָתוֹ שֶׁל נֹחַ.

10. AND THIS IS HOW THOU SHALT MAKE IT (6:15). R. JUDAN SAID: AND THIS [IS WRITTEN WHERE], THIS [WOULD HAVE SUFFICED]: [GOD INTIMATED]: ANOTHER IS DESTINED TO MEASURE WITH THY CUBIT, AS IT IS WRITTEN, THE LENGTH OF THE BUILDING AFTER THE ANCIENT [LIT. 'FIRST'] MEASURE WAS TWENTY CUBITS, AND THE BREADTH TWENTY CUBITS (II CHRON. 3:3). AND WHY IS IT [THE CUBIT] CALLED TIBIKON? R. HUNA SAID: BECAUSE IT COMES FROM THEBES. THE RABBIS SAID: ON ACCOUNT OF NOAH'S TEBAH (ARK).

T he *midrashic* sages noted the additional ו – *vav*, in the scriptural verse describing the ark. Usually, the conjunction *vav* describes something which is stated previously. This is not so in our text and it is interpreted as referring to the fact that in the future a sacred institution will be created, namely, the Temple in Jerusalem, using similar terminology of cubits (*amot*) in the establishment of measures. References made in the details about the building of the Temple, that the measurements were to be made, במדה הראשונה – *bamidah harishonah*, with the "first measurement," which refers to the measurements of Noah's ark.

'שְׁלֹשׁ מֵאוֹת אַמָּה אֹרֶךְ הַתֵּבָה, חֲמִשִּׁים אַמָּה רָחְבָּהּ, וּשְׁלֹשִׁים אַמָּה קוֹמָתָהּ' בַּר חַטְיָא אָמַר, (תהלים קיט, טו) 'בְּפִקּוּדֶיךָ אָשִׂיחָה', (שם שם, טז) 'בְּחֻקֹּתֶיךָ אֶשְׁתַּעֲשָׁע', לְמֶדְתָךְ תּוֹרָה דֶּרֶךְ אֶרֶץ, שֶׁאִם יַעֲשֶׂה אָדָם סְפִינָה שֶׁתְּהֵא עוֹמֶדֶת בַּלָּמִין, יַעֲשֶׂה רָחְבָּהּ אֶחָד מִשִּׁשָּׁה בְּאָרְכָּהּ, וְגָבְהָהּ אֶחָד מֵעֲשָׂרָה בְּאָרְכָּהּ.

THE LENGTH OF THE ARK THREE HUNDRED CUBITS, ETC. BAR HUTA QUOTED: I WILL MEDITATE ON THY PRECEPTS . . . I WILL DELIGHT MYSELF IN THY STATUTES (PS. 119:15): THE TORAH TEACHES YOU PRACTICAL KNOWLEDGE, THAT IF A MAN BUILDS A SHIP WHICH IS TO STAND

UPRIGHT IN HARBOR, HE MUST MAKE ITS BREADTH A SIXTH [OF ITS
LENGTH] AND ITS HEIGHT A TENTH.

The second half of this *midrash* deals with the measurements in a
lighter fashion. Quoting the verse in Psalm 119, about how king David
loved the laws of God, he makes the point that very often, verses in the
Torah, including these very special measurements, can convey practical
information to the reader. Thus, if one follows the proportions of the
measurements of the ark, it will help anyone to build a boat that can be
operated safely in both shallow and deep waters. This is referred to as
derech eretz, meaning practical advise for ordinary living.

Seed Thoughts

The *Midrash* ends by quoting a verse from Psalms, which it uses in order
to show that the Torah teaches practical wisdom. Thus from the dimensions of the ark, one could learn how to build a boat and operate it in
safety.

So far, so good. But the verse that is quoted ranges way beyond the
level of practical wisdom. It speaks of *chukim*, the statutes, for which the
Torah gives no reason. But it does tell us that king David delighted in
them. When it is stated that the statutes are not given a reason, it does
not mean that they are illogical or irrational. It simply means that the
Torah did not give the real reason for it. God knows the reason. It is
simply not shared with us.

The lack of a revealed reason has continued to irk certain people, and
thinkers of every generation try to figure out some of these reasons.
Searching for טעמי המצוות – *ta'amei hamitzvot*, meaning reasons for the
commandments, including those of the *chukim*, has been a popular
pastime throughout the generations. Over the years, many seekers have
found all kinds of reason for the statutes, and even though one cannot
prove their authenticity, they can be a source of great inspiration.

Kashrut, for example, is a *chok*, a statute, without a given reason.
The Torah does say that it is meant to add to the holiness of the Jewish
people, but that can apply to just about every commandment of the Torah. All kinds of reasons have been offered for *kashrut* and many of them
seem to be valid. For example, the dietary laws have been interpreted
as helping us experience God in the very act of eating or as a way of
respecting the animal world, since only a limited number of animals are

permitted by dietary laws. Since eating is so central to our lives kashrut helps strengthen the bonds of the Jewish people through a similar life-style. Some are able to see in the dietary laws health regulations and various other forms of lessons on life. We do not know which of these interpretations were intended by the Divine, but if it helps strengthen the spirituality of Judaism, then they are of tremendous importance.

David, the psalmist, understood this phenomenon and therefore he delighted in the *chukim,* the statutes without a revealed reason, even more than many a commandment for which reasons were given. It is as though God is expressing His faith in us by saying, "Please do this for Me, even if you do not understand it." By the same token, we are ex-pressing our love for God, "We gladly fulfill Your request, even though we do not completely understand it." The *chukim* are the love songs of the Jewish people to God.

Additional Commentary

The additional vav

It would have been enough for the verse to have said *zeh,* meaning "this" is the manner in which the ark should be built. But the text says *vezeh,* "*and* this . . ." The inclusion of this "and" is interpreted to mean that some time in the future, an edifice would be built by the same cubit measure-ments as the ark, and the reference is to the Temple of Solomon. That text uses the expression "במדה הראשונה" – *bemidah harishonah,* meaning that the "first scheme of measurement" should be used. The ark of Noah was, of course, the first such measurement in Scripture. This fortifies a teaching in the previous *midrash,* that the ark of Noah was like its own sanctuary, as it is written, "Planted in the house of the Lord," which refers to the spirit that God planted in Noah's ark. (Aryeh Mirkin)

Why is it called tibikin?

R. Huna said that this is because it comes from the city Thebes in Egypt. The Greek word *tibikin* means "from the city of Thebes." (Aryeh Mirkin)

A mystical interpretation of the ark

Tikunei Zohar, a Tractate of Jewish mysticism in the Zoharic writings, states that the dimensions of the ark are intended to convey the thought that God wanted to spread over the entire new universe His *sukat shalom*, His tabernacle of peace. The concept of God is expressed in Hebrew by many terms, two of which are הו-י-ה, the Tetragramaton, and the term אדני – *Adona-i*. The first term is meant to imply that God is ever-present and ever-renewing of the world. The second term teaches that God's Providence guards and conducts the world. The numerical value of these terms is equal to that of *sukah*, meaning tabernacle. But from the same terms, we can also derive the concept of "Shalom," following these directions: If you multiply the ו – *vav* of *Havay-ah* with the נ – *nun* of *Adonai*, the result is 300, which is the length of the ark. Multiply the last letter of *Havay-ah* (ה – *heh*) with the last letter of *Adonai* (י – *yud*), and the result is fifty, which is the width of the ark. Then, with the remaining letters, if you multiply the י – *yud* of *havay-ah* with the א – *aleph* of *Adonai*, the result of which is ten, then add that to the product of the ה – *heh* of *Havay-ah* (5) times the ד – *daled* of *Adonai* (4), which is twenty, the sum of these two is thirty, referring to the ark's height of thirty cubits. The total sum of these calculations is 380, which is equivalent to the numerical value of שלום – *shalom* when four (the number of letters in *Havay-ah*, *also called the "four-letter name of God"*) is added to it.

Inasmuch as the calculation of the measurements reflect *sukat shalom*, the function of the ו – *vav* of *vezeh* as an 'addition' is to indicate or hint at the idea that not only the ark, but also the Temple of Solomon should be built in such a way that it, too, would spread over us the tabernacle of God's peace. (*Tiferet Tzion*)

"I will meditate on Thy precepts (*pikudim*) ... I will delight myself in Thy statutes (*chukim*)" (Psalms 119:15) There is a difference between the term *pikudim* and the term *chukim*. *Pikudim*, precepts, refers to those commandments that help us remember particular incidences or experiences. The term *chukim*, statutes, on the other hand, refers to those commandments for which the Torah does not give a reason. In the verse quoted, it mentions that his (David's) reflections about the *pikudim* remind him of the many things that should be a part of his awareness. But then he adds, in connection with the statutes, that even though they are commandments without a given reason, he delights in them. He discovers all the kinds of nuances in the statutes and they help him remember God's commandments. It is hard for an ordinary person to remember the various statutes because they do not have a given reason. However, David was able to find many reasons that delighted him because he had the ability to think creatively about religious things. (*Tiferet Tzion*)

יא. (טז) 'צֹהַר תַּעֲשֶׂה לַתֵּבָה' רַבִּי חוּנְיָא וְרַבִּי פִּינְחָס, רַבִּי חָנִין וְרַבִּי הוֹשַׁעְיָא לָא מְפָרְשִׁין, רַבִּי אַבָּא בַּר כַּהֲנָא וְרַבִּי לֵוִי מְפָרְשִׁין, רַבִּי אַבָּא בַּר כַּהֲנָא אָמַר חַלּוֹן, רַבִּי לֵוִי אָמַר מַרְגָּלִיּוֹת, רַבִּי פִּינְחָס מָשׁוּם רַבִּי לֵוִי אָמַר, כָּל שְׁנֵים עָשָׂר חֹדֶשׁ שֶׁהָיָה נֹחַ בַּתֵּבָה לֹא צָרִיךְ לֹא לְאוֹר הַחַמָּה בַּיּוֹם, וְלֹא לְאוֹר הַלְּבָנָה בַּלַּיְלָה, אֶלָּא מַרְגָּלִית הָיְתָה לוֹ, וְהָיָה תוֹלֶה אוֹתָהּ, וּבְשָׁעָה שֶׁהִיא כֵהָה הָיָה יוֹדֵעַ שֶׁהוּא יוֹם וּבְשָׁעָה שֶׁהָיְתָה מַבְהֶקֶת הָיָה יוֹדֵעַ שֶׁהוּא לַיְלָה, אָמַר רַבִּי הוּנָא, עֲרִיקִין הֲוֵינַן מִן קוּמֵי גֻנְדָּא בְּהָדָא בּוֹטִיטָה דִטְבֶרְיָה, וְהָיָה בְיָדֵינוּ נֵרוֹת, בְּשָׁעָה שֶׁהָיוּ כֵהִים, הָיִינוּ יוֹדְעִים שֶׁהוּא יוֹם, וּבְשָׁעָה שֶׁהָיוּ מַבְהִיקִים, הָיִינוּ יוֹדְעִים שֶׁהוּא לַיְלָה.

11. A LIGHT (ZOHAR) SHALT THOU MAKE TO THE ARK (6:16). R. HUNIA AND R. PHINEHAS, R. HANAN AND R. HOSHAYA COULD NOT EXPLAIN [THE MEANING OF ZOHAR]; R. ABBA B. KAHANA AND R. LEVI DID EXPLAIN IT. R. ABBA B. KAHANA SAID: IT MEANS A SKYLIGHT; R. LEVI SAID: A PRECIOUS STONE. R. PHINEHAS SAID IN R. LEVI'S NAME: DURING THE WHOLE TWELVE MONTHS THAT NOAH WAS IN THE ARK HE DID NOT REQUIRE THE LIGHT OF THE SUN BY DAY OR THE LIGHT OF THE MOON BY NIGHT, BUT HE HAD A POLISHED GEM WHICH HE HUNG UP: WHEN IT WAS DIM HE KNEW THAT IT WAS DAY, AND WHEN IT SHONE HE KNEW THAT IT WAS NIGHT. R. HUNA SAID: ONCE WE WERE TAKING REFUGE FROM [ROMAN] TROOPS IN THE CAVES OF TIBERIAS. WE HAD LAMPS WITH US: WHEN THEY WERE DIM WE KNEW THAT IT WAS DAY, AND WHEN THEY SHONE BRIGHTLY WE KNEW THAT IT WAS NIGHT.

Some of the commentators wonder why some of the names of the sages listed could not interpret the meaning of *tzohar*. Possibly, it might mean that they went along with whatever was the popular interpretation and had nothing to add that was original. Or, their names were included since they took part in the general discussion of these verses in the academy. We still do not know from these interpretations which of the translations of *tzohar* is correct. However, in a later verse, the word "window" is actually used (Genesis 8:6).

'וְאֶל אַמָּה תְּכַלֶּנָּה מִלְמַעְלָה', רַבִּי יְהוּדָה וְרַבִּי נְחֶמְיָה, רַבִּי יְהוּדָה אוֹמֵר, שְׁלשׁ מֵאוֹת וְשִׁשִּׁים קִילִין הָיוּ בָהּ, עֶשֶׂר אַמּוֹת עַל עֶשֶׂר אַמּוֹת, וּשְׁתֵּי פְלָטִיּוֹת, שֶׁל אַרְבַּע אַמּוֹת, קִילִין מִכָּאן וְקִילִין

מִכָּן, וְקֵילִין מִכָּן וְקֵילִין מִכָּן, וּשְׁתֵּי אַמּוֹת לַצְּדָדִים. רַבִּי נְחֶמְיָה אָמַר, תֵּשַׁע מֵאוֹת קֵילִין הָיוּ
בָּהּ, וְקֵיל, שֵׁשׁ אַמּוֹת עַל שֵׁשׁ אַמּוֹת, וְשָׁלֹשׁ פְּלַטְיוֹת, שֶׁל אַרְבַּע אַרְבַּע, וְקֵיל מִכָּן וְקֵיל מִכָּן,
וּשְׁתֵּי אַמּוֹת לַצְּדָדִים. עַל דַּעְתֵּהּ דְּרַבִּי יְהוּדָה לָא נִיחָא, וְעַל דַּעְתֵּהּ דְּרַבִּי נְחֶמְיָה לָא נִיחָא,
רַבִּי יְהוּדָה וְרַבִּי נְחֶמְיָה, רַבִּי יְהוּדָה אוֹמֵר, כְּאַמָּתָהּ מִלְּמַטָּה כָּךְ אַמָּתָהּ מִלְמַעְלָה, 'וְאֶל אַמָּה
תְּכַלֶּנָּה מִלְמַעְלָה', רַבִּי נְחֶמְיָה אָמַר, כְּמִין קוֹמָרוֹטוֹן הָיְתָה, וְהָיָה מַשְׁקִיף בָּהּ, וְעוֹלֶה, וּמַשְׁקִיף
בָּהּ וְעוֹלֶה, עַד שֶׁהֶעֱמִידָהּ עַל אַמָּתָהּ, שֶׁנֶּאֱמַר 'וְאֶל אַמָּה. וְגו'''.

AND TO A CUBIT SHALT THOU FINISH IT UPWARD. R. JUDAH AND R.
NEHEMIAH DISAGREE. R. JUDAH SAID: IT CONTAINED THREE HUNDRED
AND THIRTY COMPARTMENTS, EACH COMPARTMENT BEING TEN CUBITS
SQUARE, AND TWO CORRIDORS EACH FOUR CUBITS WIDE; THE COM-
PARTMENTS RAN ALONG EACH SIDE [OF THE CORRIDOR], AND THERE
WERE TWO CUBITS AT THE [OUTER] SIDES [OF THE COMPARTMENTS]. R.
NEHEMIAH SAID: IT CONTAINED NINE HUNDRED COMPARTMENTS, EACH
BEING SIX CUBITS SQUARE, AND THREE CORRIDORS OF FOUR CUBITS
BREADTH, COMPARTMENTS RUNNING ALONG EACH SIDE AND LEAVING
TWO CUBITS AT THE [OUTER] SIDES. ON THE VIEW OF R. JUDAH THERE IS
NO DIFFICULTY; BUT ON R. NEHEMIAH'S VIEW, THERE IS A DIFFICULTY?[1]
AS WAS ITS CUBIT BELOW SO WAS ITS CUBIT ABOVE: AND TO A CUBIT
SHALT THOU FINISH IT UPWARD. R. NEHEMIAH SAID: IT WAS LIKE A
VAULTED CARRIAGE, AND HE BUILT IT SLOPING INWARDS SO THAT IT
TAPERED TO A CUBIT.

Apparently, the ark was built in such a way that the bottom floor was
very wide, but as the construction moved upward, everything narrowed
until at the very top, the width was only one cubit. R. Judah and R.
Nechemiah disagree about how these facts should be interpreted. R.
Judah felt that each floor was of similar size and that the upward movement did not become narrower and narrower. In R. Judah's view, there
were 360 rooms. In R. Nechemiah's view there were 900 rooms or compartments and they did gradually taper up to a narrow width at the top.

'וּפֶתַח הַתֵּבָה בְּצִדָּהּ תָּשִׂים' אָמַר רַבִּי יִצְחָק, לִמְּדָתְךָ תּוֹרָה דֶרֶךְ אֶרֶץ שֶׁאִם עוֹשֶׂה אָדָם עוֹשֶׂה טְרַקְלִין
עֶשֶׂר עַל עֶשֶׂר, יְהֵא עוֹשֶׂה פִּתְחוֹ מִן הַצַּד.

AND THE DOOR OF THE ARK SHALT THOU SET IN THE SIDE THEREOF. R.
ISAAC SAID: THE TORAH TEACHES YOU PRACTICAL KNOWLEDGE, THAT
WHEN YOU MAKE A CHAMBER TEN CUBITS SQUARE, YOU SHOULD SET ITS
DOOR AT THE SIDE.

---

1. Note from Rabbi Shuchat: The literal translation is, "In the view of R. Judah
there is no difficulty and in the view of R. Nechemiah there is also no difficulty."

There is another example here of the *Midrash* giving over practical advice. In building a structure with rooms, it is important not to allow the entrance to affect either the purpose of or the activities in any particular room. The way to ensure this is not to have an entrance in the middle of the room, but rather on the side.

'תַּחְתִּים שְׁנִים וּשְׁלֹשִׁים תַּעֲשֶׂהָ' תַּחְתִּיִּים לַזְּבָלִים, שְׁנִיִּים לוֹ וּלְבָנָיו וְלַטְּהוֹרִים, וְהָעֶלְיוֹנִים לַטְּמֵאִים. וְיֵשׁ מַחֲלִיפִין, תַּחְתִּיִּים לַטְּמֵאִים, שְׁנִיִּים לוֹ וּלְבָנָיו וְלַטְּהוֹרִים, וְהָעֶלְיוֹנִים לַזְּבָלִים, כֵּיצַד הָיָה עוֹשֶׂה, אֶלָּא, כְּמִין קָטָרַקְטִין, הָיָה לוֹ, פּוֹסְסָן מִן הַצַּד.

WITH LOWER, SECOND, AND THIRD STORIES SHALT THOU MAKE IT: THE BOTTOM STOREY FOR GARBAGE, THE SECOND FOR HIMSELF AND FAMILY AND THE CLEAN ANIMALS, AND THE THIRD FOR THE UNCLEAN [ONES]. OTHERS REVERSE IT: THE BOTTOM STOREY FOR THE UNCLEAN ANIMALS, THE SECOND FOR HIMSELF AND FAMILY AND THE CLEAN ANIMALS, AND THE TOP FOR THE GARBAGE. HOW THEN DID HE MANAGE? HE ARRANGED A KIND OF TRAPDOOR THROUGH WHICH HE SHOVELED IT SIDEWAYS.

All the commentators agree that the ark was divided in three floors and that Noah and his family, together with the clean animals, would always be on the middle floor. There is difference of opinion as to the other floors. Some say that the unclean animals should be on the first floor and garbage on the third. Others recommend the opposite and affirm that passage ways between the third and first floors were built so that Noah and his family would not be disturbed either by the traffic that traveled through them or by the stench that may have occurred.

'תַּעֲשֶׂהָ', אַף הִיא הָיְתָה מְסַיַּעַת, אֶת עַצְמָהּ.

SHALT THOU MAKE IT. IT HELPED [TO BUILD] ITSELF.

There is an interesting play on words here. Some say a *yud* is missing before the *heh*, rendering the meaning, "You shalt create it." Some say the vocalization should be read differently: instead of תעשה – *ta'aseha*, it should be תעשה – *tei'aseh, meaning, "it will be done."* In other words, one could imagine Noah complaining that the work was too great and the answer received was, "not to worry, you will be helped and things will happen by themselves."

Seed Thoughts

One can start out with a commentary on this *midrash* by asking whether anyone is really interested in the detailed description of Noah's ark. After all, God, Who created the entire world, can certainly arrange to create an ark. On the other hand, however, Scripture does tell us a few things about how the ark should be built. That seems to be indicative of the fact that God wanted man to build the ark, in particular, Noah.

The more one studies the details of the ark, the more one is impressed by its vastness. According to R. Nechemiah, the ark consisted of 900 rooms or compartments, not counting the various halls and passage ways. There is no modern comparison. One would have to think of large ships like the Queen Mary and the Queen Elizabeth of the Canard lines of the twentieth century. Even those beautiful ships were not of the same vastness. After all, the ark was to contain the entire world in miniature.

An additional question one can ask is, who would build the ark? Noah was only one person. Who were his staff? Did they consist of sinners who eventually would drown in the Flood, or were they part of his extended family who were destined to be saved? The *Midrash* has not yet discussed that, but it did hint that something was going on in connection with the construction of the ark. The play on the word *ta'aseha* as *tei'aseh* and the suggestion that much of the ark was built by itself, so to speak, gives us a hint as to the nature of *midrashic* teaching. The building of the ark was miraculous. Not all of it was miraculous, however. Much hard work and planning went into the effort. But when human wisdom fell short, God entered the picture and as the *Midrash* puts it, it was finished by itself.

—

Additional Commentary

On the word *tzohar*

Some say the word *tzohar* is related to the word *tzahorayim*, which refers to midday, or the mid-day meal, which is a symbol of brightness. Others say that the letter *tzaddik* and the letter *zayin* are interchangeable, and therefore, *tzohar* becomes *zohar*, meaning brightness. (Maharzu)

Four who could not explain (A)

These four sages did not offer an explanation for the word *tzohar,* either because they were not certain of the true meaning of the word, or because it had a popular interpretation with which they did not disagree. On the other hand, R. Abba and R. Levi did have their own interpretations. Both of them saw in the word *tzohar* the word *zohar* as having a connection with "light." But R. Abba felt that the light was through a window and R. Levi felt that the light was from a gem. (Aryeh Mirkin)

Four who could not explain(B)

What the lack of interpretation means is that from the point of view of their understanding, these four sages were willing to accept the translation of either a window or a gem. Nevertheless, they did not offer an interpretation because the meaning was not sufficiently clear to them, intellectually. In this respect, the *Midrash* has taught us a very important lesson, namely, not to express an opinion, especially on a text, unless it is absolutely clear to our intelligence, as clear as the mid-day sun or as clear as is our own sister, whom we know is forbidden to us. Without this clarity, an opinion should not be expressed. (*Tiferet Tzion*)

To a cubit shalt thou finish it upward

If this translation means that the ark came to a point at the top of one cubit squared, it was not acceptable to R. Judah nor was it acceptable to R. Nechemiah. If the ark were slanted, it would mean that the area of the first floor would differ from that of the second and third floors, and the total of the square areas would not be 360, as promulgated by R. Judah, nor would it be 900 rooms, as promulgated by R. Nechemiah. In the view of R. Nechemiah, the areas remain the same on all floors. In his view, the upper part of the ark was slightly adjusted, but in the end, there were the same 900 rooms. (*Tiferet Tzion*)

It helped (to build) itself

This is similar to what was said about the building of the *Mishkan* or the tabernacle. Noah's ark was looked upon as having the stamp of sanctity, just as did the *Mishkan,* according to the Zohar. This interpretation is based on the word *ta'aseha,* which is written without the *yud.* It is written with only three Hebrew letters – *taf, ayin* and *shin* – but is pronounced as though there were a *tzereh* under the *taf,* a *kamatz* under the *ayin* and a *segol* under the *shin.* Thus, it would be pronounced *tei'aseh,* meaning that it was completed by itself, just as was the Menorah, made for the Mishkan and the Holy Temple. (*Tiferet Tzion*)

יב. (יז) 'וַאֲנִי הִנְנִי', הִנְנִי מַסְכִּים לְדִבְרֵי מַלְאָכִים שֶׁהָיוּ אוֹמְרִין, (תהלים ח, ה) 'מָה אֱנוֹשׁ כִּי תִזְכְּרֶנּוּ'. 'אֶת הַמַּבּוּל מַיִם', מַיִם הָיוּ, וְכֵיוָן שֶׁהָיוּ יוֹרְדִין הָיוּ נַעֲשִׂים מַבּוּל. 'לְשַׁחֵת כָּל בָּשָׂר, כֹּל אֲשֶׁר בָּאָרֶץ יִגְוָע', יִצְמֹק.

12. AND I, BEHOLD (6:17): I AGREE WITH THE ANGELS WHO URGED,
WHAT IS MAN, THAT THOU ART MINDFUL OF HIM? (PS. 8:5). BEHOLD,
I DO BRING THE FLOOD OF WATERS. THEY WERE FIRST WATERS, AND
AS SOON AS THEY DESCENDED ON THE EARTH THEY BECAME A FLOOD.
[EVERYTHING THAT IS IN THE EARTH] YIGWA [E.V. 'SHALL PERISH']: I.E.,
SHALL SHRIVEL UP.

The *Midrash* notes that the verse quoted begins with a *vav*, called *vav hachibbur*, which indicates connection with another idea. It means here that the Holy One, Blessed be He, said, "I also agree with the angels who criticized the creation of man," as discussed in a previous *midrash* (8:6). The *Midrash* now justifies the order of the text, which says, *hamabul mayim*, meaning the water that became a Flood – and it does not say "the Flood of water" or "the waters of the Flood." It makes a very delicate point that had the Flood waters come first, in their torrential power, the ark would not have be able to survive it. What happened was that the rains came down in the usual manner, and ultimately, they rose to Flood the earth and the ark was able to float on the waters (*Tiferet Tzion*). The comment on the word *yigva*, "shall perish," is that it is usually used in connection with an entity that possesses life, whether human or animal. This does not, however, apply to vegetation, which is why they immediately interpreted it as *yitzmok*, "shall shrivel up." On the other hand, why was the term *yigva* used in the first place? Because even vegetation has an element of growth within it that is equivalent to life.

(יח) 'וַהֲקִמֹתִי אֶת בְּרִיתִי אִתָּךְ', בְּרִית אַתָּה צָרִיךְ, מִפְּנֵי הַפֵּרוֹת שֶׁאַתָּה כוֹנֵס, שֶׁלֹּא יִרְקְבוּ וְשֶׁלֹּא יִתְעַפְּשׁוּ וְשֶׁלֹּא יִשְׁתַּנּוּ, בְּרִית אַתָּה צָרִיךְ הַגְּבוֹרִים, הָיָה אֶחָד מֵהֶם נוֹתֵן רַגְלוֹ, עַל הַתְּהוֹם וְסוֹתְמוֹ, נוֹתֵן יָדוֹ עַל הַחַלּוֹן וְסוֹתְמָהּ, הָיָה בָא לִכָּנֵס לַתֵּבָה, הָיוּ רַגְלָיו מִתְעַרְכְּלוֹת, הֲדָא הוּא

דִּכְתִיב, (איוב כו, ה) 'הָרְפָאִים יְחוֹלָלוּ מִתַּחַת מַיִם וְשֹׁכְנֵיהֶם', אֲרֵי הֲוָה בָא לְכָנֵס לַתֵּבָה, וְהָיוּ שִׁנָּיו קֵהוֹת, הָדָא הוּא דִכְתִיב, (שם ד, י) 'שַׁאֲגַת אַרְיֵה, וְקוֹל שָׁחַל, וְשִׁנֵּי כְפִירִים נִתָּעוּ'.

BUT I WILL ESTABLISH MY COVENANT WITH THEE, ETC. (6:18). THOU NEEDEST A COVENANT FOR THE SAKE OF THE PRODUCE, THAT IT SHOULD NOT DECAY OR ROT. THOU NEEDEST A COVENANT: THE GIANTS SET THEIR FEET ON THE [OPENING OF THE] DEEP AND CLOSED IT UP, THEN EACH ATTEMPTED TO ENTER THE ARK, WHEREUPON HIS FEET BECAME ENTANGLED [IN THE WATER], AS IT IS WRITTEN, THE GIANTS [E.V. 'SHADES'] TREMBLE BENEATH THE WATERS AND THE INHABITANTS THEREOF – SHOKENEHEM (JOB 26:5). [READ] SHEKENEHEM (THEIR NEIGHBORS): A LION WOULD COME TO THE ARK AND HIS TEETH WOULD LOOSEN, AS IT IS WRITTEN, THE LION ROARETH, AND THE FIERCE LION HOWLETH AND THE TEETH OF THE YOUNG LIONS ARE BROKEN (IBID., 4:10).

The word *brit* as covenant is used in this context for those elements in life which cannot be sustained merely by natural means. Therefore, God promises to establish a covenant of protection so that not only Noah and his family, but all living beings and their supplies, should be protected. Many areas of this great operation had to be protected. First, the fruits so that they should not spoil; secondly, the ark-dwellers needed protection from intruders in that generation, such as those tribes known as giants. The *Midrash* even mentions certain individuals who tried to enter the ark, including wild animals. However, with the covenant established by God the ark was miraculously saved.

אָמַר רַבִּי חִיָּא בַּר אַבָּא, נַגָּר הָיִיתָ, וְאִלּוּלֵי בְרִיתִי שֶׁהָיְתָה אִתָּךְ לֹא הָיִיתָ יָכוֹל לִכָנֵס לַתֵּבָה, הָדָא הוּא דִכְתִיב, 'וַהֲקִמֹתִי בְּרִיתִי אִתָּךְ', אֵימָתַי לִכְשֶׁתִּכָּנֵס אֶל הַתֵּבָה.

R. HIYYA B. ABBA EXPLAINED: THOU WAST INDEED THE BUILDER, YET BUT FOR MY COVENANT WHICH STOOD THEE IN STEAD, COULDST THOU HAVE ENTERED THE ARK? THUS IT IS WRITTEN, BUT I WILL ESTABLISH MY COVENANT WITH THEE: WHEN [WILL THAT BE PROVED]? WHEN THOU ART BROUGHT INTO THE ARK.

The covenant also applied to Noah, himself. The fact that he built the ark did not guarantee his own entrance into it. That, too, was part of the special covenant that God rendered to him and his family.

'אַתָּה וּבָנֶיךָ', רַבִּי יְהוּדָה בַּר סִימוֹן, וְרַבִּי חָנִין בְּשֵׁם רַב שְׁמוּאֵל בַּר רַבִּי יִצְחָק אָמַר, נֹחַ, כְּשֶׁנִּכְנַס לַתֵּבָה נֶאֱסַר לוֹ פְּרִיָּה וּרְבִיָּה, הָדָא הוּא דִכְתִיב, 'וּבָאתָ אֶל הַתֵּבָה, אַתָּה וּבָנֶיךָ' לְעַצְמְךָ, 'וְאִשְׁתְּךָ וּנְשֵׁי בָנֶיךָ' לְעַצְמָן, כֵּיוָן שֶׁיָּצָא, הִתִּיר לוֹ, הָדָא הוּא דִכְתִיב, (בראשית ח, טז) 'צֵא מִן הַתֵּבָה, אַתָּה וְאִשְׁתְּךָ, וּבָנֶיךָ וּנְשֵׁי בָנֶיךָ'.

THOU, AND THY SONS, ETC. R. JUDAH B. R. SIMON AND R. HANAN IN THE
NAME OF R. SAMUEL B. R. ISAAC SAID: AS SOON AS NOAH ENTERED THE
ARK, COHABITATION WAS INTERDICTED TO HIM; HENCE IT IS WRITTEN,
AND THOU SHALT COME INTO THE ARK, THOU, AND THY SONS – APART;
AND THY WIFE, AND THY SONS' WIVES – APART. WHEN HE WENT OUT,
HE PERMITTED IT TO HIM, AS IT IS WRITTEN, GO FORTH FROM THE ARK,
THOU AND THY WIFE, ETC. (GEN. 8:16).

The *Midrash* notes that during the period of the ark, cohabitation was
forbidden and this can be discerned in the nature of the verse, which
separated the males from the females. Upon their leaving the ark, their
prohibition of cohabitation was removed and this, too, can be discerned
from the manner in which the verse was rendered, in which husband
and wife were mentioned together.

אָמַר רַבִּי אָבוּן, כְּתִיב (איוב ל, ג) 'בְּחֶסֶר וּבְכָפָן גַּלְמוּד', אִם רָאִיתָ חֶסָּרוֹן בָּא לָעוֹלָם, וְכָפָן בָּא
לָעוֹלָם, גַּלְמוּד, הֱוֵי רוֹאֶה אֶת אִשְׁתְּךָ כְּאִלוּ הִיא גַלְמוּדָה, שֶׁכֵּן בִּכְרַכֵּי הַיָּם קוֹרִין לַנִּדָּה גַלְמוּדָה,
אָמַר רַבִּי הוּנָא, כְּתִיב (בראשית מא, נ) 'וּלְיוֹסֵף יֻלַּד שְׁנֵי בָנִים, בְּטֶרֶם תָּבוֹא שְׁנַת הָרָעָב'.

R. ABIN QUOTED: THEY ARE LONELY IN WANT AND FAMINE (JOB 30:3):
WHEN WANT AND FAMINE VISIT THE WORLD, REGARD YOUR WIFE AS
THOUGH SHE WERE LONELY [I.E., MENSTRUOUS]. R. MUNA SAID: IT
IS WRITTEN, AND UNTO JOSEPH WERE BORN TWO SONS (GEN. 41:50):
WHEN? BEFORE THE YEAR OF FAMINE CAME (IBID.).

The lesson to be learned from the above is that cohabitation should
not be practiced during a time of famine or a crisis for humanity. The
word *galmud* is often used to mean *nidah*, which is the term applied to
a woman during her menstrual period, when cohabitation is forbidden.
It is in this respect that the translation of *galmud* is "lonely." The verse
quoted in connection with Joseph is the textual proof that he did not
cohabit during the years of famine.

—

Seed Thoughts

It is somewhat surprising to note that God agreed with the angels
who questioned the worthiness of man and the whole purpose of his
creation. We do not know and may not ever know why God created
the world and why He created man, but we do know that God created
man with the quality of freedom of choice. We will likely never know
why this is so, but the Zohar attempts to respond to this question by

saying that since it is in the nature of God always to want to do good; the most important human asset is the freedom to choose, with which man was created. It is as though God practices צמצום – *tzimtzum with regard to this realm*, meaning that He removes Himself from the area of freedom so that man may function in almost absolute terms. Whether this is good or not good for the world is not our business. The point is that this is how the earth was created and it is God's desire that His will, through the Torah, should be fulfilled voluntarily and in freedom. That is why the doers of evil have to be tolerated. The goal is, via education and understanding, to transform the evildoers into constructive members of society. Of course, God agreed with the angels in censoring the evildoers of society, but His goal for mankind was to produce *tzadikim*, righteous people, who would fulfill His purpose of creation.

—

Additional Commentary

Why does God agree with the angels?

In the text quoted, the word *hineni* is superfluous. Furthermore, *hineni* also implies that God was prepared, even at an earlier time, to agree with the angels. In the case of Abraham and Moses, the word *hineni* implied that they were prepared to do God's bidding immediately. The question of course is, why would God create the world, wanting it to be sustained and now be willing to destroy it? We now learn that even at the time of creation, God agreed with the criticism of the angels who said, "What is man that Thou regardest him?" However, this meant only the evildoers, for He would not have said such a thing about the righteous. Furthermore, we have to remember that the main ingredient in the creation of man was that he should have freedom of choice, for without that, his righteousness would not have much meaning. One, therefore, has to assume that part of the creation potential was that there would be evildoers in the world, who would voluntarily choose the way of death, which is how evil has been described. God did not want evildoers, even at the time of creation, and there has been no change in His will in terms of the destruction of evildoers, since that was His hope in the time of creation, as the world was created mainly for the sake of the righteous. (*Tiferet Tzion*)

You and your sons can enter the ark

The word *atah*, "you," appears to be superfluous. Why does He say "you" when it is obvious that He is speaking to Noah? It was enough to say, "Let your household enter." It is also interesting to note the change in style. In going to the ark, it says "You and your sons," and in leaving the ark, it says, "You and your wife . . ." This can be explained as follows: Noah, himself, had not completely fulfilled the commandment of being fruitful, since he did not have a daughter. Nor had his sons fulfilled this commandment, since they had no offspring. That, however, did not excuse them, and it was important to state that Noah and his sons, together with everyone else, were also prohibited from cohabitation during this period. This changed when they left the ark. Therefore, it is written that Noah was to leave with his wife, and his sons with their wives, respectively. (*Tiferet Tzion*)

יג. (יט) 'וּמִכָּל הַחַי מִכָּל בָּשָׂר, שְׁנַיִם, וְגוֹ'', אָמַר רַבִּי הוֹשַׁעְיָא, אֲפִלּוּ רוּחוֹת, נִכְנָסִים עִם נֹחַ אֶל
הַתֵּבָה, שֶׁנֶּאֱמַר 'מִכָּל הַחַי', מֵאוֹתָן שֶׁנִּבְרְאוּ לָהֶם נְפָשׁוֹת וְלֹא נִבְרָא לָהֶם גּוּפִין.

13. AND OF EVERY LIVING THING, OF ALL FLESH, ETC. (6:19). R. HOSHAYA
SAID: EVEN SPIRITS ENTERED THE ARK WITH NOAH; HENCE IT IS WRIT-
TEN, AND OF EVERY LIVING THING, OF ALL FLESH: I.E., OF THOSE FOR
WHOM SOULS [SPIRITS] WERE CREATED BUT NOT BODIES.

The *Midrash* is pointing out that one of the expressions seems superfluous. If *mikol hachai*, "from all the living creatures," is stated, then
why have *kol bassar*, "from all flesh," which could be included in the
first expression? The answer is that it was meant to include those spirits
whose bodies were not created, due to the interruption of the Sabbath.
(*Midrash Rabbah* 7:5)

רַבִּי יְהוּדָה וְרַבִּי נְחֶמְיָה רַבִּי יְהוּדָה אוֹמֵר, רְאֵם לֹא נִכְנַס עִמּוֹ, אֲבָל גּוּרָיו נִכְנְסוּ, רַבִּי נְחֶמְיָה
אָמַר, לֹא הוּא וְלֹא גּוּרָיו, אֶלָּא קְשָׁרוֹ נֹחַ בַּתֵּבָה, וְהָיָה מַתְלִים תְּלָמִיּוֹת, כְּמוֹ טְבֶרְיָא לְסוּסִתָא,
הֲדָא הוּא דִכְתִיב, (איוב לט, י) 'הֲתִקְשָׁר רְאֵם בְּתֶלֶם עֲבֹתוֹ, אִם יְשַׂדֵּד עֲמָקִים אַחֲרֶיךָ'.

R. JUDAH SAID: THE RE'EM (A WILD OX, A FABULOUS ANIMAL OF TRE-
MENDOUS HEIGHT) DID NOT ENTER THE ARK, BUT HIS WHELPS DID. R.
NEHEMIAH SAID: NEITHER HE NOR HIS WHELPS, BUT NOAH TIED HIM
TO THE ARK, AND HE PLOUGHED FURROWS [IN THE WATER] AS GREAT AS
FROM TIBERIAS TO SUSITHA, AS IT IS WRITTEN, CANST THOU BIND THE
WILD OX WITH HIS HAND IN THE FURROW, OR WILL HE HARROW THE
VALLEYS AFTER THEE? (JOB 39:10).

The expression, "Two of everything of all flesh," is interpreted to
mean that even the great and terrifying animals were included, and in
particular, that which is known as *re'em*, which is a wild ox of tremendous size and strength. There is a difference of opinion as to how the
ark would accommodate such large, ferocious animals. R. Judah says
that the offspring of the wild ox were accommodated in the ark, but R.
Nechemiah claims that even the offspring would be too large for this.

This wild animal, therefore, was attached to the ark from the outside. His head and nose were in the ark so that he could breathe. The rest of the animal was tied to the outside and was carried thus.

Even though the waters of the Flood were described as boiling hot, this particular animal was protected. So powerful was this wild ox, that as he was carried by the ark, he made furrows in the water. So deep and stormy that they were as large as the distance between Tiberias and Susitha, which are on either side of Lake Kineret, a distance of about one mile. The verse in the Book of Job records the scene that has just been described.

בִּימֵי רַבִּי חִיָא בַּר אַבָּא, עָלָה גּוּרָא אֶחָד לְאֶרֶץ יִשְׂרָאֵל, וְלֹא הִנִּיחַ אִילָן עַד שֶׁעֲקָרוֹ, וְעָשׂוּ תַעֲנִית, וְהִתְפַּלֵּל רַבִּי חִיָא וְגָעֵת אִמּוֹ, מִן הַמִּדְבָּר, וְיָרַד לְקוֹלָהּ.

IN THE DAYS OF R. HIYYA B. ABBA A [RE'EM'S] WHELP INVADED ERETZ ISRAEL AND DID NOT LEAVE A SINGLE TREE WHICH IT DID NOT UP-ROOT. A FAST WAS PROCLAIMED AND R. HIYYA PRAYED, WHEREUPON ITS MOTHER BELLOWED FROM THE DESERT AND IT [THE WHELP] WENT DOWN [TO THE DESERT] AT HER VOICE.

In the illustration by R. Hiyya, the wild ox continued his devastation even after the Flood, when he tore down tree after tree in the forest. The story also includes the fact that animals have either a code of their own or an instinct of their own to which they must respond. In this case, the wild ox heard the call of his mother, which reached him from the desert. He returned to her and therefore, presumably, stopped the destruction.

'זָכָר וּנְקֵבָה יִהְיוּ', אִם רָאִיתָ זָכָר רָץ אַחַר נְקֵבָה קַבְּלֵהוּ, נְקֵבָה רָצָה אַחַר זָכָר אַל תְּקַבֵּל.

THEY SHALL BE MALE AND FEMALE. [GOD INSTRUCTED NOAH]: 'IF THOU SEEST A MALE PURSUING A FEMALE, ACCEPT HIM; A FEMALE PURSUING A MALE, DO NOT ACCEPT HIM.'

The interpretation here is based on the word *yihiyu*, meaning that not only should they include creatures that are of each type, male and female, but that each, respectively, should also remain as male and female. What they mean here is that it is the accepted way of the world – not only the natural, animal world, but also, if you like, the "civilized" world, including the generation of Noah – for the male to pursue the female and not vice versa. This is meant not only as a sign of female modesty, but as a way to protect society from sexual immorality. Even though they did not live in an age such as our own, many aspects of Greek and

Roman sexual behavior made them feel that sexual initiatives taken by women would ultimately lead to sexual immorality.

—

Seed Thoughts I

This *midrash* makes the point that spirits, meaning entities without physical form, were created, and that they, too, would enter the ark. This is explained in an earlier *midrash* as related to the fact that God was about to create other human beings, but the Sabbath interrupted that work, and observance of the Sabbath is a priority even to God.

Granted the niceties of this interpretation, the question remains: how do we react to such an interpretation? It is difficult for a reader of the twenty-first century to accept the existence of a spirit or ghost, in any way other than fiction? In the classic, *A Christmas Carol*, the three spirits (of past, present and future), affect Scrooge and his experiences with these spirits change his character. But this is fiction, not reality. How did the sages of the *Midrash* react to the indication of the creation of spirits? Is it simply something they accept as being meaningless, or did they believe that there is some sort of reality attached to such an entity? We do not know. Perhaps some time in the future, answers to this problem may be found.

—

Seed Thoughts II

The *Midrash* interprets the verse that "male and female" should enter the ark as referring to those who remain male and female, respectively, in their actions as well. Their concern is the fact that the male pursuing the female for marriage, etc., is not only normal, but very desirable. The reverse, namely, female pursuit of the male, is looked upon as being potentially destructive. We can understand this in human relationships and there are many in our society today that would accept this view. It should be added, however, that there are also many who would not agree with this view. It seems quite clear that the sages of the *Midrash* did accept this interpretation; however, as I understand this *midrash*, they are making a claim that is almost beyond belief. They seem to be saying that this is not only a concept of human nature, but a concept of animal nature as well. They are saying to Noah, keep your eyes open and watch the animals as they enter the ark. If you note females pursuing males, be careful not to admit them. Is this a correct interpretation? If so, it is quite amazing.

—

Additional Commentary

How did R. Judah and R. Nechemiah differ?

Each of them followed their own point of view. R. Judah, in the preceding *midrash*, felt that the size of the room in the ark would be ten cubits squared. This kind of area could accommodate even the large offspring of the wild ox. R. Nechemiah, however, followed the view that each room was six cubits squared and, therefore, could not accommodate these offspring. (*Tiferet Tzion*)

Tying the wild ox to the ark

Two miracles were involved here: First, the wild ox allowed himself to be tied up in this manner, which is miraculous considering his size and strength. Secondly, the thrashing of the waters did not destroy the entire ark. (*Tiferet Tzion*)

יד. (כא) 'וְאַתָּה קַח לְךָ, וְגוֹ'', רַבִּי אַבָּא בַּר כָּהֲנָא אָמַר, הִכְנִיס עִמּוֹ דְבֵלָה, תְּנֵי מִשּׁוּם רַבִּי נְחֶמְיָה, רֹב מְכְנָסוֹ דְבֵלָה.

14. AND TAKE THOU UNTO THEE OF ALL FOOD THAT IS EATEN. R. ABBA B. KAHANA SAID: HE TOOK IN PRESSED FIGS WITH HIM.

The apparent problem in this *midrash* is the duplication of the words, *mikol ma'akhal asher ye'akhel*, which means, "from every food that can be eaten," rather than just saying, "from every food." The interpretation of the *midrash* is an indication that Noah took with him pressed figs known as *dveilah*, because it is a long-lasting food and can be eaten by anyone, including animals. It does not get rotten quickly and can be preserved for a long time.

רַבִּי אַבָּא בַּר כָּהֲנָא אָמַר, הִכְנִיס עִמּוֹ זְמוֹרוֹת לַפִּילִים, חֲצוּבוֹת לַצְּבָאִים, וְזוֹכִית לַנַּעֲמִיּוֹת. רַבִּי לֵוִי אָמַר, הִכְנִיס עִמּוֹ זְמוֹרוֹת לַנְּטִיעוֹת, יְחוּרִים לַתְּאֵנִים, גְּרוֹפִית לַזֵּיתִים.

IT WAS TAUGHT IN R. NEHEMIAH'S NAME: THE GREATER PART OF HIS PROVISIONS CONSISTED OF PRESSED FIGS. R. ABBA B. KAHANA SAID: HE TOOK IN BRANCHES FOR THE ELEPHANTS, HAZUBAH FOR THE DEER, AND GLASS FOR THE OSTRICHES. R. LEVI SAID: VINE-SHOOTS FOR VINE PLANTINGS, FIG-SHOOTS FOR FIG TREES, AND OLIVE-SHOOTS FOR OLIVE TREES.

R. Abba b. Kahana interprets the verse that duplicates the word "food" as indicating not necessarily that Noah prepared pressed figs, but that he also prepared special foods or special materials, which were needed for the nutrition of the various animals that are listed the *Midrash* text. R. Levi adds the interpretation that *asher ye'akhel* refers to the fact that *dveilah* can be eaten by everyone and also implies that it would be available even after they leave the ark. Some of the various plants that he introduced would be used in order to grow the appropriate fruits or vegetables after the Flood.

עַל דַּעְתֵּהּ דְּרַבִּי אַבָּא בַּר כָּהֲנָא, 'וְהָיָה לְךָ וְלָהֶם' דָּבָר שֶׁהוּא לְךָ וְלָהֶם, וְעַל דַּעְתֵּהּ דְּרַבִּי לֵוִי, 'וְהָיָה לְךָ וְלָהֶם', אַתָּה עִקָּר, וְהֵם טְפֵלִים לָךְ, 'וְאָסַפְתָּ אֵלֶיךָ' אֵין אָדָם כּוֹנֵס דָּבָר שֶׁאֵינוֹ צָרִיךְ לוֹ.

IN THE VIEW OF R. ABBA B. KAHANA: AND IT SHALL BE FOR THEE, AND FOR THEM IMPLIES SOMETHING THAT IS FOR THEE AND FOR THEM. IN THE VIEW OF R. LEVI AND IT SHALL BE FOR THEE, AND FOR THEM IMPLIES, THOU ART THE PRINCIPAL AND THEY ARE OF SECONDARY IMPORTANCE; AND GATHER IT TO THEE: A MAN DOES NOT GATHER [STORE] ANYTHING UNLESS HE NEEDS IT [FOR LATER].

In the view of R. Abba b. Kahana, the expression, "for you and for them" implies that Noah had to provide special foods that would be appropriate for the various types of animals. R. Levi, however, felt the interpretation was that the food had to be appropriate for Noah, who was the most important person on the ark, and, if necessary, would be available for the others as well, the general principle being that a person like Noah would only introduce into the ark those things that were appropriate to him, because he came first.

כב) 'וַיַּעַשׂ נֹחַ כְּכֹל אֲשֶׁר צִוָּה אֹתוֹ אֱלֹהִים כֵּן עָשָׂה', זֶה, שִׁכּוּן לַעֲשִׂיַּת הַתֵּבָה (בראשית ו,

THUS DID NOAH; ACCORDING TO ALL THAT GOD COMMANDED HIM, SO DID HE (6:22). THIS TEXT REFERS TO THE CONSTRUCTION OF THE ARK.

The expression, "Thus did Noah" is used twice, Gen. 6:22 and Gen. 7:5. The explanation is that the verse we are dealing with had to do with the completion of the ark. The second verse that is quoted farther on was Noah's entrance into the ark, together with his family and the entire family of the animal world.

—

Seed Thoughts

Many years ago, I saw a wonderful painting that had to do with Noah's ark. It showed the different kinds of animals coming from all over the earth as far as the horizon and wending their way to Noah's ark. The artist was conveying the message that all this was done by Divine decree. After all, how could Noah, a mere mortal, gather together all of the animals of the world? Only God could do that. At His signal, all the appropriate animals made their way to the ark. This is only one of the many miracles associated with the building of the ark. We have read intricate descriptions of the ark's interior: three levels with 900 rooms according to one opinion and 630 rooms according to another opinion.

This task was far beyond the capacity of one individual and required Divine intervention. As the Zohar puts it, the holiness of the ark was equal to the holiness of the *Mishkan*, the sanctuary of the wilderness.

The conclusion appears to be that the ark was the symbol of a microcosmic world. Is there something that we can learn from it? We do not live in a generation where Divine miracles seem to occur in an obvious fashion. Nor are any of us in the position to make decisions that would affect the entire world. The best we can do is to try to achieve what may be described as human miracles, which are the the the unexpected events within nature.

There are many things that we can learn from the ark. One of them has to do with the relationship of the human being to the animal world. Whatever God's reasons for creating animals, it is our duty to protect them and take care of them. A second thing we learn is from the fact that the inhabitants of the ark were prohibited from acts of reproduction. This value system was accepted by all, which teaches us that a community requires a moral consensus in order to maintain its viability. The third thing we learn is the importance of preparing for the future. The people in the ark were well prepared, in terms of the food that was brought in, and in terms of the plantings and other items that were mentioned. The main point, however, is that even the lesson of the Flood did not cure the world of evil. The challenge of the moral life is perpetual, and has to be faced by every generation, including our own and those of our offspring.

―

Additional Commentary

For him and for them

According to R. Abba b. Kahana, the expression, "for him and for them" seems to be superfluous, because for what other reason would Noah have brought the food? However, there is here revealed a difference of opinion. It is the view of R. Abba b. Kahana (*Midrash Rabbah* 28), that even Noah was not sufficiently worthy to survive the Flood, but was saved because he found favor in the eyes of God and he needed the help of the animal world to justify his survival. This is the meaning of the verse, "*Adam ubehemah toshiya Hashem*," which could be interpreted to mean that because of the merit of the animals does God redeem man. That is why we read later on, even in the *Machzor*, "*vayizkor et Noach ve'et kol hachaiyah*," that God remembered Noah and all of the animal world because of their *zekhut*. He, therefore, could not choose foods merely for himself, but for the animal life as well.

On the other hand, R. Levi followed the view of R. Nehemiah, that even if Noah had lived in another generation, he would have been considered a *tzaddik gamur*, an outstandingly righteous person. Therefore, the deliverance was because of him. Therefore, it says "for you and for them" because he came first and all of the blessings of the food were due to *his* merit. (*Tiferet Tzion*)

PARASHAH THIRTY-TWO, *Midrash One*

א. (ז, א) 'וַיֹּאמֶר ה' לְנֹחַ, בֹּא אַתָּה וְכָל בֵּיתְךָ אֶל הַתֵּבָה'

1. AND THE LORD SAID UNTO NOAH: COME THOU AND ALL THY HOUSE
INTO THE ARK, ETC. (7:1).

What the *Midrash* noticed is the change in the name of God from *Elokim* to *Hashem*. The explanation will eventually be revealed as we get to the conclusion of this *midrash*.

כְּתִיב, (תהלים ה, ז) 'תְּאַבֵּד דֹּבְרֵי כָזָב, אִישׁ דָּמִים וּמִרְמָה'

IT IS WRITTEN, THOU DESTROYEST THEM THAT SPEAK FALSEHOOD, ETC.
(PS. 5:7): THIS REFERS TO DOEG AND AHITOPHEL: 'THEM THAT SPEAK
FALSEHOOD': THEM AND THEIR SPEECH. R. PHINEHAS SAID: THEM AND
THEIR COMPANY. THE MAN OF BLOOD AND DECEIT (IBID.):

The expression *dovrei khazav*, is written without a *vav*. Not only does it refer to the false words that they spoke, but the word *dovrei* with a *vav* makes reference to the leaders, such as Doeg and Ahitophel, who were responsible for so much deceit. The word *damim* refers to bloodshed and the word *mirma* refers to sexual immorality.

יִתְעֵב ה'' מְדַבֵּר בְּדוֹאֵג וַאֲחִיתֹפֶל 'דֹּבְרֵי כָזָב' הֵן וְדִבּוּרָן, רַבִּי פִּינְחָס אָמַר, הֵן וּמְדַבְּרוֹתֵיהֶן,
'אִישׁ דָּמִים וּמִרְמָה', זֶה הִתִּיר גִּלּוּי עֲרָיוֹת וּשְׁפִיכַת דָּמִים, וְזֶה הִתִּיר גִּלּוּי עֲרָיוֹת וּשְׁפִיכַת דָּמִים,
שֶׁנֶּאֱמַר בַּאֲחִיתֹפֶל, (ש"ב טז, כא) 'בֹּא אֶל פִּלַגְשֵׁי אָבִיךָ', וּשְׁפִיכַת דָּמִים דִּכְתִיב, (שם יט, ב) 'וְאָבוֹא
עָלָיו וְהוּא יָגֵעַ וּרְפֵה יָדַיִם', וּכְתִיב (שם שם, שם) 'וְהִכֵּיתִי אֶת הַמֶּלֶךְ לְבַדּוֹ', וְזֶה הִתִּיר גִּלּוּי עֲרָיוֹת
וּשְׁפִיכַת דָּמִים

THE ONE PERMITTED INCEST AND BLOODSHED, AND THE OTHER PER-
MITTED INCEST AND BLOODSHED. THE ONE [AHITOPHEL] PERMITTED
INCEST AND BLOODSHED, [WHEN HE COUNSELED ABSALOM], GO IN
UNTO THY FATHER'S CONCUBINES (II SAM. 16:21). THE OTHER [DOEG]
PERMITTED INCEST: [WHERE DO WE FIND THIS]?

It is difficult to figure out how the *Midrash* is able to state that the verse refers to Doeg and Ahitophel. The only reason that is given is the fact that the verse begins with the plural and ends with the singular. So are Doeg and Ahitophel. These are two personalities whose talents and whose Torah knowledge were very great, but despite this, they were guilty of serious crimes in society. The seriousness of the term *pilegesh* has to be understood as meaning something more than the English translation of "concubine." The *pilegesh* was not a prostitute. She was the mistress of only one man. There is an argument as to whether or not she was a *mekudeshet*, sacred as a second wife, but even if not, she was *be'ulat ba'al*, meaning she had an exclusive sexual relationship with Abshalom's father, which meant she was prohibited from him. Aside from that fact, she is also considered as the king's woman, and therefore is prohibited to all others, including Abshalom.

נַחְמָן בְּרֵה דְּרַבִּי שְׁמוּאֵל בַּר נַחְמָנִי, אָמַר לְשָׁאוּל, וְכִי יֵשׁ אִישׁוּת לְדָוִיד, הֲלוֹא מוֹרֵד בַּמַּלְכוּת הוּא, וְחָשׁוּב כַּמֵּת, וְעַכְשָׁו הַתֵּר קוּגְעָתוֹ וַעֲשֵׂה אוֹתוֹ זִיטִיוְטוֹס, וּכְאִלּוּ הוּא מֵת, וְדָמוֹ מֻתָּר וְאִשְׁתּוֹ מֻתֶּרֶת, עָמַד שָׁאוּל וְנָתַן מִיכַל אֵשֶׁת דָּוִד עַל פִּיו לְפַלְטִי בֶן לַיִשׁ. וּשְׁפִיכַת דָּמִים דִּכְתִיב, (ש"א כב, יז) 'וְלֹא אָבוּ עַבְדֵי שָׁאוּל לִשְׁלֹחַ יָד בְּכֹהֲנֵי ה'', אֲבָל דּוֹאֵג הָרָגָן, שֶׁנֶּאֱמַר (שם שם, יח) 'וַיִּסֹּב דּוֹאֵג הָאֲדֹמִי וַיִּפְגַּע בְּכֹהֲנֵי ה''. 'יְתָעֵב ה'', שֶׁאֵינָן לֹא חַיִּים, וְלֹא נִדּוֹנִים

SAID R. NAHMAN B. SAMUEL B. NAHMANI: HE ANNULLED HIS [DAVID'S] CITIZEN RIGHTS AND DECLARED HIM AN OUTLAW AND AS ONE DEAD, SO THAT HIS BLOOD WAS PERMITTED AND HIS WIFE WAS PERMITTED. THE LORD ABHORRETH (PS. LOC. CIT.): THIS MEANS THAT THEY WILL NEITHER BE RESURRECTED NOR JUDGED.

This was done by King Saul on the advice of Doeg in order to punish David by arranging for his wife to be transferred to another husband.

(תהלים שם, ח) 'וַאֲנִי', כַּאֲשֶׁר עָשׂוּ, כֵּן עָשִׂיתִי, וּמַה בֵּינִי לְבֵינָם, אֶלָּא, שֶׁגְּמַלְתָּ עָלַי וְאָמַרְתָּ לִי, (ש"ב יב, יג) 'גַּם ה' הֶעֱבִיר חַטָּאתְךָ, וְגוֹ''.

BUT AS FOR ME (IBID., 8): AS THEY HAVE ACTED SO HAVE I ACTED; YET WHAT IS THE DIFFERENCE BETWEEN ME AND THEM? ONLY THAT THOU HAST SHOWN ME LOVE AND SAIDST TO ME, THE LORD ALSO HATH PUT AWAY THY SIN: THOU SHALT NOT DIE (II SAM. 12:13).

In the Psalm being quoted in this *midrash*, king David, despite his opposition to Doeg and Ahitophel, realizes that he is the first to be guilty of these horrible deeds. It was he who brought Bat Sheva into his home and arranged for her husband Uriah to fall in battle. The difference is that when David was accosted by the prophet Nathan, he immediately confessed his sins and sought forgiveness. Whereas, Doeg and Ahitophel believed in the very evil that they were doing.

דָּבָר אַחֵר, 'תְּאַבֵּד דֹּבְרֵי כָזָב' מְדַבֵּר בְּדוֹר הַמַּבּוּל, הֵן וְדִבּוּרָן כָּזָב, רַבִּי פִּינְחָס אָמַר, הֵן וּמִדַּבְּרוֹתֵיהֶן, 'אִישׁ דָּמִים' שֶׁנֶּאֱמַר (איוב כד, יד) 'לָאוֹר יָקוּם רוֹצֵחַ, יִקְטֹל עָנִי וְאֶבְיוֹן, וּבַלַּיְלָה יְהִי כַגַּנָּב', 'וּמִרְמָה', שֶׁנֶּאֱמַר (בראשית ו, יג) 'כִּי מָלְאָה הָאָרֶץ חָמָס מִפְּנֵיהֶם', 'יְתָעֵב ה'', שֶׁאֵינָם לֹא חַיִּים, וְלֹא נִדּוֹנִים, 'וַאֲנִי', כַּאֲשֶׁר עָשׂוּ כֵן עָשִׂיתִי, וּמַה בֵּינִי לְבֵינָם, אֶלָּא, שֶׁגְּמַלְתַּנִי טוֹבָה וְאָמַרְתָּ לִי, 'בֹּא אַתָּה וְכָל בֵּיתְךָ אֶל הַתֵּבָה'.

[ANOTHER INTERPRETATION]: IT REFERS TO THE GENERATION OF THE FLOOD: 'THOU DESTROYEST THEM THAT SPEAK FALSEHOOD': THEM AND THEIR SPEECH. 'THE MAN OF BLOOD,' AS IT IS WRITTEN, THE MURDERER RISETH WITH THE LIGHT, ETC. (JOB 24:14); 'AND DECEIT,' AS IT IS WRITTEN, FOR THE EARTH IS FILLED WITH VIOLENCE (GEN. 6:13). 'THE LORD ABHORRETH': THEY [THE GENERATION OF THE FLOOD] WILL NEITHER BE RESURRECTED NOR JUDGED. 'BUT AS FOR ME' [NOAH]: AS THEY HAVE ACTED SO HAVE I ACTED, YET WHAT IS THE DIFFERENCE BETWEEN ME AND THEM? ONLY THAT THOU SHOWEDST LOVE TO ME AND SAIDST TO ME: COME THOU AND ALL THY HOUSE INTO THE ARK.

A second interpretation attributes this verse, *"va'ani" as referring* to Noah. Granted that he lived in the generation of the Flood and was surrounded by all the evil of that generation. Nevertheless, God singled him out for a special consideration. Noah was a righteous man. The only criticism of him in the *Midrash* was that he did not try hard enough to save others in his generation. But in all other respects, he found favor in the eyes of God. Therefore, the invitation to him and his family to enter the ark and be saved is a sign of Gods love for him and therefore, the name "Hashem" is used, which refers to God's love and mercy, rather than the name "Elokim," which is found throughout the Creation story.

—

Seed Thoughts

The *Tiferet Tzion* has a most unusual comment. He quotes R. Phinehas as saying that the Holy One, Blessed be He created two evil inclinations. One of them was idolatry, meaning the worship of strange or pagan gods, and the other was sexual immorality (זנות – *znut*). The sage then added that of the two, the evil inclination toward idolatry was far more difficult and far more threatening than that of sexual immorality. R. Phinehas interpreted this as meaning עיקר היצה"ר אינו אלא לזנות וכל מה שעבדו ע"ז לא

היה אלא בשביל להתיר להם זנות – *ikar hayetzer harah eino ela liznut vekhol ma she'avdu avodah zarah lo hayah ela bishvil lehatir lahem znut.* "Even the most evil people, including those for whom sexual permissiveness is an important part of their way of life, somehow do not wish to rely on their own personal conviction, but always look for a way to legitimize their behavior." They, therefore, reach out to various cults and various pagan types as their form of religion. Many aspects of ancient Greek religion, including many of those cults described in Tractate *Avodah Zarah,* all seem to have a provision for some kind of sexual permissiveness, which attracted many people to it. Voltaire was once quoted as saying that people needed religion to prevent them from killing each other or engaging in some other aspect of delinquent behavior. That does not mean that one should choose a religion that helps create morality. To do so would make God secondary to human behavior. What it does mean, however, is that when religious authority breaks down, sexual permissiveness becomes very dominant in all societies. We should be grateful that in our religion, the Judge of all the earth does justice and that we serve Him by means of holiness and righteousness.

—

Additional Commentary

The righteousness of Noah (A)

Heaven forbid that we should think, about a righteous man such as Noah, that he would accept behavior such as stealth and the spilling of blood. Even those who interpret the fact that in another generation he might not have been as great as, perhaps, Abraham never felt that he would be guilty of anything unethical. The explanation is that he did not protest sufficiently about the evil of his time and could have done more to ask God's mercy upon the generation. In all other respects, however, he was a righteous man. (Yefei To'ar)

The righteousness of Noah (B)

In the text that is being quoted, the term used is "*Hashem,*" whereas previously in the creation story, He was referred to as "*Elokim.*" So the interpretation is that when God told Noah to enter the ark, that was a sign of God's great love. (*Tiferet Tzion*)

The self-criticism of King David (A)

The *vav* of the word *va'ani*, "and I," should be interpreted as meaning something additional. David was acknowledging some of the terrible acts committed during his reign, especially those of Doeg and Ahitophel. But then he realizes *"va'ani,"* meaning, "I, myself, did some of the terrible things that they did." (Maharzu)

The self-criticism of King David (B)

David said, "I, too, stumbled: in the area of sexual immorality with Bat Sheva, and in the spilling of the blood of Uriah. But God showed mercy to me. Therefore, I will continue to go into His House and bow down in His holy place." Since he mentioned the sins of his enemies, he had to acknowledge his own sins. But he also added that there is a difference between his behavior and theirs. The difference is that David acknowledged that he had sinned before God and received forgiveness. But as for Doeg and Ahitophel, the sin came from their hearts and, therefore, there was no remorse and no regret on their part; no feeling that they had done anything wrong. Everything was done by them willingly and it is in that respect that the Psalm said, "Let the deceitful leaders be obliterated." (*Tiferet Tzion*)

PARASHAH THIRTY-TWO, *Midrash Two*

ב. דָּבָר אַחֵר 'בֹּא אַתָּה, וְגוֹ'', כְּתִיב (תהלים יא, ז) 'כִּי צַדִּיק ה' צְדָקוֹת אָהֵב, יָשָׁר יֶחֱזוּ פָנֵימוֹ'
2. FOR THE LORD IS RIGHTEOUS, HE LOVETH RIGHTEOUSNESS; THE UP-
RIGHT SHALL BEHOLD HIS FACE (PS. 11:7).

It does not say that God says to Noah that he is a tzaddik, but rather,
he has watched and seen him function as a righteous person. In other
words, God is the Righteous One par excellence, and His great satisfaction is to find a human being who strives to be righteous, and this is
what God found in Noah.

רַבִּי תַּנְחוּמָא בְּשֵׁם רַבִּי יְהוּדָה בַּר סִימוֹן, רַבִּי מְנַחֲמָא בְּשֵׁם רַבִּי אֶלְעָזָר בַּר יוֹסֵי, אָמְרוּ, אֵין לְךָ
אָדָם אוֹהֵב בֶּן אֻמָּנָתוֹ, אֲבָל הֶחָכָם אוֹהֵב בֶּן אֻמָּנָתוֹ, כְּגוֹן, רַבִּי חִיָּא דְרַבִּי הוֹשַׁעְיָא, וְרַבִּי הוֹשַׁעְיָא
דְרַבִּי חִיָּא, וְהַקָּדוֹשׁ בָּרוּךְ הוּא, אוֹהֵב אֶת בֶּן אֻמָּנָתוֹ, שֶׁנֶּאֱמַר 'כִּי צַדִּיק ה', צְדָקוֹת אָהֵב'. 'יָשָׁר
יֶחֱזוּ פָנֵימוֹ' זֶה נֹחַ, שֶׁנֶּאֱמַר 'וַיֹּאמֶר ה' אֶל נֹחַ, בֹּא אַתָּה. וְגוֹ''.
R. TANHUMA IN R. JUDAH'S NAME AND R. MENAHEM IN R. ELEAZAR'S
NAME SAID: NO MAN LOVES HIS FELLOW CRAFTSMAN. A SAGE, HOW-
EVER, LOVES HIS COMPEER, E.G., R. HIYYA LOVES HIS COLLEAGUES AND
R. HOSHAYA HIS. THE HOLY ONE, BLESSED BE HE, ALSO LOVES HIS FEL-
LOW-CRAFTSMAN: HENCE, 'FOR THE LORD IS RIGHTEOUS, HE LOVETH
RIGHTEOUSNESS; THE UPRIGHT SHALL BEHOLD HIS FACE' APPLIES TO
NOAH, AS IT IS WRITTEN, AND THE LORD SAID UNTO NOAH: COME THOU
... FOR THEE HAVE I SEEN RIGHTEOUS BEFORE ME.

It is generally assumed that people in the same profession or calling or
trade are in a competitive situation with each other. This is not so for
those who are engaged in learning, in particular, in the field of Torah.
The example is given of R. Hiyya and R. Hoshaya. It so happens that
their opinions differ on most subjects having to do with Jewish law, despite which, they loved each other very much. Their homes were open
to each other, as were the students whom they taught. Since God saw in
Noah a *tzaddik*, a righteous person, and God, by definition, is the most

Righteous of all, He found in Noah a kindred spirit and invited him into the ark as a colleague in righteousness.

Seed Thoughts

The relationship between R. Hiyya and R. Hoshaya is a very beautiful one. Even though they differed on subjects that were quite serious in their implications, they loved and respected each other very much. The ability to respect one another despite differences of opinion is a tremendous asset and not everyone is capable of doing that. In a comment that you will find elsewhere, the *Tiferet Tzion* suggests that this was due to the fact that both were interested in the truth and that the Torah contained the truth that they were seeking. However, one has to point out that not all the sages shared this spirit of tolerance and understanding. In the Ethics of the Fathers (2:15), we are warned on the one hand to find warmth in their learning, but on the other hand, not to get too close, because we can be consumed by their fire and their intellectual bites, meaning attacks and criticism. Despite these warnings, the idea of mutual respect by individuals who differ substantially in their opinions is an important model for human behavior. The real challenge is whether this ideal can be applied to groups of people. Is it possible for us to learn to respect our neighbors' religion, culture and/or language, even though they may differ substantially from our own? As these words are being written, the province of Quebec is deeply involved in questions of a reasonable accommodation between social groupings and, in particular, between new immigrants and the local population. The great challenge of societies all over the world is for groups to learn the lessons of R. Hiyya and R. Hoshaya, to love each other even when they differ.

Additional Commentary

God is Righteous

The intent of this verse is to give a reason for the special invitation to Noah and his family to enter the ark. But why was it needed? After all, the whole intention of the building of the ark was to save Noah and his family. Even in saying, "You and your family," the "you" is superfluous. All that was need to be said was, "Your family." However, it should now be explained that just as the *Mishkan*, the tabernacle, had levels of sanctity, such as the courtyard, the hall and the Holy of Holies. Similarly, they had such levels of sanctity in the ark, as explained in the Zohar. Therefore, God said to Noah, "*Bo atah*, I want you to enter into that special place with a special holiness where My presence is felt." That is the reason why it says, "You are the one whom I recognized as the righteous one." (*Tiferet Tzion*)

People are competitive

When two people share the same trade, they may love each other, but it is not due to the nature of their work. Ordinarily, being engaged in the same trade leads to hostility and competition, and it therefore depends on other factors for them to feel close to each other. But sages of the Torah can and do love each other on the basis of their profession, which is the Torah, even though they may differ completely in their interpretations of Jewish law. The examples of R. Hiyya and R. Hoshaya fit this bill very well, for they always differed in their *halakhic* opinions and they continued to respect each other. The same can be said of the schools of Shammai and Hillel in their relationship to each other. The reason for this is that they were united by their love of truth; the Torah is the source of truth. Whoever studies Torah truthfully merits the name *chakham*, meaning wise one, or sage, and becomes identified with the search for truth, as he occupies himself with Torah. Since one sage knows that the other is also seeking the truth of the Torah, they love each other, and the Holy One, Blessed be He loves the righteous for the same reason – even in those cases where the righteous argued with God, such as Abraham at Sodom and Moses at the scene of the golden calf. (*Tiferet Tzion*)

PARASHAH THIRTY-TWO, *Midrash Three*

ג. כְּתִיב (שם שם, ה,) 'ה' צַדִּיק יִבְחָן, וְרָשָׁע וְאֹהֵב חָמָס שָׂנְאָה נַפְשׁוֹ', אָמַר רַבִּי יוֹנָתָן, הַיּוֹצֵר הַזֶּה, אֵינוֹ בוֹדֵק קַנְקַנִּים מְרוֹעָעִים, שֶׁאֵינוֹ מַסְפִּיק לָקוּשׁ עֲלֵיהֶם אַחַת, עַד שֶׁהוּא שׁוֹבְרָם, וּמִי הוּא בוֹדֵק, בְּקַנְקַנִּים יָפִים, אֲפִלּוּ מַקִּישׁ עֲלֵיהֶם כַּמָּה פְעָמִים אֵינָם נִשְׁבָּרִים, כָּךְ, אֵין הַקָּדוֹשׁ בָּרוּךְ הוּא מְנַסֶּה אֶת הָרְשָׁעִים, אֶלָּא אֶת הַצַּדִּיקִים. שֶׁנֶּאֱמַר 'ה', צַדִּיק יִבְחָן', וּכְתִיב, (בראשית כב, א) 'וְהָאֱלֹהִים נִסָּה אֶת אַבְרָהָם'

3. THE LORD TRIETH THE RIGHTEOUS; BUT THE WICKED AND HIM THAT LOVETH VIOLENCE HIS SOUL HATETH (PS. 11:5). R. JONATHAN SAID: A POTTER DOES NOT TEST DEFECTIVE VESSELS, BECAUSE HE CANNOT GIVE THEM A SINGLE BLOW WITHOUT BREAKING THEM. SIMILARLY THE HOLY ONE, BLESSED BE HE, DOES NOT TEST THE WICKED BUT ONLY THE RIGHTEOUS: THUS, 'THE LORD TRIETH THE RIGHTEOUS.'

This verse comes from the same Psalm as quoted in the previous *midrash* and is the verse quoted just before this text. God tests the righteous before He determines that He is dealing with a *tzaddik* and then extends His love to him. He only tests those whom He regards as righteous or potentially as righteous. The others, He knows in advance, are not worthy of this test. This is similar to the potter who only tests the good vessels, very often in the presence of the purchaser, in order to prove that the vessel is in good shape. All the others are discarded.

אָמַר רַבִּי יוֹסֵי בֶּן חֲנִינָה, הַפִּשְׁתָּנִי הַזֶּה, בְּשָׁעָה שֶׁהוּא יוֹדֵעַ שֶׁהַפִּשְׁתָּן שֶׁלּוֹ יָפָה, כָּל שֶׁהוּא כוֹתְשָׁהּ הִיא מִשְׁתַּבַּחַת, וְכָל זְמַן שֶׁהוּא מַקִּישׁ עָלֶיהָ הִיא מִשְׁתַּמֶּנֶת, וּבְשָׁעָה שֶׁהוּא יוֹדֵעַ שֶׁהַפִּשְׁתָּן שֶׁלּוֹ רָעָה, אֵינוֹ מַסְפִּיק לָקוּשׁ עָלֶיהָ אַחַת, עַד שֶׁהִיא פוֹקַעַת, כָּךְ, אֵין הַקָּדוֹשׁ בָּרוּךְ הוּא מְנַסֶּה אֶת הָרְשָׁעִים, אֶלָּא אֶת הַצַּדִּיקִים, שֶׁנֶּאֱמַר 'ה', צַדִּיק יִבְחָן'.

R. JOSE B. R. HANINA SAID: WHEN A FLAX WORKER KNOWS THAT HIS FLAX IS OF GOOD QUALITY, THE MORE HE BEATS IT THE MORE IT IMPROVES AND THE MORE IT GLISTENS; BUT IF IT IS OF INFERIOR QUALITY, HE CANNOT GIVE IT ONE KNOCK WITHOUT ITS SPLITTING. SIMILARLY, THE LORD DOES NOT TEST THE WICKED BUT ONLY THE RIGHTEOUS, AS IT SAYS, "THE LORD TRIETH THE RIGHTEOUS."

The second parable is another example where only the good flax materials are tested, and not the others.

אָמַר רַבִּי אֶלְעָזָר, מָשָׁל, לְבַעַל הַבַּיִת שֶׁהָיָה לוֹ שְׁתֵּי פָרוֹת, אַחַת כֹּחָהּ יָפֶה, וְאַחַת כֹּחָהּ רַע, עַל מִי הוּא נוֹתֵן אֶת הָעֹל לֹא עַל זֹאת שֶׁכֹּחָהּ יָפֶה, כָּךְ, הַקָּדוֹשׁ בָּרוּךְ הוּא מְנַסֶּה אֶת הַצַּדִּיקִים, שֶׁנֶּאֱמַר 'ה', צַדִּיק יִבְחָן'. 'ה' צַדִּיק יִבְחָן' זֶה נֹחַ, שֶׁנֶּאֱמַר 'וַיֹּאמֶר ה' לְנֹחַ ... כִּי אֹתְךָ רָאִיתִי צַדִּיק לְפָנַי'.

R. ELEAZAR SAID: WHEN A MAN POSSESSES TWO COWS, ONE STRONG AND THE OTHER FEEBLE, UPON WHICH DOES HE PUT THE YOKE? SURELY UPON THE STRONG ONE. SIMILARLY, THE LORD TESTS NONE BUT THE RIGHTEOUS: HENCE, 'THE LORD TRIETH THE RIGHTEOUS.' ANOTHER INTERPRETATION: 'THE LORD TRIETH THE RIGHTEOUS' APPLIES TO NOAH: HENCE, AND THE LORD SAID UNTO NOAH: COME THOU AND ALL THY HOUSE INTO THE ARK; FOR THEE HAVE I SEEN RIGHTEOUS, ETC.

The third illustration is an example of the same teaching, where only the good cow is relied upon to carry burdens.

אָמַר רַבִּי אֶלְעָזָר בֶּן עֲזַרְיָה, מָצִינוּ שֶׁאוֹמְרִים מִקְצָת שִׁבְחוֹ שֶׁל אָדָם, בְּפָנָיו, וְכֻלּוֹ, שֶׁלֹּא בְּפָנָיו, שֶׁכֵּן הוּא אוֹמֵר בְּנֹחַ, (בראשית ו, ט) 'אִישׁ צַדִּיק תָּמִים הָיָה' שֶׁלֹּא בְּפָנָיו, וּכְתִיב, 'כִּי אֹתְךָ רָאִיתִי צַדִּיק לְפָנַי', בְּפָנָיו. רַבִּי אֱלִיעֶזֶר, בְּנוֹ שֶׁל רַבִּי יוֹסֵי הַגְּלִילִי, אָמַר, מָצִינוּ, שֶׁאוֹמְרִים מִקְצָת שִׁבְחוֹ שֶׁל מִי שֶׁאָמַר וְהָיָה הָעוֹלָם, בְּפָנָיו, שֶׁנֶּאֱמַר (תהלים סו, ג) 'אִמְרוּ לֵאלֹהִים, מַה נּוֹרָא מַעֲשֶׂיךָ', שֶׁלֹּא בְּפָנָיו אוֹמֵר, (שם קלו, א) 'הוֹדוּ לַה' כִּי טוֹב כִּי לְעוֹלָם חַסְדּוֹ'.

R. ELEAZAR B. AZARIAH SAID: WE FIND THAT A PORTION OF A MAN'S MERITS MAY BE DECLARED IN HIS PRESENCE, BUT ALL OF THEM ONLY IN HIS ABSENCE. FOR THUS IT SAYS IN REFERENCE TO NOAH, FOR THEE HAVE I SEEN RIGHTEOUS, WHEREAS IN HIS ABSENCE IT SAYS, A MAN RIGHTEOUS AND WHOLE-HEARTED (GEN. 6:9). R. ELIEZER B. R. JOSE THE GALILEAN SAID: WE FIND THAT WE UTTER BUT A PORTION OF THE PRAISE OF HIM AT WHOSE WORD THE WORLD CAME INTO BEING, FOR IT IS SAID, SAY UNTO GOD: HOW TREMENDOUS IS THY WORK! (PS. 66:3), AND IT SAYS, O GIVE THANKS UNTO THE LORD, FOR HE IS GOOD (IBID., 118:1).

There is a saying that one should only tell of a small portion of a person's abilities and achievements in his presence. But all of it can be said about him in his absence. The lesson here is to emphasize the qualities of modesty and humility, which are the hallmarks of a good person. The surprising development of this *midrash* is that the same saying should be applied to the Holy One, Blessed be He. In petitioning the Holy One to help remove an evil or difficult decree, the verse says, "How awesome are Your works!" This is what is said in God's presence, namely, in prayer. But in speaking about God, the verse says, "For His mercies endureth forever," which is much higher praise.

─

Seed Thoughts

In the beautiful interpretation of the *Tiferet Tzion* quoted below, God knows and recognizes the inner struggle of the good person to maintain his ethical and moral standards. We humans do not have the Divine ability to penetrate each person's mind, but we do have the experience and the ability to realize that every person faces internal challenges. It is the hardest thing in the world to be a good person. It is so easy to conform to the permissive standards of our society. The good person does not easily conform. He looks for the ethical and moral principle and does his best to follow it, proclaim it and most importantly of all, live in accordance with this standard.

The Kotzker Rebbe was known by his contemporaries as a *tzaddik*. The Kotzker Rebbe would not accept this designation. "I am not a *tzaddik*," he would say to his contemporaries. "Even if I had a dream and in that dream the Holy One, Blessed be He would appear and would say to me, 'Rebbe, you are a *tzaddik*,' I would believe Him, but only for those few minutes. How do I know whether or not I would transcend the most immediate temptation and not succumb to it?"

To be a good man or woman is the most difficult task in the world. The Nobel prize for righteousness has not yet been established. But the moral and ethical person of whatever tradition and whatever location who strives to lead the moral life is the ideal human being, after whom we should model ourselves.

─

Additional Commentary

The Holy One tests the righteous

In what respect does God test the righteous? Our verse says, "For you have I seen as righteous." Why does it not simply say, "You are righteous"? The answer is that only God knows the inner thoughts of a person. He knows how much a good person has to struggle with his evil inclinations and his temptations that occur at any hour and any day.

That is why it says, "You, have I seen to be righteous," meaning, "I know of your inner struggle and I know that you have succeeded and declare you to be a righteous one." (*Tiferet Tzion*)

How can this teaching apply to God?

R. Eliezer claims that the advice to recite only partial praise of an individual in his presence applies to God as well. This is derived from the fact that when God is referred to directly, i.e., in second person (לשון נוכח – *lashon nokhach*) in Scripture, it seems as though His praise is limited. However, when the scriptural text praises God indirectly, in third person (לשון נסתר – *lashon nistar*) – which, when it refers to humans would mean not in the person's presence – then, the verse says, "Praise the Lord, for He is good and His mercy endures forever. (Psalms 118:1)" (*HaMidrash HaMevo'ar*)

ד. (ב) 'מִכֹּל הַבְּהֵמָה הַטְּהוֹרָה, וְגוֹ'', רַבִּי יוּדָן בְּשֵׁם רַבִּי יוֹחָנָן, וְרַבִּי בֶּרֶכְיָה בְּשֵׁם רַבִּי אֶלְעָזָר, וְרַבִּי יַעֲקֹב דִּכְפַר חָנִין בְּשֵׁם רַבִּי יְהוֹשֻׁעַ בֶּן לֵוִי, מָצִינוּ שֶׁעִקֵּם הַקָּדוֹשׁ בָּרוּךְ הוּא, שְׁתַּיִם וְשָׁלֹשׁ תֵּבוֹת בַּתּוֹרָה, כְּדֵי שֶׁלֹּא לְהוֹצִיא, דָּבָר טְמֵאָה מִתּוֹךְ פִּיו, הָדָא הוּא דִכְתִיב, 'מִכֹּל הַבְּהֵמָה הַטְּהוֹרָה תִּקַּח לְךָ שִׁבְעָה שִׁבְעָה אִישׁ וְאִשְׁתּוֹ', וּמִן הַבְּהֵמָה הַטְּמֵאָה אֵין כְּתִיב כָּאן, אֶלָּא 'אֲשֶׁר לֹא טְהֹרָה הִוא'. אָמַר רַבִּי יוּדָן בַּר רַבִּי מְנַשֶּׁה, אַף כְּשֶׁבָּא לוֹמַר לָהֶם סִמָּנֵי בְהֵמָה טְמֵאָה, לֹא פָּתַח לָהֶם, אֶלָּא, בְּסִמָּנֵי בְהֵמָה טְהוֹרָה, (ויקרא יא, ד) אֶת הַגָּמָל, כִּי לֹא מַפְרִיס פַּרְסָה אֵין כְּתִיב כָּאן, אֶלָּא, 'כִּי מַעֲלֵה גֵרָה', (שם שם, ה) אֶת הַשָּׁפָן, כִּי אֵינֶנּוּ מַפְרִיס פַּרְסָה אֵין כְּתִיב כָּאן, אֶלָּא, 'כִּי מַעֲלֵה גֵרָה', (שם שם, ו) וְאֶת הַחֲזִיר, כִּי אֵינֶנּוּ מַעֲלֵה גֵרָה אֵין כְּתִיב כָּאן, אֶלָּא, 'כִּי מַפְרִיס פַּרְסָה הוּא'.

4. OF EVERY PURE BEAST THOU SHALT TAKE TO THEE ... AND OF THE BEASTS THAT ARE NOTPURE, ETC. (7:2). R. JUDAN IN R. JOHANAN'S NAME, R. BEREKIAH IN R. ELEAZAR'S NAME, AND R. JACOB IN R. JOSHUA'S NAME SAID: WE FIND THAT THE HOLY ONE, BLESSED BE HE, EMPLOYED A CIRCUMLOCUTION OF THREE WORDS IN ORDER TO AVOID UTTERING AN IMPURE [INDELICATE] EXPRESSION: IT IS NOT WRITTEN, 'AND OF THE IMPURE BEASTS,' BUT ... THAT ARE NOT PURE. R. JUDAN SAID: EVEN WHEN [SCRIPTURE] COMES TO ENUMERATE THE SIGNS OF IMPURE ANIMALS, IT COMMENCES FIRST WITH THE SIGNS OF PURITY [WHICH THEY POSSESS]: IT IS NOT WRITTEN, 'THE CAMEL, BECAUSE HE PARTETH NOT THE HOOF,' BUT, BECAUSE HE CHEWETH THE CUD AND PARTETH NOT THE HOOF (LEV. 11:4); THE ROCK-BADGER, BECAUSE HE CHEWETH THE CUD BUT PARTETH NOT THE HOOF (IBID., 5); THE HARE, BECAUSE SHE CHEWETH THE CUD BUT PARTETH NOT THE HOOF (IBID., 6); THE SWINE, BECAUSE HE PARTETH THE HOOF, AND IS CLOVEN-FOOTED, BUT CHEWETH NOT THE CUD (IBID., 7).

The full text is as follows: "Of every pure beast thou shalt take to thee seven and seven, each with his mate; and of the beasts that are not pure, two [and two], each with his mate" (Genesis 7:2). Those animals that are described as *tamei*, meaning impure, are not referred to directly in this manner, but rather as *lo tehorah*, meaning *not* being pure or clean. In other words, The Almighty deliberately changed the style of the verses

rather than have them short, straight and to the point, by having the
animals described as "impure"; He, instead, added three additional
words and in other places, two additional words, simply to indicate that
these animals did not possess those features that would render them
pure and therefore, acceptable for certain uses. The goal was to teach
all of us good manners, to keep us away from the negative, even in our
ordinary conversation, let alone in terms of our actions.

In the verse that was quoted, three words were added to make this
point. In a subsequent verse, Genesis 7:8, two additional words are
added. Thus, in the verse in our *midrash*, it does not say "unclean animals," but rather "those animals that are not clean." This method of the
Midrash also points out that Scripture mentions first those qualities that
even the impure animals share with the clean ones, and only afterward
does it add those aspects where they differ and render the other animals
as not being pure, either for the purpose of eating or for the purpose of
sacrificial offerings. The lesson, of course, is that we should try always
to begin our conversations בלשון נקיה – *belashon nekiyah*, meaning with
wholesome, positive conversation, and only later on to add whatever
criticism we may have in mind.

(ג) 'גַּם מֵעוֹף הַשָּׁמַיִם שִׁבְעָה שִׁבְעָה', אִם תֹּאמַר שִׁבְעָה מִכָּל מִין, נִמְצָא אֶחָד מֵהֶן שֶׁאֵין לוֹ בֶן
זוּג, אֶלָּא, שִׁבְעָה זְכָרִים וְשִׁבְעָה נְקֵבוֹת.
OF THE FOWL ALSO OF THE AIR, SEVEN EACH – E.V. 'SEVEN AND SEVEN'
(7:3). IF YOU SAY THAT IT MEANS SEVEN OF EACH KIND, ONE OF THEM
WOULD LACK A MATE; HENCE IT MEANS SEVEN MALES AND SEVEN FE-
MALES;

The point here is that the "seven" does not refer merely to individual
birds. If they were only seven, equally divided between females and
males, one would be without a mate. It has to be understood, therefore,
as requiring fourteen birds, which we could define as seven couples,
even though they would be of different species of birds.

לֹא שֶׁאֲנִי צָרִיךְ לָהֶם, אֶלָּא 'לְהַחֲיוֹת זֶרַע עַל פְּנֵי כָל הָאָרֶץ'.
'NOT THAT I NEED THEM' [SAID GOD], 'BUT TO KEEP SEED ALIVE UPON
THE FACE OF ALL THE EARTH.'

The use of the term, "Not that I need them," has to be understood.
By definition, God does not need anything, ever. The expression,
therefore, should be translated not as what God needs, but as what God
desires. The midrash is aware that the request to preserve many more

pure animals over the impure kind, could bring one to think that God desires more animals in order that they be offered as sacrifices to Him. Therefore it states emphatically that this is not His desire at all. All He wants is for the animals and human beings to multiply and create a full and abundant life upon earth, which is why the animals in general were saved.

―

Seed Thoughts

The main lesson of this *midrash* is the importance of speech in the development of the human being. What exactly does that mean? In the first place, it means clean speech. The absence of what might be described as swear words or curse words. Swear words and curse words may make a person feel hurt, but do nothing to explain a situation or convey information. There is not a single swear word that could not be improved upon by the proper use of any language, properly directed to the situation at hand. This is an important consideration, because clean speech is a very important springboard to a moral and ethical position. The moment a person finds himself in the middle of a world of cursing and swearing, he is already within the boundaries of corruption and it would not take long before he would compromise even more with moral ideas and principles. However, more than clean speech is involved here. It is also a matter of accentuating the positive. In the verses quoted where God added certain words, the message was the same. The difference, however, is that the words were presented in a more gentil and acceptable way.

To accentuate the positive and avoid the negative can also mean to stand up for your ideals and relate to all things in life in light of the principles in which you believe. There are many people in life, be it public or private, who are full of criticism, whether of individual behavior or public policy. But when they are asked to present their own program, or their own affirmations, words often fail them. In my younger days, I took a course in homiletics with Professor Mordecai Kaplan. He used to say that it was not his role to teach us how to speak in public. That is the domain of others. His biggest help would be to help us have something to say. Having what to say is most important, not only in public speech, but in private thought as well. Having what to say, however, must be couched in language that is positive, truthful, and always having in mind to hurt the other as little as possible.

―

Additional Commentary

The unclean animal

In connection with the pig, it does not say that this particular animal does not chew its cud and therefore is unfit. This would be the concise and direct way of saying what has to be said. But Scripture does not approach the subject that way. Instead, it starts off by saying that the hoof of the pig is parted, which is the symbol of the pure animal, and only then goes on to add that it does not chew its cud and therefore is impure and cannot be eaten. This structure is used in reference not only to the pig, but also to the camel and others, all of which are meant to teach us to be careful with our words, and to try as much as possible to begin by accentuating the positive. (*HaMidrash HaMevo'ar*)

ה. (ד) 'כִּי לְיָמִים עוֹד שִׁבְעָה, וְגוֹ'', אָמַר רַבִּי שִׁמְעוֹן בֶּן יוֹחַאי, הֵן עָבְרוּ עַל הַתּוֹרָה, שֶׁנִּתְּנָה
לְאַרְבָּעִים יוֹם, לְפִיכָךְ 'אַרְבָּעִים יוֹם וְאַרְבָּעִים לָיְלָה'.

5. FOR YET SEVEN DAYS, ETC. (7:4). R. SIMEON B. YOHAI SAID: THEY
HAVE TRANSGRESSED THE TORAH WHICH WAS GIVEN AFTER FORTY
DAYS, THEREFORE I WILL CAUSE IT TO RAIN . . . FORTY DAYS AND FORTY
NIGHTS.

One of the questions that arises is, how can we speak of the Torah
in connection with the generation of the Flood, since the Torah was
given many generations later? The *Midrash*, elsewhere, does say that the
Torah existed long before the creation of the world, at least in theory.
In the case of the generation of the Flood, they knew about such commandments as those against idolatry, immorality, murder and theft, as
we saw from previous *midrashim*. If they had been careful to observe
these major commandments, they would have been brought closer
to the other commandments as well. The use of the term "*anokhi*" in
the text quoted is a reminder of the "*Anokhi*" in the first line of the Ten
Commandments. Since they disobeyed the first "*Anokhi*," they will be
punished by the second "*anokhi*."

אָמַר רַבִּי יוֹחָנָן בֶּן זַכַּאי, הֵם קִלְקְלוּ אֶת הַצּוּרָה, שֶׁנִּתְּנָה לְאַרְבָּעִים יוֹם, לְפִיכָךְ 'אַרְבָּעִים יוֹם
וְאַרְבָּעִים לָיְלָה'.

R. JOHANAN SAID: THEY CORRUPTED THE FEATURES WHICH TAKE SHAPE
AFTER FORTY DAYS, THEREFORE I WILL CAUSE IT TO RAIN . . . FORTY
DAYS AND FORTY NIGHTS.

One of the teachings of the traditions is during the first forty days of a
woman's pregnancy, the character of the fetus is influenced by the Holy
One, Blessed be He. If after these forty days, a pregnant woman des-
ecrates her life by having relations with another man, the *tzurah* – the
character – of the embryo is completely changed. Since this happened
so many times during the generation of the Flood, the generation was

punished measure for measure, for the forty-day periods after which pregnancy had been corrupted.

'וּמָחִיתִי אֶת כָּל הַיְקוּם' רַבִּי בֶּרֶכְיָה אָמַר, קִיּוּמֵהּ, רַבִּי אָבוּן אָמַר, יְקוּמִינָה, רַבִּי לֵוִי בְּשֵׁם רֵישׁ לָקִישׁ אָמַר, זֶה קַיִן, הָיָה תָּלוּי בְּרִפְיוֹן, וּבָא מַבּוּל וּשְׁטָפוֹ, שֶׁנֶּאֱמַר (בראשית ז, כג) 'וַיִּמַח אֶת כָּל הַיְקוּם'.

AND EVERY LIVING SUBSTANCE (YEKUM) THAT I HAVE MADE WILL I BLOT OUT. R. BEREKIAH SAID: THAT MEANS, WHATEVER EXISTS (KAYO-MAYA) UPON IT. R. ABIN SAID: THE ONE WHO AROSE AGAINST HIM [HIS BROTHER]. R. LEVI SAID IN THE NAME OF RESH LAKISH: HE [GOD] KEPT HIM [CAIN] IN SUSPENSE UNTIL THE FLOOD CAME AND SWEPT HIM AWAY: HENCE IT IS WRITTEN, AND HE BLOTTED OUT EVERY ONE THAT HAD ARISEN (GEN. 7:23).

The main concern of the *Midrash* at this point is the interpretation of the word *yekum*. If it means to refer to the entire universe, why was that word used and not others? There are several interpretations: R. Berekiah says it comes from the root word *kayam*, survival, and means that the entire universe would not survive. R. Abin sees in the term a connotation of one rising against his brother, and interprets it as a reference to Cain, which is then elaborated upon. Another idea is the connection with the word *yekuminiyah*, that which sustains a person, referring mainly to his money or possessions, implying that all of these would be destroyed in the Flood. The reference to Cain by R. Levi is based on the fact that the word is used earlier in Scripture to describe Cain's murder of Abel, where it says, "and Cain arose (*vayakom*) ..." .." Theis also indicates that Cain was put to death at the time of the Flood.

(ה.) 'וַיַּעַשׂ נֹחַ כְּכֹל אֲשֶׁר צִוָּהוּ ה'', זֶה שִׁכּוּן לְכָנוּס לְכָנוּס בְּהֵמָה חַיָּה וָעוֹף.
AND NOAH DID ACCORDING UNTO ALL, ETC. (7:5). THE PRESENT VERSE REFERS TO THE TAKING IN OF THE ANIMALS, BEASTS, AND BIRDS.

In connection with the text, it says that Noah did whatever he was commanded. This is not a repetition of a similar verse earlier, which referred to Noah's completion of the ark. The present quotation refers to the fact that the animal world was properly guided into the ark.

Seed Thoughts

One of the earliest questions that was directed to me in the rabbinate, by a well-known physician, was my opinion about the meaning of לוז – *luz*. I had never before heard of this term and the physician, who had scholarly interest in both medicine and Judaism, explained to me that there is a tradition in many circles in Judaism that after a person's death, the body disintegrates and is completely absorbed by the earth, with the exception of an item known as *luz*. No one knows for certain which particular limb or part of the body *luz* is, though we do have sources that associate it with the vertebrae of the backbone (see Midrash Rabbah above, 28:3). The luz does not merely retain its strength; it is also the means by which God authorizes and accomplishes the resurrection of the human body in the time to come

I am reminded of this first contact by the fact that one of the commentators to our *midrash* makes mention of the term *luz*. The *Tiferet Tzion* maintains that the views of R. Berakiah and R. Abin reflect their difference of opinion as found in an earlier *Midrash*. There, R. Berekiah maintained that there was no future at all for the generation of the Flood, not even in terms of the next world, and that everything of theirs in this world would be destroyed, including the *luz* of each person. R. Abin, on the other hand, believed that the punishment of the generation of the Flood was a cleansing process and that they would be entitled to a life in the World to Come. Therefore, the existence of the *luz* in each person was, and remained, vitally present.

Naturally, this use of the term *luz* implies belief that the resurrection would actually be a restoration of the human body in all of its physical manifestations.

—

Additional Commentary

The Torah and the Flood (A)

In theory, the Torah preceded the creation of the world, but from the human perspective, it was given to us at Mount Sinai. In actual fact, some of the Torah's laws, such as, idolatry, sexual immorality, murder, stealth, etc., became known even before its revelation at Mount Sinai, as a result of personal experience. It is also maintained that people knew about what are known as the seven Noachide laws. Had they observed these minimum obligations, a good part more of the Torah would have opened up for them. (*HaMidrash HaMevo'ar*)

The Torah and the Flood (B)

There is a tradition that before a child is born, the entire Torah is revealed to him, or at least as much of the Torah as was felt to be his capacity to absorb (Talmud *Nidah* 30b). Just before the child is born, an angel intercedes and what has been revealed becomes forgotten. However, what this Torah learning does do during these forty days is that it determines the character and personality of the individual. This is something that applies to all individuals, even before the giving of the Torah at Mount Sinai. It was these forty days of Torah in utero that were desecrated by the people of the Flood and they were, therefore, punished measure for measure by the Flood, whose rains lasted forty days. (*Tiferet Tzion*)

The luz and the world

R. Berekiah finds a difficulty in the presence of the word *yekum* rather than other terms to describe the world in this context, and feels that it has to do with the word *kayam*, the very survival of the universe, which God now intended to destroy. Destroying the universe meant destroying לוז השדרה – *luz hashidrah*, the *luz* of the spine, which is the source of the person's existence in the World to Come. R. Abin, on the other hand, felt that even the generation of the Flood would be entitled to the World to Come, because not all of them were complete sinners and they would have already received the terrible punishment. One would, therefore, have to say that the *luz* of their spines remained with them, through which the human being would be able to live in the World to Come. (*Tiferet Tzion*)

PARASHAH THIRTY-TWO, *Midrash Six*

(ו) 'וְנֹחַ בֶּן שֵׁשׁ מֵאוֹת שָׁנָה, וְהַמַּבּוּל הָיָה מַיִם, וְגוֹ'', רַבִּי יְהוּדָה וְרַבִּי נְחֶמְיָה, רַבִּי יְהוּדָה אוֹמֵר, שְׁנַת הַמַּבּוּל אֵינָה עוֹלָה מִן הַמִּנְיָן, אָמַר לוֹ רַבִּי נְחֶמְיָה, אַף עַל פִּי שֶׁאֵינָה עוֹלָה מִן הַמִּנְיָן, עוֹלָה הִיא, בַּתְּקוּפוֹת וּבַחֶשְׁבּוֹנוֹת.

6. AND NOAH WAS SIX HUNDRED YEARS OLD, ETC. (7:6). R. JUDAH SAID: THE YEAR OF THE FLOOD IS NOT COUNTED IN THE NUMBER [OF NOAH'S YEARS]. SAID R. NEHEMIAH TO HIM: IT IS COUNTED IN THE CHRONO-LOGICAL RECKONING.

The year of the Flood was not counted in terms of Noah's age. But in all other respects, such as the time span of the Flood and the calculation of the calendar, it definitely was counted. Why is this? One of the reasons why the year was not counted toward Noah's years was because it was a year of hardship and suffering – not only for the world at large, but for Noah, in particular, who had to go through this strenuous preparation having to do with the building of the ark and the preparation of the animals for the ark. The calculation of the years can be explained as follows: One verse says that Noah was 600 years old at the time of the Flood – but the Flood itself lasted one complete year. Then, there is a verse that describes Noah after the Flood as having lived another 350 years. The total of his age before the Flood, plus the one year of the Flood and the three hundred and fifty years Noah lived after the Flood would make Noah 951 years old. But Scripture, later on, says, "And Noah lived 950 years and then he died." From this is derived the thought that the year of the Flood was not counted, only in terms of Noah's age.

(ז) 'וַיָּבֹא נֹחַ וּבָנָיו וְאִשְׁתּוֹ וְגוֹ'', אָמַר רַבִּי יוֹחָנָן, נֹחַ, מְחֻסַּר אֲמָנָה הָיָה, אִלּוּלֵי שֶׁהִגִּיעוּ הַמַּיִם עַד קַרְסֻלָּיו לֹא נִכְנַס לַתֵּבָה.

AND NOAH WENT IN, AND HIS SONS, ETC . . . BECAUSE OF THE WATERS OF THE FLOOD (7:7), R. JOHANAN SAID: HE LACKED FAITH: HAD NOT THE WATER REACHED HIS ANKLES HE WOULD NOT HAVE ENTERED THE ARK.

The claim here is made that because Noah waited until he felt the waters reach his ankles, he was lacking in faith, in that he did not believe that the waters would come until they actually came.

———

Seed Thoughts

The contention that Noah showed lack of faith by not entering the ark until the waters were felt by him can also be argued. It seems to be at least as possible that Noah believed, or rather, he hoped that the waters of the Flood would never come. His hope was that the people would repent and since God accepts repentance, even at the last moment, he delayed entering the ark. Very often, repentance does not occur until the very last chance. Noah thought that at the moment the people saw waters gathering from the rain, they would realize that what he was telling them was true and that they would repent in their ways and ask forgiveness from God. One can maintain, therefore, not only that Noah did not lack faith, but that his faith in the possibilities of the repentance of the sinner and God's willingness to accept such repentance was very strong. Unfortunately, this repentance never happened.

The argument against this development is that since the people showed no signs of repentance during the entire 120 years that Noah was building the ark, surely a few extra days would not have made a difference. But human nature does not always work out according to preconceived rules. Noah seemed to have been hoping for the best and should be given credit for that hope.

———

Additional Commentary

Noah was lacking in faith

It says in the verse that Noah entered in the ark because of the waters of the Flood. It did not say that he entered the ark because God had commanded him to, as it was later said when he arranged for the animals to enter. One can conclude from this that Noah had many doubts about whether the Flood would actually come. He thought at first that the possibility of a flood was only a warning or a threat, and even the first waters would also fulfill that same purpose. It was only when the flood waters began to rise that he realized that the Flood was a reality and that is when he entered the ark. (Yefei To'ar)

The year of the Flood was not included

The year that the Flood occurred was not included in Noah's age because it was thought to be a cursed year. The *Midrash* interprets the year of the Flood to a similar verse in Job, "Let it not be joined to the days of the year, let it not come into the number of the months." (Job 3:6) (Maharzu)

PARASHAH THIRTY-TWO, *Midrash Seven*

(י) 'וַיְהִי לְשִׁבְעַת הַיָּמִים, וּמֵי הַמַּבּוּל', מְלַמֵּד שֶׁתָּלָה לָהֶם הַקָּדוֹשׁ בָּרוּךְ הוּא, שִׁבְעַת יְמֵי אֲבֵלוּת שֶׁל מְתוּשֶׁלַח הַצַּדִּיק, כְּדֵי שֶׁיַּעֲשׂוּ תְשׁוּבָה, וְלֹא עָשׂוּ.

7. AND IT CAME TO PASS AFTER THE SEVEN DAYS (7:10). THIS TEACHES THAT THE HOLY ONE, BLESSED BE HE, GAVE THEM A RESPITE DURING THE SEVEN DAYS' MOURNING FOR THE RIGHTEOUS METHUSALEH, SO THAT THEY MIGHT REPENT, YET THEY DID NOT.

The main challenge of the *Midrash here* is to interpret what the phrase *leshiv'at hayamim* is intended to convey. Most notable was the letter *hey at the beginning* of the word *hayamim*, indicating that there was something special, specific, about this particular set of seven days. That special factor was the fact that Metushelah, the most righteous man of that generation, having reached the age of 969, had just died, and the seven-day delay of the Flood was attributed to him, as a way of observing *shivah, the traditional seven-day mourning period,* for him. It was also hoped that this might lead to a responsive repentance, but that did not happen.

דָּבָר אַחֵר, 'וַיְהִי לְשִׁבְעַת הַיָּמִים', אָמַר רַבִּי יְהוֹשֻׁעַ בֶּן לֵוִי, שִׁבְעָה יָמִים נִתְאַבֵּל הַקָּדוֹשׁ בָּרוּךְ הוּא, עַל עוֹלָמוֹ, קֹדֶם שֶׁיָּבֹא מַבּוּל לָעוֹלָם, מַאי טַעְמָא, (בראשית ו, ו) 'וַיִּתְעַצֵּב אֶל לִבּוֹ', וְאֵין עֲצִיבָה אֶלָּא אֲבֵלוּת, שֶׁנֶּאֱמַר (ש"ב יט, ג) 'נֶעֱצַב הַמֶּלֶךְ עַל בְּנוֹ'.

ANOTHER INTERPRETATION: AND IT CAME TO PASS AFTER THE SEVEN DAYS: R. JOSHUA B. LEVI SAID: SEVEN DAYS THE HOLY ONE, BLESSED BE HE, MOURNED FOR HIS WORLD BEFORE BRINGING THE FLOOD, THE PROOF BEING THE TEXT, AND IT GRIEVED HIM (GEN. 6:6), WHILE ELSEWHERE WE READ, THE KING GRIEVETH FOR HIS SON (II SAM. 19:3).

This interpretation is based on the verse that says that God was sad in His heart. The same word for "sad" appears also among the verses about king David regarding the death of his son Absalom. It implies the sadness of mourning.

אָמַר רַבִּי יוֹסֵי בֶּן דּוּרְמַסְקִית, הֵם חָטְאוּ בְּגַלְגַּל הָעַיִן, שֶׁהוּא דוֹמֶה לַמַּיִם, אַף הַקָּדוֹשׁ בָּרוּךְ
הוּא, לֹא פָרַע מֵהֶם אֶלָּא בַּמַּיִם, אָמַר רַבִּי לֵוִי, הֵם קִלְקְלוּ סִילוֹנִית שֶׁלָּהֶם, אַף הַמָּקוֹם שִׁנָּה
לָהֶם סִדּוּרוֹ שֶׁל עוֹלָם, דֶּרֶךְ אֶרֶץ, הַמָּטָר יוֹרֵד וְהַתְּהוֹם עוֹלֶה, דִּכְתִיב, (תהלים מב, ח) 'תְּהוֹם
אֶל תְּהוֹם קוֹרֵא לְקוֹל צִנּוֹרֶיךָ', בְּרַם הָכָא, 'נִבְקְעוּ כָּל מַעְיְנוֹת תְּהוֹם רַבָּה', וְאַחַר כָּךְ 'וַאֲרֻבֹּת
הַשָּׁמַיִם נִפְתָּחוּ'.

ON THE SAME DAY WERE ALL THE FOUNTAINS OF THE GREAT DEEP
BROKEN UP, ETC. (7:11). R. JOSE B. DURMASKITH SAID: THEY SINNED
THROUGH THE EYEBALL, WHICH IS LIKE WATER, THEREFORE THE HOLY
ONE, BLESSED BE HE, PUNISHED THEM BY WATER. R. LEVI SAID: THEY
ABUSED THEIR FOUNTAINS, THEREFORE THE LORD REVERSED THE
NATURAL ORDER: THE NATURAL ORDER IS FOR RAIN TO DESCEND AND
THE DEEP TO COME UP, BUT HERE, DEEP CALLETH UNTO DEEP (PS. 42:8).

There are a number of ways in which this section has been interpreted.
One of the difficulties present here is that the waters of the Flood did
not come from the sea. It would have been the most natural thing for
the waters of the oceans, which are more plentiful than the land or the
earth, should have been used for the waters of the Flood. But that did
not happen. What happened was that the various springs and water
wells of the earth produce water that shot up into the air, after which
rain fell from the clouds and the heavens and joined together. Usually,
the rain comes downward first and then it is met by sources of water
from within the earth. In this case, however, the process was reversed.
The well springs of the earth rose first and then were met by the rains
that came down. How can one explain this anomaly?

The word *ayin* means a well, but the same word also means the eye.
The people of the generation of the Flood were betrayed by their eyes,
as it is written, "The sons of the gods fell for the beauty of the maidens
of the earth and therefore, had relations with whomever they chose."
We are also told that the females responded with the same degree of
immorality. Since their eyes had so betrayed them and caused them to
act in a way other than that which God had intended, so, too, the storms
and tempest that produced the Flood changed their procedure. The
lower waters reached up to the upper waters without waiting for them
to come down.

Seed Thoughts

One of the interpretations of the seven-day delay in the oncoming of
the Flood was that God was saddened at the prospect of destroying

the world and was mourning its disappearance. One might ask, how can one mourn before the disaster takes place? God was able to do so because He knew what was going to happen. That being the case, could not God have prevented the catastrophe? The answer is that this is not how He created the world. Human beings were created with the gift of freedom. It was that freedom that caused the disaster, but it was that very same freedom that can raise the human being to the very highest reaches of his talents and his personality. God was grieving because the human beings whom He had created did not truly understand the blessings of freedom and did not create a good world in which to have an opportunity to elevate themselves. He could not interfere by virtue of the very laws and restrictions that He had created, even for Himself. His hope was that the new world, under the leadership of Noah and his successors, would fulfill His goal in greater measure.

—

Additional Commentary

The death of a righteous man

The fact that the Flood was delayed to give time to commemorate the passing of Metushelah teaches us that giving eulogy and mourning for the righteous can prevent the coming of punishment, whether to individuals or to the world. Indeed, God created conditions during that week that made it appear as though people were living in the World to Come. All this was done so that people should understand the value and the worth of the person now taken from them. (*HaMidrash HaMevo'ar*)

PARASHAH THIRTY-TWO, *Midrash Eight*

ח. (יג) 'בְּעֶצֶם הַיּוֹם הַזֶּה, בָּא נֹחַ', אָמַר רַבִּי יוֹחָנָן, אָמַר הַקָּדוֹשׁ בָּרוּךְ הוּא, אִם נִכְנָס נֹחַ לַתֵּבָה בַּלַּיְלָה, עַכְשָׁו יִהְיוּ כָּל דּוֹרוֹ אוֹמְרִים, כָּךְ, לֹא הָיִינוּ יוֹדְעִים בּוֹ, וְאִלּוּ הָיִינוּ יוֹדְעִים בּוֹ לֹא הָיִינוּ מַנִּיחִין אוֹתוֹ לְכָנֵס, אֶלָּא, 'בְּעֶצֶם הַיּוֹם הַזֶּה בָּא נֹחַ' דִּרְגִּישׁ לֵהּ יְמַלֵּל.

8. IN THE SELFSAME DAY ENTERED NOAH (7:13). R. JOHANAN SAID: HAD NOAH ENTERED THE ARK AT NIGHT HIS WHOLE GENERATION WOULD HAVE SAID, 'WE DID NOT KNOW WHAT HE WAS DOING, BUT HAD WE KNOWN WE WOULD NOT HAVE PERMITTED HIM TO ENTER.' HENCE HE ENTERED IN THE SELFSAME DAY [WITH THE CHALLENGE], 'LET HIM WHO OBJECTS SPEAK OUT!'

The *Midrash* points to the fact that Noah entered the ark in mid-day for a special reason. The people of his generation were very suspicious in the work of building the ark. They did not understand its purpose, and when they were told about an impending Flood, they did not believe it. Had Noah entered the ark secretly at night, it would have confirmed their feelings that a great conspiracy was brewing and they might have tried to break the ark. By entering in mid-day, however, they saw that it was the same person and family who built the ark, who are now entering it and that seemed acceptable.

(יד-טז) 'הֵמָּה וְכָל הַחַיָּה', 'הֵמָּה' עִקָּר, וְהַכֹּל טְפֵלָה לָהֶם.

THEY, AND EVERY BEAST AFTER ITS KIND, ETC. (7:14). THEY WERE THE PRINCIPALS AND ALL OTHERS WERE SECONDARY.

The point is made again and again that the principle characters in the world were human beings. While everything in the ark was geared to the accommodation and preservation of the animal world, it was done only to serve man. Man is the goal of creation and everything else is secondary to him.

'כֹּל צִפּוֹר כָּל כָּנָף', אָמַר רַבִּי אֶלְעָזָר בְּשֵׁם רַבִּי אַסִי, לְחַבְרָיָה, פְּרָט לְמוֹרַטַיָּא, וּלְקַטְעַיָּא, שֶׁהֵם פְּסוּלִין, לְקָרְבְּנוֹת בְּנֵי נֹחַ.

EVERY BIRD OF EVERY WING. R. ELEAZAR SAID: R. JOSE INTERPRETED
THIS TO HIS COLLEAGUES: THIS EXCLUDES THOSE WHICH WERE MOULT-
ING OR MAIMED AS UNFIT FOR THE SACRIFICES OF THE NOACHIDES.

The term "bird" is used twice in this verse, as is the word כל – *kol*,
which means of "everything" or "every part" of the bird world. Birds that
were maimed, or crippled in whatever form, were excluded from the
ark, since they were unacceptable as sacrifices in the sanctuary.

'וְהַבָּאִים, זָכָר וּנְקֵבָה' אָמַר רַבִּי אַסִּי, פְּרָט לִסְרוּחִין, וְלִמְחֻסְּרֵי אֵבָרִים, שֶׁפְּסוּלִים לְקָרְבָּן בְּנֵי
נֹחַ. וְהַבָּאִים זָכָר וּנְקֵבָה', אָמַר לֵהּ נֹחַ, וְכִי קֵינִיגִי אֲנָא, אָמַר לֵהּ מָה אִכְפַּת לָךְ, מוּבָאִים אֵין
כְּתִיב, אֶלָּא 'הַבָּאִים' מֵאֵלֵיהֶן הָיוּ בָאִים, רַבִּי יוֹחָנָן אָמַר, (ישעיה לד, טז) 'דִּרְשׁוּ מֵעַל סֵפֶר ה'
וּקְרָאוּ', וּמַה אִם לְהִסָּגֵר בַּתֵּבָה שְׁנֵים עָשָׂר חֹדֶשׁ, הָיוּ בָאִים מֵאֵלֵיהֶן, לְהִפָּטֵם מִבְּשַׂר גִּבּוֹרִים
עַל אַחַת כַּמָּה וְכַמָּה, הֲדָא הוּא דִכְתִיב, (יחזקאל לט, יז-יח) 'בֶּן אָדָם, כֹּה אָמַר ה' אֱלֹהִים, אֱמֹר
לְצִפּוֹר כָּל כָּנָף, וּלְכֹל חַיַּת הַשָּׂדֶה, הִקָּבְצוּ וָבֹאוּ, הֵאָסְפוּ מִסָּבִיב עַל זִבְחִי אֲשֶׁר אֲנִי זֹבֵחַ לָכֶם,
זֶבַח גָּדוֹל עַל הָרֵי יִשְׂרָאֵל, וַאֲכַלְתֶּם בָּשָׂר וּשְׁתִיתֶם דָּם, בְּשַׂר גִּבּוֹרִים תֹּאכֵלוּ, וְדַם נְשִׂיאֵי הָאָרֶץ
תִּשְׁתּוּ, אֵילִים כָּרִים וְעַתּוּדִים, פָּרִים מְרִיאֵי בָשָׁן כֻּלָּם'.

AND THEY THAT WENT IN, WENT IN MALE AND FEMALE OF ALL FLESH
(7:16). SAID HE TO HIM: 'AM I A HUNTER!' 'DOES THAT MATTER TO YOU,'
HE RETORTED; IT IS NOT WRITTEN, 'AND THEY THAT WERE BROUGHT,'
BUT, AND THEY THAT WENT IN – OF THEIR OWN ACCORD. R. JOHANAN
QUOTED: SEEK YE OUT OF THE BOOK OF THE LORD, AND READ (ISA.
34:16): IF THEY CAME OF THEIR OWN ACCORD IN ORDER TO BE SHUT
UP TWELVE MONTHS IN THE ARK, HOW MUCH THE MORE [WILL THEY
COME] TO GORGE ON THE FLESH OF TYRANTS! HENCE IT IS WRITTEN,
AND THOU, SON OF MAN, THUS SAITH THE LORD GOD: SPEAK UNTO THE
BIRDS OF EVERY SORT, AND TO EVERY BEAST OF THE FIELD: ASSEMBLE
YOURSELVES, AND COME; GATHER YOURSELVES ON EVERY SIDE TO MY
FEAST THAT I DO PREPARE FOR YOU, EVEN A GREAT FEAST, UPON THE
MOUNTAINS OF ISRAEL, THAT YE MAY EAT FLESH AND DRINK BLOOD.
THE FLESH OF THE MIGHTY SHALL YE EAT, AND THE BLOOD OF THE
PRINCES OF THE EARTH SHALL YE DRINK, ETC. (EZEK. 39:17).

There is an expression in the biblical verses to the effect that Noah was
called upon to bring animals or to take animals, and it seemed as though
he was personally expected to gather them from all parts of the world.
Noah protested that he was not a hunter and not capable of gathering
these animals. He was then told that this role was not expected of him,
since the animals would come of their own accord, or rather, because
God motivated them to come. That is why it uses the expression, הבאים
– *habayim*, which means those who are in the process of coming. The

interpretation is that they would come of their own accord. The *Midrash*
brings a quote from the prophet Ezekiel that something similar will happen in the terrible apocalyptical war between Gog and Magog, where
the fate of Israel will ultimately be settled and redeemed. Ezekiel called
for the birds of the world to come together on the mountains of Israel
and to feed on the defeated armies of Gog. If the birds were able to come
of their own accord in the days of the ark, how much more so will they
agree to come in the end of days, when they will be promised such a
feast and such a celebration.

'וַיִּסְגֹּר ה' בַּעֲדוֹ', אָמַר רַבִּי לֵוִי. לְשֶׁר שֶׁקָּבַע דְּרוֹלוֹמוֹסְיָא שֶׁלּוֹ בַּמְּדִינָה, וְנָטַל אוֹהֲבוֹ וַחֲבָשׁוֹ
בְּבֵית הָאֲסוּרִין, נָתַן סְפַּרְגּוֹס שֶׁלּוֹ עָלָיו, כָּךְ, 'וַיִּסְגֹּר ה' בַּעֲדוֹ'. בִּקְשׁוּ לַהֲפֹךְ הַתֵּבָה, וְהִקִּיפָהּ
אֲרָיוֹת, שֶׁלֹּא יִגְּעוּ בוֹ.

AND THE LORD SHUT HIM IN. R. LEVI SAID: THIS MAY BE COMPARED TO A
KING WHO DECREED A GENERAL EXECUTION IN A COUNTRY, BUT TOOK
HIS FRIEND, IMMURED HIM IN PRISON, AND SET HIS SEAL UPON HIM.
EVEN SO, AND THE LORD SHUT HIM IN.

The problem that the *Midrash* noticed is that instead of using the
phrase that God arranged for Noah to enter the ark, it used the expression that He "shut him in" to the ark. What does this mean? The
answer comes in the form of this parable, brought by R. Levi: There
was a king who was experiencing an insurrection and a civil war. He
was afraid that his beloved friend might suffer a terrible fate because of
these circumstances, so he safeguarded him by locking him in one of his
prisons. Was that the only way out? Could he not have used his private
army to protect his friend? Apparently, the rebels were savage and cruel
and would have killed the beloved friend in any way they could, merely
because of his relationship to the king. The king understood that and
placed him where he could not be reached, namely, in his prison, where
he was looked after very well.

The meaning behind the parable is that the beloved friend was Noah.
God was afraid that when the people of his generation understood that
a real Flood was coming to the world, they would do everything to
break the ark and attack Noah, merely because of his relationship to the
King. God shut Noah in the ark so that he could not go out, all for his
own protection. Furthermore, lions were placed on guard to prevent the
rebels from attacking and breaking the ark.

Seed Thoughts I

Angels are a phenomenon that we read about all throughout rabbinic literature. It is difficult to know who they are or what they are. Are they real? Are they people? Are they disembodied beings? In a short phrase in this *midrash,* they are described as spirits. A spirit is an inclination or an idea that grips a person or an idea that influences a person's life. The verse that is quoted is from Psalms (104:4), עושה מלאכיו רוחות – *oseh malakhav ruchot,* He makes of his angels spirits. The *Midrash HaMevo'ar* quotes the *Pirkei D'Rabbi Eliezer* in response to the question of how did the animals come of their own decision? The answer is that God sent His angels. They are interpreted as "spirits" and these spirits are the inclinations that entered the animal world and motivated them to enter the ark.

—

Seed Thoughts II

Why did God have to shut Noah into the ark so that he would not leave? The answer is that although Noah was a good man, he was a little too good in the sense of being naive as well. He did not realize the power of the insurrectionists and rebels who were opposing the ark and its meaning. He felt that even his generation was basically good and felt that when they saw the waters rising, they would eventually repent. God knew that they would not repent, so He took his beloved one, Noah, and shut him in the ark for his own protection. When we remember the various ways in which previous *midrashim* had criticized Noah, it is quite remarkable to note that he has now reached the stage where he is the beloved one of God, the one who must be protected for the sake of the future of the world.

—

Additional Commentary

Why Noah was shut in

Why could Scripture not say that he "entered" the ark instead of having said that he was "shut in"? Furthermore, the parable that is used to answer this question seems to be not only too complicated, but unrealistic. If a king wishes to protect his friend, why would he put him in jail? Could he not have been protected by his elite bodyguards? The answer is that the king knew that the rebellion was fierce and savage. He was afraid that the elite guards could not sufficiently handle the problem and that the rebels would still try ferociously to kill the friend as a way of harassing the king. Only the prison was safe, and of course, the king would ensure that his friend would certainly not be treated as a prisoner.

The application of this parable, the נמשל – *nimshal*, is that the "king" is God and the beloved friend is Noah. When the people began to realize that a Flood was coming to destroy them, their ruthlessness would be savage and brutal. They would do anything to destroy the ark and Noah, reacting irrationally, as if this would eliminate the Flood. God realized that His beloved Noah was too good a person to comprehend what was happening. His love for his neighbors and friends motivated him to feel that they would repent and change. God realized that this would not happen and therefore, He shut Noah and his family into the ark so that they would not leave until the Flood was over. (*Tiferet Tzion*)

Parashah Thirty-Two, *Midrash Nine*

ט. (יז) 'וַיְהִי הַמַּבּוּל אַרְבָּעִים יוֹם עַל הָאָרֶץ', רַבִּי פִּינְחָס בְּשֵׁם רַבִּי לֵוִי, אָמַר, כָּךְ הָיְתָה תֵּבָתוֹ שֶׁל נֹחַ מְשֻׁקַּעַת בַּמַּיִם, כַּסְּפִינָה הַזּוֹ, שֶׁהִיא מְשֻׁקַּעַת, וְעוֹמֶדֶת בַּלְּמֵין.

9. AND THE WATERS INCREASED, AND BORE UP THE ARK, ETC. (7:17). R. PHINEHAS SAID IN R. LEVI'S NAME: NOAH'S ARK THUS SANK IN THE WATER LIKE A SHIP STANDING IN HARBOR.

The second part of the verse seems to indicate that the ark was lifted up from its lifting place to the top of the waters. That is not so, according to R. Phinehas. The ark rested lightly similar to a ship at anchor in its harbor.

(יח) 'וַיִּגְבְּרוּ הַמַּיִם, וְגוֹ'', אָמַר רַבִּי פִּינְחָס מִשּׁוּם רַבִּי לֵוִי, כָּךְ הָיְתָה תֵּבָתוֹ שֶׁל נֹחַ שָׁטָה עַל פְּנֵי הַמַּיִם כְּעַל שְׁתֵּי קוֹרוֹת, כְּמִן טְבֶרְיָא לְסוּסִתָא.

AND THE WATERS PREVAILED . . . AND THE ARK WENT UPON THE FACE OF THE WATERS (7:18). R. PHINEHAS SAID IN R. LEVI'S NAME: THE ARK THUS FLOATED UPON THE WATER AS UPON TWO PLANKS [COVERING A DISTANCE] AS FROM TIBERIAS TO SUSITHA.

Even though the Flood was stormy, the ark was given the ability to rest leisurely in the waters, protected from the storm. Indeed, its voyage was as comfortable as a ship or boat traveling between the two opposite sides of Lake Kineret, which is known as a body of water that is usually calm.

—

Seed Thoughts

How are we to understand the latest miracle as described in our present *midrash*? It probably means to inform us that just as God was concerned with the punishment of the sinful generation of the Flood, so was He concerned with the welfare of the new world about to be created. This new world was contained within the ark, with its representation of human beings and its representation of the animal world. The miracle consisted of the fact that the ark was protected from the buffeting of waves and the stormy waters. The new world had to be protected, and the inhabitants, both animal and man, had to be shown that God had special interest in their behavior during their present situation and in their future possibilities. It was God's hope that this very special help to them would register, especially in the minds of the human family, who would then do their best to create a world of justice and peace.

Additional Commentary

How the ark traveled

It should not be imagined that the ark floated along the water as an ordinary ship. Because of the Flood, the sea was very stormy. An ordinary ship would have been tossed from side to side, would have been carried along with a strong wave, and would have gone down when the wave would have receded. The ship would have been shaken because of the overpowering strength of the Flood waters. But the method with which the ark voyaged was entirely different. It is as though it traveled on a floor especially prepared for it, as comfortably as traveling along the Kineret, whose waters are always calm. Tiberias is on the west side of the Kineret, and Susitha is on the east side. The distance between them is more or less one half of the length of the Kineret. According to Nachmanides, the Flood was stormy, and some say, even boiling. But everything cooled off as the ark approached. (*HaMidrash HaMevo'ar*)

י. (יט) 'וְהַמַּיִם גָּבְרוּ מְאֹד מְאֹד עַל הָאָרֶץ, וְגוֹ'', רַבִּי יוֹנָתָן, סְלַק לְמִצְלֵי בִּירוּשָׁלַיִם, עֲבַר בְּהָדֵין פְּלָטָאנִים, וַחֲמָתֵי חַד שַׁמְרַיי, אֲמַר לֵהּ, לְהֵיכָן אַתְּ אָזֵל, אֲמַר לֵהּ לְמִסַּק לְמִצְלֵי בִּירוּשָׁלַיִם, אֲמַר לֵהּ, לָא טַב לָךְ לְמִצְלֵי בְּהָדֵין טוּרָא בְּרִיכָא, וְלָא בְּהַהוּא בֵּיתָא קַלְקַלְתָּא, אֲמַר לֵהּ, לְמָה הוּא בְּרִיךְ, אֲמַר לֵהּ, דְּלָא טָף בְּמוֹי דְּמַבּוּלָא, נִתְעַלְּמָה

10. AND THE WATERS PREVAILED . . . AND ALL THE HIGH MOUNTAINS WERE COVERED (7:19). R. JONATHAN WAS GOING UP TO WORSHIP IN JERUSALEM, WHEN HE PASSED THE PALATINUS AND WAS SEEN BY A SA-MARITAN, WHO ASKED HIM, 'WHITHER ARE YOU GOING?' 'TO WORSHIP IN JERUSALEM,' REPLIED HE. 'WOULD IT NOT BE BETTER TO PRAY AT THIS HOLY MOUNTAIN THAN AT THAT DUNGHILL?' HE JEERED. 'WHEREIN IS IT BLESSED?' INQUIRED HE. 'BECAUSE IT WAS NOT SUBMERGED BY THE FLOOD.'

The Samaritans were a people brought into Israel by the Assyrians when they invaded Jerusalem and exiled the Jewish people. It was the practice of emperors to exchange populations in order to prevent revolutions from taking place.

R. Jonathan was approached by a Samaritan and asked where he was going; when he answered that his goal was to reach Jerusalem to pray, the Samaritan asked why he didn't just pray there, at the holy mountain of Gerizim, which is particularly blessed because of the fact that it was not covered by the Flood. The Samaritan could have based his view on the verse by Ezekiel (22:24), which reads, "Son of man, say to her, 'You are the land that is not cleansed, nor rained upon in the day of indignation.'" The Rabbis disagreed with the interpretation of this verse and some maintained that it proved that the waters of the Flood did not cover the mountains in Eretz Israel. This being the case, R. Jonathan did not have a good answer to retort to the Samaritan at that particular moment.

מֵעֵינֵי רַבִּי יוֹנָתָן וְלֹא הֱשִׁיבוֹ לַשָּׁעָה, אֲמַר לֵהּ חַמָּרֵהּ, רַבִּי, תַּרְשֵׁנִי וַאֲנִי מְשִׁיבוֹ אָמַר לֵהּ הֵן, אֲמַר לֵהּ אִן מִן טוּרַיָּא רָמַיָּא הוּא הָא הוּא כְתִיב, 'וַיְכֻסּוּ כָּל הֶהָרִים הַגְּבֹהִים', וְאִן מִן מָכַיָּא הוּא לָא אַשְׁגַּח בֵּהּ קְרָיָא וְלָא אַחְשְׁבֵהּ כְּלוּם

NOW R. JONATHAN MOMENTARILY FORGOT THE TEACHING [ON THE SUBJECT], BUT HIS ASS-DRIVER SAID TO HIM, 'RABBI, WITH YOUR PERMISSION I WILL ANSWER HIM.' 'DO,' SAID HE. 'IF IT IS OF THE HIGH MOUNTAINS,' HE ANSWERED, 'THEN IT IS WRITTEN, AND ALL THE HIGH MOUNTAINS WERE COVERED. WHILE IF IT IS OF THE LOW ONES, SCRIPTURE IGNORED IT.'

At this point, R. Jonathan's donkey driver asked permission to answer the Samaritan. He quoted our present verse in Scripture, which indicated that the ark covered all of the high mountains, and that would certainly include Mount Gerizim. The Samaritan had no response to this argument and R. Jonathan was so impressed that he rewarded the donkey driver by having him sit on the donkey on his own seat of honor and he, himself, led the animal.

מִיָּד יָרַד לוֹ רַבִּי יוֹנָתָן מֵעַל הַחֲמוֹר וְהִרְכִּיבוֹ, שְׁלֹשָׁה מִילִין, וְקָרָא עָלָיו שְׁלֹשָׁה מִקְרָאוֹת, (דברים ז, יד) 'לֹא יִהְיֶה בְךָ עָקָר וַעֲקָרָה וּבִבְהֶמְתֶּךָ', אֲפִלּוּ בְּבֶהֱמוֹת שֶׁבָּכֶם, (שיר ד, ג) 'כְּפֶלַח הָרִמּוֹן רַקָּתֵךְ, מִבַּעַד לְצַמָּתֵךְ' הָרֵיקָין שֶׁבָּכֶם רָצוּף תְּשׁוּבוֹת כָּרִמּוֹן, הָדָא הוּא דִכְתִיב, (ישעיה נד, יז) 'כָּל כְּלִי יוּצַר עָלַיִךְ לֹא יִצְלָח וְכָל לָשׁוֹן תָּקוּם אִתָּךְ לַמִּשְׁפָּט תַּרְשִׁיעִי, זֹאת נַחֲלַת עַבְדֵי ה', וְגוֹ''.

R. JONATHAN IMMEDIATELY DESCENDED FROM HIS ASS AND MADE HIM [THE DRIVER] RIDE THREE MILES AND APPLIED THREE VERSES TO HIM: (I) THERE SHALL NOT BE MALE OR FEMALE BARREN AMONG YOU, OR AMONG YOUR CATTLE (DEUT. 7:14) – I.E., EVEN AMONG YOUR CATTLE DRIVERS; (II) RAKKATHEK [E.V. 'THY TEMPLES'] IS LIKE A POMEGRANATE SPLIT OPEN (S.S. 4:3): EVEN THE EMPTIEST (REKANIM) AMONG YOU ARE AS FULL OF ANSWERS AS A POMEGRANATE [IS OF SEEDS]; AND THUS IT IS WRITTEN, (III) NO WEAPON THAT IS FORMED AGAINST THEE SHALL PROSPER; AND EVERY TONGUE THAT SHALL RISE AGAINST THEE IN JUDGMENT THOU SHALT CONDEMN (ISA. 54:17).

R. Jonathan then offers three verses, each of which is a blessing to the donkey driver. The first verse emphasized a blessing to his animals. The second verse maintains the hope that even the lowest of his colleagues might be blessed with the knowledge of Torah and the ability to do mitzvot. Finally, the last blessing that was offered is that this donkey driver have a good and peaceful future.

Seed Thoughts

R. Jonathan's admiration for his donkey driver's knowledge conforms to the teachings of the Ethics of the Fathers (6:3), "Whoever learns from his friend one chapter, one law, one verse or even one letter, should treat this friend as a teacher with great respect." R. Jonathan's behavior toward his donkey driver is a good example of this teaching. But it means more than what is stated.

Let me tell you a personal anecdote. When I was a rabbinical student, I was sent for a weekend to assist a congregation in Albany, whose Rabbi had been called to the chaplaincy. The first day that I arrived, I was informed that the mother of the president of the congregation had died and that I was expected to conduct the funeral. Although I had studied some of the laws of burial, I had never actual participated in a funeral, and hoped that everything would turn out all right. When I arrived at the funeral home, the funeral director took me aside and said, "I am sure that you have officiated at other funerals, but I want you to know that every community has its own particular customs." He then spent a half hour going over with me every possible detail that would take place at the funeral, so that even an infant would have been able to conduct it. Several years later, I returned to Albany for a conference, and there I met my friend the funeral director. I then said to him, "Dear friend, do you remember when I conducted my first funeral in Albany?" He told me that he remembered it very well. "I now want to tell you," I added, "that until that moment, I had never officiated at any funeral before." The funeral director then laughed very heartily, "Of course I knew that," he replied, "as did every member of my staff. You were so green, so nervous that I spent a half hour with you. Do you think that I do that at every funeral?"

I will never forget this wonderful man. Not only did he help me, he did so with the greatest possible respect, never once hinting that I should not be doing anything for which I was not properly trained. That is the great lesson of the Ethics of the Fathers. Not merely to be grateful to anyone from whom you learn something, but to be especially grateful when it reaches you with respect, tolerance and great understanding.

Additional Commentary

He was unable to answer

R. Jonathan, for that moment, was not able to answer the remark of the Samaritan as to why he did not pray at Mount Gerizim. The reason was that he had learned that the waters had spread from elsewhere to cover even the mountains of Israel, and that therefore, they were not especially holy.

If the view is held that Mount Gerizim is holy because of its height, how would one explain the fact that God seemed to favor lower mountains, such as Sinai? Furthermore, the lower mountains were destroyed by the Flood, and Mount Gerizim was the setting for the blessing of the tribes and was also the place where Jacob buried the idols that he gathered from his contemporaries, but nevertheless, nowhere in the Tanach is there ever a mention that Mount Gerizim is holy. This is what R. Jonathan did not remember at the moment. (*Tiferet Tzion*)

PARASHAH THIRTY-TWO, *Midrash Eleven*

יא. (כ) 'חֲמֵשׁ עֶשְׂרֵה אַמָּה, וְגוֹ'', רַבִּי יְהוּדָה וְרַבִּי נְחֶמְיָה, רַבִּי יְהוּדָה אוֹמֵר, חֲמֵשׁ עֶשְׂרֵה אַמָּה בָּהָר, וַחֲמֵשׁ עֶשְׂרֵה אַמָּה בַּבִּקְעָה, רַבִּי נְחֶמְיָה אָמַר, חֲמֵשׁ עֶשְׂרֵה אַמָּה בָּהָר, אֲבָל בַּבִּקְעָה, כָּל שֶׁהֵן.

11. FIFTEEN CUBITS UPWARD DID THE WATERS PREVAIL (7:20). R. JUDAH SAID: FIFTEEN CUBITS OVER THE MOUNTAINS AND FIFTEEN CUBITS OVER THE PLAINS. R. NEHEMIAH SAID: FIFTEEN CUBITS OVER THE MOUNTAINS, BUT OVER THE PLAINS, ANY HEIGHT.

Even though the height of all the mountains and plains are not similar, R. Judah offers a rough estimate that the water rose fifteen cubits above the mountains. Furthermore, the waters remained there as a result of a miracle. Thus, it was possible for the waters to remain fifteen cubits above the plains and the mountains. R. Nechemiah followed the view that waters cannot remain in this kind of separation, and that while the waters reached fifteen cubits above the mountains, they were at different heights, depending on the topography of the plains.

(כא-כב) 'וַיִּגְוַע כָּל בָּשָׂר הָרֹמֵשׂ וְגוֹ'', כֹּל אֲשֶׁר נִשְׁמַת רוּחַ חַיִּים בְּאַפָּיו, וְגוֹ', רַבִּי שְׁמוּאֵל, חַתְנֵהּ דְּרַבִּי חֲנִינָא, חַבְרְהוֹן דְּרַבָּנָן, אוֹמֵר, כָּאן הוּא עוֹשֶׂה נְשָׁמָה רוּחַ, וּלְהַלָּן הוּא עוֹשֶׂה נְשָׁמָה נֶפֶשׁ, מְנַיִן לִתֵּן אֶת הָאָמוּר כָּאן לְהַלָּן, וְאֶת הָאָמוּר לְהַלָּן כָּאן, תַּלְמוּד לוֹמַר, חַיִּים, חַיִּים, לִגְזֵרָה שָׁוָה.

AND ALL THE FLESH PERISHED . . . ALL IN WHOSE NOSTRILS WAS THE BREATH OF (NISHMATH) THE SPIRIT OF (RUAH) LIFE, ETC. (7:21). R. SAMUEL THE SON-IN-LAW OF R. HANINA THE COLLEAGUE OF THE RABBIS SAID: HERE THE NESHAMAH IS MADE IDENTICAL WITH RUAH, WHEREAS IN AN EARLIER PASSAGE THE NESHAMAH IS IDENTIFIED WITH NEFESH. HOW DO WE KNOW THAT WE SHOULD APPLY THE TEACHING OF EACH PASSAGE TO THE OTHER? BECAUSE 'LIFE' IS WRITTEN IN BOTH PLACES, PROVING THAT THEY ARE ANALOGOUS.

In our *midrash*, the word "life" is associated with the expression נשמת רוח – *nishmat ruach*, meaning the breath of the spirit of life. The word נשמה – *neshamah* is here derived from the word נשימה – *neshimah*, meaning breath. In an earlier midrash (14:9), the word חיים – *chayim*, life, is associated with נפש – *nefesh*, which means "soul." How do we know that both are connected and that both represent the same phenomenon? Because the word *chayim* appears twice, allowing us to learn about it via an analogy גזירה שוה – *gzeirah shavah*.

(כג) 'וַיִּמַח אֶת כָּל הַיְקוּם וַיִּשָּׁאֶר אַךְ נֹחַ', רַבִּי הוּנָא בְּשֵׁם רַבִּי יוֹסֵי, 'אַךְ' מֵעוּט, שֶׁאַף הוּא, הָיָה גוֹנֵחַ, דָּם, מִפְּנֵי הַצִּנָּה.

WHATSOEVER WAS IN THE DRY LAND, DIED. THIS EXCLUDES FISH. BUT SOME MAINTAIN THAT THEY TOO WERE INCLUDED AMONG THOSE WHO WERE TO BE GATHERED INTO [THE ARK], BUT THEY FLED TO THE OCEAN [THE MEDITERRANEAN]. AND HE BLOTTED OUT EVERY LIVING SUBSTANCE . . . AND NOAH ONLY (*AKH*) WAS LEFT (7:23): *AKH* IS A DIMINISHING PARTICLE: HE TOO COUGHED BLOOD ON ACCOUNT OF THE COLD.

There was one exception to the extinction of the animal world due to the Flood, and this exception was the fish. Though water is their natural element, they would have had difficulty in those areas of the Flood where the waters were supposed to have been boiling. This was not so in and around the ark. The fish either gathered in those areas or fled to the ocean (probably to the Mediterranean), where they had a measure of freedom. Since no sin was ascribed to the fish, they had the freedom to escape and save themselves.

The word אַךְ – *akh*, is usually used to diminish a concept. Here, it is applied to Noah, meaning that even *he* suffered during the Flood, with cold and various ailments. They were the sacrifice he needed to redeem his imperfections.

———

Seed Thoughts

The text brings to our attention three important concepts, which are expressed in three words: *nefesh* (body or soul), *ruach* (spirit) and *neshamah* (breath or soul). The reason for the two-fold translation of these words are due to the differences in their meaning in the written Torah and the oral Torah. Rendered in simplified fashion, the written Torah is "this-worldly" in its interpretation of life. It does have reference to the World to Come, but only in indirect fashion. The oral Torah is completely immersed in the concept of the World to Come. The sages of the Talmud lived and breathed the World to Come, mentioned it as frequently as possible and were tremendously comforted by its meaning. However, it is to the credit of the midrashic writers, who were among the most talented interpreters of the oral Torah, that they understood the differences that we have just described. In the oral Torah, the word *neshamah* means a soul and has to do with that aspect of the human person, which is eternal and therefore related to the World to Come. In the written Torah, and especially in the scriptural text quoted in the Midrash, the word *neshamah* comes from the word *neshimah*, which means "breath" and has to do with the breath of life, pertaining not only to human beings, but to the animal kingdom as well. The sages of the Midrash found no difficulty in relating to both the written and the oral Torah, and they were very careful to respect the differences in their interpretations and to learn from them. We should try to do the very same ourselves.

—

Additional Commentary

R. Shmuel's interpretation

R. Shmuel explains that the intent of the verse, "And man became a *nefesh chayah*," was to inform us that even the concept of *nefesh* reaches us through the *neshamah*. R. Shmuel offers as evidence the verse, "כל אשר נשמת רוח חיים – *kol asher nishmat ruach chayim*," asserting that *nefesh* comes from the concept of *neshamah*. This concept can be given two meanings. The first is the *neshamah* that God breathed into man and His creation, which is נצחית – *nitzchit*, eternal. The second interpretation is the breath, which we inhale and exhale all the time, and which applies to the whole animal world, as it is written, "לא תחיה כל נשמה – *lo techayeh kol neshamah*" – do not keep alive whoever breathes. Therefore, the verse we are speaking about can be interpreted as the very same breath that we and every animal breathes. Therefore, R. Shmuel uses the *gzeirah shavah*, to show that the reference in the verse is the second meaning, which is the breath that God put into all of us, and at the same time, the *nefesh* and the *ruach* have their source in the *neshamah*. (*Tiferet Tzion*)

א. (ח, א) 'וַיִּזְכֹּר אֱ-לֹהִים אֶת נֹחַ וְאֵת כָּל הַחַיָּה, וְגוֹ'', וּכְתִיב (תהלים לו, ז) 'צִדְקָתְךָ כְּהַרְרֵי אֵל,
מִשְׁפָּטֶיךָ תְּהוֹם רַבָּה, אָדָם וּבְהֵמָה תוֹשִׁיעַ ה''

1. AND GOD REMEMBERED NOAH, AND EVERY LIVING THING, AND ALL
THE CATTLE, ETC. (8:1). THY RIGHTEOUSNESS IS LIKE THE MOUNTAINS
OF GOD; THY JUDGMENTS ARE LIKE THE GREAT DEEP; MAN AND BEAST
THOU PRESERVEST, O LORD (PS. 36:7).

The question that will ultimately be resolved by the Midrash is why
Noah was associated at this point with the animal world, both domestic
and wild. It would have been enough to say that God had remembered
Noah and the remembrance of him would have included everyone else.

רַבִּי יִשְׁמָעֵאל, וְרַבִּי עֲקִיבָא, רַבִּי יִשְׁמָעֵאל אוֹמֵר, בִּזְכוּת הַצַּדִּיקִים שֶׁקִּבְּלוּ אֶת הַתּוֹרָה, שֶׁנִּתְּנָה
מֵהַרְרֵי אֵל, אַתְּ עוֹשֶׂה עִמָּהֶם צְדָקָה עַד כְּהַרְרֵי אֵל, אֲבָל רְשָׁעִים שֶׁלֹּא קִבְּלוּ אֶת הַתּוֹרָה
שֶׁנִּתְּנָה מֵהַרְרֵי אֵל אַתְּ מְדַקְדֵּק עִמָּהֶם, עַד תְּהוֹם רַבָּה

R. ISHMAEL INTERPRETED: TO THE RIGHTEOUS WHO ACCEPTED THE TO-
RAH WHICH WAS REVEALED ON THE MOUNTAINS OF GOD THOU SHEWEST
RIGHTEOUSNESS [I.E., LOVE] REACHING UNTO THE MOUNTAINS OF GOD;
BUT AS FOR THE WICKED, WHO DID NOT ACCEPT THE TORAH WHICH
WAS REVEALED ON THE MOUNTAINS OF GOD, THOU DEALEST STRICTLY
WITH THEM, EVEN TO THE GREAT DEEP.

R. Ishmael interprets this verse from Psalms as separating the righteous from the wicked. The righteous are like the mountains of God.
They reach upward and upward. The wicked represent the lowest of the
low.

רַבִּי עֲקִיבָא אוֹמֵר, אֵלּוּ וְאֵלּוּ מְדַקְדֵּק עִמָּהֶם עַד תְּהוֹם רַבָּה, מְדַקְדֵּק עִם הַצַּדִּיקִים, וְגוֹבֶה מֵהֶם
מִעוּט מַעֲשִׂים רָעִים שֶׁעָשׂוּ בָּעוֹלָם הַזֶּה, כְּדֵי לְהַשְׁפִּיעַ לָהֶם שַׁלְוָה, וְלִתֵּן לָהֶם שָׂכָר טוֹב לָעוֹלָם
הַבָּא, מַשְׁפִּיעַ שַׁלְוָה לָרְשָׁעִים וְנוֹתֵן לָהֶם שָׂכַר מִצְווֹת קַלּוֹת שֶׁעָשׂוּ בָּעוֹלָם הַזֶּה, כְּדֵי לְהִפָּרַע
מֵהֶן לֶעָתִיד לָבוֹא

R. AKIBA SAID: HE DEALS STRICTLY WITH BOTH, EVEN TO THE GREAT
DEEP. HE DEALS STRICTLY WITH THE RIGHTEOUS, CALLING THEM TO
ACCOUNT FOR THE FEW WRONGS WHICH THEY COMMIT IN THIS WORLD,
IN ORDER TO LAVISH BLISS UPON THEM AND GIVE THEM A GOODLY
REWARD IN THE WORLD TO COME; HE GRANTS EASE TO THE WICKED
AND REWARDS THEM FOR THE FEW GOOD DEEDS WHICH THEY HAVE
PERFORMED IN THIS WORLD IN ORDER TO PUNISH THEM IN THE FUTURE
WORLD.

R. Akiva's views are quite different. This verse discusses both the
righteous and the wicked. The righteous are punished for whatever
misdeeds they have created in this world, no matter how small those
sins might be. Their reward for their good deeds is scheduled for the
World to Come and they will be eternal. The wicked are given a reward
even for those minor commandments they may have observed. This
reward takes place in this world. But as for the World to Come, they
would receive nothing but punishment, which is the interpretation here
of תהום – *tehom*, "great deep."

אָמַר רַבִּי לֵוִי, מָשָׁל אֶת הַצַּדִּיקִים בְּדִירָתָן, וְאֶת הָרְשָׁעִים בְּדִירָתָן, אֶת הַצַּדִּיקִים בְּדִירָתָן,
שֶׁנֶּאֱמַר (יחזקאל לד, יד) 'בְּמִרְעֶה טוֹב אֶרְעֶה אוֹתָם, וּבְהָרֵי מְרוֹם יִשְׂרָאֵל יִהְיֶה נְוֵהֶם', וְאֶת
הָרְשָׁעִים בְּדִירָתָן, (שם לא, טו) 'כֹּה אָמַר ה' אֱ-לֹהִים, בְּיוֹם רִדְתּוֹ שְׁאוֹלָה הֶאֱבַלְתִּי, כִּסֵּיתִי עָלָיו
אֶת הַתְּהוֹם

R. LEVI SAID: IT [SCRIPTURE] GIVES A SIMILE FOR THE RIGHTEOUS IN
THEIR DWELLING, AND FOR THE WICKED IN THEIR DWELLING. THE
RIGHTEOUS IN THEIR DWELLING: I WILL FEED THEM IN A GOOD PAS-
TURE, AND UPON THE HIGH MOUNTAINS OF ISRAEL SHALL THEIR FOLD
BE (EZEK. 34:14) – THE WICKED IN THEIR DWELLING: IN THE DAY WHEN
HE WENT DOWN TO THE NETHERWORLD I CAUSED THE DEEP TO MOURN
AND COVER ITSELF FOR HIM (IBID., 31:15).

R. Levi interprets this verse as referring to the ultimate destiny of both
the righteous and the wicked. The ultimate destiny of the righteous will
be to return to the land of Israel in the World to Come and experience
the joy of the mountains of Israel, which are such a great blessing to the
life of the people. The destiny of the wicked is also in the World to Come,
but their environment will be the worst of the worst, the ultimate depth
of darkness and hell (*Gehinnom*). He adds that the terrible location
for the wicked will always be a source of mourning for the world, for it
demonstrates the failure of the wicked to live up to the goal of creation.

רַבִּי יְהוּדָה בַּר רַבִּי אָמַר, הוֹבַלְתִּי כְתִיב, אֵין עוֹשִׂין כִּסוּי לַגִּיגִית, לֹא שֶׁל כֶּסֶף, וְלֹא שֶׁל זָהָב, וְלֹא שֶׁל נְחֹשֶׁת, אֶלָּא חֶרֶס, לְאוֹתָם שֶׁהֵם מִמִּינָה, כָּךְ, רְשָׁעִים חֹשֶׁךְ, גֵּיהִנָּם חֹשֶׁךְ, תְּהוֹם חֹשֶׁךְ, הוֹבַלְתִּי רְשָׁעִים לְגֵיהִנָּם וְכִסִּיתִי עֲלֵיהֶם אֶת הַתְּהוֹם, חֹשֶׁךְ יְכַסֶּה חֹשֶׁךְ

R. JUDAH SAID: HOBALTI (I BROUGHT) IS WRITTEN: A LID FOR A VAT IS
MADE NOT OF GOLD OR SILVER BUT OF EARTHENWARE, WHICH IS THE
SELFSAME MATERIAL. THUS THE WICKED ARE DARKNESS, GEHENNA
IS DARKNESS, AND THE DEEP IS DARKNESS: HENCE I BROUGHT THE
WICKED TO GEHENNA AND COVERED THEM WITH THE DEEP: LET DARK-
NESS COVER DARKNESS.

What has happened at this point is a change in the word האבלתי –
he'evalti, in which the א – *aleph*, is replaced with a ו – *vav*, and therefore
it becomes הובלתי – *hovalti*. One may question the authority of the
Midrash to change the letters of a Torah word. This is a good subject for
another discussion. For the moment, it should merely be stated that the
Midrash does this very often. It is as though it has a sort of poetic license
to render a thought more meaningful at the result of these editorial
changes. In our present Midrash, it means that the use of the term "great
deep" is meant to indicate that this is the place to which the evildoers
will be brought as they face their serious punishment.

רַבִּי יוֹנָתָן בְּשֵׁם רַבִּי יֹאשִׁיָּה, מְסָרֵס קְרָא, צִדְקָתְךָ עַד מִשְׁפָּטֶיךָ, כְּהַרְרֵי אֵל עַד תְּהוֹם רַבָּה, מַה הָרִים הַלָּלוּ אֵין לָהֶם סוֹף, אַף הַצַּדִּיקִים אֵין לָהֶם סוֹף לְמַתַּן שְׂכָרָן, מַה הָרִים הַלָּלוּ, נִכְבָּשִׁים לַתְּהוֹם שֶׁלֹּא יַעֲלֶה וְיָצִיף אֶת הָעוֹלָם, כָּךְ הֵם הַצַּדִּיקִים נִכְבָּשִׁים עַל הַפֻּרְעָנוּת, שֶׁלֹּא יֵצְאוּ וְיִשְׂרְפוּ אֶת הָעוֹלָם, וּמַה הָרִים הַלָּלוּ נִזְרָעִים, וְעוֹשִׂים פֵּרוֹת כָּךְ מַעֲשֵׂיהֶם שֶׁל צַדִּיקִים עוֹשִׂים פֵּרוֹת. הֲדָא הוּא דִכְתִיב, (ישעיה ג, י) 'אִמְרוּ צַדִּיק כִּי טוֹב, וְגו'', וּמַה תְּהוֹם זֶה, אֵין לוֹ חֵקֶר כָּךְ אֵין לְפֻרְעָנוּתָן שֶׁל רְשָׁעִים חֵקֶר, הֲדָא הוּא דִכְתִיב, (שם שם, יא) 'אוֹי לְרָשָׁע רָע'', וּמַה הַתְּהוֹם הַזֶּה לֹא נִזְרָע וְלֹא עוֹשֶׂה פֵרוֹת, כָּךְ אֵין מַעֲשֵׂיהֶן שֶׁל רְשָׁעִים עוֹשִׂים פֵּרוֹת, שֶׁאִלּוּ הָיוּ עוֹשִׂין פֵּרוֹת הָיוּ מַחֲרִיבִין אֶת הָעוֹלָם

R. JONATHAN IN R. JOSIAH'S NAME TRANSPOSED THE VERSE; THY RIGH-
TEOUSNESS [I.E., MERCY] IS ABOVE THY JUDGMENTS, JUST AS THE MOUN-
TAINS OF GOD ARE ABOVE THE GREAT DEEP: AS THE MOUNTAINS ARE
ENDLESS, SO ARE THE RIGHTEOUS ENDLESS ; AND AS THE MOUNTAINS
PRESS BACK THE DEEP SO THAT IT SHOULD NOT ASCEND AND INUNDATE
THE WORLD, SO DO THE RIGHTEOUS PRESS BACK PUNISHMENT, LEST
IT GO FORTH AND BURN UP THE WORLD; AND AS THE MOUNTAINS ARE
SOWN AND YIELD FRUIT, SO DO THE DEEDS OF THE RIGHTEOUS YIELD
FRUIT; AND AS THE DEEP IS UNFATHOMABLE, SO IS THE PUNISHMENT
OF THE WICKED UNFATHOMABLE [I.E., IMMEASURABLE]. AND AS THE
DEEP CANNOT BE SOWN TO YIELD FRUIT, SO THE DEEDS OF THE WICKED

DO NOT PRODUCE FRUIT, FOR IF THEY PRODUCED FRUIT THEY WOULD
DESTROY THE WORLD.

R. Jonathan interprets this verse from Psalms as a panegyric (an elabo-
rate praise) of righteousness. The greatest achievement of the good life
is morality and ethics. That is why it is compared to the mountains,
which go upward and upward. As you look at them with the naked eye,
they appear endless. Even the punishment of the wicked is a tribute
to morality and ethics. It takes more than reason to achieve the good
life. It entails the involvement of the entire body, soul and personality
of a human being. That is why the Midrash says that an analysis of the
meaning of righteousness is beyond our capacity and an analysis of why
people become wicked is also beyond human comprehension. We are
fortunate that the Torah offers us a way to go that can lead us to the
good life, with or without the ability to philosophize about it.

רַבִּי יְהוֹשֻׁעַ בֶּן לֵוִי סְלִיק לְרוֹמִי, חֲמָא תַמָּן, עַמּוּדִים מְכֻסִּים בְּטַפִּיסִין, בַּצִּנָּה, שֶׁלֹּא יִקְרְשׁוּ,
וּבַשָּׁרָב, שֶׁלֹּא יִתְבַּקְּעוּ, וְכִי הֲוָה מְהַלֵּךְ בְּשׁוּקָא חֲמָא חַד מִסְכֵּן מְכָרִיךְ בַּחֲדָא מַחְצְלָא, וְאִית
דְּאָמְרִין, פַּלְגָא מַרְדַּעַת דַּחֲמָרָא, עַל אוֹתָן הָעַמּוּדִים קָרָא, 'צִדְקָתְךָ כְּהַרְרֵי אֵל', הָן דִּיהַבְתְּ
אַשְׁפַּע, עַל אוֹתוֹ הֶעָנִי קָרָא, 'מִשְׁפָּטֶיךָ תְּהוֹם רַבָּה', הָן דִּמְחֵית גַּיִּת

WHEN R. JOSHUA B. LEVI VISITED ROME HE SAW THERE PILLARS COVERED
WITH TAPESTRY, IN WINTER SO THAT THEY SHOULD NOT CONTRACT,
AND IN SUMMER THAT THEY SHOULD NOT SPLIT. AS HE WAS WALKING
IN THE STREET, HE ESPIED A POOR MAN WRAPPED IN A MAT – OTHERS
SAY, IN HALF AN ASS'S PACK-SADDLE. TO THOSE PILLARS HE APPLIED
THE VERSE, 'THY RIGHTEOUSNESS IS LIKE THE MIGHTY MOUNTAINS'
– WHERE THOU GIVEST, THOU GIVEST IN ABUNDANCE; WHILE TO THE
POOR MAN HE APPLIED THE VERSE, 'THY JUDGMENTS ARE LIKE THE
GREAT DEEP' – WHERE THOU SMITEST, THOU SMITEST WITH FORCE.

This should not be looked upon as an attack against Rome. Rather, as
the behavior of all people, who put their materialistic concerns above
their spiritual responsibilities. In this particular story, preserving the
marble pillars was more important to the political authorities than saving the life of a starving person. This is not the Torah way and this is
something we should always remember.

אֲלֶכְּסַנְדְּרוֹס־מָקְדּוֹן, אֲזַל לְגַבֵּי מַלְכָּא קַצְיָא, לַאֲחוֹרֵי הָרֵי חֹשֶׁךְ, וּשְׁלַח לֵהּ, נְפַק לֵהּ וְהוּא טָעֵן
גִּידוּמֵי דִּדְהַב בְּגוֹ דִּסְקוּס דִּדְהַב, אֲמַר לֵהּ לְמָמוֹנָךְ אֲנָא צְרִיךְ, אֲמַר לֵהּ וְלָא הֲוָה לָךְ מַה מֵּיכוֹל
בְּאַרְעָךְ דַּאֲתֵית לָךְ לְהָדֵין, אֲמַר לֵהּ לָא אֲתֵית אֶלָּא בְּעֵיָא לְמֵידַע הֵיךְ אַתּוּן דָּיְנִין, יָתִיב גַּבֵּהּ,

יוֹמָא חֲדָא אֲתָא חַד בַּר נָשׁ קָבֵל עַל חַבְרֵהּ, אֲמַר, הָדֵין גַּבְרָא זַבַּן לִי חֲדָא קִילְקַלְתָּא וְאַשְׁכָּחִית
בְּגַוָּהּ סִימָתָא, הַהוּא דְזָבִין אֲמַר, קִילְקַלְתָּא זְבִינִת, סִימָתָא לָא זְבִינִית, וְהַהוּא דְזַבֵּן אֲמַר,
קִילְקַלְתָּא וּמַה דִּבְגַוָּהּ זַבִּינִית, אֲמַר לְחַד מִנֵּיהוּ, אִית לָךְ בַּר דְּכַר, אֲמַר לֵהּ הֵן, וַאֲמַר לְאוֹחֲרָנִי,
אִית לָךְ בְּרַתָּא נְקֵבָא, אֲמַר לֵהּ הֵן, אֲמַר לְהוֹן, זִיל אַסֵּיב דֵּין לְדֵין וְהַוֵי מָמוֹנָא לְתַרְוֵיהוֹן, חֲמָתֵהּ
יָתֵב תָּמַהּ, אֲמַר לֵהּ, מַה, לָא דַּיָּינִית טָב, אֲמַר לֵהּ הֵן, אֲמַר לֵהּ אִלּוּ הָיָה גַבְּכוֹן, הֵיךְ הֲוֵיתוּן דַּיְנִין,
אֲמַר לֵהּ קָטְלִין דֵּין וְדֵין, וּמַלְכוּתָא נָסְבָא מָמוֹנָא דְתַרְוֵיהוֹן, אֲמַר לֵהּ, אִית גַּבְּכוֹן מְטַר נָחֵת,
אֲמַר לֵהּ הֵן, אֲמַר לֵהּ אִית גַּבְּכוֹן שִׁמְשָׁא דָנַח, אֲמַר לֵהּ הֵן, אֲמַר לֵהּ אִית גַּבְּכוֹן בְּעִיר דַּקִיק,
אֲמַר לֵהּ הֵן, אֲמַר לֵהּ תִּפַּח רוּחֵהּ דְּהַהוּא גַּבְרָא, לָא בִּזְכוּתְכוֹן נָחֵת מְטַר, וְלָא בִּזְכוּתְכוֹן שִׁמְשָׁא
דָנְחָה עֲלֵיכוֹן, אֶלָּא בִּזְכוּתֵהּ דִּבְעִירָא, דִּכְתִיב, 'אָדָם וּבְהֵמָה תּוֹשִׁיעַ ה'', אָדָם, בִּזְכוּת בְּהֵמָה,
תּוֹשִׁיעַ ה'.

ALEXANDER OF MACEDON VISITED KING KAZIA BEYOND THE DARK
MOUNTAINS. HE CAME FORTH, OFFERING HIM GOLDEN BREAD ON A
GOLDEN TRAY. 'DO I THEN NEED YOUR GOLD?' HE DEMANDED. 'HAD YOU
THEN NOTHING TO EAT IN YOUR OWN COUNTRY THAT YOU HAVE COME
HERE?' HE RETORTED. 'I CAME ONLY BECAUSE I WISHED TO SEE HOW YOU
DISPENSE JUSTICE,' WAS THE REPLY. AS HE SAT WITH HIM A MAN CAME
WITH A COMPLAINT AGAINST HIS NEIGHBOR. 'THIS MAN,' HE STATED,
'SOLD ME A DUNGHILL AND I FOUND A TREASURE IN IT.' THE BUYER AR-
GUED, 'I BOUGHT A DUNGHILL ONLY,' WHILE THE VENDOR MAINTAINED,
'I SOLD THE DUNGHILL AND ALL IT CONTAINED.' SAID HE [THE KING] TO
ONE: 'HAVE YOU A SON?' 'YES,' REPLIED HE. 'AND HAVE YOU A DAUGH-
TER?' HE ASKED THE OTHER, 'YES,' WAS THE ANSWER. 'THEN MARRY
THEM AND LET THE TREASURE BELONG TO BOTH.' HE NOTICED HIM [AL-
EXANDER] SITTING ASTONISHED, AND ASKED HIM, 'HAVE I THEN NOT
JUDGED WELL?' 'YES,' HE REPLIED. 'HAD THIS HAPPENED AMONG YOU,
HOW WOULD YOU HAVE JUDGED?' 'I WOULD HAVE SLAIN BOTH AND KEPT
THE TREASURE FOR MYSELF.' 'DOES RAIN DESCEND IN YOUR COUNTRY?'
HE ASKED. 'YES.' 'DOES THE SUN SHINE?' 'YES.' 'HAVE YOU SMALL CATTLE
[SHEEP AND GOATS]?' 'YES,' HE REPLIED. 'BY HEAVEN!' HE EXCLAIMED,
'IT IS NOT FOR YOUR SAKE BUT FOR THE SAKE OF THE CATTLE, AS IT IS
WRITTEN, MAN AND BEAST THOU PRESERVEST, O LORD: MAN FOR THE
SAKE OF BEAST THOU PRESERVEST, O LORD.'

This beautiful story is found in many other sections of the midrashic
literature. In the present text, it seems to have taken place in Carthage.
(According to Aryeh Mirkin, King Kazia is actually Carthage.) In other
parts of the Midrash, the location is somewhere in Israel. Where it takes
place is not of the greatest importance. What is important is that in the
minds and hearts of the Talmudic sages, the behavior of the participants
of this story represents the highest level of personal and business ethics.

רַבִּי יְהוּדָה בַּר סִימוֹן פָּתַר קְרָיָה בְנֹחַ, אָמַר הַקָּדוֹשׁ בָּרוּךְ הוּא, צְדָקָה שֶׁעָשִׂיתִי עִם נֹחַ בַּתֵּבָה
לֹא עָשִׂיתִי עִמּוֹ, אֶלָּא עִם 'הַרְרֵי אֵל', שֶׁנֶּאֱמַר (בראשית ח, ד) 'וַתָּנַח הַתֵּבָה בַּחֹדֶשׁ הַשְּׁבִיעִי, וְגוֹ'',
'מִשְׁפָּטֶיךָ תְּהוֹם רַבָּה', יִסּוּרִין שֶׁהֵבֵאתִי עַל דּוֹרוֹ לֹא הֵבֵאתִי עֲלֵיהֶן אֶלָּא מִתְּהוֹם רַבָּה, שֶׁנֶּאֱמַר
(שם ז, יא) 'נִבְקְעוּ, וְגוֹ'', וּכְשֶׁזְכַרְתִּי לוֹ, לֹא לוֹ לְבַדּוֹ הִזְכַּרְתִּי, אֶלָּא לוֹ וּלְכָל שֶׁיֵּשׁ עִמּוֹ בַּתֵּבָה, הֲדָא
הוּא דִכְתִיב, 'וַיִּזְכֹּר אֱ-לֹהִים אֶת נֹחַ, וְאֵת כָּל הַחַיָּה, וְגוֹ''.

R. JUDAH B. R. SIMON REFERRED THE VERSE TO NOAH. THE HOLY ONE,
BLESSED BE HE, SAID: 'THE RIGHTEOUSNESS [MERCY] WHICH I SHOWED
TO NOAH IN THE ARK I SHOWED HIM NOWHERE SAVE ON THE MIGHTY
MOUNTAINS': AS IT IS WRITTEN, AND THE ARK RESTED IN THE SEVENTH
MONTH, ON THE SEVENTEENTH DAY OF THE MONTH, UPON THE MOUN-
TAINS OF ARARAT (GEN. 8:8). 'THY JUDGMENTS ARE LIKE THE GREAT
DEEP': THE CHASTISEMENT WHICH I BROUGHT ON HIS GENERATION,
I BROUGHT FROM NOWHERE ELSE THAN THE GREAT DEEP, AS IT IS
WRITTEN, ON THE SAME DAY WERE ALL THE FOUNTAINS OF THE GREAT
DEEP BROKEN UP (IBID., 7:11). AND WHEN I REMEMBERED HIM, NOT HIM
ALONE DID I REMEMBER, BUT HIM AND ALL THAT WERE WITH HIM IN
THE ARK, AS IT IS WRITTEN, AND GOD REMEMBERED NOAH, AND EVERY
LIVING THING, ETC.

What the verse, relating the entire discussion to Noah, is trying to
achieve, is to show that the ark came to its conclusion by means of natural laws and not as a result of a miracle. The second half of the verse from
Psalms, which discusses the great deep, indicates the source from which
the Flood waters arose. The verse even tells us that the waters came from
the "great deep." The first half of the verse, however, implies that it was
God's justice that the ark should alight on a mountain. In Noah's case,
the mountain of Ararat. This meant the ark was freed from the turbulent
waters at a very early stage because of the height of the mountain. Had
the ark alighted on a lower plain, it might have been destroyed due to
the stones and other items that may have accumulated in the Flood
waters. It was God's judgment, therefore, that Noah and his ark should
alight on a mountain and this is what is meant when it said that God
remembered Noah and the animal world that was with him. At the very
end of the Flood, he saw to it that the ark would alight on the mountain
and this would protect Noah and all of His animal kingdom. This is the
meaning of the verse as it applied to Noah, 'Thy righteousness are as the
mountains of the Lord and Thy laws are like the very great deep.'

Seed Thoughts I

Our Midrash consists of a number of interpretations of Psalms, "Thy righteousness is like the mountains of the Lord and Thy judgments are like the great deep"' – To these interpretations, I shall like to add one that is very personal to me and would be easily understood by the reader.

In the same week that my youngest child was born, my dear mother died. There was a difference of two or three days between these events. While these contrasting emotional events were taking place, I received a note from a rabbinical colleague, which I have since treasured as the most meaningful note I have ever received. All he wrote in the note was the beautiful verse that we had been discussing: צדקתך כהררי אל משפטיך תהום רבה – *tzidkat'kha keharerei Kel mishpatekha tehom rabbah.* It did not require an explanation.

I knew exactly what he meant. The birth of my daughter represented the highest moments of God's blessing, symbolized by the mountains of the Lord, which reach upward and upward. Whereas, the death of my mother represented the Divine Judgment of us as being mortal beings whose earthly destiny is the great deep. If the sages of the Midrash had had this kind of experience, they might very well have included it along with the other opinions. This would have been immediately understood.

—

Seed Thoughts II

The story that our Midrash includes about Alexander the Great is one of the greatest literary achievements of midrashic writings. The special wisdom of the judge in solving the problem before him by advocating the marriage of the son and daughter of the opposing litigants is, of course, of great interest. The real message of the story, however, is something else. A piece of land was sold, which provoked a legal question. The buyer said that he bought the land and found in it a treasure. He wished to return the treasure, but the seller refuses to accept it. The seller said that he sold the land and everything in it. This included the treasure, which belongs to the purchaser just as everything else relating to the land. The claims of both sides are the exact opposite of what we might expect in modern courts, where each one is concerned with his own material benefit and tries to exact for himself the best possible deal. Both the buyer and the seller of this story acted in terms of the highest possible ethical principles. The buyer did not want the treasure, if it belonged to someone else rightly; the seller refused to accept the treasure, even though the loss to him would be very great, because it did not belong to him anymore, but to the purchaser. Alexander the Great not only marveled at this decision, but pointed out that in his country, both the buyer and the seller would have been killed and he, the emperor, would have taken the property. At this point, the king who told the story made the observation that if the sun and the moon were present in his country, it could only have been due to the animal world that lived there and not to the inhumanity displayed by man to man. This was the interpretation he gave to the verse in the Psalm that we have been discussing, 'אדם ובהמה תושיע ה – *adam ubehemah toshiya Hashem*. Both man and the beasts are helped and delivered by God, because they need each other.

Additional Commentary

Noah and animal life (A)

The Rabbis interpreted the verse from Psalms as relating to Noah. The Holy One, Blessed be He said, "The justice which I had performed with Noah in the ark and my deliverance of him from the Flood was possible by means of the mountains of God." When the ark reached the high mountains, and Noah left the ark in peace, it became obvious that the suffering of the generation of the Flood was produced by the great deep. "When I remembered to save Noah at the end," said the Holy One, "I remembered not only Noah, but the animals, domestic and wild, that were with him." (*HaMidrash HaMevo'ar*)

Noah and animal life (B)

The Holy One, Blessed Be He is letting us know how great is His love for the righteous. But he also wants us to know that we should be influenced by the laws of nature rather than through miracles. When you are recipients of miracles, the rule is whoever receives his abundance through miracles is deprived that much of his reward in the World to Come. This does not apply to natural laws, and therefore, God pointed out that the justice extended to Noah in the ark was done with the help of the Lord. At the creation of the world, all the waters of the world were gathered together in one miraculous stroke. God did not want to do this at the conclusion of the Flood because the ark would have been shattered. Instead, the ark alighted on Mount Ararat and the waters gradually moved down to their places. The same rule applied to the beginning of the Flood. That is why the waters did not rain from heaven, which would have destroyed the ark, but came up from the deep. Therefore, at the time of deliverance, God remembered Noah and the animals to save them in a natural and gradual way so that the rewards in the World to Come would not be diminished. (*Tiferet Tzion*)

The following is an additional interpretation of the verse, "And God remembered Noah, and every living thing, and all the cattle, etc." (8:1). The question thus remains as to why Noah's name was associated with all the other living things.

ב. דבר אחר, הֲדָא הוּא דִכְתִיב (קהלת ט, יד) 'עִיר קְטַנָּה, וַאֲנָשִׁים בָּהּ מְעָט, וּבָא אֵלֶיהָ מֶלֶךְ גָּדוֹל', 'עִיר קְטַנָּה' זֶה הָעוֹלָם, 'וַאֲנָשִׁים בָּהּ מְעָט' זֶה דוֹר הַמַּבּוּל, 'וּבָא אֵלֶיהָ מֶלֶךְ גָּדוֹל וְסָבַב אֹתָהּ' זֶה הַקָּדוֹשׁ בָּרוּךְ הוּא, 'וּבָנָה עָלֶיהָ מְצוֹדִים גְּדוֹלִים', עֲקְמָן וּכְמָנֶן, (שם שם, טו) 'וּמָצָא בָהּ אִישׁ מִסְכֵּן וְחָכָם' זֶה נֹחַ

2. ANOTHER INTERPRETATION: THERE WAS A LITTLE CITY (ECCL. 9:14): THIS ALLUDES TO THE WORLD; AND FEW MEN WITHIN IT (IBID.), TO THE GENERATION OF THE FLOOD; AND THERE CAME A GREAT KING AGAINST IT, AND BESIEGED IT (IBID.) – TO THE HOLY ONE, BLESSED BE HE; AND BUILT GREAT BULWARKS AGAINST IT (IBID.) – AMBUSHES AND SNARES. NOW THERE WAS FOUND IN IT A MAN POOR AND WISE (IBID., 15), VIZ. NOAH;

Since the text in Ecclesiastes speaks of a city, the term "city" must include much more than people. It includes also animal life of all descriptions, as well as the food, the bread, the vegetation required to sustain the city. That justifies the comparison of the city with the world. The man of wisdom was Noah and the king is interpreted as referring to the Holy One, Blessed be He. This justifies an analogy, in which the city and its people were used as a source of comparison to Noah and his world. As a sample of Noah's wisdom, there is the reference to the pure animals that he offered to God, as it continues:

'וּמִלַּט אֶת הָעִיר בְּחָכְמָתוֹ', (בראשית ח, כ) 'וַיַּעַל עֹלֹת בַּמִּזְבֵּחַ'
AND HE BY HIS WISDOM DELIVERED THE CITY (IBID.), AS IT IS WRITTEN, AND HE TOOK OF EVERY PURE BEAST, ETC. (GEN. 8:20).

The instructions to Noah were that seven couples of each clean animal were to be admitted to the ark, whereas only two unclean couples were to be admitted. Noah wondered why this would be so, and he concluded that the purpose was to offer animal sacrifices to the Lord the moment the ark alighted on the ground. This was a remarkable insight and marked him as a person with wisdom.

'וְאָדָם לֹא זָכַר אֶת הָאִישׁ הַמִּסְכֵּן הַהוּא', אָמַר הַקָּדוֹשׁ בָּרוּךְ הוּא, אַתּוּן, לֵית אַתּוּן מַנְהָרִים לֵהּ, אֲנָא מַנְהַר לֵהּ, שֶׁנֶּאֱמַר 'וַיִּזְכֹּר אֱ־לֹהִים אֶת נֹחַ'.

YET NO MAN REMEMBERED THAT SAME POOR MAN (ECCL. LOC. CIT.): SAID THE HOLY ONE, BLESSED BE HE: 'SINCE NONE OF YOU REMEMBER HIM, I WILL REMEMBER HIM, I WILL REMEMBER HIM': HENCE, AND GOD REMEMBERED NOAH, ETC.

It has happened so often in the history of mankind that the person who does the most good is belittled and forgotten. Noah was denied the appreciation of his contemporaries. But that did not matter since God remembered him and salvaged his reputation.

—

Seed Thoughts I

The city and Noah

One of the questions that students of the Midrash ask themselves is why a particular verse is chosen to illustrate the problems of a text. Although that question can certainly arise in connection with this midrash, the answer appears to be quite obvious. The sages were very sensitive to the criticism of Noah, which we read about in earlier midrashim. How could it be conceived that The Almighty would choose a lesser person to engage in the most important act of creation, the renewal of civilization? Though Noah was, indeed, criticized – not only by his generation, but by sages who interpreted that he might have been a hero in his generation but not in the generation of those who were superior to him, such as Abraham – in our midrash, Noah's reputation is not only elevated, but he is described as a חכם – *chakham*, a person of extraordinary wisdom, who saved the world by renewing civilization. He was by all counts a fitting representative.

—

Seed Thoughts II

An additional thought: The style of the Midrash can be very captivating. Rather than list some of these unique styles in a special chapter, it seems to me more important to comment on them when they arise. In our present midrash, we have the expression, "An additional thought." This stylistic comment is found countless times in the midrashic and talmudic literature. There is no such thing as biblical text that is so understood that it elicits no additional comment. There is always something more to say and that requires additional thinking from many other sources. Sometimes the additional thought is a further elaboration of the central idea. Other times, however, it could be what might even be considered a repudiation of the second idea. To discover these truths is an exciting challenge and makes the Midrash a source to be treasured even more.

Additional Commentary

The city and the world

During the days when evil people controlled the world, it appeared small and unimportant. And the many people appeared to be few and juvenile and of lesser importance. This justifies the comparison between the verse in Ecclesiastes and the story of Noah. (Maharzu)

ג. (תהלים קמה, ט) 'טוֹב ה' לַכֹּל וְרַחֲמָיו עַל כָּל מַעֲשָׂיו'

3. THE LORD IS GOOD TO ALL, AND HIS TENDER MERCIES ARE OVER ALL
HIS WORKS (PS. 145:9).

This verse is quoted as another interpretation of the scriptural verse
that has been the text for several midrashim up to this point, namely,
that God remembered Noah and the animal world with him. The verse
that God is good to all is something that requires interpretation. If God
is good to all, then where is there room for the evil inclination and the
fact that the wicked had to be punished? (Aryeh Mirkin). This problem
will now be addressed.

אָמַר רַבִּי לֵוִי, טוֹב ה' לַכֹּל עַל הַכֹּל, שֶׁהוּא מַעֲשָׂיו, אָמַר רַבִּי שְׁמוּאֵל, טוֹב ה' לַכֹּל, וְרַחֲמָיו, עַל
הַכֹּל שֶׁהֵן מִדּוֹתָיו, הוּא מְרַחֵם, רַבִּי יְהוֹשֻׁעַ דְּסִכְנִין בְּשֵׁם רַבִּי לֵוִי, אָמַר, טוֹב ה' לַכֹּל, וּמֵרַחֲמָיו
הוּא נוֹתֵן לִבְרִיּוֹתָיו

R. JOSHUA B. LEVI TRANSLATED: THE LORD IS GOOD TO ALL, AND HIS
TENDER MERCIES ARE OVER ALL, BECAUSE THEY ARE HIS WORKS. R.
SAMUEL B. NAHMAN INTERPRETED: THE LORD IS GOOD TO ALL, AND HIS
TENDER MERCIES ARE OVER ALL, FOR IT IS HIS NATURE TO BE COMPAS-
SIONATE. R. JOSHUA INTERPRETED IN R. LEVI'S NAME: THE LORD IS GOOD
TO ALL, AND HE INSPIRES MANKIND WITH HIS [SPIRIT OF] COMPASSION.

R. Joshua b. R. Levi emphasizes the second part of the verse, that God's
mercy is related to His deeds or creations. In other words, those who
retain the humanity implanted in them receive God's goodness. Those
who do not, such as the generation of the Flood, receive His punishment. R. Shmuel makes the point that God's mercy includes everyone,
including the sinners. From his point of view, as stated elsewhere, even
the generation of the Flood will have a place in the World to Come. R.
Joshua makes the point that God implanted His goodness into the human being. This does not manifest itself automatically, but the human
being has the ability to choose to use that goodness that is implanted

in him, and God wants that goodness to be shared by all human beings
with each other.

רַבִּי תַּנְחוּמָא וְרַבִּי אַבָּא בַּר אָבִין, בְּשֵׁם רַב אַחָא, לְמָחָר שְׁנַת בַּצֹּרֶת בָּאָה, וְהַבְּרִיּוֹת מְרַחֲמִין
אֵלּוּ עַל אֵלּוּ, וְהַקָּדוֹשׁ בָּרוּךְ הוּא מִתְמַלֵּא עֲלֵיהֶן רַחֲמִים, בְּיוֹמֵי דְרַבִּי תַּנְחוּמָא, הָיוּ צְרִיכִין
יִשְׂרָאֵל לְתַעֲנִית, אָתוֹן לְגַבֵּהּ אָמְרִין לֵהּ רַבִּי, גְּזֹר תַּעֲנִיתָא, גְּזַר תַּעֲנִיתָא, יוֹם קַדְמָאי, יוֹם ב', יוֹם
ג', וְלָא נְחַת מִטְרָא, עָאל, וּדְרַשׁ לְהוֹן, אָמַר לְהוֹן, בָּנַי, הִתְמַלְּאוּ רַחֲמִים אֵלּוּ עַל אֵלּוּ, וְהַקָּדוֹשׁ
בָּרוּךְ הוּא מִתְמַלֵּא עֲלֵיכֶם רַחֲמִים, עַד שֶׁהֵן מְחַלְּקִין צְדָקָה לַעֲנִיֵּיהֶם, רָאוּ אָדָם אֶחָד נוֹתֵן
מָעוֹת לִגְרוּשָׁתוֹ, אָתוֹן לְגַבֵּהּ וַאֲמָרוּ לֵהּ, רַבִּי, מָה אֲנַן יָתְבִין הָכָא וַעֲבֵרְתָּא הָכָא, אָמַר לְהֶן, מָה
רְאִיתֶם, אָמְרוּ לוֹ, רָאִינוּ אָדָם פְּלוֹנִי נוֹתֵן מָעוֹת לִגְרוּשָׁתוֹ, שְׁלַח בַּתְרֵיהוֹן וְאַיְתְנוּן לְגוֹ צִבּוּרָא,
אָמַר לֵהּ מַה הִיא לָךְ זוֹ, אָמַר לוֹ, גְּרוּשָׁתִי הִיא, אָמַר לוֹ, מִפְּנֵי מַה נָתַתְּ לָהּ מָעוֹת, אָמַר לוֹ,
רַבִּי, רָאִיתִי אוֹתָהּ בְּצָרָה, וְהִתְמַלֵּאתִי עָלֶיהָ רַחֲמִים, בְּאוֹתָהּ שָׁעָה הִגְבִּיהַּ רַבִּי תַּנְחוּמָא פָּנָיו
כְּלַפֵּי מַעְלָה, וְאָמַר, רִבּוֹן כָּל הָעוֹלָמִים, מָה אִם זֶה, שֶׁאֵין לָהּ עָלָיו מְזוֹנוֹת, רָאָה אוֹתָהּ בְּצָרָה,
וְנִתְמַלֵּא עָלֶיהָ רַחֲמִים, אַתָּה, שֶׁכָּתוּב בְּךָ (שם שם, ח) 'חַנּוּן וְרַחוּם', וְאָנוּ בְּנֵי יְדִידֶיךָ, בְּנֵי אַבְרָהָם
יִצְחָק וְיַעֲקֹב, עַל אַחַת כַּמָּה וְכַמָּה שֶׁתִּתְמַלֵּא עָלֵינוּ רַחֲמִים, מִיָּד יָרְדוּ גְשָׁמִים, וְנִתְרַוְּה הָעוֹלָם.

R. ABBA SAID: SHOULD A YEAR OF FAMINE COMMENCE TOMORROW
AND MEN SHOW COMPASSION TO EACH OTHER, THEN THE HOLY ONE,
BLESSED BE HE, WILL ALSO BE FILLED WITH COMPASSION FOR THEM. IN
THE DAYS OF R. TANHUMA ISRAEL HAD NEED OF A FAST, SO THEY WENT
TO HIM AND REQUESTED: 'MASTER, PROCLAIM A FAST.' HE PROCLAIMED
A FAST, FOR ONE DAY, THEN A SECOND DAY, AND THEN A THIRD, YET
NO RAIN FELL. THEREUPON HE ASCENDED [THE PULPIT] AND PREACHED
TO THEM, SAYING: 'MY SONS! BE FILLED WITH COMPASSION FOR EACH
OTHER, AND THEN THE HOLY ONE, BLESSED BE HE, WILL BE FILLED WITH
COMPASSION FOR YOU.' NOW WHILE THEY WERE DISTRIBUTING RELIEF
TO THE POOR THEY SAW A MAN GIVE MONEY TO HIS DIVORCED WIFE,
WHEREUPON THEY WENT TO HIM [R. TANHUMA] AND EXCLAIMED, 'WHY
DO WE SIT HERE WHILE SUCH MISDEEDS ARE PERPETRATED!' 'WHAT
THEN HAVE YOU SEEN?' HE INQUIRED. 'WE SAW SO-AND-SO GIVE HIS
DIVORCED WIFE MONEY.' HE SUMMONED THEM AND ASKED HIM, 'WHY
DID YOU GIVE MONEY TO YOUR DIVORCED WIFE?' 'I SAW HER IN GREAT
DISTRESS,' REPLIED HE, 'AND WAS FILLED WITH COMPASSION FOR HER.'
UPON THIS R. TANHUMA TURNED HIS FACE UPWARD AND EXCLAIMED:
'SOVEREIGN OF THE UNIVERSE! THIS MAN, UPON WHOM THIS WOMAN
HAS NO CLAIM FOR SUSTENANCE, YET SAW HER IN DISTRESS AND WAS
FILLED WITH PITY FOR HER. SEEING THEN THAT OF THEE IT IS WRIT-
TEN, THE LORD IS FULL OF COMPASSION AND GRACIOUS (PS. 103:8),
WHILE WE ARE THY CHILDREN, THE CHILDREN OF THY BELOVED ONES,
THE CHILDREN OF ABRAHAM, ISAAC, AND JACOB, HOW MUCH THE MORE
SHOULDST THOU BE FILLED WITH COMPASSION FOR US!' IMMEDIATELY
THE RAIN DESCENDED AND THE WORLD ENJOYED RELIEF.

There now follows a series of stories whose purpose it is to show the necessity to be sensitive to each other, because only in this manner will God's compassion be extended and realized. The first story speaks of compassion to one's divorced wife. Many other examples acts of sensitivity will now follow.

רַבֵּינוּ, הֲוָה יָתֵב לָעֵי בְּאוֹרַיְתָא קַמֵּי כְּנִשְׁתָּא דְבַבְלָאֵי דְבַצְפּוֹרִין, עֲבַר חַד עֵגֶל קוֹדְמוֹי אֲזַל לְמִתְנְכָסָה וְשָׁרֵי גָּעֵי כְּמֵימַר שֶׁזְּבְנִי, אֲמַר לֵהּ, וּמָה אֲנִי יָכוֹל לְמֶעֱבַד לָךְ, לְכָךְ נוֹצַרְתָּ, וְחָשַׁשׁ רַבִּי אֶת שִׁנָּיו שְׁלֹשׁ עֶשְׂרֵה שָׁנָה, אָמַר רַבִּי יוֹסֵי בַּר אָבִין, כָּל אוֹתָן שְׁלֹשׁ עֶשְׂרֵה שָׁנָה שֶׁהָיָה חוֹשֵׁשׁ רַבִּי אֶת שִׁנָּיו לֹא הִפִּילָה עֻבָּרָה בְּאֶרֶץ יִשְׂרָאֵל, וְלֹא נִצְטַעֲרוּ הַיּוֹלְדוֹת, בָּתַר יוֹמִין, עֲבַר חַד שֶׁרֶץ קַמֵּי בְּרַתֵּהּ וּבְעָא לְמִקְטְלָא, אֲמַר לָהּ, בְּרַתִּי, שַׁבְקֵיהּ, דִּכְתִיב, 'וְרַחֲמָיו עַל כָּל מַעֲשָׂיו'.

OUR TEACHER WAS SITTING AND STUDYING THE TORAH IN FRONT OF THE BABYLONIAN SYNAGOGUE IN SEPPHORIS, WHEN A CALF PASSED BEFORE HIM ON ITS WAY TO THE SLAUGHTER AND BEGAN TO CRY OUT, AS THOUGH PLEADING, 'SAVE ME!' SAID HE TO IT, 'WHAT CAN I DO FOR YOU? FOR THIS YOU WERE FASHIONED.' [AS A PUNISHMENT FOR HIS HEARTLESSNESS] OUR TEACHER SUFFERED TOOTHACHE FOR THIRTEEN YEARS. DURING THESE THIRTEEN YEARS NO WOMAN MISCARRIED IN ERETZ ISRAEL, AND NONE SUFFERED PAIN IN CHILDBIRTH. AFTER THIS PERIOD A CREEPING THING RAN PAST HIS DAUGHTER. SHE WAS ABOUT TO KILL IT, WHEN HE SAID TO HER, 'MY DAUGHTER, LET IT BE, FOR IT IS WRITTEN, AND HIS TENDER MERCIES ARE OVER ALL HIS WORKS.'

The two illustrations of this kind of sensitivity are now described. The first shows the suffering that insensitivity can cause in the case of the calf that did not want to be slaughtered. In the second, the story of the insect whose life was saved, is the reward that comes to those with great sensitivity. This kind of behavior is not expected by the average person, but it is expected by those whose lives are immersed in Torah.

רַבֵּינוּ, הֲוָה עַנְוְתָן סַגִּי, וַהֲוָה אָמַר, כָּל מַה דְּיֵאמַר לִי בַר נָשׁ אֲנָא עָבֵד, חוּץ מִמַּה שֶּׁעָשׂוּ בְּנֵי בְתֵירָא לִזְקֵנִי, שֶׁיָּרְדוּ מִגְּדֻלָּתָן, וְהֶעֱלוּ אוֹתוֹ, וְאִין סָלֵיק רַבִּי הוּנָא רֵישׁ גָּלוּתָא לְהָכָא אֲנָא קָאֵם לִי מִן קוֹדְמוֹהִי, לָמָּה, דְּהוּא מִן יְהוּדָה וַאֲנָא מִן בִּנְיָמִין, וְהוּא מִן יְהוּדָה דִיהוּדָאָה וַאֲנָא מִן נָקְבָתָא, אֲמַר לֵהּ רַבִּי חִיָּא רַבָּה, וַהֲרֵי הוּא עוֹמֵד בַּחוּץ, נִתְכַּרְכְּמוּ פָנָיו שֶׁל רַבִּי, וְכֵיוָן שֶׁרָאָה שֶׁנִּתְכַּרְכְּמוּ פָנָיו, אֲמַר לֵהּ אֲרוֹנוֹ הוּא, אֲמַר לֵהּ פּוּק חֲזֵי מַאן בָּעֵי לָךְ לְבָרָא, נְפַק וְלָא אַשְׁכַּח בַּר נָשׁ, וִידַע דְּהוּא נָזוּף, וְאֵין נְזִיפָה פְּחוּתָה מִשְּׁלֹשִׁים יוֹם, אָמַר רַבִּי יוֹסֵי בַּר רַבִּי אָבִין, כָּל אוֹתָן שְׁלֹשִׁים יוֹם שֶׁהָיָה רַבִּי חִיָּא רַבָּה נָזוּף מֵרַבֵּינוּ, אַלֵּף לְרַב בַּר אֲחָתֵהּ כָּל כְּלָלֵי דְאוֹרַיְתָא, וְאֵלֵּין אִנּוּן כְּלָלַיָּא דְאוֹרַיְתָא הִלְכָתָא דְבַבְלָאֵי, לְסוֹף תְּלָתִין יוֹמִין, אָתָא אֵלִיָּהוּ זָכוּר לַטּוֹב, בִּדְמוּתֵהּ דְּרַבִּי חִיָּא רַבָּה אֵצֶל רַבֵּינוּ, וִיהַב יְדֵהּ עַל שִׁנֵּהּ וְאִתַּסֵּי, כֵּיוָן דַּאֲתָא דְרַבִּי חִיָּא רַבָּה לְגַבֵּי רַבֵּינוּ, אֲמַר לֵהּ מָה עֲבַדְתְּ בְּשִׁנָּךְ, אֲמַר לֵהּ מִן עוֹנָתָא דִיהַבְתְּ יְדָךְ עֲלוֹהִי אִתְנְשִׁמֵית, אֲמַר לֵהּ לֵית אֲנָא הֲוָה

יָדַע מַה הוּא, כֵּיוָן דִּשְׁמַע כֵּן שָׁרֵי נָהֵג בֵּהּ יְקָרָא, וְקָרֵב תַּלְמִידִים וּמְעַיֵּל לֵהּ מִלְּגָאו, אָמַר רַבִּי
יִשְׁמָעֵאל בַּר רַבִּי יוֹסֵי, וְלִפְנִים מִמֶּנִּי, אָמַר לֵהּ חָס וְשָׁלוֹם, לֹא יֵעָשֶׂה כֵן בְּיִשְׂרָאֵל

OUR TEACHER WAS VERY MODEST, AND HE USED TO SAY, 'I AM PREPARED
TO DO WHATEVER ANY PERSON TELLS ME, EXCEPT WHAT THE FAMILY
OF BATHYRA DID FOR MY ANCESTOR [HILLEL], FOR THEY RELINQUISHED
THEIR HIGH OFFICE AND PROMOTED HIM. AND IF R. HUNA, THE RESH
GALUTHA, WERE TO COME UP HERE [PALESTINE], I WOULD RISE BEFORE
HIM, FOR HE IS DESCENDED FROM JUDAH, WHEREAS I AM FROM BEN-
JAMIN; HE IS DESCENDED ON THE MALE SIDE, WHILE I AM DESCENDED
[FROM JUDAH] ON THE FEMALE SIDE.' SAID R. HIYYA THE ELDER TO HIM,
'BEHOLD, HE HAS COME!' AT THIS RABBI'S FACE TURNED PALE. 'HIS COF-
FIN HAS COME,' HE ADDED. 'GO AND SEE WHO WANTS YOU WITHOUT,' HE
ORDERED. HE WENT OUT AND FOUND NO ONE, WHEREUPON HE TREATED
HIMSELF AS BANNED FOR THIRTY DAYS. R. JOSE [ASSI] REMARKED: DUR-
ING THESE THIRTY DAYS OF HIS EXCOMMUNICATION HE TAUGHT RAB,
HIS SISTER'S SON, ALL THE [EXEGETICAL] PRINCIPLES OF THE TORAH,
WHILE HE [RAB] TAUGHT HIM THE LAWS OF THE BABYLONIANS. AT THE
END OF THE THIRTY DAYS ELIJAH, OF BLESSED MEMORY, CAME BEFORE
RABBI DISGUISED AS R. HIYYA THE ELDER, LAID HIS HAND UPON HIS
TEETH, AND CURED HIM. WHEN R. HIYYA SUBSEQUENTLY VISITED RABBI
HE ASKED HIM, 'HOW IS YOUR TOOTH?' 'SINCE YOU LAID YOUR HAND
UPON IT, IT IS CURED,' HE ANSWERED. 'I KNOW NOTHING ABOUT IT,'
SAID HE. ON HEARING THIS RABBI SHOWED HIM HONOR AND SET HIM
ON THE INNER [BENCH]. SAID R. ISHMAEL B. R. JOSE TO HIM, 'EVEN BE-
FORE ME?' 'HEAVEN FORFEND,' REPLIED HE, 'LET SUCH A THING NOT BE
DONE IN ISRAEL!'

We have in this story a further example of the sensitivity of *talmidei
chakhamim* to each other. Especially in the relationship of R. Judah the
Prince to R. Hiyya, who was a very great scholar. The story emphasizes
the blessings and rewards that came from these expressions of mutual
love and respect.

רַבֵּינוּ, הֲוָה מְתַנֵּי שְׁבָחֵהּ דְּרַבִּי חִיָּא רַבָּה קַמֵּהּ דְּרַבִּי יִשְׁמָעֵאל בַּר רַבִּי יוֹסֵי, אָמַר לֵהּ אָדָם
גָּדוֹל, אָדָם קָדוֹשׁ, חַד זְמַן חֲמִיתֵהּ בֵּי בָנֵי וְלָא אִתְכְּנַע מִנֵּהּ, אָמַר לֵהּ הַהוּא תַּלְמִידָךְ דַּהֲוַת
מִשְׁתַּבַּח בֵּהּ חֲמִיתֵהּ בֵּי בָנֵי וְלָא אִתְכְּנַע מִנַּאי, אָמַר לֵהּ וּלְמָה לָא אִתְכְּנַעַתְּ מִנֵּהּ, אָמַר לֵהּ רַבִּי
חִיָּא מִסְתַּכֵּל הָיִיתִי בְּאַגָּדַת תְּהִלִּים, כֵּיוָן דִּשְׁמַע כֵּן, מְסַר לֵהּ תְּרֵין תַּלְמִידוֹי וַהֲווֹ עָיְלִין עִמֵּהּ
לְאַשׁוּנָה, דְּלָא יִשְׁהֵי וְתַזְעַר נַפְשֵׁהּ.

OUR TEACHER WAS SINGING THE PRAISES OF R. HIYYA THE ELDER TO R.
ISHMAEL B. R. JOSE. SAID HE [R. ISHMAEL B. R. JOSE] TO HIM: 'ONE DAY
I SAW HIM [R. HIYYA THE ELDER] AT THE BATHS BUT HE DID NOT MAKE

AN OBEISANCE BEFORE ME.' 'WHY DID YOU NOT BOW BEFORE HIM?'
INQUIRED HE [OUR TEACHER]. 'I WAS MEDITATING ON AN AGGADAH
OF THE PSALMS,' HE ANSWERED. ON HEARING THIS HE GAVE HIM TWO
DISCIPLES WHO USED TO GO IN WITH HIM TO THE VAPOR ROOM, LEST HE
SHOULD STAY TOO LONG THERE AND BECOME ENFEEBLED.

On the one hand a reader can be forgiven if he notes with surprise
that a great sage like R. Ishmael should be so sensitive to the recognition
and respect that he wanted from others, in this case, R. Hiyya. From R.
Hiyya's point of view, we learn that it is not enough to do the right thing.
We also have to be concerned with appearance, that it should appear to
others to be the right thing as well. This is known in Hebrew as מְרָאִית
עַיִן – *marit ayin*, the concept that things have to look right as well as be
right.

דָּבָר אַחֵר, 'טוֹב ה' לַכֹּל, וְגוֹ', 'וַיִּזְכֹּר אֱ־לֹהִים אֶת נֹחַ, וְגוֹ'', אָמַר רַבִּי שְׁמוּאֵל בַּר נַחְמָנִי, אוֹי לָהֶם
לָרְשָׁעִים שֶׁהֵם הוֹפְכִים מִדַּת רַחֲמִים לְמִדַּת הַדִּין, בְּכָל מָקוֹם שֶׁנֶּאֱמַר ה', מִדַּת רַחֲמִים, (שמות
לד, ו) 'ה' ה' אֵל רַחוּם וְחַנּוּן', וּכְתִיב, (בראשית ו, ה) 'וַיַּרְא ה' כִּי רַבָּה רָעַת הָאָדָם בָּאָרֶץ' (שם שם,
ו) 'וַיִּנָּחֶם ה' כִּי עָשָׂה אֶת הָאָדָם' (שם שם, ז) 'וַיֹּאמֶר ה' אֶמְחֶה, וְגוֹ'', אַשְׁרֵיהֶם הַצַּדִּיקִים שֶׁהֵן
הוֹפְכִים מִדַּת הַדִּין לְמִדַּת רַחֲמִים, בְּכָל מָקוֹם שֶׁנֶּאֱמַר אֱ־לֹהִים, הוּא מִדַּת הַדִּין, (שמות כב, כו)
'אֱ־לֹהִים לֹא תְקַלֵּל', (שם שם, ח) 'עַד הָאֱ־לֹהִים יָבֹא דְּבַר שְׁנֵיהֶם', וּכְתִיב, (שם ב, כד) 'וַיִּשְׁמַע
אֱ־לֹהִים אֶת נַאֲקָתָם וַיִּזְכֹּר אֱ־לֹהִים אֶת בְּרִיתוֹ, וְגוֹ'', (בראשית ל, כב) 'וַיִּזְכֹּר אֱ־לֹהִים אֶת רָחֵל,
וְגוֹ'', 'וַיִּזְכֹּר אֱ־לֹהִים אֶת נֹחַ', מַה זְּכִירָה נִזְכַּר לוֹ, שֶׁזָּן וּפִרְנֵס אוֹתָם כָּל שְׁנֵים עָשָׂר חֹדֶשׁ בַּתֵּבָה,
'וַיִּזְכֹּר אֱ־לֹהִים אֶת נֹחַ', וְהַדִּין נוֹתֵן, מִזְּכוּת הַטְּהוֹרִים שֶׁהִכְנִיס עִמּוֹ בַּתֵּבָה. רַבִּי אֶלְעָזָר אוֹמֵר,
לְשֵׁם קָרְבָּנוֹ נִקְרָא, שֶׁנֶּאֱמַר (שם ח, כא) 'וַיָּרַח ה' אֶת רֵיחַ הַנִּיחֹחַ', רַבִּי יוֹסֵי בַּר חֲנִינָא, לְשֵׁם נַחַת
הַתֵּבָה, נִקְרָא, שֶׁנֶּאֱמַר (שם שם, ד) 'וַתָּנַח הַתֵּבָה בַּחֹדֶשׁ הַשְּׁבִיעִי, וְגוֹ''. רַבִּי יְהוֹשֻׁעַ אוֹמֵר, 'לֹא
יִשְׁבֹּתוּ' מִכְּלָל, שֶׁשָּׁבְתוּ, אָמַר רַבִּי יוֹחָנָן, לֹא שִׁמְּשׁוּ מַזָּלוֹת, כָּל שְׁנֵים עָשָׂר חֹדֶשׁ, אָמַר לֵהּ רַבִּי
יוֹנָתָן, שִׁמְּשׁוּ, אֶלָּא שֶׁלֹּא הָיָה רְשׁוּמָן נִכָּר. ר' אֱלִיעֶזֶר וְר' יְהוֹשֻׁעַ – ר' אֱלִיעֶזֶר אוֹמֵר: לֹא יִשְׁבֹּתוּ
(בר' ח, כב) – מִכָּאן שֶׁלֹּא שָׁבְתוּ. ר' יְהוֹשֻׁעַ אוֹמֵר: לֹא יִשְׁבֹּתוּ – מִכָּאן שֶׁשָּׁבְתוּ.

ANOTHER INTERPRETATION: 'THE LORD IS GOOD TO ALL, AND HIS TEN-
DER MERCIES ARE OVER ALL HIS WORKS.' AS IT IS WRITTEN, AND GOD
REMEMBERED NOAH, ETC. AND ELOKIM (GOD) REMEMBERED NOAH. R.
SAMUEL B. NAHMAN SAID: WOE TO THE WICKED WHO TURN THE ATTRI-
BUTE OF MERCY INTO THE ATTRIBUTE OF JUDGMENT. WHEREVER THE
TETRAGRAMMATON ['LORD'] IS EMPLOYED IT CONNOTES THE ATTRI-
BUTE OF MERCY, AS IN THE VERSE, THE LORD, THE LORD GOD, MERCIFUL
AND GRACIOUS (EX. 34:6), YET IT IS WRITTEN, AND THE LORD SAW THAT
THE WICKEDNESS OF MAN WAS GREAT (GEN. 6:5), AND IT REPENTED THE
LORD THAT HE HAD MADE MAN (IBID., 6), AND THE LORD SAID: I WILL
BLOT OUT MAN (IBID., 7). HAPPY ARE THE RIGHTEOUS WHO TURN THE
ATTRIBUTE OF JUDGMENT INTO THE ATTRIBUTE OF MERCY. WHEREVER

ELOKIM (GOD) IS EMPLOYED IT CONNOTES THE ATTRIBUTE OF JUDG-
MENT: THUS: THOU SHALT NOT REVILE ELOKIM-GOD (EX. 22:27); THE
CAUSE OF BOTH PARTIES SHALL COME BEFORE ELOKIM-GOD (IBID., 8);
YET IT IS WRITTEN, AND ELOKIM HEARD THEIR GROANING, AND ELOKIM
REMEMBERED HIS COVENANT (IBID., 2:24); AND ELOKIM REMEMBERED
RACHEL (GEN. 30:22); AND ELOKIM REMEMBERED NOAH.

WHAT DID GOD REMEMBER IN HIS [NOAH'S] FAVOR? THAT HE PROVIDED
FOR [THE ANIMALS] THE WHOLE TWELVE MONTHS IN THE ARK, HENCE
AND GOD REMEMBERED NOAH, AND THE SPIRIT OF JUSTICE APPROVES
IT, FOR THE SAKE OF THE CLEAN ANIMALS THAT WERE WITH HIM IN
THE ARK. R. ELEAZAR SAID: HE WAS CALLED [NOAH] ON ACCOUNT OF
HIS SACRIFICE, AS IT IS WRITTEN, AND THE LORD SMELLED THE SWEET
(NIHOAH) SAVOR (GEN. 8:21). R. JOSE B. R. HANINA SAID: ON ACCOUNT
OF THE RESTING OF THE ARK, AS IT IS WRITTEN, AND THE ARK RESTED
– VATTANAH (IBID., 4). R. JOHANAN SAID: THE PLANETS DID NOT FUNC-
TION THE WHOLE TWELVE MONTHS. SAID R. JONATHAN TO HIM, THEY
DID FUNCTION, BUT THEIR MARK WAS IMPERCEPTIBLE. R. ELIEZER AND
RABBI JOSHUA [ARGUED] – R. ELEAZAR SAID: THEY SHALL NOT CEASE
(IBID., 22) IMPLIES THAT THEY NEVER CEASED. R. JOSHUA DEDUCED:
'THEY SHALL NOT CEASE': HENCE IT FOLLOWS THAT THEY HAD CEASED.

We now come to the purpose for which all these stories were included. These stories indicate that Noah shared all these important
sensitivities and good deeds. Noah" special attribute consisted of the
fact that he not only showed consideration to the humans, his family
members, in the ark, but also to the entire animal world, wild and domestic, which he looked after carefully during the twelve months of the
Flood. Not only that, but in so far as the clean animals and the birds, he
arranged for them to share the same quarters occupied by him and his
family because of their special needs. Furthermore, the first thing he
did upon alighting from the ark was to offer sacrifices of thanksgiving
to God. The Midrash ends with a play on words with the name Noah,
showing his endearment to God. When the ark alighted, Scripture says,
ותנח התיבה – *vatanach hateivah*, that the word for "it rested" is based on
the same grammatical root as is "Noah." His name, therefore, symbolized the rest that came to the world. At the same time, the name Noah
is explained as meaning that he brought נחת רוח – *nachat ruach* to God.
This means he brought to Him abundant spiritual satisfaction.

Seed Thoughts

This Midrash is a triumphant proclamation of the goodness of God in the world. Of course evil exists and evildoers have to be punished, but to quote the words that we recite at the *Ne'ilah* service on the Day of Atonement, "God does not desire the death of the sinner, but only that he turn to God and live." The two most important aspects of this teaching is that God wants His goodness to be transferred to man and that this was the main purpose of creation. Man was created to be a moral being – that means freedom. It even means freedom from God's interference with man, because it is the exercising of moral choices that makes a moral human being. This is the hardest lesson to learn and after all these centuries, it still has not been grasped by the majority of people. The Jewish people were created in order to dramatize this teaching and give evidence, via their lifestyle, not only that it works, but that it makes life most meaningful. Unfortunately, an important segment of the Jewish people have not accepted this heritage and compromised on it – sometimes beyond recognition. The Midrash urges us to return to this goal and to this purpose. "God is good to all, and His mercy is over all His creatures," which I believe means that He has given to man the concept of compassion and it is up to us to live by this concept at its highest level.

—

Additional Commentary

Man's humanity

R. Levi points out that the word מעשיו – *ma'asav*, from the verse, "His mercies are over all His creatures" is superfluous. Can we possibly say that there is anything in this world that is not part of His creation or His accomplishments? Would it not have been enough to say, "His mercies are on everything"? This is what prompted R. Levi to say as follows: "To whom does God show mercy? To the one who did not destroy his being or his humanity from what God created at the beginning of the world." This excludes those who have destroyed this humanity by means of their evil deeds, such as the generation of the Flood. They destroyed man's humanity by their behavior, such as sexual relations with animals and other animalistic behavior that does not befit human beings. So their human character became animal character. In general, human life is affected by one's behavior. Even human nature is affected by one's behavior and sometimes that differs from what the King of the Universe originally intended. That is what is implied by the words, "All flesh destroyed their way," meaning their humanity, which God created for them. It is for this reason that He did not show compassion to them. (*Tiferet Tzion*)

ד. (ב) 'וַיִּסָּכְרוּ מַעְיְנוֹת תְּהוֹם' אָמַר רַבִּי אֶלְעָזָר, לְרָעָה (שם ז, יא) 'בַּיּוֹם הַזֶּה נִבְקְעוּ כָּל מַעְיְנוֹת
תְּהוֹם רַבָּה, וְגוֹ'', אֲבָל לְטוֹבָה, 'וַיִּסָּכְרוּ מַעְיְנוֹת תְּהוֹם', אֲבָל לֹא 'כָּל מַעְיְנוֹת', חוּץ מִמַּעְיַן
טְבֶרְיָה, וְאַבְלוֹנִים, וּמְעָרַת פַּמְיָ"ס. (ד) 'וַתָּנַח הַתֵּבָה בַּחֹדֶשׁ הַשְּׁבִיעִי בְּשִׁבְעָה עָשָׂר וְגוֹ'', עַל
טוּרֵי קַרְדּוּנְיָא.

4. THE FOUNTAINS ALSO OF THE DEEP AND THE WINDOWS OF HEAVEN
WERE STOPPED (8:2). R. ELEAZAR SAID: IN CONNECTION WITH PUNISH-
MENT IT IS WRITTEN, ON THE SAME DAY WERE ALL THE FOUNTAINS OF
THE GREAT DEEP BROKEN UP (IBID., 7:11); BUT IN CONNECTION WITH
GOOD IT IS WRITTEN, THE FOUNTAINS ALSO OF THE DEEP . . . WERE
STOPPED, BUT NOT ALL THE FOUNTAINS, THE EXCEPTIONS BEING THE
GREAT WELL [OF BIRAM], THE GULF [OF GADDOR], AND THE CAVERN
SPRING OF PANEAS. AND THE ARK RESTED IN THE SEVENTH MONTH . . .
UPON THE MOUNTAINS OF ARARAT (8:4): I.E., UPON THE MOUNTAIN
RANGE CORDYENE.

—

Seed Thoughts

One beautiful way to interpret this midrah is a play on words for the
term ותנח – *vattanach*, which tells us that the ark "rested." The beautiful
insight is that when you look at the word *vattanach*, you see the name
Noach. It is as though the story of the ark concludes with the signature of
Noah in the last verse before the ark alighted. All the doubts and hesita-
tions described in previous midrashim are now eliminated. The debate
over whether Noah was or was not a righteous man is now over. He was,
indeed, a righteous man, and this signature at the end proves it. He was a
person dedicated to God, ready and waiting to do His bidding. He would
not leave the ark without God's permission. This, too, is the meaning
of this signature," which concludes the story of the ark. The Almighty
found in Noah a true leader and disciple. Noah remained the captain,
the builder, the provider and the leader of the generation of the ark.

—

Additional Commentary

Tveriah

The nature of the Flood was such that more than water turned out to be dangerous. Some of the waters were hot to the boiling point. Many of them included underwater areas of tremendous heat, equivalent to what would be described today as steam saunas and the power of wet heat. It is of interest that the Midrash describes this development as being the origin of what we today refer to as *Chamei Tveriah*, the hot water pools of Tiberius, which are so popular in our time. In addition to what we describe as *Chamei Tveriah*, there is also the heated well spring known as *Chamat Gader*, which is also known in our time. It also includes the caves of Pamias. It is fascinating to note that the Midrash describes these natural phenomena, which are popular even today, as being the leftovers of the great catastrophe of the Flood. (*HaMidrash HaMevo'ar*)

PARASHAH THIRTY-THREE, *Midrash Five*

ה. (ו) 'וַיְהִי מִקֵּץ אַרְבָּעִים יוֹם, וַיִּפְתַּח נֹחַ', הָדָא מְסַיְּעָא לְהַהוּא דַאֲמַר רַבִּי אַבָּא בַּר כָּהֲנָא, חַלּוֹן.
5. AND IT CAME TO PASS AT THE END OF FORTY DAYS, THAT NOAH
OPENED THE HALON [E.V. 'WINDOW'] OF THE ARK (8:6). THIS SUPPORTS
THE VIEW THAT IT WAS A WINDOW [TRAPDOOR].

The word "window" resolves the difference of opinion in a previous
Midrash, where one sage said that a צוהר – *tzohar* was a window and
the other said it was some kind of jewel that reflected. Apparently, it
was a kind of window that can only be opened from the outside, and
this could only happen after the ark alighted on Mount Ararat (*Tiferet
Tzion*).

(ז) 'וַיְשַׁלַּח אֶת הָעֹרֵב' הָדָא הוּא דִכְתִיב, (תהלים קה, כח) 'שָׁלַח חֹשֶׁךְ וַיַּחְשִׁךְ'.
AND HE SENT FORTH A RAVEN (8:7): THUS IT IS WRITTEN, HE SENT
DARKNESS, AND IT WAS DARK (PS. 105:28).

From the text, it can be concluded that the raven did not accomplish
very much on its mission. The verse as quoted is meant to indicate a lesson that if you choose a messenger, make sure it is appropriate and one
liable to fulfill the task. On the other hand, the *Tiferet Tzion* maintains
that only the raven was suitable for this first flight because there was a
terrible odor in the atmosphere as a result of the ark and its inhabitants,
and only the raven was able to withstand it.

'וַיֵּצֵא יָצוֹא וָשׁוֹב' רַבִּי יוּדָן בְּשֵׁם רַבִּי יוּדָה בַּר רַבִּי סִימוֹן, הִתְחִיל מְשִׁיבוֹ תְּשׁוּבוֹת, אָמַר לוֹ מִכָּל
בְּהֵמָה חַיָּה וָעוֹף שֶׁיֵּשׁ כָּאן, אֵין אַתָּה מְשַׁלֵּחַ אֶלָּא לִי, אָמַר לוֹ מַה צֹּרֶךְ לָעוֹלָם בָּךְ, לֹא לַאֲכִילָה
לֹא לְקָרְבָּן, רַבִּי בֶּרֶכְיָה בְּשֵׁם רַבִּי אַבָּא בַּר כָּהֲנָא, אָמַר, אָמַר לוֹ הַקָּדוֹשׁ בָּרוּךְ הוּא, קַבְּלוֹ,
שֶׁעָתִיד הָעוֹלָם לְהִצְטָרֵךְ לוֹ, אָמַר לוֹ, אֵימָתַי, אָמַר לוֹ, 'עַד יְבֹשֶׁת הַמַּיִם מֵעַל הָאָרֶץ' עָתִיד
צַדִּיק אֶחָד לַעֲמֹד, וּלְיַבֵּשׁ אֶת הָעוֹלָם, וַאֲנִי מַצְרִיכוֹ לוֹ, הָדָא הוּא דִכְתִיב, (מ"א יז, ו) 'וְהָעֹרְבִים
מְבִיאִים לוֹ לֶחֶם וּבָשָׂר בַּבֹּקֶר וְלֶחֶם וּבָשָׂר בָּעָרֶב'.
AND IT WENT FORTH TO AND FRO (YAZO WA SHOB). R. JUDAN SAID IN
THE NAME OF R. JUDAH B. R. SIMON: IT BEGAN ARGUING WITH HIM:

'OF ALL THE BIRDS THAT THOU HAST HERE THOU SENDEST NONE BUT
ME!' 'WHAT NEED THEN HAS THE WORLD OF THEE?' HE RETORTED; 'FOR
FOOD? FOR A SACRIFICE?' R. BEREKIAH SAID IN R. ABBA'S NAME: THE
HOLY ONE, BLESSED BE HE, SAID TO HIM [NOAH]: 'TAKE IT BACK, BE-
CAUSE THE WORLD WILL NEED IT IN THE FUTURE.' 'WHEN?' HE ASKED.
'WHEN THE WATERS DRY OFF FROM ON THE EARTH' (IBID.). HE REPLIED:
'A RIGHTEOUS MAN WILL ARISE AND DRY UP THE WORLD, AND L WILL
CAUSE HIM TO HAVE NEED OF THEM [THE RAVENS],' AS IT IS WRITTEN,
AND THE RAVENS (ORBIM) BROUGHT HIM BREAD AND FLESH, ETC. (I
KINGS 17:6).

The importance of the raven was not its value in the ark, but its potential for the future, since it was the raven who was called upon to feed
Elijah the prophet. According to the *Tiferet Tzion*, Elijah did something
that might be considered quite cruel in his prophecy. He warned the
people and the king that if they did not repent, rain would not fall and
there would be famine in the land. The raven was described as one of
the cruelest of all the animals and it seemed appropriate that it would
be the one to feed Elijah. Even those who sometimes do cruel things
are enabled to change and do something positive and helpful to others.

רַבִּי יְהוּדָה וְרַבִּי נְחֶמְיָה, רַבִּי יְהוּדָה אוֹמֵר, עִיר הִיא בִּתְחוּם בֵּית שְׁאָן, וּשְׁמָהּ עַרְבִי, רַבִּי נְחֶמְיָה
אָמַר, עוֹרְבִים מַמָּשׁ הָיוּ, וּמֵהֵיכָן הָיוּ מְבִיאִים לוֹ, מִשֻּׁלְחָנוֹ שֶׁל יְהוֹשָׁפָט.
R. JUDAH SAID: IT REFERS TO A TOWN WITHIN THE BORDERS OF BASHAN
CALLED ARBO. R. NEHEMIAH SAID: RAVENS LITERALLY ARE MEANT, AND
WHENCE DID THEY BRING HIM [FOOD]? FROM JEHOSHAPHAT'S TABLE.

Since we never heard about this town again, it seems more appropriate
that the literal interpretation of "ravens" as birds seems to fit the text
more adequately. The Midrash adds that the ravens brought the food
from king Jehoshephat from Judah, who was a righteous person and
therefore his meat and bread could be eaten by Elijah.

דָּרַשׁ רַבִּי עֲקִיבָא מַעֲשֵׂה דוֹר הַמַּבּוּל, בְּגִנְזָק שֶׁל מָדַי, וְלֹא בָכוּ, וְכֵיוָן שֶׁהִזְכִּיר לָהֶם, מַעֲשֵׂה
אִיּוֹב מִיָּד בָּכוּ, וְקָרָא עֲלֵיהֶם, הַמִּקְרָא הַזֶּה, (איוב כד, כ) 'יִשְׁכָּחֵהוּ רֶחֶם מְתָקוֹ רִמָּה עוֹד לֹא יִזָּכֵר
וַתִּשָּׁבֵר כָּעֵץ עַוְלָה' 'יִשְׁכָּחֵהוּ רֶחֶם' הֵן שִׁכְחוּ רַחֲמֵי מִן הַבְּרִיּוֹת, אַף הַקָּדוֹשׁ בָּרוּךְ הוּא שָׁכַח
רַחֲמָיו מֵהֶם, 'מְתָקוֹ רִמָּה' שֶׁמְּתָקוּ רִמָּה מֵהֶן, 'עוֹד לֹא יִזָּכֵר וַתִּשָּׁבֵר כָּעֵץ עַוְלָה' אָמַר רַבִּי אַבָּהוּ,
תֵּעָקֵר אֵין כְּתִיב, אֶלָּא 'תִּשָּׁבֵר', כְּדָבָר שֶׁנִּשְׁבָּר, וְאֵינוֹ מַעֲלֶה חֲלִיפִין, וְאֵיזֶה, זֶה דוֹר הַפְּלָגָה.
R. AKIBA PREACHED IN GINZAK ON THE THEME OF THE FLOOD, AND THE
AUDIENCE DID NOT WEEP, BUT WHEN HE MENTIONED THE STORY OF THE
RAVEN THEY WEPT. HE THEN QUOTED THIS VERSE: THE WOMB (REHEM)

FORGETTETH HIM; THE WORM FEEDETH SWEETLY ON HIM; HE SHALL
BE NO MORE REMEMBERED; AND UNRIGHTEOUSNESS IS BROKEN AS A
TREE (JOB 24:20). 'REHEM FORGETTETH': THEY [THE GENERATION OF
THE FLOOD] FORGOT TO BE MERCIFUL TO THEIR FELLOW MEN, THERE-
FORE THE HOLY ONE, BLESSED BE HE, MADE HIS MERCY FORGET THEM.
'THE WORM FEEDETH SWEETLY ON HIM': THE WORM BECAME SWEET
THROUGH [FEEDING ON] THEM. 'HE SHALI BE NO MORE REMEMBERED,
AND UNRIGHTEOUSNESS IS BROKEN AS A TREE': R. AIBU SAID: IT IS
NOT WRITTEN, 'IS UPROOTED,' BUT 'IS BROKEN': I.E., LIKE SOMETHING
WHICH IS BROKEN, YET PRODUCES ANOTHER STOCK IN EXCHANGE; AND
TO WHAT DOES THAT ALLUDE? TO THE GENERATION OF THE DIVSION
[OF PEOPLES].

The people did not weep when R. Akiva described the sufferings of
the generation of the Flood, because they had no compassion for each
other and therefore deserved whatever punishment was meted out to
them. The sufferings of Job may not have been as painful as those of the
generation of the Flood, but he was described as a righteous man who
acted with compassion, mercy and justice in all his dealings. When the
people learned of his suffering, they wept very much. With the analogy of the tree, the text indicates that the generation of the Flood were
much too evil to be "replanted" and start again, as a tree is sometimes
uprooted and planted elsewhere. Instead, they simply perished and
were ultimately replaced by the generation of the Division of peoples
דור הפלגה – *dor haflagah*).

Seed Thoughts

In explaining his experience while teaching about the Flood, R. Akiva
quotes a verse from Job that says speaks of the womb (*rechem*), but uses
the term רחם – *rechem*, in the sense of רחמים – *rachamim*, which means
mercy or compassion. It is not, therefore, the womb that forgot them,
but rather they who forgot to be compassionate. The Midrash, here and
elsewhere, expresses the fact that compassion was a quality that God
gave to the human being at his birth in the very womb in which he was
created. Compassion is one of God's gift to man and we are called upon
to be compassionate with one another. The generation of the Flood was
not compassionate at all and that was its undoing. When R. Akiva noted
that his audience did not weep or show any emotion for the suffering
of the generation of the Flood, he understood their feeling. They had

no compassion for each other. When there is no compassion, only evil could follow and the perpetrators deserve their punishment. In the case of Job, however, he was righteous and compassionate and merciful during all his endeavors, and for him to suffer was a terrible act, which grieved R. Akiva's listeners very much and made them cry.

Compassion is one of the great virtues that Judaism has given to us. It should become a priority in all of our dealings. If that were to happen, just about all the other good things that are possible would fall into place.

—

Additional Commentary

Sending the raven

The question may be asked, why was it necessary to send the raven and only afterward the dove? Two purposes had to be achieved. The first was the condition of the atmosphere and the air, which might affect the breathing of animal life. This was why the raven was sent; it had the strength to survive many of the difficulties of the atmosphere. When it became clear that birds and animals could leave the ark safely, only then was it important to investigate the condition of the land and to see when it was safe in that respect for the inhabitants to leave the ark. This was the function of the dove. When it brought back the branch, that was proof to Noah that the earth could now, again, be inhabited. (*Tiferet Tzion*)

PARASHAH THIRTY-THREE, *Midrash Six*

ו. (ח-ט) 'וַיְשַׁלַּח אֶת הַיּוֹנָה, וְגוֹ'', וְלֹא מָצְאָה הַיּוֹנָה מָנוֹחַ וְגוֹ', יְהוּדָה בַּר נַחְמָן בְּשֵׁם רַבִּי שִׁמְעוֹן
אָמַר, אִלּוּ מָצְאָה מָנוֹחַ, לֹא הָיְתָה חוֹזֶרֶת, וְדִכְוָתָהּ, (איכה א, ג) 'הִיא יָשְׁבָה בַגּוֹיִם לֹא מָצְאָה
מָנוֹחַ', אִלּוּ מָצְאָה מָנוֹחַ, לֹא הָיוּ חוֹזְרִים, וְדִכְוָתָהּ, (דברים כח, סה) 'וּבַגּוֹיִם הָהֵם לֹא תַרְגִּיעַ וְלֹא
יִהְיֶה מָנוֹחַ, וְגוֹ'', הָא אִלּוּ מָצְאָה מָנוֹחַ לֹא הָיוּ חוֹזְרִים.

6. AND HE SENT FORTH A DOVE . . . BUT THE DOVE FOUND NO REST, ETC.
(8:8): R. JUDAH B. NAHMAN SAID IN THE NAME OF RESH LAKISH: HAD IT
FOUND A PLACE OF REST, IT WOULD NOT HAVE RETURNED. SIMILARLY,
SHE DWELLETH AMONG THE NATIONS, SHE FINDETH NO REST (LAM.
1:3): BUT HAD SHE [THE NATION] FOUND REST, THEY WOULD NOT HAVE
RETURNED [TO GOD]. AGAIN, AND AMONG THESE NATIONS SHALT THOU
HAVE NO REPOSE, AND THERE SHALL BE NO REST FOR THE SOLE OF THY
FOOT (DEUT. 28:65): BUT HAD THEY FOUND IT, THEY WOULD NOT HAVE
RETURNED.

The expression ולא מצאה מנוח – *velo matzah manoach*, "and found no
rest," seems superfluous. It would have been enough for the verse to
have said that the dove returned to the ark because there was still water
on the earth. If, therefore, it included the expression that the dove found
no rest, it could only have been because the text wanted to make a point
of interpretation. The dove found no rest, but if it did find rest, it would
not have returned. This point is broadened to include the Jewish people,
based on the verse in Lamentations that says, "She dwells among the
nations, she finds no rest." Here, too, had the Jewish people found rest,
they would not have returned. The meaning here is either they would
not have returned to the land of Israel or they would not have returned
to God. This point is strengthened with the verse in Deuteronomy,
28:65: "And among these nations shalt thou have no repose, and there
shall be no rest for the sole of thy foot."

(י-יא) 'וַיָּחֶל עוֹד שִׁבְעַת יָמִים' רַבִּי יוֹסֵי אָמַר, שְׁלֹשָׁה שָׁבוּעוֹת יָמִים.

AND HE STAYED YET ANOTHER SEVEN DAYS (8:10). R. JOSE B. R. HANINA
SAID: THERE WERE THREE PERIODS OF SEVEN DAYS IN ALL.

The Midrash would then point out that what is now being described took place over a three-week period. There was one week between the time of the return of the raven to the dispatching of the dove. There was a second week that dated from the return of the dove to its second dispatching. Finally, the third was the time when the dove was sent out to the world and did not return.

'וַיֹּסֶף שַׁלַּח אֶת הַיּוֹנָה, וַתָּבֹא אֵלָיו הַיּוֹנָה וְגוֹ'', טָרָף בְּפִיהָ, וְגוֹ', מַהוּ 'טָרָף', קָטִיל, הֵיךְ מַה דְּאַתְּ אָמַר, (בראשית לז, לג) 'טָרֹף טֹרַף יוֹסֵף', אָמַר לָהּ, אִלּוּ שָׁבַקְתֵּהּ, אִילָן רַב הֲוָה מִתְעֲבֵד, מֵהֵיכָן הֵבִיאָה אוֹתוֹ, רַבִּי אַבָּא בַּר כָּהֲנָא אָמַר, מִשַּׁבְשׁוּשִׁין שֶׁבְּאֶרֶץ יִשְׂרָאֵל הֵבִיאָה אוֹתוֹ, רַבִּי לֵוִי אָמַר, מֵהַר הַמִּשְׁחָה, הֵבִיאָה אוֹתוֹ, דְּלָא טִפַּת אַרְעָא דְּיִשְׂרָאֵל בְּמַבּוּלָא, וְהוּא שֶׁהַקָּדוֹשׁ בָּרוּךְ הוּא אוֹמֵר לִיחֶזְקֵאל, (יחזקאל כב, כד) 'אֶרֶץ לֹא מְטֹהָרָה הִיא, וְלֹא גֻשְׁמָהּ בְּיוֹם זָעַם', רַב בֵּיבַי אָמַר, נִפְתְּחוּ לָהּ שַׁעֲרֵי גַן עֵדֶן וְהֵבִיאָה אוֹתוֹ, אָמַר רַבִּי אַבָּהוּ, אִלּוּ, מִגַּן עֵדֶן הֵבִיאָה אוֹתוֹ, לֹא הָיְתָה מְבִיאָה דָבָר מְעֻלֶּה, אוֹ קִנָּמוֹן, אוֹ פַּלְסָמוֹן, אֶלָּא, רֶמֶז רָמְזָה לוֹ, אָמְרָה לוֹ לְנֹחַ, מוּטָב מַר מִזֶּה, וְלֹא מָתוֹק מִתַּחַת יָדֶיךָ.

AND AGAIN HE SENT FORTH THE DOVE . . . AND THE DOVE CAME IN TO HIM . . . AND LO IN HER MOUTH AN OLIVE-LEAF FRESHLY PLUCKED (TARAF). WHAT DOES TARAF MEAN? KILLED [SLAIN], AS YOU READ, JOSEPH IS WITHOUT DOUBT TORN IN PIECES – TAROF TORAF (GEN. 37:33). HE SAID TO HER: 'HAD YOU LEFT IT, IT WOULD HAVE GROWN INTO A GREAT TREE.' WHENCE DID SHE BRING IT? R. ABBA SAID: SHE BROUGHT IT FROM THE YOUNG SHOOTS OF ERETZ ISRAEL. R. LEVI SAID: SHE BROUGHT IT FROM THE MOUNT OF OLIVES, FOR ERETZ ISRAEL WAS NOT SUBMERGED BY THE FLOOD. THUS THE HOLY ONE, BLESSED BE HE, SAID TO EZEKIEL: SON OF MAN, SAY UNTO HER: THOU ART A LAND THAT IS NOT CLEANSED, NOR RAINED UPON ON THE DAY OF INDIGNATION (EZEK. 22:24). R. BIRAI SAID: THE GATES OF THE GARDEN OF EDEN WERE OPENED FOR HER, AND FROM THERE SHE BROUGHT IT. SAID R. ABBAHU: HAD SHE BROUGHT IT FROM THE GARDEN OF EDEN, SHOULD SHE HAVE NOT BROUGHT SOMETHING BETTER, E.G., CINNAMON OR THE BALSAM LEAF? BUT IN FACT SHE GAVE HIM A HINT, SAYING TO HIM [IN EFFECT]: 'NOAH, BETTER IS BITTERNESS FROM THIS SOURCE [GOD], THAN SWEET-NESS FROM YOUR HAND.'

The use of the word טְרַף – *tarof* is a source for much speculation. The leaf was not whole and the question was, did it come from a tree affected by the Flood, or did it come from a tree not affected by the Flood?! If it came from a tree not affected by the Flood, it could only have been from the land of Israel, which, according to one view, was not affected by the Flood. According to another view, the land of Israel was infiltrated by some of the hot waters of the Flood, and that might have produced a leaf that would have lost its shape. The fact that the leaf seemed to be damp is interpreted to mean that it was an olive leaf and that it probably came from the Mount of Olives, as referred to by the Midrash, הר המשחה – *har hamishcha*. The reference to the Garden of Eden is a metaphor, as though to say, better the bitterness from God that the sweetness from flesh and blood.

(יב) 'וַיִּיָּחֶל עוֹד שִׁבְעַת יָמִים אֲחֵרִים', הָדָא מְסַיְּעָא לְהָא דַאֲמַר רַבִּי יוֹסֵי בַּר חֲנִינָא, שְׁלֹשָׁה שָׁבוּעוֹת יָמִים, 'וַיְשַׁלַּח אֶת הַיּוֹנָה וְלֹא יָסְפָה שׁוּב אֵלָיו עוֹד'.

AND HE STAYED YET OTHER SEVEN DAYS, ETC. (8:12). THIS SUPPORTS WHAT R. JOSE B. R. HANINA SAID: [HE WAITED] THREE SEVEN-DAY PERIODS IN ALL.

As indicated above, there was a period of three weeks between the departure of the raven and the departure of the dove for the third time.

—

Seed Thoughts

Commenting on the verse that the dove did not find a resting place for itself and had to return to the ark, the Midrash goes on to say that if it had found a resting place, chances are that it would not have returned to the ark. The text then goes on to apply this teaching to the Jewish people in general, saying that the Jews found no rest in the diaspora. However, if they had found such a rest, the chances are that they would not have returned to the land of Israel.

This message is repeated in the verse in Deuteronomy that describes certain terrible things that would happen some time in the future, not clearly dated. Here, too, it goes on to make the point that if they had found a resting place, or a suitable place to live in contentment, they would not have returned to their homeland. This can be looked upon as a very depressing teaching. Does it mean that the Jewish love for the land of Israel is a limited love, that could easily be discarded if things go well elsewhere? If that were to happen, what would our future be? Would we not disappear? The answer is that God intervenes and He sees to it that the people would find enough discomfort, both materially and spiritually, to motivate them with a longing to return to the land of Israel.

If we are dealing here not merely with a love for the land of Israel, but also with the question of doing *tshuvah*, meaning engaging in repentance, which leads to the transformation of an individual, the teaching is much more powerful. It would mean that if there is too much comfort in our lives, the Jewish people would lose the desire to come closer to God and the Torah. What happens is that God intervenes at such a moment and sees to it that enough things happen to interfere with the Jewish spiritual and material security, especially in the countries of the diaspora, and this tends to motivate the Jewish people to return to God and the Jewish nation.

It should be noted that the verses that have been quoted were from times when the Jews were experiencing the destruction of the Temples. The Book of Lamentations deals with the destruction of the first Temple. The verse in Deuteronomy refers to a time in the future, undated, but could, by the same token, be a reference to the destruction of the Second Temple, which was the most serious crisis facing Jewry.

This is not a happy message. It helps to point out, however, that as this book is being printed, we are approaching the anniversary of Israel's 64th Yom Ha'atzma'ut, 2012/5772. With the establishment of the state of Israel, everything has changed for the better. It is as though all the Jewish people, religious and secular, have done *tshuvah*. The majority of the Jewish people do not yet live in Israel. But that figure should be reached in several years. Granted that Israel still suffers from the challenge of terrorism and the hostility of its neighbors, but it has created a wonderful state in a short period of time with an economy and technology that is recognized for its excellence everywhere in the world. Israel still needs development, socially and ethically, and in uniting the various diaspora communities that have come to live in Israel and share its fate and its faith.

Let us hope that with the establishment of the state of Israel, the Jewish people will find *manoach*, true rest and peace not only in the state of Israel, but wherever in the world Jewish communities are created. Let us hope that we will never allow ourselves to have spiritual rest, but that we will always look to do *tshuvah*, which means to elevate ourselves as individuals and as a nation to our highest moral potentials.

—

Additional Commentary

Finding rest

Why was it necessary for the biblical verse quoted to include the phrase that the dove found no rest? It seemed completely superfluous. It would have been enough to say that the dove returned to the ark because there was still water on the earth, the discovery of which was the main point of the mission. Therefore, R. Judah says, the whole point of the inclusion of this phrase was to make the point that if the dove had found a resting place, it would not have returned. This is meant to teach all of us that no matter how comfortable we are with our material possessions, we must make sure not to lose sight of the goals of the spiritual life of Judaism. (*Tiferet Tzion*)

The day of the month

"And it came to pass in the 601st year, in the first month, the first day of the month, the waters were dried up from off the earth; and Noah removed the covering of the ark and looked, and behold, the face of the ground was dried." (Genesis 8:13) A main point of the verse was to indicate that the third and final time that the dove was sent by Noah was on the 601st year on the first day of the month. We are told that this was the tenth month, which was the month of Av. After forty days, this brings us to the tenth day of Elul. This was the day that Noah sent the raven. After this, Noah sent the dove twice. In the end, twenty-one days had gone by, and this would lead us to the first day of Tishrei. (*Tiferet Tzion*)

ז. (י:י-יד) 'וַיְהִי בְּאַחַת וְשֵׁשׁ מֵאוֹת שָׁנָה, בָּרִאשׁוֹן בְּאֶחָד לַחֹדֶשׁ'. תְּנִינַן, מִשְׁפַּט דּוֹר הַמַּבּוּל,
שְׁנֵים עָשָׂר חֹדֶשׁ, הָא כֵּיצַד, (בראשית ז, יא) 'בִּשְׁנַת שֵׁשׁ מֵאוֹת שָׁנָה לְחַיֵּי נֹחַ, בַּחֹדֶשׁ הַשֵּׁנִי
בְּשִׁבְעָה עָשָׂר לַחֹדֶשׁ', וּכְתִיב, (שם שם, יב) 'וַיְהִי הַגֶּשֶׁם עַל הָאָרֶץ אַרְבָּעִים יוֹם וְאַרְבָּעִים לָיְלָה',
זֶה מַרְחֶשְׁוָן וְכִסְלֵו, (שם שם, כד) 'וַיִּגְבְּרוּ הַמַּיִם עַל הָאָרֶץ חֲמִשִּׁים וּמְאַת יוֹם', הֲרֵי טֵבֵת וּשְׁבָט,
אֲדָר וְנִיסָן וְאִיָּר, (שם ח, ד) 'וַתָּנַח הַתֵּבָה בַּחֹדֶשׁ הַשְּׁבִיעִי בְּשִׁבְעָה עָשָׂר יוֹם לַחֹדֶשׁ עַל הָרֵי
אֲרָרָט' זֶה סִיוָן, שֶׁהוּא שְׁבִיעִי לְהַפְסָקַת גְּשָׁמִים, לְשִׁשָּׁה עָשָׂר יוֹם חָסְרוּ, אַמָּה לְאַרְבַּעַת יָמִים,
טֶפַח וּמֶחֱצָה בְּכָל יוֹם, וְנִמְצֵאתָ אוֹמֵר שֶׁהָיְתָה הַתֵּבָה מְשֻׁקַּעַת, בַּמַּיִם אַחַת עֶשְׂרֵה אַמָּה,
וְכֻלָּהֶם לְשִׁשִּׁים יוֹם חָסְרוּ, הֲדָא הוּא דִכְתִיב, (שם שם, ה) 'וְהַמַּיִם הָיוּ הָלוֹךְ וְחָסוֹר עַד הַחֹדֶשׁ
הָעֲשִׂירִי', זֶה אָב, שֶׁהוּא עֲשִׂירִי לִירִידַת גְּשָׁמִים.

7. AND HE SENT FORTH THE DOVE, AND SHE RETURNED NOT AGAIN
TO HIM ANY MORE, AND IT CAME TO PASS IN THE SIX HUNDRED AND
FIRST YEAR, IN THE FIRST MONTH, THE FIRST DAY OF THE MONTH. WE
LEARNED: THE JUDGMENT OF THE GENERATION OF THE FLOOD LASTED
TWELVE MONTHS. HOW IS THIS DEDUCED? (I) IN THE SIX HUNDREDTH
YEAR OF NOAH'S LIFE, IN THE SECOND MONTH, ON THE SEVENTEENTH
DAY OF THE MONTH ... THE WINDOWS OF HEAVEN WERE OPENED (GEN.
7:11); AND IT IS WRITTEN, (II) AND THE RAIN WAS UPON THE EARTH
FORTY DAYS AND FORTY NIGHTS (IBID., 12): THIS EMBRACES THE REST
OF MARHESHWAN AND KISLEW; (III) AND THE WATERS PREVAILED
UPON THE EARTH A HUNDRED AND FIFTY DAYS (IBID., 24): THIS COVERS
TEBETH, SHEBAT, ADAR, NISAN, AND IYAR; (IV) AND THE ARK RESTED IN
THE SEVENTH MONTH, ON THE SEVENTEENTH DAY, UPON THE MOUN-
TAINS OF ARARAT (IBID. 8:4): THAT MEANS SIVAN, THE SEVENTH MONTH
FROM THE DESCENT OF THE RAIN. FOR SIXTEEN DAYS THE WATER DI-
MINISHED AT THE RATE OF A CUBIT PER FOUR DAYS, WHICH IS ONE AND
A HALF HANDBREADTHS PER DAY. YOU MAY THUS INFER THAT THE ARK
WAS ELEVEN CUBITS IN THE WATER, AND IT ALL DRAINED OFF IN SIXTY
DAYS. THUS YOU READ, AND THE WATERS DECREASED CONTINUALLY
UNTIL THE TENTH MONTHS (IBID., 5): THAT IS AB, THE TENTH FROM
THE DESCENT OF THE RAIN.

It should be noted that the use of the term "the first day of the first month" here refers to the first of Tishrei. The use of Nisan as the first month did not happen until the exodus from Egypt, followed by the revelation at Mount Sinai. Since it was during the month of Nisan that the children of Israel were delivered, so Scripture states that Nisan became the first month. The English translation renders the Midrash very clear. Incidentally, the scriptural verse indicates that the Flood began on what we call today Rosh Hashanah and that it also ended on Rosh Hashanah.

דָּבָר אַחֵר, 'וַיְהִי בְּאַחַת וְשֵׁשׁ מֵאוֹת שָׁנָה בָּרִאשׁוֹן בְּאֶחָד לַחֹדֶשׁ חָרְבוּ הַמַּיִם מֵעַל הָאָרֶץ', נַעֲשֵׂית כְּמִין טָפִיחַ, 'וּבַחֹדֶשׁ הַשֵּׁנִי בְּשִׁבְעָה וְעֶשְׂרִים לַחֹדֶשׁ יָבְשָׁה הָאָרֶץ', נַעֲשֵׂית כַּגְּרִיד, זָרְעוּ אוֹתָהּ וְלֹא צָמְחָה, לָמָּה, שֶׁהָיָה סַמָּן קְלָלָה, וְאֵין סַמָּן קְלָלָה הֲוֵי לִבְרָכָה, וְהִמְתִּינוּ עַד שֶׁיָּרְדוּ גְּשָׁמִים, וְזָרְעוּ.

ANOTHER INTERPRETATION: (V) AND IT CAME TO PASS IN THE SIX HUNDRED AND FIRST YEAR, IN THE FIRST MONTH [I.E., TISHRI], ON THE FIRST DAY OF THE MONTH, THE WATERS WERE DRIED UP FROM OFF THE EARTH (IBID., 8:13): IT BECAME LIKE A MARSH. (VI) AND IN THE SECOND MONTH, ON THE SEVEN AND TWENTIETH DAY OF THE MONTH, WAS THE EARTH DRY (IBID., 8:14): IT BECAME LIKE PARCHED SOIL, WHICH THEY SOWED, BUT NOTHING WOULD GROW. WHY WAS THAT? BECAUSE IT [THE FLOOD] HAD COME AS A CURSE, AND A CURSE CANNOT TURN INTO A BLESSING; SO THEY WAITED UNTIL THE NEXT RAINFALL AND THEN THEY SOWED.

The use of the term דבר אחר – *davar acher*, meaning a different interpretation, has been eliminated from some of the manuscripts. The reason why it was eliminated has to do with the fact that even if it deals with the same two verses as above, it is discussing the difference between חרבו המים – *charvu hamayim* and יבשה הארץ – *yavshah ha'aretz*, both of which mean that the earth was desolate and/or that it dried up, which was not a topic that was discussed before. Nevertheless, our midrash and many others do include the term "another interpretation," since even if a new opinion has been introduced, it still refers to the same verses (Yefei To'ar). In the interval of approximately two months, between the expression "the waters dried up" and the expression "the land dried up," no vegetation was able to grow. The reason for this was that that the remaining waters and/or mud, even if a small amount, were a leftover of the Flood, which was regarded as a terrible curse on mankind. A curse cannot become a source of blessing and therefore, the vegetation was not produced again until all of the leftover waters had disappeared. (Maharzu)

לָא הֲוָה צְרִיךְ קְרָא לְמֵימַר אֶלָּא, בְּשִׁשָּׁה עָשָׂר יוֹם לַחֹדֶשׁ יוֹם הַשֵּׁנִי יָבְשָׁה הָאָרֶץ, וּמַה תַּלְמוּד לוֹמַר, 'בְּשִׁבְעָה וְעֶשְׂרִים יוֹם לַחֹדֶשׁ הַשֵּׁנִי יָבְשָׁה הָאָרֶץ', אֶלָּא, אֵלּוּ אַחַד עָשָׂר יוֹם שֶׁיְּמוֹת הַחַמָּה יְתֵרִים עַל יְמוֹת הַלְּבָנָה, אָמַר רַבָּן שִׁמְעוֹן בֶּן גַּמְלִיאֵל, כָּל מִי שֶׁהוּא רוֹצֶה לֵידַע שֶׁיְּמוֹת הַחַמָּה יְתֵרִים עַל יְמוֹת הַלְּבָנָה אַחַד עָשָׂר יוֹם, יִסְרוֹט לוֹ סְרִטָה בַכֹּתֶל, בִּתְקוּפַת תַּמּוּז, וְלַשָּׁנָה הַבָּאָה בְּאוֹתוֹ הַזְּמַן, אֵין הַשֶּׁמֶשׁ מַגַּעַת לְשָׁם עַד אַחַד עָשָׂר יוֹם, וּמִכָּאן אַתָּה יוֹדֵעַ שֶׁיְּמוֹת הַחַמָּה יְתֵרִים עַל יְמוֹת הַלְּבָנָה אַחַד עָשָׂר יוֹם.

NOW SHOULD NOT SCRIPTURE HAVE SAID, 'ON THE SIXTEENTH DAY OF THE MONTH WAS THE EARTH DRY`: WHY THEN IS IT STATED, 'AND IN THE SECOND MONTH, ON THE SEVEN AND TWENTIETH DAY OF THE MONTH, WAS THE EARTH DRY'? BECAUSE OF THE ELEVEN DAYS BY WHICH THE SOLAR YEAR EXCEEDS THE LUNAR YEAR. R. SIMEON B. GAMALIEL SAID: IF YOU WISH TO PROVE FOR YOURSELF THAT THE SOLAR YEAR EXCEEDS THE LUNAR YEAR BY ELEVEN DAYS, MAKE A MARK ON A WALL ON THE DAY OF THE SUMMER SOLSTICE; THE FOLLOWING YEAR AT THAT SEASON THE SUN WILL NOT REACH IT UNTIL ELEVEN DAYS LATER, AND FROM THIS YOU MAY KNOW THAT THE SOLAR YEAR EXCEEDS THE LUNAR YEAR BY ELEVEN DAYS.

That is astonishing. There is an anomaly here in the dates of the closing days of the Flood. On the one hand, the waters disappeared on the sixteenth day of the month, where it says that the earth was dry. On the other hand, it repeats that the earth was dry on the 27th. The difference of eleven days is explained as the difference between the days of the lunar year and the days of the solar year. As R. Simeon b. Gamliel points out in the text, the lunar year is not reliable as a guide, because each year it appears at a different time. Since the intercalation of the Jewish calendar did not happen until many centuries later, this midrash has to be understood based on a solar year and the other dates have to be understood accordingly.

—

Seed Thoughts

Our midrash has a development that can only be described as somewhat astonishing. The difference between the dates in the verses that describe the drying up of the earth as being on the sixteenth day and the twenty-seventh day respectively, is interpreted as being accounted for by the difference between the length of the lunar year and that of the solar year. The difference, as we know by now, is eleven days. Although it may solve the problem of the text, it does raise many other questions. How, for example, do we know when or whether Scripture is dealing with the solar year or the lunar year? How are we able to find out? These questions become very important once the Midrash makes use of the difference between the solar and lunar systems. Let us hope that some day these questions will be answered.

—

Additional Commentary

The twenty-seventh day of the month: Rashi's Summary

The downflow of the waters is described as taking place in the second month, until the end of the sixteenth day (the seventeenth of the month was the first dry day). Why the difference between this date and the twenty-seventh? The answer is that the solar year is longer than the lunar year by eleven days. Hence, the calculation of the generation of the Flood was based on a complete year, שנה תמימה – *shanah tmimah*, a solar year. (Rashi on Genesis 8:14)

א. (ח, טו-טז) 'וַיְדַבֵּר אֱ־לֹהִים אֶל נֹחַ לֵאמֹר, צֵא מִן הַתֵּבָה'

1. AND GOD SPOKE UNTO NOAH, SAYING: GO FORTH FROM THE ARK, ETC.
(8:15).

What stopped Noah from leaving the ark? Why did he need a command from the Holy One, Blessed be He, for him to do so? The answer
is that he was locked into the ark, as the verse reads in Genesis 7:16, "And
God shut him in." He, therefore, was not able to leave on his own accord
and he prayed to be released from his confinement and wanted the opportunity to thank God by means of a thanksgiving offering. (Aryeh
Mirkin)

(תהלים קמב, ח) 'הוֹצִיאָה מִמַּסְגֵּר נַפְשִׁי לְהוֹדוֹת אֶת שְׁמֶךָ, בִּי יַכְתִּרוּ צַדִּיקִים כִּי תִגְמֹל עָלָי',
'הוֹצִיאָה מִמַּסְגֵּר נַפְשִׁי' זֶה נֹחַ, שֶׁהָיָה סָגוּר בַּתֵּבָה, שְׁנֵים עָשָׂר חֹדֶשׁ, 'לְהוֹדוֹת אֶת שְׁמֶךָ'

IT IS WRITTEN, BRING MY SOUL OUT OF PRISON, THAT I MAY GIVE
THANKS UNTO THY NAME; THE RIGHTEOUS SHALL CROWN THEMSELVES
BECAUSE OF ME; FOR THOU WILT DEAL BOUNTIFULLY WITH ME (PS.
142:8). 'BRING MY SOUL OUT OF PRISON' ALLUDES TO NOAH, WHO WAS
IMPRISONED TWELVE MONTHS IN THE ARK; 'THAT I MAY GIVE THANKS
UNTO THY NAME': TO GIVE THANKS TO THINE [AWE-INSPIRING] NAME;'

The Psalm from which this verse (142:8) is quoted begins with the
expression משכיל לדוד – *maskil leDavid*. In this Psalm, he writes, "Deliver
my soul from its confinement [or imprisonment]." But nowhere in the
biography of David do we find that he was locked up in such a way that
he needed to be freed. It was for this reason that the commentators
transferred the meaning of this section to apply to Noah, about whom
the Torah states that God confined him, inside the ark. It should be
noted that Noah was completely and utterly involved in the work of
the ark. He slept very little and suffered from chills and colds and the
tremendous stench coming from the animals. It is for this reason that

he prayed to be released from his confinement, at which time he would offer thanksgiving to God. (RZWE)

לָתֵת הוֹדָיָה לִשְׁמֶךָ, 'בִּי יַכְתִּרוּ צַדִּיקִים', יִתְכַּלְּלוּן בִּי צַדִּיקַיָּא, 'כִּי תִגְמֹל עָלָי' שֶׁנְּמַלְתָּ עָלַי, וְאָמַרְתָּ לִי, 'צֵא מִן הַתֵּבָה'.

'THE RIGHTEOUS SHALL CROWN THEMSELVES BECAUSE OF ME': THE
RIGHTEOUS SHALL GLORY IN ME. 'FOR THOU WILT DEAL BOUNTIFULLY
WITH ME': THOU DIDST DEAL BOUNTIFULLY WITH ME AND SAY UNTO
ME: GO FORTH FROM THE ARK.

The first interpretation, as mentioned above, was that Noah was locked in the ark and had to be released. The second interpretation is of an entirely different nature. Noah was so overwhelmed by God's miracle, in particular, from his own personal deliverance from the Flood, that he resolved only to do God's bidding and not rely on his own choices. God had ordered him to enter the ark with his family and he would remain there until God ordered him to leave. When that order came, Noah left the ark happily and thankfully.

—

Seed Thoughts

What we have in this Midrash is an outpouring of thanksgiving. Noah was grateful to God, not only for the miracles that he experienced with the Flood, but also for the plain and ordinary laws of nature, which might also be construed as the greatest miracle of all, and which had now returned to their normal pattern. He had worked tremendously hard on the ark for a period of twelve months, and his achievements were considerable. There are many ways of expressing thanksgiving and words alone are only one form. Sometimes the way a person acts is the greatest form of thanksgiving. Much as Noah wanted to leave the ark at the conclusion of the Flood, for the work was hard and the confinement of the ark was difficult, he would not do so until God asked him to leave. The Flood was God's doing and its conclusion was dependent on His decision. This attitude of humility on Noah's part was a major form of thanksgiving. The rabbis interpreted his behavior as *shvuat Noach*. Noah's sacred reminder to all the generations was one of the highest forms of religious behavior. (See additional commentary).

—

Additional Commentary

Noah's prayer

Noah's tremendous desire to offer thanksgiving to God upon his release from the confinement of the ark was interpreted by the sages of Israel as a precedent to all Jews to be engaged in the process of thanksgiving whenever they complete an achievement or a struggle. It does not matter who helps us in terms of these achievements, it is only to God that our thanksgiving should be rendered. The sages introduced this concept into our prayers and interpreted the last verse of the second paragraph of the *Shema* (which begins with the words, *vehayah im shamoa*) as being שבועת נח – *shvuat Noach*, which should be translated not so much as the vow of Noah, but as his challenge or request to all future generations. The last verse begins with, למען ירבו ימיכם – *lema'an yirbu yemei'hem* and ends with the words, כימי השמים על הארץ – *k'yimei hashamayim al ha'aretz*, "In order to prolong your days ... like the days of the Heaven on the Earth." (RZWE)

Parashah Thirty-Four, *Midrash Two*

ב. (שם יא, ה) 'ה' צַדִּיק יִבְחָן, וְרָשָׁע וְאֹהֵב חָמָס שָׂנְאָה נַפְשׁוֹ'

2. THE LORD TRIETH THE RIGHTEOUS, ETC. (PS. 11:5).

The Midrash will explain that it interprets the verse as referring to Noah. In what respect is Noah being tested? The question to be determined is whether Noah will make the decision to leave the ark of his own volition, or will he wait for a commandment from God, inviting him to leave the ark.

אָמַר רַבִּי יוֹנָתָן, הַיּוֹצֵר הַזֶּה, אֵינוֹ בּוֹדֵק קַנְקַנִּים מְרוֹעָעִים, שֶׁאֵינוֹ מַקִּישׁ עֲלֵיהֶם אַחַת, עַד שֶׁהִיא פּוֹקַעַת, וּמַה הוּא בּוֹדֵק קַנְקַנִּים יָפִים, שֶׁאֲפִלּוּ הוּא מַקִּישׁ עָלָיו כַּמָּה פְעָמִים אֵינוֹ נִשְׁבָּר, כָּךְ, אֵין הַקָּדוֹשׁ בָּרוּךְ הוּא מְנַסֶּה, אֶלָּא אֶת הַצַּדִּיקִים. אָמַר רַבִּי יוֹסֵי, הַפִּשְׁתָּנִי הַזֶּה, בְּשָׁעָה שֶׁהוּא יוֹדֵעַ שֶׁהַפִּשְׁתָּן שֶׁלּוֹ יָפָה, כָּל שֶׁהוּא כוֹתְשָׁהּ הִיא מִשְׁתַּבַּחַת, וְכָל שֶׁהוּא מַקִּישׁ עָלֶיהָ הִיא מִשְׁתַּמֶּנֶת, וּבְשָׁעָה שֶׁהוּא יוֹדֵעַ שֶׁפִּשְׁתָּנוֹ רָעָה, אֵינוֹ מַסְפִּיק לְהַקִּישׁ עָלֶיהָ עַד שֶׁהִיא פּוֹקַעַת, כָּךְ, אֵין הַקָּדוֹשׁ בָּרוּךְ הוּא מְנַסֶּה, אֶלָּא אֶת הַצַּדִּיקִים, שֶׁנֶּאֱמַר 'ה' צַדִּיק יִבְחָן' רַבִּי אֱלִיעֶזֶר אָמַר, לְבַעַל הַבַּיִת שֶׁהָיוּ לוֹ שְׁתֵּי פָרוֹת, אַחַת כֹּחָהּ יָפֶה, וְאַחַת כֹּחָהּ רַע, עַל מִי הוּא נוֹתֵן הָעֹל לֹא עַל אוֹתָהּ שֶׁכֹּחָהּ יָפֶה, כָּךְ, אֵין הַקָּדוֹשׁ בָּרוּךְ הוּא מְנַסֶּה אֶלָּא הַצַּדִּיק, שֶׁנֶּאֱמַר 'ה' צַדִּיק יִבְחָן'.

R. JONATHAN SAID: A POTTER DOES NOT TEST DEFECTIVE VESSELS, BECAUSE HE CANNOT GIVE THEM A SINGLE BLOW WITHOUT BREAKING THEM. SIMILARLY, THE HOLY ONE, BLESSED BE HE, DOES NOT TEST THE WICKED BUT ONLY THE RIGHTEOUS: THUS, 'THE LORD TRIETH THE RIGHTEOUS.' R. JOSE B. R. HANINA SAID: WHEN A FLAX WORKER KNOWS THAT HIS FLAX IS OF GOOD QUALITY, THE MORE HE BEATS IT THE MORE IT IMPROVES AND THE MORE IT GLISTENS; BUT IF IT IS OF INFERIOR QUALITY, HE CANNOT GIVE IT ONE KNOCK BUT IT SPLITS. SIMILARLY, THE LORD DOES NOT TEST THE WICKED BUT ONLY THE RIGHTEOUS, AS IT SAYS: 'THE LORD TRIETH THE RIGHTEOUS.' R. ELIEZER SAID: WHEN A MAN POSSESSES TWO COWS, ONE STRONG AND THE OTHER FEEBLE, UPON WHICH DOES HE PUT THE YOKE? SURELY UPON THE STRONG ONE. SIMILARLY, THE LORD TESTS NONE BUT THE RIGHTEOUS; HENCE, 'THE LORD TRIETH THE RIGHTEOUS.'

T he three parables that are listed in the Midrash each have different
conclusions. In the first parable, the sufferings that the righteous experience are to the credit of the tzaddik when he withstands them. Whereas,
the reaction of the evil person to this kind of suffering is to make him
rebel even more. That is why only the righteous one is tested in this
manner. The second parable is meant to indicate that suffering is meant
to purify the righteous one from his sins and help him rise to a higher
level. In the third parable, the suffering is to benefit the world, because
the righteous person becomes known and is singled out for his special
behavior, whereas the evil person cannot stand up to this challenge and
is therefore not even tested. (Aryeh Mirkin)

דָּבָר אַחֵר, 'ה' צַדִּיק יִבְחָן' זֶה נֹחַ, שֶׁנֶּאֱמַר 'צֵא מִן הַתֵּבָה'.

ANOTHER INTERPRETATION: 'THE LORD TRIETH THE RIGHTEOUS' AP-
PLIES TO NOAH [WHO STAYED IN THE ARK UNTIL GOD SAID TO HIM]: GO
FORTH FROM THE ARK.

T he verse that says, "God tests the righteous" is interpreted here as
referring to Noah. This test began when Noah was invited to enter the
ark, because on that occasion it stated אותך ראיתי צדיק – *ot'kha ra'iti tzaddik*, I watched your behavior and know that you are a tzaddik. He did
not simply say, "You are righteous." He said, "I watched your behavior,"
which meant that the tzaddik has to become a model so that when his
behavior becomes known, it can be emulated. The testing of Noah was
completed only after he left the ark, because during the course of the
Flood, he was able to stand up to all the suffering that his leadership
engendered in terms of the hard work in feeding the animals and the
various illnesses that the Midrash tells us.

Seed Thoughts

Why is it necessary for God to test the righteous? After all, He is all-
knowing and is defined as One Who knows the inner thoughts of a
human being. The answer is that God does not need this test for Himself, but needs it for the world. The world has to know that there are
righteous people living in it who should be known and singled out. As
in the case of Noah where it says, "I watched your behavior, and I know
and others will know that you are righteous.'"

There is a saying in the Talmud, which is very difficult to translate and very difficult to understand. It reads, כל מי שגדול מחבירו יצרו גדול ממנו – *kol mi shegadol mechavero yitzro gadol mimeno*, and it means that whoever is greater than his fellow, his passion or desire or ambition is also greater than that of his fellow." What does this mean? The word *yetzer* is usually associated with the concept of *yetzer harah*, which is the evil inclination. What we are talking about here is not necessarily evil, but an alternative to the righteous life. A tzaddik is a person of tremendous talent, leadership and self-confidence. He can look around at the world and become aware that there are areas in the industrial life and in the various professions where the rewards are tremendous and which his talent could easily master. The challenge could become a great temptation. But the one who transcends this challenge and chooses the Torah, with all of its material limitations, is the real tzaddik. The world does not always know about the inner struggle, but God knows and He sees to it that the righteous will be singled out for good, if not in this world, then certainly in the World to Come. In connection with this notion, the *Yefei To'ar* has a beautiful interpretation of the verse that our midrash is quoting, ה' צדיק יבחן. He says that we should translate this phrase as though it were written, ה' צדיק יבחר, God does not simply *test* the righteous, He *chooses* them with His approval and singles them out for this world and the World to Come.

Please see Seed Thought to parashah 32, midrash 3 for more insight.

—

Additional Commentary

The three parables

In connection with the parable of the vessels, the owner of the vessels is not interested in testing them for himself, but only for potential buyers, to show which ones are good. Thus, the Holy One does not bother testing the evil ones, but only the righteous, to demonstrate their spiritual strength so that the world will learn how to revere God. The testing is not to help the Holy One, Himself, but to help the world.

In the parable of the flax, R. Jose does not disagree with R. Jonathan. R. Jonathan was dealing with one who is a complete tzaddik, whereas R. Jose was concerned with a person who had not yet reached that level. That is why he used the illustration of the flax, maintaining that the more it was beaten, the more it improved. Similarly, suffering helps a good person improve his faith and overcome whatever bad habits he may have.

The third parable indicates that there is an aspect to the righteous person that the world does not really know, only God knows. There is an inner struggle in the life of a righteous person to achieve the good life. God knows how much a good person has to fight in order to fulfill a commandment or keep away from sin. God helps the righteous in this struggle, which is the meaning of the verse that says, "I have seen in your behavior that you are a tzaddik." Only God can recognize these attributes, since only He knows the inner battles that the good inclination has to wage with the evil inclination. (*Tiferet Tzion*)

ג. רַבִּי יוּדָן, בְּשֵׁם רַבִּי אַיְבוּ, פָּתַח,

3. R. JUDAN COMMENCED IN R. AIBU'S NAME:

This Midrash is intended as a continuation to the phrase, "Leave the ark," which God addressed to Noah.

משלי יב, יג) 'בְּפֶשַׁע שְׂפָתַיִם מוֹקֵשׁ רָע וַיֵּצֵא מִצָּרָה צַדִּיק', מִמֶּרֶד שֶׁמָּרְדוּ דּוֹר הַמַּבּוּל בְּהַקָּדוֹשׁ בָּרוּךְ הוּא, בָּאת לָהֶם תַּקָּלָה, 'וַיֵּצֵא מִצָּרָה צַדִּיק' זֶה נֹחַ, שֶׁנֶּאֱמַר 'צֵא מִן הַתֵּבָה'.

IN THE TRANSGRESSION OF THE LIPS IS A SNARE TO THE EVIL MAN (PROV. 12:13): THROUGH THE REBELLION OF THE GENERATION OF THE FLOOD AGAINST THE HOLY ONE, BLESSED BE HE, THEY WERE BROUGHT TO GRIEF. BUT THE RIGHTEOUS COMETH OUT OF TROUBLE (IBID.): THIS APPLIES TO NOAH: HENCE, GO FORTH FROM THE ARK.

Elsewhere in the rabbinic writings (Sanhedrin 57a), the generation of the Flood is described as in rebellion against God. They would say, as described by the verse in Job 21:15 (which is often described as referring to the generation of the Flood), "Who is God that we should worship Him?" or "How do we benefit that we pray to Him?" It is out of this rebellion that the people of the generation of the Flood were removed from the world. But out of this terrible crisis, a righteous man emerged, whose name was Noah. He then received the command to leave the ark, which was intended to mean, "Begin your leadership of the new world."

—

Additional Commentary

Leave the ark

The purpose of R. Judan's comment is to explain the scriptural text, "Leave the ark." Why is this a problem? Look at it this way: When Reuven wants Shimon to leave the house, it depends upon what his main goal is. If there is an emergency, he would probably wish to say to him, "Leave the house." However, if he merely wants him to go outside, he would simply say, "Go outside." In the case of Noah, the Holy One, Blessed be He had a special purpose. He wanted him to leave the ark for the sake of the survival of the world, to engage in reproduction, et cetera. For this, it would be enough to say, "Go outside." However, Noah was involved with the generation of the Flood, who were in rebellion against God. And in the case of most rebels against God, suffering only makes them hate God all the more. Noah was never part of this rebellion and he used the suffering and the tribulation of his experience as a way of doing *tshuvah*. According to Rashi, all the forty days in which the rain flooded the world could have been used as an opportunity for repentance, and the Flood would have immediately stopped. But those in rebellion are not capable of this kind of penitence. Noah, however, used the tragedy to transform his life, character and personality, and he emerged as a truly righteous personality. The order from God to leave the ark was meant to emphasize the word "ark" and to show that both the ark itself and Noah's struggles within the ark had made it possible for him to emerge from the ark as God's representative after the Flood. (*Tiferet Tzion*)

Leave the ark

After the verse that reads, "[God] regretted having created mankind" (Gen 6:6), it then says that Noah had found favor (ibid., v. 8). Despite the regret, God favored Noah. The interpretation is not so much that Noah was a full-fledged tzaddik, but that he was sufficiently worthy to find God's favor. The sufferings and sacrifices that he made during the twelve months of the Flood atoned for all his previous misdemeanors and sins. As it was written in midrash 31:09, "Just as the bird's nest [קן – *ken*] purified the leper, so did the ark purify Noah." It was with this in mind that God said, "Go forth from the ark," thus, informing him that what now would be upon him, in terms of the responsibilities of the new world, are due entirely to the ark that purified his life and raised him to his present level. (*Tiferet Tzion*)

Seed Thoughts

The average reader of the text would never be bothered by a phrase such as, "Leave the ark." But the sages of the Midrash were deeply involved with the meaning of every word. It was important to them to know why a particular phrase was used and not its alternative, which appeared to be simpler. The *Tiferet Tzion* made a major effort to explain this particular midrash. If, for example, Reuven wants to ask Shimon to leave his house, it would depend upon the purpose of his leaving. If it were an emergency, he would say something like, "Leave the house immediately." If, however, the purpose was merely social, he would simply say, "Go outside, I would like to talk to you." The biblical text could have said, צא החוצה – *tze hahutzah*, meaning, "go outside." After all, the Flood was over and the earth had become dry again. There was nothing to keep Noah inside the ark. However, there was another consideration. There is a view mentioned several times in previous midrashim that Noah was only partially righteous. He could not be compared, as say some of the sages, to Abraham or to others in other generations who were at the height of spiritual exaltation. However, what happened in the ark changed all of that. Noah's work with the animals, his care and love for them, his illnesses from which he suffered from time to time, all contributed to his purification. He may have entered the ark as only partially righteous, but he left the ark as a full-fledged righteous personality, capable of leading the new world. The verse, therefore, should be interpreted to mean, "Noah, you are now ready to leave the ark, which has fulfilled its purpose in proving and improving your character and personality. You can now leave the ark and enter the world."

PARASHAH THIRTY-FOUR, *Midrash Four*

ד. דָּבָר אַחֵר, 'צֵא מִן הַתֵּבָה', כְּתִיב (קהלת י, ד) 'אִם רוּחַ הַמּוֹשֵׁל תַּעֲלֶה עָלֶיךָ מְקוֹמְךָ אַל תַּנַּח',
מְדַבֵּר בְּנֹחַ, אָמַר נֹחַ, כְּשֵׁם שֶׁלֹּא נִכְנַסְתִּי בַתֵּבָה אֶלָּא בִּרְשׁוּת, כָּךְ אֵין אֲנִי יוֹצֵא אֶלָּא בִּרְשׁוּת,
(בראשית ז, א) 'בֹּא אֶל הַתֵּבָה', (שם שם, ז) 'וַיָּבֹא נֹחַ', 'צֵא מִן הַתֵּבָה', (שם ח, יח) 'וַיֵּצֵא נֹחַ'.

4. IF THE SPIRIT OF THE RULER RISE UP AGAINST THEE, LEAVE NOT THY
PLACE (ECCL. 10:4). THIS REFERS TO NOAH. NOAH ARGUED: JUST AS I
ENTERED THE ARK ONLY WHEN I WAS PERMITTED, SO MAY I NOT GO OUT
SAVE WITH PERMISSION. R. JUDAH B. R. ILAI SAID: HAD I BEEN THERE I
WOULD HAVE BROKEN IT AND GONE OUT! NOAH, HOWEVER, SAID: I EN-
TERED WITH PERMISSION AND I WILL LEAVE WITH PERMISSION. THUS:
COME THOU INTO THE ARK – AND NOAH WENT IN; GO FORTH FROM THE
ARK – AND NOAH WENT FORTH.

This Midrash is also based on the text wherein God told Noah to leave
the ark. The point is that Noah did not leave the ark of his own accord,
but waited until he received a commandment to do so. The Midrash tries
to explain this passage by reference to Ecclesiastes, which deals with the
ruler of a country, presumably with dictatorial powers, such that if he
places you in a situation of his choosing, the best advice for you is not
to leave until that same ruler gives you permission. That explains Noah's
behavior in the sense that he entered the ark at God's command and he
left the ark at God's command.

⁓

Seed Thoughts

Rashi, on the verse in Ecclesiastes, makes the point that the ruler is a
metaphor for God. If, therefore, God places you in a certain situation,
you are certainly well advised not to leave that situation without His
permission. What is involved here on Noah's part is a great sense of
responsibility. He felt that he was doing God's work in the ark and could
not leave until the work was completed. He would not accept the fact
that his work was completed merely by what he saw and heard. It had to

be by direct command. Perhaps there were other obligations that God had in store for him, so he deduced that he had to wait. The personality of Noah, therefore, becomes an important symbol of responsibility.

—

Additional Commentary

The spirit of the ruler

The intention of the Midrash is to explain why Noah felt he had to receive an explicit command from God in order to justify his going out of the ark. The verse from Ecclesiastes is brought in order to explain this behavior. Many of the commentators on this verse, including Rashi, identify the ruler as representing the Holy One, Blessed be He. The spirit of the ruler can also be defined as the spirit of prophecy. Prophecy is usually granted to extraordinary individuals whose lives have been sanctified to the point where they can sometimes make their own spiritual decisions. We know that Moses made three important decisions of his own, which were later approved by God; for example, he added one day of abstinence before the giving of the Torah (*Shabbat* 87a). Noah was not on this level of prophecy, therefore, he felt dependent on the decisions of the "ruler," who is, of course, God. For him to have left the ark of his own accord would have been to make a decision without the approval of the Divine Ruler, which was something he would not do. This notion that Noah was not capable of being an initiator is in accordance with the view of R. Yehudah (Midrash 30:10), that Noah was righteous only in his generation, but was not righteous to be compared with those who are prophets. (*Tiferet Tzion*)

ה. דָּבָר אַחֵר, 'צֵא מִן הַתֵּבָה', כְּתִיב (קהלת ז, יט) 'הַחָכְמָה תָּעֹז לֶחָכָם, מֵעֲשָׂרָה שַׁלִּיטִים אֲשֶׁר
הָיוּ בָּעִיר', 'הַחָכְמָה תָּעֹז לֶחָכָם' זֶה נֹחַ, 'מֵעֲשָׂרָה שַׁלִּיטִים' מֵעֲשָׂרָה דוֹרוֹת מֵאָדָם וְעַד נֹחַ,
וּמִכֻּלָּם לֹא דִבַּרְתִּי, עִם אֶחָד מֵהֶם, אֶלָּא עִמָּךְ, 'וַיְדַבֵּר אֱ-לֹהִים אֶל נֹחַ'.

5. WISDOM IS A STRONGHOLD TO THE WISE MAN MORE THAN TEN RUL-
ERS (ECCL. 7:19): THIS ALLUDES TO NOAH [TO WHOM GOD SAID]: 'OF
THE TEN GENERATIONS FROM ADAM TO NOAH I SPOKE WITH NONE BUT
THEE': HENCE, AND GOD SPOKE UNTO NOAH, SAYING.

T he unusual aspect of this verse is that it uses the verb וידבר – *vaydaber*
in addressing Noah, whereas up to this point, the word for speech was
always a form of the word אמור – *emor*. The use of this different verb
gives a special importance to Noah, because it was only used later in
connection with Moses and the prophets. It is in this respect that the
verse from Ecclesiastes is brought, indicating that a leader with wisdom
is far more important than the council of ten, all of whom may not have
such qualifications. Noah is here identified as that type of wise leader.
This special wisdom Noah had enabled him to look after the needs of
all the living creatures in the ark, whose needs and demands were quite
variegated. Noah learned how to handle all of them. This wisdom also
taught him to abide by the rules of the ark, which were God's rules,
and not to leave it except with His permission. One of the additional
proofs that Noah's wisdom was greater than that of the ten generations
between him and Adam was the fact that only with him was communication with God referred to with the verb *vaydaber*. *Vaydaber* is used in
the conversation to give it special importance.

—

Seed Thoughts

Tradition ascribes the authorship of the Book of Ecclesiastes to King
Solomon, who is reputed to be the wisest of men. When the verse

states that the wise man is more important than the council of ten, the reference must surely have been to King Solomon, himself (see Mirkin below). By applying this verse to Noah, he is very considerably raised in importance. That is the special contribution made by the three midrashim that we are now studying that begin with the expression, "*Davar acher*," meaning, "an additional interpretation." The ordinary expression of "Go out from the ark" has been given one sophisticated interpretation after the other. In our present Midrash, Noah declined to leave the ark until the last moment in order to wait for God's permission. He was concerned that at the last moment there might be additional information, instruction or meaning conveyed to him.

—

Additional Commentary

With no other "dibarti" (did I speak)

The text differentiates between the verbs *amira* and *dibur* for speech. Very often, *amira* is used in the sense of giving an order or expressing an obligation. For example, in Deuteronomy 26:17, את ה' האמרת היום – *et Hashem he'emarta hayom*, means, "You chose God to be your God." By the same token, ה' האמירך היום – *Hashem he-emirkha hayom*, means, "God chose you to be His people."

By contrast, the word *dibur* seems to be used for plain, ordinary conversation between one person and another. The peculiar aspect of God's message to Noah is that it is conveyed with neither a sense of obligation nor one of giving permission, but it is simply a plain and ordinary request to leave the ark. (Aryeh Mirkin)

The ten rulers

King Solomon, the author of Ecclesiastes according to the Talmud, may have very well been referring to himself where he writes that one wise man is better than ten rulers, considering that many thousands of sayings and proverbs were attributed to him. The use of the expression "ten rulers" is also significant. King Solomon had close relations with Hiram, the king of Tyre, and we know that the king of Tyre was helped by ten rulers who acted as an advisory council. This idea of ten rulers can also be found in Plato's Republic, which was the basis of the legal systems of both ancient Greece and ancient Rome. While the purpose of the council was to advise the king and prevent bad decisions, and while it is true that no one person can be perfect, still, Ecclesiastes makes the point that one wise leader knows what he is doing is better than a council of ten, many of whom may have been merely average in their leadership. (Aryeh Mirkin)

ו. דָּבָר אַחֵר, כְּתִיב (שם ג, א) 'לַכֹּל זְמָן, וְעֵת לְכָל חֵפֶץ תַּחַת הַשָּׁמָיִם', זְמָן הָיָה לְנֹחַ לִכָּנֵס לַתֵּבָה, שֶׁנֶּאֱמַר (בראשית ז, א) 'בֹּא אַתָּה וְכָל בֵּיתְךָ אֶל הַתֵּבָה', וּזְמָן הָיָה לוֹ שֶׁיֵּצֵא מִמֶּנָּה, שֶׁנֶּאֱמַר 'צֵא מִן הַתֵּבָה',

6. TO EVERYTHING THERE IS A SEASON, AND A TIME TO EVERY PURPOSE
(ECCL. 3:1): THERE WAS A TIME FOR NOAH TO ENTER THE ARK, AS IT IS
WRITTEN, COME THOU AND ALL THY HOUSE INTO THE ARK (GEN. 7:1),
AND A TIME FOR HIM TO LEAVE IT: GO FORTH FROM THE ARK.

This Midrash interprets the expression וידבר – *vaydaber* as indicating harsh or strong language, as opposed to *vayomer*, which is a softer
form of speech. Thus, "Leave the ark" is interpreted as a very strong and
determined order by God to Noah. The verse in Ecclesiastes that says
that there is a time for everything is, therefore, also interpreted harshly.
Noah was ordered to enter the ark at a certain time, whether he wanted
to or not. He actually did want to enter in order to escape the Flood.
Nevertheless, he was not given the option of remaining. In terms of
leaving the ark, that, too, happened in its special time and he also was
ordered to leave the ark, whether he wanted to or not. Therefore, the
use of the term *vaydaber* translates as, "And God ordered Noah to leave
the ark."

מָשָׁל, לְפַרְנָס שֶׁיָּצָא מִן הַמָּקוֹם, וְהוֹשִׁיב אַחֵר תַּחְתָּיו, כֵּיוָן שֶׁבָּא, אָמַר לוֹ, צֵא מִמְּקוֹמֶךָ.
HE MAY BE COMPARED TO AN ADMINISTRATOR WHO DEPARTED FOR A
CERTAIN SPOT, PUTTING SOMEONE IN HIS PLACE. ON HIS RETURN HE
SAID TO THE OTHER, 'LEAVE YOUR POSITION.'

This is explained by a series of parables. The first one tells of a permanent administrator, who appointed a replacement while he had to be
away, but when he returned, the replacement was dismissed. In the case
of Noah, God was the "administrator" and He appointed Noah to look
after the affairs of the ark until the Flood subsided. After this time, God,
the true Administrator, took over again.

מָשָׁל, לְסוֹפֵר, שֶׁיָּצָא לְמָקוֹם אַחֵר. וְהוֹשִׁיב אַחֵר תַּחְתָּיו, כֵּיוָן שֶׁבָּא, אָמַר לוֹ, צֵא מִמְּקוֹמָךְ, כָּךְ
נֹחַ. 'צֵא מִן הַתֵּבָה',

THIS COULD ALSO BE COMPARED TO A SPECIAL EXPERT [A TEACHER
OF CHILDREN, ACCORDING TO ARYEH MIRKIN] WHO DEPARTED TO AN-
OTHER SPOT, PUTTING SOMEONE IN HIS PLACE. ON HIS RETURN HE SAID
TO THE OTHER, 'LEAVE YOUR POSITION.'

The second parable deals with the *sofer*, interpreted as being an expert.
In the ark, this would refer to one who knew about the behavior of the
animals in the ark and their needs in terms of time and space. Noah was
not this kind of expert at the beginning of the Flood, but he had become
one by the end of the Flood. He had learned much from the pressure of
his experiences. Still, at the end, God came and replaced him and told
him that the time for him to leave had arrived.

וְלֹא קִבֵּל עָלָיו, לָצֵאת, אָמַר, אֵצֵא וְאֶהְיֶה פָּרֶה וְרָבֶה לַמְּאֵרָה, עַד שֶׁנִּשְׁבַּע לוֹ הַמָּקוֹם שֶׁאֵינוֹ
מֵבִיא מַבּוּל לָעוֹלָם, שֶׁנֶּאֱמַר (ישעיה נד, ט) 'כִּי מֵי נֹחַ זֹאת לִי, אֲשֶׁר נִשְׁבַּעְתִּי מֵעֲבֹר מֵי נֹחַ'.

2 BUT HE [NOAH] WAS RELUCTANT TO GO OUT, SAYING, 'AM I TO GO OUT
AND BEGET CHILDREN FOR A CURSE?' UNTIL THE HOLY ONE, BLESSED BE
HE, SWORE TO HIM THAT HE WOULD NOT BRING ANOTHER FLOOD UPON
THE WORLD, AS IT SAYS, FOR THIS IS THE WATERS OF NOAH UNTO ME;
FOR AS I HAVE SWORN THAT THE WATERS OF NOAH SHOULD NO MORE
GO OVER THE EARTH, ETC. (ISA. 54:9): THOU WILT INDEED BE FRUITFUL
AND MULTIPLY.

This midrash explains that despite the strength of this order, Noah did
not accept the order to leave the ark. He wanted to be convinced that
another flood would not emerge. Of what good would it be to produce
children if they were to be drowned in another disaster? He refused to
leave until God gave him an assurance that such a thing would never
happen, at which time Noah did, indeed, leave the ark.

Seed Thoughts

We have already noted that one of the additional teachings of the last
three midrashim is to raise the importance of Noah. For one thing, he
is a tzaddik, a righteous man, as mentioned in midrash 4; he was also a
chakham, a wise man, as mentioned in midrash 5 as well as a true leader
of humanity, since he would not leave the ark until the future of humanity was guaranteed by God, as mentioned in midrash 6. The contrast

between the interpretation of Noah in the early verses – such as the one claiming that he was righteous only in comparison to his generation – and the ones we are now reading in our present midrashim is quite dramatic. According to R. Nechemiah, if Noah lived in the generation of Moses, he would have been greater than Moses. This is probably an exaggeration, but we can see from this statement the development of the views of the rabbis, in which the rabbinic view of Noah seems to be far more generous than the plain meaning of the biblical text. The meaning of all this is not merely for us to learn how Noah developed. The real meaning is that if Noah was able to emerge as such a fully developed character and a personality that deserves imitation, so should we be able to do the same if we try hard enough, learn enough, and if our faith maintains its sincerity and purity.

—

Additional Commentary

He did not accept to leave

We learn that Noah was reluctant to leave the ark from the fact that God said, "Go out from the ark, you and your wife, etc." (Genesis 8:16). But when he actually left the ark, it was written, "And Noah went forth, and his sons, etc." (Ibid.,18). He did not leave with his wife, who came out together with the wives of his children. From this we learn that he did not accept the obligation or the commandment to be fruitful and multiply until he was assured that humanity would never again have a flood. (*Tiferet Tzion*)

Until He promised

We learn that the Holy One, Blessed be He, promised that there would not be another flood. Who motivated God to do so? Quite appropriately, it was Noah, who personally experienced the devastation of the Flood and through whom God preserved the world in miniature. (*Tiferet Tzion*)

Parashah Thirty-Four, *Midrash Seven*

ז. 'אַתָּה וְאִשְׁתְּךָ, וּבָנֶיךָ וּנְשֵׁי בָנֶיךָ' רַבִּי יוּדָן בַּר רַבִּי סִימוֹן וְרַבִּי חָנָן בְּשֵׁם רַבִּי שְׁמוּאֵל בַּר רַבִּי יִצְחָק, נֹחַ, כֵּיוָן שֶׁנִּכְנַס לַתֵּבָה נֶאֶסְרָה לוֹ פִּרְיָה וְרִבְיָה, הָדָא הוּא דִכְתִיב, (בראשית ו, יח) 'וּבָאתָ אֶל הַתֵּבָה, אַתָּה וּבָנֶיךָ' לְעַצְמָךְ, (שם שם, שם) 'וְאִשְׁתְּךָ וּנְשֵׁי בָנֶיךָ' לְעַצְמָן,

7. THOU, AND THY WIFE, ETC. R. JUDAH B. R. SIMON AND R. HANAN IN THE NAME OF R. SAMUEL B. R. ISAAC SAID: AS SOON AS NOAH ENTERED THE ARK, COHABITATION WAS FORBIDDEN TO HIM, HENCE IT IS WRITTEN, AND THOU SHALT COME INTO THE ARK, THOU, AND THY SONS (GEN. 6:18) – APART; AND THY WIFE, AND THY SONS' WIVES – APART.

It was not only Noah and his family, but the whole animal kingdom that were forbidden – and in the case of the animals, prevented – from procreation. The *Midrash HaMevo'ar* states that the reason for this will be found at the end of this midrash. There, as we will shortly read, the reason is that we are not supposed to engage in cohabitation during times of suffering and tragedy. But surely there is a more obvious reason: it was not possible for the ark to contain an additional population, either human or animal.

וְכֵיוָן שֶׁיָּצָא הֶתִּירוֹ, הָדָא הוּא דִכְתִיב, 'צֵא מִן הַתֵּבָה, אַתָּה וְאִשְׁתְּךָ'.

WHEN HE WENT OUT, HE PERMITTED IT TO HIM, AS IT IS WRITTEN, GO FORTH FROM THE ARK, THOU AND THY WIFE.

The commandment to Noah to leave the ark differed from the commandment that he received to enter the ark. Upon entering the ark, the command was, "You and your sons [separately], and your wife and their wives [separately]." This was done in order to make cohabitation impossible. Upon leaving the ark, the instructions were altered: "You and your wife [together] with your sons and their wives," the phrasing of which indicated that the prohibition was removed.

אָמַר רַבִּי אַיְבוּ, (איוב ל, ג) 'בְּחֶסֶר וּבְכָפָן גַּלְמוּד', אִם רָאִיתָ חֹסֶר בָּא לָעוֹלָם, וְכָפָן בָּא לָעוֹלָם,

'גַּלְמוּד', הֲוֵי רוֹאֶה אֶת אִשְׁתְּךָ כְּאִלּוּ גַלְמוּדָה, אָמַר רַבִּי הוּנָא, כְּתִיב (בראשית מא, נ) 'וּלְיוֹסֵף יֻלַּד
שְׁנֵי בָנִים', אֵימָתַי (שם שם, שם) 'בְּטֶרֶם תָּבוֹא שְׁנַת הָרָעָב'.

R. ABIN QUOTED: THEY ARE LONELY IN WANT AND FAMINE (JOB 30:3):
WHEN WANT AND FAMINE VISIT THE WORLD, REGARD YOUR WIFE AS
THOUGH SHE WERE LONELY [I.E., MENSTRUOUS]. R. HUNA SAID: IT
IS WRITTEN. AND UNTO JOSEPH WERE BORN TWO SONS (GEN. 41:50):
WHEN? BEFORE THE YEAR OF FAMINE CAME (IBID.).

The second section of the Midrash tries to establish the behavior
in the ark as a principle. The principle is that in a time of suffering or
tragedy, one should refrain from cohabitation and the birth of children.
A proof text is offered from Joseph, where it says that his two sons were
born before the years of famine occurred.

—

Seed Thoughts I

This midrash gives us an opportunity to examine another one of the
unique literary styles of the Midrash. Notice what is written: "R. Yehudah b. R. Simon and R. Hanan in the name of R. Samuel b. R. Isaac
[offered an opinion]." The question is, why are these views attributed
to other scholars in addition to the ones speaking? Several reasons can
be offered for this development. The first is a statement in the Ethics of
the Fathers, where it says that whoever quotes a saying in the name of
the original person from whom he had heard it brings redemption to
the world: כל המביא בשם אמרו, מביא גאולה לעולם – *kol hamevi beshem omro,
mevi geulah la'olam.* The sages looked upon this giving of credit as being
of tremendous importance. It offers a person a spiritual reward which
may last forever.

There is a second reason that can be offered for this behavior. Many
of the sages quoted in this literature were young and needed the authority of a scholar whose reputation was accepted. By giving their opinion,
which was substantiated by a great and known scholar, their own authority would be taken more seriously.

There is yet another reason for this style. The authors of the Midrash and other rabbinic literature thought it important that every
sage involved in the creation of the oral law should be remembered in
permanent form. This is the real "Honor Roll" of Judaism. It does not
acknowledge material achievements, rather, it acknowledges חידושי תורה
– *chiddushei Torah*, new insights that help keep the Torah fresh and alive.

Seed Thoughts II

This Midrash affirms that one should not cohabit during a time of suffering and tragedy. It brings the example of Joseph, whom Scripture
describes as having sons born before the years of famine. We also have
the example of Noah, in a previous midrash, refusing to leave the ark
and engage in cohabitation unless he was given an assurance that there
will never be another flood. He did not wish to produce children whose
lives would be cursed and shortened. The *Tiferet Tzion*, however, brings
another example, which makes us hesitate in terms of this teaching. It
brings the example of Moses, who was conceived and born while Pharaoh's decree to kill every male child was in force. Also, during the years
of the Holocaust, Jewish children were born as an act of affirmation of
life. No contrary opinions to these are recorded. This teaching may be
an important ideal, but it is very difficult to carry out and usually impossible to enforce. This kind of teaching might be put into the category
of דרוש וקבל שכר – *drush vekabel sakhar* – that is to say, it is a very fine
and idealistic teaching, for which hopefully we will be rewarded with
approval, but it remains in the category of theory and not that of general
practice.

ח. (יז) 'וְכָל הַחַיָּה אֲשֶׁר אִתְּךָ, וְגוֹ'', אָמַר רַבִּי יוּדָן, 'הוֹצֵא', כְּתִיב, 'הַיְצֵא' קְרִי,

8. BRING FORTH (HAYTZE) WITH THEE EVERY LIVING THING THAT IS
WITH THEE. "THAT THEY MAY SWARM IN THE EARTH" (8:18). R. JUDAN
SAID: IT IS WRITTEN *HOTZE*, BUT IT IS READ *HAYTZE*

In our text, there is a difference between כתיב – *ktiv*, the manner in
which a word is written, and קרי – *kri*, the manner in which the word is
pronounced. This development means that there are two kinds of interpretation and two different areas of significance. The difference seems to
be that in the *kri*, which indicates that this word should be read orally as
though it contained a *yud*, *Haytze*, there is nothing for Noah to do other
than open the gates of the ark and let everyone leave. The meaning of the
ktiv, reading the word as printed, with a *vav*, *Hotze*, seems to be an order to
Noah to supervise the הוצאה – *hotza'ah*, the exodus from the ark, personally so that everything would be done in proper order and in proper form.

'וְשָׁרְצוּ בָאָרֶץ' וְלֹא בַתֵּבָה, 'וּפָרוּ בָאָרֶץ' וְלֹא בַתֵּבָה. (יט) 'כָּל הַחַיָּה וְכָל הָרֶמֶשׂ, וְגוֹ'', 'כֹּל
רוֹמֵשׂ', אָמַר רַבִּי אַיְבוּ, 'רוֹמֵשׂ' מָלֵא, פְּרָט לְכִלְאָיִם, 'לְמִשְׁפְּחֹתֵיהֶם' פְּרָט לְסֵרוּס, עַל שִׁבְעָה
דְבָרִים נִצְטַוּוּ בְּנֵי נֹחַ, עַל עֲבוֹדַת כּוֹכָבִים, וְעַל גִּלּוּי עֲרָיוֹת, וְעַל שְׁפִיכוּת דָּמִים, וְעַל בִּרְכַּת הַשֵּׁם,
וְעַל הַדִּין, וְעַל הַגֶּזֶל, וְעַל אֵבָר מִן הֶחָי,

THAT THEY MAY SWARM IN THE EARTH – BUT NOT IN THE ARK; AND
BE FRUITFUL AND MULTIPLY UPON THE EARTH-BUT NOT IN THE ARK.
EVERY BEAST, EVERY CREEPING THING, AND EVERY FOWL, WHATSOEVER
MOVETH (KOL ROMES) UPON THE EARTH (8:19). R. AIBU SAID: *KOL ROMES*
IS WRITTEN FULLY. AFTER THEIR FAMILIES: THIS FORBADE HETEROGE-
NEOUS BREEDING AND EMASCULATION. THE CHILDREN OF NOAH WERE
ENJOINED CONCERNING SEVEN THINGS: IDOLATRY, INCEST, MURDER,
CURSING THE DIVINE NAME [BLASPHEMY], CIVIL LAW, AND A LIMB TORN
FROM A LIVING ANIMAL.

R. Aibu noticed that the word רומש – *romes* is written fully, which
means that it includes the letter *vav*. This differs from the previous verse,

where the word הרמש – *haremes* is written without a *vav*. The *vav* is interpreted to include a prohibition against heterogeneous breeding, which
means mixing one species with another or creating a new form that does
not resemble its precursors. The word למשפחותיהם – *lemishpechoteihem*
(i.e., in their family units) is interpreted as hinting to the prohibition
of emasculation (sometimes referred to as vasectomy). The source for
this prohibition is the description of the animals in family units, which
implies allowing them the ability to produce families.

רַבִּי חֲנִינָא בֶּן גַּמְלִיאֵל אוֹמֵר, אַף עַל הַדָּם מִן הֶחָי, רַבִּי אֱלִיעֶזֶר אוֹמֵר, אַף עַל הַכִּלְאָיִם, רַבִּי
שִׁמְעוֹן בֶּן יוֹחַאי אוֹמֵר, אַף עַל הַכְּשָׁפִים, רַבִּי יוֹחָנָן בֶּן בְּרוֹקָא אוֹמֵר אַף עַל הַסֵּרוּס, אָמַר רַבִּי
אַסֵי עַל כָּל הָאָמוּר בַּפָּרָשָׁה נִצְטַוּוּ בְנֵי נֹחַ, (דברים יח, י) "לֹא יִמָּצֵא בְךָ מַעֲבִיר בְּנוֹ וּבִתּוֹ, וְגוֹ'",
וּכְתִיב בָּתְרֵהּ, (שם שם, יב) 'כִּי תוֹעֲבַת ה' כָּל עֹשֵׂה אֵלֶּה'.

R. HANINA SAID: ALSO CONCERNING BLOOD FROM A LIVING ANIMAL.
R. ELIEZER SAID: ALSO AGAINST CROSS-BREEDING. R. SIMEON SAID:
ALSO AGAINST WITCHCRAFT. R. JOHANAN SAID: ALSO AGAINST EMAS-
CULATION. R. ISSI [ASSI] SAID: THE CHILDREN OF NOAH WERE ENJOINED
CONCERNING EVERYTHING STATED IN THE FOLLOWING PASSAGE: THERE
SHALL NOT BE FOUND AMONG YOU ANY ONE THAT MAKETH HIS SON OR
HIS DAUGHTER TO PASS THROUGH THE FIRE, ETC. (DEUT. 18:10).

It should not be understood that these additional comments by the
various sages at the end of the midrash are meant to add to the laws
of Noah. They do not mean that instead of seven laws there should be
seven plus their own suggestions. What they mean is that their concerns
should be subsumed, that is to say, included under the categories of the
seven laws of Noah and in particular, that of עבודה זרה – *avodah zarah*,
idolatry or the worship of strange gods.

—

Seed Thoughts

The seven commandments of Noah are among the greatest documents
we have in Judaism. The oral tradition attributes the first six of these laws
to Adam, the first man. When they were renewed by Noah, He added
the seventh, אבר מן החי – *ever min hachai*, tearing off and eating any limb
of a live animal. Over the years, many writers have suggested that in the
seven laws of Noah, we have the makings of a universal religion, which
all human beings of whatever culture could and should approve of and
arrange for their lives to be bound by.

In the end of the nineteenth century, a well-known Catholic priest,

Aimee Palliera, converted to Judaism. He described the spiritual crisis in his life and the pros and cons of his eventual conversion to Judaism in a book called *The Unknown Sanctuary*. There, he describes a visit he paid to an outstanding rabbinic scholar, R. Elijah Benamozegh. The way the rabbi responded to him was most interesting: "If you convert to Judaism, we will end up having one more Jew, which is very fine, especially one who is of very high quality, such as yourself. But could you not use this tremendous transformation of your life to do something very great for the world? We have in our tradition the seven commandments of Noah, which could be the basis for the spiritual transformation of the world. Why don't you start a new movement called 'The sons of Noah' and establish chapters all over the world? That would contribute to the moral transformation of our society." ʿAimee Palliera thought the proposal was magnificent, but did not feel that he had the strength and the will to further such a major project.

It is interesting to note that during the last decade of his life, the Lubavitcher Rebbe, Menachem Mendel Schneerson, devoted the main burden of his *farbrengen*, his regular assemblies with his Chassidim, to the theme of the Noachide laws. This, he affirmed, should be the manner in which we approach the non-Jewish world. Our goal should be not to convert the world to the mission of Judaism, but to convert them to the seven commandments of Noah, which have within them the power to change the world for the better.

Additional Commentary

The general principle

The six laws given to Adam, which became seven laws at the time of Noah, were meant to be the Torah in miniature and it would be possible to deduce all of the other laws from these six or seven. This is similar to the Ten Commandments, which were given at the time of the Revelation of the Torah at Mount Sinai. The Ten Commandments also represented the Torah in miniature. It is possible – and many attempts were made – to derive the entire Torah from the Ten Commandments. By the same token, it could be said that the Torah in miniature was given to Adam in the form of six commandments, and then given to Noah at the creation of the new world in the form of the seven commandments. (*Tiferet Tzion*)

ט. (כ) 'וַיִּבֶן נֹחַ מִזְבֵּחַ לַה'', 'וַיָּבֶן' כְּתִיב, נִתְבּוֹנֵן, אָמַר, מִפְּנֵי מַה צִוַּנִי הַקָּדוֹשׁ בָּרוּךְ הוּא, וְרִבָּה בַטְּהוֹרִים יוֹתֵר מִן הַטְּמֵאִים, אֶלָּא לְהַקְרִיב מֵהֶן קָרְבָּן, מִיָּד, 'וַיִּקַּח מִכֹּל הַבְּהֵמָה הַטְּהוֹרָה. וְגו''. רַבִּי אֶלְעָזָר בֶּן יַעֲקֹב אוֹמֵר, עַל מִזְבֵּחַ הַגָּדוֹל שֶׁבִּירוּשָׁלַיִם, שֶׁשָּׁם הִקְרִיב אָדָם הָרִאשׁוֹן, שֶׁנֶּאֱמַר (תהלים סט, לב) 'וְתִיטַב לַה' מִשּׁוֹר פָּר מַקְרִן מַפְרִיס'.

9. AND NOAH BUILDED (WAYYIBEN) AN ALTAR UNTO THE LORD (8:20).
WAYYABEN (HE UNDERSTOOD) IS WRITTEN: HE CONSIDERED THE MAT-
TER, REASONING: FOR WHAT REASON DID THE HOLY ONE, BLESSED BE
HE, ORDER MORE CLEAN ANIMALS [TO BE PRESERVED] THAN UNCLEAN?
SURELY BECAUSE HE DESIRED THAT SACRIFICES SHOULD BE OFFERED
TO HIM OF THEM. STRAIGHTWAY, AND TOOK OF EVERY CLEAN BEAST,
ETC. AND HE OFFERED BURNT-OFFERINGS ON THE ALTAR. R. ELAZAR B.
JACOB SAID: THAT MEANS ON THE GREAT ALTAR IN JERUSALEM, WHERE
ADAM SACRIFICED, AS IT IS WRITTEN, AND IT SHALL PLEASE THE LORD
BETTER THAN A BULLOCK THAT HATH HORNS AND HOOFS (PS. 69:32).

Aryeh Mirkin, in his comment on this aspect of the Midrash, questions
why Noah would want to build an altar and why he would slaughter
animals. He had spent the entire year caring for the animals in a very
loving way; why would he now want to slaughter the animals? The conclusion is that the word ויבן – *vayiven* should not be translated as a form
of the word for "building," but rather, as להתבונן – *lehitbonen*, meaning
"to reflect" about what God's intentions were.

'וַיָּרַח ה' אֶת רֵיחַ הַנִּיחֹחַ', רַבִּי אֱלִיעֶזֶר וְרַבִּי יוֹסֵי בַּר חֲנִינָא, רַבִּי אֱלִיעֶזֶר אוֹמֵר, הִקְרִיבוּ בְּנֵי נֹחַ שְׁלָמִים, רַבִּי יוֹסֵי בַּר חֲנִינָא אוֹמֵר, עוֹלוֹת הִקְרִיבוּ, אֵתִיב רַבִּי אֱלִיעֶזֶר לְרַבִּי יוֹסֵי בַּר חֲנִינָא, וְהָכְתִיב (בראשית ד, ד) 'וְהֶבֶל הֵבִיא גַם הוּא מִבְּכֹרוֹת צֹאנוֹ וּמֵחֶלְבֵהֶן' מִדָּבָר שֶׁחֶלְבּוֹ קָרֵב, מֶה עָבַד לֵהּ רַבִּי יוֹסֵי, מִן שַׁמְעֲנִיהוֹן, אֵתִיב רַבִּי אֱלִיעֶזֶר לְרַבִּי יוֹסֵי בַּר חֲנִינָא, וְהָא כְּתִיב (שמות כד, ה) 'וַיִּשְׁלַח אֶת נַעֲרֵי בְּנֵי יִשְׂרָאֵל, וַיַּעֲלוּ עֹלֹת וַיִּזְבְּחוּ שְׁלָמִים, וְגו'', מֶה עָבַד לֵהּ רַבִּי יוֹסֵי, שְׁלָמִים בְּעוֹרָן, בְּלָא הֶפְשֵׁט וְנִתּוּחַ, אֵתִיב רַבִּי אֱלִיעֶזֶר לְרַבִּי יוֹסֵי בַּר חֲנִינָא, וְהָא כְּתִיב (שם יח, יב) 'וַיִּקַּח יִתְרוֹ חֹתֵן מֹשֶׁה עֹלָה וּזְבָחִים', מֶה עָבַד לֵהּ רַבִּי יוֹסֵי בַּר חֲנִינָא, לְאַחַר מַתַּן תּוֹרָה בָּא יִתְרוֹ. אָמַר רַבִּי הוּנָא, אִתְפַּלְּגוּן רַבִּי יַנַּאי וְרַבִּי חִיָּא רַבָּה, רַבִּי יַנַּאי אוֹמֵר, קֹדֶם מַתַּן תּוֹרָה בָּא, רַבִּי חִיָּא רַבָּה אָמַר, לְאַחַר מַתַּן תּוֹרָה בָּא, אָמַר רַבִּי חֲנִינָא, וְלָא פְּלִיגֵי, מַאן דְּאָמַר קֹדֶם

מַתַּן תּוֹרָה בָא יִתְרוֹ, הִקְרִיבוּ בְנֵי נֹחַ שְׁלָמִים, וּמַאן דְּאָמַר אַחַר מַתַּן תּוֹרָה בָא יִתְרוֹ, עוֹלוֹת
הִקְרִיבוּ, וְדָא מְסַיֵּעַ לְרַבִּי יוֹסֵי בַּר חֲנִינָא, דִּכְתִיב (שיר ד, טז) 'עוּרִי צָפוֹן וּבוֹאִי תֵימָן', 'עוּרִי צָפוֹן'
זֶה הָעוֹלָה, שֶׁהָיְתָה נִשְׁחֶטֶת בַּצָּפוֹן, וּמַה הוּא 'עוּרִי', דָּבָר שֶׁהָיָה יָשֵׁן וְנִתְעוֹרֵר, 'וּבוֹאִי תֵימָן'
אֵלּוּ הַשְּׁלָמִים שֶׁהָיוּ נִשְׁחָטִים בַּדָּרוֹם, וּמַהוּ 'בוֹאִי', דָּבָר שֶׁל חִדּוּשׁ, רַבִּי יְהוֹשֻׁעַ בְּשֵׁם רַבִּי לֵוִי
אָמַר, קְרָא, מְסַיְּעָא לֵהּ לְרַבִּי יוֹסֵי בַּר חֲנִינָא, (ויקרא ו, ב) 'זֹאת תּוֹרַת הָעֹלָה, הִוא הָעֹלָה', שֶׁהָיוּ
בְנֵי נֹחַ מַקְרִיבִין, וְכִי אָתְיָא לִשְׁלָמִים, כְּתִיב (שם ז, יא) 'זֹאת תּוֹרַת זֶבַח הַשְּׁלָמִים' אֲשֶׁר הִקְרִיבוּ,
אֵין כְּתִיב כָּאן, אֶלָּא אֲשֶׁר יַקְרִיבוּ מִכָּן וּלְהַבָּא.

AND THE LORD SMELLED THE SWEET SAVOUR. R. ELEAZAR AND R.
JOSE B. R. HANINA DIFFER. R. ELEAZAR SAID: THE CHILDREN OF NOAH
BROUGHT [EVEN] PEACE-OFFERINGS; R. JOSE B. R. HANINA SAID: THEY
OFFERED BURNT-OFFERINGS [ONLY]. R. ELEAZAR SOUGHT TO RE-
FUTE R. JOSE B. R. HANINA: BUT IT IS WRITTEN, AND ABEL, HE ALSO
BROUGHT OF THE FIRSTLINGS OF HIS FLOCK AND OF THE FAT THEREOF
(GEN. 4:4), IMPLYING THAT OF WHICH THE FAT IS OFFERED. HOW DID
R. JOSE B. R. HANINA ANSWER HIM? IT MEANS, OF THE FAT ONES [I.E.,
THE BEST]. R. ELEAZAR SOUGHT TO REFUTE R. JOSE B. R. HANINA: BUT
IT IS WRITTEN, AND HE SENT THE YOUNG MEN OF THE CHILDREN OF
ISRAEL, WHO OFFERED BURNT-OFFERINGS, AND SACRIFICED PEACE-
OFFERINGS (SHELAMIM) UNTO THE LORD (EX. 24:5)? HOW DOES R.
JOSE B. R. HANINA EXPLAIN THIS? IT MEANS THAT THEY WERE WHOLE
(SHELEMIM) IN THEIR HIDE, NOT HAVING BEEN FLAYED OR CUT UP. R.
ELEAZAR OBJECTED TO R. JOSE B. R. HANINA: BUT IT IS WRITTEN, AND
JETHRO, MOSES' FATHER-IN-LAW, TOOK A BURNT-OFFERING AND SACRI-
FICES (IBID., 17:12)? HOW DOES R. JOSE B. R. HANINA EXPLAIN THIS? IN
ACCORDANCE WITH THE VIEW THAT JETHRO CAME AFTER REVELATION.
R. HUNA SAID: R. JANNAI AND R. HIYYA THE ELDER DIFFER IN THIS: R.
JANNAI SAID: JETHRO CAME BEFORE REVELATION; R. HIYYA THE ELDER
SAID: JETHRO CAME AFTER REVELATION. R. HANINA OBSERVED: YET
THEY DO NOT DIFFER [IN AN INDEPENDENT CONTROVERSY]: HE WHO
SAYS THAT JETHRO CAME BEFORE REVELATION HOLDS THAT THE CHIL-
DREN OF NOAH MIGHT OFFER PEACE-OFFERINGS; WHILE HE WHO SAYS
THAT JETHRO CAME AFTER REVELATION HOLDS THAT THEY MIGHT OF-
FER BURNT-OFFERINGS [ONLY]. THE FOLLOWING SUPPORTS R. JOSE B. R.
HANINA: AWAKE, O NORTH WIND (SONG OF SONGS 4:16): THIS ALLUDES
TO THE BURNT-OFFERING, WHICH WAS KILLED AT THE NORTH [SIDE OF
THE ALTAR]. TO WHAT DOES 'AWAKE' APPLY? TO SOMETHING WHICH WAS
ASLEEP AND NOW AWAKES. AND COME, THOU SOUTH (IBID.) ALLUDES TO
PEACE-OFFERINGS, WHICH WERE KILLED [EVEN] AT THE SOUTH [SIDE
OF THE ALTAR]. TO WHAT DOES 'COME' APPLY? TO A NEW PRACTICE. R.
JOSHUA OF SIKNIN SAID IN R. LEVI'S NAME: THIS VERSE TOO SUPPORTS
R. JOSE B. R. HANINA: THIS IS THE LAW OF THE BURNT-OFFERING: THAT

IS THE BURNT-OFFERING (LEV. 6:2) – VIZ. WHICH THE NOACHIDES USED
TO OFFER. BUT WHEN IT TREATS OF PEACE-OFFERINGS, VIZ. AND THIS
IS THE LAW OF THE SACRIFICE OF PEACE-OFFERINGS (IBID., 7:11), IT IS
NOT WRITTEN, 'WHICH THEY OFFERED,' BUT, 'WHICH THEY WILL OFFER'
(IBID.) – IN THE FUTURE.

This discussion seems to be clear-cut as it is rendered by the translation.

'וַיָּרַח ה' אֶת רֵיחַ הַנִּיחֹחַ', הֵרִיחַ רֵיחוֹ שֶׁל אַבְרָהָם אָבִינוּ עוֹלֶה מִכִּבְשַׁן הָאֵשׁ, 'וַיָּרַח' רֵיחַ שֶׁל
חֲנַנְיָה מִישָׁאֵל וַעֲזַרְיָה עוֹלִין מִכִּבְשַׁן הָאֵשׁ

AND THE LORD SMELLED THE SWEET SAVOR. HE SMELLED THE SAVOR OF
THE PATRIARCH ABRAHAM ASCENDING FROM THE FIERY FURNACE; HE
SMELLED THE SAVOR OF HANANIAH, MISHAEL AND AZARIAH ASCEND-
ING FROM THE FIERY FURNACE.

The beauty of this section is that the beautiful scent is not interpreted
as a material perfume, but as reflecting the character of outstanding human beings who, in the eyes of God, are the ones who really provide the
beautiful scent to human life.

מָשָׁל לְאוֹהֲבוֹ שֶׁל מֶלֶךְ, שֶׁכִּבְּדוֹ, וְשָׁלַח לוֹ דוֹרוֹן נָאֶה, דִּיסְקוֹס נָאֶה, וְעָמַד בְּנוֹ וְלֹא כִבְּדוֹ, עָמַד
בֶּן בְּנוֹ וְכִבְּדוֹ, אָמַר לוֹ, מַה דְּמֵי דוֹרוֹן דִּידָךְ לְדוֹרוֹן דְּסָבָךְ, 'וַיָּרַח ה'' הֵרִיחַ רֵיחַ דוֹרוֹן שֶׁל שָׁמַד

THIS MAY BE COMPARED TO A KING'S FRIEND, WHO, TO PAY HIS RESPECTS,
SENT THE KING A FINE GIFT, VIZ. SOME EXCELLENT BRISKET ON A BEAU-
TIFUL PLATE. THEN HIS SON CAME AND DID NOT SHOW HIM HONOR.
THEN HIS GRANDSON CAME AND SHOWED HIM HONOR; WHEREUPON HE
[THE KING] SAID TO HIM, 'YOUR GIFT IS LIKE YOUR GRANDFATHER'S.' HE
SMELLED THE SAVOR OF THE GENERATION OF DESTRUCTION.

רַב שָׁלוֹם בְּשֵׁם רַבִּי מְנַחֲמָא בַּר זְעֵירָא אָמַר, מָשָׁל לְמֶלֶךְ שֶׁהָיָה מְבַקֵּשׁ לִבְנוֹת לוֹ פָּלָטִין עַל
הַיָּם, וְלֹא הָיָה יוֹדֵעַ הֵיכָן לִבְנוֹתָה, וּמָצָא צְלוֹחִית שֶׁל פְּפוֹלְסָמוֹן, וְהָלַךְ וֶהֱרִיחָהּ, וּבָנָה אוֹתָהּ
עָלֶיהָ, הֲדָא הוּא דִכְתִיב, (תהלים כד, ב) 'כִּי הוּא עַל יַמִּים יְסָדָהּ וְעַל נְהָרוֹת יְכוֹנְנֶהָ', בְּאֵיזֶה זְכוּת,
בִּזְכוּת (שם שם, ו) 'דוֹר דֹּרְשָׁיו מְבַקְשֵׁי פָנֶיךָ יַעֲקֹב סֶלָה'.

R. SHILUM SAID IN THE NAME OF R. MENAHAMA B. R. ZE'IRA: IMAGINE A
KING WHO WISHED TO BUILD A PALACE BY THE SEA, BUT DID NOT KNOW
WHERE TO BUILD IT. FINDING A PHIAL OF FOLIATUM, HE FOLLOWED
ITS SCENT AND BUILT IT THERE. THUS IT IS WRITTEN, FOR HE HATH
FOUNDED IT UPON THE SEAS (PS. 24:2): FOR WHOSE SAKE? FOR THE
SAKE OF [THOSE OF WHOM IT IS WRITTEN], SUCH AS THE GENERATION

OF THEM THAT SEEK AFTER HIM, THAT SEEK THY FACE, EVEN JACOB, SELAH (IBID., 6).

Seed Thoughts

The sages were bothered by the fact that not only was God willing to destroy the entire world and the entire generation, but for what? For the renewal of the world through one particular person, Noah, who, for all his good points, was not universally approved, either by his generation or by the commentators. It was not felt that he could direct the world into its proper direction. That is why the Midrash, ultimately, brings to our attention the lives of Abraham and Chananyah, Mishael and Azariah, examples of individuals who were willing to give their lives for the sake of God. For, such people would be worthy to have a new world created for them, and they would be able to develop appropriate leaders who could be responsible for it.

Additional Commentary

The building of the altar (A)

Even though the word is written as *vayiven*, meaning "built," the Torah is devoid of vowels and so it can be read as *vayaven*, meaning that "he understood," from the same root as the word *nitbonen*, meaning to reflect. This hints to us that it is through reflection and deep thinking that Noah deduced that he should build an altar and offer sacrifices, even though he was not commanded to do so. He reflected upon the fact that he was ordered to include in the ark many more clean animals than unclean ones, and he concluded that the only purpose for this was to make it possible for him to offer sacrifices to God. (*HaMidrash HaMevo'ar*)

The building of the altar (B)

Noah was not able to offer sacrifices to God because a lion had attacked him in the ark and had broken his leg while he was exiting the ark. Therefore, his son Shem took his place in offering the sacrifice. It follows, then, that the word *vayiven*, which could also be translated as "he built," must not mean this here, since, even though it says *vayiven Noach*, implying that Noah did the building, in actual fact, the building was carried out by his children – in particular, by his son Shem. Therefore, Noah's name need not have been included. We can now understand the midrashic teaching that *vayiven Noah* should be read as "Noah reflected." One connotation of *vayiven* refers to Noah, implying that he *reflected* on his desire to offer a sacrifice. But the other connotation of *vayiven* implies his desire to build the alter which in actuality was done by his children.

Another thought: The word *vayiven* came to us from Sinai in that particular punctuated form so that it should be interpreted both as a כתיב – *ktiv*, meaning read as it is written, and also as a קרי – *kri*, meaning that it can be vocalized a different way. According to the *ktiv*, *vayiven Noach* should be interpreted as from the same root as *binah*, as in "reflection." But according to the *kri*, it should be interpreted as בנין – *binyan*, meaning "building." (*Tiferet Tzion*)

The sweet savor

Throughout the Torah script, we see the words ריח ניחוח – *reiyach nichoach*, meaning "sweet savor." Here, however, the expression is slightly different: ריח הניחוח – *reiya'h **hani'hoa'h***, with the addition of the informative *hey*. This is meant as a hint, an implied reference to a particular special person, and this special person could only have been Abraham, who offered his life to God in the most dedicated way, and via him, it could also additionally refer to personalities like Chananyah, Mishael and Azariah, who duplicated Abraham's dedication with their own willingness to surrender their lives to God. (*Tiferet Tzion*)

The parable

The point of the parable is to explain why the character of Noah by itself was not enough for God to establish His covenant for the survival of the world, until He was able to perceive the merit of Abraham as well as that of Chananyah, Mishael and Azariah and the generations of those who suffered for the sake of God. This is the meaning of the parable wherein the king did not build his palace in the sea until he found an area where the turbulent waters did not reach. The sea represents the turbulence of the world and it is precisely in and near that turbulence that God's palace has to be established in order to uplift the world to the Divine ideals. Noah's character by itself was not sufficiently powerful to do this job; but the character and personality of Abraham and those who followed him *were* strong enough not to be affected by the turbulence of the world and even had the ability to influence that turbulence for the positive as well. (*Tiferet Tzion*)

The other parable

The sages interpret as if God was worrying whether or not the new world would succeed. Noah, by himself, could not renew the world, and his sons possessed neither the talent nor the dedication to do what had to be done. The parable is meant to offer a more optimistic view of the succeeding generations. The king had a helper who helped him in wondrous ways. The helper's son who succeeded him, though, did not do so at all, and had a judgment been rendered at this point, it would have been fatal to the king's helper's lineage. However, the grandson of the original helper restored all the good graces of his grandfather and the king was highly pleased.

The interpretation of the parable is that even though after Abraham, we have no immediate record of those who sacrificed their lives for God, it did, thankfully, happen later on, when Chananyah, Mishael and Azariah offered their lives for the sake of God and were miraculously saved. The same can be said for the ten scholars who were killed by the Romans and whose memory we recall in the recitation of the liturgy. These events an displays of self-sacrifice "encouraged" God – Who is represented by the king in the parable – to feel that in the succeeding generations, more righteous people would emerge who would renew the world in accordance with its spiritual purpose. This is how the verse from Psalms is interpreted, מבקשי פניך יעקב סלה זה דור דורשיו – that generations will arise who will forever seek the Lord and hope for His approval. (*HaMidrash HaMevo'ar*)

י. 'וַיֹּאמֶר ה' אֶל לִבּוֹ', הָרְשָׁעִים הֵן בִּרְשׁוּת לִבָּן, (שם יד, א) 'אָמַר נָבָל בְּלִבּוֹ', (בראשית כז, מא) 'וַיֹּאמֶר עֵשָׂו בְּלִבּוֹ', (מ"א יב, כו) 'וַיֹּאמֶר יָרָבְעָם בְּלִבּוֹ', (אסתר ו, ו) 'וַיֹּאמֶר הָמָן בְּלִבּוֹ', אֲבָל הַצַּדִּיקִים לִבָּן בִּרְשׁוּתָן, (ש"א א, יג) 'וְחַנָּה הִיא מְדַבֶּרֶת עַל לִבָּהּ', (שם כז, א) 'וַיֹּאמֶר דָּוִד אֶל לִבּוֹ', (דניאל א, ח) 'וַיָּשֶׂם דָּנִיֵּאל עַל לִבּוֹ', 'וַיֹּאמֶר ה' אֶל לִבּוֹ'. 'לֹא אֹסִף' לֹא אֹסֵף, לְסָגֵי לְסַגֵּי, וְרַבָּנָן אָמְרִין, 'לֹא אֹסִף' לִבְנֵי נֹחַ, 'לֹא אֹסִף' לַדּוֹרוֹת.

10. AND THE LORD SAID TO HIS HEART. THE WICKED STAND IN SUBJEC-
TION TO THEIR HEART [I.E., PASSIONS. THUS IT SAYS], THE FOOL HATH
SAID IN HIS HEART (PS. 14:I); AND ESAU SAID IN HIS HEART (GEN. 27:41);
AND JEROBOAM SAID IN HIS HEART (I KINGS 12:25); NOW HAMAN SAID
IN HIS HEART (EST. 6:6). BUT THE RIGHTEOUS HAVE THEIR HEARTS UN-
DER THEIR CONTROL; HENCE IT IS WRITTEN, NOW HANNAH, SHE SPOKE
AT HER HEART (1 SAM. 1:13); AND DAVID SAID TO HIS HEART (IBID., 27:1);
BUT DANIEL PURPOSED TO HIS HEART (DAN. 1:8); AND THE LORD SAID
TO HIS HEART. I WILL NOT AGAIN CURSE THE GROUND, ETC.: LET THAT
INDEED SUFFICE. THE RABBIS INTERPRETED: I WILL NOT AGAIN CURSE-
THE CHILDREN OF NOAH; NEITHER WILL I AGAIN SMITE, ETC. – FUTURE
GENERATIONS. FOR THE IMAGINATION OF MAN'S HEART IS EVIL.

The Midrash points out a difference in the uses of terms such as בלבו – *belibo*, meaning "in his heart," and אל לבו – *el libo*, meaning "to his heart." Their point is that wherever "in his heart" is used, the intention is negative and is spoken by one who is either foolish or whose intentions are disruptive. On the other hand, when *el libo* is used, the intention and the meaning is very positive. The Midrash includes various proof texts in support of this idea.

The repetition of לא אוסיף – *lo osiph* is meant to strengthen God's intention as stated in our text. The first appearance means that He shall no longer send a flood to this generation. The second one emphasizes that this will apply to all generations. (*HaMidrash HaMevo'ar*)

אָמַר רַבִּי חִיָּא רַבָּה, עֲלוּבָה הִיא הָעִסָּה, שֶׁנַּחְתּוֹמָהּ מֵעִיד עָלֶיהָ שֶׁהִיא רָעָה, 'כִּי יֵצֶר לֵב הָאָדָם רַע מִנְּעֻרָיו', אַבָּא יוֹסֵי הַתּוֹרְתִּי אוֹמֵר, עֲלוּב הוּא הַשְּׂאוֹר שֶׁמִּי שֶׁבְּרָא אוֹתוֹ מֵעִיד עָלָיו שֶׁהוּא

רַע, שֶׁנֶּאֱמַר (תהלים קג, יד) 'כִּי הוּא יָדַע יִצְרֵנוּ, זָכוּר כִּי עָפָר אֲנָחְנוּ'. רַבָּנָן אָמְרִי, עֲלוּבָה הַנְּטִיעָה שֶׁמִּי שֶׁנְּטָעָהּ מֵעִיד עָלֶיהָ שֶׁהִיא רָעָה, שֶׁנֶּאֱמַר (ירמיה יא, יז) 'וַה' צְבָאוֹת הַנּוֹטֵעַ אוֹתָךְ דִּבֶּר עָלַיִךְ רָעָה'.

R. HIYYA THE ELDER SAID: HOW WRETCHED MUST BE THE DOUGH WHEN THE BAKER HIMSELF TESTIFIES IT TO BE POOR! [THUS MAN'S CREATOR SAYS] FOR THE IMAGINATION OF MAN'S HEART IS EVIL – ABBA JOSE THE POTTER SAID: HOW POOR MUST BE THE LEAVEN WHEN HE WHO KNEADED IT TESTIFIES THAT IT IS BAD! THUS: FOR HE KNOWETH OUR [EVIL] PASSIONS [E.V. – 'FRAME'], HE REMEMBERETH THAT WE ARE DUST (PS. 103:14). THE RABBIS SAID: HOW INFERIOR MUST BE THE PLANT WHEN HE THAT PLANTED IT TESTIFIES THAT IT IS BAD; THUS, FOR THE LORD OF HOSTS, THAT PLANTED THEE, HATH SPOKEN EVIL OF THEE (JER. 11:17).

The Midrash acknowledges how sad it is when, for example, a baker disparages his own product, and similarly, how sad it is when God disparages man, whom He created. On the other hand, it is not a complete disparagement, it is only a recognition of how powerful and dangerous the יצר הרע – *yetzer harah*, the evil inclination can be.

שָׁאַל אַנְטוֹנִינוֹס אֶת רַבֵּינוּ, אָמַר לוֹ, מֵאֵימָתַי יֵצֶר הָרַע נָתוּן בָּאָדָם, מִשֶּׁיֵּצֵא מִמְּעֵי אִמּוֹ, אוֹ עַד שֶׁלֹּא יָצָא מִמְּעֵי אִמּוֹ, אָמַר לוֹ, עַד שֶׁלֹּא יָצָא מִמְּעֵי אִמּוֹ, אָמַר לוֹ, לָאו, שֶׁאִלּוּ הָיָה נָתוּן בּוֹ עַד שֶׁהוּא בִמְּעֵי אִמּוֹ, הָיָה חוֹטֵט אֶת בְּנֵי מֵעֶיהָ וְיוֹצֵא, וְהוֹדָה לוֹ רַבִּי, שֶׁהִשְׁוָה לְדַעַת הַמִּקְרָא, שֶׁנֶּאֱמַר 'כִּי יֵצֶר לֵב הָאָדָם רַע מִנְּעֻרָיו', רַבִּי יוּדָן אָמַר 'מִנְּעָרָיו' כְּתִיב, מִשָּׁעָה שֶׁהוּא נִנְעָר לָצֵאת מִמְּעֵי אִמּוֹ. וְעוֹד שָׁאַל אַנְטוֹנִינוֹס אֶת רַבֵּינוּ, אָמַר לוֹ, מֵאֵימָתַי נְשָׁמָה נִתְּנָה בָּאָדָם, מִשֶּׁיֵּצֵא מִמְּעֵי אִמּוֹ, אוֹ עַד שֶׁלֹּא יָצָא מִמְּעֵי אִמּוֹ, אָמַר לוֹ, מִשֶּׁיֵּצֵא מִמְּעֵי אִמּוֹ, אָמַר לוֹ, לָאו, מָשָׁל, אִם תַּנִּיחַ בָּשָׂר שְׁלֹשָׁה יָמִים בְּלֹא מֶלַח מִיָּד הוּא מַסְרִיחַ, וְהוֹדָה לוֹ רַבִּי, שֶׁהִשְׁוָה דַעְתּוֹ לְדַעַת הַמִּקְרָא, שֶׁנֶּאֱמַר (איוב י, יב) 'חַיִּים וָחֶסֶד עָשִׂיתָ עִמָּדִי, וּפְקֻדָּתְךָ שָׁמְרָה רוּחִי', מֵאֵימָתַי נָתַתָּ בִּי אֶת הַנְּשָׁמָה מִשֶּׁהִפְקַדְתָּנִי.

ANTONINUS ASKED OUR TEACHER: 'WHEN IS THE EVIL URGE PLACED IN MAN?' 'AS SOON AS HE IS FORMED [IN EMBRYO],' HE REPLIED. 'IF SO,' HE OBJECTED, 'HE WOULD DIG THROUGH THE WOMB AND EMERGE; RATHER IS IT WHEN HE EMERGES [FROM THE WOMB].' RABBI AGREED WITH HIM, BECAUSE HIS VIEW CORRESPONDS WITH THAT OF SCRIPTURE, VIZ. FOR THE IMAGINATION OF MAN'S HEART IS EVIL FROM HIS YOUTH (MINE'URAW). R. JUDAN SAID: THIS IS WRITTEN MINE'ARAW (FROM HIS AWAKENING), WHICH MEANS, FROM WHEN HE AWAKES TO THE WORLD. HE ASKED HIM FURTHER: 'WHEN IS THE SOUL PLANTED IN MAN?' 'WHEN HE LEAVES HIS MOTHER'S WOMB,' REPLIED HE. 'LEAVE MEAT WITHOUT SALT FOR THREE DAYS,' SAID HE, 'WILL IT NOT PUTREFY? RATHER, WHEN HIS DESTINY IS DETERMINED.' OUR TEACHER AGREED WITH HIM, FOR

SCRIPTURE TOO SUPPORTS HIM: ALL THE WHILE MY SOUI [E.V. ('BREATH')
IS IN ME, AND THE SPIRIT OF GOD IS IN MY NOSTRIL (JOB 27:3), WHILE IT
IS WRITTEN, AND THY PROVIDENCE HATH PRESERVED MY SPIRIT (IBID.
10:L2): HENCE, WHEN DIDST THOU PLACE THE SOUL IN ME? WHEN THOU
DIDST DETERMINE MY FATE.

Additional Commentary

The difference between belibo *and* el libo

Evil people are slaves to their heart. Their evil inclination dominates
their lives. This is reflected by the use of *belibo*, which implies that it was
the heart that dominated the character and actions. The righteous, however, are able to transcend their evil inclinations, and this is reflected
by expressions like *el libo* or *al libo*, to indicate that the heart is ruled
by another quality, often one's intellect or strength of character. *El libo*
is used in relation to God, but since God does not have an evil inclination, the reference probably has to do with His overpowering His *midat
hadin*, the concept of justice.

One has to say about this entire interpretation that it is not necessarily
so, or, as the Hebrew language puts it, לאו דוקא – *lav davka*. For instance,
in the case of Abraham our father (Genesis 17:17) it says, *vayomer belibo*.
Also, in Ecclesiastes 2:15, from the first-person voice of King Solomon,
it says *ve'amarti ani belibi*. In Zecharia 12:5, it says, *ve'amru alufei Yehudah
belibam*, meaning that "the leaders of Judah said [something] in their
hearts." This shows that *belibo* and *belibam* can be used for positive
thoughts as well. (Mirkin)

—

Seed Thoughts

It will be noted from the additional commentary by Aryeh Mirkin that
there are other proof texts available that the expression *belibo* can also
be used to imply good things. However, even though the proof text may
not be absolute, the central teaching remains the same and should be
underlined and taught. The head should always direct the heart and not
vice versa. This is the teaching of *el libo – to* the heart. Emotions are very
important and so is passion, but they have to be directed to a goal that
is intellectually sound.

—

יא. (כב) 'עֹד כָּל יְמֵי הָאָרֶץ, זֶרַע וְקָצִיר, וְקֹר וָחֹם, וְגוֹ'', רַבִּי יוּדָן, מִשֵּׁם רַבִּי שְׁמוּאֵל, מַה סְבוּרִים
בְּנֵי נֹחַ, שֶׁבְּרִיתָן כְּרוּתָה, עוֹמֶדֶת לָעַד, אֶלָּא, כָּל זְמָן שֶׁהַשָּׁמַיִם וְהָאָרֶץ קַיָּמִין, בְּרִיתָן קַיֶּמֶת,
לִכְשֶׁיָּבוֹא אוֹתוֹ יוֹם שֶׁכָּתוּב בּוֹ (ישעיה נא, ו) 'כִּי שָׁמַיִם כֶּעָשָׁן נִמְלָחוּ, וְהָאָרֶץ כַּבֶּגֶד תִּבְלֶה',
בְּאוֹתָהּ שָׁעָה, (זכריה יא, יא) 'וַתֻּפַר בַּיּוֹם הַהוּא', וְגוֹ'

11. WHILE THE EARTH REMAINETH, SEED TIME AND HARVEST, AND COLD
AND HEAT, AND SUMMER AND WINTER, AND DAY AND NIGHT SHALL
NOT CEASE (8:22). R. JUDAN SAID IN R. AHA'S NAME: WHAT DID THE
CHILDREN OF NOAH THINK: THAT THE COVENANT MADE WITH THEM
WOULD ENDURE TO ALL ETERNITY? THAT IS NOT SO, BUT ONLY AS LONG
AS THE HEAVEN AND EARTH ENDURE WILL THEIR COVENANT ENDURE.
BUT WHEN THAT DAY COMETH, OF WHICH IT IS WRITTEN, FOR THE
HEAVENS SHALL VANISH AWAY LIKE SMOKE, AND THE EARTH SHALL BE
WORN OUT LIKE A GARMENT (ISA. 51:6), THEN [SHALL THE VERSE BE
FULFILLED], AND IT [SC. THE COVENANT] WILL BE BROKEN ON THAT
DAY (ZECH. 11:11).

אָמַר רַבִּי אַחָא, מִי גָרַם לָהֶם שֶׁיִּמְרְדוּ בִי, לֹא עַל יְדֵי שֶׁהָיוּ זוֹרְעִין וְלֹא קוֹצְרִין יוֹלְדִין וְלֹא קוֹבְרִין,
מִכָּן וְאֵילָךְ, 'זֶרַע וְקָצִיר' יוֹלְדִין וְקוֹבְרִין, 'קֹר וָחֹם' חַמָּה חַכְאֲבִית, 'קַיִץ וָחֹרֶף', מְקַיֵּץ אֲנִי עֲלֵיהֶם
אֶת הָעוֹף, הֵיךְ מַה דְּאַתְּ אָמַר, (ישעיה יח, ו) 'וְקָץ עָלָיו הָעַיִט, וְכָל בֶּהֱמַת הָאָרֶץ עָלָיו תֶּחֱרָף'.

R. AHA COMMENTED: WHAT WAS RESPONSIBLE FOR THEIR REBELLING
AGAINST ME? WAS IT NOT BECAUSE THEY SOWED BUT DID NOT CUT
DOWN, I.E., THEY GAVE BIRTH BUT DID NOT BURY? THEREFORE HENCE-
FORTH THERE SHALL BE SOWING AND CUTTING DOWN: THEY SHALL
BEAR AND BURY. COLD AND HEAT: [THEY SHALL SUFFER] FEVER AND
AGUE. SUMMER (KAYYIZ) AND WINTER (HOREF): I WILL CAUSE THE
BIRDS TO SUMMER UPON THEM, AS YOU READ, AND THE RAVENOUS
BIRDS SHALL SUMMER UPON THEM, AND ALL THE BEASTS OF THE EARTH
SHALL WINTER UPON THEM (ISA. 18:6).

מַעֲשֶׂה הָיָה בְּאֶחָד מִגְּדוֹלֵי הַדּוֹר. שֶׁהָיָה חוֹשֵׁשׁ אֶת רֹאשׁוֹ, וְאִית דְּאָמַר רַבִּי שְׁמוּאֵל בַּר נַחְמָן
הָיָה אוֹמֵר, חֲמֵי מַה עֲבַד לָן דָּרָא דְמַבּוּלָא.

IT ONCE HAPPENED THAT ONE OF THE GREAT MEN OF HIS TIME – SOME
SAY THAT IT WAS R. SAMUEL B. NAHMAN – WAS SUFFERING WITH HEAD-
ACHE, AND HE LAMENTED: THIS IS WHAT THE GENERATION OF THE
FLOOD DID FOR US!

דָּבָר אַחֵר, 'עֹד כָּל יְמֵי הָאָרֶץ', רַבִּי הוּנָא בְּשֵׁם רַבִּי אַחָא, מַה סְבוּרִים בְּנֵי נֹחַ, שֶׁבְּרִיתָן כְּרוּתָה
וְעוֹמֶדֶת לָעַד, כָּךְ אָמַרְתִּי לָהֶם, 'עֹד כָּל יְמֵי הָאָרֶץ וְגוֹ'", אֶלָּא, כָּל זְמָן שֶׁהַיּוֹם וְהַלַּיְלָה קַיָּמִין
בְּרִיתָן קַיֶּמֶת, וּכְשֶׁיָּבוֹא אוֹתוֹ הַיּוֹם, שֶׁכָּתוּב בּוֹ (זכריה יד, ז) 'וְהָיָה יוֹם אֶחָד הוּא יִוָּדַע לַה', לֹא יוֹם
וְלֹא לַיְלָה', בְּאוֹתָהּ שָׁעָה, (שם יא, יא) 'וַתֻּפַר בַּיּוֹם הַהוּא', אָמַר רַבִּי יִצְחָק, מִי גָרַם לָהֶם שֶׁיִּמְרְדוּ
בִי, לֹא עַל שֶׁהֵן זוֹרְעִין וְלֹא קוֹצְרִין, דְּאָמַר רַבִּי יִצְחָק, אַחַת לְאַרְבָּעִים שָׁנָה הָיוּ זוֹרְעִים, וּמְהַלְּכִין
מִסּוֹף הָעוֹלָם וְעַד סוֹפוֹ לְשָׁעָה קַלָּה, וּמַתְלִישִׁין אַרְזֵי לְבָנוֹן בַּהֲלִיכָתָן, וְהָיוּ אֲרָיוֹת וּנְמֵרִים
חֲשׁוּבִים בְּעֵינֵיהֶם כְּנִימָה בִּבְשָׂרוֹ, הָא כֵּיצַד הָיָה לָהֶם אֲוִיר יָפֶה כְּמוֹ כְּמוֹ הַפֶּסַח וְעַד הָעֲצֶרֶת.

ANOTHER INTERPRETATION OF WHILE THE EARTH REMAINETH, ETC.:
R. HUNA SAID IN R. AHA'S NAME: WHAT DO THE CHILDREN OF NOAH
THINK:, THAT THE COVENANT MADE WITH THEM WILL ENDURE TO ALL
ETERNITY? [NO, FOR] THUS SAID I TO THEM: WHILE THE EARTH RE-
MAINETH. BUT AS LONG AS DAY AND NIGHT ENDURE, THEIR COVENANT
WILL ENDURE. YET WHEN THAT DAY COMETH OF WHICH IT IS WRITTEN,
AND THERE SHALL BE ONE DAY WHICH SHALL BE KNOWN AS THE LORD'S,
NOT DAY, AND NOT NIGHT (ZECH. 14:7), AT THAT TIME [SHALL BE FUL-
FILLED THE VERSE], 'AND IT WILL BE BROKEN IN THAT DAY.' R. ISAAC
COMMENTED: WHAT WAS RESPONSIBLE FOR THEIR REBELLING AGAINST
ME? WAS IT NOT BECAUSE THEY SOWED WITHOUT HAVING TO REAP? FOR
R. ISAAC SAID: THEY USED TO SOW ONCE IN FORTY YEARS, AND THEY
TRAVELED FROM ONE END OF THE WORLD TO THE OTHER IN A BRIEF
PERIOD, CUTTING DOWN THE CEDARS OF LEBANON IN THEIR COURSE,
MAKING NO MORE OF THE LIONS AND LEOPARDS THAN OF THE VERMIN
IN THEIR SKIN. HOW IS THIS TO BE UNDERSTOOD? THEY ENJOYED THE
CLIMATE [NOW USUAL] BETWEEN PASSOVER AND PENTECOST [RIGHT
THROUGH THE YEAR].

רַבָּן שִׁמְעוֹן בֶּן גַּמְלִיאֵל אוֹמֵר, מִשּׁוּם רַבִּי מֵאִיר, וְכֵן הָיָה רַבִּי דּוֹסָא אוֹמֵר כִּדְבָרָיו, חֲצִי תִּשְׁרֵי
וּמַרְחֶשְׁוָן וַחֲצִי כִסְלֵו זֶרַע, חֲצִי כִסְלֵו וְטֵבֵת וַחֲצִי שְׁבָט חֹרֶף, חֲצִי שְׁבָט וַאֲדָר וַחֲצִי נִיסָן קֹר,
חֲצִי נִיסָן וְאִיָּר וַחֲצִי סִיוָן קָצִיר, חֲצִי סִיוָן וְתַמּוּז וַחֲצִי אָב קַיִץ, חֲצִי אָב וֶאֱלוּל וַחֲצִי תִּשְׁרֵי חֹם

R. SIMEON B. GAMALIEL SAID IN R. MEIR'S NAME, AND R. DOSA TOO SAID
THUS: [THE LATTER] HALF OF TISHRI, MARHESHWAN AND THE FIRST
HALF OF KISLEW IS SEEDTIME; THE SECOND HALF OF KISLEW, TEBETH
AND HALF OF SHEBAT ARE THE WINTER MONTHS; THE SECOND HALF OF
SHEBAT, ADAR AND THE FIRST HALF OF NISAN ARE THE COLD SEASON;
THE SECOND HALF OF NISAN, IYAR AND THE FIRST HALF OF SIWAN IS
HARVEST TIME; THE SECOND HALF OF SIWAN, TAMMUZ AND THE FIRST

HALF OF AB IS SUMMER; THE SECOND HALF OF AB, ELUL AND THE FIRST
HALF OF TISHRI ARE THE HOT SEASON.

רַבִּי יְהוּדָה מוֹנֶה, מִמַּרְחֶשְׁוָן, רַבִּי שִׁמְעוֹן מַתְחִיל מִתִּשְׁרֵי. אָמַר רַבִּי יוֹחָנָן, לֹא שִׁמְּשׁוּ מַזָּלוֹת כָּל
שְׁנֵים עָשָׂר חֹדֶשׁ, אָמַר לוֹ רַבִּי יוֹנָתָן, שִׁמְּשׁוּ, אֶלָּא שֶׁלֹּא הָיָה הֶיקָּן רְשׁוּמָן נִכָּר, רַבִּי אֱלִיעֶזֶר וְרַבִּי יְהוֹשֻׁעַ,
רַבִּי אֱלִיעֶזֶר אוֹמֵר, 'לֹא יִשְׁבֹּתוּ', לֹא שָׁבָתוּ, רַבִּי יְהוֹשֻׁעַ אוֹמֵר, 'לֹא יִשְׁבֹּתוּ' מִכְּלָל שֶׁשָּׁבָתוּ.

R. JUDAH COUNTED FROM MARHESHWAN. R. SIMEON COMMENCED WITH
[THE BEGINNING OF] TISHRI. R. JOHANAN SAID: THE PLANETS DID NOT
FUNCTION THE WHOLE TWELVE MONTHS [OF THE FLOOD]. SAID R.
JONATHAN TO HIM: THEY DID FUNCTION, BUT THEIR MARK WAS IMPER-
CEPTIBLE. R. ELIEZER SAID: THEY SHALL NOT CEASE IMPLIES THAT THEY
NEVER CEASED. R. JOSHUA DEDUCED: THEY SHALL NOT CEASE: HENCE IT
FOLLOWS THAT THEY HAD CEASED.

The point of this Midrash is to teach that one should not imagine that
with the coming of the Flood and the emergence of the new generation,
the new generation would have a free ride henceforth. On the contrary,
the moral goals of social behaviors will be even stricter because of the
experience of the generation of the Flood. And if it turns out that the en-
suing generations will be morally corrupt, then it will end – as indicated
by the prophets – in major military struggles, as in the case of the battle
of the nations of Gog and Magog.

Seed Thoughts I

One of the reasons given for the ultimate demoralization of the generation of the Flood was the feature of idleness. Not having anything to do
to spend one's time productively can lead not only to the breakdown of
the individuality of a personality, but also to the destruction of an entire
community. A person needs a challenge in order to be fulfilled. Indeed,
every human being needs a series of challenges that accompany him
throughout his life so that he will always be motivated to do as much
as he can and so that he can reap the rewards of his actions in many
aspects of his life. The Ethics of the Fathers (mishnah 2:2) states this in a
beautiful teaching. Rabban Gamliel, the son of R. Judan HaNassi, says,
יפה תלמוד תורה עם דרך ארץ שיגיעת שניהם משכחת עון – *yafeh talmud Torah im
derekh eretz sheyegi'at shneihem meshakachat avon.* Torah study is good
together with an occupation, for the exertion of them both makes sin
forgotten. A person should do his very best to occupy his time both with
spiritual things, such as the study of Torah, and material things, such as

the struggle for the earning of a livelihood. Both of these occupations are so challenging and so demanding that they take up the complete time of an individual so that he forgets sin, since he has no time for it. What this mishnah advocates is the complete opposite of idleness, which should be eliminated from human life. When an individual's time is devoted to purposes that are challenging and meaningful, a good life will surely arise.

—

Seed Thoughts II

Today we are being overwhelmed with talks about environmentalism – be it the modification of temperature or the discussion about global warming – and the accusation that all this is due to the behavior of man. The question remains, based on the verse from Isaiah, that a time will come when Heaven and Earth will complete their mission. This should be interpreted not that they will be removed from existence, but that they will be modified. Possibly, what we are experiencing today might be a modification of that mission. As for the view that it is caused by man, our position should be that it is, indeed, caused by man, but not necessarily as a result of the extensive use of gasoline. Rather, it may be a punishment for the sins of mankind, such as terrorism, genocide, sexual immorality and many other things happening in our days. The cure is repentance. Not just materially, but spiritually.

—

Additional Commentary

The covenant with Noah

Do the nations of the world actually believe that God's covenant with Noah – not to destroy the world and its inhabitants again – is something that will be forever, as powerful as the covenant with Israel, which is forever, and which will survive even the transformation of this world to another type of world? The covenant of Israel is not dependent on the mission of Heaven and Earth, but only upon the eternity of the Holy One, Blessed be He. As long as the mission of Heaven and Earth continues, so will the covenant of Noah continue. But when that day comes, when Heaven will turn into smoke and the Earth like a worn out piece of cloth, the covenant with Noah will also be annulled. But the covenant of Israel will never be annulled. (*HaMidrash HaMevo'ar*)

יב. (ט, א) 'וַיְבָרֶךְ אֱ־לֹהִים אֶת נֹחַ וְאֶת בָּנָיו, וַיֹּאמֶר לָהֶם פְּרוּ וּרְבוּ', זֶה, שֶׁכֵּן בִּזְכוּת הַקָּרְבָּנוֹת.

12. AND GOD BLESSED NOAH AND HIS SONS, AND SAID UNTO THEM: BE
FRUITFUL AND MULTIPLY (9:1). THIS [BLESSING CONFERRED] HERE WAS
A REWARD FOR THEIR SACRIFICE.

The first thing to notice is that the blessing of פרו ורבו – *pru urvu*, "be
fruitful and multiply," should not be looked upon as an additional commandment. It is, rather, an extra blessing given to Noah in appreciation
of the offerings of thanksgiving that he had just performed. The order
to Noah to leave the ark with his wife and his sons to leave with their
wives has been interpreted already as permission to restore procreation
to their lives. Therefore, *pru urvu* was not an additional requirement,
since God already commanded this to Adam and Eve, but rather, it is an
additional blessing.

'וּמוֹרַאֲכֶם וְחִתְּכֶם יִהְיֶה', מוֹרָא וְחִתִּית חָזְרוּ, וּרְדִיָּה לֹא חָזְרָה, אֵימָתַי חָזְרָה בִּימֵי שְׁלֹמֹה,
שֶׁנֶּאֱמַר (מ"א ה, ד) 'כִּי הוּא רֹדֶה בְּכָל עֵבֶר הַנָּהָר מִתִּפְסַח וְעַד עַזָּה'

AND THE FEAR OF YOU AND THE DREAD OF YOU (HITKEM) SHALL BE
UPON EVERY BEAST OF THE EARTH (9:2): FEAR AND DREAD RETURNED,
BUT DOMINION DID NOT RETURN. WHEN DID IT RETURN? IN THE DAYS
OF SOLOMON, AS IT IS WRITTEN, FOR HE HAD DOMINION OVER ALL THE
REGION (I KINGS 5:4).

The Hebrew word רדיה – *rediyah*, referring to complete control over
the animals, is not used here because in the time of Noah, there was no
such control. This kind of control did exist in the time of Adam and for
a short period of time with king Solomon. But never again. What happened in the time of Noah was that he was able to control those which
we call domestic animals, but not those of the wild.

תָּנֵי רַבִּי שִׁמְעוֹן בֶּן אֶלְעָזָר אוֹמֵר, תִּינוֹק בֶּן יוֹמוֹ חַי, מְחַלְּלִין עָלָיו אֶת הַשַּׁבָּת, אֲבָל דָּוִד מֶלֶךְ
יִשְׂרָאֵל מֵת אֵין מְחַלְּלִין עָלָיו אֶת הַשַּׁבָּת, כָּל זְמַן שֶׁאָדָם חַי מְחַלְּלִין עָלָיו אֶת הַשַּׁבָּת, אֲבָל

אִם מֵת אֵין מְחַלְּלִין עָלָיו אֶת הַשַּׁבָּת. וְכֵן רַבִּי שִׁמְעוֹן בֶּן אֶלְעָזָר אוֹמֵר, תִּינוֹק בֶּן יוֹמוֹ חַי, אֵין
מְשַׁמְּרִין אוֹתוֹ מִפְּנֵי הַחֻלְדָּה, מִפְּנֵי הַנָּחָשׁ, שֶׁלֹּא יְנַקְּרוּ אֶת עֵינָיו, אֲרִי רוֹאֶה אוֹתוֹ וּבוֹרֵחַ, נָחָשׁ
רוֹאֶה אוֹתוֹ וּבוֹרֵחַ, אֲבָל, עוֹג מֶלֶךְ הַבָּשָׁן מֵת, מְשַׁמְּרִין אוֹתוֹ מִן הַחֻלְדָּה וּמִן הָעַכְבָּרִים שֶׁלֹּא
יְנַקְּרוּ אֶת עֵינָיו, כָּל זְמַן שֶׁאָדָם חַי מוֹרָאוֹ עַל הַבְּרִיּוֹת, מֵת נִטַּל מוֹרָאוֹ מִן הַבְּרִיּוֹת, הָדָא הוּא
דִּכְתִיב, 'וּמוֹרַאֲכֶם וְחִתְּכֶם יִהְיֶה'.

IT WAS TAUGHT, R. SIMEON B. ELEAZAR SAID: FOR A LIVE INFANT ONE
DAY OLD THE SABBATH IS DESECRATED; FOR DAVID KING OF ISRAEL,
DEAD, THE SABBATH MAY NOT BE DESECRATED. AND THUS TOO DID R.
SIMEON B. ELEAZAR SAY: AN INFANT ONE DAY OLD, ALIVE, NEED NOT BE
GUARDED FROM MICE OR SERPENTS TO PREVENT THEM PICKING OUT
HIS EYES: A LION SEES HIM AND FLEES, A SERPENT SEES HIM AND FLEES.
YET OG, KING OF BASHAN, DEAD, MUST BE GUARDED! FOR AS LONG AS A
MAN IS ALIVE HIS FEAR LIES UPON THE [LOWER] CREATURES; WHEN HE
DIES, HIS FEAR IS REMOVED FROM THE LOWER CREATURES. THUS IT IS
WRITTEN, AND THE FEAR OF YOU AND THE LIFE OF YOU, ETC.

Regarding the conclusion that sometimes animals stay away from human beings, even from babies – this may happen, but is not advised for anyone to test this theory. By the same token, even Og, the powerful king of Bashan, has no power after death and has to be protected from the wild animals by those who are weaker than he.

—

Seed Thoughts I

We now have the beautiful lines that indicate how, in Judaism, life is holier than death. If a baby of even a day old needs help, even the Sabbath can be desecrated. But if David, king of Israel and the king Messiah has to be moved after death, the Sabbath may not be desecrated. Life is holier than death in a very special way that has to do with the commandments. To live in accordance with the commandments is to be truly alive. If you are eligible to perform these commandments, even if only potentially, as a little baby, the Sabbath and Yom Kippur may be broken, and any other prohibition may be transgressed for the sake of trying to preserve that life. But in death, one is not able to observe the commandments and therefore, transgression is forbidden.

—

Seed Thoughts II

This Midrash is a wonderful affirmation of the importance of the commandments, which help us realize the purpose for which life is given to man. This should be compared to a similar section in the Ethics of the Fathers, where the commandments are extolled as having a very special relationship to the Jewish people: רצה הקדוש ברוך הוא לזכות את ישראל, לפיכך הרבה להם תורה ומצות – *ratzah haKadosh Baruch Hu lezakot et Yisrael, lefikhakh hirbah lahem Torah umitzvot*, God gave the Jewish people the greatest possible asset by bestowing upon them a maximum number of commandments. How is this to be understood? The best way is to consider the various benedictions that we recite upon performing a commandment.

There are many types of benedictions. The most prevalent are those whose message is universal; for instance, the benedictions of enjoyment, "*Bircot Hanehenin*," as the one for bread and those for other food items. The prayer books list many such benedictions of a universal nature, which begin with, "Blessed art Thou God, O Lord of the universe," and which continue by stating the specific aspect of the benediction – for example, "Who bringest bread from the earth." These blessings are universal; anyone can recite them and they apply to all those who want to show reverence toward God. However, the Jewish people are not involved in eating bread, for example. in any special way, distinct from that of everyone else. The Almighty, however, wanted the Jewish people to be in a special category and so bestowed upon them commandments that relate only to them and are commanded only to them. For these commandments, we have special blessing called *Bircot Hamitzvot*.

For example, in the commandment to put on Tefillin: the benediction for this commandment also has a special style of its own – "Blessed art Thou God, O Lord of the universe, Who has sanctified us with His commandments and has commanded us to [in this case] put on Tefillin." This particular type of benediction applies to all those commandments that have as their objective the *sanctification* of the Jewish people. The fact that there are so many of these is interpreted as being a major spiritual asset to living as a Jew. This is how I interpret Rav Hannia Ben Akashia's statement based on the verse (Isaiah 42:21) stating that "God wanted Israel to justify its existence" – as a unique people, and therefore He multiplied the unique commandments particular to the Jewish people, to help us create a covenantal community. (See also the Malbim on Isaiah 42:21.)

Additional Commentary

Be fruitful and multiply

The commandment to be fruitful and multiply was given not only to the children of Noah, but to Noah, himself. However, according to the tradition, Noah did not produce other children after the Flood. One interpretation as to why this is, is that he had been attacked by one of the animals, the lion, and was never able to recover from the injuries he suffered. The blessing to be fruitful and multiply might be related to Noah in an entirely different way. He was able to recover from his injury and live for several hundred years after the Flood, and was also able to experience the arrival of Abraham – his descendant about whom one might say that he fulfilled the dream of Noah in the creation of a better world. It is calculated that Abraham was fifty-eight years old when Noah died, so perhaps this could truly have been the fulfillment of his mission. (*Tiferet Tzion*)

יג. (ג-ד) 'כָּל רֶמֶשׂ אֲשֶׁר הוּא חַי, אַךְ בָּשָׂר בְּנַפְשׁוֹ דָמוֹ' רַבִּי יוֹסֵי בַּר אִיכוּ, בְּשֵׁם רַבִּי יוֹחָנָן, אָדָם הָרִאשׁוֹן, שֶׁלֹּא הֻתַּר לְבָשָׂר תַּאֲוָה, לֹא הֻזְהַר עַל אֵבֶר מִן הֶחָי, אֲבָל בְּנֵי נֹחַ שֶׁהֻתְּרוּ לִבְשָׂר תַּאֲוָה, הֻזְהֲרוּ עַל אֵבֶר מִן הֶחָי.

13. EVERY MOVING THING THAT LIVETH SHALL BE FOR FOOD FOR YOU . . .
ONLY FLESH WITH THE LIFE THEREOF, WHICH IS THE BLOOD THEREOF,
SHALL YE NOT EAT (9:3). R. JOSE B. R. ABIN SAID IN R. JOHANAN'S NAME:
ADAM, TO WHOM FLESH TO SATISFY HIS APPETITE WAS NOT PERMITTED,
WAS NOT ADMONISHED AGAINST EATING A LIMB TORN FROM THE LIV-
ING ANIMAL. BUT THE CHILDREN OF NOAH, TO WHOM FLESH TO SATISFY
THEIR APPETITE WAS PERMITTED, WERE ADMONISHED AGAINST EATING
A LIMB TORN FROM THE LIVING ANIMAL.

The fact that the prohibition of eating a limb from a living animal
applied to Noah and not to Adam is easily understood. The first man,
Adam, was allowed to eat only fruits and vegetables. The taking of animal life for meat to eat was forbidden. Therefore, quite obviously, since
that was forbidden, surely eating the limb of a living animal was also
prohibited. This law started to apply to Noah because in his case, he was
given permission to eat meat, for the first time of anyone in the biblical
story.

(ה) 'אַךְ' לְהָבִיא אֶת הַחוֹנֵק עַצְמוֹ, יָכוֹל כְּשָׁאוּל, תַּלְמוּד לוֹמַר, 'אַךְ', יָכוֹל כַּחֲנַנְיָה מִישָׁאֵל וַעֲזַרְיָה, תַּלְמוּד לוֹמַר 'אַךְ'.

AND SURELY (WE – AK) YOUR BLOOD OF YOUR LIVES WILL I REQUIRE
(9:5). THIS INCLUDES ONE WHO STRANGLES HIMSELF. YOU MIGHT
THINK THAT EVEN ONE IN THE PLIGHT OF SAUL IS MEANT: THEREFORE
WE HAVE AK. YOU MIGHT THINK, EVEN ONE LIKE HANANIAH, MISHAEL
AND AZARIAH: THEREFORE WE HAVE AK.

The question of death by suffocation was raised because the expression "taking of blood" did not apply to it. This has to be corrected and
understood that it is death that is spoken of and prohibited by use of

this expression, and not the manner of death, such as the literal taking of blood. Similarly, suicide is also prohibited because you are not allowed to take your own life and spill your own blood in the same way you are not allowed to spill the blood of your neighbor. This prohibition, however, can be limited by the expression אַךְ – *akh*, in the sense of defining one thing and excluding another, like the term "nevertheless." This, therefore, comes to exclude cases where one gave up one's life to sanctify God's name, as with King Saul, who asked to have his life taken so that the King of Israel would not fall into enemy hands.

Two illustrations are given in the Midrash. One of them tells of king Saul, who took his own life because he felt that the kingship would be betrayed if he allowed his enemies to damage his body to a very grave extent. The Midrash also gave the example of Chananiah, Mishael and Azariah, who gave their lives for the sanctification of God's name In the last moment, their lives were divinely rescued. An act of קדוש השם – *kiddush hashem*, the sanctification of God's name, is the only allowance for taking one's own life.

'מִיַּד כָּל חַיָּה', זֶה הַמּוֹסֵר אֶת חֲבֵרוֹ לַחַיָּה לְהָרְגוֹ, 'מִיַּד אִישׁ אָחִיו' זֶה הַשּׂוֹכֵר אֶת אֲחֵרִים לַהֲרֹג אֶת חֲבֵרוֹ. דָּבָר אַחֵר, 'מִיַּד כָּל חַיָּה אֶדְרְשֶׁנּוּ' אֵלּוּ אַרְבַּע מַלְכֻיּוֹת, 'מִיַּד הָאָדָם מִיַּד אִישׁ אָחִיו' זֶה עֵשָׂו, דִּכְתִיב (בראשית לב, יב) 'הַצִּילֵנִי נָא מִיַּד אָחִי מִיַּד עֵשָׂו', 'אֶדְרֹשׁ אֶת נֶפֶשׁ הָאָדָם' אֵלּוּ יִשְׂרָאֵל, שֶׁנֶּאֱמַר (יחזקאל לד, לא) 'וְאַתֵּנָה צֹאנִי צֹאן מַרְעִיתִי אָדָם אַתֶּם'.

AT THE HAND OF EVERY BEAST WILL I REQUIRE IT: THIS REFERS TO THE FOUR KINGDOMS. AT THE HAND OF MAN (HA-ADAM): R. LEVI SAID: THAT MEANS, FROM THE HAND OF EDOM. EVEN AT THE HAND OF EVERY MAN'S BROTHER, AS IT IS WRITTEN, DELIVER ME, I PRAY THEE, FROM THE HAND OF MY BROTHER, FROM THE HAND OF ESAU (GEN. 32:12). WILL L REQUIRE THE LIFE OF MAN: THIS REFERS TO ISRAEL, AS IT IS WRITTEN, AND YE MY SHEEP, THE SHEEP OF MY PASTURE, ARE MEN (EZEK. 34:31).

The Midrash ends with a warning to all those who plot evil against Israel, such as the four empires who persecuted us, Babylon, Persia, Greece and Rome. The name for Rome is Edom, which is a play on words, and implies not to spill the blood of Adam (which has the same letters as "Edom"). The word דם – *dam* is also in that phrase, which implies that of the four empires, Edom (Rome) was the worst and destroyed the Second Temple, thus placing us in the exile which only ended recently with the rise of the state of Israel. God will see to it that the blood that was spilled on Israel will be compensated in its good time.

Seed Thoughts

Based on the additional commentary that will follow, it seems that Noah was given more commandments to do than Adam because he had many more reasons to be thankful, since he was spared from the Flood. The more that are given by God, the more obligations one should take. The 613 commandments should be looked upon in that way. If we are given more, then it is upon us to "give back" to God as much as possible.

Additional Commentary

Our obligation to thank God

Why did R. Yossi b. Aibu offer a special reason for Noah's being commanded about limbs torn from a living animal, in contrast to Adam not having been commanded regarding this matter? Why did he not question any other commandments that were given to Noah and not to Adam? The answer is that the more additional blessings a human being receives from God, the more obligated he is to thank God and commit himself to God's work. Thus, when God delivered Israel from Egypt by means of all kinds of wonders and miracles, we were commanded then to observe 613 commandments. Similarly, Noah, who was rescued from the waters of the Flood, was obligated with more mitzvot than the first Adam. The main point of R. Yossi's question, however, had to do with the tearing of a limb from a living animal. Since this kind of commandment has to do with the suffering of animals, which happened also in the time of Adam, should not Adam have been commanded about this as well? It was in this respect that R. Yossi added the explanation that the eating of meat was not permitted to Adam, and therefore, the idea of eating such a limb from any animal was not relevant. (*Tiferet Tzion*)

The derivation of limb from a living animal

The expression בשר בנפשו – *bassar benafsho*, "flesh with life thereof," is written in reference to a limb from a living animal, אבר מן החי – *ever min hachai*. When it goes on to say בנפשו דמו – *benafsho damo*, this refers to blood from a living animal. It is for that reason that the word *benafsho* is placed between the words *bassar* and *damo*. (RZWE)

The four empires

The reference to the four empires is gleaned from the verse where it says, "I will demand justice from every wild animal." It could easily have said from *any* animal, but it said from *all* animals. There is an emphasis on the expression כל חיה – *kol chayah*, and that it also carries the meaning of "all who act as though they are animals," as in the four empires. Since it also says, ומיד האדם – *umiyad ha'adam*, meaning those persecuted by man, it might very well mean, מיד האדום – *miyad ha'edom*, another name for Rome. Or the reference to *ha'adam*, meaning that well-known *adam*, i.e., Edom, which is Rome. (Mirkin)

יד. (ו-ז) 'שֹׁפֵךְ דַּם הָאָדָם, בָּאָדָם דָּמוֹ יִשָּׁפֵךְ וְגוֹ׳', אָמַר רַבִּי חֲנִינָא, כֻּלְּהֶם כַּהֲלָכוֹת בְּנֵי נֹחַ. בְּעַד אֶחָד, בְּדַיָּן אֶחָד. בְּלֹא עֵדִים, וּבְלֹא הַתְרָאָה, עַל יְדֵי שָׁלִיחַ, עַל יְדֵי עֻבָּרִים

14. WHOSO SHEDDETH MAN'S BLOOD, ETC. (9:6). R. HANINA SAID: ALL THESE ARE SPECIFICALLY NOACHIAN LAWS, [VIZ. THAT A MAN IS CONDEMNED] ON THE TESTIMONY OF ONE WITNESS, ON THE RULING OF ONE JUDGE, WITHOUT A FORMAL WARNING, [FOR MURDER COMMITTED] THROUGH AN AGENT, AND FOR [THE MURDER OF] AN EMBRYO.

All these laws were given to the sons of Noah, and they are completely different from the laws of Israel and the Torah.

בְּעַד אֶחָד, בְּדַיָּן אֶחָד, 'שֹׁפֵךְ דַּם הָאָדָם, בָּאָדָם' אֶחָד 'דָּמוֹ יִשָּׁפֵךְ'. בְּלֹא עֵדִים, וּבְלֹא הַתְרָאָה 'שֹׁפֵךְ דַּם הָאָדָם' 'דָּמוֹ יִשָּׁפֵךְ'. עַל יְדֵי שָׁלִיחַ 'שֹׁפֵךְ דַּם הָאָדָם', עַל יְדֵי אָדָם, 'דָּמוֹ יִשָּׁפֵךְ'. עַל יְדֵי עֻבָּרִים 'שֹׁפֵךְ דַּם הָאָדָם', רַבִּי יְהוּדָה בַּר רַבִּי סִימוֹן אָמַר, אַף הַחוֹנְקוֹ, 'שֹׁפֵךְ דַּם הָאָדָם, וְגוֹ׳'. אָמַר רַבִּי לֵוִי, הֲרֵי שֶׁהָרַג וְלֹא נֶהֱרַג, אֵימָתַי הוּא נֶהֱרָג, לִכְשֶׁיָּבוֹא אָדָם, 'שֹׁפֵךְ דַּם הָאָדָם בָּאָדָם דָּמוֹ יִשָּׁפֵךְ''

ON THE TESTIMONY OF ONE WITNESS AND ON THE RULING OF ONE JUDGE, FOR IT SAYS, WHOSO SHEDDETH MAN'S BLOOD, BY ONE MAN SHALL HLS BLOOD BE SHED. WITHOUT A FORMAL WARNING, AS IT SAYS, WHOSO SHEDDETH MAN'S BLOOD, BY MAN SHALL HLS BLOOD BE SHED. [HE WHO COMMITS MURDER] THROUGH AN AGENT, BECAUSE IT SAYS, WHOSO SHEDDETH MAN'S BLOOD BY MAN, SHALL HIS BLOOD BE SHED: [I.E., IF HE SLAYS] BY MEANS OF ANOTHER PERSON, HIS BLOOD SHALL BE SHED. FOR [THE MURDER OF] AN EMBRYO, FOR IT SAYS, WHOSO SHEDDETH THE BLOOD OF MAN WITHIN [ANOTHER] MAN, SHALL HIS BLOOD BE SHED. R. JUDAH B. R. SIMON SAID: ALSO HE WHO MURDERS BY STRANGLING, AND ON HIS OWN TESTIMONY, AS IT SAYS, WHOSO SHEDDETH MAN'S BLOOD [WHILE RETAINING IT] WITHIN MAN, SHALL HIS BLOOD BE SHED. R. LEVI SAID: BEHOLD, IF A MAN SLEW YET WAS NOT SLAIN, WHEN WILL HE BE SLAIN? WHEN MAN COMES [FOR FINAL JUDGMENTS; THUS IT IS WRITTEN], WHOSO SHEDDETH MAN'S BLOOD, WHEN MAN COMES SHALL HLS BLOOD BE SHED.

These interpretations are based on the fact that the word באדם –
ba'adam is mentioned in the text. The text does not say just שופך דם
האדם – *shofekh dam ha'adam*, but adds the word באדם – *ba'adam*. One
interpretation is that one witness, or a person confessing his own guilt,
is enough for a conviction in Noahide law. This is in contrast to Talmudic Law, which requires at least two witnesses. According to the laws of
Noah, an individual who hires someone to kill someone else is responsible for the murder. According to Jewish law, the one committing the
murder is held responsible and cannot say he was sent by another (see
Rashi on this midrash). The laws also differ on the question of killing
or wounding a woman bearing a child. The section ends by mentioning
that not all cases are solvable and that God will see to it that justice is
carried out in the end.

דָּרַשׁ רַבִּי עֲקִיבָא, כָּל מִי שֶׁהוּא שׁוֹפֵךְ דָּמִים, מַעֲלִים עָלָיו כְּאִלּוּ הוּא מְמַעֵט אֶת הַדְּמוּת, מַאי
טַעְמָה, 'שֹׁפֵךְ דַּם הָאָדָם בָּאָדָם דָּמוֹ יִשָּׁפֵךְ', מִפְּנֵי מָה 'כִּי בְּצֶלֶם אֱ-לֹהִים עָשָׂה אֶת הָאָדָם'.
דָּרַשׁ רַבִּי אֶלְעָזָר בֶּן עֲזַרְיָה, כָּל מִי שֶׁהוּא מְבַטֵּל פְּרִיָה וְרִבְיָה, מַעֲלֶה עָלָיו הַכָּתוּב כְּאִלּוּ הוּא
מְמַעֵט אֶת הַדְּמוּת, מַאי טַעְמָה, 'כִּי בְּצֶלֶם אֱ-לֹהִים עָשָׂה אֶת הָאָדָם', וּכְתִיב בָּתְרֵהּ, 'וְאַתֶּם
פְּרוּ וּרְבוּ וְגוֹ', שִׁרְצוּ בָאָרֶץ וּרְבוּ'. דָּרַשׁ בֶּן עַזַּאי, כָּל מִי שֶׁהוּא מְבַטֵּל פְּרִיָה וְרִבְיָה, מַעֲלֶה עָלָיו
הַכָּתוּב כְּאִלּוּ שׁוֹפֵךְ דָּמִים, וּמְמַעֵט אֶת הַדְּמוּת, מַאי טַעְמָה, 'שֹׁפֵךְ דַּם הָאָדָם', מִפְּנֵי מָה,
'כִּי בְּצֶלֶם אֱ-לֹהִים', וּמַה כְּתִיב אַחֲרָיו, 'וְאַתֶּם פְּרוּ וּרְבוּ', אָמַר לוֹ רַבִּי אֶלְעָזָר בֶּן עֲזַרְיָה, נָאִים
דְּבָרִים הַיּוֹצְאִים מִפִּי עוֹשֵׂיהֶן, בֶּן עַזַּאי, נָאֶה דּוֹרֵשׁ וְלֹא נָאֶה מְקַיֵּם, אָמַר לוֹ, אֲנִי, לְפִי שֶׁחָשְׁקָה
נַפְשִׁי בַּתּוֹרָה, אֲבָל, יִתְקַיֵּם הָעוֹלָם בַּאֲחֵרִים.

R. AKIBA LECTURED: HE WHO SHEDS BLOOD IS REGARDED AS THOUGH
HE HAD IMPAIRED [GOD'S] LIKENESS. WHAT IS THE PROOF? WHOSO
SHEDDETH MAN'S BLOOD, ETC. WHAT IS THE REASON? FOR IN THE IM-
AGE OF GOD MADE HE MAN R. ELAZAR B. AZARIAH LECTURED: HE WHO
REFRAINS FROM PROCREATION IS AS THOUGH HE IMPAIRED [GOD'S]
IMAGE. WHAT IS THE PROOF? FOR IN THE IMAGE OF GOD MADE HE MAN,
WHICH IS FOLLOWED BY, AND YOU, BE YE FRUITFUL, AND MULTIPLY.
BEN AZZAI LECTURED: HE WHO REFRAINS FROM PROCREATION IS AS
THOUGH HE SHED BLOOD AND IMPAIRED [GOD'S] LIKENESS. WHAT IS
THE PROOF? WHOSO SHEDDETH MAN'S BLOOD, ETC.; WHY? FOR IN THE
IMAGE OF GOD MADE HE MAN, WHICH IS FOLLOWED BY, AND YOU, BE
YE FRUITFUL, AND MULTIPLY. SAID R. ELAZAR B. AZARIAH TO HIM:
TEACHINGS ARE BECOMING WHEN THEY ARE UTTERED BY THOSE WHO
PRACTICE THEM, BUT YOU, SON OF AZZAI, PREACH WELL, BUT DO NOT
FULFIL YOUR TEACHING! THAT IS BECAUSE I DESIRE TO STUDY TORAH,
HE PLEADED, WHILE THE WORLD CAN BE PRESERVED THROUGH OTHERS.

Since the human being is created in the image of God, when a human life is taken, it is as though the image of God has been affected in that it is less present in the world. By the same token, one who refrains from the commandment to be fruitful and multiply also diminishes the influence of the image of God in the world, rendering it quite a serious matter. It is of interest to note that the commentators do not accept the apology of Ben Azzai and his claim that his total involvement in the study of Torah justifies the fact that he did not participate in the act to be fruitful and multiply.

—

Seed Thoughts I

One main theme to consider is the concept of the image God. It is not something physical. It is something moral and spiritual. It should be understood in light of the text that says, מה הוא רחום אף אתה רחום – *mah hu rachum af atah rachum,* just as He is merciful, so should you be merciful. This is called *imitatio Dei,* Latin for "imitation of God." This is the true goal of the Judaic person and the way for him to become a moral human being.

—

Seed Thoughts II

Another theme here involves the rabbis' responses to Ben Azzai's statement as to why he did not get married and have children. Based on his statement, this is a good opportunity to talk about the meaning of marriage, its importance and its furtherance in the Jewish community. Ben Azzai was probably right. His concentration on Torah may have been such that he did not learn how to behave socially, how to speak with the opposite sex and how to take the initiative in creating the possibility of a life partnership for himself. He could have and should have asked for help from others, but may have been too embarrassed to do so or, as it seems to be a unique case, he was just too involved in his studies for this world.

Every community ought to have arrangements whereby every Jewish single can meet each other in an atmosphere of respect and mutual honor. The best proof attesting to the importance of this is that there are two significant dates on the Jewish calendar; Yom Kippur and the fifteenth of Av, which were used by the Jewish people, in ancient times, as occasions when Jewish singles could meet each other for the purpose of marriage. This was taken very seriously, and we can infer this from the fact that it was the most sacred day in the Jewish calendar that was used for this purpose, as it is the week after the ninth of Av, the day commemorating the destruction of the Temple and of Jerusalem – as though to indicate that only through marriage and a family can the Jewish people renew itself. This shows the intention of the Torah, and intimates how important it is for all of us to do what we can to help every Jewish man and woman to have the opportunity for a lifetime marriage.

Parashah Thirty-Four, *Midrash Fifteen*

טו. 'וְאַתֶּם פְּרוּ וּרְבוּ', אָמַר רֵישׁ לָקִישׁ, בְּרִית נֶחְלְקָה לָאֲוִירוֹת, רַבִּי שִׁמְעוֹן בֶּן לָקִישׁ הֲוָה יָתֵב
לָעֵי בְּאוֹרַיְתָא בַּחֲדָא אִילְטִיס דִּטְבֶרְיָה, נְפַקּוּן תַּרְתֵּין נְשִׁין מִן תַּמָּן, אֲמָרָה חֲדָא לַחֲבֶרְתַּהּ,
בְּרִיךְ דְּאַפְּקָן מִן הָדֵין אֲוִירָא בִישָׁא, צְוַח לְהוֹן וַאֲמַר לְהוֹן, מָה הָן אַתּוּן אֲמָרִין, מִן מָזְגָא, אֲמַר,
אֲנָא חָכַם מִן מָזְגָא, וְלֵית בַּהּ אֶלָּא תַּרְתֵּין עַמּוּדִין, אֲמַר, בָּרוּךְ שֶׁנָּתַן חֵן לְמָקוֹם עַל יוֹשְׁבָיו. חַד
תַּלְמִיד מִן דְּרַבִּי יוֹסֵי הֲוָה יָתֵב קוֹדָמוֹי, הֲוָה מַסְבַּר לֵהּ וְלָא סָבַר לֵהּ, אֲמַר לֵהּ לָמָה לֵית אַתּ
סָבַר, אֲמַר לֵהּ, דַּאֲנָא גָּלֵי מֵאַתְרָאי, אֲמַר לֵהּ מֵהֵיכָן אַתָּר אַתְּ, אֲמַר לֵהּ מִן גּוּבַת שַׁמַּאי, אֲמַר
לֵהּ וּמַה אִנּוּן אֲוִירָא דְּתַמָּן, אֲמַר לֵהּ, כַּד יָנוֹקָא מִתְיְלִיד, אֲנָא גָבְלִין לֵהּ אֲדַמִדְמָנֵי, וְטוֹשִׁין מוֹחֵהּ
דְּלָא יְכָלוֹנֶה יְתוּשַׁיָּה, אֲמַר, בָּרוּךְ שֶׁנָּתַן חֵן מָקוֹם בְּעֵינֵי יוֹשְׁבָיו.

15. AND YOU, BE YE FRUITFUL, AND MULTIPLY; SWARM IN THE EARTH,
AND MULTIPLY THEREIN (9:7). RESH LAKISH SAID: A COVENANT HAS
BEEN MADE IN FAVOR OF CLIMATES. RESH LAKISH WAS SITTING AND
STUDYING TORAH IN A SMALL FOREST OF TIBERIAS, WHEN TWO WOMEN
CAME OUT FROM THERE, ONE SAYING TO THE OTHER, 'PRAISED BE HE
WHO HAS LED US OUT FROM THAT BAD CLIMATE.' 'WHENCE DO YOU
COME?' HE CALLED OUT TO THEM. 'FROM MAZGA,' THEY REPLIED. 'I
KNOW ABOUT MAZGA,' HE OBSERVED, 'AND IT CONTAINS NO MORE THAN
TWO DWELLING HOUSES! BLESSED IS HE WHO INSPIRETH THE INHABIT-
ANTS OF A TOWN WITH LOVE FOR IT!' A DISCIPLE OF R. ISSI WAS SITTING
BEFORE HIM AND COULD NOT COMPREHEND WHAT HE WAS EXPLAINING
TO HIM. 'WHY CANNOT YOU GRASP IT?' HE ASKED, 'BECAUSE I AM AN
EXILE FROM HOME,' HE REPLIED. 'WHENCE ARE YOU?' INQUIRED HE.
'FROM GABATH SHANIMAI,' HE REPLIED. 'WHAT IS ITS CLIMATE?' HE
ASKED. 'WHEN A CHILD IS BORN THERE WE HAVE TO CRUSH SPICES AND
SMEAR HIS HEAD WITH IT, LEST INSECTS SHOULD EAT HIM,' HE REPLIED.
'BLESSED IS HE WHO INSPIRETH THE INHABITANTS OF A PLACE WITH
LOVE FOR IT!' HE EXCLAIMED.

The interpretation is needed because of the expression, "swarm in
the land." It seems obvious that if people were to multiply, they would
multiply on the earth and nowhere else. The inclusion of the word הארץ
– *ha'aretz*, the earth, must have a special meaning. It is interpreted as
meaning that God wants every aspect of earth to be inhabited. Even

those places that are less comfortable than others and require much sacrifice.

אַף לֶעָתִיד לָבוֹא כֵּן, שֶׁנֶּאֱמַר (יחזקאל לו, כו) 'וַהֲסִרֹתִי אֶת לֵב הָאֶבֶן מִבְּשַׂרְכֶם, וְגוֹ', לֵב בָּשָׂר' לֵב בּוֹסֵר שֶׁל חֲבֵרוֹ.

IN THE FUTURE TOO IT WILL BE THUS: AND I WILL TAKE AWAY THE STONY HEART OUT OF YOUR FLESH, AND I WILL GIVE YOU A HEART OF FLESH – LEB BASAR (EZEK.36:26), I.E., A HEART WHICH HAS NO DESIRE OF (BOSER) HIS NEIGHBOR'S PORTION.

In order to fulfill the requirement of having every aspect of earth occupied by people, local pride has to be developed. This local pride depends upon the population being less impressed by the material things in life and more interested in each other and each other's welfare. This is the prediction of what will happen in the World to Come. The evil inclination will be eliminated, gradually, and human beings will learn to love each other and live among each other with mutual respect.

—

Seed Thoughts

Several times in our Midrash, phenomena that we regard as natural and ordinary are looked upon with "religious eyes," so to speak, and our attention is called to the fact that these may actually be miracles that have been divinely implanted in us or around us. For example, the manner in which the human body is formed has inspired several midrashim extolling the brilliance of the composition of the human body. Only God could have done it. Here, we have an example of finding significance in seemingly trivial phenomena. Local pride, while being a human phenomenon, has a deeper goal. God has an interest in cultivating local pride because it helps inhabit places that are relatively challenging for human beings to live, such as the Arctic or the torrid zones or the desert. While it is not an instinct and human beings can rebel against it, as shown in our Midrash, still, there are enough people whose local pride make all parts of the earth not only inhabited, but also habitable and relatively comfortable.

—

Additional Commentary

The covenant of climate

The covenant of climate is hinted at in the verse that says, "Be fruitful and multiply," but then goes on to say, "swarm in the earth and multiply in it." By doubling the expression of reproduction in the verse, the intention is that wherever people live and wherever they are born, that is the place that they should continue living. The air and the atmosphere, the very climate of different places is different and has an influence on the people living there. The reason behind this development is that people should be encouraged to live not only in the most comfortable of places. As the Book of Isaiah states, לא תהו בראה לשבת יצרה – *lo tohu be-arah lashevet yatzrah*, the world was created to be inhabited and not desolate. Every place in the world is suitable for human habitation. But it is expected of an individual to learn to become accustomed to his location and to accept it. The result will be that his local environment will even find favor in his eyes. (Mirkin)

א. (ט, ח-ט) 'וַיֹּאמֶר אֱ-לֹהִים אֶל נֹחַ וְאֶל בָּנָיו, וְגוֹ'', 'וַאֲנִי הִנְנִי מֵקִים', רַבִּי יְהוּדָה וְרַבִּי נְחֶמְיָה,
רַבִּי יְהוּדָה אָמַר, לְפִי שֶׁעָבַר עַל הַצִּוּוּי, לְפִיכָךְ נִתְבַּזָּה, וְרַבִּי נְחֶמְיָה אָמַר, הוֹסִיף עַל הַצִּוּוּי וְנָהַג
בִּקְדֻשָּׁה, לְפִיכָךְ זָכָה הוּא וּבָנָיו לְדִבּוּר, 'וַיֹּאמֶר אֱ-לֹהִים אֶל נֹחַ וְאֶל בָּנָיו'.

1. AND GOD SPOKE UNTO NOAH, AND TO HIS SONS WITH HIM, SAYING:
AS FOR ME, BEHOLD, I ESTABLISH MY COVENANT WITH YOU, ETC. (9:8,
9). R. JUDAH SAID: BECAUSE HE TRANSGRESSED [GOD'S] COMMAND HE
WAS PUT TO SHAME. R. NEHEMIAH SAID: HE WENT BEYOND [GOD'S] COM-
MAND AND ACTED WITH SELF-RESTRAINT. THEREFORE HE AND HIS SONS
WERE FAVORED WITH [GOD'S] ALLOCUTION, AS IT IS WRITTEN, AND GOD
SPOKE UNTO NOAH AND TO HIS SONS, ETC.

The difference of opinion between R. Yehudah and R. Nechemiah
has to do with whether Noah should be looked upon with favor or
disfavor. This debate is a continuation of their disagreement, which we
read about first in parashah 30, midrash 9. R. Yehudah is very critical of
Noah. In our particular midrash, he criticizes Noah for not obeying the
commandment of reproduction immediately upon his emergence from
the ark. For this reason, Noah was punished in the sense that God's word
did not come exclusively to him, but also to his children. R. Nechemiah
thought entirely differently. He felt that an attitude of holiness should
prevail even after leaving the ark, as it did during the gender separation
in the ark, but only for a while. His reward was that God spoke to him
and his children in a very special and private way.

—

Seed Thoughts

R. Yehudah criticized Noah for the fact that he did not engage in procreation immediately upon leaving the ark. He had been commanded to
do so and there is no reference of children being born to him after the
Flood. What did R. Yehudah expect, that Noah would look upon this
as a major priority? The fact that he and everyone else were prohibited

from sexual activity during the days of the Flood was looked upon by Noah as a sacred mission. One cannot immediately move from a sacred mission to a life of indulgence; that, too, had to be approached with some sense of cooperating with The Divine. The more we analyze the behavior of Noah in relationship to these personal events, the more we learn to admire his character and to realize that he did not deserve the critical evaluation that so many of the commentators seem to have. This, of course, is the opinion of R. Nechemiah.

—

Additional Commentary

Because he transgressed the commandment

In most cases where God communicated with Noah, it was to him alone. Only in two cases it is described that He spoke to him and his children. The inclusion of his children is generally looked upon as something derogatory, that Noah was not worthy, in such instances, to be spoken to alone. The reason for this, in our midrash, is that Noah was described as being derelict for not performing the commandment of procreation immediately upon his leaving the ark – this is according to the view of R. Yehudah. R. Nechemiah, however, interprets this as a praiseworthy act. Noah overcame his lust and concentrated on sexual separation for a while, as did his children. Therefore, the children were included with him in the special communication with the Almighty. They all merited this special communication by the very virtue of their modesty, and there is nothing derogatory about this for Noah. As for the inclusion of his children in the communication, from Noah's perspective, it is said that a person is never jealous, either of his son or of his pupil. (Mirkin)

ב. (יב) 'וַיֹּאמֶר אֱ-לֹהִים זֹאת אוֹת הַבְּרִית אֲשֶׁר אֲנִי נֹתֵן בֵּינִי וּבֵינֵיכֶם וְגוֹ', לְדֹרֹת עוֹלָם' אָמַר
רַבִּי יוּדָן, 'לְדֹרֹת' כְּתִיב, פְּרָט לִשְׁנֵי דוֹרוֹת, לְדוֹרוֹ שֶׁל חִזְקִיָּהוּ, וּלְדוֹרוֹ שֶׁל אַנְשֵׁי כְנֶסֶת הַגְּדוֹלָה

2. AND GOD SAID: THIS IS THE TOKEN OF THE COVENANT . . . FOR
PERPETUAL GENERATIONS – LEDOROTH (9:12). R. JUDAN SAID: THIS IS
WRITTEN LE-DORATH, WHICH THUS EXCLUDES TWO GENERATIONS, THE
GENERATION OF HEZEKIAH AND THAT OF THE GREAT SYNAGOGUE.

Usually the word *dorot* in its various forms, such as *ledorotei'hem* or
ledorot appears with either one or two appearances of the letter *vav*. But
in this case, it appears without any *vav*, as דרת. This is interpreted to
mean that there were two generations so well learned and so observant
that they did not require any reminder of God's covenant, i.e., the rainbow. These were the generation of Hezekiah and that of the men of the
Great Assembly. One of the reasons why the generation of Hezekiah
was mentioned was because our tradition tells us that he placed someone with a sword at the door of the study hall saying that all must either
observe the commandments or suffer the fate of the sword (*Sanhedrin*
94b). The tradition continues and tells us that a survey that took place
several years later showed that there was not a single person among
Israel who was not a scholar in the time of Hezekiah. (*Tiferet Tzion*)

רַבִּי חִזְקִיָּה מוֹצִיא דוֹרָן שֶׁל אַנְשֵׁי כְנֶסֶת הַגְּדוֹלָה, וּמֵבִיא דוֹרוֹ שֶׁל רַבִּי שִׁמְעוֹן בֶּן יוֹחַאי.

R. HEZEKIAH OMITTED THE GENERATION OF THE MEN OF THE GREAT
SYNAGOGUE AND SUBSTITUTED THAT OF R. SIMEON B. YOHAI.

One of the reasons given for this action was his opinion that a true
righteous person was on a higher level that one who is a *baal tshuvah*
who has just become religious. The men of the Great Assembly succeeded in having their generation swear allegiance to the Torah, but
that was not as good as being under the leadership of someone like R.
Shimon b. Yohai, who was a great tzaddik. (*Tiferet Tzion*)

אֵלִיָּהוּ זָכוּר לַטּוֹב, וְרַבִּי יְהוֹשֻׁעַ בֶּן לֵוִי, הָווֹ יָתְבִין תָּנְיִן בַּחֲדָא, מָטוֹן שְׁמוּעָה מִן דְּרַבִּי שִׁמְעוֹן בֶּן יוֹחַאי, אֲמַרִי, הָא מָרֵא דִשְׁמַעְתָּא, נֵעוּל וְנִשְׁיְלֵהּ, עַל אֵלִיָּהוּ זָכוּר לַטּוֹב לְגַבֵּהּ, אָמַר לֵהּ מַן עִמָּךְ, אָמַר לֵהּ גְּדוֹל הַדּוֹר, רַבִּי יְהוֹשֻׁעַ בֶּן לֵוִי. אָמַר לֵהּ נִרְאֲתָה הַקֶּשֶׁת בְּיָמָיו, אָמַר לֵהּ הֵן, אָמַר, אִם נִרְאֲה הַקֶּשֶׁת בְּיָמָיו לֵית הוּא כְדַאי לְמֶחֱמֵי סְבַר אַפָּאִי

ELIJAH OF BLESSED MEMORY AND R. JOSHUA B. LEVI WERE SITTING AND
STUDYING TOGETHER, WHEN THEY CAME TO A RULING OF R. SIMEON
B. YOHAI. SAID ONE: 'HERE IS THE AUTHOR OF THE RULING: LET US GO
AND QUESTION HIM ABOUT IT.' SO ELIJAH OF BLESSED MEMORY WENT
TO HIM, 'WHO IS WITH YOU?' HE ASKED. 'THE GREATEST OF HIS GENERA-
TION, R. JOSHUA B. LEVI,' HE ANSWERED. 'HAS THE RAINBOW APPEARED
IN HIS DAYS?' HE INQUIRED; 'IF IT HAS, HE IS NOT WORTHY OF BEING
RECEIVED BY ME.'

Here is a most interesting and possibly a most disturbing view that
the appearance of the rainbow is a sign that a community is lacking in
piety. This section has Elijah the prophet giving his approval of this
thought and considering it important enough to prevent R. Joshua b.
Levi from visiting him.

רַבִּי חִזְקִיָּה בְּשֵׁם רַבִּי יִרְמְיָה אָמַר, כָּךְ אָמַר רַבִּי שִׁמְעוֹן בֶּן יוֹחַאי, בִּקְעָה בִּקְעָה אִמְּלַאי דִּינָרֵי זָהָב, וְנִתְמַלְאָה

R. HEZEKIAH RELATED IN R. JEREMIAH'S NAME: R. SIMEON B. YOHAI
HAD BUT TO SAY, 'O FIELD, O FIELD, BE FILLED WITH GOLD DINARS,' AND
IT WAS FILLED.

This is the first of several ways in which R. Hezekiah adds to his praise
of R. Shimon b. Yohai. R. Shimon b. Yohai was trying to demonstrate
to his students that the attainment of gold is possible in life, and for
some people it could even come to them relatively easily; however, one
should note that choosing gold comes at the expense of one's share in
the World to Come. The true work of a Jew in this world is the work of
Torah and that is the only occupation that will guarantee you a place in
the World to Come. (*Tiferet Tzion*)

רַבִּי חִזְקִיָּה בְּשֵׁם רַבִּי יִרְמְיָה אָמַר, כָּךְ אָמַר רַבִּי שִׁמְעוֹן בֶּן יוֹחַאי, אִי בָּעֵי אַבְרָהָם לְמַקְרְבֵי מִן גַּבֵּהּ וְעַד גַּבִּי, וַאֲנָא מַקְרַב מִגַּבֵּי עַד מַלְכָּא מְשִׁיחָא, וְאִן לָא בָּעֵי יִצְטָרַף אֲחִיָּה הַשִּׁילוֹנִי עִמִּי, וַאֲנָן מַקְרְבִין מִן אַבְרָהָם עַד מַלְכָּא מְשִׁיחָא

R. HEZEKIAH RELATED IN R. JEREMIAH'S NAME: THUS DID R. SIMEON B.
YOHAI SAY: IF ABRAHAM IS WILLING, HE CAN EFFECTIVELY INTERCEDE
FOR [ALL GENERATIONS] FROM HIS DAYS UNTIL MINE, WHILE I CAN IN-
TERCEDE FOR [ALL GENERATIONS] FROM MY TIME UNTIL THE ADVENT

OF MESSIAH. WHILE IF HE IS NOT WILLING, LET AHIJAH THE SHILONITE
UNITE WITH ME, AND WE CAN INTERCEDE FOR ALL FROM THE DAYS OF
ABRAHAM UNTIL THOSE OF MESSIAH.

This midrash now includes a series of paragraphs whereby R. Hezekiah, in R. Jeremiah's name, praises R. Shimon b. Yohai, saying that he
and Abraham, together (provided Abraham was willing) could intercede on behalf of the Jewish people throughout the generations. And if
Abraham were not willing, then he (R. Shimon) would join up with the
prophet Ahijah the Shilonite. The reason why the latter was chosen was
because he had suffered greatly during the time of Jeroboam.

רַבִּי חִזְקִיָּה בְּשֵׁם רַבִּי יִרְמְיָה אָמַר, כָּךְ אָמַר רַבִּי שִׁמְעוֹן בֶּן יוֹחַאי, אֵין הָעוֹלָם יָכוֹל לַעֲמֹד בְּפָחוּת
מִשְּׁלֹשִׁים צַדִּיקִים כְּאַבְרָהָם אָבִינוּ, אִי תְּלָתִין אִנּוּן אֲנָא וּבְרִי תְּרֵי מִנְּהוֹן, וְאִם עֶשְׂרִים אִנּוּן אֲנָא
וּבְרִי מִנְּהוֹן וְאִם עֲשָׂרָה אִנּוּן אֲנָא וּבְרִי מִנְּהוֹן, וְאִם חֲמִשָּׁה אִנּוּן אֲנָא וּבְרִי מִנְּהוֹן, וְאִם תְּרֵין אִנּוּן
אֲנָא וּבְרִי הֵן, וְאִם חַד הוּא אֲנָא הוּא.

R. HEZEKIAH SAID IN R. JEREMIAH'S NAME: THUS DID R. SIMEON B. YO-
HAI SAY: THE WORLD POSSESSES NOT LESS THAN THIRTY MEN AS RIGH-
TEOUS AS ABRAHAM. IF THERE ARE THIRTY, MY SON AND I ARE TWO OF
THEM; IF TEN, MY SON AND I ARE TWO OF THEM; IF FIVE, MY SON AND I
ARE TWO OF THEM; IF TWO, THEY ARE MY SON AND I; IF THERE IS BUT
ONE, IT IS I.

One could, of course, express a certain amount of shock at the arrogance that is shown in these last several paragraphs. On the other hand,
let us suggest that these thoughts were not really said by R. Shimon b.
Yohai, but attributed to him by R. Hezekiah in R. Jeremiah's name. This
was meant to be a high tribute to R. Shimon b. Yohai on how outstanding was his spiritual leadership.

—

Seed Thoughts

From my first contact with the biblical text, the story of the rainbow
always made a tremendous impact upon me. God used the very materials of the natural world – the sun, clouds and rain – to be the stage from
which a moral lesson is proclaimed to the world. That moral lesson is
the covenant that God would not destroy the world again, which is a
positive sign and a lasting reminder to human beings to devote themselves to the moral life with the best of their ability. Not only did the
message appear once, it was repeated whenever climatic events were so

arranged to make a rainbow possible. It can, therefore, appear several times a year, several times a month or even several times a day. If the rainbow were purely a natural phenomenon, we could take it or leave it. But the moment that there is an interpretation that its appearance is a covenant between God and man, it becomes a very profound teaching, which has to be taken seriously. Or so I thought, until the advent of this midrash. Here we have a midrash that tells us exactly the opposite. If there is a rainbow in the sky, it is a negative sign that there is something wrong with that generation – they are not sufficiently pious. If they were truly sensitive to the commandments of God, they would not need reminders. They would not have to be told again and again that God has a covenant with the world. They would know it and live it without requiring its repetition.

Perhaps the Midrash is right. Maybe, in an ideal world, we should not require reminders of God's good intentions and of the good news and tidings that He has prepared for the good people of this earth. But we do not live in an ideal world. We are people of flesh and blood. We have our successes and our failures. We have our memories and our forgetfulness. It is, therefore, important for us not only to know that God has a covenant with mankind, but to have it repeated again and again as often as possible for it to become something that we will never forget.

—

Additional Commentary

The generations of Hezekiah and the men of the Great Assembly (A)

The rainbow was not seen in two particular generations (*Sanhedrin* 94b). It says that in the time of Hezekiah, a survey was made from Dan to Be'er Sheva and one did not find anyone who was ignorant of Jewish Law (ibid.). In the generation of the men of the Great Assembly, the entire community was involved in an oath to follow God's Torah and to observe all of His commandments. All these people were, therefore, not in need of the special sign as a reminder, which was the rainbow. (Mirkin)

The generations of Hezekiah and the men of the Great Assembly(B)

The fact that the word דרת – *dorot* is spelled minus the two *vav*s that appear in the usual spelling (דורות), hints at the intention of the text, which is to indicate that the covenant would not apply to those two generations, mentioned above. It should also be added that it would not apply even in the case of a generation that identified itself with even one of the generations that have been described in the Midrash. If there would have been the same merit as even one of these special generations, it would have been enough to stop the Flood.

The Flood occurred because of two things: The first and prime reason of the ultimate destruction of the world was brought on because of the sin of sexual immorality. (See the verse that describes that "the sons of God" saw the daughters of man.) As a result of this, God decided, essentially, "I will no longer waste My time judging these people, and their years will be limited to 120." The second reason to destroy the world was due to ethical wickedness in general, as it is written, "God said to Noah: 'The end of all flesh has come before me because the earth is filled with wickedness.'"

It is because of what happened in the two righteous generations mentioned that the *vavs* were removed from the word *dorot*. When a generation lacks the ethical attributes of the two generations hinted at by the lack of a *vav*, some type of destruction is inevitable. But when it possesses similar ethical attributes, the covenant applies. Since the two values whose desecration produced the Flood were sexual immorality and wickedness, it follows that the Midrash would set aside two generations that practiced complete virtue in these fields, namely, the generation of Hezekiah and that of the men of the Great Assembly.

The people of Hezekiah's generation were very careful to guard themselves against wickedness and were able to do so because they had trained themselves to be satisfied with less, מסתפקים במועט – *mistapkim bemu'at*. Other generations used to feel that one cannot control wickedness in general because humans are creatures of flesh and blood. But the generation of Hezekiah, when necessary, would abandon the cultivation of their vineyards instead of abandoning the study of Torah, even when their loss of profit thereby would be great. Since they were able to do this, it was quite obvious that they would never desire or exploit anything that did not belong to them.

In the generation of the men of the Great Assembly, they obligated themselves and their wives, their sons and their daughters, by oaths and vows to be extremely careful to guard themselves concerning the areas of sexual immorality – more so than in any other generation, as it is written in Nechemiah, chapter ten. It, therefore, says that the generation of Hezekiah and the men of the Great Assembly were extremely strict in the areas of wickedness and sexual immorality, more than any other generation. When the word לדרת – *ledorot* is spelled missing two – *vavs*, it was most certainly pointing to them; they certainly did not need the sign of the covenant, namely, the rainbow. (*Tiferet Tzion*)

PARASHAH THIRTY-FIVE, *Midrash Three*

ג. (יג) 'אֶת קַשְׁתִּי נָתַתִּי', קִישׁוּתִי, דָּבָר שֶׁהוּא מָקֵשׁ לִי, אֶפְשָׁר כֵּן, אֶלָּא, קַשִּׁין דְּפֵירֵי.

3. I HAVE SET MY BOW (KASHTI) IN THE CLOUD (9:13): THAT MEANS, MY
LIKENESS (KISHUTHI), SOMETHING THAT IS COMPARABLE TO ME. IS
THAT REALLY POSSIBLE? IN TRUTH, [THE BOW RESEMBLES GOD] AS THE
STRAW RESEMBLES THE GRAIN.

The question that is raised by the commentators is why the word
קשתי – *kashti, my bow*, is used, rather than simply the word קשת – *keshet,
the* bow, as found in the verse in Ezekiel (*HaMidrash HaMevo'ar*). The
answer seems to be that the word *keshet* has the additional meaning of
an identity. It does not represent God, but it hints at His presence in the
same way that the skin of a fruit sometimes offers a clue as to the shape
of the fruit (see additional commentary.)

וְהָיָה בְּעַנְנִי עָנָן עַל הָאָרֶץ', רַבִּי יוּדָן, בְּשֵׁם רַבִּי יוּדָן בַּר סִימוֹן, לְאֶחָד שֶׁהָיָה בְיָדוֹ קָלוּב קָלוּב רוֹתֵחַ,
בִּקֵּשׁ לִתְּנוֹ עַל בְּנוֹ, וּנְתָנוֹ עַל עַבְדּוֹ.

AND IT SHALL COME TO PASS, WHEN I BRING CLOUDS UPON THE EARTH
(9:14). R. JUDAN SAID IN NAME OF R. JUDAH B. R. SIMON: THIS MAY
BE COMPARED TO A MAN WHO WAS HOLDING IN HIS HAND SOME HOT
FLOUR, AND WAS GOING TO GIVE IT TO HIS SON, BUT GAVE IT TO HIS
SERVANT INSTEAD.

This parable is explained by the *Midrash HaMevo'ar* as follows. The
bow can be used as a military instrument with deadly consequences.
The idea of a rainbow appearing in the clouds indicates that the clouds
represent darkness and therefore the possibility of punishment. One
might think that God uses this rainbow to affect the punishment of
mankind, but instead of the bow facing downward toward the earth,
it faces upward so that it is harmless to man. The father redirects the
punishment originally intended for the son to the servant (the cloud).
It is as if the cloud is the servant of the earth.

וְהָיְתָה הַקֶּשֶׁת בֶּעָנָן וּרְאִיתִיהָ לִזְכֹּר בְּרִית עוֹלָם', 'בֵּין אֱ־לֹהִים' זוֹ מִדַּת הַדִּין שֶׁלְּמַעְלָה, 'וּבֵין
כָּל נֶפֶשׁ חַיָּה, וְגוֹ'', רַבִּי יִצְחָק וְרַבִּי יוֹחָנָן וְרַבִּי יוּדָן, גִּיּוֹרֵי, הָלְכוּ לִשְׁמֹעַ תּוֹרָה מֵרַבִּי שִׁמְעוֹן בֶּן
יוֹחַאי, אִית דְּאָמְרֵי, פָּרְשַׁת נְדָרִים, וְאִית דְּאָמְרֵי, פָּרְשַׁת נְסָכִים, וְנָטְלוּ הֵימֶנּוּ רְשׁוּת, וְהִמְתִּינוּ
שָׁם עוֹד יוֹם אֶחָד, אָמְרוּ, צְרִיכִים אָנוּ לִטֹּל מִמֶּנּוּ רְשׁוּת פַּעַם שְׁנִית, חַד מִנְּהוֹן דְּרַשׁ וַאֲמַר לְהוֹן,
כְּבָר כְּתִיב, (יהושע, כב, ו) 'וַיְבָרְכֵם יְהוֹשֻׁעַ וַיְשַׁלְּחֵם וַיֵּלְכוּ לְאָהֳלֵיהֶם' מַה תַּלְמוּד לוֹמַר, (שם שם,
ז) 'גַּם כִּי שִׁלְּחָם יְהוֹשֻׁעַ אֶל אָהֳלֵיהֶם וַיְבָרֲכֵם', אֶלָּא, בְּשָׁעָה שֶׁהָיוּ יִשְׂרָאֵל מְכַבְּשִׁים וּמְחַלְּקִים
אֶת הָאָרֶץ, הָיָה שֵׁבֶט רְאוּבֵן וְגָד עִמָּהֶם, וְעָשׂוּ אַרְבַּע עֶשְׂרֵה שָׁנָה, נָטְלוּ רְשׁוּת מִן יְהוֹשֻׁעַ לָלֶכֶת
לְאָהֳלֵיהֶם, וְשָׁהוּ שָׁם עוֹד יָמִים אֲחֵרִים, וְחָזְרוּ וְנָטְלוּ מִמֶּנּוּ רְשׁוּת עוֹד פַּעַם שְׁנִיָּה, לְכָךְ נֶאֱמַר,
'וְגַם כִּי שִׁלְּחָם, וְגוֹ'', אָמַר רַבִּי יוּדָן, שֵׁבֶט רְאוּבֵן וְגָד, בְּנֵי פָמַלְיָא שֶׁל יְהוֹשֻׁעַ, וְלִוָּה אוֹתָן עַד
הַיַּרְדֵּן, וְכֵיוָן שֶׁרָאוּ שֶׁנִּתְמַעֲטָה פָמַלְיָא שֶׁלּוֹ, חָזְרוּ וְלִוּוּ אוֹתוֹ עַד בֵּיתוֹ, הַבְּרָכָה הָאַחֲרוֹנָה הָיְתָה
גְדוֹלָה מִן הָרִאשׁוֹנָה, הֲדָא הוּא דִכְתִיב, (שם שם, ח) 'וַיֹּאמֶר לָהֶם לֵאמֹר, בִּנְכָסִים רַבִּים שׁוּבוּ אֶל
אָהֳלֵיכֶם וּבְמִקְנֶה רַב מְאֹד בְּכֶסֶף וּבְזָהָב וּבִנְחֹשֶׁת וּבְבַרְזֶל וּבִשְׂלָמוֹת הַרְבֵּה, חִלְּקוּ שְׁלַל אֹיְבֵיכֶם
עִם אֲחֵיכֶם'. וְאוֹחֲרָנָא דְּרַשׁ, כְּבָר כְּתִיב, (מ"א ח, סו) 'בַּיּוֹם הַשְּׁמִינִי שִׁלַּח אֶת הָעָם וַיְבָרֲכוּ אֶת
הַמֶּלֶךְ', מַה תַּלְמוּד לוֹמַר, (דה"ב ז, י) 'וּבְיוֹם עֶשְׂרִים וּשְׁלֹשָׁה לַחֹדֶשׁ הַשְּׁבִיעִי שִׁלַּח אֶת הָעָם
וַיְבָרֲכוּ אֶת הַמֶּלֶךְ', אֶלָּא, נָטְלוּ מִמֶּנּוּ רְשׁוּת, וְהִמְתִּינוּ שָׁם יָמִים אֲחֵרִים, וְחָזְרוּ וְנָטְלוּ מִמֶּנּוּ
רְשׁוּת פַּעַם שְׁנִיָּה, לְכָךְ נֶאֱמַר, 'בְּיוֹם עֶשְׂרִים וּשְׁלֹשָׁה לַחֹדֶשׁ הַזֶּה שִׁלַּח אֶת הָעָם'.

AND THE BOW SHALL BE IN THE CLOUD, [THAT IMAGE WAS MEANT AS A
REMINDER OF THE COVENANT FOR THE WORLD BETWEEN GOD (ELOKIM)
[WHICH REFERS TO THE ATTRIBUTE OF JUSTICE OF THE UPPER WORLD]
AND IN BETWEEN ALL LIVING THINGS (9:16). IT ONCE HAPPENED THAT
R. ISAAC, R. JONATHAN AND R. JUDAN B. GIYORI WENT TO HEAR AN EX-
POSITION OF THE TORAH – SOME SAY OF THE CHAPTER ON VOWS AND
SOME SAY OF THE CHAPTER ON LIBATIONS-FROM R. SIMEON B. YOHAI.
THEN THEY TOOK THEIR ADIEUS FROM HIM, BUT STAYED ON ANOTHER
DAY. SAID THEY: WE MUST BID HIM FAREWELL A SECOND TIME. ONE OF
THEM THEN EXPOUNDED [A SCRIPTURAL PASSAGE], SAYING TO THEM:
SINCE IT IS ALREADY WRITTEN, SO JOSHUA BLESSED THEM, AND SENT
THEM AWAY; AND THEY WENT UNTO THEIR TENTS (JOSH. 22:6), WHY IS
IT FURTHER STATED, MOREOVER WHEN JOSHUA SENT THEM AWAY UNTO
THEIR TENTS, HE BLESSED THEM (IBID., 7)? THE REASON IS BECAUSE
WHEN THE ISRAELITES WERE ENGAGED IN CONQUERING AND DIVID-
ING THE LAND, THE TRIBES OF REUBEN AND GAD WERE WITH THEM
AND LIKEWISE SPENT FOURTEEN YEARS THERE IN CONQUERING AND
DIVIDING THE COUNTRY. AFTER THE FOURTEEN YEARS THEY RECEIVED
PERMISSION FROM JOSHUA TO RETURN HOME, BUT THEY STAYED THERE
ANOTHER FEW DAYS, AND THEN ASKED PERMISSION A SECOND TIME.
THEREFORE IT SAYS, 'MOREOVER, WHEN JOSHUA SENT THEM AWAY,' ETC.
R. JUDAN SAID: THE TRIBES OF REUBEN AND GAD FORMED JOSHUA'S
PERSONAL RETINUE, AND HE ACCOMPANIED THEM TO THE JORDAN [ON
THEIR RETURN HOME]. WHEN THEY SAW THAT HIS RETINUE WAS THUS
DIMINISHED, THEY TURNED BACK AND ESCORTED HIM TO HIS HOME.

HIS LAST BLESSING WAS GREATER THAN THE FIRST, AS IT IS WRITTEN, AND HE SPOKE UNTO THEM, SAYING: RETURN WITH MUCH WEALTH TO YOUR TENTS, ETC. (IBID., 8).

ANOTHER EXPOUNDED THUS: SINCE IT IS WRITTEN, ON THE EIGHTH DAY HE SENT THE PEOPLE AWAY, AND THEY BLESSED THE KING (I KINGS 8:66), WHY IS IT STATED, AND ON THE THREE AND TWENTIETH DAY OF THE SEVENTH MONTH HE SENT THE PEOPLE AWAY, AND THEY BLESSED THE KING (I CHRON. 7:10)? THE REASON, HOWEVER, IS THAT THEY OB-TAINED PERMISSION [TO GO ON THE TWENTY-SECOND DAY], WAITED A COUPLE OF DAYS, AND THEN RECEIVED PERMISSION A SECOND TIME; THEREFORE IT IS SAID, AND ON THE THREE AND TWENTIETH DAY OF THE SEVENTH MONTH, ETC.

The rainbow is here interpreted as a covenant between God (*Elokim*) and all living things. However, the expression "all living things" (*kol nefesh chayah*) differs from the manner in which this was first described in the Torah text. At the same time, the Tiferet Zion commentary is bothered by the fact that the word *adam*, "man," is not used. He has interpreted the verse in the following manner: When this verse uses the expression *Elokim* for God, it refers to the attribute of Justice in the upper world without any participation or influence of the attribute of Mercy. When the verse says that the covenant is between the attribute of Justice and all living things, the reference is to the attribute of Justice as it is expressed in the *lower* world, meaning our world, in which some type of compassion is necessary, which is the method by which God operates when He deals with people of flesh and blood.

The discussions between the three sages mentioned – R. Isaac, R. Jonathan and R. Judan b. Giyori – have to do with how to take leave of a leader or a teacher, and examples are brought from Joshua and the tribes as well as from King Solomon at the dedication of the Temple. The conclusion seems to be that one should take leave of one's teacher twice. In both examples, a blessing was received upon the students' departure, and the second was always greater than the first.

אָמַר רַבִּי לֵוִי, כְּתִיב (שם שם, ט) 'כִּי חֲנֻכַּת הַמִּזְבֵּחַ עָשׂוּ שִׁבְעַת יָמִים, וְהֶחָג שִׁבְעַת יָמִים', וְאֵין לְךָ ז' לִפְנֵי הֶחָג שֶׁאֵין בָּהֶן שַׁבָּת וְיוֹם הַכִּפּוּרִים, וְאוֹתָן שִׁבְעַת יָמִים, הָיוּ יִשְׂרָאֵל אוֹכְלִים וְשׁוֹתִים וּשְׂמֵחִים וּמַדְלִיקִין נֵרוֹת, וּבַסּוֹף חָזְרוּ וְנִצְטַעֲרוּ עַל הַדָּבָר, אָמְרוּ, תֹּאמַר שֶׁיֵּשׁ בְּיָדֵינוּ עָוֹן שֶׁחִלַּלְנוּ שַׁבָּת, וְלֹא הִתְעַנִּינוּ בְּיוֹם הַכִּפּוּרִים, וּכְדֵי לְפַיְּסָן, שֶׁרָצָה הַקָּדוֹשׁ בָּרוּךְ הוּא מַעֲשֵׂיהֶם, יָצְתָה בַּת קוֹל וְאָמְרָה לָהֶן, כֻּלְּכֶם מִבְּנֵי הָעוֹלָם הַבָּא, וְהַבְּרָכָה אַחֲרוֹנָה הָיְתָה גְּדוֹלָה מִן הָרִאשׁוֹנָה, שֶׁנֶּאֱמַר (מ״א שם, שם) 'וַיֵּלְכוּ לְאָהֳלֵיהֶם שְׂמֵחִים וְטוֹבֵי לֵב', אָמַר רַבִּי יִצְחָק,

'שְׂמֵחִים', שֶׁמָּצְאוּ נְשׁוֹתֵיהֶם טְהוֹרוֹת, 'וְטוֹבֵי לֵב' שֶׁנִּתְעַבְּרוּ זְכָרִים, אָמַר רַבִּי לֵוִי, יָצְאָה בַת
קוֹל וְאָמְרָה לָהֶם, כֻּלְּכֶם מִבְּנֵי הָעוֹלָם הַבָּא

R. LEVI SAID: IT IS WRITTEN, FOR THEY KEPT THE DEDICATION OF THE
ALTAR SEVEN DAYS AND THE FEAST [SC. TABERNACLES] SEVEN DAYS
(IBID., 9). NOW THE SEVEN DAYS BEFORE THE FESTIVAL MUST INCLUDE
THE SABBATH AND THE DAY OF ATONEMENT, YET DURING [ALL] THESE
SEVEN DAYS THE ISRAELITES ATE, DRANK, REJOICED AND LIT LAMPS.
SUBSEQUENTLY, HOWEVER, THEY WERE SMITTEN WITH REMORSE, SAY-
ING, 'PERHAPS WE HAVE DONE WRONG BY DESECRATING THE SABBATH
AND EATING ON THE DAY OF ATONEMENT?' IN ORDER TO TRANQUILLIZE
THEM AND ASSURE THEM THAT THE HOLY ONE, BLESSED BE HE, HAD AP-
PROVED THEIR ACTIONS, THERE CAME FORTH A HEAVENLY VOICE AND
DECLARED TO THEM, 'YE ARE ALL WORTHY OF THE HEREAFTER.' THE
LAST BLESSING WAS GREATER THAN THE FIRST; HENCE IT SAYS, AND
THEY WENT UNTO THEIR TENTS JOYFUL AND GLAD OF HEART (I KINGS,
LOC. CIT.). R. ISAAC OBSERVED: 'JOYFUL,' BECAUSE THEY FOUND THEIR
WIVES CLEAN, AND 'GLAD OF HEART' BECAUSE THEY CONCEIVED MALE
CHILDREN. R. LEVI SAID: THERE WENT FORTH A HEAVENLY VOICE AND
PROCLAIMED, 'YE ARE ALL WORTHY OF THE HEREAFTER.'

The seven days of celebration in connection with the Temple in Jerusalem included one Sabbath and the day of Yom Kippur. Neither of
these days affected the celebration. When it was over, the participants
felt a sense of great guilt at having desecrated the Sabbath and Yom
Kippur. However, a heavenly voice relieved their tension when it proclaimed that they are all worthy of the World to Come.

וְאוֹחֲרָנָא דְּרַשׁ, כְּבָר כְּתִיב, (מ"ב ד, ה) 'וַתֵּלֶךְ מֵאִתּוֹ', 'וַתֵּלֶךְ מֵאִתּוֹ', מַה תַּלְמוּד לוֹמַר, (שם שם, ז) 'וַתָּבֹא וַתַּגֵּד
לְאִישׁ הָאֱ-לֹהִים', אֶלָּא, (שם שם, ו) 'וַיַּעֲמֹד הַשָּׁמֶן', שֶׁהוּקַר הַשֶּׁמֶן, וּבָאת לִשְׁאֹל, אִם תִּמְכֹּר אִם
לֹא תִמְכֹּר, הַבְּרָכָה הָאַחֲרוֹנָה הָיְתָה גְדוֹלָה מִן הָרִאשׁוֹנָה, (שם שם, ז) 'וְאַתְּ וּבָנַיִךְ תִּחְיִי בַּנּוֹתָר',
עַד שֶׁיִּחְיוּ הַמֵּתִים.

THE THIRD EXPOUNDED: IT IS ALREADY WRITTEN, SO SHE WENT FROM
HIM (II KINGS 4:5); WHY THEN IS IT STATED FURTHER, THEN SHE CAME
AND TOLD THE MAN OF GOD (IBID., 7)? THE REASON, HOWEVER, IS
BECAUSE IT SAYS AND THE OIL STAYED (IBID., 6), WHICH MEANS THAT
THE MARKET PRICE ADVANCED, AND SHE CAME TO ASK HIM WHETHER
TO SELL NOW OR NOT. HIS SECOND BLESSING WAS GREATER THAN THE
FIRST, VIZ. AND LIVE THOU AND THY SONS OF THE REST (IBID., 7):
WHICH MEANS, UNTIL THE RESURRECTION OF THE DEAD.

The story of Elisha and the woman who needed help is another example of the fact that seeking permission a second time is beneficial.
In the case of the woman, her second visit was not to say goodbye, but
to seek his advice on how to act, since the price of oil had risen. He
told her to continue the sale, as the income so provided would help her
throughout her lifetime.

וְכֵיוָן שֶׁרָאָה אוֹתָן שֶׁהֵן בְּנֵי אָדָם שֶׁל יִשּׁוּב, שָׁלַח עִמָּהֶם זוּג אֶחָד שֶׁל תַּלְמִידֵי חֲכָמִים, לֵידַע
מָה הֵם דּוֹרְשִׁין בַּדֶּרֶךְ, וְחַד מִנְּהוֹן דְּרַשׁ, כְּבָר כְּתִיב, (שמות יד, יט) 'וַיִּסַּע מַלְאַךְ הָאֱ־לֹהִים הַהֹלֵךְ
לִפְנֵי מַחֲנֵה יִשְׂרָאֵל וַיֵּלֶךְ מֵאַחֲרֵיהֶם', מַה תַּלְמוּד לוֹמַר, (שם שם, שם) 'וַיִּסַּע עַמּוּד הֶעָנָן מִפְּנֵיהֶם
וַיַּעֲמֹד מֵאַחֲרֵיהֶם', אֶלָּא, אוֹתוֹ מִדַּת הַדִּין שֶׁהָיְתָה מְתוּחָה כְּנֶגֶד יִשְׂרָאֵל, הֲפָכָהּ הַקָּדוֹשׁ בָּרוּךְ
הוּא וּמְתָחָהּ כְּנֶגֶד הַמִּצְרִים

WHEN HE [R. SIMEON B. YOHAI] SAW THAT THEY WERE MEN OF SUCH
CULTURE, HE SENT A COUPLE OF SCHOLARS WITH THEM, TO HEAR WHAT
THEY WOULD TEACH ON THE ROAD. ONE OF THEM EXPOUNDED THUS: IT
WAS ALREADY WRITTEN, AND THE ANGEL OF GOD, WHO WENT BEFORE
THE CAMP OF ISRAEL, REMOVED AND WENT BEHIND THEM (EX. 14:19);
WHY THEN IS IT FURTHER STATED, AND THE PILLAR OF CLOUD REMOVED
FROM BEFORE THEM, AND STOOD BEHIND THEM (IBID.)? IT MEANS THAT
THAT VERY ATTRIBUTE OF JUDGMENT, WHICH THREATENINGLY CON-
FRONTED ISRAEL, WAS TURNED ROUND BY THE HOLY ONE, BLESSED BE
HE, AND DIRECTED AGAINST THE EGYPTIANS.

Although we have the expression מַלְאַךְ אֱלֹקִים – *malakh Elokim*, an angel
of God, it should be understood that the word "angel" in this text is not
an angel in a literal sense, but rather, in a metaphorical sense. After the
narrative of the golden calf, there is a verse that says, "I will send before
you an angel." But the angel turned out to be the pillar of cloud. The
verse refers to the pillar of cloud as being an angel of God, meaning a
messenger of God. Therefore, here, when we see the expressions "angel
of God" and "pillar of cloud," they can be understood interchangeably,
and both together represent the quality of Justice, for which the Divine
Name *Elokim* always stands. The pillar of cloud was always stretched
over Israel for as long as they were in Egypt, a reminder of the prophecy
that the Egyptians would persecute them and force the Hebrews to
serve them. Here, however, in the verse with which we are now dealing,
the Holy One, Blessed be He, changed all of that and directed the cloud
against Egypt.

וְאָחֲרָנָא דָּרַשׁ, כְּתִיב, 'וְהָיְתָה הַקֶּשֶׁת בֶּעָנָן וּרְאִיתִיהָ לִזְכֹּר בְּרִית עוֹלָם בֵּין אֱלֹהִים וּבֵין כָּל
נֶפֶשׁ חַיָּה, וְגוֹ'', 'בֵּין אֱלֹהִים' זוֹ מִדַּת הַדִּין שֶׁלְּמַעְלָה, 'וּבֵין כָּל נֶפֶשׁ חַיָּה' זוֹ מִדַּת הַדִּין שֶׁל
מַטָּה, מִדַּת הַדִּין שֶׁל מַעֲלָה, קָשָׁה, וּמִדַּת הַדִּין שֶׁל מַטָּה, רָפָה. וְחַד מִנְּהוֹן דָּרַשׁ, כָּתוּב אֶחָד
אוֹמֵר, (משלי ח, יא) 'וְכָל חֲפָצִים לֹא יִשְׁווּ בָהּ', וְכָתוּב אֶחָד אוֹמֵר, (שם ג, טו) 'וְכָל חֲפָצֶיךָ לֹא יִשְׁווּ
בָהּ', 'חֲפָצִים' אֵלּוּ מִצְוֹת וּמַעֲשִׂים טוֹבִים, 'חֲפָצֶיךָ' אֵלּוּ אֲבָנִים טוֹבוֹת וּמַרְגָּלִיּוֹת, רַבִּי אֲחָא,
בְּשֵׁם רַבִּי תַּנְחוּם בַּר רַבִּי חִיָּא חֲפָצַי, וַחֲפָצֶיךָ, לֹא יִשְׁווּ בָהּ, (ירמיה ט, כג) 'כִּי אִם בְּזֹאת יִתְהַלֵּל
הַמִּתְהַלֵּל הַשְׂכֵּל וְיָדֹעַ אוֹתִי, כִּי אֲנִי ה' עוֹשֶׂה חֶסֶד מִשְׁפָּט, וְגוֹ'

A SECOND EXPOUNDED: AND THE BOW SHALL BE IN THE CLOUD; AND I WILL LOOK UPON IT, THAT I MAY REMEMBER THE EVER LASTING COVENANT BETWEEN ELOKIM (GOD): THIS REFERS TO THE ATTRIBUTE OF HEAVENLY JUDGMENT ABOVE; AND EVERY LIVING CREATURE OF ALL FLESH THAT IS UPON THE EARTH: THIS REFERS TO JUDGMENT BELOW: THE JUDGMENT ABOVE IS RIGID WHILE THE JUDGMENT BELOW IS PLIABLE. A THIRD EXPOUNDED: ONE VERSE SAYS, [FOR WISDOM IS BETTER THAN RUBIES,] AND ALL THINGS DESIRABLE ARE NOT TO BE COMPARED UNTO HER (PROV. 8:11); WHEREAS ANOTHER VERSE SAYS, AND ALL THY DESIRABLE THINGS ARE NOT TO BE COMPARED UNTO HER (IBID., 3:15)? 'THINGS DESIRABLE' CONNOTES RELIGIOUS ACTS AND GOOD DEEDS; 'THY DESIRABLE THINGS,' GEMS AND PRECIOUS STONES. R. AHA EXPLAINED IT IN THE NAME OF R. TANHUMA B. R. HIYYA: MY DESIRABLE THINGS AND THY DESIRABLE THINGS ARE NOT TO BE COMPARED UNTO HER, FOR, BUT LET HIM THAT GLORIETH GLORY IN THIS, THAT HE UNDERSTANDETH, AND KNOWETH ME (JER. 9:23).

The interpretation of the bow in the cloud is well expressed. Based on the two verses from Proverbs, one would have to conclude that one cannot put aside the study of Torah in order to look after one's own particular needs or to acquire wealth. These verses, from Proverbs 3 and 8, do not contradict each other. On the one hand, the verse talks about commandments that others can fulfill for you, and these commandments can be put aside in order for you to study Torah. On the other hand, the other verse is referring to commandments that cannot be fulfilled by others for you; therefore, these have to be observed, even at the expense of Torah learning. In other words, if it is for your own private materialistic purposes, you cannot set aside the study of Torah. But if it is for the needs of Heaven, meaning for commandments that others cannot perform for you, in such cases only can the study of Torah be put aside. (*HaMidrash HaMevo'ar*)

אַרְטְבָן, שָׁלַח לְרַבֵּינוּ, מַרְגָּלִית אַטִימִיטוֹן, אָמַר לֵהּ שְׁלַח לִי מִילֵּי טָבָא דְּכַוָּתַהּ, שָׁלַח לֵהּ
חֲדָא מְזוּזָה, שָׁלַח וַאֲמַר לֵהּ אֲנָא שְׁלַחִית לָךְ מִלָּה דְּלֵית לֵהּ טִימִי, וְאַתְּ שְׁלַחַת לִי מִילֵּי דְּטָבָא

חַד פּוֹלָר, אָמַר לֵהּ חֲפָצַי וַחֲפָצֶיךָ לֹא יִשְׁווּ בָהּ, וְלֹא עוֹד, אֶלָּא, שְׁלַחַתְּ מִלָּא דַאֲנָא צָרִיךְ מִנְטַר
לֵהּ, וַאֲנָא שְׁלָחִית לָךְ מִלָּא דְאַתְּ דָּמֵךְ וְהִיא מִנְטְרָא לָךְ, שֶׁנֶּאֱמַר (משלי ו, כב) 'בְּהִתְהַלֶּכְךָ תַּנְחֶה
אֹתָךְ' בָּעוֹלָם הַזֶּה, (שם שם, שם) 'בְּשָׁכְבְּךָ תִּשְׁמֹר עָלֶיךָ' בִּשְׁעַת הַמִּיתָה, (שם שם, שם) 'וַהֲקִיצוֹתָ
הִיא תְשִׂיחֶךָ' לֶעָתִיד לָבוֹא.

[NOT INCLUDED IN THE SONCINO BUT AS A NOTE: ARTEBAN (THE LAST PARTHIAN KING) SENT OUR TEACHER (R. JUDAH HA-NASI) A PRICELESS GEM, WITH THE REQUEST, 'LET ME HAVE IN RETURN AN ARTICLE AS VALUABLE AS THIS.' SO HE SENT HIM A MEZUZAH. HE SENT BACK WORD: 'I GAVE YOU A PRICELESS OBJECT, WHEREAS YOU RETURNED ME SOMETHING WORTH BUT A FOLAR' (A SMALL DEBASED COIN). 'MY DESIRABLE THINGS AND THY DESIRABLE THINGS ARE NOT TO BE COMPARED UNTO HER,' HE RETORTED (THE MEZUZAH SYMBOLIZING THE KNOWLEDGE OF GOD). 'MOREOVER, YOU SENT ME SOMETHING WHICH I MUST GUARD, WHEREAS I SENT YOU SOMETHING WHICH GUARDS YOU WHILE YOU SLEEP AT EASE, AS IT SAYS, WHEN THOU WALKEST, IT SHALL LEAD THEE (PROV. 6:22) — IN THIS WORLD; WHEN THOU LIEST DOWN, IT SHALL WATCH OVER THEE (IBID.) — IN THE HOUR OF DEATH; AND WHEN THOU WAKEST, IT SHALL TALK WITH THEE (IBID.) — IN THE HEREAFTER.']

The two verses in Proverbs pointed to different valuable assets of mankind. One is spiritual, having to do with commandments and good deeds, and the other is material, as in, for example, precious stones. As to which is more valuable, the Midrash includes the verse from Jeremiah 9:23, "'But let him that glorieth glory in this, that he understandeth, and knoweth Me . . . for these do I desire,' saith the Lord." This is beautifully illustrated in the story of Arteban, the Parthian king, who was friendly with R. Yehudah the Prince, who, in addition to his spiritual prowess, was a man of wealth. Arteban sent R. Yehudah a precious gem and asked him in return something of equal value that he could cherish. R. Yehudah sent him a mezuzah. He was highly insulted in light of the fact that a mezuzah is relatively inexpensive as compared to a priceless gem. R. Yehudah explained that he would have to go to much expense and effort to protect the precious jewel sent to him, whereas Arteban could sleep peacefully now possessing a mezuzah, which has the power to guard man. This is the spirit of the verse in Jeremiah, that the Torah not only gives us fulfillment in this world, but watches over us and assures our entry into the World to Come (*Braita deRabbi Meir*, Pirkei Avot 6:9).

Seed Thoughts

The efforts made by the sages to indicate, on the one hand, that the word *keshet*, bow, has some kind of a relationship to God, seems to be undermined at the same time by suggesting that the *keshet* is only something peripheral and external. However, I should like to add my own interpretation of this midrash and the meaning of its struggle to define what the bow implies or does not imply. On the one hand, the occurrence of the rainbow is a function of the natural world. The Malbim, in his commentary of the Torah, goes into great elaboration and description of the rainbow as a natural phenomenon. However, when the Book of Genesis associates the rainbow with the concept of a covenant between God and mankind, it is no longer possible for a religious person to confine the story of the rainbow to merely a natural phenomenon. My understanding of this phenomenon is that, through it, God is proclaiming His existence in the world. The story of the rainbow tells us that God exists, but His existence is not a casual item of belief. It is a demanding existence. It demands the moral transformation of the world as the only guarantee against its ultimate destruction. This interpretation gives tremendous power to the rainbow's story. Every time the beautiful rainbow appears, always within a cloud, which represents, metaphorically, the difficulties of the world, and also by the light of the sun, which represents the happier possibilities of the world, God is saying to the entire world, "I exist, I am here, I must be taken seriously."

—

Addtional Commentary

My bow (A)

The word קשתי – *kashti*, my bow, is used instead of the simple expression *keshet*, meaning *the* bow. This seems to have the meaning of a resemblance, as though the bow resembles God in some fashion, as the verse says, כמראה הקשת – *kemareh hakeshet*, "like the appearance of the bow" (Ezekiel 1:28), which resembles the glory of God. At this point a serious question has to be asked: Can we say that there is something or anything that resembles the appearance of God? Did we not learn (Deuteronomy 4:15), "Take therefore good heed to yourselves; for you saw no manner of form on the day when the Lord spoke to you in Horeb out of the midst of the fire"? The answer has to be that whether we use the term "resemblance" or the concept of an external skin to a fruit, we are speaking of some kind of metaphoric resemblance and has no relationship whatsoever to the essence of the Divine. It is for this reason that the sages prohibited looking directly at the rainbow, lest it be understood as a form of a false god. (*HaMidrash HaMevo'ar*)

My bow (B)

The term *kashti* is used even though the noun *keshet* has not yet appeared. It gives the impression that God possesses a bow that somehow has a relationship to Him. That is why the commentators go out of their way to suggest that it indicates a resemblance, but one only of something distant, such as the skin or crust of a fruit, which has no intrinsic relationship to the fruit itself. For this reason, there are many restrictions in *halakha* preventing one from drawing a picture of the rainbow, lest it be used as an *avodah zarah*, worship of a strange god.

The two tractates of R. Shimon b. Yohai

R. Isaac, R. Jonathan and R. Judan b. Giyori went to study with R. Shimon Bar Yochai. One view is that they wanted to study the tractate of *Nedarim* (Vows) with R. Shimon b. Yochai. A second view is that they wanted to study the tractate of *Nesakhim* (Libations). There are at least two precious assets that the Torah possesses in relation to evil of the heart. One is that it is a sort of cure for the evil inclination, as it is written by the sages, "The Holy One, Blessed be He said, 'I created the evil inclination but I also created the Torah as a cure for it.'" By means of the Torah, the *yetzer harah* loses its power to dominate man. The second attribute of the Torah is, if a person stumbled and was involved in sin, the Torah possesses the amazing power to cleanse the stains and impurities from the human being. The method prescribed is that if a person is accustomed to learn one page a day, let him learn two, etc. Even though the whole Torah has been described as a cure for the evil inclination, nevertheless, the tractate of *Nedarim* possesses a spiritual power in this respect that is greater than other portions of the Torah. It helps a person motivate himself to be separate from negative values in a community. As the sages say, the study of Torah helps a person separate himself from all evil urges. (*Brakhot* 5a)

The person who studies the section on *korbanot*, sacrifices, is looked upon as though he, himself, offered those sacrifices (Hosea 14:3, Bamidbar Rabbah 18:17). The best section to learn that can help a person purify himself from evil deeds is the portion known as *Nesakhim*, which means "libations." It is interesting to note that after the sin of the spies – whose sin was so great that God punished them by not allowing them entry into the Land of Israel – they were ordered to offer libations, which have the power to influence all areas of spiritual life in this world and the next. (*Tiferet Tzion*)

א. (ט, יח) 'וַיִּהְיוּ בְנֵי נֹחַ הַיֹּצְאִים מִן הַתֵּבָה', (איוב לד, כט) 'וְהוּא יַשְׁקִט וּמִי יַרְשִׁעַ, וְיַסְתֵּר פָּנִים וּמִי
יְשׁוּרֶנּוּ, וְעַל גּוֹי וְעַל אָדָם יָחַד', דָּרַשׁ רַבִּי מֵאִיר, 'וְהוּא יַשְׁקִט' מֵעוֹלָמוֹ, 'יַסְתֵּר פָּנִים' לְעוֹלָמוֹ,
כַּדַּיָּן שֶׁמּוֹתְחִין כִּלָּה עַל פָּנָיו, וְאֵינוֹ יוֹדֵעַ מַה נַּעֲשֶׂה מִבַּחוּץ, כָּךְ אָמְרוּ דוֹר הַמַּבּוּל, (שם כב, יד)
'עָבִים סֵתֶר לוֹ, וְלֹא יִרְאֶה'

1. AND THE SONS OF NOAH, THAT WENT FORTH FROM THE ARK, WERE
SHEM, AND HAM, AND JAPHETH (9:18) IT IS WRITTEN, WHEN HE GIVETH
QUIETNESS, WHO THEN CAN CONDEMN, ETC. (JOB 34:29)? R. MEIR INTER-
PRETED IT: HE QUIETETH HIMSELF FROM HIS WORLD, AND HE HIDETH
HIS FACE (IBID.) FROM HIS WORLD, LIKE A JUDGE BEFORE WHOM A
CURTAIN IS SPREAD, SO THAT HE DOES NOT KNOW WHAT IS HAPPENING
WITHOUT. THIS IS WHAT THE GENERATION OF THE FLOOD SAID (IBID.,
22:14): "CLOUDS SURROUND HIM AND HE DOES NOT SEE."

W hat is bothering the Midrash at this point is to understand why this
text, which describes the fact that Noah left the ark with his three sons, appears in the Torah. After all, we had all of this information before. All of the
discussions that follow will eventually lead to the answer to this problem.

It is very difficult to interpret this text. It begins with, "When He
giveth quietness, who then can condemn?" The Holy One, Blessed be
He, supervises His world, and there is no one competent to criticize.
The verse from Job is then brought, which says, "And He hideth His
face" – if so, then how can He know what is happening? In other words,
God is hiding His face from the world and is not supervising it? Does
this means that He remains concealed in connection with His world and
does not at all care what happens to it? Apparently, there were places
where a judge would have his face covered, either to protect him from
charges of favoritism or to protect him from those condemned by his
decisions. Here, the clouds function as the covering for God's vision, so
to speak. This is the interpretation of R. Meir. (Aryeh Mirkin)

אָמְרוּ לוֹ, דַּיָּךְ מֵאִיר, אָמַר לָהוֹן, וּמָה הוּא דִכְתִיב, 'וְהוּא יַשְׁקִט וּמִי יַרְשִׁעַ וְגוֹ'', אָמַר, נָתַן
שַׁלְוָה לְדוֹר הַמַּבּוּל וּמִי בָא וְחִיְּבָן, וּמָה שַׁלְוָה נָתַן לָהֶם, (שם כא, ח) 'זַרְעָם נָכוֹן לִפְנֵיהֶם עִמָּם,

וְצֶאֱצָאֵיהֶם לְעֵינֵיהֶם', (שם שם, יא) 'יְשַׁלְּחוּ כַצֹּאן עֲוִילֵיהֶם, וְגוֹ'', רַבִּי לֵוִי וְרַבָּנָן, רַבִּי לֵוִי אָמַר,
לִשְׁלֹשָׁה יָמִים הָיְתָה אִשְׁתּוֹ מְעֻבֶּרֶת, שֶׁנֶּאֱמַר כָּאן 'נָכוֹן', וְנֶאֱמַר לְהַלָּן, (שמות יט, טו) 'הֱיוּ נְכֹנִים',
מַה נָכוֹן, שֶׁנֶּאֱמַר לְהַלָּן 'לִשְׁלֹשֶׁת יָמִים' אַף נָכוֹן שֶׁנֶּאֱמַר כָּאן לִשְׁלֹשֶׁת יָמִים, וְרַבָּנָן אָמְרִין, לְיוֹם
אֶחָד הָיְתָה אִשָּׁה מְעֻבֶּרֶת וְיוֹלֶדֶת, נֶאֱמַר כָּאן 'נָכוֹן', וְנֶאֱמַר לְהַלָּן 'נָכוֹן', (שם לד, ב) 'וֶהְיֵה נָכוֹן
לַבֹּקֶר', מַה נָכוֹן שֶׁנֶּאֱמַר לְהַלָּן יוֹם אֶחָד אַף כָּאן יוֹם אֶחָד. 'וְצֶאֱצָאֵיהֶם לְעֵינֵיהֶם' שֶׁהָיוּ רוֹאִים
בְּנֵיהֶם וּבְנֵי בְנֵיהֶם. 'יְשַׁלְּחוּ כַצֹּאן עֲוִילֵיהֶם' אָמַר רַבִּי לֵוִי, בַּעֲרָבְיָא צָוְחִין לְיָנוֹקָא, עֲוִילָה, (איוב
שם, שם) 'וְיַלְדֵיהֶן יְרַקֵּדוּן' כְּאִלֵּין שֵׁדַיָּא, הֵיךְ מַה דְאַתְּ אָמַר, (ישעיה יג, כא) 'וּשְׂעִירִים יְרַקְּדוּ שָׁם'.
כְּשֶׁהָיְתָה אַחַת מֵהֶם יוֹלֶדֶת בַּיּוֹם, הָיְתָה אוֹמֶרֶת לִבְנָהּ, צֵא וְהָבֵא לִי צֹר לַחְתֹּךְ טַבּוּרָא, בַּלַּיְלָה
הָיְתָה אוֹמֶרֶת לִבְנָהּ, צֵא הַדְלֵק לִי נֵר, לַחְתֹּךְ טַבּוּרָא דִילָךְ. עוֹבָדָא הֲוָה בַּחֲדָא אִתְּתָא דִּילְדַת
בַּלַּיְלָה, אָמְרָה לִבְרָא זִיל אַדְלֵק בּוֹצִינָא דְּנִקְטַע שׁוּרָךְ, נְפַק וּפְגַע בֵּהּ שֵׁדָא שִׁימָדוֹן, אָמַר לֵהּ זִיל
גְּלוֹג לְאִמָּךְ דְּקָרָא תַרְנְגוֹלָא, וְאִלְמָלֵא דְקָרָא תַרְנְגוֹלָא הֲוֵינָא מָחֵיתָךְ וְקָטֵלְתָּךְ, אָמַר לֵהּ זִיל
אַתְּ גְּלוֹג לְאִמָּךְ דְּלָא קְטַעַת אִמָּא שׁוּרִי, דְּאִלְמָלֵא דִּקְטַעְתֵּהּ הֲוֵינָא מָחֵי יָתָךְ וְקָטֵל יָתְיךְ, הָדָא
הוּא דִכְתִיב, (איוב שם, ט) 'בָּתֵּיהֶם שָׁלוֹם מִפָּחַד', מִן הַמַּזִיקִין

LET THAT SUFFICE THEE, MEIR, SAID THEY TO HIM. THEN WHAT IS
MEANT BY, 'WHEN HE GIVETH QUIETNESS, WHO CAN CONDEMN?' HE
DEMANDED. WAS NOT EASE GIVEN TO THE GENERATION OF THE FLOOD;
WHO THEN CAN CONDEMN THEM? THEY REPLIED. AND WHAT EASE WAS
GIVEN TO THEM? THEIR SEED IS ESTABLISHED (NAKHON) IN THEIR SIGHT
WITH THEM, AND THEIR OFFSPRING BEFORE THEIR EYES (IBID., 21:8);
THEY SEND FORTH THEIR LITTLE ONES LIKE A FLOCK, ETC. (IBID., 11). R.
LEVI SAID: THEIR WIVES WERE PREGNANT BUT THREE DAYS AND THEN
BORE: FOR 'NAKHON' IS STATED HERE, WHILST ELSEWHERE IT IS SAID,
BE READY (NEKHONIM, PL. OF NAKHON) AGAINST THE THIRD DAY (EX.
19:15): JUST AS 'NAKHON' THERE MEANS FOR THREE DAYS, SO 'NAKHON'
HERE MEANS FOR THREE DAYS. THE RABBIS SAID: EVEN AFTER ONE DAY,
FOR 'NAKHON' OCCURS HERE, WHILE ELSEWHERE IT IS SAID, AND BE
READY (NAKHON) BY THE MORNING (IBID., 34:2): JUST AS 'NAKHON'
THERE MEANS IN ONE DAY, SO HERE TOO IT MEANS ONE DAY. 'AND THEIR
OFFSPRING BEFORE THEIR EYES' MEANS THAT THEY SAW THEIR CHIL-
DREN'S CHILDREN. 'THEY TEND FORTH THEIR LITTLE ONES (AWILEHEM)
LIKE A FLOCK': R. LEVI SAID: IN ARABIA A CHILD IS CALLED AWILA. AND
THEIR CHILDREN DANCE (IBID.) – LIKE DEMONS, AS YOU READ, AND
SATYRS SHALL DANCE THERE (ISA. 13:21). WHEN ONE OF THEM GAVE
BIRTH BY DAY SHE WOULD SAY TO HER SON, 'GO AND BRING ME A FLINT
TO CUT YOUR NAVEL CORD.' IF AT NIGHT, SHE WOULD SAY TO HER SON,
'GO AND LIGHT A LAMP TO CUT [BURN] THROUGH YOUR NAVEL CORD.' IT
ONCE HAPPENED THAT A WOMAN WHO GAVE BIRTH AT NIGHT SAID TO
HER SON, 'GO AND LIGHT ME A CANDLE TO CUT THROUGH YOUR NAVEL
CORD.' HE WENT OUT, AND THE DEMON SHIMADON [LIT. 'DESTRUCTION']
MET HIM AND SAID TO HIM, 'GO AND INFORM YOUR MOTHER THAT THE
COCK HAS CROWED, BUT IF THE COCK HAD NOT CROWED YET, I WOULD

HAVE SMITTEN AND KILLED YOU.' 'GO AND INFORM YOUR MOTHER THAT
MY MOTHER HAD NOT YET CUT MY NAVEL CORD,' HE RETORTED, 'BUT
HAD MY MOTHER CUT MY NAVEL CORD, I WOULD HAVE SMITTEN AND
KILLED YOU.' THUS IT IS WRITTEN, THEIR HOMES ARE SAFE, WITHOUT
FEAR (JOB 21:9) – OF DEMONS:

They said to R. Meir, essentially "Enough already. You are exaggerating with your interpretation." Maybe they objected to what R. Meir was saying because it appeared as though he was defending the generation of the Flood. This means that if that generation had known that there truly was providential care in the universe, they may not have departed from the proper path. As for the interpretation of the rabbis, they felt that the Holy One Blessed be He gave the generation of the Flood quiet and rest without demanding obligations from them, and despite that, they sinned.' (Aryeh Mirkin)

The Midrash then specifies the various ways in which nature was tampered with to make things much easier for the generation of the Flood, such as the absence of pain during childbirth and so on. All of these things are well listed in the translation.

(שם שם, שם) 'וְלֹא שֵׁבֶט אֱלוֹהַ עֲלֵיהֶם' מִן הַיִּסּוּרִים, וּכְשֶׁהִסְתִּיר פָּנָיו מֵהֶם, מִי אָמְרוּ לוֹ, שֶׁלֹּא עָשִׂיתָ כַשּׁוּרָה, וּמַה הִסְתִּיר פָּנָיו מֵהֶם, שֶׁהֵבִיא עֲלֵיהֶם הַמַּבּוּל, הֲדָא הוּא דִכְתִיב, (בראשית ז, כג) 'וַיִּמַח אֶת כָּל הַיְקוּם, וְגוֹ'', 'עַל גּוֹי וְעַל אָדָם יָחַד' 'עַל גּוֹי' זֶה דּוֹר הַמַּבּוּל, 'וְעַל אָדָם' זֶה נֹחַ, 'יָחַד' שֶׁמִּמֶּנּוּ הֻשְׁתַּת הָעוֹלָם, וְיֵשׁ לוֹ לְהַעֲמִיד עוֹלָמוֹ מֵאֻמָּה שְׁלֵמָה, וּמֵאָדָם אֶחָד, שֶׁנֶּאֱמַר 'וַיִּהְיוּ בְנֵי נֹחַ הַיֹּצְאִים'.

NEITHER IS THE ROD OF GOD UPON THEM (IBID.) – THEY ARE SPARED
SUFFERINGS. YET WHEN HE HID HIS FACE FROM THEM, WHO SAID TO
HIM, 'THOU HAST NOT DONE WELL'? AND WHY DID HE HIDE HIS FACE
FROM THEM? [BECAUSE AS IT IS WRITTEN], WHETHER IT BE DONE
UNTO A NATION OR UNTO A MAN, ALIKE – YAHAD (JOB 34:29): 'UNTO
A NATION' REFERS TO THE GENERATION OF THE FLOOD; 'AND UNTO A
MAN,' TO NOAH; 'ALIKE': FOR FROM HIM [NOAH] WAS THE WORLD ESTAB-
LISHED, AND HE CAN SET UP HIS WORLD FROM A NATION, AND HE CAN
ESTABLISH HIS WORD FROM A SINGLE PERSON, AS IT IS WRITTEN, AND
THE SONS OF NOAH, ETC.

When it comes to creating a new world, there are no rules that apply to God. He can achieve this by means of preserving a nation or He can do so through an individual. He chose an individual, namely Noah, who eventually was the progenitor of all generations. That is why his name is mentioned again, together with his three sons, they all were the creators of the new world and its progenitors. For this, they deserve to be mentioned again and again.

—

Seed Thoughts

When we come to a midrash like this, which appears more fantastic than real, one is forced to ask a number of questions. Did the sages really believe that a woman could be pregnant for only one day or three days? Why should God create laws in Nature and "have to" change them? And if the Rabbis did not believe such things, then why are these opinions included in the Midrash and why do they become the focal points for debates and differences of opinion? There are no explanations that are conclusive, but I would like to make a suggestion that the readers will hopefully approve.

The more we read the story of the Flood in *Midrash Rabbah*, the more we come to realize that the sages were very sensitive to the idea of the destruction of the world. They seem to have some kind of theological guilt. How could God do such a thing? Surely not everyone in that generation was equally evil and guilty. Could it be, as Rashi said, that there were only nine good people and that the world could not be saved in only their merit, as Sodom and Gemorah could not be saved? (See Rashi to Parsha *Vayerah*,18:32.)

In order to demonstrate God's justness in destroying the generation of the Flood, the rabbis described a whole series of evil doings of which the generation of the Flood were guilty – terrible evils all of which were mentioned in the early parshiyot. However, that in itself may not have been enough. What they are now saying is that these evils took place at a time where all of them were granted what one can only describe as complete rest, relaxation and a multiple of good things happening to all of them. Nature itself was changed on their behalf so that all of its difficulties were removed in order for them to find fulfillment. The pain of childbirth was mostly removed. Children never died while their parents were alive and this was extended to six generations. To do evil things within the challenges of a normal world is bad enough. But to do evil things when the entire universe has been changed for your benefit deserves the most terrible punishment. This seems to be what the sages were aiming to achieve in terms of their own conscience. This totally justified, in their view, the destruction of the world.

—

Additional Commentary

The view of the sages

Eve was cursed with the punishment that she and those who would live after her would suffer in childbirth. However, just as the punishment of the first man ended with the birth of Noah, as it is written in *Tanhumah* that when Noah was born, Lemech said, "He will comfort us." The same thing applied with the curse of Eve, which ended with the generation of the Flood, in order to give them peace and rest beyond nature. However, after the Flood, all these past punishments were restored. (*Tiferet Tzion*)

Creators of humanity

Even though the sons of Noah who left the ark were three, the Midrash speaks of rebuilding the world from one man since Noah begat his sons, so they have to be looked upon as one unit. God wanted the world to be repopulated within a short period of time, and indeed, there were some cases where sextuplets were born. Still, it is from Noah and his three sons that all of humanity emerged. (*Tiferet Tzion*)

ב. (איוב לד, כד) 'יָרֹעַ כַּבִּירִים לֹא חֵקֶר, וְגוֹ'', הֵרֵעוּ, אַנְשֵׁי דוֹר הַמַּבּוּל בְּמַעֲשֵׂיהֶם הָרָעִים, 'וְאֵין חֵקֶר' אֵין חֵקֶר בְּמַעֲשֵׂיהֶם הָרָעִים, (שם שם, שם) 'וַיַּעֲמֵד אֲחֵרִים תַּחְתָּם', אֵלּוּ בְנֵי נֹחַ 'וַיִּהְיוּ בְנֵי נֹחַ, שֵׁם חָם וָיָפֶת'.

2. MIGHTY MEN DO EVIL THAT IS UNFATHOMABLE (JOB 34:24): THE MEN
OF THE GENERATION OF THE FLOOD DID EVIL WITH THEIR WICKED
DEEDS; 'THAT IS UNFATHOMABLE': THEIR WICKED DEEDS WERE UN-
FATHOMABLE [ENDLESS]. AND HE SETTETH OTHERS IN THEIR STEAD
(IBID.): VIZ., THE CHILDREN OF NOAH; HENCE AND THE SONS OF NOAH,
ETC.

The Midrash here concerns itself with two problems. The first has
to do with the text that says that Noah left the ark with his three sons;
since this verse was mentioned earlier, why was it repeated? The second
problem that concerns the rabbis, according to Mirkin, is the expression
וַיִּהְיוּ – *vayihiyu*, "there will be" – even though it is grammatically correct,
since the *vav* changes the tense from future to past, still, the fact that
yihiyu is in future tense seems to hint to a different future, as we will
explain in the next paragraph. In attempting to resolve these questions,
a verse from Job is introduced. As we note from earlier midrashim, several verses from Job have been interpreted as relating to the Flood. This
particular verse seems to indicate that the generation is evil and that
God will destroy them as a punishment until they disappear. The word
used is יָרֹעַ – *yaro'a*, meaning, "they will become evil." It also means to
break. In the case of the generation of the Flood, it is as though they
were evil in a much more inappropriate way beyond any generation
before or since. Therefore, they were broken up and destroyed.

The answer concerning the second problem seems to be that since
the generation of the Flood were replaced, by Noah and his three sons,
only the accomplishments of Noah and his sons will lead into the future,
as is suggested by the expression *yihiyu*, in futuristic terms. As for the
expression אֵין חֵקֶר – *ein kheker*, "unfathomable," the evil of the genera-

tion of the Flood was so evil and terrible that they had no way of finding any rationale for it to even come close to possibly understanding it.

(ישעיה מג, יג) 'גַּם מִיּוֹם אֲנִי הוּא, וְאֵין מִיָּדִי מַצִּיל', מֵאֻמּוֹת הָעוֹלָם, (שם שם, שם) 'אֶפְעַל וּמִי
יְשִׁיבֶנָּה', כָּל פְּעֻלּוֹת וּמַחֲשָׁבוֹת, שֶׁפָּעַלְתִּי עִם דּוֹר הַמַּבּוּל, מִי אָמַר לִי, לֹא עָשִׂיתִי כַשּׁוּרָה, אֲבָל
נֹחַ, נִכְנַס בְּשָׁלוֹם, וְיָצָא, בְּשָׁלוֹם, 'וַיִּהְיוּ בְנֵי נֹחַ הַיֹּצְאִים. וְגוֹ''.

YEA, SINCE THE DAY WAS I AM HE, AND THERE IS NONE THAT CAN DELIVER
OUT OF MY HAND (ISA. 43:13): NONE CAN DELIVER ANY OF THE WORLD
NATIONS OUT OF MY HAND. I WILL WORK, AND WHO CAN REVERSE IT
(IBID.)? IN ALL THE WORKS AND DESIGNS WHICH I EXECUTED UPON THE
PEOPLE OF THE GENERATION OF THE FLOOD, WHO COULD SAY TO ME,
'THOU HAST NOT DONE RIGHTLY'? BUT NOAH ENTERED [THE ARK] IN
PEACE AND LEFT IT IN PEACE: THUS, AND THE SONS OF NOAH, ETC.

The second section of this Midrash, just mentioned, begins with a
verse in Isaiah. "Even from that very day, I am the only One [the only
God of the universe]." It is of interest that the *Midrash Ha-Mevo'ar*, following Rashi, explains this verse as referring to the revelation at Sinai
and it indicates that just as God was alone and decisive at the revelation
at Sinai, so was He alone and decisive at the time of the Flood. There
was no one before or after the Flood who could criticize the actions
of His decision and will. It is of interest to note that Aryeh Mirkin, in
his commentary, attributes this idea to a different verse. He attributes it
to the following verse, Genesis 6:17: "And I will bring a flood upon the
earth." There is no one among the nations who can interfere with God's
ways or change His will. Indeed, the previous Midrash describes how
the people of that generation were trying to harass Noah and prevent
him from completing the ark, and then, once it was completed, they
tried to take the leadership away from him. But they could not succeed.
They were all decimated and Noah and his family replaced them. This is
the meaning of the verse that says that Noah, when he left the ark, was
blessed with his three sons; and the use of the word *vayihiyu* there is
appropriate, since they were to be the beginning of a new world. This is
also why the verse is repeated, to indicate that something new has been
added to the story.

'וְחָם הוּא אֲבִי כְנָעַן', אֲבוּי דִּפְחָתָא. 'שְׁלֹשָׁה אֵלֶּה בְּנֵי נֹחַ', וּמֵאֵלֶּה נָפְצָה כָל הָאָרֶץ', לָמָּה הַדָּבָר
דּוֹמֶה, לְדָגָה גְדוֹלָה, דְּנָפְצָה עֻבְּרַהּ וּמָלְאָה אַרְעָא.

AND HAM IS THE FATHER OF CANAAN: HE WAS THE SOURCE OF DEGRADA-
TION. THESE THREE WERE THE SONS OF NOAH, AND OF THESE WAS THE

WHOLE EARTH OVERSPREAD (9:19), AS BY A HUGE FISH THAT SPAWNED
ITS EGGS AND FILLED THE EARTH.

Here, the Midrash is concerned that only the offspring of Ham were mentioned and not those of Shem and Japheth. Also, why was Canaan not described as the son of Ham, but rather Ham described as the father of Canaan? The answer is that Canaan turned out to be a son of lesser ability, someone who is, one might say, no good. Therefore, Ham is described as the father of "the no-good one." The section ends with the repetition of the verse telling of Noah leaving with his three sons. The reason for this is that they were to repopulate the entire earth, in quite a miraculous way. In the same way that a fish allows its eggs to enter the waters, so, in some fashion, were the three sons of Noah and their offspring – probably aided by the Divine design – able to repopulate the world – in a way that can be described as very quickly. So the verse says that Noah left the ark with his three sons, who were most important because they were responsible for the repopulation of the world.

———

Seed Thoughts

This seed thought is based on a commentary by RZWE. There is a remarkable statement in *Exodus Rabbah* (29:5), which tells us that God intended to give the Torah to the generation of the Flood. Proof text for this is in a psalm, which contains the words, ה' למבול ישב – *Hashem lamabul yashav*. The translation of the full verse is, "God sat enthroned at the deluge, the Lord will strengthen His people, the Lord will bless His people with peace" (Psalms 29:10). The word "strengthen" is usually interpreted as referring to Torah. In other words, the second part of the verse, which followed the statement that God was enthroned at the Flood, should be translated as, "The Lord will give His Torah to the people and thereby, He would be blessing them with peace."

This is quite a remarkable statement; but what does it mean? It seemed that it was God's intention that the generation of the Flood should have been the forbears of the real and permanent world, and everything intended for the permanent world should have been a part of that generation, including the giving of the Torah and the creation of a moral dimension in the universe. We are forced to conclude that the Flood and its punishment represented not only the failures of mankind, but perhaps to say also, in as respectful way as possible, the failure of God's plan for mankind. Since the Almighty created man with freedom of will, that is to say, God released some of His power and placed it within the responsibility of man in such a way that it would not be controlled by Him. Therefore, it was not only the failure of man, but since man's freedom was given by God, one would have to say that in a certain respect there was a failure of the Divine plan, which is probably dramatized by the expression toward the end of the first Torah portion of Genesis, that the Lord "regretted" His creation of man.

This failure of the Divine plan, as it were, comes to teach us something. The creation story ends with *asher barah Elokim la'asot*, God created in order for man to complete. Man, therefore, has a share in the creation of the world. By knowing what happened in the story of the Flood, we have to be ultra careful that it does not happen again. We have a great responsibility. We have to see to it that God's plan for mankind should be successful, that the freedom of will given to us should be used responsibly and as a result of that behavior, we praise His name forever.

Additional Commentary

The future tense and Noah

The verse quoted from the Book of Job reads, "Mighty men do evil that is unfathomable," and the reference is to the people of the generation of the Flood. It says in our text, about Noah and his sons, *vayihiyu*, the word in the future tense, "they will become," instead of the term we might have expected, "they became." This means that they became the new founders of mankind. The sages are trying to affirm a new development, namely, that the sons of Noah replaced the leaders of the generation of the Flood. The Holy One, Blessed be He, is the One Who broke up and destroyed that leadership and established the sons of Noah instead. (Aryeh Mirkin)

Parashah Thirty-Six, *Midrash Three*

ג. 'וַיָּחֶל נֹחַ אִישׁ הָאֲדָמָה', נִתְחַלֵּל וְנַעֲשָׂה חֻלִּין, לָמָּה 'וַיִּטַּע כָּרֶם', לֹא הָיָה לוֹ לִטַּע דָּבָר אַחֵר,
שֶׁל תַּקָּנָה, לֹא יְחוּר אֶחָד, וְלֹא גְרוֹפִית אַחַת, אֶלָּא 'וַיִּטַּע כָּרֶם'. וּמֵהֵיכָן הָיָה לוֹ, אָמַר רַבִּי אַבָּא
בַּר כַּהֲנָא, הִכְנִיס עִמּוֹ זְמוֹרוֹת וּנְטִיעוֹת, וְיִחוּרִים שֶׁל תְּאֵנָה, וּגְרוֹפִיּוֹת לְזֵיתִים, הֲדָא הוּא דִכְתִיב,
(בראשית ו, כא) 'וְאָסַפְתָּ אֵלֶיךָ', אֵין אָדָם כּוֹנֵס דָּבָר אֶלָּא אִם כֵּן הָיָה צָרִיךְ לוֹ.

3. AND NOAH THE HUSBANDMAN BEGAN-WAY – YAHEL (9:20) – HE WAS
DEGRADED (NITHHALLEL) AND DEBASED (HULLIN). WHY? BECAUSE HE
PLANTED A VINE-YARD (IBID.). SHOULD HE HAVE NOT PLANTED SOME-
THING OF USE, SUCH AS A YOUNG FIG-SHOOT OR A YOUNG [OLIVE-]
SHOOT? INSTEAD OF WHICH HE PLANTED A VINEYARD. AND WHENCE
DID HE PROCURE IT? SAID R. ABBA B. KAHANA: HE TOOK INTO THE ARK
WITH HIM VINE SHOOTS FOR PLANTING, AND YOUNG SHOOTS FOR FIG
TREES AND OLIVE TREES, AS IT IS WRITTEN, AND THOU SHALT GATHER
TO THEE (GEN. 6:21): A MAN GATHERS IN ONLY WHAT HE WILL NEED [IN
THE FUTURE].

This section begins by stating that Noah planted the vineyard, and
this causes the sages to react. However, that is not exactly what was
said. The verse begins with ויחל – *vayechal* Noah, which is interpreted as
meaning not only that "he began" something, but it also implies that he
did something that has to do with *chillul Hashem*, that is to say, profan-
ing the Divine name. It must be understood that he brought into the ark
many other things, which we will soon find out, but the first thing he did
was plant the vineyard, which produces wine. Wine has the potential,
unfortunately, to bring devastation to the lives of individuals. As we will
see, the Torah brings examples that wine, in moderation, can be a good
thing; but in excess, it can lead to alcoholism, a very serious disease. For
Noah to have begun his new life work after the Flood by building the
vineyard is very much criticized in our midrash.

The next question raised is, where could Noah have gotten the vines
to plant his vineyard? He brought them with him into the ark. We know
this from the verse that says that he brought things with him which are

to be eaten, among these, small branches, seedlings, which consisted of vines, figs and olives.

'אִישׁ הָאֲדָמָה', שְׁלֹשָׁה הֵם שֶׁהָיוּ לְהוּטִים אַחַר הָאֲדָמָה, וְלֹא נִמְצָא בָהֶם תּוֹעֶלֶת, וְאֵלוּ הֵן, קַיִן, נֹחַ, וְעֻזִּיָּהוּ, קַיִן, (שם ד, ב) 'הָיָה עֹבֵד אֲדָמָה', נֹחַ, 'אִישׁ הָאֲדָמָה', עֻזִּיָּהוּ, (דה"ב כו, י) 'וְאִכָּרִים וְכֹרְמִים בֶּהָרִים וּבַכַּרְמֶל, כִּי אֹהֵב אֲדָמָה הָיָה'. 'אִישׁ אֲדָמָה' שֶׁעָשָׂה פָנִים לָאֲדָמָה, וְשֶׁבִּשְׁבִילוֹ נִתְלַחְלְחָה הָאֲדָמָה, וְשֶׁמִּלֵּא כָּל פְּנֵי הָאֲדָמָה. 'אִישׁ הָאֲדָמָה' בּוֹרְגָר לְשֵׁם בּוּרְגָרוּת

THE HUSBANDMAN. THREE HAD A PASSION FOR AGRICULTURE, AND NO GOOD WAS FOUND IN THEM: CAIN, NOAH, AND UZZIAH. CAIN WAS A TILLER OF THE GROUND (IBID., 4:2); NOAH: AND NOAH, THE HUSBANDMAN, BEGAN; UZZIAH: AND HE HAD HUSBANDMEN AND VINEDRESSERS IN THE MOUNTAINS AND IN THE FRUITFUI FIELDS, FOR HE LOVED HUSBANDRY (I CHRON. 26:10). A HUSBANDMAN [LIT. A MAN OF THE GROUND: HE WAS SO TERMED] BECAUSE HE SAVED THE FACE OF THE GROUND, SINCE FOR HIS SAKE THE GROUND WAS PRESERVED; AND BECAUSE HE FILLED THE FACE OF THE GROUND – A MAN OF THE GROUND: JUST AS A CASTLE-GUARD IS CALLED BY THE NAME OF THE CASTLE.

אָמַר רַבִּי בֶּרֶכְיָה, חָבִיב מֹשֶׁה, מִנֹּחַ, נֹחַ, מִשֶּׁנִּקְרָא (בראשית ו, ט) 'אִישׁ צַדִּיק'. נִקְרָא 'אִישׁ אֲדָמָה', אֲבָל מֹשֶׁה, מִשֶּׁנִּקְרָא (שמות ב, יט) 'אִישׁ מִצְרִי', נִקְרָא (דברים לג, א) 'אִישׁ הָאֱ-לֹהִים'.

R. BEREKIAH SAID: MOSES WAS MORE BELOVED THAN NOAH. NOAH, AFTER HAVING BEEN CALLED A RIGHTEOUS MAN (GEN. 6:9), IS CALLED A MAN OF THE GROUND; BUT MOSES, AFTER HAVING BEEN CALLED AN EGYPTIAN MAN (EX. II, 19), WAS THEN CALLED THE MAN OF GOD (DEUT. 33:1). HE WAS MORE BELOVED THAN NOAH, WHO ENDED AS A CASTRATE.

In this section a comparison is made between Moses and Noah in a very dramatic way. Moses began as an אִישׁ מצרי – *ish mitzri*, an Egyptian, and then later classified as אישׁ אלוהים – *ish Elokim*, man of God. Noah, on the other hand, was described as an אישׁ צדיק – *ish tzaddik*, a righteous man, especially due to his deeds at the time of the Flood, and at the end of his life he was considered an אישׁ אדמה – *ish adamah*, man of the earth, which is quite a descent.

'וַיִּטַּע כֶּרֶם' בְּשָׁעָה שֶׁהָיָה הוֹלֵךְ לְטַע כֶּרֶם, אַפְגַע בּוֹ שֵׁדָא שִׁימָדוֹן, אָמַר לֵהּ שֻׁתָּפִי עִמָּךְ, אֶלָּא, אִזְדַּהַר בָּךְ, דְּלָא תֵעוֹל לְחָלְקִי, וְאִם עַלְתְּ בְּחָלְקִי אֲנָא חָבֵל בָּךְ.

AND PLANTED A VINEYARD. AS HE WAS GOING TO PLANT THE VINEYARD THE DEMON SHIMADON MET HIM AND PROPOSED, 'COME INTO PARTNERSHIP WITH ME [IN THIS VINEYARD], BUT TAKE CARE NOT TO ENTER INTO MY PORTION, FOR IF YOU DO I WILL INJURE YOU.'

This section is quite interesting; it talks about the chief of the demons speaking with Noah, advising him to drink only in moderation, lest he become like the demon himself. Interesting that in his commentary, Aryeh Mirkin says that this story is an allegory; but the truth of the matter is that when one becomes drunk, one does act as a demon, and will be treated as such. That was Noah's fate.

⁓

Seed Thoughts

This midrash is one of the few examples of the rabbis not only criticizing excessive drinking of wine, but also attacking the people who would do so in a very strong manner. It is very true that there are many places in the Bible that describe the joy of wine, how it adds simchah to a person's life and is related to enjoyment, but this is only when consumed in moderation. When it is taken in excess, it can produce terrible reactions. A person can become an alcoholic and the "cure" can be very difficult and not always successful. When I was young, I used to think that Jews were protected from alcoholism. Even at the Kiddush of the Sabbath and festivals, the intake of wine would be limited, but still permitted. I was disillusioned by a number of physicians, who told me that there were many cases of Jews who became alcoholics. Whether they were Jews who made Kiddush or Jews who had never heard of Kiddush, there was apparently not too much of a difference. The warning against excessive drinking certainly remains very much in order in our day as well. And in our day, the real danger is not so much wine, but hard liquor, which apparently was not that well known in ancient times, but is certainly well known today. Making a *l'chayim* is a very joyful religious act, and in Chassidic circles in particular, they make a great deal of them. But we have to be very careful, because even with *l'chayim*s, if one drinks in excess, it can lead to addiction with all its negativity. Let us make our drinking of wine a true *l'chayim* dedicated to life in its fullest, in its joy and in its moderation.

⁓

Additional Commentary

The man of the earth

The meaning of this expression is similar to that which we find in the Book of Ruth, with the expression איש נעמי – *ish Na'omi*, "the husband of Naomi," which can also be interpreted as the protector of Naomi or somebody very special to Naomi. Therefore, you could say that Noah was a "protector" of the earth. We see this is so in three ways: Firstly, in terms of what he did regarding plowing the earth, sowing seeds and various other good agricultural works; secondly, he could be called *ish adamah* because it was through his merit that God arranged for rain to descend on the earth and The third reason he can be called "man of the earth" is because the sons who followed him were responsible for repopulating the world. (*Tiferet Tzion*)

Noah as transgressor

The verse could have read that Noah, the man of the earth, went about to plant the vineyard and the word *vayechal* would mean that he began to plant this vineyard. However, the verse reads that the verb *vayechal* is followed by another verb ויטע כרם – *vayit'a kerem*. That makes the translation difficult, because the word *vayechal*, in this rendering, could not be translated as beginning. This has to be seen as a different verb entirely, נתחלל – *nitchallel*, he debased himself. It was not proper for Noah, for his first act after the ark, to plant the vineyard, or do something which could bring calamity to the world. There are other things he could have planted and that was ascribed to him as a negative behavior. (Aryeh Mirkin)

And he planted a vineyard

Why is it important to note that he planted a vineyard? There is no doubt that he also planted other fruit trees. Because of the fact, however, that he planted the vineyard first and the vineyard also has certain negative consequences, even though we know from other verses that wine can make man and God rejoice. Nevertheless, sometimes wine can lead to drunkenness. Such things can not happen with other fruit trees, which have no negative consequences associated with them. It is for this reason that the word *vayechal* is interpreted as a critical expression. That Noah debased himself. This is discussed differently in *Midrash Tanhumah*. (*Yefei To'ar*)

ד. 'וַיֵּשְׁתְּ מִן הַיַּיִן' 'וַיֵּשְׁתְּ' 'וַיֵּשְׁתְּ' שָׁתָה שֶׁלֹּא בְמִדָּה וְנִתְבַּזָּה

4. AND HE DRANK OF THE WINE, AND WAS DRUNKEN (9:21). HE DRANK
IMMODERATELY, BECAME INTOXICATED, AND WAS THUS PUT TO SHAME.

Here we are told that Noah did not drink in moderate proportion.
The expression מן היין – *min hayayin* is interpreted to mean that he drank
all the wine that was at his disposal, and that led to his drunkenness,
which, in turn, led to his humiliation, as described in the Torah text.

אָמַר רַבִּי חִיָּא בַּר אַבָּא, בּוֹ בַיּוֹם נָטַע, בּוֹ בַיּוֹם שָׁתָה, בּוֹ בַיּוֹם נִתְבַּזָּה. 'וַיִּתְגַּל בְּתוֹךְ אָהֳלֹה', רַבִּי
יְהוּדָה אָמַר רַבִּי חָנִין בְּשֵׁם רַבִּי שְׁמוּאֵל בַּר יִצְחָק, וַיִּגַּל אֵין כְּתִיב כָּאן, אֶלָּא 'וַיִּתְגַּל', גָּרַם גָּלוּת
לוֹ וְלַדּוֹרוֹת, עֲשֶׂרֶת הַשְּׁבָטִים לֹא גָלוּ אֶלָּא בִּשְׁבִיל יַיִן, הָדָא הוּא דִכְתִיב, (עמוס ו, ו). 'הַשֹּׁתִים
בְּמִזְרְקֵי יַיִן', וּכְתִיב (ישעיה ה, יא) 'הוֹי מַשְׁכִּימֵי בַבֹּקֶר שֵׁכָר יִרְדֹּפוּ וְגוֹ'', שֵׁבֶט יְהוּדָה וּבִנְיָמִין לֹא
גָלוּ אֶלָּא בִּשְׁבִיל הַיַּיִן, שֶׁנֶּאֱמַר (שם כח, ז) 'וְגַם אֵלֶּה בַּיַּיִן שָׁגוּ וּבַשֵּׁכָר תָּעוּ'

R. HIYYA B. ABA SAID: HE PLANTED IT, DRANK THEREOF, AND WAS HU-
MILIATED ALL ON ONE AND THE SAME DAY. AND HE WAS UNCOVERED
(WAYYITHGAL) WITHIN HIS TENT. R. JUDAH B. R. SIMON AND R. HANAN
IN THE NAME OF R. SAMUEL B. R. ISAAC SAID: NOT WAYYGAL IS WRIT-
TEN BUT WAYYITHGAL: HE WAS THE CAUSE OF EXILE FOR HIMSELF
AND SUBSEQUENT GENERATIONS. THE TEN TRIBES WERE EXILED ONLY
BECAUSE OF WINE, AS IT IS WRITTEN, 'WHO DRINK WINE IN BOWLS,'
(AMOS 6:6) AND 'WOE UNTO THEM THAT RISE UP EARLY IN THE MORN-
ING, THAT THEY MAY FOLLOW STRONG DRINK' (ISA. 5:11). THE TRIBES
OF JUDAH AND BENJAMIN WERE EXILED ONLY ON ACCOUNT OF WINE,
AS IT IS WRITTEN, BUT THESE ALSO [VIZ. JUDAH AND BENJAMIN] ERRED
THROUGH WINE (IBID., 28:7).

In this section if it had been the intention of the text to say that Noah
drank wine, it would have been written that way, that he drank wine. But
instead, it says he planted a vineyard and looked after it and the text uses
a series of verbs describing these events, implying they all happened the
same day, including the excessive drinking. In other words, the impres-

sion given by the phrasing is that Noah lusted after this wine and felt he could not wait for it; these so-called miraculous events described are intended to dramatize the fact.

The commentators note the use of the word ויתגל – *vayitgal* – meaning that his nakedness "was uncovered" – as being reflexive. That is to say, his nakedness was not uncovered, but *he* uncovered his nakedness and he contributed to his humiliation. He was responsible for all this. It should be noted that the word *vayitgal* contains the letters of גלות – *galut*, exile. Much will be made of this in the lessons about this particular midrash that follow. The series of connections that the commentators make with Noah, seem to cite him as being responsible for the exile of many future generations. His drunkenness contributed to much personal humiliation and in the future, the fact that other generations resorted to drunkenness, which led to humiliation, produced those sins that ultimately led to the exile of the Jewish people.

Two biblical verses are brought to our attention in the text to prove that wine was the cause of the exiles of our history. The first text is from the prophet Amos. He was close enough to the Assyrian domination to state the basis of the verse that wine was a cause of the exile of the Ten Tribes in the sense that drunkenness contributed to the numerous sins that accumulated in their midst, such as sexual licentiousness and various other forms of immorality. The second text brought here is from the prophet Isaiah; although he came before the exile of the tribes of Judah and Benjamin, he prophesied that wine would be their exile as well and would lead to the various types of sin for which exile was the only form of atonement.

'בְּתוֹךְ אָהֳלוֹ' 'אָהֱלָה' כְּתִיב, בְּתוֹךְ אָהֳלָה שֶׁל אִשְׁתּוֹ, אָמַר רַבִּי הוּנָא בְּשֵׁם רַבִּי אֱלִיעֶזֶר בְּנוֹ שֶׁל רַבִּי יוֹסֵי הַגְּלִילִי, נֹחַ, כְּשֶׁיָּצָא מִן הַתֵּבָה הִכִּישׁוֹ אֲרִי וּשְׁבָרוֹ, וּבָא לְשַׁמֵּשׁ מִטָּתוֹ, וְנִתְפַּזֵּר זַרְעוֹ וְנִתְבַּזָּה

WITHIN HIS TENT (AHALOH): THIS IS WRITTEN AHALAH (HER TENT), VIZ. HIS WIFE'S TENT. R. HUNA SAID IN R. ELIEZER'S NAME: WHEN NOAH WAS LEAVING THE ARK A LION STRUCK AND MUTILATED HIM. NOW HE WENT TO COHABIT, BUT HIS SEMEN WAS SCATTERED AND HE WAS HUMILIATED.

Here is an interesting example of biblical literature that has כתיב – *ktiv* and קרי – *kri*, where a Hebrew word is written in one manner, but orally read in another manner. Here, the word is אהלו – *ohalo*, which means "his tent" is written with a feminine ending, אהלה – *ohalah*, thus meaning "*her* tent." This could be interpreted as saying that Noah, in his drunken stupor, was headed for his wife's tent in order to fulfill his marital obligations, having forgotten that as a result of his injuries, he was no longer able to have any children. As our text describes it, he had failed in his sexual attempt and felt completely humiliated.

אָמַר רַבִּי יוֹחָנָן, לְעוֹלָם לֹא תְהִי לָהוּט אַחַר הַיַּיִן, שֶׁכָּל פָּרָשַׁת הַיַּיִן כְּתִיב בָּהּ וי"ן אַרְבַּע עֶשְׂרֵה פְעָמִים, הָדָא הוּא דִכְתִיב, 'וַיָּחֶל נֹחַ', 'וַיִּטַּע כָּרֶם', 'וַיֵּשְׁתְּ מִן הַיַּיִן', 'וַיִּתְגַּל', 'וַיַּרְא חָם', 'וַיַּגֵּד לִשְׁנֵי אֶחָיו', 'וַיִּקַּח שֵׁם וָיֶפֶת', 'וַיָּשִׂימוּ עַל שְׁכֶם שְׁנֵיהֶם', 'וַיֵּלְכוּ אֲחֹרַנִּית', 'וַיְכַסּוּ אֵת עֶרְוַת אֲבִיהֶם וּפְנֵיהֶם אֲחֹרַנִּית וְעֶרְוַת אֲבִיהֶם, וְגוֹ'', 'וַיִּיקֶץ נֹחַ', 'וַיֵּדַע אֵת אֲשֶׁר עָשָׂה לוֹ', 'וַיֹּאמֶר אָרוּר כְּנַעַן עֶבֶד עֲבָדִים, וְגוֹ''.

R. JOHANAN SAID: BEWARE OF A PASSION FOR WINE, BECAUSE IN THIS PASSAGE ON WINE WAY (WOE) IS WRITTEN FOURTEEN TIMES, AS IT IS WRITTEN, AND NOAH THE HUSBANDMAN BEGAN (WAYYAHEL), AND PLANTED (WAYYITTA) A VINEYARD, AND HE DRANK (WAYYESHT) OF THE WINE, AND WAS DRUNKEN (WAYYISHKAR); AND HE WAS UNCOVERED (WAYYITHGAL). AND HAM SAW (WAYYAR) . . . A. . AND TOLD (WAYYAGGED) HIS TWO BRETHREN, AND SHEM AND JAPHETH TOOK (WAYYIKHAH) A GARMENT, AND LAID IT (WAYYASIMU) UPON BOTH THEIR SHOULDERS, AND WENT (WAYYELEKU) BACKWARD, AND COVERED (WAYYEKASSU) . . . A. . AND NOAH AWOKE (WAYYIKKEZ) . . . A. . AND KNEW (WAYYEDA') WHAT HIS YOUNGEST SON HAD DONE UNTO HIM. AND HE SAID (WAYYOMER): CURSED BE CANAAN (GEN. 9:20–25).

This last section notes that the entire episode of Noah, his wine and his drinking, is described with a series of verbs, each beginning with the letters וי – *vav yud*, which is also the way to spell the Hebrew word for "woe" or to express suffering. In other words, the verbs themselves tell the story that wine, when consumed in excess, contributes to terrible things, both for the individual and for society. Fourteen of these verbs are used here, helping to illustrate, as much as the teachings themselves, the kind of calamitous behavior that alcoholism can produce.

—

Seed Thoughts

We can accept the fact, as stated in the previous midrash, that wine has to be taken in moderation, for if it is not, then many negative things can occur as a result of drunkenness. The present midrash presents this thought in a much more serious fashion. It might even appear to be exaggerated. It claims that drunkenness is so bad that it influenced and promoted the two great exiles of the Jewish people. One was the exile of the ten tribes during the time of the king of Assyria, and the other was during the time when Judah and Benjamin were exiled in the time of Nebuchadnezzar. The question that ought to bother all of us is hinted at in the statement that the exile was due to drunkenness. How do we explain the fact that over the past several thousand years, either drunkenness was not regarded as a major problem, or there simply has not been a large-scale concerted effort by the Jewish people to stop it or find ways of eliminating it?

We know that there were times when the Christian community made abstinence from liquor a major religious factor. Such a thing never happened in Judaism. On the contrary, we have an idea of a לחיים – *l'chayim*, drinking "to life," which has taken root in many places and been very much emphasized among certain elements of the Chassidic movement. What could be the reason for this lack of historical opposition to the drinking of wine? The answer seems to be that an opposing interpretation can be found in the many aspects of the Psalms and the many aspects of our literature, praising wine as a source of joy and that God and man can rejoice in drinking it. A balance had to be found between the criticism beginning with Noah and the fact that other expressions of the Bible tolerate wine for the purpose of rejoicing and enjoyment on the festivals.

Maybe this tolerance to wine developed from the fact that the rabbis went to great pains in establishing rules for Kiddush and Havdalah that the Havdalah glass should be overflowing and that even the amount of wine in the Kiddush cup should be above a certain minimum. Maybe the fact that wine was *not* outlawed contributed to the fact that, at least until modern generations, sobriety was a hallmark of Jewish behavior. Indeed, there are many songs, particularly in Yiddish, that extol the fact that average Jewish behavior "under the influence" was very sober in contrast to the drunkenness that was often displayed by their persecutors.

———

Additional Commentary

How could a man like Noah allow himself to be drunk?

It is very difficult for a reader to accept the fact that a man like Noah, who was described as a most righteous man, could have succumbed to drunkenness so soon after leaving the ark. Let us examine some of the events that may allow for an interpretation: While Noah was in the ark, he and the others were protected from the animals and never attacked by any of them. However, when Noah left the ark, he was attacked by a lion and injured. It should be added at this point that the main commandment given to Noah and his children was to propagate the earth with people. As a result of his injury, Noah discovered that he was no longer able to have children. Upon this realization, Noah was horrified and separated himself from his wife. He did not know – and could not have known – that this was not a reason to separate, for sexual activity in marriage is mandatory even when children are not in the offing. In Hebrew, this is called עונה – *onah*. What happened then was that Noah was either told, or he felt, that wine had certain medicinal powers, so that he thought by drinking wine, his ability to produce children might be restored. This explains his heavy drinking. In fact, the text even attributes his nakedness to his drinking. At that time, he tried to have marital relations with his wife, but unfortunately, being drunk did not allow him to have any control and the relations were unfruitful. (RWZE)

ה. (כב) 'וַיַּרְא חָם אֲבִי כְנַעַן', אָמַר לְהוֹן וַאֲגַד לְהוֹן, אָמַר לְהוֹן, אָדָם הָרִאשׁוֹן שְׁנֵי בָנִים הָיוּ לוֹ, וְעָמַד אֶחָד מֵהֶן וְהָרַג אֶת חֲבֵרוֹ, וְזֶה יֶשׁ לוֹ שְׁלֹשָׁה וְהוּא מְבַקֵּשׁ לַעֲשׂוֹתָן אַרְבָּעָה, אָמַר לְהוֹן וַאֲגַד לְהוֹן

5. AND HAM, THE FATHER OF CANAAN, SAID . . . AND TOLD (WAYYAGGED)
HIS TWO BRETHREN WITHOUT (9:22). HE SAID TO HIS BRETHREN: ADAM
HAD BUT TWO SONS, YET ONE AROSE AND SLEW HIS BROTHER; AND THIS
MAN [NOAH] HAS THREE SONS AND YET HE WANTS FOUR! HE SPOKE TO
THEM, AND PERSUADED THEM.

The sages note here that the ordinary expression to indicate speaking, ויאמר – *vayomer*, is not the one used to describe how Ham spoke to
his brothers about their father's condition. The word used instead was
ויגד – *vayaged*, which seems to imply not only that he spoke to them,
but that he tried very much to influence them to his way of thinking.
He mentioned to them the case of Adam, whose sons, as Noah's, were
to inherit the entire world. Adam had two sons, one of whom killed
the other, and as a result, that one inherited everything. Similarly, in the
case of Noah, he had three sons due to inherit the world, and still, he
was trying his best to propagate the world by adding a fourth, which
would mean that the three will be deprived by receiving a lesser portion
of the inheritance. One of the commentators noted that Ham spoke to
his brothers outside the tent. The reason for this is that he was hoping
that while his father was not injured, his son Canaan would see to it by
means of an injury that he would inflict that Noah should be incapable
of having any more children. (*Tiferet Tzion*)

אָמַר רַבִּי יַעֲקֹב בַּר זַבְדִּי, מַה טַּעַם, עֶבֶד יוֹצֵא בְשֵׁן וָעַיִן, מֵהָכָא, 'וַיַּרְא' 'וַיַּגֵּד'.

R. ABBA B. ZABDI SAID: WHY DOES A SLAVE GO FREE FOR THE LOSS OF A
TOOTH OR AN EYE? IT FOLLOWS FROM THIS: AND . . . HE SAW, AND TOLD.

This section is quite difficult. One of the rules involving slavery is that
a slave could only be freed by permission from his master, by the means

of a document, which the master would give to him or his sponsor. The exception to this procedure, as mentioned in the Torah, is if, through some physical contact, whether a beating or something accidental, the slave gets injured either in his eye or his tooth; then, the slave automatically goes free and requires no document. Even though our sages see an eye and a tooth as representing the loss of any of the twenty-four limbs of the body (see Rashi on Exodus 21:26), the tooth and the eye are the symbols the Torah text uses. In this particular case in our midrash, Ham and his son Canaan were condemned to be perpetual slaves to Ham's brothers, Shem and Japheth. However, in their behavior, they were guilty of ראיה – *reiyah*, which is a sin of the eyes, having their brothers look at their father's nakedness and humiliation, and they were also guilty of a sin of speech, trying to influence the others by telling them the example of Adam, trying to prove that it would be a good thing if Noah could be prevented from having more children. Thus, this sin of speech, which is very similar to having an injury done to their teeth, in addition to the sin of sight regarding their father's nakedness, which relates to the eyes, brought upon them Noah's curse of slavery. The idea of future slaves being freed for damage to an eye or a tooth reminds us of this story. See the additional commentary.

Seed Thoughts

This midrash is one of the saddest documents in the entire story of Noah. Here we have the generation that experienced the tragedy of the Flood, followed by the deliverance of the family of Noah from the destruction of the Flood and the hope that Noah and his sons and their families would be the beginning of a new world. Instead of this new hope, what do we have? Ham, the youngest son of Noah, and his son Canaan, the grandson of Noah, seemed not to have been satisfied with the idea of inheriting one quarter of the entire world, which would have been the case were Noah to have had another child. They wanted the full one third that they were already eligible for. Hence, they felt motivated to do anything possible to see to it that Noah would not have another son, who would share in the inheritance. They were ready to use violence and whatever else it might take to injure him so that his capacity for propagation would be removed. Can anything be more despicable than that? It is quite true that in the centuries and millenia since this story, horrible things have happened in the universe, climaxed by the Holocaust, which many in my generation have experienced. The terrible things that happen over the millenia do not generally take place on the background of miracles as they did with the sons of Noah. We know that Noah and his sons experienced miracles. They experienced personal deliverance from the Flood; they experienced privileges that no human was ever given or will ever be given again. What was the result? The hatred in all those terrible things that are associated with self-interest of the worst sort. All of this puts into jeopardy the struggle for hope and faith and peace, but this is the course that we must follow, despite the Hams and the Canaans and any other unworthy human beings that have dotted the landscape of humanity.

—

Additional Commentary

The shameful behavior of Ham and his son Canaan

Noah's younger son, Ham, wanted to influence his brothers, Shem and Japheth, to his way of thinking, so he invited them to join him and go outside, away from the presence of their father. He wanted to do this in order to give his son Canaan freedom of the place so that he could injure Noah, if necessary, so that he should not have the ability to propagate. This is a terrible act – even reprehensible – which did not even have to be done, since Noah had already been injured. This demonstrates to what lengths Ham and Canaan were willing to go to achieve their ignoble ends. (*Tiferet Tzion*)

The concept of tooth and eye

The main reason for the punishment of Ham was because he abused the power of his vision and of his speech. In the case of the slave master, if the master damaged the tooth or eye of the slave, the slave was immediately redeemed from slavery. The rule is בשן ועין יצא – *beshen ve'ayin yotze*. The slave achieves his freedom through the abuse of any of his limbs, symbolized in the Torah text by his tooth or his eye, without requiring a freedom document. (*Tiferet Tzion*)

ו. (כג) 'וַיִּקַּח שֵׁם וָיֶפֶת אֶת הַשִּׂמְלָה', אָמַר רַבִּי יוֹחָנָן, שֵׁם הִתְחִיל בַּמִּצְוָה תְּחִלָּה וּבָא יֶפֶת וְנִשְׁמַע לוֹ, לְפִיכָךְ זָכָה שֵׁם לְטַלִּית, וְיֶפֶת לְפַיָּילָא.

6. AND SHEM AND JAPHETH TOOK A GARMENT. R. JOHANAN SAID: SHEM COMMENCED THE GOOD DEED, THEN JAPHETH CAME AND HEARKENED TO HIM. THEREFORE SHEM WAS GRANTED A TALLITH AND JAPHETH A PALLIUM.

The sages note two anomalies in this section. The first is that the word ויקח – *vayikach*, "and he took," is written in the singular, whereas it refers to the *two* sons, Shem and Japheth. They also noted that the name of Shem appears before Japheth, whereas Japheth was the older one. These observations prompted them to conclude that it was Shem who took the initiative in protecting their father from shame. Japheth merely followed the leadership of his younger brother. As a result, they were given different categories of rewards. The Tallit and its tzitzit are themselves a commandment and a reminder to us of all the other commandments, therefore, the full extent of Shem's reward was that מצוה גוררת מצוה – *mitzvah goreret mitzvah*, that one commandment leads to the opportunity to do another. Japheth was given an honorary reward of a different kind: the cloak, possibly a toga, worn by the nobility of the ancient Greek civilization. This comes from the fact that Yavan, a descendant of Japheth, is the Hebrew name for Greece.

'וַיָּשִׂימוּ עַל שְׁכֶם שְׁנֵיהֶם, וַיֵּלְכוּ אֲחֹרַנִּית וַיְכַסּוּ אֶת עֶרְוַת אֲבִיהֶם', מִמַּשְׁמַע שֶׁנֶּאֱמַר 'וַיֵּלְכוּ אֲחֹרַנִּית' אֵינִי יוֹדֵעַ שֶׁעֶרְוַת אֲבִיהֶם לֹא רָאוּ', אֶלָּא', מְלַמֵּד, שֶׁנָּתְנוּ יְדֵיהֶם עַל פְּנֵיהֶם, וְהָיוּ מְהַלְּכִין לַאֲחוֹרֵיהֶם, וְנָהֲגוּ בוֹ כָּבוֹד, כְּמוֹרָא הָאָב עַל הַבֵּן.

AND LAID IT UPON BOTH THEIR SHOULDERS. NOW SINCE IT IS SAID, AND WENT BACKWARDS, DO WE NOT KNOW THAT THEY SAW NOT THEIR FATHER'S NAKEDNESS? THIS, HOWEVER, TEACHES THAT THEY HID THEIR FACES WITH THEIR HANDS AND WALKED BACKWARD, GIVING HIM THE RESPECT DUE FROM A SON TO A FATHER.

It is quite true that walking backwards may have helped the sons in not seeing their father's nakedness; however, peripheral vision often plays visual tricks on us. That is why they kept their hands over their eyes, as an additional effort to be respectful to their father.

אָמַר הַקָּדוֹשׁ בָּרוּךְ הוּא לְשֵׁם, אַתָּה כִּסִּיתָ עֶרְוָתָא דַאֲבוּךְ, חַיֶּיךָ, שֶׁאֲנִי פּוֹרֵעַ לָךְ, (דניאל ג, כא) 'בֵּאדַיִן גֻּבְרַיָּא אִלֵּךְ כְּפִתוּ בְּסַרְבָּלֵיהוֹן'. רַבִּי יוּדָן וְרַבִּי הוּנָא, רַבִּי יוּדָן אָמַר, בְּגֵלֵיהוֹן, רַבִּי הוּנָא אָמַר, בְּמוֹקְסֵיהוֹן

SAID THE HOLY ONE, BLESSED BE HE, TO SHEM: 'THOU DIDST COVER THY FATHER'S NAKEDNESS: BY THY LIFE! I WILL REWARD THEE WHEN THESE MEN ARE BOUND IN THEIR CLOAKS (BE-SARBELEHON),' ETC. (DAN. 3:21). (R. JUDAN AND R. HUNA [DIFFERED AS TO THE MEANING OF 'BE-SARBELEHON']: R. JUDAN SAID: IT MEANS IN THEIR PRAYER CLOAKS; R. HUNA SAID: IT MEANS IN THEIR ROBES OF STATE.)

In addition to their immediate reward, the descendants of Shem will eventually receive a very great reward. The reference is in the Book of Daniel, in the story of Chananya, Mishael and Azariah, who are condemned to be burned to death by Nebuchadnezzar. They were dressed in the clothes of nobility, at Nebuchadnezzar's orders, to show a specific kind of respect. They were, of course, descendants of Shem. Not only were they saved from the burning fire, but their clothing was not touched at all, nor was there any smell of fire in their garments or any stench in any aspect of their behavior. It was a tremendous miracle and great reward to Shem.

אָמַר הַקָּדוֹשׁ בָּרוּךְ הוּא לְיֶפֶת, אַתָּה כִּסִּיתָ עֶרְוַת אָבִיךָ, חַיֶּיךָ, שֶׁאֲנִי פּוֹרֵעַ לָךְ, (יחזקאל לט, יא) 'בַּיּוֹם הַהוּא אֶתֵּן לְגוֹג מְקוֹם שָׁם קֶבֶר בְּיִשְׂרָאֵל גֵּיא הָעֹבְרִים קִדְמַת הַיָּם וְחֹסֶמֶת הִיא אֶת הָעֹבְרִים וְקָבְרוּ שָׁם אֶת גּוֹג וְאֶת כָּל הֲמוֹנֹה וְקָרְאוּ גֵּיא הֲמוֹן גּוֹג'

THE HOLY ONE, BLESSED BE HE, SAID TO JAPHETH: 'THOU DIDST COVER THY FATHER'S NAKEDNESS: BY THY LIFE, I WILL REWARD THEE, FOR IT SHALL COME TO PASS ON THAT DAY, THAT I WILL GIVE UNTO GOG A PLACE FIT FOR BURIAL IN ISRAEI' (EZEK. 39:2).

God also rewarded Japheth's future: In the terrible struggle between Gog and Magog, Gog, who was king of the nations in those days, was a descendant of Japhet, as recorded in Genesis 10. Not only was the terrible force of the enemy defeated, but the dead were buried in the Land of Israel to honor Gog and that victory was attributed to Japheth as a reward for the respect he gave to his father.

אָמַר הַקָּדוֹשׁ בָּרוּךְ הוּא לְחָם, אַתָּה בִּזִּיתָ עֶרְוַת אָבִיךָ, חַיֶּיךָ, שֶׁאֲנִי פּוֹרֵעַ לָךְ, (ישעיה כ, ד) 'כֵּן
יְנְהַג מֶלֶךְ אַשּׁוּר אֶת שְׁבִי מִצְרַיִם וְאֶת גָּלוּת כּוּשׁ נְעָרִים וּזְקֵנִים עֲרוֹם וְיָחֵף וַחֲשׂוּפֵי שֵׁת עֶרְוַת
מִצְרָיִם'.

THE HOLY ONE, BLESSED BE HE, SAID TO HAM: 'THOU DIDST BRING THY
FATHER'S NAKEDNESS INTO DISGRACE: BY THY LIFE, I WILL REQUITE
THEE: SO SHALL THE KING OF ASSYRIA LEAD AWAY THE CAPTIVES OF
EGYPT, AND THE EXILES OF ETHIOPIA, YOUNG AND OLD, NAKED AND
BAREFOOT, AND WITH BUTTOCKS UNCOVERED TO THE SHAME OF EGYPT'
(ISA. 20:4).

The Holy One, Blessed be He, then informed Ham that he would be
punished because of the disrespect he showed to his father. This punishment took place when the king of Assyria defeated Kush and Mitzrayim
(Egypt), who are listed in the Book of Genesis as descendants of Ham.
They were defeated in an ignoble way, suffered terribly and were buried
in a difficult experience. All of this was a punishment to Ham.

Seed Thoughts

It is to be noted that the fifth commandment of the Ten Commandments did not order us to *love* our father and mother, but to *honor* them.
This is a very important distinction, because in certain respects, honor
goes beyond love. One could probably assume that the children of
Noah were not particularly happy with their father's drunkenness and
the fact that he exposed himself in preparation for a sexual act, which
of course was humiliating to his children. Still, he was their father and
they respected him and they knew that he deserved honor, so they ran
to cover his nakedness and behave in such a way as to maintain their
father's reputation and stature in his eyes and in the eyes of his children
and extended family circle. The question as to whether parents have to
earn the love of their children is something that is debatable; However,
parents do not have to earn honor. It is built into their home and their
place in society.

It is noteworthy that only in relationship to a father and mother does
the Torah offer this type of special commandment, because parents
are in a special category. Of course we have to love our fellow human
being and of course there has to be mutual respect and of course we
must love neighbors as ourselves, but the treatment of a mother and a
father goes beyond the love and respect due to any Jew or the average
person. The role of parents in life is to be the creators of human beings,

the creators of a family circle, creators of that unit which is the most important aspect of human society. In some instances, the parents look after their children in the first half of life, and in the second half, children look after their parents. Perhaps this is the way it should be. All of us can learn a tremendous lesson from Shem and Japheth, that the honor due to parents is one of the most important principles of human life and human experience.

—

Additional Commentary

God's blessing of Shem

In the category of the commandments known as those "between man and man," there are two specific types of good deeds involved. The first is the fact that we are fulfilling the will of God, Who commanded us to act in this good way. Secondly, performing deeds from this category tends to contribute to a feeling of satisfaction, as it agrees with our natural moral consciousness and brings us favor in the eyes of our fellow human beings. In so far as the first aspect, whereby God's commandment is fulfilled, the reward will only be in the World to Come. As for the fact that someone benefits and receives satisfaction, that reward is related to this world. The rabbis express these same sentiments elsewhere. These are things of which a person derives the fruits in this world but the principles remain in the World to Come. In the case of Shem, his good deed fulfilled both aspects: For one, he fulfilled God's commandment to honor one's father and mother, and he will, therefore, receive a reward in the World to Come. In the second place, his actions immediately benefited his father, so he, therefore, was rewarded also in this world. It is of interest to note that the reward he received was the Tallit because the Tallit itself combines both aspects discussed here: it, too, is a commandment of God; but not only is it a particular commandment, it is also a reminder of all the other commandments, which are of benefit to all of us. (*Tiferet Tzion*)

ז. (כד) 'וַיִּיקֶץ נֹחַ מִיֵּינוֹ', נִתְפָּרֵק יֵינוֹ מֵעָלָיו.

7. AND NOAH AWOKE FROM HIS WINE (9:24): HE WAS SOBERED FROM HIS WINE.

The verse begins with the statement that Noah awoke from his wine. It does not say that he awoke from his sleep, because that may have meant that he was still in a drunken state. None of his curses would have been taken seriously. Saying that he woke from his wine means that all the affects of the wine had disappeared and he was now sufficiently sober for his words to be taken seriously.

'וַיֵּדַע אֵת אֲשֶׁר עָשָׂה לוֹ בְּנוֹ הַקָּטָן', הַפָּסוּל, הֲדָא הוּא דִכְתִיב, (מ"א ח, סד) 'כִּי מִזְבַּח הַנְּחֹשֶׁת קָטֹן מֵהָכִיל, וְגוֹ''.

AND KNEW WHAT HIS YOUNGEST SON HAD DONE UNTO HIM. HERE IT MEANS, HIS WORTHLESS SON, AS YOU READ, BECAUSE THE BRAZEN ALTAR THAT WAS BEFORE THE LORD WAS TOO LITTLE TO RECEIVE THE BURNT-OFFERING, ETC. (I KINGS 8:64).

In this section, Ham is being described as קטן – *katan*, which ordinarily means either "small" or "young." But he was not the youngest son; he was older than Shem. So the interpretation of *katan*, very often, is used in the sense of פסול – *pasul*, meaning "rejected" or "not qualified."

'וַיֹּאמֶר אָרוּר כְּנָעַן עֶבֶד עֲבָדִים יִהְיֶה לְאֶחָיו' חָם חָטָא, וּכְנַעַן נִתְקַלֵּל, אַתְמָהָא, רַבִּי יְהוּדָה וְרַבִּי נְחֶמְיָה, רַבִּי יְהוּדָה אָמַר, לְפִי שֶׁכָּתוּב, (בראשית ט, א) 'וַיְבָרֶךְ אֱ־לֹהִים אֶת נֹחַ וְאֶת בָּנָיו', וְאֵין קְלָלָה הֲוָה בִמְקוֹם בְּרָכָה, לְפִיכָךְ 'וַיֹּאמֶר אָרוּר כְּנָעַן', רַבִּי נְחֶמְיָה אָמַר, כְּנַעַן רָאָה וְהִגִּיד לָהֶם, לְפִיכָךְ תוֹלִין אֶת הַקְּלָלָה בִמְקֻלָּל.

AND HE SAID: CURSED BE CANAAN (9:25): HAM SINNED AND CANAAN IS CURSED! R. JUDAH AND R. NEHEMIAH DISAGREED. R. JUDAH SAID: SINCE IT IS WRITTEN, AND GOD BLESSED NOAH AND HIS SONS (GEN. 9:1), WHILE THERE CANNOT BE A CURSE WHERE A BLESSING HAS BEEN GIVEN, CONSEQUENTLY, HE SAID: CURSED BE CANAAN. R. NEHEMIAH

EXPLAINED: IT WAS CANAAN WHO SAW IT [IN THE FIRST PLACE] AND
INFORMED THEM, THEREFORE THE CURSE IS ATTACHED TO HIM WHO
DID WRONG.

The Midrash goes on to say that Canaan was punished, though it was
Ham, his father, who sinned. Why should this be? There are a number
of answers. One of them is that when the family left the ark, God blessed
Noah and his sons, and a human curse is not functional in the face of a
blessing by God. This is the view of R. Yehudah. R. Nechemiah offers
a different opinion. He says that Canaan had great culpability because
he was the first to see his grandfather, Noah, in his humiliated state. He
was the one who told Ham, who later brought it to the attention of the
brothers.

אָמַר רַבִּי בֶּרֶכְיָה, הַרְבֵּה צַעַר נִצְטַעֵר נֹחַ בַּתֵּבָה שֶׁלֹּא הָיָה לוֹ בֵן קָטָן שֶׁיְּשַׁמְּשֶׁנּוּ, אָמַר, לִכְשֶׁאֵצֵא
אֲנִי מַעֲמִיד לִי בֵן קָטָן שֶׁיְּשַׁמְּשֵׁנִי, כֵּיוָן שֶׁעָשָׂה לוֹ חָם אוֹתוֹ מַעֲשֶׂה, אָמַר, אַתָּה מָנַעְתָּ אוֹתִי
מִלְהַעֲמִיד לִי בֵן קָטָן שֶׁיְּשַׁמְּשֵׁנִי, לְפִיכָךְ יִהְיֶה אוֹתוֹ הָאִישׁ עֶבֶד לְאֶחָיו, שֶׁהֵן עֲבָדִים לִי

R. BEREKIAH SAID: NOAH GRIEVED VERY MUCH IN THE ARK THAT HE
HAD NO YOUNG SON TO WAIT ON HIM, AND DECLARED, 'WHEN I GO OUT
I WILL BEGET A YOUNG SON TO DO THIS FOR ME.' BUT WHEN HAM ACTED
THUS TO HIM, HE EXCLAIMED, 'YOU HAVE PREVENTED ME FROM BEGET-
TING A YOUNG SON TO SERVE ME, THEREFORE THAT MAN [YOUR SON]
WILL BE A SERVANT TO HIS BRETHREN!'

There are several opinions as to why Noah developed hostility toward
Ham. For one, according to R. Berekiah, Noah complained that Ham
prevented him from producing a young child, who would help him in
so many ways.

רַבִּי הוּנָא בְּשֵׁם רַבִּי יוֹסֵף, אָמַר לוֹ, אַתָּה מָנַעְתָּ אוֹתִי מִלְהַעֲמִיד בֶּן רְבִיעִי, לְפִיכָךְ אֲנִי מְאָרֵר
בֶּן רְבִיעִי שֶׁלָּךְ

R. HUNA SAID IN R. JOSEPH'S NAME: [NOAH DECLARED], 'YOU HAVE
PREVENTED ME FROM BEGETTING A FOURTH SON, THEREFORE I CURSE
YOUR FOURTH SON.'

Another interpretation was that Noah was prevented from having a
fourth son. Therefore, Ham's punishment would be that his own fourth
son, Canaan, would be cursed.

רַבִּי הוּנָא בְּשֵׁם רַבִּי יוֹסֵף אָמַר, אַתָּה מָנַעְתָּ אוֹתִי מִלַּעֲשׂוֹת דָּבָר שֶׁהוּא בָאֲפֵלָה, לְפִיכָךְ יִהְיֶה
אוֹתוֹ הָאִישׁ כָּעוּר וּמְפָחָם

R. HUNA ALSO SAID IN R. JOSEPH'S NAME: 'YOU HAVE PREVENTED ME
FROM DOING SOMETHING IN THE DARK [SC. COHABITATION], THERE-
FORE YOUR SEED WILL BE UGLY AND SOILED BY HARD LABOR [LIT. BY
SOOT].'

R. Huna suggested Noah was saying that since Ham prevented him
from doing the act of propagation, which takes place in the darkness, so
he would be punished by having his face darkened by hard labor.

אָמַר רַבִּי חִיָּא בַּר אַבָּא, חָם וְכֶלֶב שִׁמְּשׁוּ בַּתֵּבָה, לְפִיכָךְ יָצָא חָם מְפֻחָם, וְכֶלֶב מְפֻרְסָם
בְּתַשְׁמִישׁוֹ. אָמַר רַבִּי לֵוִי, לְאֶחָד שֶׁקָּבַע מוֹנִיטִין שֶׁלּוֹ, בְּתוֹךְ אָהֳלוֹ שֶׁל מֶלֶךְ, אָמַר הַמֶּלֶךְ, גּוֹזֵר
אֲנִי שֶׁיִּתְפַּחֲמוּ פָּנָיו, וְיִפָּסֵל מַטְבְּעוֹ, כָּךְ, חָם וְכֶלֶב שִׁמְּשׁוּ בַּתֵּבָה, לְפִיכָךְ יָצָא חָם מְפֻחָם, וְכֶלֶב
מְפֻרְסָם בְּתַשְׁמִישׁוֹ.

R. HIYYA SAID: HAM AND THE DOG COPULATED IN THE ARK, THEREFORE
HAM CAME FORTH BLACK-SKINNED WHILE THE DOG PUBLICLY EXPOSES
ITS COPULATION. R. LEVI SAID: THIS MAY BE COMPARED TO ONE WHO
MINTED HIS OWN COINAGE IN THE VERY PALACE OF THE KING, WHERE-
UPON THE KING ORDERED: I DECREE THAT HIS EFFIGY BE DEFACED AND
HIS COINAGE CANCELED. SIMILARLY, HAM AND THE DOG COPULATED IN
THE ARK AND WERE PUNISHED.

The final interpretation is somewhat different. In this interpretation,
R. Levi brings in the fact that Ham was the only person who did not
obey the prohibition against sexual activity in the ark. Indeed, one of the
commentators suggested that Canaan was born out of this illegitimate
activity. That was one of the reasons that Ham was punished. He could
not be spared here because the activity in the ark took place before the
blessing of God to the children of Noah. Therefore, he was eligible to
have his face darkened. The illustration of the king is an allegory to the
ark. If a person acts anti-socially in his own home, he merits criticism.
But to act this way in the palace of a king makes this behavior something out of proportion. Similarly, according to the Zohar, the ark was
the palace of the Holy One, Blessed be He. For Ham to have rebelled
against the orders of his father, in the palace of the Holy One, Blessed
be He, was a negative act of great proportions, something that deserved
punishment.

~

Seed Thoughts

We interpreted "mefuham" as "darkened from hard labor," which relates to the curse that Ham would be a servant to his brothers. The word "Mefuham" means "soiled by soot" and is a play on the name of Ham as well. There are interpretations that render this as "black," since Mitzrayim and Kush were the children of Ham, and today, these are known as the countries of Egypt and Ethiopia, respectively. By these interpretations, it is possible for a person reading this material for the first time to charge our ancestors with racism and to say that the punishment of Ham, in which his features were changed from light to dark, may seem to indicate that all people with similar dark coloring must have shared in this punishment. This is incorrect. Only Ham was punished with his skin changing from white to dark. This has nothing to do with his descendants. Their color or shade was God's decision, how He created the world. Maybe He created us with differing externals in order for us to learn tolerance and acceptance of each other. We may never know the reason. What is certain, however, is that there is variety in God's creation and all of us are human beings regardless of the color of our skin. Ham was punished deservedly, but only he was punished, and the darkening of his skin was only considered a punishment for him. We cannot generalize this to assume that a similar coloring is also a punishment to his descendants; they did nothing wrong and besides this, in general, color is not a punishment.

—

Additional Commentary

The sin of Ham

The reason for the punishment of Ham was not necessarily his behavior toward his father, but for his behavior in the ark. There was a prohibition against sexual activity, which everyone followed with the exception of Ham among the humans and the dog among the animals. It was the result of his sexual activity in the ark that gave birth to Canaan. (*Yefei To'ar*)

The sin of Ham

As was mentioned above, Ham was culpable for engaging in sexual activity in the ark against the prohibition of Noah, who was afraid he would not be able to accommodate new births on the ark. However, Ham sinned in this regard and he was punished by having his face blackened. The reason why he was punished was because all this took place before God's blessing to Noah and his sons. Therefore, the punishment was not canceled out by the blessing. (*Tiferet Tzion*)

When Noah awoke from his sleep

In actual fact, Noah was not asleep. He was in a drunken stupor. When the wine and its affects had disappeared, he then awakened. It is important to make this distinction because if the curses of Noah were made while he was in his stupor, they would not have been effective. But when it says that he awoke from his intoxication, he was completely sober and whatever he said was to be taken seriously. (Aryeh Mirkin)

The sin of Ham, why punish Canaan?

The truth of the matter is that if Canaan did not sin, he would not at all be responsible for any aspect of his father's behavior. However, he was guilty. He was the first to notice Noah's humiliating condition. It was he who informed his father, who then informed his own brothers and after that, whatever ensued is history. Canaan was, in fact, guilty, himself; but the reason that he was the only one punished here was because his father was protected by the blessing of God to Noah and his children. (Aryeh Mirkin)

ח. ('וַיֹּאמֶר בָּרוּךְ ה' אֱלֹהֵי שֵׁם' אָמַר רֵישׁ לָקִישׁ, אַף מִיֶּפֶת עָמְדוּ בְּאָהֳלֵי שֵׁם, 'וַיֹּאמֶר בָּרוּךְ ה'
אֱלֹהֵי שֵׁם, וִיהִי כְנַעַן'. 'יַפְתְּ אֱ-לֹהִים לְיֶפֶת' זֶה כֹּרֶשׁ, שֶׁהוּא גוֹזֵר שֶׁיִּבָּנֶה בֵּית הַמִּקְדָּשׁ, אַף עַל
פִּי כֵן 'וְיִשְׁכֹּן בְּאָהֳלֵי שֵׁם' אֵין שְׁכִינָה שׁוֹרָה אֶלָּא בְּאָהֳלֵי שֵׁם.

8. AND HE SAID: BLESSED BE THE LORD, THE GOD OF SHEM. RESH LAKISH
SAID: EVEN FROM JAPHET CAME [CONVERTS] TO THE TENTS OF SHEM
. . . MAY GOD ENLARGE JAPHET (9:26) – THIS ALLUDES TO CYRUS WHO
ORDERED THE TEMPLE TO BE REBUILT; YET EVEN SO, AND HE SHALL
DWELL IN THE TENTS OF SHEM: THE SHECHINAH DWELLS ONLY IN THE
TENTS OF SHEM.

Although the verse says, "Blessed be the God of Shem," it concludes
by saying that Canaan was a servant למו – *lamo*, which is the plural of
לו – *lahem*, to him. This means that he shall serve both Shem and Japhet.
"Blessed be the God of Shem," therefore, includes many strangers and
proselytes who were descended from Japheth but who joined the Jewish people, the descendants of Shem.

The second section, which begins, יפת אלהים ליפת – *yaft Elokim leYaphet*,
is interpreted to mean that God broadened the outreach of the world
of Japheth, so that it included many outsiders who helped the Jewish
people. One of the most important of these was Cyrus, king of Persia.
The connection to the Jewish people is through חירם – *Hiram*, who was
the representative of the Jewish people in that era. Cyrus (a descendant
of Japheth) ordered the building of the Second Temple,,however, the
Shekhinah rests only in the House of Shem, among the people of Israel.

בַּר קַפָּרָא אָמַר, יִהְיוּ דִבְרֵי תוֹרָה, נֶאֱמָרִים בִּלְשׁוֹנוֹ שֶׁל יֶפֶת בְּתוֹךְ אָהֳלֵי שֵׁם

BAR KAPPARA EXPLAINED IT: LET THE WORDS OF THE TORAH BE UT-
TERED IN THE LANGUAGE OF JAPHETH [SC. GREEK] IN THE TENTS OF
SHEM.

Bar Kappara gave a different and very profound interpretation of this
verse. He explains it to mean that the tradition of Japheth is now broad-

ened so that its language can be used to translate and even interpret the words of the Torah that was given to Israel, who are the descendants of Shem. The translation of the words of the Torah into the language of Japheth can now be accepted in the tents of Shem, meaning in the houses of study of the Jewish people. Thus it is written in Tractate *Megillah* that the scrolls of the Torah can be written in the language of the people. R. Gamliel said that this is not so. We are only permitted to translate the Torah into Greek, as יון – *Yavan* is one of the descendants of Japheth and is the name in Hebrew for Greece (Genesis 10:2).

רַבִּי יוּדָן אָמַר, מִכָּאן לְתַרְגּוּם מִן הַתּוֹרָה, הֲדָא הוּא דִכְתִיב, (נחמיה ח, ח) 'וַיִּקְרְאוּ בַסֵּפֶר תּוֹרַת הָאֱ-לֹהִים' זֶה הַמִּקְרָא, (שם שם, שם) 'מְפֹרָשׁ' זֶה תַּרְגּוּם, (שם שם, שם) 'וְשׂוֹם שֶׂכֶל' אֵלּוּ הַטְּעָמִים, (שם שם, שם) 'וַיָּבִינוּ בַּמִּקְרָא' אֵלּוּ רָאשֵׁי הַפְּסוּקִים, רַבִּי הוּנָא בֶּן לוּלְיָאנִי אוֹמֵר, אֵלּוּ הַהַכְרָעוֹת, וְהָרְאָיוֹת, רַבָּנָן דְּקֵיסָרִין אָמְרִי, מִכָּן לַמָּסֹרֶת

R. JUDAN SAID: FROM THIS WE LEARN THAT A TRANSLATION [OF THE BIBLE IS PERMITTED]. THUS IT IS WRITTEN, AND THEY READ IN THE BOOK, IN THE LAW OF GOD (NEH. 8:8): THIS REFERS TO SCRIPTURE; DISTINCTLY (IBID.): TO A TRANSLATION; AND THEY GAVE THE SENSE (IBID.) – I.E., THE PUNCTUATION ACCENTS; AND CAUSED THEM TO UNDERSTAND THE READING (IBID.)-THIS REFERS TO THE BEGINNINGS OF THE VERSES. R. HIYYA B. LULIANUS SAID: IT REFERS TO THE GRAMMATICAL SEQUENCE [OF WORDS]. THE RABBIS OF CAESAREA SAID: HERE WE HAVE AN ALLUSION TO THE TRADITIONAL TEXT.

In the same Tractate *Megillah*, the question was asked, why was the Greek language chosen above all others as the language into which we could translate the Torah? The answer is that Greek was regarded as the most beautiful of all languages. It was later established that Targum Onkelos, even though it was in Aramaic, was also acceptable as a translation and interpretation of the Torah. For one, the Targum's Aramaic was very close to Hebrew as it is a semitic language and Aramaic is found in the Bible in Genesis, Jeremiah and Daniel.

One of the best examples of these developments in biblical interpretation is found in connection with Ezra and Nechemiah, when all Israel gathered to listen to the words of the Torah. The text there says, "So they read in the book in the Torah of God, distinctly [*meforash*] and gave the sense [*vesom sechel*], and caused them to understand the reading [*vayavinu bamikra*]" (Nehemiah 8:8). The Talmud (*Megillah* 3a) explains this to mean, "They read in the book of the Torah of God" – this is the Bible. The verse then continues with the word מפורש – *mephorash* (distinctly), which is said to refer to "targum," meaning a translation of the text. The next words in the text are, ושום שכל – *vesom sekhel* ("and gave the sense"), which refers to the end of verses. Then it continues, "and caused them to understand" – which is understood to refer to the טעמים – *te'amim*, the cantillation for the reading of the Torah. Many parts of the Torah are difficult to understand and have to be seen in relationship to what came first and what comes after. This was the work of the sages of Israel during the time of Ezra and Nechemiah during the time of the Second Temple.

רַבִּי זְעֵירָא וְרַבִּי חֲנַנְאֵל בְּשֵׁם רַבִּי, אֲפִלּוּ אָדָם, רָגִיל בַּתּוֹרָה כְּעֶזְרָא, לֹא יְהֵא קוֹרֵא מִפִּיו וְכוֹתֵב, וְהָא תְנֵי, מַעֲשֶׂה שֶׁהָיָה רַבִּי מֵאִיר בְּאַסְיָא, וְלֹא הָיָה שָׁם מְגִלַּת אֶסְתֵּר, וְקָרָא לוֹ מִפִּיו, וּכְתָבָהּ, תַּמָּן אָמְרִין, שְׁתֵּי מְגִלּוֹת כָּתַב, גָּנַז אֶת הָרִאשׁוֹנָה, וְקִיֵּם אֶת הַשְּׁנִיָּה.

R. ZERA AND R. HANANEL SAID: EVEN IF A MAN IS AS WELL-VERSED IN THE TORAH AS EZRA, HE MUST NOT READ IT FROM MEMORY AND WRITE IT. BUT IT WAS TAUGHT: IT ONCE HAPPENED THAT R. MEIR VISITED ASIA MINOR, AND FINDING THERE NO SCROLL OF ESTHER, HE READ IT FROM MEMORY AND WROTE IT? THERE [IN BABYLONIA] THEY SAY: HE WROTE TWO SCROLLS, SUPPRESSED THE FIRST AND KEPT THE SECOND AS VALID [FOR USE].

R. Zeira adds the thought that no one, not even the most accomplished scholar of the Bible, has the right either to read or study it by heart or write it from memory. One must always use the text and look at it. From the story of R. Meir, we learn that this rule is important, but cannot always be observed. Sometimes the demands of life enter the picture and force even great scholars to modify this rule temporarily. Thus, since R. Meir could not find a copy of the Megillah from which to read, he wrote his own from memory, even though he knew that this was generally not considered acceptable behavior.

Seed Thoughts

When the Torah is lifted up in the synagogue during *hagbah*, we proclaim, "This is the Torah that Moses placed before the people of Israel, according to God, by the hand of Moses." Based on the above midrash, it seems it might have been more accurate to say, " . . . g . . given by God by the hand of Moses *and* the sages of Israel." Without the activity of the sages of Israel, beginning with Ezra and Nechemiah and continuing into the second century, the Jewish people would never have properly understood the Torah, nor would they have been able to follow it.

Notice that the midrash gives the example "even if one is well versed in the Torah as Ezra." Ezra was almost like a second Moses according to the Talmud, since he re-established the written tradition, removing mistakes from the tradition. God gave the Torah, but the human element was in the area of preserving the Torah so that it could remain as authentic as possible and be relevant over all the centuries. This is a possible way to interpret the story of Rabbi Meir, who recalled the scroll of Esther by heart and then wrote it down. The scroll of Esther was written, according to our tradition (*Megillah* 7a), by Divine inspiration (*ruach hakodesh*), but preserving that tradition, along with that of the whole Bible, is the task of all the generations.

Our midrash deals with the question of translation, which is of tremendous importance. The translations of the Torah were originally very limited and guarded, permitted only in the Greek language, for instance, the Septuagint, and then later, the Aramaic language was also used, such as Targum Onkelos. That gradually expanded to other languages as well, based on the principle of the beauty of Japheth in the tents of Shem.

―

Additional Commentary

Some thoughts on the Torah

It is possible to understand Bar Kappara's position that one is forbidden to write or to quote the Torah in any other language besides Hebrew, and only in the style of print known as Ashuri. However, to interpret the Torah, either in written fashion or oral, by means of a different language is permitted. What is the source of this permission? The verse that says, *yeft Elokim leYafet veyishko be'ohaleh Shem* – God made Japheth beautiful and he dwelled in the tents of Shem. What it means is that the true resting place of Torah is in the tents of Shem alone, but interpreting its beauty is permitted in other languages and it also helps more of us understand the teachings that we find in the Prophets and the Writings. (Aryeh Mirkin)

The two Megillot of R. Meir

The first Megillah, R. Meir wrote from his own memory. The second one, he analyzed very carefully, changed it, and improved it. The first was discarded because it was not acceptable since it was from memory. (Aryeh Mirkin)

א. 'בְּנֵי יֶפֶת גֹּמֶר וּמָגוֹג' אָמַר רַבִּי שְׁמוּאֵל בַּר אַמִּי, זוֹ אַפְרִיקָה וְגֶרְמַנְיָא, וּמָדַי, וּמַקְדוֹנְיָא,
אִיסַנְיָא. וְתוּבֵיָה, 'תִּירָס' רַבִּי סִימוֹן אָמַר, זוֹ פָּרָס, רַבָּנָן אָמְרִי, תוּרְקִי.(ג) 'וּבְנֵי גֹמֶר אַשְׁכְּנַז וְרִיפַת
וְתֹגַרְמָא' אַסְיָא, וְהַדְיָף, וְגֶרְמַנְיָא, רַבִּי בֶּרֶכְיָה אָמַר, גֶּרְמָנִיקְיָא.

1. THE SONS OF JAPHETH: GOMER, AND MAGOG, ETC. (10:2). R. SAMUEL
B. AMMI SAID: THESE ARE AFRICA, GERMANIA, MEDIA, MACEDONIA AND
MYSIA. AND TIRAS: R. SIMON SAID: THAT IS THE EUPHRATES REGION;
THE RABBIS SAID: IT IS THRACE. AND THE SONS OF GOMER: ASHKENAZ,
AND RIPHATH AND TOGARMAH (10:3): I.E., ASIA, ADIABENE, AND GER-
MANIA. R. BEREKIAH SAID: GERMANICIA.

In this midrash, the sages attempt to find the connection between the
verse describing the children of Japheth and the development of some
of the countries or civilizations in either their contemporary time or in
the development of these nations up to their present state. We have, in
the beginning, Gomer, who is interpreted as being Africa, though in the
Talmud, it is Germany. There is a note by the commentaries that the
Africa mentioned here is not the same one as we know, the continent
south of the Mediterranean, but rather, it refers to north of the Mediterranean, which we know as the countries of Italy, Romania, etc. The text
tries to establish the connection with some of these countries. Yosiphon
notes that *Germania* is what we, today, call France. There is a certain
amount of difference of opinion here among the sages. For example, regarding the country called Tiras, R. Simon claims this is Persia, whereas
the rabbis claim that it refers to Turkey. How do any of them prove this?
From the name Tiras itself – the last two letters, that is to say, רס, makes
R. Simon feel that it has to do with פרס – *Paras*, meaning Persia. On
the other hand, the rabbis feel that it has to do with the first two letters
תי, referring to Turkey. The connection between Gomer and *Germania*
could also be made, as Germany was settled by the Goths, and there is a
certain connection between Gomer and Gothic.

'וּבְנֵי יָוָן אֱלִישָׁה וְתַרְשִׁישׁ' אֶלְקִיסְטְרוֹס, אִיטַלְיָא, דַּרְדַנְיָא, כָּתוּב אֶחָד אוֹמֵר, 'וְדֹדָנִים' וְכָתוּב
אֶחָד אוֹמֵר, (דה"א א, ז) 'וְרוֹדָנִים, רַבִּי סִימוֹן וְרַבִּי חָנִין, רַבִּי סִימוֹן אָמַר, 'דוֹדָנִים', שֶׁהֵם בְּנֵי
דוֹדִין שֶׁל יִשְׂרָאֵל, 'רוֹדָנִים', שֶׁהֵן בָּאִים וְרוֹדִין אוֹתָם, אָמַר רַבִּי חֲנִינָא, בְּשָׁעָה שֶׁיִּשְׂרָאֵל נְתוּנִים
בַּעֲלִיָּה אָנוּן אָמְרִין לְהוֹן, בְּנֵי דוֹדְכֶן אֲנַן, וּבְשָׁעָה שֶׁהֵם נְתוּנִין בִּירִידָה הֵם בָּאִים וְרוֹדִין אוֹתָם.

AND THE SONS OF JAVAN: ELISHAH, AND TARSHISH, KITHIM, AND
DODANIM (10:4): I.E., HELLAS AND TARAS [TARANTUM], ITALIA, AND
DARDANIA. ONE VERSE CALLS THEM DODANIM, WHILE ANOTHER VERSE
CALLS THEM RODANIM (I CHRON. 1:7)? R. SIMON SAID: THEY ARE CALLED
DODANIM BECAUSE THEY ARE THE DESCENDANTS OF ISRAEL'S KINSMEN
(DODIM); 'RODANIM,' BECAUSE THEY COME AND OPPRESS (RODIM)
THEM. R. HANAN SAID: WHEN ISRAEL ARE ELEVATED THEY SAY TO THEM,
'WE ARE THE DESCENDANTS OF YOUR KINSMEN,' BUT WHEN THEY ARE
LOW THEY COME AND OPPRESS THEM.

In this section, there is a midrash contrasting two words. One of the place names of the children of Japheth and the children of Yavan, is "Dodanim." But this name appears elsewhere, in the Book of Chronicles, where it begins with a ר, making it Rodanim. The word *dodanim* means those that are close to us, friendly, almost part of the family. The word *rodanim* means those more authoritative, persecutors, etc. Over the years, there were certain countries that were *dodanim* for the Jews, and others were largely *rodanim*, such as Rome, which caused the ultimate destruction of the Second Temple and the exile of the Jewish people.

―

Seed Thoughts

Contrasting the relationship between the word *dodanim* in the Torah and *rodanim* in the Book of Chronicles lends itself to an important, yet unfortunate aspect of Jewish history. Let us begin with the example taken from the text itself. There are many places in the Talmud describing the relationships between the leaders and scholars of the Jewish people as well as their Roman contemporaries. There are many stories also of outstanding women, described in the Torah as distinguished people, from whose behavior we have much to learn. When the rabbis spoke of and commented on Roman law, at this stage they were as *dodanim* – friendly and in close contact. Yet, this was the same civilization that later destroyed the Temple and contributed to the Jewish exile of the past 2000 years. They were *rodanim*. Even after the Roman empire disappeared, the same type of fate continued up until our times. Many times, the Jews achieved great significance in their respective communities, even up to the Second World War. They were outstanding in German life and professions. Great scholars emerged. And yet, this civilization created the Holocaust. The *dodanim* became *rodanim*. Now, Germany has begun to move back and has become an ally of Israel. Maybe they will be once again *dodanim* to the Jewish people. There is another example: The tenth to the fifteenth centuries was a great time in the Spanish community, as many things began to evolve and be created. They describe these years as the Golden Age It was a great time for humanity in general as well, as it brought in the Renaissance. We have many examples of *dodanim* converting to *rodanim* and dragging other people along out of fear. Sometimes the people fear their authorities, and sometimes they succumb to propaganda. This is unfortunate. Many cultures are becoming as *rodanim*, persecutors. Hopefully, these people will see that they are merely succumbing to fear and will return to be *dodanim* and help improve this world in a peaceful way.

ב. 'וּבְנֵי חָם כּוּשׁ וּמִצְרַיִם וּפוּט וּכְנָעַן' אָמַר רַבִּי שִׁמְעוֹן בֶּן לָקִישׁ, הָיִינוּ סְבוּרִים שֶׁנִּתְבַּלְעָה
מִשְׁפַּחְתּוֹ שֶׁל פּוּט, בָּא יְחֶזְקֵאל וּפֵרֵשׁ, (יחזקאל ל, ה) 'כּוּשׁ וּפוּט וְלוּד וְכָל הָעֶרֶב וּבְנֵי אֶרֶץ
הַבְּרִית אִתָּם בַּחֶרֶב יִפֹּלוּ'.

2. AND THE SONS OF HAM: CUSH, AND MIZRAIM, AND PUT, AND CANAAN
(10:6). RESH LAKISH SAID: WE MIGHT HAVE THOUGHT THAT THE FAMILY
OF PUT WAS ABSORBED, HAD NOT EZEKIEL COME AND EXPLICITLY ENU-
MERATED HIM: ETHIOPIA, AND PUT, AND LUD, AND ALL THE MINGLED
PEOPLE . . . SHALL FALL (EZEK. 30:5).

T he text did not include the genealogy of Put. This prompted the sages
to feel that his family must have been absorbed (literally, "swallowed
up") by the other families through marriages and other relationships.
This view was corrected by the prophet Ezekiel, who included Put as a
separate family during his time.

'וְכוּשׁ יָלַד אֶת נִמְרֹד', הֲדָא הוּא דִכְתִיב, (תהלים ז, א) 'שִׁגָּיוֹן לְדָוִד אֲשֶׁר שָׁר לַה' עַל דִּבְרֵי כוּשׁ בֶּן
יְמִינִי' רַבִּי יְהוֹשֻׁעַ בַּר נְחֶמְיָה, בְּשֵׁם רַבִּי חֲנִינָה בֶּן יִצְחָק, כְּנֶגֶד בִּימָה שֶׁל רָשָׁע אֲמָרוֹ, וְכִי כוּשִׁי
הֲוָה, אֶלָּא שֶׁעָשָׂה כְּמַעֲשֵׂה נִמְרוֹד, הֲדָא הוּא דִכְתִיב, עַל כֵּן יֵאָמַר נִמְרֹד גִּבּוֹר צַיִד לִפְנֵי ה' אֵין
כְּתִיב כָּאן, אֶלָּא 'כְּנִמְרֹד גִּבּוֹר צַיִד', מַה זֶה, צָד אֶת הַבְּרִיּוֹת בְּפִיהֶם, אַף זֶה, צָד אֶת הַבְּרִיּוֹת
בְּפִיהֶם, לָא גְנַבְתְּ, מַן גְּנַב עִמָּךְ, לָא קְטַלְתְּ, מַן קְטַל עִמָּךְ.

AND CUSH BEGOT NIMROD (10:8). THIS EXPLAINS THE TEXT, SHIGGAION
OF DAVID, WHICH HE SANG UNTO THE LORD, CONCERNING CUSH A BEN-
JAMITE ISH YEMINI (PS. 7:1). R. JOSHUA B. R. NEHEMIAH SAID IN THE
NAME OF R. HANINA B. ISAAC: HE [DAVID] COMPOSED THIS WITH REF-
ERENCE TO THE SEAT OF JUDGMENT OF THAT WICKED MAN. WAS THEN
ESAU A CUSHITE? [HE IS SO CALLED] BECAUSE HE ACTED LIKE NIMROD.
HENCE IT IS WRITTEN, LIKE NIMROD A MIGHTY HUNTER BEFORE THE
LORD (10:9): IT IS NOT WRITTEN, NIMROD [WAS A MIGHTY HUNTER],
BUT LIKE NIMROD: JUST AS THE ONE SNARED PEOPLE BY THEIR WORDS,
SO DID THE OTHER [ESAU, I.E., ROME] SNARE PEOPLE BY THEIR WORDS,
SAYING, '[TRUE,] YOU HAVE NOT STOLEN, [BUT TELL US] WHO WAS YOUR

PARTNER IN THE THEFT; YOU HAVE NOT KILLED, BUT WHO WAS YOUR
ACCOMPLICE IN THE MURDER.'

Many of the commentators (Matnot Kehuna and RZWE) suggest
that Cush in this text refers to Esav. Accordingly, *yemini* refers to Isaac.
One of the reasons for this interpretation is that Esav is often compared
to Nimrod. The text describes certain people as behaving כנמרוד – *ke-
Nimrod*, "like Nimrod." One of the problems is that there is a text which
says that Cush was the father of Nimrod. The commentators make many
efforts to reinterpret the word ילד – *yalad* here as not being "begot," but
rather as being from the word תולדות – *toladot*, meaning that Cush and
Nimrod were simply identified with each other. There is a line in the
Talmud saying that Cush, Nimrod and Amraphel were one and the
same person. These are difficult passages to comprehend. The sages use
the expression "like Nimrod" to show a spiritual connection between
Nimrod and Esav. Both are being described as being outstanding as
hunters of animals.

Furthermore, Esav was known as Edom (from the word "red") based
on the fact that his complexion and hair was reddish. But Edom in the
midrash refers to Rome, and in this respect, the expression ציד בפיו –
tzayid befiv, applies to both Nimrod and Esav. It takes the concept of a
hunter of animals and applies it to human beings, in terms of harassment
with one's speech. The identification of Nimrod with Esav was meant to
imply that these verbal snares and questioning trickery were used by the
Romans in their judicial courts. To harass Jews who appeared before
them for judgment, (Aryeh Mirkin)

⁓

Seed Thoughts

The concept of *tzayid befiv*, harassment by means of the mouth or
speech, is a very dramatic description. One can be a "hunter" of human
beings, as suggested by this concept, which in this context means being willing to use every questioning technique to trick an unsuspecting
victim and force him even to confess to a crime without his realizing
that this is what the "hunter" was saying or trying to do.

The important lesson that emerges out of all of this is that speech is
not only one of God's greatest gifts to mankind, the *abuse* of speech can
become one of the most severe dangers facing the human being. The
abuse of speech can take many forms, not only in the legal situation of

courts of law, but in ordinary, everyday relationships of human beings. One person cursing another, for example, is an abominable abuse of speech. The use of swear words in any language probably has its origin in cursing. Using such words never enhances an argument, but it does have the result of hurting another person. Speech is one of God's greatest gifts; it should never be used as a weapon, but only as a blessing.

Additional Commentary

What difference does it make for the Put family to have been absorbed?

The Torah detailed the descendants of Japheth and Ham in order to inform us that seventy nations made up the world at that time. They included fourteen nations from the descendants of Japheth, thirty nations from the descendants of Ham and twenty-six from the descendants of Shem. By the same token, seventy princes and generals and heads of state descended from Abraham. Corresponding to them, there were seventy who descended from Jacob. These were the roots of all Israel, as explained by Rabbi Yitzchak Luria, of blessed memory, known as the Holy Ari, in his book called *Sefer haGilgulim*. Therefore, it is important that all these seventy nations should be accounted for, in order to sustain the world. That is why the prophet Ezekiel emphasized that Cush and Put were to be included. Put was included to inform us that it was a nation in itself; however, because it was a weak kingdom, it became secondary to the members of the Cush family and this is why it was not mentioned in its own right. (*Tiferet Tzion*)

Who are Cush and Nimrod

The Talmud maintains that Cush, himself, was Nimrod. It uses three names for the same person: Cush, Nimrod and Amraphel. How, then, do we explain the verse that reads, "Cush begot Nimrod"? Cush introduced rebellion into the world. As it says later on, he was called Nimrod because of this, since the Hebrew word for rebellion is *mered*, which shares the same root as Nimrod. As for why the term "begot" was used, very often this term is used to describe the transmission of certain spiritual values. The term *toladot* is often used to describe this concept as well, since it comes from the same root as *yalad*, begot, and refers to that which is inherited from others. For example, it says, "These are the generations [*toladot*] of Noah, Noah was a righteous man" – his righteousness was described as his *toladot*, his spiritual offspring, his good deeds. In the case of Cush, he will always be associated with *mered*, rebellion.

The Midrash interprets things this way because if Nimrod were truly the son of Cush, he would have been included in the preceding verse, where it lists the sons of Cush. We cannot accept the interpretation that Nimrod was not included because he did not have a family. In all other cases, all the descendants were included whether or not they had their own families. If we accept the fact that Cush was Nimrod, it helps us to explain the verse that was quoted, *"shigayon leDavid."* The problem is that nowhere in Scripture do we find a person whose name was Cush ben Yemini, from whom David prayed to be protected. It has been interpreted that the person referred to was Esav, who followed in the pattern of Nimrod – whose real name was Cush – and who was called "ben Yemini" because he lived in the south of Eretz Yisroel. (*Tiferet Tzion*)

ג. 'הוּא הָיָה גִבֹּר צַיִד לִפְנֵי ה'', חֲמִשָּׁה, 'הוּא' לְטוֹבָה, וַחֲמִשָּׁה, 'הוּא' לְרָעָה, 'הוּא הָיָה גִבֹּר צַיִד
לִפְנֵי ה'', (בראשית לו, מג) 'הוּא עֵשָׂו אֲבִי אֱדוֹם', (במדבר כו, ט) 'הוּא דָתָן וַאֲבִירָם', (דה"ב כח, כב)
'הוּא הַמֶּלֶךְ אָחָז', (אסתר א, א) 'הוּא אֲחַשְׁוֵרוֹשׁ', וַחֲמִשָּׁה הֵם לְטוֹבָה, (דה"א א, כז) 'אַבְרָם הוּא
אַבְרָהָם', (שמות ו, ו) 'הוּא מֹשֶׁה וְאַהֲרֹן', (שם שם, כו) 'הוּא אַהֲרֹן וּמֹשֶׁה', (עי' דה"ב לב, ל) 'הוּא
חִזְקִיָּה הַמֶּלֶךְ', (עזרא ז, ו) 'הוּא עֶזְרָא עָלָה מִבָּבֶל'

3. HE (HU) WAS A MIGHTY HUNTER, ETC. FIVE TIMES 'HU' IS FOUND
DENOTING A WICKED CHARACTER, AND FIVE TIMES DENOTING A GOOD
ONE. IT IS EMPLOYED FIVE TIMES TO DENOTE A WICKED CHARACTER: HE
(HU) WAS A MIGHTY HUNTER; THIS (HU) IS ESAU THE FATHER OF THE
EDOMITES (GEN. 36:43); THESE ARE (HU) THAT DATHAN AND ABIRAM
(NUM. 26:9); THIS SAME (HU) KING AHAZ (II CHRON. 28:22); THIS IS (HU)
AHASUERUS (EST. 1:1). FIVE TIMES 'HU' DENOTES A GOOD CHARACTER:
ABRAM – THE SAME IS (HU) ABRAHAM (I CHRON. 1:27); THESE ARE (HU)
THAT MOSES AND AARON (EX. 6:27); THESE ARE (HU) THAT AARON AND
MOSES (IBID., 26); THIS SAME (HU) HEZEKIAH (II CHRON. 32:30); THIS
(HU) EZRA WENT UP (EZRA 7:6).

One of the problems that aroused the interest of the sages was that
every time הוּא – *hu*, "he," was mentioned in the verses quoted, it was
seemingly superfluous. Each of these verses could easily have been
understood without the word *hu*. Seeing, therefore, that *hu* does occur,
there must be a reason for it. This midrash explains the reason.

How do we understand the fact that the people in the circumstances
were described either as evil or as good? And, why were these particular individuals singled out? The interpretation seems to be that the
people who are described as evil here are those that were consistently
evil until the very end, and, similarly, those who are described as good
or righteous are deemed so from the beginning of their lifetime until
the very end, without interruption or compromise. The commentators
spent a lot of time proving these contentions and disputing much of the
criticism that some of the evildoers were not always evil, and some of
the righteous ones were not always righteous. Nevertheless, this is the

interpretation that all agree explains these statements most authentically.

רַבִּי בֶּרֶכְיָה בְּשֵׁם רַבִּי חָנִין, אַף אִית לָן חַד 'הוּא' טָבָא מִן כֻּלְּהוֹן, (תהלים קה, ז) 'הוּא ה' אֱלֹהֵינוּ', שֶׁמַּדַּת רַחֲמָיו לְעוֹלָם.

R. BEREKIAH SAID IN THE NAME OF THE RABBIS OF THE OTHER COUNTRY [I.E., BABYLONIA]: WE HAVE ANOTHER THAT IS BETTER THAN ALL: HE IS (HU) THE LORD OUR GOD (PS. 105:7), TEACHING THAT HIS MERCY ENDURES FOR EVER.

Whereas the appearances of *hu* in the previous verses – whether referring to the five good names or the five evil names – are linguistically superfluous, there is one verse wherein this word is not only not superfluous, but it is very important, very meaningful and very necessary. That is the *Hu* that applies to The Holy One, Blessed be He. God transcends the world. Good and evil cannot possibly apply to Him in any way. The only concepts that might apply to Him are reward and punishment, and this, only in relation to how He behaves toward mankind.

—

Seed Thoughts

In an Additional Commentary section that follows, the *Yefei To'ar* offers five reasons why people who do evil continue to do so and people who try to live righteously continue to do so. When we examine the arguments that are offered, the wording may seem different, but the reasons why evil people tend to remain evil seem to be very similar to the reasons why good people generally continue to remain good. In other words, our behavior is not determined by instincts that we cannot control or by certain influences of society and the world, forcing our response. It has to do with choices. Evil people remain evil because they choose to. Conversely, good people tend to do good because they make the right choices. The ability to make choices is one of the most precious assets of freedom. To be taught how to make those choices that are moral ought to be the main thrust of education. Good people can be produced. So can evil people, unfortunately. Our job, as lovers of Torah, must be to teach the right choices and to motivate young an old to see these choices as the greatest gift to mankind.

—

Additional Commentary

Motivations that are used to change evil to good or good to evil

There are five ways that seem to be successful in influencing an evil person to choose good.

The first way is knowledge and understanding. In one's hurry to act, one can make mistakes and make the wrong choices. Therefore, correct knowledge and understanding can affect the person's abillity to choose wisely. In this vein, it is said that even though Nimrod knew about God – as the rabbis interpreted the phrase "before God" to mean that he had some understanding of the meaning of God – nevertheless, his knowledge and intelligence did not help him. He remained with his evil ways all of his days.

The second way is via old age and physical weakness, which often make a person wish to repent. However, it is said about Esav that even though sleep and weakness fell upon him, nevertheless, he remained attached to his evil ways.

The third way of motivating a person to leave his evil ways might be if good people criticize him, warn him or try to improve him with the hope that with their intervention, he would return to the good path. This brings to mind Dathan and Aviram, about whom we read that even though Moshe visited them in their tents to set them straight, and even to appease them, nevertheless, they turned their backs upon him and made their disagreement permanent.

The fourth way is through the experience of suffering and difficulties, which one would think would humble a person and encourage him to return to God, as is often the case. This was not the case, however, regarding Ahaz, the king of Israel, according to the Midrash. Even though Ahaz and his people were in great trouble, as described by Isaiah, he still did not change his evil ways. The more sorrows he had, the more he transgressed against God.

The fifth way occurs when a person reaches a status of importance and his reputation becomes significant to him to the point that he would be embarrassed to be discovered doing evil things. Nevertheless, in this respect, King Ahashverosh, before he became king, was in charge of the horses of Nebuchadnezzar, and even as he grew in rank and authority, he still did not elevate his standards of behavior, but acted the very same way with the people in his court as he did with the horses of Nebuchadnezzar.

By the same token, there are five ways which one may think to

Parashah Thirty-Seven, Midrash Three 397

change a person from a good way to a bad way, God forbid. The first, similarly, has to do with knowledge and intelligence. Unfortunately, we have the example of Elisha b. Abuyah, who, as a result of his intense research, forsook the basic tenets of Judaism. Nevertheless, Abraham our father also did tremendous thinking, but in his case, it blessed him with tremendous revelation, to the point that all the kings of his time sought his advice, help and encouragement. Despite all this prestige and recognition, he remained faithful to God and did not allow himself to be influenced to follow false ways. In fact, he guarded his covenant with God until the last day of his life.

The second challenge to the good life is if a person is overcome by old age or weakness in either heart or mind, which can influence his or her behavior. The example is brought of Yochanan the High Priest, who became bitter in his old age. On the other hand, Moshe and Aharon, even though they were in their eighties, showed tremendous leadership in Torah and faith in God.

The third challenge to living a life of goodness is if one loses the teacher who is most influential to his life. This is what the sages said about King Solomon. He did not marry the daughter of Pharaoh until after Shimi b. Gera was no longer alive. However, in the case of Ezra, even though he lost his great teacher, Baruch b. Niryah, nevertheless, he remained righteous and his love of Eretz Yisroel remained strong.

The fourth challenge to the ethical life is experience of suffering and poverty, which embitters a person's life. However, Hizkiyahu, even though he was suffering, never lost his faith in God and His ultimate salvation.

The fifth way that a person may change his ways and stray from the good path is if he achieves a status of importance. He may become very proud and forget about God. However, the Midrash recalls David, who was described as "the little one" when Samuel anointed him as king, and who always remained humble, both before and even after becoming king. (*Yefei To'ar*)

ד. 'וַתְּהִי רֵאשִׁית מַמְלַכְתּוֹ בָּבֶל וְאֶרֶךְ וְאַכַּד וְכַלְנֵה', חֶרֶן, וּנְצִיבִין, וְקַטוֹסְפִין. 'בְּאֶרֶץ שִׁנְעָר'
זוֹ בָבֶל, לָמָּה נִקְרֵא שְׁמָהּ שִׁנְעָר, אָמַר רֵישׁ לָקִישׁ, שֶׁשָּׁם נִנְעֲרוּ מֵתֵי דוֹר הַמַּבּוּל. דָּבָר אַחֵר,
'שִׁנְעָר' שֶׁהִיא מְנֹעֶרֶת מִן הַמִּצְווֹת, בְּלֹא תְרוּמָה וּבְלֹא מַעַשְׂרוֹת, וּבְלֹא שְׁבִיעִית. דָּבָר אַחֵר,
'שִׁנְעָר' שֶׁהֵם מֵתִים בְּתַשְׁנִיק, בְּלֹא נֵר, וּבְלֹא מֶרְחָץ. דָּבָר אַחֵר, 'שִׁנְעָר' שֶׁשָּׂרֶיהָ מֵתִים נְעָרִים.
דָּבָר אַחֵר, 'שִׁנְעָר', שֶׁשָּׂרֶיהָ מַבִּיטִין בַּתּוֹרָה עַד שֶׁהֵן נְעָרִים. דָּבָר אַחֵר, 'שִׁנְעָר' שֶׁהֶעֱמִידָה
שׂוֹנֵא וְעָר, לְהַקָּדוֹשׁ בָּרוּךְ הוּא, וְאִי זֶה, זֶה נְבוּכַדְנֶצַּר.

**4. AND THE BEGINNING OF HIS KINGDOM WAS BABEL, AND ERECH, AND
ACCAD, AND CALNEH (10:10): I.E., EDESSA, NISIBIS, AND CTESIPHON. IN
THE LAND OF SHINAR: THIS IS BABYLONIA. SHINAR CONNOTES THAT IT
IS EMPTIED (SHEMENU'ERETH) OF PRECEPTS, LACKING THE PRECEPTS
OF TERUMAH, TITHES, AND THE SABBATICAL YEAR. SHINAR CONNOTES
THAT ITS INHABITANTS DIE IN ANGUISH, WITHOUT A LIGHT AND WITH-
OUT A BATH. SHINAR CONNOTES THAT ITS PRINCES (SARIM) DIE YOUNG
(NE'ARIM). SHINAR FINALLY CONNOTES THAT ITS PRINCES STUDY THE
TORAH IN THEIR YOUTH.**

The first section of this midrash offers many various translations and
interpretations for the name Shinar. The Hebrew, שנער – *Shin'ar*, is the
name for the entire region we are now discussing. In English it would
probably be described as Babylonia. Babel or Babylon was the name of
the important city that arose in that region. The various names and interpretations are well translated in the English and are self-explanatory.

'מִן הָאָרֶץ הַהִוא יָצָא אַשּׁוּר', מִן הָעֵצָה הַהִיא יָצָא אַשּׁוּר, כֵּיוָן שֶׁרָאָה אוֹתָן בָּאִים לַחֲלֹק עַל
הַקָּדוֹשׁ בָּרוּךְ הוּא, פָּנָה מֵאַרְצוֹ, אָמַר לוֹ הַקָּדוֹשׁ בָּרוּךְ הוּא, אַתְּ יָצָאתָ לְךָ מֵאַרְבַּע, חַיֶּיךָ, שֶׁאֲנִי
פּוֹרֵעַ לְךָ, וְנוֹתֵן לְךָ אַרְבַּע, 'וַיִּבֶן אֶת נִינְוֵה, וְאֶת רְחֹבֹת עִיר, וְאֶת כָּלַח, וְאֶת רֶסֶן', תְּלָתְסָר, וְלֹא
עָשָׂה, אֶלָּא, כֵּיוָן שֶׁבָּא וְנִשְׁתַּתֵּף עִמָּהֶן בְּחָרְבַּן בֵּית הַמִּקְדָּשׁ, אָמַר לוֹ הַקָּדוֹשׁ בָּרוּךְ הוּא, אֶתְמוֹל
אֶפְרוֹחַ עַכְשָׁו בֵּיצָה, אֶתְמוֹל מַפְרִיחַ מִצְווֹת וּמַעֲשִׂים טוֹבִים, עַכְשָׁו מְכוֹנָן כַּבֵּיצָה, אֶתְמְהָא,
לְפִיכָךְ, (תהלים פג, ט) 'הָיוּ זְרוֹעַ לִבְנֵי לוֹט סֶלָה', לְלוֹט.

**OUT OF THAT LAND WENT FORTH ASSHUR (10:11): FROM THAT SCHEME
ASSHUR DISSOCIATED HIMSELF. WHEN HE SAW THEM COME TO WAGE
WAR AGAINST THE HOLY ONE, BLESSED BE HE, HE QUITTED HIS COUN-**

TRY. SAID GOD TO HIM: 'THOU HAST DEPARTED FROM FOUR PLACES; BY
THY LIFE! I WILL GIVE THEE FOUR'; HENCE, AND BUILDED NINEVEH,
AND REHOBOTH-IR, AND CALAH, AND RESEN, [THE LAST-NAMED BEING]
TALSAR. YET HE [ASSHUR] DID NOT REMAIN CONSTANT [IN HIS RIGH-
TEOUSNESS], AND WHEN HE CAME AND JOINED THEM IN DESTROYING
THE TEMPLE GOD SAID TO HIM: 'YESTERDAY A CHICKEN AND TO-DAY AN
EGG! YESTERDAY THOU DIDST SOAR ALOFT WITH RELIGIOUS ACTIONS
AND NOBLE DEEDS, WHILST NOW THOU ART SHUT UP LIKE [A CHICKEN
IN] AN EGG'; THEREFORE, THEY HAVE BEEN AN ARM TO THE CHILDREN
OF LOTT (PS. 83:9), WHICH MEANS, FOR A CURSE (LE-LEWAT).

There are a number of interesting points in this section. For one thing,
the biblical text deals with the children of Ham. But Asshur is descended
from Shem. This may explain his behavior, when he refused to go along
with the decisions of his peers to build the tower of Babel, looking upon
that development as a rebellion against God. He, therefore, did not accept that course of action and removed himself to another area. This was
the original behavior of Asshur, the patriarch of his family. His children
and grandchildren, however, did not follow in this way and one of his
descendants, Nebuchadnezzar, destroyed the first Temple.

'וְאֶת רֶסֶן בֵּין נִינְוֵה וּבֵין כָּלַח, וְגוֹ'", אֵין אָנוּ יוֹדְעִים אִם 'רֶסֶן' הִיא הַגְּדוֹלָה, וְאִם 'נִינְוֵה' הִיא
הַגְּדוֹלָה, מִן מַה דִּכְתִיב, (יונה ג, ג) 'וְנִינְוֵה הָיְתָה עִיר גְּדוֹלָה לֵאלֹהִים מַהֲלַךְ שְׁלֹשֶׁת יָמִים', הֱוֵי,
נִינְוֵה הִיא הַגְּדוֹלָה.

THE SAME IS THE GREAT CITY. WE DO NOT KNOW WHETHER RESEN IS
THE GREAT CITY OR NINEVEH; SINCE, HOWEVER, IT IS WRITTEN, NOW
NINEVEH WAS AN EXCEEDING GREAT CITY (JONAH 3:3), IT FOLLOWS
THAT NINEVEH IS THE GREAT CITY.

What prompted this discussion is that the word הגדולה – hagdolah,
seems to be misplaced in that sentence and could be understood by
some as referring to Resen as the big city. The verse of Jonah, however,
is conclusive and establishes firmly that only Nineveh deserves the title
of a great city.

—

Seed Thoughts

This midrash contains a most unusual parable or proverb. It has to do
with a chicken and an egg. Strictly speaking, the word אפרוח – ephro'ah
does not necessarily refer to a fully grown chicken, but to what we nor-

mally refer to as a chick or a very young chicken, ultimately to become a fully grown fowl. This parable is used to refer to Asshur, who started his career in this midrash as a tzaddik, defending the will of God, and ended as a *rasha*, an evil one, when his descendents collaborated with the Babylonians in the destruction of the first Temple. The verse says that this egg started out by being a chick, with hope it would develop into a fowl, but instead, it reverted back to an egg, meaning back to nothing. There are two ways of understanding these symbols: Once a chick leaves an egg, that ends the life of the egg and brings spirit to the chick. What happened with Asshur was that in reverting back to his origins, it was as though he reverted back to the egg, giving up all life, content and meaning to his spiritual existence.

Here is the second another interpretation: An egg is protected by its shell, as a result of which, the embryo cannot leave until its time has come. Thus, by reverting back to the status of an egg, there was no way for Asshur to change his behavior or improve it. He could no longer leave the egg, so to speak, and remain; therefore, that ended his spiritual progress. (*HaMidrash HaMevo'ar*)

—

Additional Commentary

A candle and a bathing pool (A)

It seems as though Babylon or Babel, for all its political power later on, was often suffering from poverty. There is a saying that if the poverty of the world could be divided into ten units, nine would be shared by Babylon and the last tenth by the rest of the world. Babylon even lacked candles, because there was a scarcity in oil. The result was that there could be no studying at night or staying up at night for any other purpose. That is one of the many interpretations of the name Shinar, "one can sleep without being awoken." They also lacked a bathing pool, which was very important in that century and in that climate. The problem was a lack of wood for fuel to warm the baths. There were no cedars in Babylon, so it was difficult for the masses of the population to wash themselves properly and indeed they were described as a people with negative bodily odors. (*HaMidrash HaMevo'ar*)

A candle and a bathing pool (B)

There is another interpretation that asserts that the lack of candle light and bathing pool should not be ascribed to poverty. What happened was the prevalence of a disease, which we might call Tremors. It was discovered that the lack of oil candles and bathing pools were very dangerous for Tremors and encouraged their growth and their spread. (*Yefei To'ar*)

ה. 'וּמִצְרַיִם יָלַד אֶת לוּדִים וְגוֹ'", אָמַר רַבִּי אַבָּא בַּר כָּהֲנָא, אָמַר רַבִּי יְהוֹשֻׁעַ בֶּן קָרְחָה, כָּל מוֹנִיטָא שֶׁל מִצְרַיִם, אֵינָהּ אֶלָּא בַּיָּם, 'לוּדִים' לוּדֵי יָם, 'עֲנָמִים' עֲנָמֵי יָם, כִּשְׁמָן, 'לְהָבִים' לַהַב יָם, 'נַפְתֻּחִים' נַפְתּוּחֵי יָם. 'פַּתְרֻסִים' פַּרְוִיטוֹת, 'כַּסְלֻחִים' פְּקוּסִים. אָמַר רַבִּי אַבָּא בַּר כָּהֲנָא, פַּתְרֻסִים וְכַסְלֻחִים הָיוּ מַעֲמִידִין הוֹטְלִיסוֹן, הָיוּ אֵלּוּ מְגַנְּבִין נְשׁוֹתֵיהֶן שֶׁל אֵלּוּ, וְאֵלּוּ מְגַנְּבִין נְשׁוֹתֵיהֶן שֶׁל אֵלּוּ, מַה יָּצָא מֵהֶן, 'פְּלִשְׁתִּים' גְּבוֹרִים, 'כַּפְתֹּרִים' נַּסִים.

5. AND MIZRAIM [I.E., EGYPT] BEGOT, ETC. (10:13). R. ABBA B. KAHANA SAID: THE MOTTO OF EGYPT IS THE SEA: LUDYM – LUD YAM [YAM – MEANING SEA]; ANAMYM, ANAMEI YAM, AS THEIR NAME; LEHAVYM – LEHAVEI YAM; NAPHTUHYM – NAPHTUHEI YAM. PATHRUSIM – PARVITOT [SAILORS], CASLUHIM – PAKUSIM [COVERED IN SOOT FROM WORKING ON THE BOAT]. R. ABBA B. KAHANA SAID: THE PATHRUTHIM AND CASLUHIM SET UP BAZAARS WHERE THEY STOLE EACH OTHER'S WIVES. WHAT CAME FORTH FROM THEM? THE PHILISTINES AND CAPHTORIM (10:14): THE PHILISTINES WERE MIGHTY MEN, WHILE THE CAPHTORIM WERE DWARFS.

Usually, names in the Bible are singular. When you look at the names of the offspring of Mitzrayim, they seem to be in the plural because of the end, יﬦ – *yud*, then *mem sofit*. That, however, is not so. There is one theme that seems to dominate Egyptian life, and that is water. Egypt is on the sea and the sea in Hebrew is יﬦ – *yam* and, therefore, the suffix *yam* has been added to all these names. For example, לודים – *Ludim* is really made up of *ludei yam*, and the name ענמים – *Anamim* is derived from ענמי יﬦ – *anamei yam*. The Midrash includes many more examples.

There are two words mentioned in this midrash that require more detail and explanation. One of them is פתרוסים – *patrusim*. The word *patrusim* is similar to the word פרוויטות – *parvitot*, a Greek word close to the modern-day פירטים – *piratim*, meaning pirates or sailors of the sea. The Midrash seems to feel that the use of this term in connection with the Philistines and the Caphtorim – in particular, that they descended from both the Patrusim and the Caslusim – indicates that they were born out of wedlock and their society was guilty of sexual behavior most inappropriate.

Seed Thoughts

In midrashim 4 and 5, one may be inclined to say that the sages of the Midrash were not objective in their descriptions and their evaluations. It is true that at first, Asshur was a good man who refused to join a rebellion against God. But his children participated in the destruction of the First Temple. The people of Babylon were deprived of oil for candles and bathing facilities, despite which they became a great power. One could, indeed, find ways of admiring this kind of achievement, if not for the fact that Nebuchadnezzar took the initiative to destroy the First Temple in order to take over all of Israel. Our sages of the Midrash could not seem to relate the names of the children of Ham, nor even those of Shem, in the Bible without mentioning what their children had done to the Jewish people and Jewish history. They had to express their hurt in these descriptions, which was a form of protest. Egypt was a great power and the Bible tells us specifically not to despise the Egyptians (Deut. 23:8) even though they enslaved us, but the sages of the Midrash, who were intense "Jewish nationalists," could not prevent themselves from expressing their hurt. The Jewish people were hurt by the Egyptians during the period of their slavery and they were hurt by the Philistines and the Cypriots. They expressed this hurt in asserting that Egypt worshiped the Nile as a God and therefore their moral and sexual behavior was completely unprincipled. As for the Philistines, they came to the world through immoral process that could only be described as debasing.

ו. (טו-יח) 'וּכְנַעַן יָלַד אֶת צִידֹן', 'וְאֶת הַחִוִּי' חַלְדִּין, 'וְאֶת הָעַרְקִי' אַרְקָא דְלִיבְנָן, 'אֶת הַסִּינִי' אָרְתּוֹסְיָה, 'אֶת הָאַרְוָדִי' אַרְוָד, 'אֶת הַצְּמָרִי' חֶמֶץ, וְלָמָּה הוּא קוֹרֵא אוֹתָהּ צְמָרִי, יְהוּדָה בַּר רַבִּי אָמַר, שֶׁהֵן עוֹשִׂין בַּצֶּמֶר, 'אֶת הַחֲמָתִי' פִּיפָנִי. (יט) 'וַיְהִי גְבוּל הַכְּנַעֲנִי מִצִּידֹן, וְגוֹ'', עַד קָלָדָה.

6. AND CANAAN BEGOT ZIDON HIS FIRSTBORN, ETC. (10:15–18). THE
HIVITE: THE INHABITANTS OF HILDINS; THE ARKITE: I.E., ARKAS OF
THE LEBANON. THE SINITE: ORTHOSIA. THE ARVADITE: ARADUS. THE
ZEMARITE: HAMATS; AND WHY IS IT CALLED ZEMARITE? BECAUSE WOOL
(ZEMER) IS MANUFACTURED THERE. THE HAMATHITE: EPIPHANIA. AND
THE BORDER OF THE CANAANITE WAS . . . UNTO LASHA (10:19): I.E., AS
FAR AS CALLIRRHOE.

This Midrash continues the style of the previous ones, trying to identify names and places that might have had their origin in the names of
the children of Noah. In the case of the place known as חלדין – *Childin*,
it comes from the root חלד – *cheled*, which means "earth," or, as some
say, "a serpent." Either way, people of that place lived in caves within
the earth, so it is as though they lived in darkness most of the time. In
the case of the town named צמרי – *Tzimri*, it is named for the fact that
its inhabitants work with צמר – *tzemer*, wool. The Midrash that follows
debates the question of whether it is more appropriate to name places
or people after events or after one's ancestors.

———

Seed Thoughts

The verses we have been reading in the past several midrashim have to
do with the children of Noah and their descendants. These fifteen verses
were preceded by one significant verse describing the death of Noah:
"And all of the days of Noah were nine hundred and fifty years; and he
died" (Genesis 9:29). The Midrash, which finds important lessons in so
many details that escaped the average reader, had nothing to say on this
significant verse, which informs us that Noah died. One might say that

the *Midrash Rabbah* said so much about Noah in the preceding sections that their opinions had already been expressed. However, that rarely happens in Midrash; the sages almost always have more to say.

I discussed this observation with a young scholar working in the field of Midrash. He told me not to be too surprised at this kind of discovery. Midrash is a collection of rabbinic material by the sages of the first several centuries of the common era. There are several such major collections and more may yet follow, as there is much as yet undiscovered material – we do not know what may or may not have been left out. Every few years, some scholar would report the discovery of a document previously unknown, which might be the whole *Midrash Rabbah* or some other collection, or merely a section of one of the midrashic collections. Such a discovery happens often and is very exciting. It may very well be that someone might produce a document that might include some of the eulogies of the sages on this particular verse describing the death of Noah. With Midrash, the story is never over. There is always the possibility of more to come.

PARASHAH THIRTY-SEVEN, *Midrash Seven*

ז. 'וּלְשֵׁם יֻלַּד גַּם הוּא, אֲבִי כָּל בְּנֵי עֵבֶר, וְגוֹ'", אֵין אָנוּ יוֹדְעִין אִם שֵׁם הוּא הַגָּדוֹל, אִם יֶפֶת הוּא הַגָּדוֹל, מִן מַה דִּכְתִיב, (בראשית יא, י) 'אֵלֶּה תּוֹלְדֹת שֵׁם, שֵׁם בֶּן מְאַת שָׁנָה וַיּוֹלֶד אֶת אַרְפַּכְשַׁד שְׁנָתַיִם אַחַר הַמַּבּוּל', הֲוֵי יֶפֶת הוּא הַגָּדוֹל.

7. AND UNTO SHEM, THE FATHER OF ALL THE CHILDREN OF EBER, THE
ELDER BROTHER OF JAPHETH, TO HIM ALSO WERE CHILDREN BORN
(10:21). WE DO NOT KNOW FROM THIS VERSE WHETHER SHEM OR JA-
PHETH WAS THE ELDER. BUT SINCE IT IS WRITTEN, NOW THESE ARE THE
GENERATIONS OF SHEM. SHEM WAS A HUNDRED YEARS OLD, AND BEGOT
ARPACHSHAD TWO YEARS AFTER THE FLOOD (GEN. 11:10), IT FOLLOWS
THAT JAPHETH WAS THE ELDER.

The first problem this midrash addresses is to ascertain which of
Noah's sons was the oldest. The verse says, "the brother of Japheth, the
elder." The way it is stated, we do not know whether it is Shem who
is older or Japheth. Some of the biblical dates in connection with the
Flood helps us solve this problem. It is said that Shem fathered a son
two years after the Flood, at which time he was a hundred years old.
That means that he was ninety-eight at the time of the Flood, which
makes him younger than Japheth.

'וּלְעֵבֶר יֻלַּד שְׁנֵי בָנִים, שֵׁם הָאֶחָד פֶּלֶג כִּי בְיָמָיו נִפְלְגָה הָאָרֶץ', רַבִּי יוֹסֵי וְרַבָּן שִׁמְעוֹן בֶּן גַּמְלִיאֵל, רַבִּי יוֹסֵי אוֹמֵר, הָרִאשׁוֹנִים, עַל יְדֵי שֶׁהָיוּ מַכִּירִים אֶת יְחוּסֵיהֶם, הָיוּ מוֹצִיאִין שְׁמָן, לְשֵׁם הַמְּאֹרָע, אֲבָל אָנוּ, שֶׁאֵין אָנוּ מַכִּירִים אֶת יְחוּסֵינוּ, אָנוּ מוֹצִיאִין לְשֵׁם אֲבוֹתֵינוּ, רַבָּן שִׁמְעוֹן בֶּן גַּמְלִיאֵל אוֹמֵר, הָרִאשׁוֹנִים, עַל יְדֵי שֶׁהָיוּ מִשְׁתַּמְּשִׁין בְּרוּחַ הַקֹּדֶשׁ, הָיוּ מוֹצִיאִין, לְשֵׁם הַמְּאֹרָע, אֲבָל אָנוּ, שֶׁאֵין אָנוּ מִשְׁתַּמְּשִׁין בְּרוּחַ הַקֹּדֶשׁ, אָנוּ מוֹצִיאִין, לְשֵׁם אֲבוֹתֵינוּ, אָמַר רַבִּי יוֹסֵי בֶּן חֲלַפְתָּא, נָבִיא גָּדוֹל הָיָה עֵבֶר שֶׁהוֹצִיא לְשֵׁם הַמְּאֹרָע, הֲדָא הוּא דִכְתִיב, 'וּלְעֵבֶר יֻלַּד שְׁנֵי בָנִים, וְגוֹ'"

AND UNTO EBER WERE BORN TWO SONS; THE NAME OF THE ONE WAS
PELEG [I.E., DIVISION], FOR IN HIS DAYS WAS THE EARTH DIVIDED (10:25).
R. JOSE SAID: THE ANCIENTS, SINCE THEY KNEW THEIR GENEALOGY,
NAMED THEMSELVES IN REFERENCE TO THE EVENTS [OF THEIR DAYS].
BUT WE WHO DO NOT KNOW OUR GENEALOGY NAME OURSELVES BY OUR

FATHERS. R. SIMEON B. GAMALIEL SAID: THE ANCIENTS, BECAUSE THEY
COULD AVAIL THEMSELVES OF THE HOLY SPIRIT, NAMED THEMSELVES IN
REFERENCE TO [FORTHCOMING] EVENTS; BUT WE WHO CANNOT AVAIL
OURSELVES OF THE HOLY SPIRIT ARE NAMED AFTER OUR FATHERS. R.
JOSE B. R. HALAFTA SAID: EBER MUST HAVE BEEN A GREAT PROPHET,
SEEING THAT HE NAMED HIS CHILD IN REFERENCE TO A [FUTURE] INCI-
DENT, AS IT IS WRITTEN, AND UNTO EBER WERE BORN TWO SONS, ETC.

There is an interesting debate on the question of how places and
people should be named. Should it be based on events that happened or
should it be based upon honoring our ancestors? R. Jose says that it is
better to name our children after our ancestors rather than after events,
so that we may honor them and remember them. However, the problem
is that the generations after Noah lived for many hundreds of years,
knew each others' backgrounds and were automatically remembered
without any special efforts being made. As a result of this, they began
naming people after events that happened. Most of us, however, do not
understand our *yichus* very well, since very few people live even to the
age of a hundred. Therefore, it is important for us to create some form
of remembrance of our ancestors. Regardless, R. Shimon b. Gamliel
is of the the opinion that it is more important to name people after
events rather than after ancestors. The problem is that the preceding
generations were blessed with the holy spirit of prophecy and knew
which event should be commemorated. We, however, do not have this
special relationship to prophecy, sowe do not know which events to
commemorate. We, therefore, have no other recourse but to name our
children after our ancestors. R. Jose b. Halafta is quoted as saying in his
volume *Seder Olam* (*HaMidrash HaMevo'ar*) that Eber must have been
a great prophet because he named his child Peleg, for his generation was
divided, even though this did not take place until the end of Peleg's life.

לָמָּה נִקְרָא שְׁמוֹ 'יָקְטָן', שֶׁהָיָה מַקְטִין אֶת עַצְמוֹ וְאֶת עֲסָקָיו, וּמֶה זָכָה, זָכָה לְהַעֲמִיד שְׁלֹשׁ
עֶשְׂרֵה מִשְׁפָּחוֹת, וּמָה אִם הַקָּטָן, שֶׁהוּא מַקְטִין עֲסָקָיו כָּךְ, גָּדוֹל שֶׁהוּא מַקְטִין אֶת עֲסָקָיו עַל
אַחַת כַּמָּה וְכַמָּה, וְדִכְוָתַהּ, (שם מה, יד) 'וַיִּשְׁלַח יִשְׂרָאֵל אֶת יְמִינוֹ וַיָּשֶׁת עַל רֹאשׁ אֶפְרַיִם וְהוּא
הַצָּעִיר', אָמַר רַבִּי הוּנָא, וְכִי מִן הַתּוֹלָדוֹת, אֵין אָנוּ יוֹדְעִין שֶׁהוּא הַצָּעִיר, אֶלָּא, שֶׁהָיָה מַצְעִיר
אֶת עֲסָקָיו, וּמֶה זָכָה, זָכָה לַבְּכוֹרָה, וּמָה אִם הַצָּעִיר, עַל יְדֵי שֶׁהָיָה מַצְעִיר אֶת עֲסָקָיו, זָכָה
לַבְּכוֹרָה, גָּדוֹל שֶׁהוּא מַצְעִיר אֶת עֲסָקָיו, עַל אַחַת כַּמָּה וְכַמָּה.

AND WHY WAS THE OTHER CALLED 'JOKTAN'? BECAUSE HE MINIMIZED
(MAKTIN) [THE IMPORTANCE OF]HIS AFFAIRS. WHAT DID HE THEREBY
EARN? HE WAS PRIVILEGED TO FOUND THIRTEEN FAMILIES. NOW IF A
YOUNGER IS THUS REWARDED BECAUSE HE MINIMIZES HIS AFFAIRS,

HOW MUCH MORE SO WHEN A GREAT MAN MINIMIZES HIS IMPORTANCE!
SIMILARLY, AND ISRAEL STRETCHED OUT HIS RIGHT HAND, AND LAID
IT UPON EPHRAIM'S HEAD, WHO WAS THE YOUNGER [ELDER] (GENESIS
48:14). SAID R. HUNA: DO WE NOT KNOW FROM THE BIRTH RECORDS
THAT HE WAS THE YOUNGER. BUT YOUNGER (ZA'IR) MEANS THAT HE
MINIMIZED (MAZ'IR) HIS IMPORTANCE. WHAT DID HE THEREBY EARN?
HE ATTAINED THE BIRTHRIGHT. NOW IF THE YOUNGER IS THUS RE-
WARDED BECAUSE HE MINIMIZES HIS IMPORTANCE, HOW MUCH THE
MORE SO WHEN AN OLDER MINIMIZES HIS IMPORTANCE!

The name of Eber's second child was Yoktan. This name teaches us a lesson of humility. Why was he called Yoktan? He minimized his personal achievements and was awarded for this humility by the fact that he founded thirteen families, all of whom contributed much to the spread of the Jewish religion. This midrash contains a beautiful interpretation of the fact when Jacob blessed his grandchildren, Ephraim was described as the young one. We already knew, however, from previous verses that he was the younger one, so why was this repeated? The word צעיר – tza'ir, "the young one" is now interpreted as meaning he minimized himself. The lesson here is that if an ordinary person minimizes himself and receives a reward, how much more significant would it be if a great and important person acts with humility; how much more so should he be rewarded?

—

Seed Thoughts

"Why was the other called יקטן – Yoktan? Because he minimized the importance of his affairs." We are talking about humility; although this is one of the highest personality traits to aspire to, it is very much misunderstood. Let us begin with a short list of what humility is not: It is not withdrawal. It does not call upon anybody to withdraw either from his word or from his leadership for fear of asserting himself. It also is not remaining silent when you have something important to say for fear of people to think that you are only interested in publicity. The Torah says that Moses was the most humble man in the world. What makes this statement so revolutionary was that Moses was also the most important achiever of the Torah. He was probably the greatest achiever of the Jewish people or of any other people. He was involved in every struggle that came to his attention and even argued with God when necessary. How could such a man be described as humble? There is only one reason and this is to be found in the early stages of his career, as expressed in the Torah. When God called upon him to lead the Jewish people, his answer was מי אנכי – *mi anokhi*, who am I to speak to Pharaoh to lead the Jewish people? This attitude of lessening one's ego, of controlling it and, if necessary, eliminating it, this is what humility is all about. To quote another rabbinic saying, "Let others praise you and not yourself."

Additional Commentary

R. Jose and R. Shimon b. Gamliel

Their disagreement is not over the fact that Eber gave his son a name in relationship to an event. Eber was the fourth generation from Noah. All the members of the four generations were alive. Furthermore, beyond four generations, we do not use the term אבות – *avot*, as it says in the Ten Commandments, "He punishes the sin of the fathers up to the third and fourth generations," meaning not beyond. That is why there is a proverb that says that the compassion of a father only goes up to four generations. R. Jose and R. Shimon were not concerned with Eber, but with the names of the tribes. Jacob did not call even one of his children by the name of Abraham. In connection with the tribes of Israel, not one was called Yitzhak. The Midrash later mentions that Eber must have been a prophet to name his son Peleg because of an event yet to come; this is why R. Jose and R. Shimon debated the question of how places and people were named in the book of Genesis. (*Tiferet Tzion*)

R. Jose says

R. Jose did not take names very seriously. He did not believe that a name has an effect on the behavior of a person. He says that some people have beautiful names and their behavior is despicable, whereas other people have horrible names and their behavior is beautiful. He said that the *Rishonim* had no special policy in connection with names, but that it was convenient for them to be named after an event. The fact that they did not name after their ancestors was because the family's pedigree was already widely known due to their achievements. It was looked upon as somewhat degrading to name a child after such great people, as though they would never be remembered other than the name given to this child. After all, we say that we do not require remembrances for the righteous. What they said and did became their true remembrance.

R. Shimon b. Gamliel, on the other hand, believed that a name does influence a person's behavior. He claimed that the reason why the Rishonim named their children after events was because they had a prophetic insight as to what would happen. Sometimes an event influenced a person to call their child by a specific name; for example, Leah called her son Reuven because he was born at a time when she longed for a child. The name expressed the wonder of his birth. However, since we are not blessed with the gift of prophecy, we have no recourse but to name our children after our ancestors, with the hope that the good behavior of our ancestors will be an example to our children. (*Tiferet Tzion*)

ח. 'וְיָקְטָן יָלַד אֶת אַלְמוֹדָד וְאֶת שָׁלֶף, וְאֶת חֲצַרְמָוֶת', רַבִּי הוּנָא אָמַר, מָקוֹם הוּא שֶׁשְּׁמוֹ חֲצַר מָוֶת שֶׁהֵן אוֹכְלִין כְּרֵישִׁים, וְלוֹבְשִׁים כְּלֵי פַּפְּיָר, וּמְצַפִּים לַמִּיתָה בְּכָל יוֹם. רַבִּי שְׁמוּאֵל אָמַר, אֲפִלּוּ כְּלֵי פַּפְּיָר אֵין לָהֶם.

8. AND JOKTAN BEGOT . . . AND HAZARMAVETH (10:26). R. HUNA SAID: IT REFERS TO A PLACE CALLED HAZAR MAWETH, WHERE PEOPLE EAT LEEKS, WEAR GARMENTS OF PAPYRUS, AND HOPE DAILY FOR DEATH. SAMUEL SAID: THEY DID NOT EVEN HAVE GARMENTS OF PAPYRUS.

The question arises as to why anyone would call their town חצר מות – *Chatzar Mavet,* which includes the word "death" in it. The interpretation of the *Midrash HaMevo'ar* is that the residents of this town lived in abject poverty in terms of their clothes, their food, their homes and just about every other aspect of their lives. The word *chatzer* sometimes read as though it were *chatzir,* which means leek – a vegetable that resembles an onion but without the bitter taste, which grows in many parts of Israel and is very often one of the main food items for those living in abject poverty.

'וַיְהִי מוֹשָׁבָם מִמֵּשָׁא' אֶלְעָזָר בֶּן פִּינְחָס אָמַר, מִישָׁה מִיתָה, מָדַי חוֹלָה, עֵילָם גּוֹבְבֵי גוֹסְסוֹת, חֲבָל יַמָּא, תְּכֶלְתָּא דְבָבֶל, צוֹר, צָיַר, תְּכֶלְתָּא דַחֲבֵל יַמָּא, רַבִּי יְהוּדָה אוֹמֵר, בֵּין הַנְּהָרוֹת, כַּגּוֹלָה, לְיַחוּסִים. 'בֹּאֲכָה סְפָרָה' טָפָרֵי. 'הַר הַקֶּדֶם' טוּרֵי מַדִינְחָא.

AND THEIR DWELLING WAS FROM MESHA (10:30). R. EIEAZAR B. PAPPOS SAID: MESENE IS DEAD; MEDIA IS SICK, AND ELAM IS DYING. HABIL YAMMA IS THE GLORY OF BABYLON. ZUZIRA IS THE GLORY OF HABIL YAMMA. R. JUDAH SAID: BETWEEN THE RIVERS IS AS THE EXILE [SC. BABYLON] IN RESPECT OF GENEALOGY. AS THOU GOEST TOWARD SEPHAR: I.E., TAPHAR; UNTO THE MOUNTAIN OF THE EAST: I.E., THE MOUNTAINS OF THE EAST.

Seed Thoughts

The idea of a town bearing the word death in its name is a serious matter. The *Midrash HaMevo'ar* attributes this development to the abject poverty of the town's residents. The *Tiferet Tzion* has a different approach. It claims that the residents of *Chatzar Mavet* believed so strongly in the World to Come and its promise of immortality for the righteous that life in this world had no importance for them. The Ethics of the Fathers says that this world is but a passage way for the World to Come. The people of *Chatzar Mavet* took this seriously. They disparaged life on Earth and could not wait for death to come. One should not be surprised that they lived in poverty, for to change that would mean investing in the life in this world. They might have even felt that poverty would accelerate their death and thus would be a good thing in that way as well.

This view is completely contrary to Judaism. The fact that this world is a passage way to the World to Come does not diminish its importance. Without this special passage way, one could not reach the World to Come. In fact, it is written in Ethics of the Fathers, "Rabbi Yaakov said: Better one hour of repentance and good deeds in this world than the entire life of the World to Come; and better one hour of spiritual bliss in the World to Come than the entire life of this world" (4:22). The World to Come has to be earned; we do not achieve it automatically. It has to be earned in this world, not only through commandments and good deeds, but also through the challenge of building a better world and using our brains and knowledge to bring out the very best of what this world and this life is capable of. That is why, despite our belief in the afterlife, we are looked upon as a "this-worldly" religion, since we believe that our deeds in this world have not only intrinsic value, but also entitle us to a place in the World to Come.

Additional Commentary

The town that was called 'Death'

It is very difficult to comprehend that somebody would name their son *Chatzarmavet*, meaning "garden of death." After all, we have a saying that nobody should open their mouth to Satan and wish bad things on anyone. We have to acknowledge, therefore, that this name shows us how strongly the father felt that the whole purpose of man was to exist after death and that this world is only a lobby for the World to Come.

As the Ethics of the Fathers says, "This world is like a lobby before the main room." That is why the man called his son *Chatzar Mavet*, so that with this name, he could internalize the idea that the focus of this world should be with the next world in mind, and then he could teach all of his children about this and about life after death. He probably was successful in teaching this idea, because there was a place or a town called *Chatzar Mavet*. There, they ate leeks, they did not cultivate the land and everything about their way of life prepared them for death. (*Tiferet Tzion*)

'וַיְהִי כָל הָאָרֶץ שָׂפָה אֶחָת, וְגוֹ'", אֶלְעָזָר בַּר רַבִּי יוֹסֵי בַּר זִמְרָא פָּתַח, (תהלים נט, יב) 'אַל תַּהַרְגֵם,
פֶּן יִשְׁכְּחוּ עַמִּי הֲנִיעֵמוֹ בְחֵילְךָ וְהוֹרִידֵמוֹ, (כי מרו בה)' רַבָּנָן פָּתְרֵי קְרָיָה בְּדוֹאֵג וּבַאֲחִיתֹפֶל, אָמַר
דָּוִד אַל תַּהֲרֹג דּוֹאֵג וַאֲחִיתֹפֶל, 'פֶּן יִשְׁכְּחוּ עַמִּי' פֶּן יִשְׁכְּחוּ הַדּוֹרוֹת הַבָּאִים אַחֲרֵיהֶם, 'הֲנִיעֵמוֹ
בְחֵילְךָ' טַלְטְלֵמוֹ, 'וְהוֹרִידֵמוֹ' הוֹרִידֵמוֹ מִגְּדֻלָּתָן

1. AND THE WHOLE EARTH WAS OF ONE LANGUAGE, ETC. (11:1). R. ELA-
ZAR COMMENCED HIS DISCOURSE IN THE NAME OF R. JOSE B. ZIMRA
WITH THE TEXT: SLAY THEM NOT, LEST MY PEOPLE FORGET, MAKE THEM
WANDER TO AND FRO BY THY POWER, AND BRING THEM DOZEN, O LORD,
OUR SHIELD (PS. 59:12). THE RABBIS RELATE THE VERSE TO DOEG AND
AHITOPHEL: DAVID SAID, 'SLAY NOT DOEG AND AHITOPHEL, LEST MY
PEOPLE FORGET,' I.E., LEST THE GENERATIONS THAT FOLLOW THEM
FORGET. 'MAKE THEM WANDER TO AND FRO BY THY POWER,' I.E., CAST
THEM ABOUT; 'AND BRING THEM DOWN' FROM THEIR GREATNESS;

In the verse from Psalms that is quoted, King David prays, in connection with those who have hurt him the most, that they do not die
a normal death, but that, instead, they should first be reduced from
their positions of grandeur and suffer humiliation before reaching their
earthly end. He had in mind, in particular, two men who had betrayed
him: Doeg and Ahitophel.

וְלָנוּ מַה יַּעֲשֶׂה (שם שם, שם) 'מָגִנֵּנוּ ה'', (שם שם, יג) 'חַטַּאת פִּימוֹ דְּבַר שְׂפָתֵימוֹ', זֶה הִתִּיר גִּלּוּי
עֲרָיוֹת וּשְׁפִיכוּת דָּמִים, זֶה הִתִּיר גִּלּוּי עֲרָיוֹת וּשְׁפִיכוּת דָּמִים, זֶה הִתִּיר גִּלּוּי עֲרָיוֹת וּשְׁפִיכוּת
דָּמִים, שֶׁנֶּאֱמַר (ש"ב טז, כא) 'בֹּא אֶל פִּלַגְשֵׁי אָבִיךָ', (שם יז, ב) 'וְאָבוֹא עָלָיו וְהוּא יָגֵעַ וּרְפֵה יָדַיִם',
וְזֶה הִתִּיר גִּלּוּי עֲרָיוֹת וּשְׁפִיכוּת דָּמִים, נַחְמָן בְּרֵהּ דִּשְׁמוּאֵל, אָמַר, הַתֵּר קוּנְעָתוֹ מִמֶּנּוּ, וַעֲשֵׂה
אוֹתוֹ זִיטִיוְטוֹיס, וּכְמוֹ שֶׁהוּא מֵת, דָּמוֹ מָתָּר, וְאִשְׁתּוֹ מֻתֶּרֶת.

BUT FOR US, LET 'THE LORD BE OUR SHIELD' FOR THE SIN OF THEIR
MOUTH, AND THE WORDS OF THEIR LIPS (IBID., 13): THIS ONE PERMIT-
TED INCEST AND BLOODSHED, AND THAT ONE PERMITTED INCEST
AND BLOODSHED. THIS ONE [AHITOPHEL] PERMITTED THEM, [FOR HE
COUNSELLED], GO IN UNTO THY FATHER'S CONCUBINES (II SAM. 16:21);
[WHILE HE FURTHER SAID], AND I WILL COME UPON HIM WHILE HE IS

WEARY AND WEAK-HANDED . . . AND I WILL SMITE THE KING (IBID., 17:2).
AND THE OTHER [DOEG] PERMITTED THEM: NAHMAN B. SAMUEL SAID:
HE ANNULLED HIS [DAVID'S] CITIZEN RIGHTS AND DECLARED HIM AN
OUTLAW AND AS ONE DEAD, SO THAT HIS BLOOD WAS PERMITTED [HIS
LIFE WAS FORFEIT] AND HIS WIFE PERMITTED.

The Midrash goes on to explain how these men had betrayed David.
Both were guilty of sexual immorality and the shedding of blood. In the
case of Ahitophel, he had advised Absalom, who was rebelling against
his father, David, to copulate with his father's concubines, and he did
so. This was certainly sexual immorality. He also advised him to wait
until David was alone and weary, for that would be a good time to take
his life. In the case of Doeg, he had lied to King Saul that David had
intended to kill him and also told the king that he, Saul, had the power
of a legislator, so he could decree that his daughter, who was married
to David, was free to marry someone else – and she did so, which, of
course, is immoral according to Jewish law.

רַבִּי אֶלְעָזָר, בְּשֵׁם רַבִּי יוֹסֵי בַּר זִמְרָא, פָּתַר בְּדוֹר הַפְּלָגָה, אָמְרוּ יִשְׂרָאֵל, אַל תַּהֲרֹג דּוֹר הַפְּלָגָה,
'פֶּן יִשְׁכְּחוּ עַמִּי' פֶּן יִשְׁכְּחוּ הַדּוֹרוֹת הַבָּאִים אַחֲרֵיהֶם, 'הֲנִיעֵמוֹ בְחֵילְךָ וְהוֹרִידֵמוֹ' טַלְטְלֵמוֹ,
וְהוֹרִידֵמוֹ מִלְמַעְלָן לְמַטָּן, וְלָנוּ מַה יַּעֲשֶׂה 'מָגִנֵּנוּ ה'', 'חַטַּאת פִּימוֹ' מֵחֲטָיָה שֶׁהוֹצִיאוּ מִפִּיהֶם,
אָמְרוּ, אֶחָד לְאֶלֶף וְתַרְנ"וּ שָׁנָה הָרָקִיעַ מִתְמוֹטֵט, אֶלָּא, בּוֹאוּ וְנַעֲשֶׂה סָמוֹכוֹת, אֶחָד מֵהַצָּפוֹן,
וְאֶחָד מֵהַדָּרוֹם, וְאֶחָד מֵהַמַּעֲרָב, וְזֶה שֶׁכָּאן, סוֹמְכוֹ מִן הַמִּזְרָח, 'דְּבַר שְׂפָתֵימוֹ', 'וַיְהִי כָל הָאָרֶץ
שָׂפָה אֶחָת, וּדְבָרִים אֲחָדִים'.

R. ELAZAR IN THE NAME OF R. JOSE B. ZIMRA RELATED THE VERSE TO
THE GENERATION OF THE DIVISION [OF PEOPLES]. ISRAEL SAID: 'SLAY
NOT THE GENERATION OF DIVISION, LEST MY PEOPLE FORGET: LEST THE
GENERATIONS THAT FOLLOW THEM FORGET. 'MAKE THEM WANDER TO
AND FRO BY THY POWER: CAST THEM AWAY, 'AND BRING THEM DOWN
FROM ABOVE TO BELOW. BUT FOR US, MAY 'THE LORD BE OUR SHIELD.
FOR THE SIN OF THEIR MOUTH: FOR THE SIN WHICH THEY UTTERED
WITH THEIR MOUTH. THEY SAID: ONCE IN ONE THOUSAND SIX HUN-
DRED AND FIFTY-SIX YEARS THE FIRMAMENT TOTTERS; THEREFORE LET
US GO AND MAKE SUPPORTS, ONE IN THE NORTH, ONE IN THE SOUTH,
ONE IN THE WEST. WHILST AT THIS SPOT [SC. BABYLONIA] WILL BE ITS
EASTERN SUPPORT. 'AND THE WORD OF THEIR LIPS: THUS IT IS WRIT-
TEN, AND THE WHOLE EARTH WAS OF ONE LANGUAGE, ETC.

The Midrash now contends that the verse with which king David
prayed that his enemies should suffer before their death can also be used
in connection with the Tower of Babel. It is not enough that this genera-

tion be eliminated as were the generation of the Flood. It is important that they go through humiliation to show that their ideas had no basis in reality and that their limited knowledge had caused their disaster.

⁓

Seed Thoughts

Our Midrash begins with a text that opens the Tower of Babel story. Namely, "And the whole earth was of one language and one speech [*devarim achadim*]." This verse can be interpreted homiletically to apply to many situations in life that go beyond the context of the Tower of Babel story. One would think that it is a good thing that all the inhabitants shared one language;. but, in fact, they had very little to talk about. They had no real agenda, no real cause and no real challenge. Of what good is one universal language if you have nothing of importance to say to each other or for the generation to accomplish? Perhaps this can tell us something about what motivated the generation of the Tower of Babel.

They had rebelled against God and became a secular society. But every human being in any social group needs some meaning. This was probably what they were striving for in the building of the tower. But their knowledge was so limited – based, as it was, on a false conception of what the earth consisted of – and they wanted to protect themselves from what they thought was an imminent end to the world as they understood it. They were, of course, completely wrong in their evaluation. The punishment they suffered may not have been a real punishment. They were forced to move from where they lived to different parts of the world and that, of course, was a source of humiliation and exile. But they also were forced to have more than one language. It is a big question whether or not that was a punishment. Most languages are able to produce a culture and a literature which is meaningful for those who speak it. This would certainly eliminate דברים אחדים – *devarim achadim*, that they would be limited to certain themes. On the contrary, this could be understood as a blessing, since language is the vehicle that can make thought, ideas, challenges and hopes meaningful and significant.

⁓

Additional Commentary

One language

According to our verse, the whole world at the time of the Tower spoke one language. The Midrash interprets this as meaning that all of them were united to rebel against God. Their sin, therefore, seems to have been much greater than that of the generation of the Flood. In the case of the generation of the Flood, humanity was virtually destroyed because of the sin of חמס – *chamas* [theft]. But the sin of *chamas* is not a more grave offense than rebelling against God; so why is it that that generation's punishment seems so much less severe than that of the generation of the Flood? The answer of the Midrash seems to be that precisely because their sin was greater than that of the generation of the Flood, it was important to do something to make sure that the generation that followed would be warned against this kind of behavior. It was important, therefore, not to exterminate them, but to humiliate them so that they would learn from this experience and future generations might be dissuaded from the sin of rebellion. (Aryeh Mirkin)

Once in 1656 years (A)

From Adam to Noah, there was a time gap of 1056 years; between the time of Noah and the time of the Flood was 600 years – the total was 1656. Part of the sin of the generation of the Tower of Babel was believing that the Flood was not caused by Divine decree, but by natural law. And according to their calculation of the years, this might happen again in accordance with natural law. Therefore, they decided to build the tower to protect them. Since all of them were of one language, meaning that they all shared the same ideas and conviction, they all agreed that the Flood was a natural event. (*Tiferet Tzion*)

Once in 1656 years (B)

How was the number 1656 reached? From Adam to Shet, there were 130 years; from Shet to Enosh, 105 years; from Enosh to Keinan, 90 years; from Keinan to Mehalelel, 70 years; from Mehalelel to Yared, 65 years; from Yared to Hanoch, 162 years; from Hanoch to Metushelah, 65 years; from Metushelah to Lemech, 187 years; from Lemech to Noah, 182 years, to which we have to add that when Noah reached the age of 600, the Flood began. The total, therefore, is 1656 years. (Aryeh Mirkin)

ב. רַבִּי אַבָּא פָּתַח, (משלי כז, כב) 'אִם תִּכְתּוֹשׁ אֶת הָאֱוִיל בַּמַּכְתֵּשׁ, בְּתוֹךְ הָרִיפוֹת בַּעֱלִי, לֹא
תָסוּר מֵעָלָיו אִוַּלְתּוֹ', אָמַר רַבִּי אַבָּא בַּר כַּהֲנָא, כְּזֶה שֶׁהוּא כּוֹתֵשׁ אֶת הַשְּׂעוֹרִים בַּמַּלְבֵּן, סָבוּר
שֶׁהוּא מְבִיאָן לִידֵי מוּטָב, וְעַד הוּא סָלֵק וְעַד הוּא נָחֵת, 'לֹא תָסוּר מֵעָלָיו אִוַּלְתּוֹ', כָּךְ דּוֹר
הַמַּבּוּל, וְדוֹר הַפְּלָגָה, (בראשית יא, י) (שְׁנָתַיִם) אַחַר הַמַּבּוּל', 'וַיְהִי כָל הָאָרֶץ שָׂפָה אֶחָת וּדְבָרִים
אֲחָדִים'.

2. R. ABBA B. KAHANA BEGAN THUS: THOUGH THOU SHOULDEST BRAY
A FOOL IN A MORTAR WITH A PESTLE AMONG GROATS, ETC. (PROV.
27:22). SAID R. ABBA B. KAHANA: LIKE A MAN WHO POUNDS BARLEY IN
A FRAME; SO HE [WHO CHASTISES THE FOOL] THINKS TO IMPROVE HIM,
YET EVEN AS IT [THE PESTLE] RISES AND FALLS, YET WILL HIS FOOLISH-
NESS NOT DEPART FROM HIM (IBID.). THUS THE GENERATION OF THE
FLOOD WAS REMOVED FROM THE GENERATION OF DIVISION, BUT [TWO
YEARS, AS IT IS WRITTEN, SHEM BEGOT ARPACHSHAD TWO YEARS AF-
TER THE FLOOD (GEN. 11:10), YET, AND THE WHOLE EARTH WAS OF ONE
LANGUAGE, ETC.

The text here reads "After the Flood" (Gen. 11:10). This series of
midrashim are expressions of surprise at the fact that the story of the
generation of Division (Tower of Babel) appears in the Torah right after
the end of the Flood story. It is not that they were close time-wise, since
there was a difference of about 300 years between these two stories,
but the juxtaposition highlights that the original members of the latter
generation actually experienced the effects of the Flood, and hence,
should have acted more wisely. What the verse in Proverbs teaches us
is that fools are not influenced by wisdom or even by experience. They
were determined to build their tower to support the heavens that they
believed were destined to fall eventually, and no counter-intelligence
would convince them otherwise. A fool remains a fool.

—

Seed Thoughts I

The Seed Thought of the previous Midrash idealized the concept of nationhood as it has evolved to modern times. This idealization even suggested that the punishment of the multiplication of languages and cultures could be understood from a certain sophisticated point of view as a blessing and not actually as a punishment at all. This, however, was not the intention of Scripture. The text makes it clear that the multiplication of languages, cultures and religions made confrontation inevitable. There have been language wars in every succeeding generation, including our own. Religious wars have been even more prevalent than language wars. Some of the religious wars in Europe lasted for several centuries. There are religious wars in several places today, particularly in the Muslim world; for example, the Shiites versus the Sunnis. The struggle for language purity, religious purity has become the obsession of many states, cultures and groupings. In this respect at least, we would have to say that the world has suffered grievously as a result of the rebellion of the generation of the Tower of Babel.

Seed Thoughts II

When I graduated high school, I remember there was a guest speaker at the ceremony whose name I do not recall, but whose message was electrifying. This is what he said: " Do not saw sawdust, saw wood." When he began illustrating his thought, I could not get over the reality of his message, which I, myself, had experienced. People too often spend the most precious amounts of their energy, time and effort in trivialities that are essentially worthless. They think that what they are doing immediately has merit until they discover at a later stage that their work was valueless. They sawed sawdust instead of having sawed wood. Our midrash reflects this teaching. The verse in Proverbs about the fool and the illustration of grinding the barley are also parallels of people who think they are achieving something, but are actually sawing sawdust instead of sawing wood.

How could the generation of the Tower of Babel have acted the way they did? They were of intellectually sound mind – how could they have imagined that the skies, or the heavens, were solid to the point where they could be held up by a tower in one corner so that the world might be protected from a future destruction? One need not be a scientist to realize the utter foolishness of this entire concept. One can only imagine that when people rebel against God and have lost their sense of meaningfulness, they are willing to accept even an irrational false god if it gives them the feeling of temporary security. It is a sad chapter in the story of the creation of the world.

———

Additional Commentary

After the Flood

The main point of the midrashic discussion is to explain the meaning of how the nations were divided after the Flood. It is the purpose of the text and the commentary to let us know the reason why God punished that generation by dispersing them over the entire earth, so that they would have different languages and different religions, for this remains a punishment for every generation. It creates for them permanent disagreement. Disagreement, division and debate bear the seeds of war due to the changeability of religion and languages, which is very difficult for human beings to accept. The generation of the Tower of Babel sinned, but the future generations are still bearing that punishment. That generation did not learn any of the terrible lessons of the generation of the Flood; their intent was to rebel against God. Therefore, it was necessary to punish them with a terrible, long-enduring punishment – a punishment that continues to affect not only groups and cultures, but also the individual. (*Tiferet Tzion*)

ג. רַבִּי יוֹחָנָן פָּתַח, (משלי יז, יג) 'מֵשִׁיב רָעָה תַּחַת טוֹבָה, לֹא תָמוּשׁ רָעָה מִבֵּיתוֹ', אָמַר רַבִּי יוֹחָנָן,
אִם קְדָמְךָ חֲבֵרְךָ בַּעֲדָשִׁים, קַדְּמֵנּוּ בְּבָשָׂר, לָמָּה שֶׁהוּא גָּמַל עָלֶיךָ תְּחִלָּה.

3. R. JOHANAN BEGAN THUS: WHOSO REWARDETH EVIL FOR GOOD, EVIL
SHALL NOT DEPART FROM HIS HOUSE (IBID., 17:13). SAID R. JOHANAN:
IF YOUR NEIGHBOR [FIRST] ENTERTAINED YOU WITH LENTILS AND
YOU [SUBSEQUENTLY] ENTERTAINED HIM WITH MEAT, YOU ARE STILL
INDEBTED TO HIM; WHY? BECAUSE HE SHOWED HOSPITALITY TO YOU
FIRST.

The proximity in time of the Tower of Babel to the events of the generation of the Flood makes the former's behavior almost inexplicable.
Those who were born right after the Flood saw with their own eyes the
nature of the destruction. Were they not grateful to be alive? Should they
not have been thankful to God for having saved them via the ark? Why
would they respond to this ultimate goodness with such ultimate evil?
As the Book of Proverbs says, when you respond to goodness with evil,
the evil remains and does not disappear. It is not good enough to return
lentils to those who gave you lentils. All you are doing is acknowledging
the original gift, but are doing nothing to thank the giver for his gift.
Whereas, if you acknowledge his gift of lentils with your gift of meat,
you are responding to his goodness with your goodness.

אָמַר רַבִּי שִׁמְעוֹן בַּר אַבָּא, לֹא סוֹף דָּבָר, 'מֵשִׁיב רָעָה תַּחַת טוֹבָה', אֶלָּא אֲפִלּוּ מֵשִׁיב רָעָה תַּחַת
רָעָה, 'לֹא תָמוּשׁ רָעָה מִבֵּיתוֹ'. אָמַר רַבִּי אֲלֶכְסַנְדְּרִי, 'מֵשִׁיב רָעָה תַּחַת טוֹבָה' שֶׁאָמְרָה תוֹרָה,
(שמות כג, ה) 'כִּי תִרְאֶה חֲמוֹר שֹׂנַאֲךָ רֹבֵץ תַּחַת מַשָּׂאוֹ, וְחָדַלְתָּ מֵעֲזֹב לוֹ, עָזֹב תַּעֲזֹב עִמּוֹ', עָלָיו
הוּא אוֹמֵר, 'מֵשִׁיב רָעָה, תַּחַת טוֹבָה לֹא תָמוּשׁ. וְגוֹ'"

R. SIMEON B. ABBA SAID: NOT ONLY 'WHOSO REWARDETH EVIL FOR
GOOD,' BUT EVEN HE WHO REWARDETH EVIL FOR EVIL, 'EVIL SHALL NOT
DEPART FROM HIS HOUSE.' R. ALEXANDRI COMMENTED ON THE VERSE
'WHOSO REWARDETH EVIL FOR GOOD': NOW THE TORAH SAID: IF THOU
SEE THE ASS OF HIM THAT HATETH THEE LYING UNDER ITS BURDEN,
THOU SHALT FORBEAR TO PASS BY HIM; THOU SHALT SURELY RELEASE IT

WITH HIM (EX. 23:5): OF SUCH SCRIPTURE SAITH, 'WHOSO REWARDETH
EVIL FOR GOOD, EVIL SHALL NOT DEPART,' ETC.

There are occasions when evil has to be responded to with good. The
best example is the commandment in the Torah to help unload the
donkey of your enemy when it is overloaded with a heavy burden. If
you help him, you will be blessed. If you do not act this way, but respond
to evil with evil, it will remain with you forever.

רַבִּי בֶּרֶכְיָה, פָּתַר קְרָיָה בַּדּוֹרוֹת הַלָּלוּ, דּוֹר הַמַּבּוּל וְדוֹר הַפְּלָגָה, דִּכְתִיב 'אַחַר הַמַּבּוּל', 'וַיְהִי כָל
הָאָרֶץ שָׂפָה אֶחָת וּדְבָרִים אֲחָדִים'.

R. BEREKIAH RELATED THE VERSE TO THESE GENERATIONS. NOW THE
GENERATION OF THE FLOOD WAS REMOVED FROM THE GENERATION OF
DIVISION BUT [TWO YEARS, AS IT IS WRITTEN, 'SHEM BEGOT ARPACH-
SHAD] TWO YEARS AFTER THE FLOOD' (GEN. 11:10), YET, AND THE WHOLE
EARTH WAS OF ONE LANGUAGE, ETC.

From the words of R. Berekiah, one deduces that the generation of the
Tower of Babel responded to the goodness that saved them from the
Flood by the evil of rebelling against God. They responded to good with
evil and therefore will evil remain with them throughout the generations.

—

Seed Thoughts

In the section describing the person who received lentils and was about
to respond with lentils, a key concept seems to be missing. Only when
we understand what may be missing will we understand the power of
this teaching. What was not mentioned in this discussion is חסד – *chesed*,
which is often translated as "love." The person who received lentils was
given them as an act of *chesed*. The only way to respond to an act of love
is with your own act of love. This could not have been accomplished
had he only returned lentils. That would have simply have been an ac-
knowledgment of the love that someone had rendered to him. Only had
he given something of the value of meat, which is worth so much more
than lentils, could this also have been understood and appreciated as an
act of love in which *chesed* was being reciprocated on its own high level.

The Midrash, of course, is concerned with interpreting the actions of
the people involved in building the Tower of Babel and how they related
to the generation of the Flood. We have already alluded to this, but we

should learn from this discussion also something for ourselves and our own lives. Even evil has to be responded to with good. That is the only way for the moral world to function. It is the only way to educate those who are less committed to the moral life. The Torah, which insists to safeguard the property of our enemy, sets the stage for an authentic moral revolution. We have to respond to evil with good. We might suffer, and in many ways, as part of this process; but it is the only way to go, and the only way to achieve a moral world – which is worthy to inhabit.

Additional Commentary

Entertained him with meat

If the original recipient also would have offered lentils back, this would not have been a proper offering, but rather a payback of lentils for lentils, without acknowledging the love that preceded and inspired the gift. If, however, he would have offered meat, which is much more expensive, he would not only be repaying for what he received, but would also be offering some love on his part. (RZWE)

ד. יְהוּדָה בַּר רַבִּי פָּתַח, (ישעיה מד, יח) 'לֹא יָדְעוּ וְלֹא יָבִינוּ, כִּי טַח מֵרְאוֹת עֵינֵיהֶם, מֵהַשְׂכִּיל
לְבֹּתָם', הֲדָא הוּא דִכְתִיב, (בראשית ו, ד) 'הַנְּפִלִים הָיוּ בָאָרֶץ בַּיָּמִים הָהֵם'

4. R. JUDAH B. RABBI COMMENCED: THEY KNOW NOT, NEITHER DO
THEY UNDERSTAND; FOR THEIR EYES ARE BEDAUBED, THAT THEY CAN-
NOT SEE, AND THEIR HEARTS, THAT THEY CANNOT UNDERSTAND (ISA.
44:18). THUS IT IS WRITTEN, THE NEPHILIM WERE IN THE EARTH IN
THOSE DAYS, ETC. (GEN. 6:4).

R. Yehudah is quoting Isaiah as his way of indicating that the people of
the generation of the Division did not really understand what was happening. They had eliminated God from their interpretation of events
– that was their undoing. They did not even understand the meaning of
the event in their generation, that the Nephilim were in the land. These
Nephilim were supposed to be some kind of super-human being, which
is, by itself, some kind of indication that there was a Divine aspect to
what was happening in that generation; but despite these occurrences,
they saw the world as devoid of a Divine dimension.

יְהוּדָה בַּר רַבִּי אוֹמֵר, לָא הֲוָה לְהוֹן לְמֵילַף מֵן קַמָּאֵי, אַתְמְהָא, דּוֹר הַמַּבּוּל מִדּוֹר אֱנוֹשׁ, דּוֹר
הַפְלָגָה, מִדּוֹר הַמַּבּוּל, דִּכְתִיב 'אַחַר הַמַּבּוּל', 'וַיְהִי כָל הָאָרֶץ'.

R. JUDAH B. RABBI COMMENTED: THE LATER GENERATIONS WOULD NOT
LEARN FROM THE EARLIER ONES; VIZ. THE GENERATION OF THE FLOOD
FROM THAT OF ENOSH, AND THE GENERATION OF THE DIVISION FROM
THAT OF THE FLOOD [FROM WHICH IT WAS BUT TWO YEARS REMOVED,
AS IT IS WRITTEN, 'SHEM BEGOT ARPACHSHAD] TWO YEARS AFTER THE
FLOOD,' YET, AND THE WHOLE EARTH WAS OF ONE LANGUAGE, ETC.

It is not that one generation did not learn from another, the problem
was that they learned the wrong things from the former generation. The
generation of Division was obsessed with the idea that everything that
happened was due to natural law and not Divine Intervention. That be-

ing the case, they felt that their own talents might be able to achieve what earlier generations did not.

⁓

Seed Thoughts

This Midrash forces us to acknowledge the failure of the creation to establish a better world. It is not the first Midrash to acknowledge this failure. But here, the failure is in triplicate. It acknowledges not only the generation of the Flood, but also the failures of the generation of Enosh and the generation of the Division. It is sad to read and even sadder to contemplate the reasons for this failure. They were not due to God, but definitely due to man. The ruination of man was the fact that he was, and is, equipped with freedom of will – one of God's greatest gifts – and that he could not handle it. Putting it this way, there is an element of hope: since the responsibility is all man's, the possibility of change is also in the purview of mankind. One is, sadly, forced to say this with pessimism since there is a human tendency to destroy and dominate instead of build and share. Why are we better than the generations that we are now describing? Having said that, if we cannot change the whole world, maybe it would be enough to change ourselves, to help change the Jewish people and to help change the people among whom we live. Maybe if this were accomplished, other parts of the world would follow suit.

⁓

Additional Commentary

Interpreting R. Yehudah

R. Yehudah's opinion is based on two concerns: For one thing, he is trying to understand why the text included the words "after the Flood." He was also concerned with the fact that God seemed to have withdrawn Himself from a personal concern for the generation after the Flood, because it said that He dispersed them among all the nations – seemingly, without any concern for what may happen to them. It would have been better if God had looked after even their punishments directly so that they would have understood that even His punishments include a measure of love that would encourage them to return. It is in this respect that he quotes the verse from Isaiah, which says that they simply did not know and did not understand. Since they insisted on believing that everything depended upon the laws of nature and accidental coincidences, they were, of course, not impressed by miracles. They should have been able to understand that the disasters in the generations of Enosh and the Flood were far beyond natural occurrences, but they were not able to do so. That is why the text uses the phrase, "after the Flood" – because that is when the first members of the generation of Division first appeared. The evidence of tremendous destruction was everywhere. Nevertheless, they refused to accept any evidence other than the function of natural law. (*Tiferet Tzion*)

ה. רַבִּי עֲזַרְיָה פָּתַח, (ירמיה נא, ט) 'רִפְּאנוּ אֶת בָּבֶל וְלֹא נִרְפָּתָה, עִזְבוּהָ עֲזְבוּהָ וְנֵלֵךְ אִישׁ אֶל אַרְצוֹ, כִּי
נָגַע אֶל הַשָּׁמַיִם מִשְׁפָּטָהּ וְנִשָּׂא עַד שְׁחָקִים', 'רִפְּאנוּ אֶת בָּבֶל' בְּדוֹר אֱנוֹשׁ, 'וְלֹא נִרְפָּתָה' בְּדוֹר
הַמַּבּוּל, 'עִזְבוּהָ וְנֵלֵךְ אִישׁ אֶל אַרְצוֹ', 'וַיְהִי כָל הָאָרֶץ שָׂפָה אֶחָת'.

5. R. AZARIAH COMMENCED: WE WOULD HAVE HEALED BABYLON, BUT
SHE WAS NOT HEALED (JER. 51:9): 'WE WOULD HAVE HEALED BABYLON'
– IN THE GENERATION OF ENOSH; 'BUT SHE WAS NOT HEALED' – IN THE
GENERATION OF THE FLOOD. FORSAKE HER, AND LET US GO EVERY ONE
INTO HIS OWN COUNTRY (IBID.) – AS IT IS WRITTEN, AND THE WHOLE
EARTH WAS OF ONE LANGUAGE, ETC.

One can ask the question, why has Babylon been featured so much in
this midrash? It should be stated that both the generation of the Flood
and the generation of Division both have a relationship to Babel (Babylon). Babylon was the area where most of the dead of the Flood were
eventually gathered. Therefore, the punishment was that much greater
for those living in that area. Maybe the sins before the Flood were that
much greater there. Furthermore, Abraham himself came from Babylon
(Ur of the Casdim), although he was ordered by God to leave. As to the
origin of the generation of Enosh, that, too, is connected to Babylon by
virtue of the Hebrew style. The use of the word הֵחֵל – *heichel*, referring
to the beginning of the calamity, is mentioned in the description of the
generation of Enosh and also in the description of the Flood and that
of the Tower of Babel. As for the expression, "we have healed Babylon,"
it means that leaders in that generation advised Babylon to repent, and
that would be its healing. The fact that the scriptural verse contained
both singular and plural shows that it refers to many generations.
(RZWE)

Seed Thoughts

This midrash makes special reference to Babylon, probably because the connection to Babylon was so close for several centuries. One might say that the Rabbis had a love-hate relationship with Babylon. On the one hand, the Jewish people lived in Babylon for a long enough period of time to create and edit the Babylonian Talmud, which has become the foundation of the spiritual life of the Jewish people. On the other hand, it was the king of Babylon, Nebuchadnezzar, who invaded Jerusalem and destroyed the First Temple. Our midrash describes the fact that although Babylon ultimately became an important power, it missed many opportunities to transform its spiritual life into something noble and exceptional. It did not draw the proper conclusions from the tragedy of the generation of the Flood, nor from that of the generation of Enosh – both periods during which the land of Babylon and its people suffered tremendously. They had the opportunity to see the hand of God in these tremendous occurrences, which would have healed them spiritually. But they did not accept them and thus, suffered the consequences.

—

Additional Commentary

Punishment for thinking

R. Azariah seemed to be concerned that the Babylonians were being punished for their thoughts even before they committed some of the terrible things for which they were later noted. This was only because they had been given an opportunity to repent and change their ways in the time of the generation of the Flood, but did not do so. They had also been given an opportunity to repent and heal themselves in the generation of Enosh and did not do so. Ordinarily, no one is punished for their thoughts unless they sin in action. Unlike man, however, God understands people's thoughts in advance and probably felt that there was no hope for Babylon in terms of changing their behavior. (*Tiferet Tzion*)

PARASHAH THIRTY-EIGHT, *Midrash Six*

ו. רַבִּי אֶלְעָזָר וְרַבִּי יוֹחָנָן, רַבִּי אֶלְעָזָר אוֹמֵר, 'וּדְבָרִים אֲחָדִים' הַבּוּרִים אֲחָדִים, מַעֲשֶׂה דוֹר
הַמַּבּוּל נִתְפָּרֵשׁ, מַעֲשֶׂה דוֹר הַפְּלָגָה לֹא נִתְפָּרֵשׁ, 'וּדְבָרִים אֲחָדִים' שֶׁאָמְרוּ דְּבָרִים חַדִּים, עַל
(דברים ו, ד) 'ה' אֱלֹהֵינוּ ה' אֶחָד', וְעַל (יחזקאל לג, כד) 'אֶחָד הָיָה אַבְרָהָם בָּאָרֶץ', אָמְרוּ, אַבְרָהָם
זֶה, פִּרְדָּה עֲקָרָה הוּא אֵינוֹ מוֹלִיד, וְעַל ה' אֱלֹהֵינוּ אָמְרוּ, לֹא כָל הֵימֶנּוּ, לָבֹר לוֹ אֶת הָעֶלְיוֹנִים,
וְלִתֵּן לָנוּ אֶת הַתַּחְתּוֹנִים, אֶלָּא, בּוֹאוּ וְנַעֲשֶׂה לָנוּ מִגְדָּל, וְנַעֲשֶׂה עֲבוֹדַת כּוֹכָבִים בְּרֹאשׁוֹ, וְנִתֵּן
חֶרֶב בְּיָדָהּ וּתְהֵא נִרְאֵית כְּאִלּוּ עוֹשָׂה עִמּוֹ מִלְחָמָה.

6. AND THE WHOLE EARTH WAS OF ONE LANGUAGE AND OF ONE SPEECH
(AHADIM). R. ELAZAR SAID: THAT MEANS, OF VEILED DEEDS, FOR THE
DEEDS OF THE GENERATION OF THE FLOOD ARE EXPLICITLY STATED,
WHEREAS THOSE OF THE GENERATION OF DIVISION ARE NOT EXPLIC-
ITLY STATED. AND OF ONE SPEECH (AHADIM): THAT MEANS THAT THEY
SPOKE AGAINST TWO WHO WERE UNIQUE [LIT. 'ONE'], VIZ. AGAINST
ABRAHAM WHO WAS ONE (EZEK. 33:24) AND AGAINST THE LORD OUR
GOD, THE LORD IS ONE (DEUT. 6:4). SAID THEY: 'THIS ABRAHAM IS A
BARREN MULE AND CANNOT PRODUCE OFFSPRING.' AGAINST 'THE LORD
OUR GOD, THE LORD IS ONE': 'HE HAS NO RIGHT TO CHOOSE THE CELES-
TIAL SPHERES FOR HIMSELF AND ASSIGN US THE TERRESTRIAL WORLD!
BUT COME, LET US BUILD A TOWER AT THE TOP OF WHICH WE WILL SET
AN IDOL HOLDING A SWORD IN ITS HAND, WHICH WILL THUS APPEAR TO
WAGE WAR AGAINST HIM.'

The main brunt of this midrash is to find out what the sin of the
generation of Division really was and why their punishment was so
much less severe than that of the generation of the Flood. After all, they
were rebelling against God, Himself, whereas the generation of the
Flood were rebelling against each other in terms of stealth and sexual
immorality.

The first half of the sentence is singular, שפה אחת – *safah achat*, and
the second is in the plural, דברים אחדים – *devarim achadim*, which means
more than one '*echad*' [one]. The first 'one' refers to Abraham, who was
dismissed because at that time he had no offspring and hence was not

a future threat. The second 'one' [*echad*] refers to God, against Whom they were rebelling.

דָּבָר אַחֵר, 'וּדְבָרִים אֲחָדִים' וּדְבָרִים אֲחוּדִים, מַה שֶּׁבְּיַד זֶה בְּיַד זֶה, וּמַה שֶּׁבְּיַד זֶה בְּיַד זֶה, רַבָּנָן
אָמְרִי, 'שָׂפָה אֶחָת', מָשָׁל לְאֶחָד שֶׁהָיָה לוֹ מַרְתֵּף שֶׁל יַיִן, פָּתַח חָבִית רִאשׁוֹנָה, וּמְצָאָהּ שֶׁל
חֹמֶץ, שְׁנִיָּה וּמְצָאָהּ שֶׁל חֹמֶץ, שְׁלִישִׁית וּמְצָאָהּ שֶׁל חֹמֶץ, הָא מַשְׁפּוֹ דְכוֹלָא בִישָׁא.
ANOTHER INTERPRETATION: AND ONE SPEECH (AHADIM) MEANS
UNITED IN POSSESSIONS, WHAT ONE POSSESSED BEING AT THE OTHER'S
DISPOSAL. THE RABBIS SAID: OF ONE LANGUAGE (SAFAH) MAY BE ILLUS-
TRATED BY THE CASE OF A MAN WHO HAD A WINE CELLAR. HE OPENED
ONE BARREL AND FOUND IT SOUR, ANOTHER AND FOUND IT SOUR, AND
A THIRD AND FOUND IT SOUR. 'THIS SATISFIES (MASHPO) ME THAT ALL
THE BARRELS ARE UNFIT,' HE REMARKED.

The point of the parable of the wine seems to be that God gave up on all three of these terrible generations. The generation of Enosh, the generation of the Flood and the generation of Division. All three wines were sour, meaning that all these three generations were unfit and un-worthy.

אָמַר רַבִּי אֱלִיעֶזֶר, אֵי זוֹ זוֹ קָשָׁה, זֶה שֶׁאוֹמֵר לַמֶּלֶךְ, אוֹ אֲנִי אוֹ אַתָּה בַּפָּלָטִין, אוֹ זֶה שֶׁאוֹמֵר, אֲנִי
בַּפָּלָטִין וְלֹא אַתָּה, בְּוַדַּאי, זוֹ קָשָׁה, שֶׁאוֹמֵר לַשַּׂר, אֲנִי בַּפָּלָטִין וְלֹא אַתָּה, כָּךְ, דּוֹר הַמַּבּוּל אָמְרוּ,
(איוב לא, טו) 'מַה שַׁדַּי כִּי נַעַבְדֶנּוּ וּמַה נּוֹעִיל כִּי נִפְגַּע בּוֹ', דּוֹר הַפְּלַגָּה אָמְרוּ, לֹא כָל הֵימֶנּוּ, שֶׁיָּבוֹר
לוֹ אֶת הָעֶלְיוֹנִים, וְלִתֵּן לָנוּ אֶת הַתַּחְתּוֹנִים, אֶלָּא, בּוֹאוּ וְנַעֲשֶׂה לָנוּ מִגְדָּל, וְנַעֲשֶׂה עֲבוֹדַת כּוֹכָבִים
בְּרֹאשׁוֹ, וְנִתֵּן חֶרֶב בְּיָדָהּ וּתְהִי נִרְאֵית כְּאִלּוּ עוֹשָׂה עִמּוֹ מִלְחָמָה
R. ELIEZER SAID: WHO IS WORSE – THE ONE WHO SAYS TO THE KING,
'EITHER YOU OR I WILL DWELL IN THE PALACE,' OR THE ONE WHO SAYS,
'NEITHER YOU NOR I WILL DWELL IN THE PALACE'? SURELY THE ONE
WHO SAYS, 'EITHER YOU OR I.' SIMILARLY, THE GENERATION OF THE
FLOOD SAID, WHAT IS THE ALMIGHTY, THAT WE SHOULD SERVE HIM?
(JOB 31:15), WHEREAS THE GENERATION OF DIVISION SAID: 'IT DOES NOT
REST WITH HIM TO CHOOSE THE CELESTIAL SPHERES FOR HIMSELF AND
ASSIGN THE TERRESTRIAL WORLD TO US. COME, RATHER, AND LET US
BUILD A TOWER AT THE TOP OF WHICH WE WILL SET AN IDOL HOLDING
A SWORD, THAT IT MAY APPEAR TO WAGE WAR WITH HIM.'

It would appear from these parables that the generation of the Tower of Babel was worse than that of the Flood. This is important to remember as we approach the conclusion of this midrash.

אוֹתָן שֶׁל דּוֹר הַמַּבּוּל, לֹא נִשְׁתַּיְּרָה מֵהֶן פְּלֵיטָה, וְאֵלּוּ שֶׁל דּוֹר הַפְּלַגָּה נִשְׁתַּיְּרָה מֵהֶם פְּלֵיטָה,
אֶלָּא, דּוֹר הַמַּבּוּל, עַל יְדֵי שֶׁהָיוּ שְׁטוּפִים בְּגָזֵל, שֶׁנֶּאֱמַר (שם כד, ב) 'גְּבוּלֹת יַשִּׂיגוּ, עֵדֶר גָּזְלוּ
וַיִּרְעוּ', לְפִיכָךְ, לֹא נִשְׁתַּיֵּיר מֵהֶן פְּלֵיטָה, אֲבָל אֵלּוּ עַל יְדֵי שֶׁהָיוּ אוֹהֲבִים זֶה אֶת זֶה, שֶׁנֶּאֱמַר
'וַיְהִי כָל הָאָרֶץ שָׂפָה אֶחָת', לְפִיכָךְ, נִשְׁתַּיְּרָה מֵהֶן פְּלֵיטָה. רַבִּי אוֹמֵר, גָּדוֹל הַשָּׁלוֹם, שֶׁאֲפִלּוּ
יִשְׂרָאֵל עוֹבְדִים עֲבוֹדַת כּוֹכָבִים, וְשָׁלוֹם בֵּינֵיהֶם, אָמַר הַמָּקוֹם, כִּבְיָכוֹל אֵינִי יָכוֹל לִשְׁלֹט בָּהֶן
כֵּיוָן שֶׁשָּׁלוֹם בֵּינֵיהֶם, שֶׁנֶּאֱמַר (הושע ד, יז) 'חֲבוּר עֲצַבִּים אֶפְרָיִם, הַנַּח לוֹ', אֲבָל מִשֶּׁנֶּחְלְקוּ, מַה
הוּא אוֹמֵר, (שם י, ב) 'חָלַק לִבָּם, עַתָּה יֶאְשָׁמוּ', הָא לָמַדְתָּ, גָּדוֹל הַשָּׁלוֹם וּשְׂנוּאָה הַמַּחֲלֹקֶת,
'וּדְבָרִים אֲחָדִים', מַעֲשֵׂה דּוֹר הַמַּבּוּל נִתְפָּרֵשׁ, אֲבָל מַעֲשֵׂה דּוֹר הַפְּלַגָּה לֹא נִתְפָּרֵשׁ

YET OF THE FORMER NOT A REMNANT WAS LEFT, WHEREAS OF THE
LATTER A REMNANT WAS LEFT! BUT BECAUSE THE GENERATION OF THE
FLOOD WAS STEEPED IN ROBBERY, AS IT IS WRITTEN, THEY REMOVE THE
LANDMARKS, THEY VIOLENTLY TAKE AWAY FLOCKS AND FEED THEM
(IBID., 24:2), THEREFORE NOT A REMNANT OF THEM WAS LEFT. AND
SINCE THE LATTER, ON THE OTHER HAND, LOVED EACH OTHER, AS IT
IS WRITTEN, AND THE WHOLE EARTH WAS OF ONE LANGUAGE, THERE-
FORE A REMNANT OF THEM WAS LEFT. RABBI SAID: GREAT IS PEACE, FOR
EVEN IF ISRAEL PRACTICE IDOLATRY BUT MAINTAIN PEACE AMONGST
THEMSELVES, THE HOLY ONE, BLESSED BE HE, SAYS, AS IT WERE, 'I HAVE
NO DOMINION OVER THEM'; FOR IT IS SAID, EPHRAIM IS UNITED IN
IDOL-WORSHIP; LET HIM ALONE (HOS. 4:17). BUT WHEN THEIR HEARTS
ARE DIVIDED, WHAT IS WRITTEN? THEIR HEART IS DIVIDED; NOW SHALL
THEY BEAR THEIR GUILT (IBID., 10:2).

A further question is being asked by this midrash: Why was nothing left of the generation of the Flood, as they were completely exterminated, while a remnant was left of the generation of the Tower of Babel, even though they rebelled against God, Himself? At this point, the Midrash responds with a view that can only be described as revolutionary. The generation of the Tower of Babel loved each other and helped each other and practiced Shalom, which is the greatest of all the Jewish values. The *midat hadin*, the attribute of mercy, is personified as saying to God, "This generation cannot be punished, for they love each other." It is this that prompted Rabbi, who was the *Nassi*, the leader of the Jewish people and editor of the Mishnah, to acknowledge how great is the power of Shalom. It can even make God ignore the theological rebellion against Him, if those who are rebelling are imbued with love and mercy and compassion toward each, which is what Shalom is all about.

דָּבָר אַחֵר, 'וּדְבָרִים אֲחָדִים' שֶׁאָמְרוּ דְּבָרִים חַדִּים, אָמְרוּ, אַחַת לְאֶלֶף וְתַרְנ"ו שָׁנָה הָרָקִיעַ
מִתְמוֹטֵט, בּוֹאוּ וְנַעֲשֶׂה סְמוֹכוֹת, אֶחָד מִן הַצָּפוֹן, וְאֶחָד מִן הַדָּרוֹם, וְאֶחָד מִן הַמַּעֲרָב, וְזֶה
שֶׁכָּאן, סוֹמְכוֹ מִן הַמִּזְרָח. הֲדָא הוּא דִכְתִיב, 'וַיְהִי כָל הָאָרֶץ שָׂפָה אֶחָת וּדְבָרִים אֲחָדִים'.

ANOTHER INTERPRETATION: AND OF ONE SPEECH (AHADIM) MEANS
THAT THEY SPOKE SHARP WORDS (HADIM), SAYING, 'ONCE IN ONE
THOUSAND SIX HUNDRED AND FIFTY-SIX YEARS THE FIRMAMENT TOT-
TERS; THEREFORE LET US GO AND MAKE SUPPORTS FOR IT, ONE IN THE
NORTH, ONE IN THE SOUTH, ONE IN THE WEST, WHILE THIS SPOT WILL
BE ITS EASTERN SUPPORT.' THUS IT IS WRITTEN, AND ALL THE EARTH
WAS ONE LANGUAGE OF SHARP WORDS.

This is another interpretation of the word אחדים – *achadim*, that should be understood as coming from the word חדים – *chadim*, which means "sharp." They knew exactly how they wanted to rebel against God. Since the Flood occurred 1656 years after Creation, it would seem to follow, by natural law, that something similar would happen the same number of years later. They thus projected the Tower of Babel in very great detail. It should be added that they never actually finished the Tower of Babel; they were punished before it was completed.

—

Seed Thoughts

The Midrash is part of rabbinic literature. Like in all ancient literature, it contains material from an earlier era, which do do not always fully understand. Those of us now in the process of reading and studying *Midrash Rabbah* can testify to similar experiences. For months, we could read material that seems to relate to circumstances different from that which we are familiar, and at other times, more frequently than expected, a gem is discovered with such meaning and inspiration that it makes all the routine efforts and other literary disappointments very much worthwhile.

The midrash we have just studied is one of those gems. It is a true message of salvation. It implies that there is no such thing as being spiritually down and out. We should never believe that we are beyond forgiveness. The generation of the Tower of Babel rebelled against God in the most blatant way. From our point of view, they seemed to have de- served the worst punishment. But God looks at these things differently. They loved each other, they helped each other and they had compassion, fairness and justice operating for each other. These words happened to have been written, quite unintentionally, on Rosh Chodesh Nisan. This is the month wherein we are called upon for spiritual renewal. Can there be any greater call for renewal than this proclamation of Shalom that has been among the greatest of all our values? In another context, there is a saying that God says: הלואי אותי עזבו ואת תורתי שמרו – *halevai oti azavu ve'et Torati shamaru*, "Would that I [God] be forsaken but My Torah be observed?!" Of course, God does not want to be forsaken and the Torah without God is hard to conceive. But, on the other hand, we are told and warned to be very careful in our criticism of each other. If people love each other and help each other, and with only noble intent, they are most worthy and we should never forget this.

—

Additional Commentary

The importance of the Tower of Babel generation

The generation of the Flood were steeped in stealth and robbery and, therefore, they could not be granted continuity. As a result, no remnants of their generation were left. Had they remained, the world could not have been sustained. This, however, did not apply to the generation of the tower, whose sin would not have dramatically affected the way people live amongst each other, although it would have affected their relationship to God. Because of their widespread distribution to different parts of the Earth, their joint rebellion against God would have been very much interfered with. (*Tiferet Tzion*)

ז. 'וַיְהִי בְּנָסְעָם מִקֶּדֶם', נָסְעוּ מִן מַדִינְחָא לְמֵיזַל לְמַדִינְחָא, אָמַר רַבִּי אֶלְעָזָר בַּר רַבִּי שִׁמְעוֹן,
הִסִּיעוּ עַצְמָן מִקַּדְמוֹנוֹ שֶׁל עוֹלָם, אָמְרוּ, אִי אֶפְשֵׁינוּ, לֹא בּוֹ וְלֹא בֶאֱלָהוּתוֹ.

7. AND IT CAME TO PASS, AS THEY JOURNEYED FROM THE EAST – MIKKE-
DEM (10:2). THEY TRAVELLED FROM FURTHER EAST TO NEARER EAST. R.
ELAZAR B. R. SIMEON INTERPRETED: THEY BETOOK THEMSELVES AWAY
FROM THE ANCIENT (KADMON) OF THE WORLD, SAYING, 'WE REFUSE TO
ACCEPT EITHER HIM OR HIS DIVINITY.'

The first question facing the sages is the meaning of the word קדם – *kedem*. If it is meant to be translated as "east," then they left to enter the valley
of Shinar, which is Babylon, and it can only mean that they left the east in
order to go east. This is pretty far-fetched. Can the answer possibly be that
the word *kedem* is actually not "east," but indicates another space or time
coordinate? The word *kedem* in this particular case refers to "Him Who is
first in the world," קדמונו של עולם – *kadmono shel olam*. The reference is to
God. This is the view of R. Elazar. They removed themselves from Him
Who is first in the world. They simply said that it was not possible for us
to believe in Him any longer – neither in Him nor His doctrine, nor in the
good things that might come from Him or the burdens that might come
from Him. They cannot recognize His spiritual Kingship.

'וַיִּמְצְאוּ בִקְעָה' רַבִּי יְהוּדָה וְרַבִּי נְחֶמְיָה, רַבִּי יְהוּדָה אוֹמֵר, הִתְכַּנְּסוּ כָּל עוֹבְדֵי כוֹכָבִים, לִרְאוֹת
אֵי זֶה בִקְעָה מַחֲזֶקֶת לָהֶם, וּבַסּוֹף מָצְאוּ, וְרַבִּי נְחֶמְיָה אָמַר, 'וַיִּמְצְאוּ', (משלי ג, לד) 'אִם לַלֵּצִים
הוּא יָלִיץ'.

THAT THEY FOUND A PLAIN. R. JUDAH SAID: ALL THE NATIONS OF THE
WORLD ASSEMBLED TO DISCOVER WHICH PLAIN WOULD HOLD THEM
ALL, AND EVENTUALLY THEY FOUND IT. R. NEHEMIAH OBSERVED: THEY
FOUND: THUS IT IS WRITTEN, IF IT CONCERNETH THE SCORNERS, HE
PERMITS THEM TO SCORN (JOB 3:34).

In the second section of this midrash, there follows an interesting difference of opinion between R. Yehudah and R. Nechemiah on what it

means when it says that they discovered this valley of Shinar and decided
to reside. According to R. Yehudah, they were looking for a place with
room and they found it. R. Nechemiah differs. He says that they did not
find it, but that it was miraculously made for them. Could it be in this
respect that, as the proverb quoted, even the לצים – *letzim*, those who are
foolish and idle, are helped by Him, so why not even the non-believers?!

וַיֵּשְׁבוּ שָׁם' אָמַר רַבִּי יִצְחָק, כָּל מָקוֹם שֶׁאַתָּה מוֹצֵא יְשִׁיבָה, הַשָּׂטָן קוֹפֵץ. אָמַר רַבִּי חֶלְבּוֹ, בְּכָל
מָקוֹם שֶׁאַתָּה מוֹצֵא נַחַת רוּחַ, הַשָּׂטָן מְקַטְרֵג, אָמַר רַבִּי לֵוִי, בְּכָל מָקוֹם שֶׁאַתָּה מוֹצֵא, אֲכִילָה
וּשְׁתִיָּה, הַשָּׂטָן מְקַטְרֵג.

AND THEY DWELT THERE. R. ISAAC SAID: WHEREVER YOU FIND DWELL-
ING MENTIONED, SATAN BECOMES ACTIVE. R. HELBO SAID: WHEREVER
YOU FIND CONTENTMENT, SATAN BRINGS ACCUSATIONS. R. LEVI SAID:
WHEREVER YOU FIND EATING AND DRINKING, THE ARCH-ROBBER
[SATAN] CUTS HIS CAPERS [IS UP TO MISCHIEF].

In the third section, the Midrash goes on to quote the end of the verse:
וישבו שם – *vayeshvu sham*, "and they settled there." It then points out that
in many places in the Torah where it says that people "settled there,"
hoping for contentment, something happens that affected them very
much. For example, in the case of Jacob, when he came to Canaan, he
settled there in contentment, until the tragedy of his son Joseph envel-
oped him. And so, it seems to happen every time there is a particular
measure of contentment, something happens. The expression used here
is שטן מקטרג – *satan mekatreg*, Satan waits with his accusing finger.

———

Seed Thoughts

How do we explain that Satan lies in wait with his accusations? The
point to be noted here is that the expression *vayeshvu sham*, "and they
resided there," is completely linguistically superfluous. It would have
been enough to say that they came into the valley of Shinar. It is obvious
that they would have settled there, so it did not have to be written in
that manner. The reason for this variation is to teach us that they were
in such a hurry to build the tower and the city that they did not realize
that the whole effort was false, misleading and would come to a very
bad end.

When the verse said that "they settled there," they settled feeling that
they had nothing else to do with their lives, no challenge whatsoever.
They hoped that they would create for themselves something that

would awaken them. But they chose the wrong thing. One of the things that we learn from all of this is that idleness contributes to the worst kind of boredom and emptiness and a feeling of life not being worth living. These are the circumstances that stood as a background to the ideas of the various sages quoted in the Midrash, explaining how such a mood leads to sin and, therefore, Satan is in wait. In light of this realization, R. Helbo added the thought that even for a person who occupies himself with Torah and important endeavors of that nature, if it results in self-satisfaction, too much of this could lead to an overly large ego, which also can lead one to sin; Satan awaits under those circumstances as well. (*Tiferet Tzion*)

Additional Commentary

How to explain the fact that Satan lies in wait with his accusations

The text reads, "And they dwelt there." R. Yitzhak said, wherever it mentions ישיבה – *yeshivah*, which means "dwelling," without any interpretation – meaning that they did not dwell there in order to achieve a special spiritual purpose – at such times, Satan lies in wait. In other words, this is a situation that will lead people to sin. They found a place in the land of Shinar and they dwelled there – simply, without any special purpose. This was a perfect setup of sin or misdirection.

In this respect, R. Helbo offered a more unique interpretation. Commenting on the word וישבו – *vayeshvu*, "and they dwelled," he saw in it the saying ישוב הדעת – *yishuv hada'at*, "contentment." They dwelled with contentment and unusual spiritual satisfaction. Whenever you find this expression in the Torah text, that is what it really means. Therefore, due to this spiritual contentment with themselves and the feeling that they have no need to improve, Satan lies in wait, and sin is almost inevitable.

Said R. Levi on the same verse, the word *yeshivah*, "dwelling," is usually used in association with eating and drinking. This means that all they did was eat and drink and indulge in material success without any special spiritual purpose. It was out of this self-contentment and indulgence that the people of the generation of the Tower of Babel built this city and that their names became known throughout history. The only real way to rebel against the Holy One, Blessed be He, is to let satisfaction and success go to one's head. It was this behavior that produced the punishment of this generation, causing them to be scattered all over the world. (*HaMidrash HaMevo'ar*)

ח. 'וַיֹּאמְרוּ אִישׁ אֶל רֵעֵהוּ', מִי אָמַר לְמִי, רַבִּי בֶּרֶכְיָה אָמַר, מִצְרַיִם, אָמַר לְכוּשׁ.

8. AND THEY SAID ONE TO ANOTHER (11:3) WHO SAID TO WHOM? SAID R. BEREKIAH: MIZRAIM SAID TO CUSH.

In connection with the phrase, "One person said to the other," the Midrash asked who said what to whom? The curiosity of the sages was aroused because of the fact that this expression appears in the singular. Therefore, it must refer to particular individuals. The conclusion the sages came to was that this statement could only have been uttered by Mitzrayim – the son of Ham – to his brother Cush. There are several reasons for this: One is the similarity in the wording. The verse concerning the Tower of Babel says הבה – *havah*, "come," let us gather material for the building process, and when the Israelites were slaves in Egypt, years later, the Torah uses the same expression: "Come, let us gather materials for the building," which, in those cases were for the building of the store cities. (*HaMidrash HaMevo'ar*)

Another interpretation of this is the similarity in style. The expression is *havah*, let us gather the materials for building, whereas in the case of the Egyptians, in their period as conquerors, it says הבה נתחכמה – *havah nitchakmah*, "Come, let us outsmart them." So the similarity in style also hinted to the sages that these words were said by Mitzrayim to his brother Cush. Another indication that this reference might be specifically to Cush is the fact that his son Nimrod was the man who began the rebellion against God.

'הבָה נִלְבְּנָה לְבֵנִים וְנִשְׂרְפָה לִשְׂרֵפָה'. עֲתִידִין אִלֵּין עַמְמַיָּא מִשְׁתָּרְפָה מִן גּוֹ עַלְמָא.

COME, LET US MAKE BRICKS, AND BURN THEM (WE-NISREFAH) THOROUGHLY: THIS IS WRITTEN WE-NISSORFAH (AND WE WILL BE BURNT): THIS PEOPLE IS DESTINED TO BE BURNT OUT OF THE WORLD.

Here, the Midrash follows the notion that Divine punishment is also measure for measure [*midah keneged midah*]. Since the building materials were processed by fire, their punishment would be to be burnt out of the world. In addition, the Midrash will later say that a third of the tower was burnt by fire.

'וַתְּהִי לָהֶם הַלְּבֵנָה לְאָבֶן, וְגוֹ'", רַבִּי הוּנָא אָמַר, הֲוַת מַצְלַחַת בִּידָן, אָתֵי לְמִבְנֵי חֲדָא הוּא בָנֵי תַרְתֵּין, אָתֵי לְמֵישׁוֹעַ תַּרְתֵּין וְהוּא מֵישׁוֹעַ אַרְבַּע. "וַיֹּאמְרוּ הָבָה נִבְנֶה לָנוּ, וְגוֹ'", אָמַר רַבִּי יוּדָן, מִגְדָּל בָּנוּ, עִיר לֹא בָנוּ, אֲתִיבוּן לֵהּ, וְהָכְתִיב, (בראשית יא, ה) 'וַיֵּרֶד ה' לִרְאֹת אֶת הָעִיר וְאֶת הַמִּגְדָּל'', אֲמַר לְהוֹן, קְרוֹן דְּבָתְרֵהּ, (שם שם, ח) וַיַּחְדְּלוּ לִבְנֹת הַמִּגְדָּל, אֵין כְּתִיב כָּאן, אֶלָּא, 'וַיַּחְדְּלוּ לִבְנֹת הָעִיר'

AND THEY HAD BRICK FOR STONE, ETC. R. HUNA SAID: THEIR WORK PROSPERED: A MAN CAME TO LAY ONE [STONE] AND HE LAID TWO; HE CAME TO PLASTER ONE [ROW] AND PLASTERED TWO. AND THEY SAID: COME, LET US BUILD US A CITY, AND A TOWER (11:4). R. JUDAN SAID: THE TOWER THEY BUILT, BUT THEY DID NOT BUILD THE CITY. AN OBJECTION IS RAISED: BUT IT IS WRITTEN,AND THE LORD CAME DOWN TO SEE THE CITY AND THE TOWER (IBID., 5)? READ WHAT FOLLOWS, HE REPLIED: AND THEY LEFT OFF TO BUILD THE CITY (IBID., 8), THE TOWER, HOWEVER, NOT BEING MENTIONED.

The third section describes the fact that the work of their building the tower was very successful. In the time it ordinarily took to produce one brick, they were able to produce two bricks, and so on (see additional commentary by Mirkin). In other words, the Holy One, Blessed be He, allowed them to be successful and have no excuses later, to think that had they done better in terms of their building, they would have not have suffered consequences. Rather, He let them be successful and later, when the time came for their punishment, they got what they deserved.

אָמַר רַבִּי חִיָּא בַּר אַבָּא, הַמִּגְדָּל הַזֶּה שֶׁבָּנוּ, שְׁלִישׁוֹ נִשְׂרַף, וּשְׁלִישׁוֹ שָׁקַע, וּשְׁלִישׁוֹ קַיָּם, וְאִם תֹּאמַר שֶׁהוּא קָטָן, רַבִּי הוּנָא בְּשֵׁם רַבִּי אִידִי אָמַר, כָּל מִי שֶׁהוּא עוֹלֶה עַל רֹאשׁוֹ רוֹאֶה דְקָלִים שֶׁלְּפָנָיו, כְּאִלּוּ חֲגָבִים.

R. HIYYA B. ABBA SAID: A THIRD OF THIS TOWER WHICH THEY BUILT SANK [INTO THE EARTH], A THIRD WAS BURNT, WHILE A THIRD IS STILL STANDING. AND SHOULD YOU THINK THAT IT [THE REMAINING THIRD] IS SMALL – R. HUNA SAID IN R. IDI'S NAME: WHEN ONE ASCENDS TO THE TOP, HE SEES THE PALM TREES BELOW HIM LIKE GRASSHOPPERS.

The next section indicates that their original intention was to build a city and then also a tower. The city is mentioned first because of its importance. What actually happened was that the tower was completed, but the city was not. As for the tower, ultimately, one third of it was burned, one third sank into the ground and one third remained intact.

'וְנַעֲשֶׂה לָּנוּ שֵׁם', תַּנֵּי רַבִּי יִשְׁמָעֵאל, אֵין 'שֵׁם' אֶלָּא עֲבוֹדַת כּוֹכָבִים. 'פֶּן נָפוּץ עַל פְּנֵי כָל הָאָרֶץ' אָמַר רַבִּי שִׁמְעוֹן בַּר רַבִּי חֲלַפְתָּא, 'פִּי כְסִיל מְחִתָּה לוֹ'. (משלי יח, ז)

AND LET US MAKE A NAME (SHEM). THE SCHOOL OF R. ISHMAEL TAUGHT: SHEM (A NAME) MEANS NOUGHT ELSE BUT AN IDOL. LEST WE BE SCATTERED ABROAD UPON THE FACE OF THE WHOLE EARTH. R. SIMEON B. HALPUTHA [HALAFTA] QUOTED: A FOOL'S MOUTH IS HIS RUIN (PROV. 18:7).

This final section of this midrash responds to the text that says, "Let us make for ourselves a name." R. Ishmael responds to this by saying that the "name" brought here can only refer to idol worship. In other words, the creators of the Tower of Babel intended to place an idol on the very top of the tower, to be at the forefront of the rebellion against God.

—

Seed Thoughts

This Midrash contains a remarkable line, which interprets the expression of the people of the Tower of Babel: "Let us make a name for ourselves." The Midrash interprets this as idol worship and tells us that the "name" they had in mind was a reputation, which they would derive by virtue of the fact that they would place an idol at the top of the tower. There is much to be said on this subject. In rabbinic literature, there is much material about names, the importance of names, what names should be, what they reflect, how they should be interpreted, and so forth. However, in some of the most famous texts dealing with moral character, the word "name" is never used by itself. It is always used with one particular adjective, namely, שם טוב – *shem tov*. The goal is to have a good name. To have a name by itself is neutral. What you do with it, how you interpret it, how you live by it is what is important. So, a good name exceeds every other characteristic of the human being.

There are other forms of names, which reflect other goals; these are not bad, but simply not at the same high level of quality. For instance, there are people who want their names, meaning themselves, to have the reputation of a celebrity, or popularity, or a person with a great following, or a politician who wants power and the reputation that comes with it. These are not terrible aspirations; but they are just not at the same exalted level and pure quality as having a *shem tov*. In the history of Judaism, the most important achiever was Moses, and yet what does it say about him?! That of all people of his generation, he was the most humble. He cared about *shem tov*. He cared very little about the grandeur that might relate to him because of his achievements. Only the good name, which is the result of good deeds, mattered to him. This is something that should also matter to us.

Additional Commentary

The making of the bricks

Their work was very successful: They intended to make one brick, yet they found they had enough material and skill to make two. When they wanted to plaster two rows, they were able to do four rows. In their work, they felt that the stones were able to be done with ease and were also much stronger. They did not have rocks, but the bricks that they were making came out as strong as rocks. So did this happen with any material that they were working with. While they did not have the equivalent of what we call cement, whatever materials they used turned out to work just as well. (*HaMidrash HaMevo'ar*)

The height of the Tower

R. Huna said that whoever went to the top of the tower would see the palm trees appearing to be the size of grasshoppers, due to the height of the tower. As described in the *Pirkei D'Rabbi Eliezer* (24), the height was seventy kilometers, which, at the equivalent of two thousand handbreadths for every kilometer, makes 140,000 handbreadths, or approximately 20,000 meters. (*HaMidrash HaMevo'ar*)

Who said what to whom?

Having asked the question, who said what to whom, the Midrash responds that Mitzrayim, who is the son of Ham, said these words to Cush, his brother. The point that they are making is that the children of Ham originated this particular sin of the Tower of Babel. There is a certain expression here that lends itself to interpretation. Here, in Genesis, it says הבה – *havah*, in the phrase, "Come, let us make bricks" (Genesis 11:3), while later on, in the Book of Exodus, the Egyptians said, *havah*, in the sentence, "Come, let us deal wisely with them" (Exodus 1:10). After all, it was the Egyptians who enslaved Israel by means of mortar and bricks. You might, therefore, say, מעשה אביהם בידיהם – *ma'asei avihem beyadeihem*, meaning they imitated the actions of their forefathers. (Aryeh Mirkin)

Parashah Thirty-Eight, *Midrash Nine*

ט. 'וַיֵּרֶד ה' לִרְאֹת אֶת הָעִיר וְאֶת הַמִּגְדָּל וְגוֹ'", תַּנֵּי רַבִּי שִׁמְעוֹן בַּר חֲלַפְתָּא, זוֹ אַחַת מֵעֶשֶׂר
יְרִידוֹת הָאֲמוּרוֹת בַּתּוֹרָה.

9. AND THE LORD CAME DOWN TO SEE, ETC. R. SIMEON B. YOHAI [SHOULD
HAVE BEEN HALAFTAH] SAID: THIS IS ONE OF THE TEN DESCENTS MEN-
TIONED IN THE TORAH.

This is one of the ten occasions where the word "descent" is used in
connection with the Holy One, Blessed be He. In every such case, there
was some need of that hour that had to be resolved.

'אֲשֶׁר בָּנוּ בְּנֵי הָאָדָם' אָמַר רַבִּי בֶּרֶכְיָה, וְכִי מַה נֹּאמַר, בְּנֵי חֲמָרַיָּא, אוֹ בְּנֵי גַמְלַיָּא, אֶלָּא בְּנוֹי
דְּאָדָם קַדְמָאָה, מָה אָדָם הָרִאשׁוֹן, אַחַר כָּל הַטּוֹבָה שֶׁעָשִׂיתִי עִמּוֹ, אָמַר (בראשית ג, יב) 'הָאִשָּׁה
אֲשֶׁר נָתַתָּה עִמָּדִי, וְגוֹ'", כָּךְ, שְׁנָתַיִם מִדּוֹר הַמַּבּוּל עַד דּוֹר הַפְלָגָה, 'וַיְהִי כָל הָאָרֶץ שָׂפָה אֶחָת'.

WHICH THE CHILDREN OF MEN (ADAM) BUILDED. R. BEREKIAH SAID:
WOULD WE THEN HAVE THOUGHT THAT ASSES OR CAMELS BUILT IT?
IT MEANS, HOWEVER, THE CHILDREN OF THE FIRST MAN [ADAM]: JUST
AS ADAM, AFTER ALL THE GOOD WHICH I BESTOWED UPON HIM, SAID,
THE WOMAN WHOM THOU GAVEST TO BE WITH ME ETC. (GEN. 3:12), SO
THOUGH THE GENERATION OF THE FLOOD [PRECEDED THAT] OF THE
DIVISION [BY BUT TWO YEARS, AS IT IS SAID], 'TWO YEARS AFTER THE
FLOOD' (IBID., 11:10), YET, AND THE WHOLE EARTH WAS OF ONE LAN-
GUAGE, ETC.

The first comment of the sages is regarding the use of the term "human beings," which in Hebrew is בני האדם – *bnei ha'adam* – who, if not
human beings, could build a tower? Surely not animals! The Midrash,
therefore, concludes that the word *adam* refers to Adam, the first human being. He was a person who, while having many astoundingly
good points, also demonstrated ingratitude. He was given a very good
woman to be his wife and companion, but at the first challenge, he
blamed her for his eating of the forbidden fruit: "The wife that You
have given me ..." Similarly, the generation of the Tower included

people who were alive during the Flood and whose lives had been saved. However, instead of being thankful, they rebelled against God and created one language and one culture and built a tower to challenge God.

'וַיֹּאמֶר ה' הֵן עַם אֶחָד וְשָׂפָה אַחַת לְכֻלָּם', רַבִּי יְהוּדָה וְרַבִּי נְחֶמְיָה, רַבִּי יְהוּדָה אוֹמֵר, הוֹאִיל וְהֵן עַם אֶחָד וְשָׂפָה אַחַת, אִם עוֹשִׂין הֵן תְּשׁוּבָה אֲנִי מְקַבְּלָן, רַבִּי נְחֶמְיָה אוֹמֵר, מִי גָרַם לָהֶם שֶׁיִּמְרְדוּ בִי, לֹא עַל יְדֵי שֶׁהֵם עַם אֶחָד, וְשָׂפָה אֶחָת.

AND THE LORD SAID: BEHOLD, THEY ARE ONE PEOPLE, ETC. (11:6). R. JUDAH INTERPRETED IT: SINCE, BEHOLD, THEY ARE ONE PEOPLE AND THEY HAVE ALL ONE LANGUAGE, IF THEY REPENT I WILL ACCEPT THEM. R. NEHEMIAH EXPLAINED IT: WHAT CAUSED THEM TO REBEL AGAINST ME? WAS IT NOT BECAUSE, BEHOLD, THEY ARE ONE PEOPLE AND OF ONE LANGUAGE?

R. Yehudah has a positive evaluation of the generation of the Tower. After all, they were united, and as we learned in a previous midrash, their unity saved them from a more severe punishment. However, according to R. Nechemiah, of what good is unity if it leads to false values and rebellions against God?

'וְעַתָּה לֹא יִבָּצֵר וְגוֹ'', אָמַר רַבִּי אַבָּא בַּר כָּהֲנָא, שֶׁפָּתַח לָהֶן הַקָּדוֹשׁ בָּרוּךְ הוּא פֶּתַח שֶׁל תְּשׁוּבָה, שֶׁנֶּאֱמַר 'וְעַתָּה', וְאֵין 'וְעַתָּה' אֶלָּא תְּשׁוּבָה, הֵיךְ מַה דְּאַתְּ אָמַר, (דברים י, יב) 'וְעַתָּה יִשְׂרָאֵל מָה ה' אֱלֹהֶיךָ שֹׁאֵל מֵעִמָּךְ כִּי אִם לְיִרְאָה', וְהֵן אָמְרִין, 'לֹא', אָמַר הַקָּדוֹשׁ בָּרוּךְ הוּא, 'יִבָּצֵר מֵהֶם כֹּל אֲשֶׁר יָזְמוּ לַעֲשׂוֹת', הַכֶּרֶם הַזֶּה, בְּשָׁעָה שֶׁאֵינוֹ עוֹשֶׂה פְּרִי, מַה בְּעָלָיו עוֹשִׂין לוֹ, מְגַמְּמִין אוֹתוֹ.

AND NOW. R. ABBA B. KAHANA SAID: THIS TEACHES THAT THE HOLY ONE, BLESSED BE HE, GAVE THEM AN OPPORTUNITY TO REPENT, FOR AND NOW INDICATES REPENTANCE, AS IT SAYS, AND NOW, ISRAEL, WHAT DOTH THE LORD THY GOD REQUIRE OF THEE, BUT TO FEAR THE LORD THY GOD, ETC. (DEUT. 10:12). BUT THEY SAID, NO!' – THEN LET ALL WHICH THEY PURPOSE TO DO BE WITHHOLDEN FROM THEM (11:6), DECREED THE LORD. WHEN A VINEYARD DOES NOT YIELD FRUIT, WHAT DOES ITS OWNER DO TO IT? HE UPROOTS IT!

The text we are now dealing with includes the expression, וְעַתָּה – *ve'atah*, meaning "and now." This is interpreted as an invitation to the people to repent, to do *tshuvah*, since in many places, the word *ve'atah* serves that function; for example, the verse, "And now Israel, what doth the Lord require of thee?" (Deut. 10:12), which is a well-known invitation to repentance. However, this invitation was not accepted by the generation of the Tower of Babel, so they were punished by being dispersed all over the world.

—

Seed Thoughts

This midrash, like so many in the Noah section, features a debate between R. Yehudah and R. Nechemiah. Their differences of opinion comprise a major feature of this section of the Midrash. It is not certain whether each of them had a consistent position, which would have been reflected in their express views; but in general, it often seems that R. Yehudah shared those views that were rather conventional, and that R. Nechemiah tended to take positions that were much more original, sometimes even startling. Similarly, in this midrash, R. Yehudah expressed a view that we already knew of, namely, that the people of the Tower of Babel generation were united, loved each other and were peaceful with each other, and that this was very important in the eyes of God, so much so that He diminished the severity of their punishment. R. Nechemiah had an entirely different view.

The generation of the Tower were of one language and of one culture. This was their downfall. Why is this? Well, close-knit groups often tend to be intolerant to others. They also tend to see the world in the same way. In addition, they had one leader, which implies that they had a dictatorship, since the people of that generation did not hear of democracy nor of various conceptions of freedom. This dictatorship was not necessarily a benevolent one. The dictator was probably Nimrod, who led the rebellion against God. Therefore, whatever good things may be discerned in their behavior, they remained with the faults of a closed, narrow-minded group with a dictatorship that had to be overthrown.

—

Additional Commentary

The ten Divine yeridot (descents) (A)

The Midrash identifies ten instances in Scripture where God is described as having "descended" to our world. These ten "Divine Descents" are as follows: (1) "And they hear the voice of the Lord God walking in the garden toward the cool of the day" (Genesis 3:8). This is inferred as well from the verse in Song of Songs, "My beloved went down to the Garden"; (2) "And the Lord came down to see the city and the tower"

(Genesis 11:5); (3) "I will go down now and see whether they have done altogether according the cry of it" (Genesis 18:21); (4) "And I am come down to deliver them out of the hands of the Egyptians" (Exodus 3:8); (5) "And he bowed the heavens, and came down" (Psalms 18:10); (6) "And the Lord came down upon Mount Sinai" (Exodus 19:20); (7) "And the Lord descended in the cloud and stood with him there" (Exodus 34:5); (8) "And the Lord came down in the cloud" (Numbers 11:25); (9) "And the Lord came down in a pillar of cloud" (Numbers 12:5); (10) "And His feet shall stand on that day upon the Mount of Olives" (Zechariah 14:4). In all these cases, the *yeridah* was for a special purpose, each at its particular time. (Aryeh Mirkin)

The ten Divine yeridot *(B)*

How does the language of "descent" have any relationship to God? After all, His majesty fills the entire universe. R. Shimon b. Halafta said that this is one of ten languages of ירידה – *yeridah* (descent) found in Scripture. The interpretation is that in nine of those descents, there was some sort of supernatural occurrence involved. For example, in the case of Sodom, fire and brimstone were poured on the city from the skies. In the case of the burning bush, it is said that the bush was not consumed by the fire upon it. In Egypt, all the plagues were beyond nature. At Sinai, it says that they *saw* the *sounds* of the shofar. In the case of splitting the rock, the whole event was supernatural, and the same can be said about God's interaction with Moses in the Tent of Meeting. Just as the sages noted, in Pirkei Avot, ten miracles that took place in the Temple in Jerusalem, so did they refer to these ten special revelations that shared in common the language of *yeridah*. By that they meant that the occurrence came from the upper worlds and was a supernatural event occurring in this world. (*Tiferet Tzion*)

PARASHAH THIRTY-EIGHT, *Midrash Ten*

י. 'הָבָה נֵרְדָה', זֶה אֶחָד מִן הַדְּבָרִים שֶׁשִּׁנּוּ לְתַלְמַי הַמֶּלֶךְ, הָבָה אֵרְדָה וְאָבְלָה.

10. COME, LET US GO DOWN (11:7). THIS IS ONE OF THE THINGS WHICH
THEY ALTERED FOR KING PTOLEMY [CHANGING IT TO] 'COME, I WILL GO
DOWN, AND THERE CONFOUND THEIR LANGUAGE.'

This midrash begins with the quotation, "Let us come down to the earth." The Talmud (*Megillah* 9a) relates the story of how Ptolemy (Philadephus 285–247 BCE) of Egypt requested a translation of the Torah into Greek. He collected seventy Jewish scholars and placed them into different rooms. Each made exactly fifteen identical changes in the text in places they thought the original might be misunderstood. The first line of this midrash, as quoted above, is one of the many verses that was changed by each of the seventy sages. The plural form "us" may give the impression that there is more than one Divine Authority of the world, which is contrary to the beliefs of Judaism. And so the seventy sages, in translating this verse, changed it to the singular form, meaning, "I [God] will go down to the earth." Many such changes were made under these circumstances. This literature is preserved for us under the name of the Septuagint.

'וְנָבְלָה שָׁם שְׂפָתָם' אָמַר רַבִּי אַבָּא בַּר כָּהֲנָא, מִשְׂפָתָם אֲעֵשֶׂה נְבֵלָה, הֲוָה חַד מִנְּהוֹן אָמַר
לְחַבְרֵהּ, אַיְתִי לִי קוֹלָב, וְהוּא הֲוָה יָהֵב לֵהּ מַגְרוֹפִי, הֲוָה מָחֵי לֵהּ וּפָצַע מוֹחֵהּ, הָדָא הוּא דִכְתִיב,
מִשְׂפָתָם אֲעֵשֶׂה נְבֵלָה.

R. ABBA INTERPRETED IT: THROUGH THEIR OWN LIPS WILL I DESTROY
THEM. THUS ONE SAID TO HIS FELLOW-WORKER, 'BRING ME WATER,'
WHEREUPON HE WOULD GIVE HIM EARTH, AT WHICH HE STRUCK HIM
AND SPLIT HIS SKULL; 'BRING ME AN AXE,' BUT HE BROUGHT HIM A
SPADE, AT WHICH HE STRUCK HIM AND SPLIT HIS SKULL. THUS IT IS
WRITTEN, THROUGH THEIR OWN LIPS I WILL DESTROY THEM.

The next section makes mention of the fact that the languages of the generation of Division were confused so that one person would have difficulty understanding another. An illustration given is of one who asked his associate to bring an axe, and instead was brought a shovel. This person was so offended that he began hitting him with it and killed him. The mixing of languages caused many misunderstandings, and even tragedies.

'וַיָּפֶץ ה' אֹתָם מִשָּׁם' רַבִּי יְהוּדָה וְרַבִּי נְחֶמְיָה, רַבִּי יְהוּדָה אָמַר, הָלְכוּ לָהֶם בְּנֵי צוֹר לְצִידוֹן, וּבְנֵי צִידוֹן לְצוֹר, מִצְרַיִם, תּוֹפֶשֶׂת לְאַרְצוֹ, רַבִּי נְחֶמְיָה אָמַר, כָּל אֶחָד וְאֶחָד, תּוֹפֵשׂ אַרְצוֹ שֶׁהָיָה תְּחִלַּת שְׁבְתּוֹ שָׁם, וּלְשָׁם הוּא חוֹזֵר, אֶלָּא מַהוּ 'וַיָּפֶץ', שֶׁנִּכְנְסוּ כָּל הָאֲרָצוֹת בְּרָאשֵׁי הֶהָרִים, וְהָיְתָה כָּל אֶחָד וְאֶחָד בּוֹלַעַת אַנְשֵׁי מְקוֹמָהּ

SO THE LORD SCATTERED THEM ABROAD – WAYYAFEZ (11:8). R. JUDAN SAID: THE TYRIANS WENT TO SIDON AND THE SIDONITES TO TYRE, WHILE MIZRAIM [EGYPT] RETAINS HIS LAND. R. NEHEMIAH SAID: ALL THE COUNTRIES ASSEMBLED WITHIN THE ANGULAR POINTS AND EACH ABSORBED ITS OWN INHABITANTS.

In this next section, the difference of opinion between R. Yehudah and R. Nechemiah can be explained as follows: Both agree that there were two dispersions of population because the word "disperse" is mentioned twice in the verse. They also both agree that after the first dispersion, the people returned either to their homes or to areas contiguous to their homes. According to R. Yehudah, after the second dispersion, they found themselves in a different country and were not able to return home. R. Nechemiah, however, states that after the second dispersion, they also returned home. This view exemplifies the tremendous power of attraction of the land of one's origin.

רַבָּנָן אָמְרֵי, אֵין 'וַיָּפֶץ', אֶלָּא, וַיָּצֶף, הֵצִיף עֲלֵיהֶן הַיָּם, וְהֵצִיף שְׁלֹשִׁים מִשְׁפָּחוֹת מֵהֶן

THE RABBIS SAID: WAYYAFEZ (SCATTERED) IS TO BE READ WAYYAZEF (SWEPT AWAY): THE SEA CAME UP AND SWEPT AWAY THIRTY FAMILIES.

There is another interpretation offered by the rabbis. It is based on an interesting play on words. Instead of the word ויפץ – *vayifetz*, to distribute, they changed the letters around so that it would be ויצף – *vayitzef*, which means to overflow. They bring this to make the point that there was an oceanic overflowing that brought havoc across the population. Many families were destroyed as a result of this flooding. Since there were only seventy descendants of Jacob, there was a major inroad made in the population.

רַבִּי לֵוִי אָמַר, אֵין לְךָ צָרָה בָאָה לָאָדָם שֶׁאֵין לָאֲחֵרִים בָּהּ רֶוַח, אוֹתָן שְׁלֹשִׁים מִשְׁפָּחוֹת מֵהֵיכָן
עָמְדוּ, מֵאַבְרָהָם, שֵׁשׁ עֶשְׂרֵה מִקְּטוּרָה, וּשְׁתֵּים עֶשְׂרֵה מִיִּשְׁמָעֵאל, וְאֵלֶּין תַּרְתֵּין חוֹרָנְיָתָא,
(בראשית כה, כג) 'וַיֹּאמֶר ה' לָהּ, שְׁנֵי גוֹיִם בְּבִטְנֵךְ'.

R. PHINEHAS SAID IN R. LEVI'S NAME: NO MISFORTUNE COMES TO A MAN
WHICH DOES NOT PROFIT SOMEBODY. WHENCE WERE THOSE THIRTY
FAMILIES REPLACED? FROM ABRAHAM, SIXTEEN FROM THE SONS OF
KETURAH AND TWELVE FROM ISHMAEL, AND AS FOR THE REMAINING
TWO – AND THE LORD SAID UNTO HER: TWO NATIONS ARE IN THY WOMB
(GEN. 25:23).

R. Levi added the thought that even after a destruction, someone profits and that the thirty families lost in this episode were replaced – by
the descendants of Abraham. Abraham lived in the midst of a rebellion
against God and prayed for the rebels hoping that their plans would not
succeed. One might say his reward was that his descendant would be
among those repopulating the world.

———

Seed Thoughts

The midrash begins by explaining how this phrase was changed by the
sages in their translation of the Torah for Ptolemy, the ruler of Egypt.
On this, the *Tiferet Tzion* asks: was it important to mention this fact? It
then answers is that it was, indeed, very important, because in present-
ing Torah to non-Jews, and to Jews who may be ignorant of their heritage, it is important that Judaism not be compromised. There are many
expressions in the Torah that can be easily misunderstood. Anything
should be done to eliminate the possibility of misunderstanding and to
make sure that the interpretations are not only convincing, but authentic. This story of the sages who interpreted the Torah to Ptolemy is only
one example of the fact that throughout history, Jews, both individually
and collectively, have been called upon to defend Judaism and interpret
it to those less aware of the true meanings of its texts and traditions.
The Ethics of the Fathers even has a statement that says we must all be
well-equipped "to know what to answer to the non-believer." This is a
very important subject and should be studied and learned by all Jews.
During the Spanish period, various debates were held between representatives of the Catholic church and others of Judaism. It is important
that there be people with the ability to defend us and our beliefs should
the need arise.

———

Additional Commentary

The sages and Ptolemy (A)

There were seventy sages who were called upon to translate the Torah into Greek. They made changes, one of which had to do with the text that we are now studying. Our text begins, "Come now and let us go down to the earth." That is written in the plural, which gives rise to the possibility that there might be more than one Supreme Authority in Judaism. Therefore, they thought it important to change the plural to the singular so that these possibilities would not arise. (Aryeh Mirkin)

The sages and Ptolemy (B)

With the reference to Ptolemy, the Midrash is telling us that whenever we are in a position with a non-Jewish person, that this particular verse should be rendered the way it was to Ptolemy, namely that the plural should be changed to the singular. Of course, more than this one thought is intended; the idea is that we should take an example from the sages who were entrusted with the responsibility of interpretation. All Jews in every generation should do the best they can to interpret Judaism in the most easily and widely understood way possible. (*Tiferet Tzion*)

R. Yehudah and R. Nechemiah

At first, the verse says, "And God scattered them from that place." Later on, there is another verse that says, "From that place, God distributed them." This means that there were two occasions or instances of dispersions. R. Yehudah has the view that the first dispersion was such that the inhabitants were able to return – if not to the exact same location, then to the one next to it; for example, those from Tzur may return to Tzidon or those from Tzidon to Tzur. As for the second dispersion to another land, R. Yehudah holds that they were never able to return from it. R. Nechemiah, however, also agrees that there were two cases of dispersion. Insofar as the first one is concerned, they met in the mountainous area and they were all together because of the fact that they were either celebrating the organization of the Tower or its completion. When it was over, they were able to return to where they came from. Regarding the second dispersion, they were able to return as well, because apparently, the land had a tremendous power of attraction for all of them. God seems to have given the land חן – *chen*, causing the inhabitants to love and be drawn to that particular land. This enabled them to return even after the second dispersion. That is also what it means when it says that their language was swallowed, "*nivla*," since the land now included all of them with their spiritual and cultural baggage. This was another of the miracles associated with this entire experience according to R. Encomia. (*Tiferet Tzion*)

The pioneer families

No real dispersion took place in this story, rather an oceanic flooding of that area of Babylon, according to the Midrash. Seventy nations existed at the time of the הפלגה – *haflagah*, Division: The children of Japheth – seven. The children of Gomer – three. The children of Yudan – four. The children of Ham – four. The children of Cush – five. The children of Raamah – two. The children of Mitzrayim – eight. The children of Canaan – eleven. The children of Shem – five. The children of Aram – four. The children of Arpachshad – one. The children of Ever – two. The children of Yoktan – thirteen. All together, this totals seventy (Genesis 10:32). There is a second counting of seventy families in Genesis. These were the sum total of the descendants of Yaakov. The midrash says that there was an oceanic flood, and that this flood destroyed thirty of the aforementioned families, but they were "replaced" by the descendants of Abraham, all of whom are named in our midrash. This is why the folk saying, as quoted, applies here, that there is someone or some group that profits from the difficulties of others. (Aryeh Mirkin)

יא. 'עַל כֵּן קָרָא שְׁמָהּ בָּבֶל', חַד תַּלְמִיד מִן דְּרַבִּי יוֹחָנָן הֲוָה יָתֵב קֳדָמוֹהִי, וַהֲוָה מַסְבַּר לֵהּ וְלֹא סָבַר, אֲמַר לֵהּ מַאי טַעְמָא לֵית אַתְּ סָבַר, אֲמַר לֵהּ דַּאֲנָא גְּלֵי מִן אַרְעָאי, אֲמַר לֵהּ מֵהֵיכָן אַרְעָא דִּידָךְ, אֲמַר לֵהּ מִן בּוֹרְסִיף, אֲמַר לֵהּ לָא תֵימַר לִי כֵן, אֶלָּא, מִן בּוֹלְסִיף, 'כִּי שָׁם בָּלַל ה' שְׂפַת כָּל הָאָרֶץ'.

11. THEREFORE WAS THE NAME OF IT CALLED BABEL (11:9). A DISCIPLE OF R. YOHANAN WAS SITTING BEFORE HIM AND COULD NOT GRASP HIS TEACHING. 'WHAT IS THE CAUSE OF THIS?' HE ASKED. 'IT IS BECAUSE I AM EXILED FROM MY HOME,' REPLIED HE. 'WHENCE DO YOU COME?' INQUIRED HE. 'FROM BORSIF,' HE ANSWERED. 'NOT THAT IS ITS NAME,' HE REJOINED, 'BUT BALSIF, IN ACCORDANCE WITH THE TEXT, BECAUSE THERE THE LORD DID CONFOUND (BALAL) THE LANGUAGE (SEFATH) OF ALL THE EARTH.'

This midrash is self-explanatory. A pupil of R. Yochanan's was not able to grasp the lesson. R. Yochanan tried to seek the reason for his inability to do so. The student blamed it on the change of atmosphere or air that he found in Tiberius, as compared to where he came from. When asked where he came from, the pupil answered that he was from בורסיף – *Borsif*, which was known to the sage as the place where remnants of the tower existed. R. Yochanan said that he was pronouncing it wrong; it is not *Borsif* but בולסיף – *Bolsif*, which is a play on words in Hebrew (*Balal safah*) meaning that their language was confused. The people who came from this town were known for their forgetfulness. It had nothing to do with the air in Tiberius, but with the culture of the town where he came from.

—

Seed Thoughts

It is very interesting to note that in this midrash, R. Yochanan, who was one of the great scholars of the Talmud, has given us a lesson about what it means to be a teacher. He was not willing to accept the fact that a pupil was not capable of learning. He analyzed the pupil's background to the best of his ability until he discovered something that helped him understand the condition of the student. Whether or not R. Yochanan accepted the tradition of forgetfulness for people from the same town of origin as this pupil of his, we do not know; but chances are that he did not accept this as an excuse or exemption, and probably did everything in his power to bring this student up to the level of his colleagues. This is something all teachers should try to remember: never give up on a student until every effort has been made to teach him.

יב. 'וְאֵלֶּה תּוֹלְדֹת תֶּרַח, תֶּרַח הוֹלִיד אֶת אַבְרָם וְגוֹ'", אָמַר רַבִּי אַבָּא בַּר כָּהֲנָא, כָּל מִי שֶׁנִּכְפַּל
שְׁמוֹ, יֵשׁ לוֹ חֵלֶק לָעוֹלָם הַזֶּה וְלָעוֹלָם הַבָּא, אֲתִיבוּן לֵהּ וְהָכְתִיב, 'אֵלֶּה תּוֹלְדֹת תֶּרַח', יֵשׁ
לוֹ בָּעוֹלָם הַזֶּה, וְיֵשׁ לוֹ לָעוֹלָם הַבָּא, אַתְמְהָא, אָמַר לְהוֹן אַף הִיא לָא תַבְרָא, דַּאֲמַר רַבִּי יוּדָן
מְשׁוּם רַבִּי אַבָּא בַּר כָּהֲנָא, (בראשית טו, טו) 'וְאַתָּה תָבוֹא אֶל אֲבֹתֶיךָ בְּשָׁלוֹם' בְּשָׂרוֹ, שֶׁיֵּשׁ לְאָבִיו
חֵלֶק לָעוֹלָם הַבָּא, (שם שם, שם) 'תִּקָּבֵר בְּשֵׂיבָה טוֹבָה', בְּשָׂרוֹ, שֶׁיִּשְׁמָעֵאל עוֹשֶׂה תְשׁוּבָה.

12. NOW THESE ARE THE GENERATIONS OF TERAH. TERAH BEGOT
ABRAM, ETC. (11:27). R. ABBA B. KAHANA SAID: WHOEVER HAS HIS NAME
THUS REPEATED HAS A PORTION IN THIS WORLD AND IN THE WORLD
TO COME. THEY RAISED AN OBJECTION TO HIM: BUT IT IS WRITTEN,
NOW THESE ARE THE GENERATIONS OF TERAH. TERAH BEGOT ABRAM,
ETC.? THAT TOO DOES NOT DISPROVE IT, REPLIED HE, FOR WHAT IS THE
MEANING OF, BUT THOU [ABRAHAM] SHALT GO TO THY FATHERS IN
PEACE (IBID., 15:15)? HE [GOD] INFORMED HIM THAT HIS FATHER HAD A
PORTION IN THE WORLD TO COME; THOU SHALT BE BURIED IN A GOOD
OLD AGE (IBID.): HE INFORMED HIM THAT ISHMAEL WOULD REPENT IN
HIS OWN DAYS.

Please refer to parashah 30, midrash 4 for an interpretation and Seed
Thought of this parallel midrash.

—

Additional Commentary

Traditional thoughts about the World to Come

The mitzvoth and Torah study that a person performs in this world prepare for him a true spiritual home in the World to Come. To the extent
that the person teaches his children and pupils the way of Torah and
good deeds, they have prepared for themselves a spiritual home in this
world and also in the World to Come, if they continue to live this way. In
the World to Come, it is not possible anymore for a person to perform
mitzvot or good deeds. As the rabbis have interpreted the verse, הַיּוֹם

לעשותם – *hayom la'asotam*, the mitzvot have to be performed "today" (in this world) and not למחר – *lemachar*, not "tomorrow." Nevertheless, it is possible for someone in the World to Come to have his status elevated from day to day by virtue of the good deeds done by his children and/or his pupils who are still living.

Why was it important for Abraham to know that his father did *tshuvah*? The sages say that R. Yochanan cried before his death because he did not know which direction he would be going. That is the reason why Abraham was told that his father, Terah, had repented, after which he was able to experience all the wonderful rewards of the World to Come.

How do we know that Ishmael did *tshuvah*? We know this because at the death of Abraham, both Ishmael and Yitzhak participated in the burial, as it is written in the Torah that he was buried by "Yitzhak and Ishmael." The fact that Yitzhak, the younger one, was mentioned first shows that Ishmael accepted his spiritual leadership and this is what is meant when Abraham was told that he would die בשיבה טובה – *beseivah tovah*, in a good age and with great fulfillment, since Ishmael would turn to the way of good. (*Tiferet Tzion*)

יג. (כח) 'וַיָּמָת הָרָן עַל פְּנֵי תֶּרַח אָבִיו' רַבִּי חִיָּא בַּר בְּרֵהּ דְּרַב אָדָא דְּיָפוֹ, תֶּרַח, עוֹבֵד צְלָמִים הָיָה, חַד זְמַן נְפַק לַאֲתַר, הוֹשִׁיב לְאַבְרָהָם, מוֹכֵר תַּחְתָּיו, הֲוָה אָתֵי בַּר אִינָשׁ בָּעֵי דְיִזְבַּן, וַהֲוָה אָמַר לֵהּ בַּר כַּמָּה שְׁנִין אַתְּ, וַהֲוָה אָמַר לֵהּ בַּר חַמְשִׁין, אוֹ שִׁתִּין, וַהֲוָה אָמַר לֵהּ וַי לֵהּ לְהַהוּא גַּבְרָא דַהֲוָה בַּר שִׁתִּין, וּבָעֵי לְמִסְגַּד לְבַר יוֹמֵי, וַהֲוָה מִתְבַּיֵּישׁ וְהוֹלֵךְ לוֹ. חַד זְמַן אֲתַת אִתְּתָא טְעִינָא בִּידָהּ חֲדָא פֵּינָךְ דְּסֹלֶת, אָמְרָה לֵהּ הֵא לָךְ, קָרֵב קֳדָמֵיהוֹן, קָם, נְסִיב בּוּקְלָסָא בִּידֵהּ וְתַבְּרִינוֹן לְכָלְהוֹן פְּסִילַיָּא, וִיהַב בּוּקְלָסָא בִּידָא דְרַבָּה דַהֲוָה בֵּינֵיהוֹן, כֵּיוָן דַּאֲתָא אֲבוּהּ אֲמַר לֵהּ מַאן עֲבִיד לְהוֹן כְּדֵין, אֲמַר לֵהּ מַה נְּכַפּוֹר מִנָּךְ, אֲתַת חֲדָא אִתְּתָא טְעִינָא לָהּ חֲדָא פֵּינָךְ דְּסֹלֶת, וַאֲמָרַת לִי, הֵא לָךְ קָרֵב קֳדָמֵיהוֹן, קָרֵבְתְּ לְקֳדָמֵיהוֹן הֲוָה דֵין אָמַר, אֲנָא אֵכוֹל קַדְמָאי, וְדֵין אָמַר, אֲנָא אֵכוֹל קַדְמָאי, קָם הָדֵין רַבָּה דַהֲוָה בֵּינֵיהוֹן, נְסַב בּוּקְלָסָא וְתַבְּרִנּוֹן, אֲמַר לֵהּ מָה אַתָּה מַפְלֶה בִּי וְיָדְעִין אִנּוּן, אֲמַר לֵהּ וְלֹא יִשְׁמְעוּ אָזְנֶיךָ מַה שֶׁפִּיךָ אוֹמֵר, נָסְבֵהּ וּמַסְרֵהּ לְנִמְרוֹד, אֲמַר לֵהּ נִסְגּוּד לְנוּרָא, אֲמַר לֵהּ אַבְרָהָם, וְנִסְגּוּד לְמַיָּא, דְּמַטְפִין נוּרָא, אֲמַר לֵהּ נִמְרוֹד נִסְגּוּד לְמַיָּא, אֲמַר לֵהּ אִם כֵּן נִסְגּוּד לַעֲנָנָא דְּטָעֵין מַיָּא, אֲמַר לֵהּ נִסְגּוּד לַעֲנָנָא, אֲמַר לֵהּ אִם כֵּן נִסְגּוּד לְרוּחָא דִּמְבַדַּר עֲנָנָא, אֲמַר לֵהּ נִסְגּוּד לְרוּחָא, אֲמַר לֵהּ וְנִסְגּוּד לְבַר אֱנָשָׁא דְּסָבֵל רוּחָא, אֲמַר לֵהּ מִלִּין אַתְּ מִשְׁתָּעֵי, אֲנִי, אֵינִי מִשְׁתַּחֲוֶה אֶלָּא לָאוּר, הֲרֵי אֲנִי מַשְׁלִיכְךָ בְּתוֹכוֹ, וְיָבוֹא אֱלוֹהַּ שֶׁאַתָּה מִשְׁתַּחֲוֶה לוֹ וְיַצִּילְךָ הֵימֶנּוּ, הֲוָה תַּמָּן הָרָן, קָאֵם פְּלוּג, אָמַר, מַה נַּפְשָׁךְ אִם נָצַח אַבְרָהָם, אֲנָא אָמַר, מִן דְּאַבְרָהָם אֲנָא, וְאִם נָצַח נִמְרוֹד אֲנָא אָמַר, דְּנִמְרוֹד אֲנָא, כֵּיוָן שֶׁיָּרַד אַבְרָהָם לְכִבְשַׁן הָאֵשׁ וְנִצּוֹל, אָמְרִין לֵהּ דְּמַאן אַתְּ, אֲמַר לְהוֹן, מִן אַבְרָהָם אֲנָא נְטָלוּהוּ וְהִשְׁלִיכוּהוּ לָאוּר, וְנֶחְמְרוּ בְּנֵי מֵעָיו, וְיָצָא, וּמֵת עַל פְּנֵי תֶּרַח אָבִיו, הֲדָא הוּא דִּכְתִיב, 'וַיָּמָת הָרָן עַל פְּנֵי תֶּרַח', וְגוֹ'.

13. AND HARAN DIED IN THE PRESENCE OF HIS FATHER TERAH (11:28). R. HIYYA SAID: TERAH WAS A MANUFACTURER OF IDOLS. HE ONCE WENT AWAY SOMEWHERE AND LEFT ABRAHAM TO SELL THEM IN HIS PLACE. A MAN CAME AND WISHED TO BUY ONE. 'HOW OLD ARE YOU?' ABRAHAM ASKED HIM. 'FIFTY YEARS,' WAS THE REPLY. 'WOE TO SUCH A MAN!' HE EXCLAIMED, 'YOU ARE FIFTY YEARS OLD AND WOULD WORSHIP A DAY-OLD OBJECT!' AT THIS HE BECAME ASHAMED AND DEPARTED. ON ANOTHER OCCASION A WOMAN CAME WITH A PLATEFUL OF FLOUR AND REQUESTED HIM, 'TAKE THIS AND OFFER IT TO THEM.' SO HE TOOK A STICK, BROKE THEM, AND PUT THE STICK IN THE HAND OF THE LARG-EST. WHEN HIS FATHER RETURNED HE DEMANDED, 'WHAT HAVE YOU DONE TO THEM?' 'I CANNOT CONCEAL IT FROM YOU,' HE REJOINED. 'A WOMAN CAME WITH A PLATEFUL OF FINE MEAL AND REQUESTED ME TO

OFFER IT TO THEM. ONE CLAIMED, "I MUST EAT FIRST," WHILE ANOTHER
CLAIMED, "I MUST EAT FIRST." THEREUPON THE LARGEST AROSE, TOOK
THE STICK, AND BROKE THEM. 'WHY DO YOU MAKE SPORT OF ME,' HE
CRIED OUT; 'HAVE THEY THEN ANY KNOWLEDGE!' 'SHOULD NOT YOUR
EARS LISTEN TO WHAT YOUR MOUTH IS SAYING,' HE RETORTED. THERE-
UPON HE SEIZED HIM AND DELIVERED HIM TO NIMROD. 'LET US WORSHIP
THE FIRE!' HE [NIMROD] PROPOSED. 'LET US RATHER WORSHIP WATER,
WHICH EXTINGUISHES THE FIRE,' REPLIED HE. 'THEN LET US WORSHIP
WATER!' 'LET US RATHER WORSHIP THE CLOUDS WHICH BEAR THE WA-
TER.' 'THEN LET US WORSHIP THE CLOUDS!' 'LET US RATHER WORSHIP
THE WINDS WHICH DISPERSE THE CLOUDS. 'THEN LET US WORSHIP THE
WIND!' 'LET US RATHER WORSHIP HUMAN BEINGS, WHO WITHSTAND
THE WIND.' 'YOU ARE JUST BANDYING WORDS,' HE EXCLAIMED; 'WE WILL
WORSHIP NOUGHT BUT THE FIRE. BEHOLD, I WILL CAST YOU INTO IT,
AND LET YOUR GOD WHOM YOU ADORE COME AND SAVE YOU FROM IT.'
NOW HARAN WAS STANDING THERE UNDECIDED. IF ABRAM IS VICTORI-
OUS, [THOUGHT HE], I WILL SAY THAT I AM OF ABRAM'S BELIEF, WHILE
IF NIMROD IS VICTORIOUS I WILL SAY THAT I AM ON NIMROD'S SIDE.
WHEN ABRAM DESCENDED INTO THE FIERY FURNACE AND WAS SAVED,
HE [NIMROD] ASKED HIM, 'OF WHOSE BELIEF ARE YOU? 'OF ABRAM'S, HE
REPLIED. THEREUPON HE SEIZED AND CAST HIM INTO THE FIRE; HIS
INNARDS WERE SCORCHED AND HE DIED IN HIS FATHER'S PRESENCE.
HENCE IT IS WRITTEN, AND HARAN DIED IN THE PRESENCE OF (AL PENE)
HIS FATHER TERAH

There are two versions of the second part of this midrash. The first is that Haran was thrown into the fire and died instantly, while his father was also present. There is another version, found in the commentary attributed to Rashi and others, that his innards were scorched, either from the fire or by some other manner, but that he did not die im-mediately. He was then taken to his father's house where he died a few days later. That is the literal meaning of our text, which says that he died either in the presence of his father or facing his father.

———

Seed Thoughts

Abraham's brother Haran was in great spiritual doubt as to whether to support Abraham his brother, or Nimrod. He was conflicted, and when his innards became inflamed as a result of his insincere support of Abra-ham, it could be looked upon as מדה כנגד מדה – *midah keneged midah,* measure-for-measure punishment. The rabbis say that no one has the right to make a choice in life that is dependent upon a miracle. Haran was not a true believer in Abraham's mission; he simply wanted to back the winner, and when Abraham emerged from the fire unscathed, he assumed that Abraham was the winner. But Haran was not. His choice was based on the expectation of a miracle happening to him, as it did to Abraham; but God does not operate the universe in this fashion. One has to commit to faith without the expectation of reward in order for it to be authentic.

יד. 'וַיִּקַּח אַבְרָם וְנָחוֹר לָהֶם נָשִׁים, וְגוֹ'', אַבְרָם הָיָה גָּדוֹל מִנָּחוֹר שָׁנָה אַחַת, וְנָחוֹר הָיָה גָּדוֹל
מֵהָרָן שָׁנָה אַחַת, נִמְצָא הָרָן גָּדוֹל מֵאַבְרָהָם שְׁתֵּי שָׁנִים, שָׁנָה לְעִבּוּרָהּ שֶׁל מִלְכָּה, וְשָׁנָה
לְעִבּוּרָהּ שֶׁל יִסְכָּה, הָרָן, מוֹלִיד לְשֵׁשׁ שָׁנִים, וְאַבְרָם, אֵינוֹ מוֹלִיד אַתְמָהָא.

14. AND ABRAM AND NAHOR TOOK THEM WIVES, ETC. (11:29). ABRAM
WAS A YEAR OLDER THAN NAHOR AND NAHOR WAS A YEAR OLDER THAN
HARAN; [HENCE ABRAM WAS] TWO YEARS OLDER [THAN HARAN]; [NOW
DEDUCT] THE YEAR OF PREGNANCY WITH MILCAH AND THE YEAR OF
PREGNANCY WITH ISCAH, AND YOU FIND THAT HARAN BEGOT CHILDREN
AT SIX YEARS OF AGE, YET YOU SAY THAT ABRAM COULD NOT BEGET A
CHILD!

There is obviously an error in the Hebrew where it says that Haran
was two years older than Abraham. That appears to be a mistake. The
Yefei To'ar gave us a plausible interpretation of the text, saying that the
word קטן – *katan* replaced the world גדול – *gadol*, which seems to imply
that Haran was two years younger than Abraham. Mistakes can occur in
just about any document, including Midrash. But why was the mistake
not corrected? While the rabbinic texts are not as sacred as is the Torah,
there is, nevertheless, a great reverence for them. The mistake was,
therefore, always acknowledged by oral tradition, but not changed in
written form.

In the light of the fact that Haran, the younger brother, had children
at such a young age, Abraham was belittled by some of his peers as not
being able to father a child.

'וַתְּהִי שָׂרַי עֲקָרָה, וְגוֹ'', אָמַר רַבִּי לֵוִי, בְּכָל מָקוֹם שֶׁנֶּאֱמַר 'אֵין לָהּ' הָוָה לָהּ, 'וַתְּהִי שָׂרַי עֲקָרָה,
אֵין לָהּ וָלָד', הָוָה לָהּ, (בראשית כא, א) 'וַה' פָּקַד אֶת שָׂרָה, וְגוֹ'', (ש"א א, ב) 'וַיְהִי לִפְנִנָּה יְלָדִים,
וּלְחַנָּה אֵין יְלָדִים', וַהֲוָה לָהּ, (שם ב, כא) 'כִּי פָקַד ה' אֶת חַנָּה וַתַּהַר וַתֵּלֶד, וְגוֹ'', (ירמיה ל, יז) 'צִיּוֹן
הִיא, דֹּרֵשׁ אֵין לָהּ', וַהֲוָה לָהּ, (ישעיה נט, כ) 'וּבָא לְצִיּוֹן גּוֹאֵל', (שם נד, א) 'רָנִּי עֲקָרָה לֹא יָלָדָה
פִּצְחִי רִנָּה וְצַהֲלִי'.

[THE REASON, HOWEVER, WAS]: AND SARAI WAS BARREN; SHE HAD NO
CHILD (IBID., 30). R. LEVI SAID: WHEREVER 'SHE HAD NOT' IS FOUND, IT

MEANS THAT EVENTUALLY SHE DID HAVE. THUS: AND SARAI WAS BAR-
REN; SHE HAD NO CHILD: EVENTUALLY SHE DID HAVE, AS IT IS WRITTEN,
AND THE LORD REMEMBERED SARAH (GEN. 21:1). AND PENINAH HAD
CHILDREN, BUT HANNAH HAD NO CHILDREN (I SAM. 1:2): EVENTUALLY
SHE DID HAVE, AS IT IS WRITTEN, AND SHE BORE THREE SONS, ETC.
(IBID., 2:21). AGAIN, SHE IS ZION, THERE IS NONE THAT CARETH FOR HER
(JER. 30:17). YET EVENTUALLY SHE WILL HAVE [ONE TO CARE FOR HER,
AS IT IS WRITTEN], AND A REDEEMER WILL COME TO ZION, AND UNTO
THEM THAT TURN FROM TRANSGRESSION, ETC. (ISA. 59:20).

—

Seed Thoughts

This is a very beautiful way to end the section on Noah. It is quite true, as the text says, that Sarai was barren. But this was not an absolute statement. She was barren only temporarily; then, later on, she was blessed with a child, Yitzhak. The same can be said about Hannah, in the Book of Samuel; she, too, was barren, but only temporarily. Eventually, she was blessed, not only with Samuel, but with two other children as well. There is a beautiful insight here, especially when it is applied to the Jewish people: The Land of Israel was also described as barren. Yet, the prophet says, רני עקרה לא ילדה – *roni akarah lo yeladah,* "Rejoice, oh barren one . . . because you will be redeemed" (Isaiah 54:1). As it is written, ובא לציון גואל – *uva letzion goel,* "And a redeemer shall come unto Zion" (Isaiah 59:20). The barrenness of the Land is only temporary, as are all other forms of Jewish suffering. It will all be changed as the years go by.

These words are being written in the midst of the celebration of the sixtieth anniversary of the establishment of the State of Israel. Already there is a population of 7.5 million, of which 5.5 million are Jewish and 1.5 million are Arab. The progress has been remarkable. The ingathering of the exiles has not been completed and I'm unsure whether it ever will be since we live in a globalized world. But one million Jews did come from the former Soviet Union and many thousands came from Ethiopia and many hundreds are continuing to arrive from various parts of the world, week in and week out. In many fields, such as economics, technology and Jewish scholarship, the State of Israel has achieved remarkable heights. All of these things were accomplished while the state was surrounded by enemies, intent on its destruction. The existence of the State of Israel is, in itself, a message of hope, and the text about barrenness there may refer to the past and to part of the present but should not be allowed to refer to the future. As it says, מוֹשִׁיבִי עֲקֶרֶת הַבַּיִת אֵם הַבָּנִים שְׂמֵחָה הַלְלוּיָהּ – *moshivi akeret habayit em habanim smeichah, halleluyah* (Psalms 113:9) – "He transforms the barren wife into a glad mother of children." This applies to the Jewish people as well, who were transformed from barrenness to fulfillment and from hopelessness to hope. Let us hope and pray that the Jewish people will be fully restored to their national home and that all of our generations, including neighbors and friends, will be blessed with lives of rejoicing and fulfillment.

BIBLIOGRAPHICAL ABBREVIATIONS

HAMIDRASH HAMEVO'AR – Under the general editorship of Rabbi Abraham Steinberger presiding over a faculty of scholars, the first four volumes, comprising *Bereishit Rabbah*, were published in 1984 in Jerusalem. The final volume of the *Midrash Rabbah* was completed fifteen years later. This commentary leaves nothing undone or unexplained. Every new interpretation is traced to its source. The use of different type styles (bold, italics, etc.) helps the reader follow the various levels of interpretation. Every volume ends with additional commentary from a plethora of sources.

MATNOT KEHUNA – This commentary is the work of Rabbi Issachar Ber ben Naftali of the town of Mishbershin in Poland. The work first appeared in the Cracow edition (1587) of the *Midrash Rabbah* and has appeared in every compilation ever since. This commentary sparkles with brevity and has been used by all who study Midrash.

MIRKIN – This commentary by Moshe Aryeh Mirkin was the first of the modern Hebrew commentaries. Published in Tel Aviv in 1968, the author emphasizes the plain meaning of the text. He leans heavily on the edition of Theodore and Albeck, then great textual scholars, and bases many of his interpretations on manuscript emendations and corrections they suggested. He has a great talent for brevity without compromising the meaning, and this is a most valuable contribution of understanding Midrash.

RZWE – These are the initials of Rabbi Zev Wolf Einhorn. His Hebrew commentary is titled מהרז״ו, which are his Hebrew initials. His commentary is a very large work and appears also in abridged form; both forms are presented side by side in the Vilna edition. His interpretation tries to apply the thirty-two hermeneutical principals of Rabbi Elazar ben Azariah. Our quotations are from the Vilna Edition.

RASHI – Rabbi Solomon Yitzhaki (1040–1105) is the great interpreter of the Bible and Talmud. According to the Vilna edition, Rashi also wrote a commentary to *Bereishit Rabbah*, but authorities diasgree and feel that the commentary is culled from his views as written in his other commentaries. There are even some scholars who argue that the commentary to *Bereishit Rabbah* was written by someone else. However, Rashi's name is associated with these ideas and probably always will be.

SONCINO – The Soncino Press, from its headquarters for many years in London, England, pioneered the translation of the great classics of Judaism into English, including the Bible, the Talmud, the Zohar and the *Midrash Rabbah*. The *Midrash Rabbah* was translated in 1939, and in the 1980s, the rights to Soncino Press were acquired by Judaica Press in New York, through whose permission their translation has been used. In addition to the translation, the Soncino editions include explanatory notes.

TIFERET TZION – The author of *Tiferet Tzion*, Rabbi Yitzhak Zev Yadler, passed away in 1917 and his great work, *Tiferet Tzion*, was not published until 1958. It is a tremendous work by one person, who, according to his own testimony, spent fourteen years of unremitting work, night and day, to produce this monumental commentary on the *Midrash Rabbah*. A pious scholar and mystic by belief, upbringing and conviction, he was able to relate to many of the difficult mystical passages of the *Midrash Rabbah* as no one else has been able to do. The present work relies heavily on his insights.

YEFEI TO'AR – This work, by Rabbi Samuel Yaffe Ashkenazi, is the most important of the early commentaries on the *Midrash Rabbah*. It appeared in 1607, more or less around the same time as the Venice edition of the *Midrash Rabbah*. Unfortunately, the author passed away ten years before its publication. Already in his day, he was interested in comparing the different texts of Midrash to be found in many manuscripts. The *Yefei To'ar* has since been included in every anthology of the *Midrash Rabbah*. Our quotations are from the Vilna edition.

ABOUT THE AUTHOR

Rabbi WILFRED SHUCHAT has been an active rabbi for over 50 years, and has studied and taught the Midrash Rabbah during his tenure as Rabbi of Shaar HaShomayim Synagogue in Montreal, Canada. His groundbreaking work in the interpretation and analysis of Midrash has made these psychological and philosophical rabbinic perspectives accessible to laymen and clergy alike.